D0107332

Celluloid Symphonies

The publisher gratefully acknowledges the generous support
of the Music in America Endowment Fund of the
University of California Press Foundation, which was established
by a major gift from Sukey and Gil Garcetti,
Michael P. Roth, and the Roth Family Foundation.

Celluloid Symphonies

Texts and Contexts in Film Music History

Edited by

Julie Hubbert

UNIVERSITY OF CALIFORNIA PRESS

Berkeley   Los Angeles   London

University of California Press, one of the most distinguished university presses in the United States, enriches lives around the world by advancing scholarship in the humanities, social sciences, and natural sciences. Its activities are supported by the UC Press Foundation and by philanthropic contributions from individuals and institutions. For more information, visit www.ucpress.edu.

University of California Press
Berkeley and Los Angeles, California

University of California Press, Ltd.
London, England

Library of Congress Cataloging-in-Publication Data

Celluloid symphonies : texts and contexts in film music history / edited by Julie Hubbert.
    p.   cm.
Includes bibliographical references and index.
ISBN 978-0-520-24101-5 (cloth : alk. paper) —
ISBN 978-0-520-24102-2 (pbk. : alk. paper)
1. Motion picture music—History and criticism.   2. Symphony.
I. Hubbert, Julia Bess.
ML2075.C455   2011
781.5'4209—dc22   2010013985

Manufactured in the United States of America

20   19   18   17   16   15   14   13   12   11
10   9   8   7   6   5   4   3   2   1

This book is printed on Cascades Enviro 100, a 100% post consumer waste, recycled, de-inked fiber. FSC recycled certified and processed chlorine free. It is acid free, Ecologo certified, and manufactured by BioGas energy.

CONTENTS

PREFACE

In the last few decades, the study of film as a unique and independent art form has flourished in scholarly communities and university curriculums. As film studies have grown in depth and detail, however, one aspect has remained significantly underappreciated and unexamined: film music. Not only has the film studies community had little to say about this integral and essential aspect of the film medium, but music historians, too, have participated in this neglect, overlooking film music both as an important part of a new, uniquely twentieth-century art form and as an important component of twentieth-century music history. Recently, a concerted attempt to correct this neglect has been initiated, most notably with several fine edited essay collections analyzing individual films. But the discipline still lacks literature that combines historical scope with a critical scholarly intent. It also lacks literature that is fundamentally interdisciplinary, with potential appeal to students and scholars in both film and music studies.

As a history of American film music, *Celluloid Symphonies* is quite different from the existing handful of histories in the literature. Some, like Roy M. Prendergast's seminal *Film Music: A Neglected Art* (1977; 2d ed. 1992), which provides commentary on films only to 1970, or Royal S. Brown's detailed but very selective study *Overtones and Undertones: Reading Film Music* (1994), are not comprehensive. Others, like Laurence E. MacDonald's *The Invisible Art of Film Music* (1998), Larry M. Timm's *The Soul of Cinema: An Appreciation of Film Music* (2002), and, to some extent, Roger Hickman's *Reel Music: Exploring 100 Years of Film Music* (2005), are not critically minded. *Celluloid Symphonies,* in contrast, aims to be comprehensive both historically and analytically. It charts the major innovations and trends that have shaped film music history from 1896 to the present and analyzes the important aesthetic choices, technological innovations, and commercial pressures that have defined the relationship between music and film over the course of film history.

To date, music historians have defined the source material for film music primarily as individual musical scores. This score-centered approach has various drawbacks. A basic logistical problem is that film scores proper are frequently unavailable for study. More philosophically, this approach has the limitation not only of privileging orchestral underscores but also of encouraging a "great composer" interpretation of film music. Film scholars, in contrast, no doubt because of varying levels of comfort analyzing musical notation, have tended to focus on texted or popular music and the performance of music in films, the film musical in particular, while eschewing discussion of composed underscores. These tendencies have all contributed to the interdisciplinary neglect of film music scholarship. *Celluloid Symphonies,* by identifying a written and aesthetic history for film music that does not require expert knowledge of music notation or theory, significantly expands the literature to include a broad community of both film and music scholars, as the subject requires.

Because of its scope and topic, this project relies on primary texts and other source documents—fifty-three articles, essays, and interviews—to outline the evolution of film music from a variety of perspectives. These primary documents reveal how composers as well as directors, producers, and industry executives have affected the sound, structure, and placement of music in films. They also describe the major practical, technical, commercial, and aesthetic concerns and innovations that have shaped the use of music in film history. While some of these documents are already known to film and music scholars, many are not. The consolidation of these documents from disparate archival sources is one of the central contributions this book hopes to make to the existing film music literature.

The book is far more than just a "reader," however, for it provides essential critical context and commentary on these source materials as well. A handful of critical studies have been especially useful in the creation of the critical introductions to the five periods of film music history covered here. Rick Altman's *Silent Film Sound* (2005) and Martin Miller Marks's *Music and the Silent Film: Contexts and Case Studies, 1895–1924* (1997) offer excellent analysis of music of the silent period; Jeff Smith's *The Sounds of Commerce: Marketing Popular Film Music* (1998) is a thorough investigation of the use of popular music from silent to contemporary film; and Claudia Gorbman's *Unheard Melodies: Narrative Film Music* (1987) provides a solid aesthetic analysis of the orchestral underscore in particular. Apart from these studies and a handful of isolated essays, however, there is little existing literature to draw from, and large parts of film music history—notably, early sound films and a vast landscape of post-1960s filmmaking—have received virtually no attention. Areas that remain relatively unexplored include the ways in which nondiegetic music was initially conceptualized in the early sound film period, the evolution of jazz as an underscore, the effects of "runaway production" on film music in the 1960s, the dramatic changes wrought by the auteur-director phenomenon on both the sound and structure of film music in the early 1970s, the impact of synthesizers on the conceptual distinction between sound and music in the early 1980s, and the effects of music videos, video games, and new sound design on the film music landscape during the last two decades.

This history has been organized into five large "periods," with each critical introduction attending to the practical, political, and aesthetic forces that affected the film industry in general and film music in particular during the period in question. The first three of these periods will be familiar in the sense that they articulate, with only minor exceptions, long-recognized periods in conventional film history: the silent period, which ends clearly with the coming of sound film in 1926; the transitional or early sound period, which I argue lasts for music until around 1935; and the celebrated Golden Age of Hollywood, which I suggest lasts until roughly 1960. The decision to describe 1960 as something of a turning point in film music history was informed not only by the abandonment of the Romantic orchestra in favor of a variety of instrumentations, including jazz, rock 'n' roll, and avant-garde classical trends like serialism and aleatoric practices, but also by the marketing of film music for the long-playing record album. A similar turning point can be seen emerging in the late 1970s and early 1980s with the self-conscious return of the thematic orchestral score. This final "postmodern" period is defined in part by the increasingly dense and allusive use of not just popular songs but also preexisting classical music in soundtrack formulas. In addition, easy access to an enormous spectrum of film, first through video and now through digital technologies, has changed how film music is perceived by allowing it to act not just as text, but as hypertext. The period is also defined by an increased blurring of the conceptual distinctions between music and sound design, and by the influence of a growing number of new film-related audiovisual formats, including the "music video" and video games.

While the intent of this reader is to be comprehensive, it is not exhaustive. It cannot describe all the changes and innovations film music history has witnessed, nor can it recognize all the technical and aesthetic developments that film itself has undergone. Instead it seeks to highlight significant trends and developments in the area of film music. Frequently, these changes have been triggered by innovations in the areas of film exhibition and production; however, as many of the documents reveal, some changes to film music have been made in response to innovations that have taken place outside of film, particularly in the concert hall.

Despite being literally connected to film, therefore, film music has uniquely and duplicitously articulated at various times both the history of film and the history of twentieth-century music.

This reader is also limited in the sense that it focuses on music as it evolved within the American film industry, particularly in the productions of the major Hollywood studios. This decision was dictated entirely by practical concerns: to discuss the musical trends and practices that have characterized individual national cinemas abroad would require not one book but many. Still, in that various national cinemas have responded directly to Hollywood innovations, the materials presented here could be very useful for initiating discussion of the musical aspects of French, German, British, Russian, Asian, and Indian film music practices. The scope of this book has also been intentionally narrowed to consider primarily narrative film. This choice also reflects considerations of space, though the concerns of less visible genres—newsreels, travelogues, documentaries, experimental films, etc.—will be seen, if only through implication, in the discussion of mainstream filmmaking as well.

ACKNOWLEDGMENTS

This book has been long in the making, and over the years I have received assistance and encouragement, both professional and personal, from a number of colleagues, friends, family members, and institutions.

My research was funded by several grants from the Office of Research at the University of South Carolina. This assistance was absolutely indispensable in helping me travel and do the archival work needed for this book. I am also indebted to the staff at several film and music libraries and archives around the country, including the University of California, Los Angeles; the University of Southern California; the University of Minnesota; the New York Public Library; and the Library of Congress. Two individuals at these institutions deserve special mention: Mike Mashon at the Film and Television Reading Room at the Library of Congress, and Jennifer Ottervik, Head Librarian at the University South Carolina. Their eagerness to help me with even the smallest details of this book was gratifying and greatly appreciated.

I would also like to thank the undergraduate and graduate students who took my film music courses over the past several years. Their discussion of the source documents included in this book, and many that are not, was invaluable and significantly influenced my selection of material for this book. Specific students also helped tremendously in the preparation of this manuscript. Graduate assistant Valerie McPhail started the massive undertaking of keying all the source documents into computer files, but most of this work was accomplished by the very capable and cheerful Connie Frigo. I also want to thank Alex Wroten and Gardiner Beson, two of the best undergraduate students I've had in recent years, for their help preparing the Sibelius files for this manuscript.

I have been very lucky to have the support of many colleagues here at the University of South Carolina and at institutions around the country. When I first contemplated working in the area of film music, two colleagues, Neil Lerner and Daniel Goldmark, were particularly welcoming and encouraging. Their excitement for this project kept me going when fatigue and discouragement ran high. My friend Ivan Raykoff also saw the potential in this project early on and provided unwavering encouragement, as did friend and former colleague Georgia Cowart. Several other film music colleagues offered well-timed support. Jim Buhler, David Neumeyer, Michael Pisani, and Jeff Smith all made me feel like this book was much needed and worthwhile. My colleagues in Film and Media Studies at the University of South Carolina have also been tremendously helpful and supportive. Susan Courtney's rigorous revision of a grant proposal I had written for this book a few years ago completely reconceptualized the scope and focus of the book and reenergized my work on it. Dan Streible and Laura Kissel were patient and persistently interested in my success. They, along with Craig Kridel, have been great friends to me and to this project over the years, and their good wishes and humor have been invaluable. My music history colleagues at the School of Music, past and present—Peter Hoyt, Sarah Williams, Rebecca Oettinger, and Kevin Karnes—also provided steady support and encouragement over the years. And to the anonymous readers who read the manuscript of this book for the University of California Press I also owe a great deal of thanks. The book has benefited enormously from their very useful comments and suggestions.

This book would not have been completed without the encouragement of my friend and editor at UC Press, Mary Francis. She artfully prodded and pushed me at just the right times, and this text is in many ways as much a result of her diligence and hard work as mine. Eric Schmidt helped with the preparation of the manuscript, and Rose Vekony and Anne Canright organized the text and copy edited my prose, a tremendous undertaking to be sure.

No one, however, can be more relieved and excited that this book is finally finished than my family. Long ago I ordered them to stop asking me "How is the book going?" and they did. But they never gave up asking how I was doing and what they could do to help. To them I owe everything, and so it is to them—to my husband Rich, daughter Eleanor, sisters Lisa, Gretchen, and Charlotte, and to my mom and dad that I dedicate this book.

PART ONE

Playing the Pictures

Music and the Silent Film (1895–1925)

INTRODUCTION

That film historians have only recently begun to recognize film not as a uniquely visual art but as a highly integrated one, one that unites the previously separate mediums of image, sound, and music, stems no doubt from a peculiarity rooted in the beginnings of film history itself. For nearly the first three decades, film was not a fully mechanized art; instead it relied on a strange simultaneity of technically disparate parts, merging mechanically reproduced moving images with live performances of music and sound. Unfortunately, this mix of real and reproduced media led instantly to a critical inequity. Because it was mechanized and represented a new technology, the visual part of the film came immediately to define the film proper. Then as now, film was prized primarily as a visual technology or art.

The history of silent film music is important not only because it challenges this visual-centric model of film, but also because it offers a new and deeper understanding of the term *silent*. Certainly, if film had been truly silent from the beginning, this section would not exist. If the following documents reveal anything, it is the irony of the most common term used to refer to early film. For in fact, the "silent" period was full of sounds—noise, music, even dialogue and narration. In qualifying the silence of early film, therefore, the documents in this section redefine that silence not as a lack of sound, but as a lack of integration. The undoing of film's silence, in other words, will come not with the *inclusion* of music and sound, but with their mechanization, the technological innovation that allowed music to be represented alongside the images.

The history conveyed by these documents of music in the silent period also challenges the assumption that the sound of film music was standardized or "classicized" by Hollywood composers of the 1930s and 1940s. Far from being the beginning of a classical tradition of wall-to-wall orchestral music, Max Steiner's "Golden Age" scoring model was, rather, the culmination of three decades of silent film music experimentation.

Like any art form, film has an extensive prehistory. Beginning as early as the sixteenth and seventeenth centuries, inventors and artists had been seeking ways not just to represent reality, but to animate it. It wasn't until the nineteenth century, however, with the invention of photography and the cinema-like experiences of the diorama and panorama, that those efforts took off, and as a result audiences were now treated to a flourishing of optical experiments. While some of these early experiments were more popular than others, none was completely successful at both animating the photograph and projecting it onto a large screen for mass viewing.[1] That distinction was achieved only at the end of the century, on December 28, 1895, when the brothers Auguste and Louis Lumière, owners of a film and photographic plate manufacturing business in Lyon, France, projected a series of short films, or *cinématographes,* as they called them, onto the wall of the *salon indien* at the Grand Café in Paris.[2]

In terms of basic technology, these films were similar to the films we watch today, although they were silent and radically shorter. Each was limited to the length of the reel, which at first was only about 25 meters, or one minute, long. These first films were also limited in subject matter. As a surviving playbill for the Paris exhibition reveals, the Lumière films were *actualités,* or proto-documentaries.[3] While many featured the Lumière family and the city of Lyon, one of the Lumière brothers' first production initiatives was to place trained cameramen in major cities and exotic locations all around the world to document life outside of France. The result was short scenics, of places like Venice, Milan, Naples, and even Melbourne. They made these short documentaries not to entertain audiences, but to advertise their film equipment company to a global market.[4]

The cinema experience for the audience at the Grand Café was more than just a visual spectacle. In an important footnote at the bottom of the playbill, musical accompaniment by the *pianiste-compositeur* Emile Maraval was announced. Little is known today of Maraval, nor does the announcement reveal what kind of music he played, whether he penned new music or simply improvised an accompaniment for each short film. Perhaps he changed the style and tempo of his music to suit the topic of each film, giving Venice and Australia different treatments. It is impossible to know.[5] Nonetheless, the presence of a musician at this first film exhibition is significant. Not only did the Lumière brothers find a way to animate photographs and project them onto a screen in larger-than-life-size form, but they also thought to integrate those images with music.

When a similar group of Lumière *cinématographes* was shown to Queen Victoria several months later, the musical part of the experience was somewhat different. As the program for this special occasion announces, the Windsor Castle exhibition was accompanied not by a pianist, but by an orchestra, specifically the Empire Theater Orchestra conducted by Leopold Wenzel.[6] Although, again, little is known of Wenzel,[7] the exhibition program yields much more information about what the musical part of the experience may have sounded like. On this occasion, not only was the accompaniment orchestral, but it relied to some extent on preexisting music, including selections previously written by Wenzel for the ballet and works by other composers such as Karl Millöcker, Olivier Metra, Ernest Gillet, and Charles Gounod. Wenzel also seems to have differentiated filmic action and subject matter through use of varying musical styles and tempi. "Hussars Passing through Dublin," for instance, was paired with a march by Métra, and the comedy "A Joke on the Gardener" with a waltz by Wenzel, while the final travelogue, "A Moving Train near Clapham Junction," was accompanied by "Metropolitan Galop" by Charles Hubans.

Not all of the earliest film exhibitions followed the Lumière exhibition format, of course, or even used the Lumière technology. In Europe, for instance, early cinema audiences were treated to Max Skladanowsky's Bioskop films;[8] in the United States, audiences watched "vitascopes," films projected by Thomas Edison's Vitascope machine.[9] While individual technologies varied, all these films appear to have been shown with musical accompaniment.

In the United States at the turn of the twentieth century, film's first home was the vaudeville theater. In this setting, films were not shown as "programs," or uninterrupted collections of short films with different subjects, as in Europe. Instead, the film was simply part of the parade of individual acts that defined the vaudeville program. A short film of a modern dancer or two men boxing, for instance, might have been sandwiched in between a juggler and a comic routine.

The isolated appearance of film in the vaudeville setting fuels the first challenge to the argument that early silent films may in fact have been silent. According to the contemporary literature, it is unclear whether music was indeed heard during the film portions of this kind of program. Some reports make no mention of music, while others indicate its clear presence. In April 1896, for instance, when Koster and Bial's Music Hall in New York City hosted the first Vitascope projections, the hall's band was said to have provided "a musical accompaniment." When the Vitascope was premiered the following year in Philadelphia, not only was a musical accompaniment provided, but it was valued as an essential aspect of the new cinema experience: "The soldiers marched to the stirring tune of the 'Marseillaise' and the scene stirred the audience to such a pitch of enthusiasm that has rarely been equaled by any form of entertainment. The playing of the 'Marseillaise' aided no little in the success of the picture. In the sham battle scene the noise and battle din created also added to the wonderful sense of realism."[10]

George Beynon, an early historian of film music, however, describes a different understanding of music for film in the vaudeville tradition. In the introductory chapter to his 1920 instruction manual *Musical Presentation of Motion Pictures,* "Evolution of the Motion Picture," Beynon insists that in the vaudeville setting music was provided for everything *but* the motion picture. If music was heard during the film sections of the program, he asserts, it was there by default rather than by design. "The film was run in silence except for the beating of the big drum outside for the purpose of drawing the crowds . . . [and] during the 'packing process' [when] the pianist regaled the seated ones with some music, mostly apropos of nothing." It was only by accident, Beynon concludes, that a conscientious musician "forgot himself as to play soft music for a particularly touching death-bed scene."[11]

Although a few current film historians, including Rick Altman, argue that early film might have been truly silent, at least on some occasions or in some venues,[12] the majority of the evidence indicates the opposite. In fact, "silent" films appear, generally speaking, to have had downright noisy. As the Philadelphia critic at the Vitascope premiere observed, in addition to the musical accompaniment, films had sound effects, and attempts were even made to include spoken dialogue. As film historian Charles Musser sums it up, "Modern-day film producers distinguish four basic kinds of sounds: music, narration, effects, and dialogue. Of these, all but the fourth were commonly used during the first year of moving pictures. But even dialogue was employed within a short time as actors or singers were placed in back of the screen."[13] Early silent film, in short, was hardly silent but instead hosted a number of additive sound features. And of all the initial accompaniments, music appears to have been most consistently included, for it gave film broad and democratic appeal, helping it to appeal to different classes of filmgoers at a variety of venues.

Over the course of the next decade, the transition of film from novelty act to independent art form brought a number of changes to both film and its exhibition. One of the most significant changes was the acquisition of an independent exhibition space devoted solely to the display of moving pictures, starting in about 1905. In the United States, storefront theaters soon became known as nickelodeons because of their nickel admission price.[14] As new spaces for film exhibition began to flourish, and a system of film rental was standardized through the establishment of film "exchanges," film production also changed. Even before the nickelodeon model began to dominate, production focus was shifting from documentary-minded films to fictional or "story" films.[15] With this shift in focus came an increase in film length. Whereas the first narrative films and actualities typically featured a single shot or "scene," emerging narrative films expanded to include multiple scenes (typically six to twelve), occupying anywhere from two or three hundred to a thousand feet of film. Longer films took up one reel and typically lasted from ten to eighteen minutes, depending both on their length and on projection speed, which were not standardized until 1909–10. Shorter films were typically half as long so that two could occupy a single reel (known as a "split reel").[16]

As films grew in length, they began to be organized by genre. The earliest films tended to fall into three categories: actuality (travelogues, newsreels, reenactments, etc.), comedy, and drama. By 1910, those genres had been expanded to include a host of subgenres: western, Indian film, war picture, detective serial, melodrama, trick film, farce or slapstick, fairy tale, biblical passion, and science fiction. It was this initial flowering, between 1905 and 1910, that saw the rise of such pioneer filmmakers as Georges Méliès, Edwin Porter, D. W. Griffith, and Cecil B. DeMille and early production companies like Pathé, Edison, Biograph, Vitagraph, Selig, Lubin, Kalem, and Essaney.[17]

Just as the expansion of narrative filmmaking encouraged the specialization of directors and genres, it also led to the standardization of exhibition practices, especially with regard to musical accompaniment. For instance, in a 1909 advice column for fellow nickelodeon owners entitled "Plain Talk to Theatre Managers and Operators" (**Document 1**), featured in the trade magazine *Motion Picture World,* theater manager F. H. Richardson describes the standard instrumentation of the musical accompaniment as piano and drums. A successful accompaniment, he notes, rested on the musicians' ability to differentiate musically not only individual film actions and episodes but film genres as well. Although Richardson does not describe particular musical selections—what one would have heard during a Civil War picture, for instance, or a western—he did say that the pianist needed to have good improvisation skills. This suggests that music for the cinema before 1910 included renditions of popular tunes and simple impromptu melodies. He also describes the placement of the musicians, at the front of the theater next to the screen, which not only allowed them to see what they were accompanying, but also helped create the illusion that their sound was emanating from the screen. A simple methodology is also available in Richardson's description. A successful accompaniment rested on the musician's ability to attentively follow and differentiate individual film actions and also larger film genres through musical style and tempo.

The musicians did more than set an appropriate mood for each film, however. As Richardson notes, they were in charge of providing *all* the sound for the film, which they did primarily by way of sound effects. In the very early days of film, the standards for "realistic" sound had been set high by traveling shows like Lyman H. Howe's High-Class Moving Pictures and Hale's Tours and Scenes of the World.[18] Because these road shows toured with a single, unchanging program of films, they had an elaborate array of sound effect devices, everything from train, truck, and tractor sounds to gunshots, chimes, electric door bells, baby cries, roosters crowing and dogs barking, the clip-clop of horses' hoofs, and wind, rain, thunder, and ocean waves. Some of these devices, like thunder sheets and wind whistles, were borrowed from the theater; others were developed just for moving pictures.[19]

Since the film fare at the storefront nickelodeon typically changed three times a week, theater musicians did not have time to compose elaborate sound accompaniments, nor did they have as elaborate an array of sound effect devices as the road shows had.[20] The nickelodeon drummer typically had some standard percussion instruments: drums, bells, gongs, woodblocks, and whistles. By 1905 or so, he or she would also have a number of additional percussive devices, or "traps." Most traps articulated common sounds, animal noises like hens' cackling; and the sounds of mechanical devices like winches, ratchets, and blacksmith anvils; and signals such as chimes and steamboat whistles. Traps were widely advertised in music and film journals of the early 1900s, and were used well into the 1920s. For those exhibitors who could not afford the expense of lots of traps or multiple persons to articulate them, sound-effect "cabinets" became available starting around 1907. Semiautomated machines, like the Ciné Multiphone Rousselot, the Excela Soundograph, and the British Allefex, consolidated many of the most popular traps or film sounds in a large tabletop device that could be operated by a single percussionist. The fact that these traps and cabinets were conceived of as percussion instruments, to be played by musicians, is a reminder that in the early cinema, sound and music were not separate. In silent film, film music was film sound.[21]

By 1910, singers had become part of cinema music, though as Richardson points out, they did not typically accompany films. Instead, they provided interstitial material—specifically, the "illustrated song," a musical interlude or sing-a-long that took place between films or while the reel was being changed on the projector. During this portion of the program the singer would stand to the side of the stage and sing while a series of pictures illustrating the text of the song, or the sheet music itself, was projected on the screen.[22] Sometimes the song was coordinated thematically with one of the films in the program, but most often the illustrated song simply promoted the sale of a new popular song. It was one of the earliest examples of using film to market a product, in this case song recordings and sheet music for home consumption.[23]

Film production companies, of course, were interested in the standardization of the musical part of films as well. By 1910, most film companies were providing written synopses of new films as part of their rental service, and as early as 1909 Edison's film company took this practice one step further, distributing "musical suggestion sheets" in its bimonthly magazine, the *Edison Kinetogram,* under the title "Incidental Music for Edison Pictures" **(Document 2).** While one column condensed the plot into numbered episodes, a corresponding column suggested an appropriate type or tempo of music to play during each episode. These early cue sheets allow us a glimpse of the specific repertoires that pianists might have played. Although the description is often general, calling simply for waltzes, marches, or "popular airs" without identifying specific compositions, titles are occasionally given as well. The early cinema was clearly full of the popular music of the day—Tin Pan Alley songs, folk songs, ballads, rags, and Sousa marches.[24]

These early cue sheets also describe a "compilation" approach to underscoring the film. After breaking a film down into individual scenes, the pianist would translate the action of each scene into a musical tempo, which was then used to specify an accompanying musical selection. Hurried actions on screen, for instance, were given fast music—jigs, allegros, marches; quieter actions like love scenes called for slower music—plaintive melodies, andantes and adagios. That each scene was distilled primarily to the tempo or rhythm of the action, with the moods or emotions of the characters performing those actions only a secondary consideration, is significant. Although the earliest film music was certainly used to enhance the screen narrative, it seems primarily to have been a rhythmic feature, emphasizing both the pace of the action on the screen and the structure of the film as a whole.

Theater musicians also took part in these early efforts to standardize the live, musical part of the film. Their participation in the discussion came primarily by way of two new critical venues. The first was the "music advice column." Film industry magazines and journals had already been encouraging some discussion of music, as exemplified by Richardson's essay. Around 1910, that effort intensified, becoming more specifically musical. That year, for instance, in *Film Index,* one of the main weeklies that serviced the motion picture industry, Clyde Martin launched a column entitled "Playing the Pictures." A few months later, *Moving Picture World* introduced a similar column called "Music for the Pictures," edited by Charles E. Sinn, the seasoned musical director for Chicago's Orpheum Theater, and Martin added an additional column, "Working the Sound Effects." Each week, in response to readers' letters, Martin and Sinn discussed the problems musicians encountered with specific films. Both also usually ended their columns with suggestions or cue sheets for newly released films **(Document 5).** In 1912 Ernst Luz, the musical director for the Loew's Theater chain, launched a column in *Moving Picture News* that, bearing various titles from "Music and the Picture" to "Musical Plots," routinely featured cue sheets but no dialogue with practicing musicians. By the mid-1910s, most of the industry serials, as well as major music journals like *Metronome,* the *Musical Courier,* and the *American Organist,* had weekly or monthly advice columns for the moving picture musician. *Metronome,* a journal devoted to practical musical occupations like wind and dance bands, was one of the first publications focused specifically on music to take notice of film music, as evidenced, for instance, by Frank Edson's long-running column "The Movies," launched in 1916. The addition of regular columns on film in more prestigious publications such as *Musical America* and the *New York Dramatic Mirror,* both of which surfaced around 1917, was a clear sign that film was beginning to be viewed as a serious art form.[25]

In the early 1910s, one of the most frequently discussed advice column topics was the execution of sound effects. In a *Motion Picture World* column from 1911 entitled "With Accompanying Noises," a guest writer, musician Emmett Campbell Hall, reveals not only how complex the musicalization of sound had become but also how troublesome.[26] Part of the problem, Hall acknowledges, stemmed from inattentive musicians. A missed or poorly timed sound could have an unintended comic effect on the appreciation of a film. Other sounds were discovered to be mechanically unreproducible (a fusillade of cannon or gunfire, for instance). A subtler part of the problem, however, lay in the conceptual equality of sounds, with no one sound, whether foreground or background, having priority over another. Likewise, there was no hierarchical distinction between sound and music. In a film with a pastoral setting, for instance, musicians might give equal priority to imitating the sound of the sheep seen in the background as to musically evoking the broken heart of the shepherdess in the foreground. Hall doesn't provide any prescriptive solution, other than to exhort musicians to use caution and taste ("cut out the sound effect or use it with brains" are his final words); nevertheless, his remarks describe the general confusion of sound and music that dominated the early cinema.

Similar observations fuel Louis Reeves Harrison's sublime satire "Jackass Music" (**Document 3**), published in *Moving Picture World* in 1911. Harrison's humorous distillation of the inattentive and unthinking drummer, the fictitious Percy Peashaker, is another reminder of the flat quality of early live sound, and of the importance of properly executed sound effects to a good musical accompaniment. As the bad example of Percy reveals, drummers were making little or no distinction between distant sounds and sounds that were at the center of the film's action. Both were typically executed at the same dynamic level, as if they existed in the same spatial dimension.[27]

Film sound was not the only aspect of the musical accompaniment in need of reform. Harrison's two other "Jackass Music" caricatures, Lily Limpwrist and Freddy Fuzzlehead, address the equally significant problem of repertoire. In both examples, we see a new criterion for selecting or improvising the music for individual scenes taking shape. Whereas before, the tempo of the screen action was the prime musical motivator, here Harrison points to another pressing consideration: the mood or emotion of the characters on the screen. Jackson couches his suggestion in the satire of the emotionally challenged Lily Limpwrist, a pianist oblivious to the appropriate tempo and mood of death, and in the example of Freddy Fuzzlehead, a "funner" pianist who often intentionally counterpoints scenes with unsuitable music or songs featuring contradictory texts.[28] Behind Harrison's artful satire, however, is an innovation of significant proportions: the idea that not just the tempo, but also the emotion and atmosphere of the scene, should drive musical selection.

Not all issues could be discussed adequately in the space of the music advice columns, of course. Some important topics, like the question of appropriate repertoire for the pianist, were dealt with in another new critical venue, the playing manual, a sort of advice column writ large. The earliest playing manuals, in fact, texts like W. Tyacke George's *Playing to Pictures* (1912), George Ahern's *What and How to Play for Pictures* (1913), and Lyle True's *How and What to Play for Motion Pictures* (1914), surfaced around the same time as the columns and featured a similar mix of methodology and analysis of individual films.[29] In general, though, they provided more theory and aesthetics than the advice column, no doubt because they had more space.

As a frequent column contributor to *Moving Picture News,* George Ahern was no doubt aware of cosmopolitan theater practices. But considering that his manual was published in the decidedly unmetropolitan town of Twin Falls, Idaho, his observations about repertoire or "appropriate music" become even more noteworthy. Like Harrison, Ahern urges a closer reading by theater pianists of both the emotions and actions of the characters on the screen. Under the chapter heading "Appropriate Music" (**Document 4**), he also advocates a subtle hierarchy in the selection process. In choosing or improvising music, he says, tempo and sound effects should yield to the more important question of the mood or atmosphere of the scene. Moreover, every mood or event should be recognized musically. This more detailed approach, which involved not only more nuanced musical interpretation but also attention to a greater number of filmic variables, in fact pointed to a minor revolution of sorts in motion picture accompaniment. Musicians were no longer just "accompanying" the film; they were now "illustrating the picture" or "playing the moods," to use two catchphrases that began to surface with greater frequency in the early 1910s. Ahern's suggestions are all in the service of building not just a theater pianist but a new breed of motion picture musician, the musical illustrator.

As for the repertoire of the early cinema, Ahern gives an idea, if only theoretically, of what pianists most likely played. Most film accompaniment, he admits, consisted of a continuous parade of popular "hits." Although he doesn't define what he means by "hits," the sample cue sheets he includes in the manual indicate that he means Tin Pan Alley tunes, Broadway songs, popular dance hall numbers, rags, and folk songs. In 1913, in other words, popular music still dominated the cinema's musical soundscape.

Not all films, however, were treated with "hits," Ahern continues. "Really good pictures," he says, are given "better" music. This category of repertoire was defined not by Mozart and Beethoven, as one might expect, but rather by lesser-known composers of operetta and light classical fare.[30] The works of the classical masters, in fact, appear to have been deliberately avoided. Most contemporary audiences, Ahern warns, are not familiar with Mozart, Beethoven, and Chopin and would not want to hear such "high-brow" selections. "People don't go to a picture show to hear a concert," he concludes, "but to see the pictures accompanied by good music." Not all audiences would have agreed with Ahern, of course, especially his murky category of "better" music. Certainly some classical music was being played, though it is true that even in 1913 the practice was not widespread.[31] Given that the cinema was still attended primarily by lower- or working-class audiences that were much more familiar with popular than classical music, Ahern's assessment about the nature of the music heard in movie theaters makes sense.[32]

In addition to the advice column and the playing manual, a third venue catering to theater musicians emerged in the early 1910s as well. While not critical or theoretical, film music "repertoire collections" and "encyclopedias" were nonetheless an important resource. These books brought together musical scores, classified and organized by mood, tempo, or geography for easy manipulation during improvisation. Gregg A. Frelinger's *Motion Picture Piano Music: Descriptive Music to Fit the Action, Character, or Scene of Moving Pictures* (1909), *The Emerson Moving Picture Music Folio* (1910), the *Orpheum Collection of Moving Picture Music* (1910), *F. B. Haviland's Moving Picture Pianist's Album* (1911), the *Carl Fischer Moving Picture Folio* (1912), and *Gordon's Moving Picture Selections* (1914) were some of the earliest such collections, along with the multivolume *Sam Fox Moving Picture Music* (1913), in which the editor, J. S. Zamecnik, arranged the musical selections according to film topics or musical styles.[33] While most of the repertoire featured in these collections was newly composed, later repertoire collections like Erno Rapee's *Motion Picture Moods for Pianists and Organists* (1924) also contained a good deal of preexisting music by well-known classical composers. These film music collections, helped musicians organize their material by mood and tempo, but they were also useful for film accompanists who wished to acquire repertoire and build their own personal libraries.

The encyclopedias in particular contained little or no discussion of selection practices, but their contents raise an important aesthetic consideration. Most relied heavily on preexisting music. Certainly, new music was being improvised and written specifically for the pictures. Zamecnik, for instance, a composer and theater pianist in Cleveland who originally studied with Dvořák, wrote a number of original pieces, or "moods," for the *Sam Fox* anthology.[34] However, an equal amount of music previously written for entirely different situations was also being recontextualized by film accompanists. Film may have relied on music's preassociations to make itself understood, but it was also, from the very beginning, repurposing existing music and giving it new associations.

By the early 1910s, cinema audiences were being treated to a fairly consistent film music experience, one that integrated the sound of live piano and percussion with visual imagery to closely "illustrating" the actions and emotions of the characters on the screen. In the next decade, this illustrative approach would prove formative in several respects. Popular music and light classics, for instance, continued to be an important part of the musician's repertoire, for comedies and newsreels especially. The practice of using music to highlight the mood on the screen remained dominant as well. However, several of the illustrator's practices were rejected by the next generation of film accompanists, and new, significant changes were proposed, especially in terms instrumentation. This next generation also distanced themselves from the illustrators by expanding the repertoire of the cinema and by labeling their new music the "better" music.

In many respects, the reforms that began to reshape film accompaniment during the 1910s were triggered, as they had been before, by changes that film itself was undergoing. The average length of a narrative film was increasing, for one thing. Before 1910, theaters typically screened a half-hour program of one-reelers, short films that were differentiated (in both production and distribution) by general typology: comedies, dramas, newsreels (weeklies), travelogues, melodramas, slapsticks, and so forth. Between 1910 and 1915, however, the "feature" film—typically meaning a drama from two to eight reels long—began to surface with increasing regularity.[35] Initially, these films were exhibited like touring "roadshow" films— that is, they were given special, stand-alone screenings with an admission cost of between ten and twenty cents instead of a nickel—but by the mid-1910s they were being incorporated into film programs. This exhibition format, with the longer film "featured" among the shorts, provided a new incentive for audiences to patronize the movie theater.

Feature films were distinctive not only because they were longer but also because they were more narratively complex. Many offered treatments of dramatic masterworks from literature or important historical events. Some imported well-known theater actors and actresses from the stage. Sarah Bernhardt, for instance, one of the most famous dramatic actresses of the early twentieth century, starred in several dramatic silent films of the early 1910s. Her appearances, together with the new multireel length of the feature film, gave the film drama in particular a new sense of maturity and artistry.[36]

The seriousness that attended the production of these new feature films also carried over into their exhibition, including their musical accompaniment. In a 1911 "Music for the Pictures" column, for instance, Charles Sinn argues that a similar "elevation" or "improvement" should mark the music as well. The only music suitable for a great actress in a classical drama, in his view, was that of the concert hall and the opera house, the great classical masters such as Wagner, Mendelssohn, Puccini, Tchaikovsky, and Grieg. This new repertoire was not to be used for all the films on the theater program, however. Comedies, slapsticks, and newsreels, for instance, still required the use of popular music. Feature films, according to Sinn, were special not only because they presented serious drama, but also because they should rely on classical concert-hall and operatic literature for the accompanying music.[37]

In another column from 1911 (**Document 5**), Sinn agitates not only for the more dedicated inclusion of classical repertoire, but also for a radically different organizational method. Drawing on the compositional techniques of opera composer Richard Wagner, Sinn proposes that the dramatic musical accompaniment be constructed around the concept of the leitmotif. In his operas, Wagner associated certain characters, ideas, and events on the stage with specific themes or melodies in the orchestra, so that each reiteration of the theme or melody would add to the meaning of the drama by recalling a previous visual context. Using such a technique with motion pictures, Sinn notes, would allow the musical accompaniment to parallel a film's larger narrative structure instead of just illustrating the moods of each scene. Yet, Sinn admits, such a technique would also be virtually impossible to execute without advance screenings of the film, a luxury rarely available to musicians in 1911.[38] Although at this point it is only a suggestion, the idea of improving dramatic film music with compositional techniques that emphasize thematic unity will shortly prove significant.[39]

While Sinn may have been one of the first to advocate "classicizing" film music—importing classical music and the compositional practices of classical composers into film accompaniment—one of the first composers to successfully execute these ideas was Joseph Carl Breil. Breil began his career writing for the theater and later wrote several operas. But by 1914, when D. W. Griffith approached him in 1914 to provide the film accompaniment for his new Civil War epic, Breil had also established a reputation as a film musician on two high-profile European films.[40] His third score, for Griffith's *Birth of a Nation* (1915), was a high-water mark both for him as a composer and for film accompaniment in general. Many of the score's distinctive features were dictated by innovations D. W. Griffith was making to the film proper. At over three hours in length, the twelve-reel *Birth of a Nation* was the longest American film yet made. Breil's accompaniment, which also clocked in at over three hours, was thus equally singular in terms of length. *Birth of a Nation* was also one of the first blockbuster films, playing in many metropolitan theaters for well over a year. As a result, Breil's accompaniment became one of the best-known and most widely circulated orchestral film scores in early film music history.[41]

Although he employed traditional compilation techniques, supporting individual scenes with well-known patriotic and Civil War tunes, for instance, Breil departed from the illustrator's approach in two significant ways. First and most noticeably, his accompaniment drew heavily from the great symphonic and operatic literature. In his compilation, Breil quotes the music of Grieg, Weber, Beethoven, Tchaikovsky, and Wagner, among others.[42] He gave Wagner's famous "Ride of the Valkyries," in fact, not only a new military context but also, considering how widely the film circulated, greater exposure than it had received in American concert halls and opera houses to that date.[43] In this regard, the *Birth of a Nation* accompaniment was an audible challenge to the traditional nickelodeon practice of using popular and light operetta repertoire to illustrate filmic action. It showed that special-event films were special to some degree because of the serious classical masterworks used in their musical accompaniment.

Breil also departed from the old approach by importing the compositional technique of the leitmotif into his score. Although a majority of the score consisted of preexisting music, in the parts Breil composed himself he used Wagnerian-type leitmotifs to refer to individual characters and events.[44] As Breil put it, addressing the specific needs of the dramatic film required awaking to the possibilities of a musical accompaniment that, like the new drama itself, emphasized "uniformity of design and construction."[45] While Breil's score fell short of this goal because of its patchwork use of preexisting music, his attempt represented an innovative emphasis on thematic unity, as opposed to episodic structure, in film accompaniment.

The lofty intentions and inspirations for this new classical and thematic approach were also reflected in the terminology Breil used. Even after acknowledging that he had composed less than half of the music for *Birth of a Nation* himself, Breil preferred to call his specially prepared accompaniments "musical scores." The term itself signaled a shift in the aesthetic sensibilities of film accompaniment. Although Breil may not have been the first to import classical sounds and techniques into film music, even in its day the *Birth of a Nation* score was seen to epitomize these improvements.[46]

This "classicization" project could not have been completed, however, without the help of exhibitors. Musicians like Breil could import classical symphonic repertoire into their "specially prepared scores," but without a specially prepared orchestra to execute them in the theater, the improvement would not have been heard. Although having an orchestra accompany the pictures was by no means unheard of in the mid-1910s, it was also not standard.[47] In most cities, the pianist still held sway, although the organ, too, was beginning to find its way into movie houses. With the inclusion of more classical repertoire and techniques, however, came the move to make the orchestra the main purveyor of cinema music. As an interview in *Moving Picture World* entitled "The Art of the Exhibition" **(Document 6)** suggests, this crusade was the territory of one exhibitor in particular, S. L. Rothapfel. Rothapfel was manager of the Strand Theater in New York City, one of the first movie theaters to employ a full-time orchestra to accompany the pictures instead of a pianist.[48]

The new dramatic epic not only required more serious, classical music, but it required the classical symphonic orchestra to play that music. Although Rothapfel was not the first to expand the instrumentation of film music beyond pianos and drummers, previous "orchestras" were chamber sized, consisting, for the most part, of two to twelve instruments.[49] Rothapfel was one of the first metropolitan movie palace managers to assemble a concert-sized, forty-piece orchestra to play for films. This instrumentation allowed movie theaters to feature specially prepared scores and more of the classical symphonic or operatic literature than before. Rothapfel's mission to "symphonicize" the film experience, to change the standard instrumentation of film music from piano to orchestra, addressed the practical aspects of the "better music" or "classical music" project. His mission to make theater music orchestral even led to a structural innovation, the symphonic prelude or orchestral overture, used to introduce the feature film.

This push to reform and elevate film accompaniment included efforts to provide films with an entirely original, often symphonic score. Much as serious actors and actresses were imported from the theater into film, directors and exhibitors sought to lend an air of sophistication to the musical accompaniment by importing well-known classically trained composers. In 1908, the great French composer Camille Saint-Saëns composed an original score for the film *L'assassinat du duc de Guise,* produced by an esteemed group of French theater actors. The film itself proved unsuccessful, however, so Saint-Saëns's efforts went fairly unnoticed. Over the next several years, the practice of composing entirely original scores was pursued only intermittently, and then primarily with big-budget historical or religious films. In 1912–13, for instance, productions of *Cleopatra, The Life of John Bunyan, The Prisoner of Zenda, Hiawatha,* and *Quo Vadis* were all advertised as having original special scores. The 1913–14 season included more historical epics, but only a few of these "special scores," by composer Manuel Klein, music director at the New York Hippodrome, and one by George Colburn, are known to survive.[50] Between 1911 and 1913, the Kalem film company also tried distributing some of its dramatic films with original scores by composer Walter Cleveland Simon, but, due to time constraints and the variations in individual theater orchestras, the effort was soon abandoned.[51]

In 1916, the highly regarded operetta composer Victor Herbert attempted to write an original score for *The Fall of a Nation*. Music expressly written for a specific picture, Herbert argued, would solve the problems of the "patchwork character" of current film accompaniment. "When the orchestra plays bits of 'Faust,' or 'Tannhäuser,' or 'Carmen' or 'Traviata,' the hearing of the music flashes pictures from those operas on the minds of the spectators, and attention is distracted from the characters in the [film] story."[52] Preexisting popular and classical music came loaded with extramusical associations, and while some compilers were skillful at manipulating those associations to good effect, some types of music—those with texts in particular, such as songs and arias—were inherently problematic. New or original music, Herbert asserted, would circumvent these problems. In the end, Herbert, hampered by a constantly changing script and last-minute editing, did not complete the score, but his experiment laid important groundwork for further attempts at original scoring in the late 1920s.[53]

While the compilation method remained the most practical solution for accompaniment in the teens, not all voices in this period sang its praises. Theater organist Blanche Greenland, for one, approached the practice with some skepticism. In a 1916 article titled "Faking in Movie Music Corrupting Public Taste," Greenland describes how the new and admirable practice of using "better" or classical music was being compromised by the widespread practice of arranging. "Do we realize," she asks, "that a juggernaut is bearing down upon the public of our moving picture theaters? Emblazoned over the front is its name, 'Faking.'" Faking, she continues, "is the deliberate mutilation of harmony by a performer with the intention of deceiving the ear of the listener. For instance, in such well-worn melodies as Rubinstein's 'Melody in F,' Mendelssohn's 'Spring Song,' and Dvořák's 'Humoresque,' horrid modulations are substituted, absurd inventions inserted, wrong chords introduced, producing something entirely wrong, which leaves its effect on the listener. . . . It is a vicious mingling of wrong combinations of notes perpetrated by an unlearned performer."[54] Greenland's concern was not that the use of classical music would fail to elevate film, but that the butchering of great music by the ubiquitous and unskilled small-town musician was cheapening classical music. Instead of edifying public musical taste, the movies were corrupting it with sloppy, simplified arrangements of concert-hall classics.

Greenland was not alone in her assessment of film's "better music" project. Concerns about the use of the classical repertoire surfaced frequently in the critical literature of the time. Some doubted that any films, dramatic or otherwise, were worthy of Bach, Beethoven, and Chopin. "There have been relatively few subjects shown on the screen which call for classical accompaniment," pronounced the author of one playing manual, the *Stolley-McGill Ten Lesson Course in Moving Picture Playing* (1916). Some saw the coming of movies as representing the destruction of serious, concert-hall literature.

Ultimately, what these repertoire concerns really reveal is how idiosyncratic film music accompaniment was in the mid-1910s. The use of the classical repertoire and its close synchronization to film was still only a wish and not a fact. Because Breil's, Griffith's, Herbert's, and Sinn's innovations continued to share space with the less sophisticated practices of small-town illustrators and funners, their suggestions would not be fully realized until the 1920s, the so-called golden age of silent film music.

If the 1910s was a transition period that brought a new aesthetic to film accompaniment, the decade that followed saw those innovations made general practice by a new generation of reformers. By the 1920s, the use of classical music and thematic compositional techniques and the replacement of the pianist by a classical orchestra were becoming quite standard. As Rick Altman has pointed out, as the orchestra came increasingly to substitute for the piano, film music began to focus more and more on published scores and classical repertoire.[55] The intensification of this classical campaign is reflected in a quartet of publications by theater musicians from the mid-1920s (**Documents 7–9 and 11**) that document the successful transition from the improvised piano accompaniment of the nickelodeon era to specially prepared, concert hall–inspired compilation scores.

As before, developments in the parameters of the musical accompaniment were influenced by changes happening in film production and exhibition. Edith Lang and George West's *Musical Accompaniment of Moving Pictures* (1920) and Erno Rapee's *Encyclopaedia of Music for Pictures* (1925) show the film program, especially as it was practiced in large metropolitan movie palaces, to have developed significantly since the teens, particularly in terms of organization. Lang and West were Boston theater organists, and Rapee was one of the most prominent New York city movie palace conductors, working first at the Rivoli and Rialto Theaters, then, from 1920 to 1923, at the five-thousand-seat Capitol Theater with its 77-member orchestra.[56] Together their texts reflect much of the range of exhibition practices that were being utilized at movie theaters around the country, with Lang and West focusing on the challenges facing the theater organist, while Rapee describes the variety of duties assumed by the music director or conductor of a large movie palace orchestra.

As part II of Lang and West's *Musical Accompaniment of Moving Pictures,* "Musical Interpretation" (**Document 7**), outlines, by 1920 an evening's program routinely consisted of a variety of short films—a comedy, a scenic, a newsreel, a documentary or educational film, and a longer feature film, typically a drama. Each type of film had a different structure—narrative versus nonnarrative, say— requiring different organizational approaches, such as thematic versus nonthematic. Each film genre, as Lang and West point out, also had different repertoire requirements. Newsreels and comedies, for instance, typically allowed inclusion of popular music or texted music. Scenics or travelogues, and newsreels to a certain extent, often relied on ethnically coded music, repertoire that consumed a large portion of the published anthologies of film music. Classical selections and newly composed music were reserved for dramas or feature films.

As Lang and West's manual reveals, anticipating the needs not just of individual films but of entire film programs was an essential aspect of film accompaniment.[57] The musical needs of the film program as a whole steer Rapee's *Encyclopaedia of Music for Pictures* as well, which devotes complete chapters to the scenic (chapter 3), the newsreel (chapter 4), and the comedy (chapter 7), for example. From the early 1910s, these shorter films were joined in the film program by the dramatic film, which was typically the longest entry and the most substantial in terms of content and budget. As the dramatic film evolved into the feature film, it demanded more separation from the rest of the film program. According to the discussion of the feature film in the section of Lang and West's manual entitled "Musical Interpretation," typically, if not uniformly, the feature film was set apart by means of a special thematic treatment, resulting in a leitmotif compilation score that required some level of rehearsal. But as Rapee points out in his chapter on the feature film **(Document 9),** another means of providing emphasis, especially in the deluxe movie palaces that maintained in-house orchestras, singers, and even dance companies, was through the musical prologue.

In his chapter entitled "Vocal or Dance Artists" **(Document 9),** Rapee further describes how a musical performance can prepare the audience for the feature film. Many theaters, he observes, have adopted the practice of employing "vocal or dance artists to build prologues to the feature film." In building these prologues, which are ordinarily inserted between the newsreel or scenic and the featured dramatic film, Rapee advises: "The question as to whether a vocal or dance prologue should be used for any particular picture depends largely upon the atmosphere and the main characters of your picture."

When using music to set off, or "feature," the long dramatic film at the center of the program, Rapee notes, lighting and sets can be employed as enhancement— for example, to create special effects such as "rain, snow, floods, waterfalls, clouds, moon," effects that are central to the atmosphere or narrative of the feature film. The fact that this essentially nonmusical task fell to the music director or conductor, which explains why Rapee included it in his manual on film music, is testimony to the importance of live musical performance in the film program by the early 1920s. Indeed, people now went to the movie theater not just for films but to hear live music as well. Most of the film listings in the weekly trade journals described not just which films were playing at which theaters in major cities around the country, but also what prelude, postlude, and interstitial music was being offered in between the films. In most metropolitan cities, in fact, the cinema was second only to the symphony and the opera in terms of articulating significant musical repertoire.[58]

Like the special-event films and historical and religious dramas of the teens, the feature film, Rapee states plainly in his manual, needed "better" music. Contradicting Ahern, who twelve years earlier was sure his patrons would not tolerate concert-hall fare, even for dramatic films, Rapee, in a chapter entitled "The Missionary of Good Music and the Motion Picture Theatre" (Document 9), asserts exactly the opposite. The works of the classical masters should form the mainstay of the film accompanist's repertoire. Rapee takes this idea a step further, speaking not just of the importance of including classical repertoire but of a "movement for better music" in film accompaniment in general.

Opera had long been a part of silent film, but with the growing standardization of the orchestra as the primary musical instrument of the movie theater came greater use of the symphonic repertoire. By the 1920s, the orchestral overtures, symphonies, and symphonic works of Beethoven, Tchaikovsky, Schubert, Schumann, Dvořák, Grieg, Liszt, Rimsky-Korsakov, Mendelssohn, MacDowell, Verdi, Wagner, Gounod, Massenet, Puccini, Offenbach, and von Suppé, among many others, were routinely heard not just in program overtures and interludes but within film accompaniments themselves. Rapee himself loudly trumpeted the first performances of Richard Strauss's complex orchestral tone poems *Till Eulenspiegel*, in 1921, and *Ein Heldenleben*, in 1922, when they were presented as "overtures" on the movie theater musical program. Just as significant, but garnering less attention, was Rapee's use of selections from Strauss and Debussy tone poems as well as modernist fare from Stravinsky and Schoenberg in the compilation score for the great German expressionist film *The Cabinet of Dr. Caligari* at the Capitol Theater in 1921.[59]

In their manual, Lang and West describe a shift in the primary repertoire of the film musician, especially for the feature film. Audiences now, they note in their chapter entitled "Mental Alertness," are "capable of much more education and cultivation than they are generally given credit for," a process that includes classical music, a new and "inexhaustible treasure trove for all who seek diligently and patiently."[60] In his 1921 manual *Musical Presentation of Motion Pictures* (the longest and least technical of the three discussed here), George Beynon, a well-known accompanist and compiler, puts it another way, saying that classical music should be used to counteract the cinema's long and close relationship with popular or, as he calls it, "cheap" music. In 1915, Beynon had been part of an early experiment on the part of movie producers and music publishers to standardize film accompaniment by providing complete specially prepared scores through the film exchange service.[61] His manual was a further effort, not just toward standardization, but also toward improvement of musical accompaniment.

As all three of these manuals reveal, unlike the nickelodeons that a decade earlier were featuring primarily light and popular selections, the picture palaces of the 1920s were serving up a steady diet of operatic and symphonic literature, especially for the long dramatic features. Popular music—Tin Pan Alley, Broadway songs, early jazz, ragtime, and folk music—was still heard in the movie theater, but it had become almost exclusively the domain of the shorter, non-featured parts of the program, the comedies, scenics, and newsreels, and so received less air time than classical music. Beynon, in his chapter entitled "Proper Presentation of Pictures: Songs as Themes" **(Document 8),** in fact cautions against excessive use of popular or texted music, while noting something new: the value of an original theme to accompany the main hero or heroine of the feature.

In addition to changing the standard repertoire of the compilation score, the general move to "classicize" and reform film accompaniment was affecting the structure of the specially prepared score. Film accompanists were still choosing their musical selections based on the emotions and actions of the characters on the screen, but now they were relying on specific musical themes or melodies to convey key information. "The kernel of the musical illustration of a picture is the *main theme*," Lang and West state in their manual. "This should be typical in mood or character of the hero or heroine. . . . [It] should be announced at the introduction . . . [and it should] be emphasized a at the first appearance of the person with whom it is linked."[62] Beynon devotes three chapters of his manual to thematization of the score. In "Proper Presentation of Pictures: The Theme and How to Use it" **(Document 8),** Beynon not only discusses ways of implementing a thematic approach, but he also acknowledges the aesthetic implications of doing so. A thematic approach to film accompaniment does more than underscore mood and tempo, he asserts; it reinforces narrative unity and structure as well. A repeated melody allows the images on the screen to be interpreted by recalling previous imagery.

The systematic deployment of musical themes in film accompaniment was not a new idea. As early as 1911, Clarence Sinn, for one, had encouraged theater musicians to use Wagnerian leitmotifs to create a sense of film unity (see **Document 5**). By the 1920s, what he could only theorize about was being executed on a regular basis. While neither Beynon nor Lang and West mention Wagner in this regard, they do describe the deployment of themes as part of a larger improvement project. In a section of their manual entitled "Thematic Development," Lang and West note that thematically coherent scores are the result of film accompaniment having imported the models of classical "symphonies and sonatas." For Beynon, the ramifications of this new technique are even bigger. In his view, the "proper presentation of pictures" involved not just conveying individual moods or tempos through compiled snatches of music; rather, it required a single composition that brought together both thematic and "incidental" music to create a structured viewing experience.

Executing the new thematic score was possible only with better synchronization techniques and tools, which the playing manual authors make frequent
mention of, Beynon especially. In the initial decades of the silent film, musicians
had addressed synchronization informally, usually through advice columns in
trade publications. Already in the early teens, "musical suggestions"—alternately
called "plots," "synopses," or "musical programs"—for selected weekly films were
commonly included at the end of these columns, tied to specific tempo markings.
Starting in the mid to late teens, the "music" columns in film journals like *Moving
Picture World* and *Motion Picture News,* and the "photoplaying" or "movies" columns in music journals like the *American Organist* and *Metronome,* began to
include not just summaries of titles and actions with corresponding repertoire
selections, but also stopwatch timings, down to the quarter-minute. In the mid-
teens, "stand–alone cue sheets" issued by studios as part of their film exchange
service also began to surface. Although the musician Max Winkler did not invent the cue sheet as he claimed, the cue sheets he began producing for Universal
in 1915 were some of the earliest produced independent of a trade journal column.[63] Winkler, who was eventually contracted by Paramount and Bluebird studios to make cue sheets for their films, was quickly joined by Beynon, who prepared cue sheets for the films made by the Famous Players, Lasky, and Morosco
studios, and S. M. Berg, who for worked for the Metro, Vitagraph, World, Selznick, and Triangle studios.

These studio-produced or film exchange cue sheets were significant, but because their repertoire selections were often guided by financial arrangements the
compilers made with music publishing companies, it was not until the early 1920s
and the advent of the commercial cue sheet service that cue sheets became a common part of film music accompaniment. Each service was launched with great
fanfare and announcements of which celebrity conductors and composers had
been secured to prepare the service's cue sheets. These included many of the most
prominent New York movie palace music directors and conductors of the 1920s,
Rapee, Rothapfel, and Hugo Riesenfeld among them, as well as popular advice
columnists such as Ernst Luz, James Bradford, J. C. Zamencik, Edward Kilyeni,
and Carli Elinor and veteran cue sheet makers Winkler, Berg, and Beynon.

The most successful of the independent commercial services was Cameo Music Service Corporation. Cameo had a distinctive patented style developed by
M. J. Mintz, the general music editor of the service. Mintz's "Thematic Music
Cue Sheet" format included not only stopwatch timings, but also a musical in-
cipit (usually ten to twenty measures long) of the melody of each suggestion.
Document 10 presents a good example of this popular style, in the first page of
the cue sheet James Bradford prepared for Cameo for the 1924 hit film *The Thief
of Bagdad.* This format also included special "Notes" to the performer that covered atypical structural requirements—instructions to repeat a section of the

melody, for example, or to play a tune arhythmically to suggest "drunkenness," or prompting a specific sound effect. Cameo also issued entirely verbal cue sheets too, as shown in the second example in **Document 10,** the cue sheet for the 1926 film *Dame Chance*. Although this cue sheet accomplishes the same thing structurally as the first one, its non-incipit format made room for a concern that became increasingly important in the preparation of cue sheets: the use of taxable or nontaxable musical repertoire—the subject of **Document 15.**[64]

Despite the increased accuracy of cue sheets, there remained one significant impediment to true synchrony, something that was beyond the control of the musician. As Beynon observes in chapter 12 of his manual, "Synchrony" (**Document 8),** the science of timings was still plagued by variations both in the speed of the film and in the "load," or electrical current, being supplied to the projector. As long as those two features remained irregular, so did film accompaniment. While a solution to this problem eluded musicians and theorists alike, the fact that such technical matters were being discussed was tacit acknowledgment of how sophisticated the improvement project had become.

Synchronization was also a concern of Rapee's. Although he does not address the issue in terms of the electrical current running the projector, he does point out how variations in the film's projection speed can affect the structure of the prepared musical accompaniment. Achieving a consistent and predetermined feet-per-minute ratio on film projectors, he notes in the chapter of his manual titled "Projection" (**Document 9),** is crucial to being able to synchronize the musical accompaniment with the film.

While much of their effort was devoted to elevating film accompaniment through the importation of classical repertoire and compositional techniques, some of the manualists of the 1920s found room to address the difficult musical problem of film sound. Lang and West's discussion of the "unit" organ is noteworthy in this regard. In the 1920s, in addition to the standard sound of an orchestra, theaters began to feature "unit" organs, an electric keyboard instrument made specifically for motion picture accompaniment.[65] As outlined in "Special Effects and How to Produce Them" (**Document 7),** part of the growing appeal of these enormous electronic organs, aside from their volume, was the wide range of special sound effects they could produce. Most unit organs had a variety of stops that could imitate everything from clock chimes, train whistles, and car horns to babies crying, dogs barking, and hurricanes raging. While traditional "traps" and sound effect devices were still being used, theaters big and small now favored the unit organ over the piano because it consolidated sound and music in a single instrument.

As the equipment for sound production became more sophisticated, however, the concept of sound itself saw an important refinement. Whereas the film "funners" and "jackass" illustrators of the previous generation had imitated all sounds equally, embedded in Lang and West's discussion of the unit organ is a tacit acknowledgment of foreground and background sound. Through the use of dynamics and selective silence, theater musicians were now adding a consideration of distance and perspective into their definition of sound. Still, a practical or even theoretical distinction between film sound and film music was not yet available. Like most of their contemporaries and predecessors, Lang and West, too, describe a fundamental conceptual equality between sound and music in the theater.

One final improvement to the film program, especially as it was practiced at the major metropolitan movie palaces, resulted directly from improvement and expansion of the theater orchestra. Part of what made a movie palace a "palace" or "deluxe" was that it maintained a full-time orchestra, in addition to employing a full-time house organist. Although, as Rapee acknowledges in his chapter titled "How to Organize and Rehearse an Orchestra" **(Document 9),** movie theaters around the country were still using a variety of instrumentations and ensembles, increasingly the New York City movie palace model, exemplified by the Capitol, Rivoli and Rialto theaters, with their orchestras of sixty pieces or more—differing from a "symphony" orchestra only in the size of the string section—was what most metropolitan theaters aspired to.[66] Moreover, the movie theater's symphonic orchestra was being allowed to flex its muscle more, not just in terms of accompanying the feature film or preparing the feature film with a musical prologue, but in preparing the entire film program with a specifically musical number: the overture. As Rapee suggests again in his discussion of this device (Document **9),** the movie theater by the mid-1920s was rivaling the symphony hall and the opera house as a venue for serious musical performances.[67]

As the first-generation reformers had foreseen, the "better music" or classicization effort was supported not just by changes in the sound, construction, and content of the specially prepared score, but also by developments in a number of exhibition and production practices. Although he never wrote a handbook or playing manual, Hugo Riesenfeld played a significant part in shaping the sound of the 1920s cinema. Born in Vienna and trained as a violinist, pianist, and composer at the Vienna Conservatory of Music, the famed music director brought the great German symphonic tradition with him to New York's best movie houses. Over the course of his career, Riesenfeld was the musical director of three of the most prestigious movie palaces—the Rialto, Rivoli, and Criterion theaters—and he was renowned for his specially prepared scores for feature films.[68] In many ways, Riesenfeld continued the discussion begun a decade earlier by S. L. Rothapfel, for he, too, was interested not only in creating complex thematic scores that drew primarily from the "better," classical music repertoire, but also in having those scores performed by large, sixty- to eighty-piece symphony orchestras that rivaled in skill the most prestigious concert-hall orchestras in the country.

By 1925, Riesenfeld and music directors like him at "deluxe" movie palaces in major metropolitan areas had access to significant exhibition resources. As his article "Music and Motion Pictures" **(Document 11)** outlines, the movie palaces had enormous music libraries, repertoire collections that were being continually refreshed with new music from an international array of publishers. Central to the accumulation of repertoire was the music librarian and a library staff who categorized new and existing music according to tempo, style, or form. If the maintenance of repertoire required a large staff, so did the compilation of each film score. Music directors at the deluxe palaces were no longer solitary compilers and composers, but coordinators of teams of supernumeraries—timers, copyists, arrangers, rehearsal conductors—who contributed to the score creation process. The division of labor that Riesenfeld describes, in fact, is remarkably similar to the Hollywood studio system that would emerge less than a decade later.

Riesenfeld also describes the improved synchronization practices that were making the complex, symphonic compilation scores possible. Where previously music directors had little time and opportunity to prescreen a film, Riesenfeld constructed scores based on multiple screenings of each film. The use of the stopwatch was still key in integrating live music with mechanized images, but what really allowed the specially prepared score to become commonplace in the 1920s was the ability of the music director to see a film several times in advance and to analyze it, stopping and replaying it at will. At Riesenfeld points out, the compilation formula had also progressed to a position where directors had several days to rehearse and refine their scores.

A few other matters of note in Riesenfeld's essay not only reflect the state of the mature compilation score, but describe the state of new music in the late 1920s as well. The author's passing reference to jazz—"for the time being jazz predominates in our film theatres"—reflects both the country's general obsession with the new style of popular music and the widespread view that jazz was not an artistic form of music. For Riesenfeld, jazz was not only of lesser quality, but also ephemeral. "It is only a matter of time," he observes, "before the wheel of public favor again turns, bringing the better type of music to the foreground again." He leaves little room for guessing at what "better" still means to compilers and accompanists, noting that "a jazz selection is old and discarded in a single season. A Beethoven overture or Chopin nocturne is eternally new."

Riesenfeld also describes the establishment of not just "better" repertoire, but better performers on the film theater's musical program. He and the other directors at the New York movie palaces now routinely engaged the services of renowned concert-hall soloists, such as pianists Jan Paderewski and Joseph Hoffman, violinists Sascha Jacobson and Efrem Zimbalist, and conductor-composers Percy Grainger and John Philip Sousa, to play during the interludes between films.

The addition of esteemed concert-hall performers added another measure of seriousness and artistry to the pursuit of music for film. This improvement went hand in hand with the general increase in both skill and pay of the orchestral musicians and organists working in the movie theaters' pits. That the very existence of the pit musician might shortly be in peril is not hinted at in Riesenfeld's discussion. In fact, he perceives the new and experimental sound film, mentioned briefly near the end of the essay, not as a threat to live film music practices but instead as a possible solution for rural communities with less sophisticated musical programs and accompaniment. Although "it is not probable that the Vitaphone will ever entirely replace the orchestra," Riesenfeld concludes, it does make possible "the finest musical accompaniment . . . where there is no orchestra available."

Something that remains unavailable in either the small-town or the deluxe cosmopolitan theater, even in the golden age of silent accompaniment, Riesenfeld notes, is the newly composed score, due to both compositional time constraints and silent film music's fundamental ephemerality. Composers in the late 1920s would "rather starve," he asserts, "with the hope of creating a great symphony that will live through the ages, than grow fat off the proceeds of an excellent but short-lived film score."

That is not to say that original scores were not being written. Several of the greatest films of this period did indeed have original scores, many by emerging concert-hall composers. European directors seemed particularly interested in testing the possibilities of collaborating with composers. In France, director Abel Gance commissioned several young composers to create scores for his films: Darius Milhaud wrote the music for *La roue* in 1923 and Arthur Honegger composed a score for his epic *Napoléon* in 1927.[69] Established eccentric Erik Satie wrote an original score for the short avant-garde film *Entr'acte,* directed by René Clair, which premiered as the interlude in Francis Picabia's 1924 ballet *Relâche.* The daring and "noisy" American composer George Antheil, working in Paris, wrote original music to accompany the 1924 French surrealist film *Ballet mécanique,* by Fernand Léger.[70] Perhaps the most successful original score from the period was one that German composer Edmund Meisel produced for Soviet director Sergei Eisenstein's 1926 masterpiece *Battleship Potemkin.* Meisel's thematic, orchestral score was so dissonant and compelling in the last reel that it was banned in parts of Germany and England for fear that it, even more than the images of revolution in the film, would incite the audience to riot.[71] A young Dmitri Shostakovich, who would go on to write more than forty film scores throughout his career, composed his first score in 1929 for the Russian silent film *New Babylon.*[72]

While filmmakers in Europe and Russia tentatively explored the possibilities of the original score, few U.S. directors made similar attempts. Other than actor Douglas Fairbanks, who entrusted several of his silent blockbusters—*The Thief of*

Bagdad (1924) and *The Black Pirate* (1926), for instance—to the young American composer Mortimer Wilson, silent film music production in the United States focused primarily on the compilation not the original score.[73] Several impediments still stood in the way of the original score becoming standard practice. A general lack of time was arguably the most problematic. Providing music for a three-hour epic was equivalent to writing an opera, yet film composers were usually given several weeks at most to complete their work. Often the director compounded the problem by editing the film literally moments before its exhibition, leaving the composer little or no time to make adjustments to the score. Thus Herbert's experiences and frustrations with *The Fall of a Nation* (1916) continued to be revisited—literally, in fact, in the case of Honegger's score for Gance's *Napoléon* a decade later.

Although the reform efforts to improve or "classicize" film music failed to produce consistent collaborations with concert-hall composers, they did succeed in standardizing the use of classical music in actual film production. Although accounts vary as to when the practice was started, music—particularly classical music—was frequently played on the set during film production.[74] On-set music helped supply emotional inspiration for the actors as they filmed, and the public announcement of actors' on-set musical preferences, suggestive of their familiarity with the classical repertoire, also enhanced their reputations.[75]

The embrace of "better" music was also encouraged by copyright laws, which dogged the use of new music in the movie theater. Through the 1910s, composers, especially popular song composers, became increasingly aware that their music was being used in film accompaniments without their permission and without royalties being paid. Several composers attempted to address this problem, most visibly and ultimately most successfully in a legal action that took place in 1917. That year Victor Herbert served a lawsuit against theaters owners, arguing not only that original film music was worthy of copyright protection, but that royalties should be paid when *any* copyrighted music was performed in movie theaters. This suit had consequences even before it was settled. Beginning in the early 1920s, the entire body of working film music literature began to be separated into two categories: copyrighted (and taxable) and noncopyrighted (or free) music. Since the majority of the classical literature fell under the public domain and was as a result nontaxable and free to use, film accompanists and music directors acknowledged including classical music more frequently in their compilations.[76]

The greater inclusion of classical music in film music was no doubt also stimulated by another lawsuit, this one from 1924. As **Document 12,** a *New York Times* article titled "Publishers Win Movie Music Suit," recounts, songwriter Irving Berlin and nine others successfully sued theater owners for compensation for all the air time their popular tunes had been getting free of charge. Although enforcing copyright protection through bans and taxes was difficult, if not impossible, especially in small-town theaters, these court cases no doubt encouraged composers to use less disputed repertoire. In any case, the neat concurrence of this string of litiga- tions and the rise in popularity of the classical repertoire in the movie theater is striking.[77]

The development of film between 1896 and 1926 was attended by great variety and experimentation. Within a short period of time, film had developed a broad range of genres and styles—from newsreels to narrative masterpieces, commer- cial advertisements to scenic travelogues, serious educational films to silly car- toons, low comedies to high drama, surreal montages to moralizing melodramas, magical tricks to unadorned realism, as well as a range of temporal lengths, from ninety-second *actualités* to fifteen-reel historical epics. The visual vocabulary and structure of silent film, from the experimentation of the nickelodeons in the 1910s to the standardization of the movie palaces in the 1920s, are well studied, primarily because it is the visual portion of these films that has survived intact. Film image-tracks can, with variations in projection speed aside, be viewed largely as they were originally intended to be. The same cannot be said of the sound that accompanied those images. The evolution of silent film sound and music is less well understood in large part because sound was an aspect of the film that was not mechanized. Music in the silent film, rather than being a fixed production element, was an ephemeral exhibition practice, and in many ways it was valued for its very lack of mechanization, for its ability to be living, flexible, and personal. Music and sound made film not only realistic but also artistic.

The documents in this section reinforce the centrality of this missing, or "silent," unmechanized part of early film. Just as directors experimented with and established visual standards for a range of film genres and lengths, musicians worked to establish standards for the structure, synchronization, and sound of film music. They experimented with a variety of repertoire—the allusive proper- ties of popular music and texted songs, and the less specific emotional qualities supplied by newly composed music. They explored instrumentation, anywhere from single upright pianos to eighty-piece orchestras. They tested the filmic effect of different tempos and meters on the perceived speed of moving images, and the way musical structure enhanced film structure and continuity. A stylistic change or abrupt musical silence could momentarily disrupt or emphasize the visual im- agery; a single musical selection could have a suturing effect, smoothing over a visual cut or scene change. Similarly, a recurring musical theme could bring large- scale continuity to familiar characters in unfamiliar scenes. Silent film musicians even experimented with turning music into ambient sound and mechanical noise.

That the parameters for most of these elements of film sound were tested and standardized to a very high degree by the 1920s reveals just how formative this earliest period was to the history of film and film music. In fact, many of the techniques and practices pioneered by the musicians of the golden age of silent film music will be revisited by future composers, and some will continue virtually uninterrupted. Musicians like Max Steiner simply transferred many aspects of the mature compilation score—its thematic construction especially—to the sound film score. In many ways, Steiner's "wall-to-wall music" model of the early Hollywood score was a literal extension of the specially prepared orchestral scores of the silent period. Other silent music practices, however, like the rendering of sound effects, will be severely limited (to occasional mimicry or "mickey-mousing") and transferred to the newly created department of film sound. The revolution that ends the silent period will not just be the technical innovation of including dialogue; it will include as well the separation of film sound from film music, and of composers from sound engineers. This separation will also lead to a redefinition of the placement of music in film. Although the classic Hollywood score will be sonically and structurally familiar, its evolving status as an "underscore" defines an entirely new concept of filmic space, one that is not visualized. Therein lies one of the clearest indications that the musical world of the silent film has been left behind.

NOTES

1. A full account of the complex history of pre-film experiments can be found in C. W. Ceram, *Archeology of the Cinema,* trans. Richard Winston (New York: Harcourt, Brace and World, [1965]).

2. For a good general history of both the *cinématographe* and the Lumière brothers' participation in the evolution of the early French cinema, see Roy Armes, *French Cinema* (London: Secker & Warburg, 1985), pp. 7–18; and also Richard Abel, *The Ciné Goes to Town: French Cinema, 1896–1914* (Berkeley: University of California Press, 1994), pp. 9–19.

3. Ceram, *Archeology of the Cinema,* pl. 224.

4. The Lumières saw their *actualités* primarily as advertisement for the photographic equipment—film, cameras, projection devices—they manufactured and sold. It was their contemporaries Georges Méliès and Léon Gaumont who first recognized the narrative potential of film to entertain and tell stories. See Armes, *French Cinema,* pp. 9–11.

5. Roger Manvel and John Huntley, *The Technique of Film Music* (London: Hastings House, 1957), p. 21. Rick Altman provides a detailed discussion of the exhibition of the Lumière films in the United States, and while both he and Martin Miller Marks mention premieres of the Lumière brothers' films, neither mentions Maravel. See Altman, *Silent Film Sound* (New York: Columbia University Press, 2004), pp. 83–87; and Martin Miller Marks, *Music and the Silent Film: Contexts and Case Studies, 1895–1924* (New York: Oxford University Press, 1997), p. 30.

6. See Ceram, *Archeology of the Cinema,* plate 228.

7. Born in Naples, Wenzel was music director for the Empire Theater of Varieties from 1889 to 1920. Before the theater showed film, Wenzel wrote music for many ballets that were staged there. See Jeffrey Richards, *Imperialism and Music: Britain, 1976–1953* (Manchester: Manchester University Press, 2002), pp. 258–60; and Marks, *Music and the Silent Film,* pp. 48–50.

8. Marks, *Music and the Silent Film,* pp. 31–48. Although Skladanowsky used a different technology than that of the Lumières to project his films, he offered similar programs of short films,

primarily documentaries, each with a different musical accompaniment. For a description of the music for one of Skladanowsky's programs, see ibid., p. 34.

9. Edison's Vitascope and his place in the history of the American cinema are described in detail by Charles Musser in *The Emergence of Cinema: The American Screen to 1907* (Berkeley: University of California Press, 1994), pp. 109–32.

10. Ibid, pp. 116, 178.

11. George W. Beynon, *Musical Presentation of Motion Pictures* (New York: Schirmer, 1921), part II: "The Evolution of Picture Music," pp. 3, 4.

12. See Rick Altman, "The Silence of the Silents," *Musical Quarterly* 80, no. 4 (1996): 648–718. Since Altman first launched his argument, others have supported the thesis that "silence" was indeed one of the possible accompaniments that early cinema received. See Francois Jost, "The Voices of Silence," and Stephen Bottomore, "The Story of Percy Peashaker: Debates about Sound Effects in Early Cinema," in *The Sounds of Early Cinema*, ed. Richard Abel and Rick Altman (Bloomington: Indiana University Press, 2001), pp. 48–56 and 129–42.

13. Musser, *Emergence of Cinema*, p. 178. In the very earliest stages of film history, Musser points out, attempts were made to automate or mechanize sound and music as well. This led first to the unsuccessful practice of playing phonographs of recorded sounds and using mechanical player pianos for film accompaniment. Since coordination between three separate machines was difficult, if not impossible, the practice (and the dream of full synchronization) was quickly abandoned in favor of a more flexible accompaniment of live music and sound. One part of this impulse to automate sound, however, survived in the sound-effects "machines," which were not only mechanical but also, it was hoped, more realistic than musicalized sound.

14. For a detailed history of the rise of the nickelodeon in early cinema exhibition, see Musser, *Emergence of Cinema*, pp. 417–447. See also Eileen Bowser, *The Transformation of Cinema, 1907–1915* (Berkeley: University of California Press, 1990), pp. 1–20.

15. Musser, *Emergence of Cinema*, pp. 335–369. Musser discusses in detail the transition to "story" films that a number of production companies made between 1903 and 1904.

16. Bowser, *Transformation of Cinema*, pp. 56.

17. Ibid., p. 21–36.

18. Altman, *Silent Film Sound*, pp. 133–55.

19. Ibid., pp. 203–26. See also Bottomore, "Story of Percy Peashaker."

20. As Musser observes, early nickelodeon exchange statistics suggest that the program was changed anywhere from two to three times a week (*Emergence of Cinema*, p. 450). According to Bowser, "While exhibitors in 1907 might run films made at any date, audiences were so motion-picture crazy that they were going repeatedly and wanted new subjects all the time. Films, like vegetables, were a perishable product" (*Transformation of Cinema*, pp. 21–22).

21. Some historians have suggested that early sound was, in fact, distinct from music, that there was a practical or functional division between musicians and sound effects personnel. Starting around 1910 in *Moving Picture World*, for instance, music and sound effects were treated in separate advice columns. See Tim Anderson, "Reforming 'Jackass Music': The Problematic Aesthetics of Early American Film Music Accompaniment," *Cinema Journal* 37, no. 1 (1997): 10–11.

22. The practice of the illustrated song is discussed in a number of sources. Altman's *Silent Film Sound*, pp. 182–193, offers the most thorough discussion. Gillian Anderson's *Music for Silent Films, 1894–1929* (Washington, D.C.: Library of Congress, 1988), pp. xiii–xviii, documents the popularity of the illustrated song well into the 1910s and 1920s. See also Bowser, *Transformation of Cinema*, pp. 15–18.

23. Jeff Smith sees the illustrated song as an early example of film marketing "synergy," a term that surfaced in the 1980s to describe the phenomenon of carefully coordinating several mediums,

film, television, and radio for instance, to sell record albums, and vice versa. See Smith, *The Sounds of Commerce: Marketing Popular Film Music* (New York: Columbia University Press, 1998), pp. 26–32.

24. For more on repertoire used in the nickelodeons, see Altman, *Silent Film Sound,* pp. 203–20.

25. For a more detailed discussion of the musical advice column, see Altman, *Silent Film Sound,* pp. 240–46; and Charles Berg, *An Investigation of the Motives for and the Realization of Music to Accompany the American Silent Film, 1896–1927* (New York: Arno Press, 1976), pp. 112–123. See also Marks, *Music and the Silent Film,* pp. 10–11.

26. Emmett Campbell Hall, "With Accompanying Noises," *Moving Picture World,* June 10, 1911, p. 1296.

27. Berg discusses the problem of music's involvement in early film sound in detail in *An Investigation,* pp. 190–97.

28. Smith discusses the ironic or "funner" accompanist in *Sounds of Commerce,* pp. 27–28, as does Berg, *An Investigation,* pp. 198–202. T. Anderson, "Reforming 'Jackass Music,'" pp. 12–14, argues that critiques of funners, like Harrison's, were part of a larger project to redefine narrative film experiences along the lines of a single master text.

29. Berg, *An Investigation,* pp. 166–67. See also Altman, *Silent Film Sound,* pp. 222–26.

30. The only elevated or "better" repertoire that Ahern specifically mentions is a piece called "Goodbye" by the Italian composer Paolo Tosti.

31. David Robinson notes that in Europe orchestra members were quicker to play in movie theaters and so were quicker to introduce symphonic and operatic repertoire; see his *Music of the Shadows: The Use of Musical Accompaniment with Silent Pictures, 1896–1936,* supplement to *Griffithiana,* no. 38/39 (October 1990), p. 10. See also Russell Sanjek, *American Popular Music and Its Business: The First Four Hundred Years,* vol. 3: *From 1900 to 1984* (New York: Oxford University Press, 1988), p. 11, describing the inclusion of classical music in American movie theater repertoire, albeit on a limited basis, as beginning around 1909. Tim Anderson, in "Reforming 'Jackass Music,'" p. 13–14, dates the limited introduction of classical music at around 1912 but points out that the new repertoire was not limited to genres; even in newsreels, "every class of music is needed from the popular to the severely classical." For a general consideration of the repertoire for the nickelodeon era, see also Altman, *Silent Film Sound,* pp. 204–8.

32. Anderson, "Reforming 'Jackass Music,'" p. 14. Charles Hoffman provides corroboration of the reliance on popular music in *Sounds for Silents* (New York: DBS Publications, 1969). In an article entitled "Music Cues—1910," silent film pianist Bert Ennis wrote that in his cue sheets he suggested following the film version of an Irish story with popular tunes like "Has Anybody Here Seen Kelly?," "Mother Machree," and "The River Shannon"; a drama or "tear-jerker" with "My Gal Sal," "I'm Tying the Leaves So They Won't Fall Down," and "A Bird in a Gilded Cage"; and a war picture with "The Blue and the Gray," "Good Bye, Dolly Grey," and "Break the News to Mother." Popular music wasn't the only repertoire used in 1910, Ennis remembers, but it certainly dominated. "We showed our class by injecting at times the classical and standard numbers . . . 'Hearts and Flowers,' 'Melody in F,' 'Traumerei,' and 'Pilgrim's Chorus'—they all helped to give helpless audiences a barrage of highbrow music before the present day experts in the writing of music scores for films discovered Debussy, Beethoven, Schubert, Mozart, Wagner and other big leaguers of the classical field" (pp. 12–13). See also Altman, *Silent Film Sound,* pp. 220–26.

33. Two other collections were used extensively by European musicians: Giuseppe Becce's *Kinothek* (1919) and *Allgemeines Handbuch der Filmmusik* (1927), edited by Becce, Hans Erdmann, and Ludwig Brav. For a discussion of these repertoire and playing manuals and their archival sources, see Marks, *Music and the Silent Film,* pp. 68–70; Altman, *Silent Film Sound,* pp. 258–65; and Berg, *An Investigation,* pp. 122–46.

34. Zamecnik's compositional skills are frequently cited in biographical sketches from the pe-riod. See Gordon Whyte, "J. S. Zamecnik," *Metronome*, Sept. 1, 1927, pp. 41, 62; and "J. S. Zamecnik, the Musical Wizard," *Motion Picture News*, May 1, 1920, p. 3834. See also contemporary biographies of Zamecnik, including Altman, *Silent Film Sound*, pp. 259–65 and 355–57; Rodney Sauer, "J. S. Zamecnik and Silent Film Music," at www.cinemaweb.com/silentfilm/bookshelf/21_bio_1.htm (consulted 9/26/2008).

35. Bowser, *Transformation of Cinema*, p. 191.

36. The works of Dante, Dickens, and Thackeray were among the favorite literature of the early feature films, as were biographies of historical figures like Christopher Columbus, Napoleon, George Washington, and Cleopatra. One of Sarah Bernhardt's earliest films featured the actress as Queen Elizabeth (1912). See ibid., pp. 204–5.

37. Clarence Sinn, "Music for the Picture," *Moving Picture World*, August 31, 1911, p. 871.

38. Musicians rarely had the opportunity to see a film before they had to create an accompani-ment for it. Exhibitors often scheduled an extra matinee for that very reason—to give the musicians a chance to devise an accompaniment. (And moviegoers often avoided the first run of a film for that same reason.) Musicians did have some prescreening tools to work with, however. Production com-panies often circulated written synopses in advance as part of their rental or exchange service. The Edison *Kinetogram,* a biweekly publication of Edison's film company, was doing this as early as 1909. Being able to preview a film before its theatrical release, however, appears not to have been a routine option for musicians until the mid-1920s.

39. Sinn's appropriation of Wagner's operatic technique is significant to film music historians, but it is problematic for Wagner scholars, who point out that many of Sinn's assumptions about the leitmotif technique are inaccurate. See Scott Paulin, "Richard Wagner and the Fantasy of Cinematic Unity: The Idea of the *Gesamtkunstwerk* in the History and Theory of Film Music," in *Music and Cinema,* ed. James Buhler, Caryl Flinn, and David Neumeyer (Hanover, N.H.: Wesleyan University Press, 2000), pp. 58–84.

40. Breil compiled and wrote music for the French four-reeler *Les amours de la reine Élisabeth* (1912), starring Sarah Bernhardt, and for the Italian blockbuster *Cabiria* (1914). While Breil certainly had an impact on the development of the great compilation score of the silent period, his claim to have written the first original film score (for *Queen Elizabeth*) was probably somewhat exaggerated, especially the claim of "original." Most of Breil's scores were compilations, some containing over 50 percent preexisting music. For Breil's biography, see Marks, *Music and the Silent Cinema*, pp. 98–108. Marks also points out that Breil was not the first to write a "specially prepared score." In the United States, little-known composers like Walter Simons, Noble Kreider, Manual Klein, and George Col-burn were writing special compilation scores for Kalem's and Universal's exchange services as early as 1910 (ibid., p. 62–108). Hoffman, *Sounds for Silents,* pp. 4–11, discusses the history of the compila-tion score, too, and includes pictures of many examples.

41. Breil was not the only composer from whom Griffith commissioned a score. When *Birth of a Nation* initially premiered in Los Angeles at Clune's Auditorium under the title *The Clansman,* it featured a score by Los Angeles composer Carli Elinor. See Marks, *Music and the Silent Cinema,* pp. 131–35.

42. For a detailed description and analysis of all the classical music quotations and excerpts in the *Birth of a Nation* score, see ibid., pp. 109–66 (especially pp. 145–48) and appendix 10, pp. 208–9.

43. Although *Birth of a Nation*'s twelve-reel length initially challenged exhibitors, it toured widely as a special exhibition film and by the early 1920s was one of the most widely seen films in the United States. In its wake, orchestral accompaniments were tried for several high-profile dramatic films. See Richard Koszarski, *An Evening's Entertainment: The Age of the Silent Feature Picture, 1915–1928* (Berkeley: University of California Press, 1994), pp. 41–44.

44. While Breil no doubt led the way, Griffith also appears to have had a hand in importing Wagnerian techniques to film accompaniment. As Lillian Gish, one of his favorite actresses remembers in her memoir *The Movies, Mr. Griffith, and Me* (Englewood Cliffs, N.J.: Prentice-Hall, 1969), pp. 152–53, it was Griffith who wanted to use not only Wagner's "Ride of the Valkyries" but also leitmotifs for each main character in *Birth of a Nation*.

45. Joseph Breil, "Moving Pictures of the Past and Present and the Music Provided for Same," *Metronome* 32, no. 11 (1916): 42.

46. The importation of classical music was a slow process that took place over a number of years starting as early as 1909–10. In 1912, for instance, one critic noted that classical music, though part of the mix, was not yet displacing popular music: "For every classical number that appears on my programmes, . . . there are . . . three or four waltzes . . . and frequently a couple of snappy tunes" (quoted in T. Anderson, "Reforming 'Jackass Music,'" p. 14). Nonetheless, if a single film can be said to have accelerated this process, it was *Birth of a Nation*. Many of Breil's contemporaries saw that film in particular as a turning point in film accompaniment. In 1920, for example, in his handbook *Musical Presentation of Motion Pictures,* George Beynon wrote that the *Birth of a Nation* score "would go down in the annals of the history of the film industry as a happening of greatest importance" (p. 11). Altman, too, discusses the changes in instrumentation and repertoire that Breil's *Birth of a Nation* score popularized; see *Silent Film Sound,* pp. 292–96,

47. See Robinson, *Music of the Shadows,* p. 11. Berg also outlines the history of the cinema orchestra in *An Investigation,* p. 150.

48. After World War I, Rothapfel dropped the "p" from his name, apparently in response to anti-German sentiment, using his appointment at the Capitol Theater in New York City to launch the new spelling. See Ben M. Hall, *Best Remaining Seats: The Story of the Golden Age of the Movie Palace* (New York: Clarkson N. Potter, 1961), p. 66; also Marks, *Music and the Silent Film,* p. 264 n. 83. Rothapfel's biography is recounted in several sources, including G. Anderson, *Music for Silent Films,* pp. xxviii–xxix; and Marks, *Music and the Silent Film,* pp. 92–98.

49. Berg, *An Investigation,* p. 150.

50. Marks, *Music and the Silent Film,* pp. 62, 88–89. Little is known about either Klein or Colburn.

51. Ibid., pp. 76–89; and Altman, *Silent Film Sound,* pp. 254–58.

52. Frank Edson, "A Moving Picture Score by Victor Herbert," *Metronome* 32, no. 6 (1916): 16.

53. Herbert's experiences and the nature of his collaboration with the film's director, Thomas Dixon, are described in Wayne Shirley, "A Bugle Call to Arms for National Defense! Victor Herbert and His Score for *The Fall of a Nation,*" in *Wonderful Inventions: Motion Picture Broadcasting and Recorded Sound at the Library of Congress,* ed. Iris Newsom (Washington D.C.: Library of Congress, 1985), pp. 173–85. Composer Victor Schertziger also composed an original score for Griffith's 1916 film *Civilization,* but it does not seem to have established a viable compositional precedent either; see Altman, *Silent Film Sound,* pp. 295–96.

54. Blanche Greenland, "Faking in Movie Music Corrupting Public's Taste," in *Musical America* 22, no. 21 (1915): 12. According to Altman (*Silent Film Sound,* pp. 256–58), strains of this problem surface even earlier. "Faking" was related to the widespread problem of amateurism in early film accompaniment; as a commentator in the New York *Dramatic Mirror* in 1911 reveals, some theater pianists "faked" repertoire because they could not read music.

55. Altman, *Silent Film Sound,* pp. 308–19.

56. Rothapfel finished his career as silent film musical director at the even larger Roxy Theater in New York City, which boasted an orchestra of 110—the largest permanent orchestra in the world at that time. Rapee's and Rothapfel's careers at the Capitol and Roxy theaters have been well documented. See Hall, *The Best Remaining Seats;* G. Anderson, *Music for Silent Films;* and Gillian Anderson, "The

Presentation of Silent Films, or, Music as Anaesthesia," *Journal of Musicology* 5, no. 2 (1987): 257–95.

57. For a good discussion of the film program and its musical tastes and needs, see Altman, *Silent Film Sound*, pp. 380–88.

58. For detailed lists of the symphonic and operatic repertoire used in the movie theaters—in both the program overtures and in the film accompaniments—see Hall, *Best Remaining Seats*, pp. 44–55; Altman, *Silent Film Sound*, pp. 308–18; G. Anderson, *Music for Silent Films*, pp. xxiv–xxvi; and Koszarski, *An Evening's Entertainment*, pp. 44–50. Between 1917 and 1920, many film and music journals, including *Moving Picture World, Motion Picture News, Musical America, The Musical Courier, The Metronome,* and *The Dominant,* established permanent columns that described the musical offerings of the New York movie palaces and, in some instances, movie palaces in other cosmopolitan cities like Los Angeles, Cincinnati, and Baltimore.

59. See Julie Hubbert, "Modernism at the Movies: The Cabinet of Dr. Caligari and a Film Score Revisited," *Musical Quarterly* 88, no. 1 (2005): 63–95.

60. Edith Lang and George West, *Musical Accompaniment of Moving Pictures* (New York: Boston Music Co., 1920), p. 3.

61. Hoping to build on the success of cue sheets, Paramount Pictures engaged Beynon, one of the most experienced film musicians writing in the 1920s, to compile and compose specially prepared orchestra scores for each of its films, which would be published by Schirmer Music Publishing and circulated with the rental of the film. The venture ultimately failed, however, mostly because it was too expensive for theater owners, but also because the instrumentation of the theater orchestra had not yet been standardized. See Berg, *An Investigation,* pp. 152–54.

62. Beynon, *Musical Presentation of Motion Pictures,* part I: "Equipment," p. 8.

63. Altman, *Silent Film Sound*, pp. 346–54.

64. In addition to Altman's discussion of cue sheets, see G. Anderson, *Music for Silent Films*, pp. xxix–xxxii.

65. Gillian Anderson's study of the silent film favors the perspective of the theater or unit organist. See *Music for Silent Films,* especially pp. xix–xxi; and "Presentation of Silent Films," pp. 265–270.

66. In 1921, exhibitors from around the country assembled in New York City to hear Rothapfel, Rapee, and Riesenfeld discuss the practical details of the New York City movie palace music model for the purpose of incorporating aspects of it, if not the practice as whole, in their own theaters in smaller cities and towns. See "Musical and Film Interests Combine at First Conference," *Musical America,* January 29, 1921, pp. 1, 3–4; and "Motion Picture and Musical Interests Meet at First National Conference," *Musical Courier,* February 3, 1921, pp. 6, 26.

67. Altman, *Silent Film Sound*, pp. 300–308.

68. G. Anderson, *Music for Silent Films*, pp. xxi–xxvi.

69. While the premiere of Gance's film *Napoléon* was a success, Honegger's accompanying score was a disaster. See Kevin Brownlow, *Napoléon: Abel Gance's Classic Film* (New York: Alfred A. Knopf, 1983), pp. 150–52.

70. Marks discusses Satie's score and its predecessors in great detail in *Music and the Silent Film,* chapter 5: "Erik Satie's Score for *Entr'Acte*," pp. 167–185. See also Doug Gallenz, "Satie's *Entr'Acte*: A Model of Film Music," *Cinema Journal* 16, no. 2 (1976): 36–50.

71. Ronald Bergan, *Eisenstein: A Life in Conflict* (New York: Overlook Press, 1999), pp. 122–24, 133, and 166–67. Meisel confirms this timeline for the *Potemkin* score, along with the details of his relationship with Eisenstein, in an essay he wrote shortly thereafter entitled "Wie schreibt man Filmmusik?" *Ufa-Magazine* (Berlin) 14, no. 1 (1927); reprinted in Werner Sudendorf, ed., *Der Stummfilmmusiker Edmund Meisel* (Frankfurt am Main: Deutsches Filmmuseum, 1984), pp. 57–60.

72. Hoffman, *Sounds for Silents,* pp. 21–33. Hoffman covers particularly well the music of high-profile international films like *Battleship Potemkin* and *The Cabinet of Dr. Caligari.* For a general overview of music in Soviet cinema, see also Tatiana Egorova, *Soviet Film Music,* trans. Tatiana Ganf and Natalia Egunova (Amsterdam: Harwood Academic Publishers, 1997), pp. 3–13.

73. G. Anderson, *Music for Silent Films,* pp. xxix–xxxii. See also Robinson, *Music of the Shadows,* pp. 14–16; Berg, *An Investigation,* p. 158–66; and Hoffman, *Sounds for Silents,* pp. 29–35. It should be noted that even in some contemporary histories, a distinction is not always clearly made between scores that are wholly newly and originally composed and compilation scores that have some originally composed sections, like Breil's *Birth of a Nation* score.

74. On the set of his great epic *Napoléon* (1927), director Abel Gance admitted, for instance, that he "always had music, not only to give the mood, but to keep everyone quiet. . . . In a scene where the young Napoleon . . . had to cry . . . he couldn't until the musicians played Beethoven's *Moonlight Sonata*" (G. Anderson, *Music for Silent Films,* p. xlii). Anderson (ibid.) suggests that the practice of on-set music began in the late teens, whereas Altman (*Silent Film Sound,* pp. 369–70) dates the practice from 1914 or before.

75. "Studio Music Inspires Players in Screen Work," *New York Times,* March 30, 1926. While the practice seems to have been international, the repertoire played on the set during filming was apparently not carried over into the compilation scores for the films in question.

76. Berg, *An Investigation,* pp. 140–48.

77. The phenomenon of taxable and nontaxable music is described in detail in Sanjek, *American Popular Music,* 3:47–57.

Plain Talk to Theater Managers and Operators

Seating/Music

F. H. Richardson

(1909)

SEATING

So far as price goes a theater may be seated with opera chairs costing from as low as $1.25 each to as high as one wishes to go, a very comfortable, substantial seat being available at about $1.40 each. Upholstered seats are not desirable in moving picture theaters from any point of view. They would be a distinct disadvantage any way one might look at it. The audience remains seated such a comparatively short time that the non-upholstered seat, provided it be properly made, is perfectly comfortable and in Summer it is much cooler also. Second-hand chairs are often available at very low figure, but you should either see them or have a guarantee in writing as to their size, condition, etc., with privilege of examination before paying if shipped from a distance. Theater seats should always have a wire hat holder beneath the seat and on the back of each seat should be affixed a very small ring or staple through which the ladies may thrust a hatpin to hold their headgear instead of being obliged to hold them in their laps. Two small staples, one one-half inch above the other, are best. You will probably have to throw a slide on the screen calling attention to the arrangement until the ladies become accustomed to it. You will find it will be highly appreciated by ladies who remove their hats. Advertisements in The Moving Picture World will put you in touch with manufacturers of theater seats who will send prices, descriptions and illustrations of the various style seats.

One very essential and important feature in seating is to utilize all available space, but at the same time not get the rows so close together that the user will experience discomfort. The requirements of Chicago will serve as a safe guide in this respect. It is as follows: 32 inches from chair back to chair back. Chicago law is good to follow in the matter of aisles also. It calls for aisles 3 feet wide if more than one and 4 feet if but one. Taking the above as a basis to measure seating capacity of a room, proceed as follows: Measure from the stage to the point you wish to locate your front row of seats. From this point measure to the point where the rear of your last row of seats will be. Multiply this measurement by 12, to reduce to inches, and divide by 32. The last result will be the number of rows. Next measure the width of the room and subtract width of the aisle, or combined width of all aisles if more than one. Multiply remainder by 12, to reduce to inches, and divide the result by width of chair you propose using, which may be 18, 19 or 20 inches. Next multiply the number of rows by the number of seats per row and the result is the seating capacity of your room. Of course if length of all rows is not the same you will have to subtract the deficiency of short rows or else measure all rows separately, adding all together and dividing by chair width. Theaters having curved rows will undoubtedly have an architect's floor plan to figure from. All theaters should have a sloped floor. The day of the flat floor is past. Such a house is hopelessly out of date and behind the times. What this slope will be will necessarily depend somewhat on how much you are able to get if the installation be in a building already erected. All the slope you can get up to the point where the rows of chairs must be on steps is an advantage. The best floor slope result the writer has seen is a newly constructed Chicago moving picture theater. The floor is of cement and the slope is about 5 feet in 50. There are two ways to getting a slope in an old flat floor room, viz.: Build an incline on top of the old floor or drop the front end of the old floor down into the basement. The latter is much the best where it can be done. The first named plan has the disadvantage of requiring a slope from the entrance up to the new floor level. Never use steps for this, since in case of panic people would certainly pile up on them and many be injured or killed. They are not likely, however, to fall on an incline, even though it be quite steep, especially if it be carpeted with heavy coarse matting, securely nailed down.

As regards seating plans, I think it would be somewhat a waste of space to elaborate upon them. The main thing is to have long rows of seats unbroken by an aisle, and so arrange your exit, which in all cases should be entirely separate from the entrance, so that there will be the least possible congestion when the crowds are passing out. It is by far the best, where it can be so arranged, to have the exit at the opposite end of the house from the entrance. This is in some cases possible where there is an ample passage between the theater building and the next adjoining, provided it be not a public alley. This plan relieves all congestion caused by interference between people coming in and those passing out. In ordinary storeroom theaters the central aisle plan is almost invariably the best. Where it is practicable to have a center aisle and one at either side, it is a most excellent plan to use the center aisle exclusively for persons passing out, the incoming ones being steered into the side aisles, none being allowed to enter the center aisle. As the people usually do not come in big bunches, the side aisles, where this plan is adopted, may be comparatively narrow. Where there are long rows of seats unbroken by an aisle, it is dangerous in case of panic; also it is annoying to patrons, in that late comers have to crowd past many seats to reach center seats in the row. In picture theaters, the further the front row of seats is from the curtain, the better, since when one is very close to the curtain, all sense of perspective is lost; moreover, the picture is little more than a blur. It is much the best to locate the piano in a pit in the center under the curtain or stage front, since the piano player then has a constant view of the picture without effort. This is essential, if he or she is to produce the best results in following the film action with music. Carpet all aisles with heavy matting or linoleum. The sound of people walking on the bare floor is very annoying to an audience. The curtain should be at such height, if possible, that the head of a man standing at the front row of seats will not interfere in the picture. As regards picture size, there is no rule. It depends on the house entirely. But it may be said that the picture should, if possible, be at least ten feet wide. A picture twelve feet wide is called life size from the fact that in this size there are a greater percentage of life-size figures than in any other. From twelve to fourteen feet in width usually makes the best appearing picture. Unless it is absolutely necessary, do not throw the top of the picture clear up to the ceiling. It does not look so well as when there is a margin of from six inches to two feet. After all other cleaning is done for the day, every seat should be carefully dusted. There is nothing more annoying to a lady in a light-colored dress than to find her costume soiled by a dusty theater seat. It amounts to an outrage.

MUSIC

Music is a matter of greater importance than many moving picture theater managers seem to imagine. Get a good piano player, who can read any music at sight and make him or her attend strictly to business. Pay a salary which will justify you in demanding the best work and then see to it that your player makes good. A piano player who cannot read music at sight has no rightful place in a moving picture theater, especially if illustrated songs are run. But the song is a comparatively small matter. Always and invariably the piano player can help out a film wonderfully if he or she wants to and knows how. Often and often have I entered a theater while the film was running and seen the piano player industriously engaged in talking to a friend, dividing her attention impartially between the friend and a wad of gum. He or she would have got busy or been fired in just one minute had I been managing the house. The piano player should have a wide range of "know it by heart" music; should watch the picture closely and play suitable music, with due attention to producing as many of the noises as is practical with that instrument. There is no reason, where a drummer cannot be employed, why an auto horn, a chime bell and a whistle cannot be manipulated by the piano player. They can easily be attached to the instrument within easy reach, and such things help. A piano player can do much if he or she wants to and mighty little if he or she don't want to and don't have to. Of course you will have to pay more for good service, but it pays to do it.

Where the house has seating capacity to justify there should always be a drummer. But get a good one. A good drummer can perform wonders in adding to the effectiveness of a film, but a poor one is worse than none. The up-to-date moving picture theater drummer has contrivances for imitating almost any sound and he knows how to use them, too. It may be safely said that any 300 capacity house which has available capacity business should have a drummer and piano player. More need not be added except in large houses. I feel that I cannot impress too strongly on managers the advisability of getting all you can out of the available music.

——————

From *Moving Picture World*, October 30, 1909, pp. 599–600.

Incidental Music for Edison Pictures

(1909)

MUSIC CUES

How the Landlord Collected His Rents

Scene 1—March, brisk
        2—Irish jig
        3—Begin with andante, finish with allegro
        4—Popular air
        5—   "   "
        6—Andante with lively at finish
        7—March (same as No. 1)
        8—Plaintive
        9—Andante (use March No. 1)

The Ordeal

Scene 1—An andante
        2—An allegro changing to plaintive at end
        3—Plaintive
        4—Adagio or march changing at end to allegro strongly marked
        5—Andante to plaintive, changing to march movement at end
        6—Lively, change to plaintive at Fantine's arrest
        7—March with accents to accompany scene finishing with andante
        8—Andante
        9—Allegro, to march at arrest
       10—March, changing to andante at end

11—Slow march, p.p.

12—Andante p.p. hurry at action of putting passport, etc in fire

13—March p., changing to f.f. at the entrance of Jean Valjean, the Mayor

14—Andante to Javert's entrance, then a hurry till the Mayor tears off the piece of iron from the bed. Adagio to end.

'Tis Now the Very Witching Time of Night

Scene 1—Lively at start, marked march at finish

2—Andante, tremolo

3—   "   "   change to pizzicato at ghosts

4—Pizzicato crescendo and decrescendo

5—Andante to donkey scene, mock march to skeletons then hurry

6—Hurry, pizzicato

7—Same as No. 1

True Love Never Runs Smoothly

At opening, Andante P.P.

Till boy gets horse loose from wagon, Hurried movement

Till buggy strikes water, Allegro

Love and War

Scene 1—Allegro

2—Andante

3—   "

4—Waltz at start, pause at entrance of orderly. Note—drum at cannon shots indicated by the start of surprise form all characters, stop the waltz and begin andante same as No. 1, till plaintive at exit of officers.

5—Same andante blending into same plaintive for finale

A Knight for a Night

Scene 1—Lively ("He's a Jolly Good Fellow")

2—   "   "   "

3—Andante at start, to pizzicato at change

4—Pizzicato

5—Allegro

6—   "

7—Hurry

8—Andante, change to hurry at finish

9—Andante to allegro at change

Why Girls Leave Home

At opening, Popular air

Till second scene, Pizzicato

Till view of orchestra seats, Regular overture

Till view of stage is shown, Waltz time

Note—Knock at door till girl starts to leave home, Home Sweet Home.

Till audience applauds, Lively music

Till Act 2, snow scene, Plaintive

Till audience applauds, Lively music

Till Act 3, bridge scene, Pizzicato

Till gallery applauds, Lively music

Till Act 4, heroine's home, Plaintive music

Till hero bursts through window, Lively, work to climax

Till next set, girl's return home, Waltz movement

From *Edison Kinetogram,* September 15, 1909, p. 12.

3

Jackass Music

Louis Reeves Harrison

(1911)

Civilization is not a crab, but theatrical managers walk sideways if not backwards when they allow their musicians to play the wrong accompaniment to the right composition whether of sound or picture. O, what a noise when the lights are turned low and Lily Limpwrist takes her place at the usual instrument of torture. With a self-conscious smirk she gives a poke to her back switch, dabs her side teasers with both patties, rolls up her sleeves and tears off "That Yiddisher Rag." She bestows a clam smile on the box-of-candy young man in the first row, but the presentation on the screen fails to divert her "I-seen-you" glances any more than if it was the point of the joke.

The chorus-girl who attempts to pose as a prima-donna with little more equipment than a tuft of bleached hair, a pair of high-heeled slippers and a cigarette voice can be tolerated, we often endure the howling and screeching of a Tommy trying to sing "Come into the garden Maud," but when Lily Limpwrist assails our unprotected organs of hearing with her loony repertoire it seems a shame to throw away ten cents on such a performance, to say nothing of the time wasted. We sit patiently through the act of an imported star, who commends to our attention the interesting intelligence "Me Rag, moy Bess used-ter droive em cryzy at the Croiterion," we submit to the inanities of the chin-whiskered pillow-paunched Dutch comedian, who says: "Vot it is, is it? Ask me," and we even tolerate the Irish comedian, shaved yesterday, who looks like an undertaker out-of-a-job when he wails in a hold-over voice: "Where thuh dear-ol Sha-hamrock gurrows," but there is a limit.

Lily is all right at home, when her mother importunes her to "play something and don't wait to be teased," or still better as a summer-eve girl on a Coney-

Island boat, but no man will ever marry a girl who plays a dance while the pictured man is in a death struggle; she would probably be *at* one when the real one was in trouble. The girl of sympathy will play music in accord with the pictured story, the girl of ambition will try to improve the quality of her work, the girl of sense will try to improve the quality of the performance, draw patronage instead of driving it away, benefit the management, and show to others who are looking for pianists that she is not a fat-wit but a woman of ideas and good taste.

The performance of Lily Limpwrist is a poetic dream compared to the diabolical dipso-mania of Freddy Fuzzlehead and Percy Peashaker when they cut loose between the "vodeveal" acts. Gee! *Non compos mentis* and *le diable au corps* for theirs and a free pass to Matteawan for what they have done to kill the box-office receipts at moving-picture shows. Percy is really a wonder. When there is water in the picture it goes to Percy's cerebrum. If there is a lake shown on the screen, no matter is it is a mile away, calm or stormy, he shakes his box of peas so that we may know that it is principally made of water. Realism become intense when a vessel appears and Percy blows a whistle "Oo-Oo" to enforce the fact that it is a steamer and not a full-rigged ship. "Bow-wow" indicates that we are looking at a dog and not a door-mat, "Honk-honk" gives one a thrilling remembrance of crossing Broadway after the theatre with fifty cow-boys taxis in full pursuit, and he is a master of such startling effects as clapping two blocks of wood together when an old nag candidate for the glue factory trots along a country road. But Percy's star act, the one that gets a laugh, is his imitation of a baby crying, no matter whether the one on the screen is nursing or merely dying. Percy is a comparatively new type of the egomaniac, but whether we must humor him or put him in a padded cell must be left to the alienists.

If you were to ask a large proportion of the audience what should be done to Freddy Fuzzlehead they would vote to shoot him, but I am in favor of slow torture, making the punishment fit the crime, put him in a room where there is another of his kind playing with the piano and let him die a lingering death. Ten thousand dollars a day is spent to amuse people with moving pictures, good, bad and indifferent, but all are bad or indifferent when Fuzzlehead does his long-eared stunt. Ten millions of people pay their nickels and dimes to see the moving pictures and these shock-headed klepto-pianoacs steal their pleasure away in order to practice the accompaniment for the song-and-dance comedians, those who come on the stage and say, "I will now sing you a little ballad entitled 'Show you are a clod-hopper by keeping time with your feet.'" The same comedian who gets no applause from the long-suffering audience and ask if they are hand-cuffed or says to the piano man, *sotto voce*, "Did y'ever s-see sucha lotta dubs?" The hall-room lobster on the stage is "great" to Fuzzlehead, the boob action exactly suits the boob at the piano, the moving pictures are rot, he could do better himself if he had time, but he would say the same thing if he was shown the treasures of the

Louvre or the Palace of Luxembourg. Ten thousand dollars a day is spent to *produce* the moving pictures, and it would be impossible to say how much more to keep going the ten thousand motion-picture theatres throughout the country. These pictures are not all masterpieces, many of them are very crude, but the whole art is in a primitive state, is constantly improving, and the exhibitions are kept alive by their production. People go every day to see the pictures, once in a while for the variety entertainment, and it is not only asinine but unbusiness-like to lower the grade of musical accompaniment when the lights are turned down. Inappropriate music may "do" for an unintelligent part of the audience, but what is the use of driving away the intelligent portion? All other parts of the theatrical working force move in harmony, like the wheels of a clock, but these fatheads against the stage apron are like the clock alarm that goes off when you don't need it and never when you do. Attention of managers to the comfort of patrons would help a great deal to get suitable music. Better music means better patronage and more of it, and superior patronage means a demand for superior photoplays. Suitable music is an essential. If the drummer can not be taught to subordinate his morbid craving for attention to the general effect, cut him out altogether and pay more for a pianist who can improvise softly during scenes of pathos or utilize operatic selections for the dramatic effects.

Bangity-bang-bang. Bing-bang-bang.

Desperate Desmond has got Claude Eclaire in a tight place, but no matter, the "rag" is on, "hit it up."

Bangity-bang-bang! Bing-bang-bang!

There is a tender-hearted mother dying in the little play, the world around her is subdued and silent, her face is pale, her frame attenuated, her respiration is heavy with sighs of sorrow and unsatisfied desire to have her children properly cared for. Tears are falling like her life illusions, she is overcome with her double burden of pain and sorrow, her eyes, inflamed by the fever of unattained hopes, turn beseechingly to the infinite power above, a last faint sigh, the eyes close forever:

Bangity-bang-gang! Bing-bang-bang!

From *Moving Picture World*, January 21, 1911, pp. 124–25.

4

Selections from *What and How to Play for Pictures*

Eugene A. Ahern

(1913)

HOW TO PLAY

These are the things I take into consideration first in playing pictures:

FIRST: If convenient to the management of the house, have the operator run the pictures through in advance of the regular show, so you will be more able to play the pictures with appropriate music.

SECOND: In selecting your music, try and remember the scenes that necessitate the change of music.

THIRD: Appropriate music of course is the first requisite in playing pictures properly.

By appropriate I mean not only music that is in keeping with the atmosphere of the picture, but music that has two or more different movements, so you won't need to make an entire change of music to fit the scenes, but just play some other movement in the same piece. A little further along I will illustrate my idea of appropriate music.

FOURTH: Second to appropriate music is keeping the tempo of your music with the action of the players. One can do this sometimes and save the trouble of a change of music.

The following is a criticism of the "Music Critic of the Motion Picture World" on a letter contributed to the Motion Picture World's Music Section by Mr. Metcalf, of Montana:

We recently showed the Reliance feature, "The Bawler Out," in three parts, also a Keystone comedy. Below is the program used for that day: Liebergarten (Schumann); Humoreske (Dvorak); Serenade (Drdla), and several others.

This is the criticism:

This is a splendid program, musically. Unfortunately, I did not see the picture in question, so cannot pass as to its fitness in regard to detail. Many leaders strive to carry out the general atmosphere of the picture, rather than try to work every little detail. This, on the whole, is much the safer plan, for, as Mr. Metcalf says, it is difficult for an orchestra to follow closely to detail. Some leaders "humor" the scenes without changing the piece of music. Unless done with skill, this is risky, although I have known violinists who could so vary the music at times by means of retards, accelerate, diminish, crescendo, etc., that their work was a joy to hear. This, of course, in scenes where the contrasts were not too pronounced. It would hardly hold good in all situations.

This is what he says in regard to following the pictures by different changes of tempo.

FIFTH: Play your music pianissimo so as not to divert the attention of the audience from the picture to the music, but loud enough to be heard all over the house.

Play the tempo with the action of whoever on the screen is the central figure, not necessarily the leading man or lady, as sometimes the heavy or villain is the person that is attracting attention. This is where some pianists will say that it will be necessary to change music, to follow the action of each player.

Appropriate Music

Here is what I mean about appropriate music:

To illustrate, here is a little scene from the picture "Notre Dame," second part of the first reel:

Scene 1. "Leading Lady is Waiting for Her Lover." Music, "Melody of Love," from "Gypsy Love" until the archdeacon appears (villain); then the first part of the same piece ("Gypsy Love,") which is in a minor key. (Tempo was moderato, but I hurried it to follow the heavy.)

Now you see I didn't make an entire change of music, but just changed from one theme to another, and both in the same piece of music. I alternated these two movements according to whoever was on the screen, leading lady or the heavy. This is what I mean by select appropriate music, secondary to selecting music that is in keeping with the atmosphere of the picture.

Therefore, one has to be well acquainted with his library of music, as you know some pieces have two or three different themes or movements, so if one knows his music it won't be necessary to get different pieces of music altogether, but just change to a different movement.

Now don't think I never change music, for I do, but not as often as some pianists, because you know it takes from 15 to 18 minutes to run one reel, and if the pianist only played one or two pieces of music it would get tiresome.

Some pianists change music as often as from ten to fifteen times in one reel or 1,000 feet of film. Here is where I don't agree with a lot of picture pianists. I believe where one changes music as often as that there isn't any real sense of music conveyed to the audience, and these are the ones we have to entertain, not ourselves—because if they weren't in the house we wouldn't be at the piano.

My idea is not to change music any oftener than is absolutely necessary, but to pick out the theme of the picture and play to it. You know there are some pictures that would drive a pianist to distraction if he or she would try to follow each scene. For instance, some of the Biograph dramas, where every four or five seconds there is a change of scenes. (I think I counted 47 scenes in this picture, "Sands o' Dee.")

. . .

Producer's Suggestions

Some of the producing companies are giving music suggestions for the picture, which in itself is all right, but I don't agree with this party when he advises about eighteen pieces of music in order to follow the picture. The pianist would have to change music every four seconds, and imagine what kind of music a person in the audience hears.

Now from the foregoing talk I don't want any one to think that you have to go into "ecstasy" in playing the pictures, but there are a lot of pictures that a pianist can make 50 per cent more impressive by appropriate music. Nor do I mean for a pianist to play the better class of music for all of the dramas, because I say there are a lot of pictures that aren't good enough to use this kind of music for.

I use only my better music, such as the "Melody in F," "Fifth Nocturne," or "Tosti's Goodbye," and the like, on only real good pictures, because you know it isn't every picture that these pieces can be fitted to. Some suggestions offered by some of the film producers, use such music for every little solemn scene in the pictures.

This is the way I arrange it: I never use such music unless I can finish playing at least half of it or more. If I can't do this, I wait until I get a scene long enough so I can play it. That way I don't spoil a good piece of music by only playing just parts of it.

Here is another thing to take into consideration in using some of this better grade or in fact any kind of music that is set to words. Take for instance "The Rosary," which nearly every one knows is very pretty, both the music and the words. And there are a lot of people who know the words, and it would be out of place to play for some scenes, say for instance where a soldier was dying, or some scene on this order; the music would suit the occasion, but the words would be out of place.

This clipping from the Motion Picture World will help to show you what I mean:

> Thomas Bruce, of the Majestic Theater, North Yakima, Wash., whose letterhead reads, "Musical Interpreter of Pictures, Pipe Organ, and Piano," writes: In the February 1st issue of Moving Picture World, under heading, "Thoughts for Pianists," in your department, Mr. Aiken says: "Picture playing does not consist as some suppose of merely fitting song titles to the scenes." I fully agree with him, for to play a modern song to some pictures would be out of place, and inartistic; on the other hand, it would be worse to play Grieg's "Ich Liebe Dich" to some light modern drama when "I'd Love to Live in Loveland" would be more suitable.
>
> Then, of course, there are pictures when no songs can be used. One I have in mind is "At Napoleon's Command" (Cines), which I improvised through entirely with the exception of "Marseilles." To have played "Just Before the Battle, Mother" at the title, "The Eve Before the Battle," would have been comedy. The summary of all this is that the picture player must have ingenuity and artistic judgment and an unlimited repertoire.

When the "Manger to the Cross" was exhibited at this house, I was asked and advised to play the "Holy City," but have to explain why this could not be used in any part of the picture. The music was appropriate enough, but not the words, and you know that it would be improper to play "Hosanna in Excelsis" for any of the picture, except at the "Entrance to Jerusalem," and especially where our singer wanted to sing it, that was "On the Way to Calvary."

Now some will probably object to this, as the management did, but these are my ideas of playing the pictures. But if the proprietor wants things done his way, do it that way. My present employers are fine men to work for, and anything in the music line is always left to me, and anything I do is O.K. with them.

Popular Music

Here is where some pianists would have some difficulty in following my ideas. As you know, there are some exhibitors who want the popular hits played incessantly, regardless of the picture on the screen. It might do in some houses, but not here. I use the popular music between reels, opening the show and closing, on weeklies, educational, travelogues, scenics, and some comedies—that is, where they fit the picture. Not criticizing, but as an illustration: In one of our nicest and most up-to-date picture palaces in the west the orchestra played "Brass Band Ephram Jones" and "By the Saskachwan" (from the Pink Lady) for a comedy, the "Punkinville Boys," a rube comedy. Here is where my idea of playing the pictures would get a severe jolt. To me it doesn't make any difference how popular a song is, I don't use it unless it can fit a picture, or be played for some of the aforesaid rules.

I have a certain piece of instrumental music in my library that I have used only three or four times, not popular, but semi-classic. When I can fit it to a picture it sounds 100 per cent better than to just play it any time just because it is pretty.

In regard to old music (popular), it is well to have quite a number of them memorized, if not all the melody, just enough to let the audience get the drift of it. I used the other evening "The Golden Hair Was Hanging Down Her Back," and you would be surprised to know the number of people in the audience that remembered it.

One can use just the title of these popular songs, or the first few lines of the chorus, as "Everybody's Doin' It," "Fiddle Up" (just that much), to a better advantage sometimes than the whole song.

I don't believe it is necessary to memorize all the late "hits" this way, but just the "big hit," as there are a lot of people who don't know all the late popular music.

In playing in small towns it is sufficient to know what are the hits just in your own locality, not what is the rage in Chicago or New York, because some pieces play out in these cities before they reach the smaller places, and especially in the west. In fact, there are lots of hits that die—we never hear them at all.

Therefore it would be useless to try and work this way of playing in such places. A pianist can play a song hit for a month or more in one of the small towns where there is no way of popularizing a song, and unless it is sung, he could never make it as popular as a singer can.

There are always some of these "high brows" criticizing the song hits and rags, but in this business one has to use them as well as the classy ones. I take them as well as the classy ones. I take the same stand as a large exhibitor in the south does. He says: "People don't go to a picture show to hear a concert, but to see the pictures, accompanied by good music."

The following is from the "Motion Picture Story Magazine":

The Appeal of "Beulah Land"
By William Lord Wright

We are told in the Arabian Nights' Entertainment that when Mr. Sinbad, the Sailor, returned from one of his particularly exciting adventures and rested, he was soothed by the sweet strains of music. When some twenty-odd millions of photo-show fans seek relaxation after the cares of the day, they also wish to be soothed by melody. To the discriminating, the music in the motion picture theatres has been anything but soothing.

During the enaction of the dignified production of Biblical times the incessant tapping of the triangle and roll of the snare-drum have rudely detracted from uplift and refining atmosphere. When Bob, the brave lieutenant who gives his life for his country, is breathing his last on the stricken battlefield, the enlivening strains of "Everybody's Doin' It" on the pianoforte has quickly sundered the chord of sentiment connecting the audience with the picture screen, and has transformed an appealing scene into incongruous comedy. But there is promise of better things.

The refining atmosphere cannot be too carefully fostered in the motion picture theatre. I frequently visit a theatre where the musical director requests the audience to name the songs. The favorite selections of children are particularly desired. One little girl the other evening asked for "Beulah Land." That song is close to the child's heart. It's an old-fashioned song; a song of the home. "Beulah Land" has beautiful words and lovely melody. It is a vision of a life Over Yonder; a dream of a joyous future; it is the strongest evidence of immortality there is.

The night "Beulah Land' was sung there immediately followed "The Star of Bethlehem." Never had the films seemed so appealing; the sacred atmosphere had been unconsciously prepared by "Beulah Land," and that large audience was made better for it all.

And there are other songs touching the life immortal that are not out of place in the motion picture theatre when morality pictures are the program. There is the "Home of the Soul," "The Sweet By and By," and a score or more like them, all of which appeal powerfully to the child's heart, and that come into the life of the most cynical with vision unobscured.

The day of the illustrated song, with its insincere sentimentality, is waning in Filmland. Musical bills-of-fare are being selected with thought and care, and this, I unhesitatingly assert, is one of the most important steps forward.

Let us taboo the "popular" songs, many of them winning by their suggestiveness, and return to the good, old-fashioned airs of everyday people, just as the pictures are turning from false standards of life to real people and human sympathy.

And it will not be long before Cinematography will be responsible for a revival of the classic light operatic music. The photo-opera is expected to make its initial bow before so very long. Then selections from "Il Trovatore," "The Bohemian Girl," "Carmen," "Faust," and the lilting airs from Gilbert and Sullivan's "Mascot," "Mikado," "Pinafore," "Patience," etc., will add tone and good taste to the motion picture show.

There is nothing as demoralizing in this world of ours as poor or suggestive music.

. . .

Effect Playing

A few of several effects that can be used by the pianist:

To imitate a violin or mandolin: Strike A and E together; strike D and G together.

Imitation of a calliope, street organ, or music box—Play Rainbow or Good Old Summer Time in treble clef, both hands; play bass real loud and jerky.

Thunder or heavy seas; can also be used for short struggle scenes—Bass clef, "right hand," F, A flat, B, sustain with loud pedal, a chromatic with left hand. To break the monotony if scenes are too long, play F sharp, A natural, and C sharp (right hand); tremolo, F sharp octave, or trill (left hand); crescendo, diminish, both, according to picture.

On comedies, if O.K. with the exhibitor, one can work quite a few effects, such as a fall, slide, or anything on this order, by making a glissando.

If you ever work with a drummer, watch him. See what he uses. There are quite a number a pianist can do himself. This is where you are playing alone.

(Note.) Don't try to work any effects if you have to stop playing any longer than half a second or so, and if not done at the proper time it will spoil the picture.

Now don't use these effects on all pictures, but just occasionally. Where there are too many of these things in a picture, like the Alkali Ike comedies, when he gets on one of his dish-breaking streaks, I never try any of these effects.

Some of these things can be used more often in the cities than in the smaller towns, for in the smaller places one has to play to the same people, and where you play for the same crowd each week one has to be careful and not do the same thing over and over again, and also the same with music, keep getting new music right along.

· · ·

SPECIMEN PROGRAM

FOUR REELS

Drama

Waltz. Mazurka or Redowa.
Nocturne.

Comedy (Split Reel)

Rag. Popular Song. Lively Waltz. Rag.

Society Drama

Novelette. Song Ballad. Waltz.

Scenic or Travelogue

Comic Opera or Standard Selections.

· · ·

The above was just gotten up to show how I arrange my music. The idea is not to have two pieces of music alike, following one another. It depends upon the pictures how each one of these movements arranges itself, in order to suit the action of the players. Where one waltz follows another they both have the same rhythm, and sound like the same piece of music, and gets monotonous. Therefore try and avoid this if possible. This holds true in all kinds of music.

DON'TS

DON'T

- Play the "Flower Song" for every pathetic scene.
- Go to sleep during a war drama. Let the ushers do that.
- Play "Everybody's Doin' It" unless two or more parties die in the same scene.
- Keep your foot on the loud pedal all evening.
- Play on one melody any longer than 20 or 30 minutes.
- Try to silence a baby's cries by playing loudly. The softer you play the sooner the mother will quiet it.
- Look at the audience all the time, as the picture requires your attention now and then.
- Chew the "rag," as there are "minors" in the "flats" above and below.
- Play so loudly the patrons can't see the picture.
- Argue with the proprietor, even if you are wrong.
- Play continuously. Give the audience a chance to think (unless requested to do otherwise.)
- Ridicule a person, by your gaze, when he is enthusiastic about the pictures.
- Play a waltz for an Indian unless a dead one, and not then.
- Come late. Be on time.

From *What and How to Play for Pictures* (Twin Falls, Idaho: Newsprint, 1913), pp. 7–12, 28–37, and 53–60.

Music for the Picture

Clarence E. Sinn

(1911)

Last week included a letter from P. C. H. Hummel, setting forth his methods of working up dramatic pictures in accordance with the thematic principles as laid down by Wagner. I made no comments on this letter, as I received it just before sending in my own, and the subject appeared to deserve more than passing mention. The letters of Richard Wagner, and his biographers, are voluminous on his methods, but I can find nothing sufficiently condensed to quote in this page, or in several pages, for the matter of that. Those who are interested, may find information in Wagner's theoretical writings, "Art and Revolution," "The Art Work of the Future," and "Opera and the Drama." His biographers also touch upon the matter, more or less. Boiled down, it amounts to something like this: To each important character, to each important action, motive or idea, and to each important object (Siegmund's sword, for example), was attached a suggestive musical theme. Whenever the action brought into prominence, any of the characters, motives, or objects, its theme or motif was sung or played. Perhaps Brother Hummel can put it better, but that, I believe, expresses the subject in a few words. Such a method of applying music to the pictures is the ideally perfect one, and if it could be universally carried out, would have nothing to be desired. At least, such is my opinion. But to apply it thoroughly, one must know his pictures thoroughly beforehand. In this, Brother Hummel is fortunate, as well as industrious. He says: "First of all, I read the stories of coming pictures, and make it my business to see them before they are shown at the places where I am employed." There you have it in a nutshell. Given an analytical mind, five years of experience, and opportunity to study the pictures beforehand, any informed pianist ought to be able to get good results. I should like to hear from others on this subject, as it seems to me there is much promising material for thought and discussion.

In addition to his leitmotifs, Wagner employed scenic or descriptive music, and this idea, too, comes well within the lines of moving picture music.

I have touched upon this thematic idea several times in previous articles, although I was merely following the old melodramatic form of attaching a certain easily-remembered melody to each of the principal characters. The germ of the idea is much the same, though of a simple and primitive form. Those who are familiar with the older melodramas, especially the English ones, may remember that the "leading lady" had some pathetic melody, which accompanied her throughout the play. Likewise, the leading man, in scenes when he was the central figure. The villain also came in for his share of "heavy" music for his entrances and big scenes. Other music was neutral, or descriptive, according to scenes and action. Now, this idea applied to pictures, though not so elaborate, as I understand Brother Hummel's to be, is much the same in essentials, and is the form I adopted on which to base these articles. The moving picture story is episodic; short and to the point by necessity. Its component parts are exemplified by the characters telling it, of which one is usually predominant. The principal theme of the story centers about the principal character, or characters, of course, and any musical themes given to these characters must be in harmony with the general tendency of the picture, else they will be out of keeping with the characters themselves. This is why I harp so much on working to the "central idea," or "impression," of the picture. When the musician has classified his picture, and grasped the general trend of it, he should have less trouble in placing his thematics, descriptives, neutrals, and "fill-ins," than if he went at it in a haphazard fashion.

There are some pictures which do not so readily work out in this manner. Some of the more active ones are just one piece of "business" after another, without developing anything in particular, until the thousand feet are up. All you can do is follow the action and not bother about motives and themes. Why should you, when the originators don't? Other pictures have a pronounced theme running right through. Lubin's *His Last Parade* is a case in point. Mr. King's Orpheum Theater Orchestra (Chicago) accompanied the picture as follows:

1. Pathetic till scene changes
2. Patriotic march ("Daughters of the American Revolution," by Lampe), this march is played loud for each marching scene, and softly for each sick-room scene. Continued without a break piano and forte, until the old man is assisted out of the ranks, then:

3. Pathetic till he falls back on his pillow, dead.
4. Then, "The Vacant Chair," till finish. If cornet and drums are in orchestra,
    "Taps" (lights out) may be used before No. 4.

From *Moving Picture World*, January 21, 1911, p. 135.

The Art of Exhibition

Rothapfel on Motion Picture Music—
Its Object and Its Possibilities

W. Stephen Bush

(1914)

One great lesson is being brought home to me by my weekly talks with Rothapfel on the art of exhibition. Exhibiting motion pictures is essentially a new profession and no previous training in any other branch in the business of amusing and entertaining the public will count for very much in the make-up of the successful exhibitor. The man who will hereafter win fame and distinction through his ability to present motion pictures must be something of a musician, something of a specialist in projection, something of an expert in the selection of programs, something of a leader and pioneer, something of an appraiser in all matters of taste, and all these abilities must be fused and blended in just the right proportion.

I know, through the pleasure of personal acquaintanceship, that there are more such exhibitors today than ever before, and when I point to Rothapfel as the best type I surely do not mean to imply that there are no others. All this leads up, naturally, to the subject of this interview, to-wit: Music and the motion picture. The Strand music has become famous, and it is well therefore to listen to the man responsible for this music.

"A book might be written on this subject of unending interest," said Rothapfel as he sat in his office and after he had thoroughly secured himself against the possibility of interruption.

"Yes, music is just as important as the screen is. I pay more attention and give more time to music than to any other accessory in my whole entertainment. The atmosphere of a theater depends in no small measure upon the character of the music. I look to the music to create the feeling of enthusiasm and sympathy in my audience. Music disposes them to accept my performance in the proper spirit. The main object of music, however, is to interpret the story on the screen. Before going any further, let me say that only in certain cases, which I will explain later, do we indulge in what is known as 'playing the pictures.'

"'Playing the pictures' is still the bane of many otherwise intelligently conducted theaters. I have heard managers say time and again how proud they were of their music, that their leader knew how to 'play the pictures.' 'Playing the pictures' is a relic of the crudest stage in the development of motion picture exhibition. We all know what it means: little 'hurries' for galloping horses, a little pathos for a touching scene, etc. At times I would observe flashes of real intelligence where the music would really begin to interpret the picture, but as a rule, it was merely an accident and my hopes were disappointed by hearing the reversion to the regular style of 'playing the pictures.'"

HE SAYS HE IS NO MUSICIAN

"As I am not a musician and afraid of being misunderstood, I will just confine myself to saying that each big picture—the feature of the program, if you will—must be interpreted musically by a general theme which characterizes the nature of the film play. To select this theme it is, of course, necessary to study the entire picture. Let me give you an example. In the play of *Such a Little Queen,* in which Mary Pickford takes the leading part, a little waltz from *Sari* appealed to me. It had a note of pathos alternating with brilliancy and I thought it typical of the character of the queen. If the selection of the theme is a happy one and the theme is capable of being counter-pointed to suit the varying emotions of the play, the effect upon the audience is undeniable. I had the original waltz played as the little queen was coming down the stairs, and it interpreted in a flash the characteristics of the leading character. I caught the atmosphere of the play and variations of the theme accompanied all the telling scenes greatly to the delight of the audience.

"I can give no hard and fast rules for the selection of such a theme. A little knowledge of musical repertoire is needed, of course, and one really cannot have too much of this. A musical memory, too, is very essential and in my case, at least, is a most useful substitute for profound technical knowledge. Now, after having chosen a general theme for my big feature, I fell at liberty to introduce incidental music which has no relation to the general theme. Such incidental music may be a march, a few bars of a popular or patriotic song, etc. This incidental music must fit episodes and situations that are not directly and intimately connected with the main character or the strict dramatic action of the photoplay."

SYMPHONIES IN PICTURES

"Some day I hope great symphonies will be illustrated with motion pictures and then we will have one of the phases of the true relation between the motion picture and music. When we hear music we see pictures. Why should we not be able to reverse this process? The theme must have a climax, that is to say, after accentuating and interpreting the play on the screen, the music must rise to a grand finale and bring out every note of pathos in the picture. This, of course, is very important. If the climax is either overdone or underdone, the effect of the theme is lost and the effort in vain. Rare judgment must be used and one's whole soul and thought must be at their best. So much for music with features.

"I think that the playing of an overture before any picture is shown on the screen is a proper way to begin the entertainment. The overture puts the audience in the proper mood. I know of no better preparation for the audience. The topical review we generally start with a march and carry it along until the first sub-title appears and then we make the music correspond to the picture.

"This, you will say, is 'playing the pictures.' Yes, quite so. But here, 'playing the pictures' is entirely proper and I know of no other way to illustrate a topical review to advantage. In showing a baseball scene, it is entirely proper to give some snappy, popular music and let the impact of ball and bat be plainly heard in the orchestra. If the thing is done properly it rings absolutely true and never fails to please the audience."

PICKING MUSIC FOR DANGEROUS AND
DOUBTFUL SPOTS

By this time it was clear to me that Mr. Rothapfel was analyzing the parts of his own program for the current week and I suggested that we go in the theater and sit down among the audience to listen and learn. I had not seen the show and I was very anxious to find out what music he had chosen for the pictures of the smoking ruins and the charred walls of the Belgian villages that had been struck by the furious God of War. Surely, it seems difficult to find music suitable to such pictures. Indeed, any music with such scenes most at first thought seem altogether incongruous. The screen showed nothing but dull desolation, oppressive in its sameness. Imagine my surprise when I heard the orchestra playing a prelude by the Russian composer Rachmaninov, which, in an almost inspired manner, illustrated and interpreted in harmonized sound the horrors of war. It was terrible, pathetic, gripping. The music supplied what the pictures failed to show: the terror-stricken men, the agonized women and children, the tramp of the pitiless conqueror. The effect of the music upon the audience was startling. As the last scene passed away, I heard a brief collective sigh go up and then a swift, short, strong burst of applause.

"Scenic pictures," continued Rothapfel, "offer one opportunities and occasionally raise such a picture to the importance of the biggest item on the program. Much, for instance, can be made of a pastoral scene. It is delightful to hear the tinkling of a bell in the distance or the fall of water or the roaring of the surf, etc. Only good music will do here, nothing trashy. The music for such pictures should never be too loud. In showing Swiss, Neapolitan, Venetian scenes or landscapes of a similar character, an aria sung behind the scenes never fails to captivate the audience. For pictures showing animal life, pathos and humor should be the dominant notes playing daintily. For scientific pictures a faint monotone, something entirely neutral, is to be preferred and where the subject touches the purely scientific, perhaps an entire stop in the music might be recommended. Comedy should be played to action, a one-step or some light air, good comic opera and musical interpolations get many a laugh when put in a good place. Here the music, of course, can aim at nothing higher than accentuating the comedy situation."

MUSIC FOR THE EXHIBITOR WITH SMALL EQUIPMENT

"In our enthusiasm for your present musical achievements," said I, "let us not forget the exhibitor who lacks your splendid equipment."

"You forget," replied Rothapfel, with one of his characteristic smiles, "that no man ever started with a more limited equipment than your humble servant. My entire musical outfit consisted of a piano. Of course, I had no experience and no training, but my ideals were the same then and even in my humble and dingy surroundings I tried to make music the big feature of my program. I was so anxious about the music that I spent a good deal of time explaining things to my pianist and I was very much worried as to whether she would carry out my ideas. To make assurance doubly sure, I rigged up an electric switchboard with six colors which she always had in sight, and which I operated from the booth where I turned the crank. Oh, yes; I was operating my own machine. We got along very well after a while. In one sense, the man who has no other music than a piano has a much easier time than the conductor of a big orchestra, for he has nothing but his instrument to control.

"Where the exhibitor is able to afford more than a piano, I think a violin might be added first and then an organ; a pipe organ, however small. With these three instruments it is possible to play almost anything. In the Hotel Astor these three instruments, night after night, render a program so varied and beautiful that you would never think that the musical outfit producing it consisted of but these three elements. I would not add anything more to these three instruments until I were able to have an orchestra of ten pieces, as follows: piano, organ, first violin, second violin, viola, 'cello, bass, clarinet, flute, drum. If I were to enlarge this orchestra I would add two French horns, another trumpet, another clarinet and more strings to meet the added increase of tone."

THE STUDY OF MOTION PICTURE
MUSIC STILL IN ITS INFANCY

"The failure of exhibitors to make the most of the musical end of their program has resulted in the closing of many a house that might otherwise have proven a success. Even now our study of this subject is far from thorough and our knowledge far from complete. I only know that I personally have restored the success and popularity of many a motion picture theater, merely by specializing in motion picture music.

"The men who render music to embellish and strengthen the picture must not only be well-trained musicians, but they must have some special qualification. I prefer young men and women who can be more easily moulded and in whom the fire of enthusiasm burns most brightly. Every motion picture musician must have the knack of improvisation, the ability to instantly adapt himself to any class of music. Men or women who are mechanically perfect but otherwise ordinary will not make good material for a first-class motion picture orchestra. I look for a spark of originality in every one of my musicians, and where I see a man or woman who does things just a little different I try to encourage them all I know how. I consider the character or rather the temperament of my musicians and find that men who have traits of good nature, who are loyal and in love with their work, are the most valuable. The kind of musicians I want to keep away from is the man who tries to subordinate the pictures to the music. After all, pictures must always remain the groundwork of our entertainment, and it just jars me when I hear an orchestra hammer away all through a picture with but small regard to the action on the screen. When a musician begins to think that the people come mainly to hear the music and that the pictures are but an incident, he has outlived his usefulness with me.

"I repeat that managers cannot evade their responsibility for the share which music must play in every motion picture entertainment. They must control and inspire the leader. The manager should have some idea as to the qualifications of the musicians and realize that one good musician is worth more than five mediocre men. Every orchestra leader should have on his finger-tips the airs of all nations, the bugle calls of all countries and know plenty of good 'hurries,' mysterioso, etc. In selecting themes it is well to keep away from the hackneyed stuff which everybody uses. There is a perfect wealth of excerpts from operas and overtures that have never been used and will be found suitable for all kinds of occasions."

MUSIC AND THE DAILY CHANGE MAN

"Of course, when a man changes every day he really cannot do the music full justice unless he has a wonderful organization. If he has the right training and a competent staff and if he will make it a point to have his pictures ready for rehearsal early in the morning he may surprise himself at what he can do. Practice of this sort is invaluable to an exhibitor. We have had emergency cases in the Strand where our whole musical program had to be changed on a few hours' notice, but nothing is impossible if you have the energy and proper assistance."

ROTHAPFEL OFTEN LEADS
THE ORCHESTRA HIMSELF

Rothapfel himself takes up the little piece of wood called a baton and takes the place of the leader. Watching him at such moments from the wings it is easy to get the right perspective of his passionate love and study of music. In his hands the baton indeed becomes a magic wand. His orchestra realizes the intimate touch between himself and them and this is a great advantage. It infuses into them a spirit of cooperation and responsibility.

Visitors to the Strand have often been struck by the quiet behavior of the musicians. One scarcely realizes that they are there. They come and disappear almost noiselessly. In many orchestras, even in big theaters, the musicians seem to be anxious to impress the public with the fact that they take none but the most perfunctory interest in their work, that they do not pretend to be artistes but merely mechanics whose chief interest centers in watching the movement of the clock. This feeling of contemptuous indifference toward their own art manifests itself in such men by loud talk, and by ill-repressed laughter suggestive of late hours in a barroom. Such an orchestra, whether at play or at rest, will never send any magnetic currents into the audience and will simply kill all atmosphere. In the management of Rothapfel's orchestra none of these evils appear and he takes care that the spell which music winds about the human heart is never broken at the Strand.

From *Moving Picture World*, October 31, 1914, pp. 627–28.

Selections from
Musical Accompaniment of Moving Pictures

Edith Lang and George West

(1920)

PART II

MUSICAL INTERPRETATION

1. *The Feature Film*

Perhaps the best way of indicating a safe procedure in the musical interpretation of a feature film is to single out one photo-play, and to suggest a musical garb that will fittingly clothe it with strains such will bring out in bolder relief the plastic curves of the story. All of the motion picture concerns issue for each of the pictures which they release a synopsis that enumerates the various characters of the cast and gives an outline of the story. This synopsis should be carefully studied and should enable the player to select music descriptive of the various situations and emotions portrayed.

Let us take as an illustration *The Rose of the World* with Elsie Ferguson.[1] The opening scenes are laid in India, at a British Army Station. This will immediately suggest the necessity of preparing certain strains of music characteristic of the Orient; also of martial music in scenes depicting the soldier life. The story is as follows. Captain S. is married to a 16-year-old girl named Rose, who is very beautiful, but as yet has not awakened to a realization of life and love. (*1. Main love theme, intensely emotional.*) The Captain is about to depart with his troops on a military expedition against rebellious natives. The film shows his leave-taking from the young wife; he tells her that if he returns alive he will teach her what love really means. The troops are seen departing in the distance, with the Captain in command, to the sound of Scottish bagpipes. (*2. Hindu motive interwoven with military march and imitation of bagpipes.*) The troops disappear, and Rose suddenly realizes her loss; she wildly longs for her husband. *(3. Main love theme repeated, with softer registration and rhythmically more agitated accompaniment.)* In the next scene, the return of the troops is shown. *(4. Same musical treatment as No. 2, going from faint to loud, and leading directly into 5. Introduction of Overture to the opera* William Tell.*)* Rose looks in vain for her husband; the officers tactfully inform her that she is left a widow and hand her a box of letters, the only thing that they are bringing back to remind her of her husband. *(6. Main love theme in the minor mode, suggestive of grief and despair.)* The next picture picks up events several years later, when Rose, believing herself a widow, has married the Viceroy of India, and a grand ball is held to celebrate the occasion. *(7. Brilliant waltz music.)* Lieut. R., a comrade of the late Captain S. appears and asks for permission to write the biography of his dead friend. *(8. "Somewhere a voice is calling.")* His request is granted. Rose's niece, a young school girl of "sentimental" age, falls in love with Lieut. R., and consequently is jealous of Rose, whose collaboration in the biography of her husband brings her much in contact with Lieut. R. The mischievous niece places a picture of the late Captain S. on the piano and begins to play and sing. *(9. Imitate school girl trying to play Grieg's "I love you.")* The niece's kitten helps in the performance by prowling leisurely over the keyboard. *(10. Imitate kitten skipping up and down the keys.)* Rose, exasperated, snatches the Captain's photo from the piano and rushes from the room. *(11. Agitated strain based on the main love motive.)* The biography has reached its closing chapter and Lieut. R. demands to see the box containing the late Captain's letters in order to make the story of the last moments complete. Rose feels that these letters are too sacred for the eyes of the outside world. *(12. Massenet's "Elégie," leading into an agitated strain.)* Her husband, the Viceroy, without regard for the delicate feelings of Rose, demands that she surrender the letters in order to help Lieut. R. in his task. Rose realizes how repulsive her present husband is to her and how much she still loves her lost hero. *(13. Suggest the inner struggle of Rose by treating main love motive in minor mode and breaking it up in short phrases which successively rise in pitch, and finally lead into a calmer transition.)* The Viceroy has left Rose's boudoir; she gets out the box of letters and tries to read some of them; her emotion overcomes her and she faints. *(14. Nevin's "The Rosary"; endeavor to make the climax of the song synchronize with the moment at which Rose faints.)* Her health gradually fails and they decide to send her to England to recuperate. *(15. Suggestion of the Hindu theme leading into "Home, Sweet Home.")* Then follow scenes on the ocean liner and of the sea-voyage. *(16. "Sailor, beware.")* Rose returns to England, to the home of her first husband. *(17. "I hear you calling me.")* There she feels nearer to him in spirit, and spends much time in reading over his letters. *(18. Main love theme, with vibrato effects in the treble, and echo registration on the organ.)* She reads of the siege, the battle scenes, and his approaching death by thirst and starvation. *(19. Suggestion of Hindu music, agitated* *strains depicting the battle, leading into a tremendous climax.)* Suddenly the Viceroy and his Hindu secretary appear in the room. Her husband chides her, and becomes more loathsome in her eyes, the quarrel ending in a violent scene at the dinner table. *(20. Snatches of the waltz played for her wedding ball, suggested in a distorted and agitated manner, leading to a brutal outburst which accompanies the final confession of Rose, at the dinner table, that she loathes the Viceroy and belongs only to her first love.)* Rose rushes from the table and seeks to seclude herself in her own rooms. *(21. Suggest "Somewhere a voice is calling.")* In the night a terrible storm comes up. *(22. Storm music from Overture to* William Tell.*)* Rose, in a frenzy, begs her Hindu maid to try an incantation that will bring back the spirit of Captain S. *(23. Over a low rumbling in the bass, suggestive of the continued storm, the weird chant of the Hindu woman rises in the treble; this leads in a big crescendo to the climax.)* At the height of the storm and incantation, Captain S. bursts into the room; he had escaped from the native prison, where he had been held a captive for three years, had managed to disguise himself as a Hindu and to find employment as the Viceroy's secretary. He had been watching to see if his wife still loved him. *(24. Main love theme.)* At the sight of the man whom she believed dead, Rose loses consciousness. Awakening the next morning, she finds her lover at her side; they are reunited, to live happily ever after. *(25. Apotheosis of main love theme.)*

Even this short exposition, briefly outlining the story, will show the variety of music required, and the manifold treatment which it needs, to depict graphically the emotions that animate each scene. Perhaps one of the most difficult things for the beginner to learn is the joining together of musical motives and strains, as enumerated in the above example. It is here that musical taste and the ability to improvise will prove most valuable. . . .

What has been said, under the general recommendations, regarding the necessity of varying constantly the time and key of the accompanying music, in order to avoid monotony, should naturally be borne in mind throughout the musical illustration of the feature film. The transition from one strain to another should be made with the aid of effective modulation. . . . Variety of registration must add color to the music. The player should follow the story closely, and keep his eyes on the film as much as possible.

2."Flash-Backs"

A peculiar feature of many films is the introduction of flash-backs. Thereby is meant the momentary interruption of the pictured story to give in a pictorial "flash" the thought of one of the actors, or to illustrate his words, or again to remind the audience of a secondary action which is supposed to go on at the same time in a different place.

Thus, for instance, a man, driven to despair, may be contemplating suicide. His emotional tension is illustrated in the music by gloomy or tragic accents. The man is about to shoot himself, when in his mind he suddenly sees the home of his childhood with his young orphan sister left to the mercies of this world, if he should destroy himself. The screen shows the old homestead, the sister in her sunbonnet picking flowers in the quaint and pretty garden. Nothing could be farther removed from the horror of the actual situation, than this picture of calm, of innocence and happiness. It fades as abruptly as it sprang up. But the thought of the consequences of his action have suddenly brought the man to realize the cowardice of his plan; he is determined to "stick it out" like a man. Now, it would be a mistake to interrupt the musical tension of the scene by introducing a few bars of "Garden music" while the girl is shown with her flowers; it would cut short the dramatic progress and foil the building up of a climax which comes when the man resolves to live and throws away his gun. Therefore the music should not change its *character* during the flash-back, but is should be very much *subdued* and be instantly softened to a mere whisper while the flash-back is shown, or burst out immediately into normal loudness when the flash-back vanishes.

Another situation in which a flash-back may be employed is the following. An actor may read, or relate to some one else, the account of something that has happened to himself or another person. To make this plain to the audience, the incident itself is often shown in the form of a flash-back. An escaped prisoner of war, standing before his own superiors, may tell how he killed the enemy guard in order to make his escape, and the actual killing of the guard may be recalled to the audience by showing a short phase of the struggle during the telling of the story. The music which accompanies the actual scene need not be changed for the moment during which the flash-back lasts; but in order to emphasize the dramatic tension of the incident, the speed and dynamic intensity of the music played should be heightened during the flash-back. In other words, a piece of moderate tempo and moderate loudness played for the scene in which the man appears before the officers should be played with greater loudness and greater speed while the flash-back lasts, to return instantly to "normal" when the flash-back vanishes. . . .

As will be seen by the above, the handling of flash-backs requires a technique of its own; practice will develop it quickly if the underlying principles are correctly understood. These principles are: in most cases *not* to *disrupt* the continuity of the music while the flash-back lasts, but to *change* the *intensity* by playing the music, characteristic of the main action, in dynamic degree of loudness or softness which befits the secondary action. . . .

3. Animated Cartoon and Slap-Stick Comedy

Many a player, who is otherwise admirably fit to give musical interpretation of moving pictures, falls down on the animated cartoons and burlesque films. This is due to an absence of the all-important sense of humor, or "comedy touch," which is needed in every-day life as much as in this particular branch of the movie entertainment. . . . A cheerful aspect of things, the faculty to laugh with and at the world, are indispensable. In no art of the pictures should the attention of the player be riveted more firmly on the screen than here. If the "point" of the joke be missed, if the player lag behind with his effect, all will be lost, and the audience cheated out of its rightful share of joy. . . .

Nowhere does success, the "getting across" of a picture, depend so much on special effects as it does here. It may be stated candidly that these effects, and the best among them, are not always purely musical. As will be pointed out in the chapter on "Special Effects," a battery of traps and other accessories are really needed to emphasize in a comic manner the action on the screen. It is often noise, more than music, that is wanted to arouse the hilarity of the audience; and the noise again may be of various kinds. It should always be broadly imitative when accompanying a fall, a hit, a slide, a whirl or flight through the air, a brawl, the whistle of an engine, the chirping of a bird, the mewing of a cat, or the barking of a dog. . . .

This part of the show is admirably adapted to the introduction of all sorts of popular songs and dances. The player should keep in touch with the publications of popular music houses, since it will repay him to establish a reputation which will make the public say: "Let's go to the Star Theatre—you always hear the latest tune there." This will prove a never-failing drawing card for the younger generation of movie-fans, and it will react most decidedly to the advantage of the organist in his relation to the box-office and his own earning power.

It is well also to keep in touch with the monthly announcements of the latest phonograph records issued. As a rule, these numbers have proved assured successes, and people like to hear their favorite tunes, either those they already have at home, or new ones which they might want to add to their collection. The player's repertoire should always be kept alive by the infusion of new and up-to-date material. . . .

4. The Comedy Drama

Much that has been said in the previous chapter also applies to this type of film. However, all effects, in general, will have to be toned down, and the methods employed will approach more nearly those of the "feature film." Sense of humor should again be the chief asset of the player. But it should be rather a sense of wit than a fondness for horse-play. Fine musical taste, a light touch, apt musical illustrations, will greatly add to the charm of the picture.

The player will here, as in the feature film, characterize the chief actors by suitable motives; there will be a main theme and the obligatory number of supplementary selections. As there is usually a love story interwoven, there will be need of some sentimental strain besides pieces of a lighter nature. For flights, escapes and chases, the player should hold in readiness various kinds of musical "hurries."[2] . . .

5. *Weekly News Pictures*

The topical character of these pictures calls, as a rule, for topical music. The audience that fills a moving picture house likes to hear the popular success of the hour, be it a song or instrumental number, well played and effectively rendered. It goes without saying that due regard must always be exercised in instances where the music and picture might clash. It will never do to launch forth on a popular dance tune which might fit one scene, showing some public happenings with which this music might agree, and to persist in playing the tune while the picture shifts to the scene of a funeral or disaster. But, as a general rule, the news section of the picture is the one that will give the best opportunity to play the lighter type of popular numbers.

Unless the picture is of such character that it would call for a specially appropriate musical illustration, the tune need not be changed for every scene that is shown. But there are certain events, of which we shall speak in the following paragraphs, that should receive special musical treatment.

Military or civic processions will require martial music. Pictures of weddings might be emphasized by a strain from Mendelssohn's or de Koven's wedding music. A funeral procession should be accompanied by the playing of Chopin's or Beethoven's funeral march. This will also be appropriate for the showing of grave or a cemetery.

Church functions will suggest the playing of a chorale or some well-known sacred music. Patriotic gatherings or the showing of statesmen and royal personages should be accompanied by patriotic music or by the national anthem of the particular country whose statesman or ruler is shown. It is against the law to play garbled versions of "The Star Spangled Banner" or paraphrase on it. If played at all, our national anthem should be given in its entirety, with spirited movement and yet in a dignified manner. However, the anthem should not be dragged in without rhyme or reason, perhaps simply because the flag is displayed in some picture. Since the audience will rise whenever the anthem is played, it should be introduced, if at all, not more than once at each performance, and only when the scene demands it.

The player should familiarize himself with the most important and common bugle signals of the Army. . . .

Frequently pictures of aëroplanes and other air-craft are thrown on the screen. These should be accompanied by light, "soaring" music (such as "Through Space" by Paul Wachs or "Butterfly Chase" by Hugo Argus). If an aëroplane makes a rapid and spectacular descent, the player might lightly glide his thumb down the keys.

Horse races or automobile races call for rapid music. If the player's technique is not sufficiently developed to execute a generally difficult composition that demands a great deal of speed, he may obtain satisfactory results by a rapid *tremolo* in the treble, punctuated by crisp chord progressions, of moderate speed, played in a lower register. . . . Football games may call for college songs. Other sportive happenings, such as baseball or tennis, seldom require special music. It is different with boat races or sailing regattas. They should not only be accompanied by music suggestive of the speed, but also of the graceful movement of the sailing boats, or of the swell of the sea. Waltzes are very appropriate for yachting scenes.

Fire scenes demand music of dramatic excitement, interspersed with *glissandi* (slides) on the keys, from bass to treble, to illustrate the leaping flames. If the fire increases or decreases in violence, the player should suggest this in his music. Should the flames become extinguished, and the scene show the rack and ruin of the place, the music should calm down and express the mournful desolation of the picture.

For launching of boats, it is advisable to add to the tension of the picture by accompanying the sliding of the boat along the ways with an appropriate tremolo in the treble, breaking into a joyous tune of a "horn-pipe" character when the boat takes the water. The player will find it useful to familiarize himself with a number of chanties or sailor songs, as they will fit in not only with "news" pictures, but in a great many feature films.

In the showing of industrial plants where hammering and the clangor of machines dominate, such pieces as the "Anvil Chorus" will often add to the enjoyment of the audience. Pictures of agricultural scenes might fittingly be accompanied by some of the "rural" songs and dances that the audience is familiar with. Scenes in the South, cotton fields, steamers on the Mississippi, etc., etc., will call for the songs of Stephen Foster, Virginia reels, Negro spirituals, etc.

Events in foreign lands, if these lands are in the Orient, will take on added significance in the minds of the audience if they are accompanied by music which suggests Oriental strains.[3] . . .

Under the heading of "news" pictures are often run films that portray the latest fashions. Such exhibitions require no special music. They call for agreeable and fluent salon music, or waltzes. . . .

6. Educational Films

More than any other pictures, educational films should absorb the whole attention of the spectators. By their very nature and purpose, they are intended to impart information or instruction of a general or special order. The music that accompanies such views should therefore be carefully calculated not to distract the attention. The player should avoid loud or showy pieces, and instead play music that will be conducive to the creation of a calm and receptive mood in the listener.

The organ registration for such pieces should be soft, nor should it be too changeful, but rather adhere to one and the same registration for some length of time.

There may be certain views, however, which by virtue of a musical emphasis will tell their lesson more vividly. In the showing of growth and development of flowers or insects, a crescendo that follows the progress of the picture might not be out of place. Certain views of animal life may suggest to the player particular effects that will be in keeping with the story being told on the screen. Scientific demonstrations rarely call for special effects.

The case is different when the education is to be imparted by means of travel pictures. These require a few words of special advice.

7. Travel Views

In dealing with travel views the player should bear in mind, first of all, that he must provide his memory or his stock of accessible music with a number of pieces that are directly intended by their composers as nature studies more or less sharply defining certain moods on land and sea, or will do so by implication. The well-stocked library of a picture player should contain various categories of music, catalogued according to the applicability of each piece, with plenty of cross references so that at a moment's notice the player may lay his hand on the desired composition. For travel views he may find it convenient to order his music according to 1, nature in general, and 2, special countries, with a possible addition of 3, particular occupations or situations.

Under the heading of "Nature in General" would come 1, landscapes and 2, water scenes. The first of these may appear in three general aspects; namely, 1, sunny, 2, cloudy, and 3, stormy. Music will be found that will fit more intimately the views of placid gardens and orchards, harmonize with undulating fields, shady woods, rugged mountains, or majestic glaciers. In each case, a certain affinity between the music and the pictured scene should be sought.

There exists a great deal of music that by its very name suggests woodland scenes, or quaint gardens (see especially the works of MacDowell, Nevin, or Grieg).

"Water scenes," on the other hand, may differentiate between views of brooks, lakes, rivers, or oceans. Here, again, any number of compositions with suggestive titles will give the player ample material to choose from. A frequent occurrence is the showing of cascades or rapids. These lend themselves admirably to musical illustration by means of brilliant arpeggios or purling runs. The seascape, in turn, may be shown in a state of utter calm, of moderate motion, or lashed by a storm. Each will require a different musical treatment.

While it is difficult to give a complete catalogue of music that will embrace all possible travel pictures, the following suggestions will at least serve to call the player's attention to some of the scenes he is likely to encounter. . . .

Among the pictures of the U.S.A. the player will have to reckon with Southern scenes (negro activities, etc.), which will call for tunes that are typical of the South, such as the songs of Stephen Foster and others. The West will furnish pictures of cowboys, round-ups, mining activities, mountain scenes, etc., which may be made more graphic by the playing of music that approximates the particular situation. Coast scenes will generally demand music that in some way suggests the water. From the North you may expect views of winter sports, such as skating, skiing, or ice-boating. The player should know a number of typically American songs and tunes, representative of various states and races.

The Orient, in general, furnishes a limited type of views. There are processions, temple scenes, dances, fête days, and the like. The player should command over a fairly representative repertoire of exotic strains, some typical of Arabia and Persia, some of India, others of China and Japan. There are distinct differences between the music of these countries, and an earnest student of the subject will try to find something characteristic of each of them. . . .

It may be well to remind the player with what variety of scenes in views of Europe he may meet. He will do well to carry in his memory some of the well-known folk-songs of England, Scotland, and Ireland, folk-dances of Italy and Spain, folk-tunes of Russia and Scandinavia, and some characteristic songs of France. It will not do always to play the national anthems of such countries except when really national events are shown. For travel pictures the folk-song literature of these countries should be drawn upon.[4]

PART III

THE THEATRICAL ORGAN

Chapter 5

Special Effects, and How to Produce Them

The best, and the only safe, way of producing special effects is to leave them in the hands of a capable trap-drummer who has provided himself with all the hundred and one noise-making apparatuses now on the market for imitating everything from a baby's cry of "Ma-ma" to a horse-laugh, "Ha-Ha"; whistles; squeals; imitations of the various sounds made by machinery, i.e. sawmills, motors (aëroplane, automobile, motor boats, steam engines, motor cycles); shots (cannon, rifle, revolver); crashes; breaking glass; crumbling of walls; falling timber; rain; thunder; surf; tramp of marching feet; knocks; raps; burlesque falls where the hero, a Charlie Chaplin or Fatty Arbuckle, comes to earth with the sound of a clap of thunder assisted by a dozen tin wash-boilers, topped off by a Chinese gong.

There has been much discussion as to whether or not such performance comes under the duties of the organist. The writers do not think so. No one can play the organ artistically and at the same time work traps. It is better therefore to let pass unnoticed such effects as cannot be produced easily and legitimately on the organ itself. Of course, on the new unit orchestra "organs," these traps are actually a part of the instrument, the organist merely pushing a button or tapping a pedal for a certain effect. The fact that these contraptions are usually out of working order takes us back to the assumption that the organist had better let the traps alone.

The following are some of the legitimate "special effects":

Rain—light string tone in quick arpeggii or tremolo.

Wind and rain—light string tone in fast chromatic scales in 3ds, 6ths, and 4ths.

Wind and rain and thunder—all the above with heavy pedal tone, holding down two pedal notes at once when rumble of thunder is desired.

Crash of thunder—any heavy chord, played *sfz* in the lower register, full organ and ped., with immediate *diminuendo*.

Whistles—a minor or augmented chord. Each organist should determine for himself a characteristic chord, by listening to the town fire whistle or to the locomotive, and deciphering the tones for himself.

Bells—Almost every theatrical organ has a set of bells; hence there is no need of imitation. On the piano, chimes may be imitated [with octaves filled in with open 5th].

Glissando—This effect is especially useful in comedy, refined and burlesque. A slip or fall is emphasized by a *glissando* with one hand followed by a *bump* with full organ, swells closed as desired. The *glissando* is produced by stiffing the thumb and dragging it up or down the length of the keyboard using the thumb nail as the point of contact. The *glissando* is used to illustrate a "slip" sudden descent of an aëroplane, whizzing of an automobile around a corner, any sliding sensation or one of intense speed.

Bump or fall—Slap the keys with the palm of the hand, lower octaves for a heavy fall, upper octaves for lighter effects.

Silence—This is one of the most important and telling effects when properly used. Any extremely tense situation is heightened by a moment's silence, just before the climax is reached. Suspense, such as when two people, searching for each other, are almost in contact yet each unconscious of the other person's nearness. In the presence of death, a "close-up" view of a dead person, *absolute silence* is the only adequate description, dramatically, pictorially and musically.

Recitative—Use recitative every now and then to lighten the musical setting, or to heighten a tension.

Xylophone—This stop is useful in comedies. Use it only as solo, very staccato, with light string acc.

Approaching a climax—Thereby is meant that tense moment when, in a great automobile sweepstakes race, the cars are approaching "death curve," or when we can see them in the distance coming into the final "home-stretch"; or where a man is on a great height and is about to fall, either to safety or destruction, etc., etc.; in such cases a low menacing rumble is of great help with soft string and 16' bourdon tones. Sometimes just a pedal rumble is the thing, produced by holding down two adjacent pedal keys. This rumble is frequently noticed in the orchestra during acrobatic acts in vaudeville.[5] When the "thriller" of the act is about to take place, the orchestra stops and the snaredrum begins its subtle, sinister rumble, increasing in volume until the successful fall or jump takes place, when the whole orchestra comes in *fortissimo* to applaud the performance.

Galloping horse—Any music Allegro 6/8 seems to convey this effect. "Light Cavalry" Overture by Suppé seems to be the most popular selection. By playing this rhythm softly the effect of distance is lent; increasing the volume of tone brings the horses nearer in the mind of the listener. A more ambitious player may also study the "Ride of the Valkyries" by Wagner, or "Mazeppa" by Liszt.

Jazz band—The only way to imitate a jazz band is to hear one of these unique organizations. . . . The general idea is to have one hand play the tune, while the other hand "jazzes" or syncopates around it, the pedals performing the drum and double bass parts.

From *Musical Accompaniment of Moving Pictures: A Practical Manual for Pianists and Organists* (New York: G. Schirmer, 1920), pp. 31–43.

NOTES

1. By kind permission of The Famous Players–Lasky Corporation.

2. Grieg's "In the Hall of the Mountain King" is particularly useful as a comedy agitator.

3. The player will find a great many pieces of general usefulness and special applicability to national events in the series of volumes published in the Boston Music Company Edition and containing representative pieces of various national schools. So far, the series comprises the following countries: America, France Russia, Scandinavia, Italy, Germany, Bohemia (Slovak countries), Spain and Finland.

4. Much useful music will be found in the volumes of various national schools contained in the Boston music Company Edition and mentioned in footnote [3].

5. By careful observance of good vaudeville performances, many ideas may be gained in the way of special effects, particularly for comedy work.

Selections from *Musical Presentation of Motion Pictures*

George Beynon

(1921)

CHAPTER VI. PROPER PRESENTATION OF PICTURES: THE THEME AND HOW TO USE IT

It may be that you too have suffered. It may have happened that you entered a theatre to see Mary Pickford or Douglas Fairbanks earn a paltry stipend. It is possible that after you had enjoyed the comedy and the Review, you settled back in your seat anticipating an hour and a quarter of unadulterated joy. As the heroine was introduced, the orchestra opened the picture with "Land of Dreams," that simple and melodic number by Driffil. You were greatly impressed, and mentally registered the musical selection as a *beautiful* one. The music changed as the picture proceeded on its way. Subsequently, the first selection was played again. It became to your mind a *nice* number. Two or three short musical selections intervened and you heard it again. It was then only a *fair* number. An agitato followed and again the same number knocked at your brain in its repetition. It was a *monotonous* number. The third reel was shown, and again you heard it. You became restless and could not understand why they played it so frequently. It palled. As the music continued, this poor little selection was dragged in by the heels whenever the star appeared in the foreground. It became fairly maddening by its persistency. Your soul rebelled and you *hate* that music forever. This innocent little musical piece that was selected for your enjoyment, and at first seemed destined to fulfill its mission, but which, through endless reiteration, caused you so much irritation, is known by photoplay musicians as the "Theme."

Notwithstanding this truthful yet painful description of the distorted situation to which the Theme may lend itself, or into which it may be pushed by the ill-advised judgment of some one who should know better, it has a definite and well-defined purpose and, if properly used, enhances the picture immeasurably. It should be selected carefully and with due consideration for the character, episode, heroine, villain or ingénue; the decision depending upon the desire to make the one character stand out prominently and impressively throughout the picture.

In a photoplay where an act is performed frequently for a purpose, the Theme may be used to denote that purpose. In an allegorical picture, it should convey the thought for which certain scenes stand. Sometimes two or more Themes are suggested, but they are totally impracticable from every standpoint in a musical setting and are not at all feasible when used in connection with a small combination of musicians. However, when played by a large orchestra, more than one Theme can be made very effective, for there is always a second man to each instrument. While the first plays, the second turns the pages and ferrets out the particular Theme wanted. This gives an opportunity to make the setting of a feature more impressive by giving a "Love Theme" to the hero or heroine and a "Sinister Theme" to the villain, if the latter be of sufficient prominence to warrant the distinction.

Organists, when playing for the picture show, have no difficulty in suiting each scene with appropriate music, and any number of Themes are possible.

Not only are they possible, but are much to be desired, as the organ provides facilities for changing the *tempo,* rhythm and color of each.

Under the proper treatment, a theme which was originally bright and used for the heroine may be played in a minor key during a scene in which she is sad. If she dies, it is possible to improvise upon the same Theme a form of dirge which will hold the atmosphere and retain the personality of the star. In fact, there is no limit to the vast resources of the organ in playing Themes.

Naturally, the selection of a Theme in the fitting of a picture becomes of vital importance. To choose a waltz as the motif for Jean Valjean in *Les Misérables* would be ridiculous, and the selection of a dramatic Theme for Rebecca in "Rebecca of Sunnybrook Farm" would be equally ill-advised. A careful study of the characters represented should be made and the dramatic value of the Theme should be understood. Then it will be selected with due consideration for the dominant feeling of the play.

If the Theme be picked for the star in a heavy drama, and her part be of a highly dramatic order, the natural selection would be a dramatic Theme, such as "Cavatina" (Böhm), "Prelude" (Damrosch), or "Prelude" (Rachmaninoff). If the plot be heavy and the entire setting cumbersome and labored, it would be well to give the Theme to the ingénue or to a lighter role, thus gaining variety of color in the picture music.

Of course, all this cannot be done at the first performance of a feature, if the leader has had no opportunity to preview the picture. In this respect the organist has a distinct advantage over the orchestra leader. Placed at the console before the screen, he readily follows the picture at its first performance and, as the question gives him no concern, is in a position to offer a creditable performance at the first attempt. The orchestra leader must depend upon a furnished cue-sheet, which may or may not suggest a number already in his library. On the other hand, the suggested number may be one that he has used but recently and is not permissible on that account. Audiences have good memories, and it is not advisable to impress upon their minds the idea that there is a dearth of music in the leader's library. But after he has seen the picture, heard his incidental music in the setting, noted the high lights in the play, and closely analyzed the situation with regard to his orchestral requirements, he can usually add a fifty per cent value to his musical presentation by a better selection of his Theme. . . .

Fox-trots, One-steps or Two-steps make poor Themes, and are seldom used as such; but they are permissible under certain conditions—for instance, in a Chaplin comedy or one that runs more than one reel. For example, if the comedian's chief stunt is to fall asleep throughout the entire picture, a good Theme to accentuate the situation would be, "Please Go 'Way and Let Me Sleep." Carrying out this principle, it is a simple matter to decide upon the Theme necessary for a comedy. Waltzes and Intermezzos are little used except for pictures in which children are starred. The Moderato movements, Allegros and Allegrettos are chiefly suggested and should be decidedly melodious and catchy, if possible, to establish the association of ideas. Andantes will fit the more serious characters, while Andantinos, Lentos and Adagios are reserved for the dramatic roles.

Owing to the nature of pictorial reviews, there is never any Theme required. The same might be said concerning scenics. Even features of mediocrity or those lacking a prominent leading role might be played without one. A safe rule to follow when in doubt is found in the definition of a Theme: *A Theme is a number emblematic and significant of the nucleus around which the silent drama is built, whether it be a principal or a principle.* If there be no reason for a Theme, do not use one. There is grave danger in setting all features along hackneyed lines, introducing a Theme without reason for its presence. Features which are strongly atmospheric or picturesque should be played without a Theme, unless under exceptional circumstances.

Frequently the predominant idea of a picture may be carried out by a repetition of the opening number to close the picture, for it brings the auditors back to that mental state in which they were when the feature commenced.

As pictures deal more extensively with psychological subjects, the Theme will be chosen to represent the trend of the play and will become in reality a motif, signifying the underlying or hidden objective. . . .

These few suggestions regarding this very important selection for the musical setting should be carefully considered. As stated at the beginning of the chapter, if the Theme is used too frequently it is detrimental to the musical interpretation of the picture, annoys the patrons of the theatre, and kills the particular selection for further use. Use long Themes, because the scene depicted may be a lengthy one and a short Theme would necessitate a tiresome repetition of the music. Use discretion in selecting the Theme. Play it according to the action, and only when a motif is required. The results will amply justify the time spent and well repay the thought given to this most important subject.

CHAPTER VII. PROPER PRESENTATION OF PICTURES: SONGS AS THEMES

As the demand for themes in picture music becomes more urgent and also more exacting, the light intermezzo or serenade, the dreamy waltz or cavatina, is forced into the background and the song-theme takes a more prominent place in presenting the virtues of the heroine. The essential attributes of a theme are melody and rhythm. These are always found in songs, because the lyrics compel rhythmic measure, and melody is what brings the song out of the muck and establishes it as a "hit."

There are many kinds of song which should be classified under separate heads in the leader's library. Those used for themes are *Classic,* which include works of the masters and near masters found in concert and recital programs, and *light opera arias* and *popular songs,* sometimes called by the discourteous "Shoo-fly music." The classic might be divided into two sections, listed as Concert Songs and Grand Opera Arias. The latter class is not used extensively; with a corner of its own it would not receive the rough handling incident to a search for choice concert numbers.

Such themes as "Asthore" (Trotère); "Still as the Night," "For All Eternity" (Mascheroni); and the two famous numbers by Tosti, "Good-bye" and "Serenade," should be found in the Concert Song group. These are only a few examples indicative of the wide field from which one may choose. . . .

Of the better known Grand Opera Arias, the most familiar themes are "My Heart at Thy Sweet Voice," from *Samson and Delilah;* "The Toreador's Song," "Habanera," and the "Don José Aria," from *Carmen;* "Valentine's Song," from *Faust;* and the "Spring Song," from *Manon.* The use of these numbers should depend entirely upon the likeness between the screen actor and the opera principal, taking into consideration also the similarity of dominant emotions prevailing in the scenes. The task of fitting pictures with themes from operas is a ticklish one. If properly chosen, they enhance the musical setting immeasurably, but if the leader is a poor guesser, that number becomes a thorn in the musical flesh of the auditors, pricking them at every appearance.

Under the heading of Grand Opera Arias should be filed those popular duets, trios, quartets and sextets which can sometimes be used to advantage. Hackneyed "has beens" like the "Trio from Faust," "Quartet from Rigoletto," and "Sextet from Lucia," should find the light of day only when that day is so wet and dreary that the patronage has completely crippled the cash box. Aside from the fact that those "Hurdy-Gurdy" favorites have traditional associations which forever bar them from depicting new ideas, no one wants to sit through a picture which he has paid to see and be regaled with music which he has frequently paid to be rid of. Have some consideration for those who pay at the wicket. You may not have played the Faust trio for some months, yet the organ-grinder that very morning chose it as his *pièce de résistance* for the neighborhood. . . .

Light Opera Arias usually carry a title that is significant of the general feeling of the song. They are known by their titles as well as by their melodies, and the masses of the musically unwashed can invariably call them by name. Therefore, it becomes comparatively safe to select light opera numbers by their titles. The principal motif in Romberg's "Blue Paradise" is a song called "Auf Wiedersehn," which freely translated means "Until We Meet Again." The title in itself holds the suggestion of parting with the hope of a safe return, and could be applied to a heroine who, in the early stages of the picture plot, is torn from her lover and after many adventures returns to him—usually in the last reel. This number can be used as an incidental selection to fit any scene denoting a sad farewell. . . .

For pictures which hold little dramatic intensity but lots of heart interest, light opera arias can be made to serve as effective themes.

Musical Comedy numbers may be regarded in the same light as light opera, and owing to their popularity are always prime favorites as themes. Use them not too often, and they become as verdant oases in the desert of heavy music. They may be catalogued with light opera selections or placed under a separate listing, according to the ideas of the musical director.

Popular music depends upon the sentiment expressed in the lyrics of the song for its adaptability as a theme. The ballad-style is used for features, while the lighter numbers can be fitted to Comedies and Pictorial Reviews.

There is a strong tendency prevalent in the average audience to hum or sing with the orchestra when they are playing something familiar. Herein lies a danger in using popular songs for themes. The orchestra leader cannot afford to embarrass some patronage by providing a vehicle of annoyance in the shape of a catchy song which is sure to be whistled. . . .

There is also a group of sacred songs which can be requisitioned frequently to good purpose. Of late, the religious aspect of pictures has been strongly developed and subtitles inserted which suggest certain hymns or sacred numbers. Besides the usual hymns, "Rock of Ages," "Nearer, My God, to Thee," "Lead, Kindly Light," etc., there are the splendid orchestrations of "The Lost Chord," "The Palms," and "The Holy City." "Onward, Christian Soldiers" should be classed under marches, as it has officially become the marching song of the Red Cross Society.

Let us not forget Folk-Songs and Patriotic numbers. They are closely allied, and yet must be listed separately, for reasons of practicability. In the former group we find "In the Gloaming," "Seeing Nellie Home," "Swanee River," "Old Kentucky Home," "Just a Song at Twilight," and many others of fond memory.

Nothing is more effective than these touching old ballads. They become the spice with which to flavor the musical interpretation of the picture, reaching the hearts of the listeners and bringing the tears to their eyes.

There is a strange peculiarity about the acceptance of these folk-songs by the average audience. They are better known than any other form of music, yet they are listened to with bated breath. No whispering or humming desecrates their sublimity. On the other hand, as a class they stand alone as an exception to our general rule regarding the choosing of material for picture settings. We have found that no number should be used that will, by its influence, detract from the picture. Every folk-song has for everybody a significance gained through hearing it during some crisis in their careers. It is closely associated with that epoch in their lives, and its repeated rendition brings back the sadness of by-gone days. Yet, in spite of the contradiction of dominant emotions, and because the song has become part of themselves, the folk-song can be used with telling effect as a theme. Its possibilities are more numerous as incidental music; but if treated as a thematic motif, it will touch the hearts of the auditors and impress the picture strongly on their minds.

The subject of the song-theme has been merely touched upon, for its magnitude carries many tentacles, the following of which would lead us far afield. We have tried to suggest a few possibilities in the thematic treatment of songs that may start a line of thought in the leader's mind, bringing greater results than we could possibly anticipate.

CHAPTER VIII. PROPER PRESENTATION OF PICTURES: THE CHOICE OF INCIDENTAL MUSIC

Many orchestra leaders regard the theme as the chief factor in a musical setting. Their energies being directed toward making it so, and in the focusing upon one musical item, they foreshorten their vision, losing the larger view of the general picture presentation. The theme then becomes a jagged rock projecting toward heaven from a drab and somewhat level ground composed of trivial and inconsequential melodies.

It is the very nature of a good theme that it should be distinctive, not only in melody but in harmonic strength and individuality; therefore, we can find no fault with the theme. The error lies with the leader who neglects to bolster it up with incidental music. . . .

The best choice of incidental music to start a musical setting is always one in which is found the general sentiment of the picture or the atmosphere in which the play is cloaked. This sometimes requires a marked degree of discretion. The leader must know his musical history and be an adept in picking out one school from the other. An experience which illustrates this occurred in the presentation of one of those super-features for which a special score was arranged and an augmented orchestra engaged. The plot was highly dramatic in character, and the arranger, wishing to prepare the minds of the audience musically for what they might expect, opened with the "España" rhapsody by Chabrier. Immediately, the patrons' minds were imbued with the idea that the picture would be Spanish in atmosphere. Much to their surprise and disgust, the first scene opened in Paris while the orchestra still played the music of Spain. Not once during the entire eight reels was there a glimpse of any location that was not French. The plot was French, the acting was French, the costumes were French, and all typically so. Later, the music became French also, but somewhat apologetically, as though feeling its guilt and fearing the censure of its auditors. . . .

Never introduce a Japanese picture by playing an Egyptian serenade, for there will surely be a son of Nippon, grinding his teeth, somewhere in the audience. An excuse that there is but little Japanese music may have some ground to stand on, but this does not make it valid, for there is certainly enough to fit one picture; and few exhibitors run two Japanese pictures in consecutive order. If the leader can fit one, he can fit all by a simple arrangement of ballads, marches, intermezzos or serenades. . . .

Allowing the picture to be screened in silence is an unforgivable offence that calls for the severest censure. No picture would begin in silence under any conditions, as will be discussed in a later chapter dealing with silence as a factor in picture playing. . . .

Secondary to suitability, the music in a setting should be varied. Without variety of *tempo*, there can be but little variety of color; and a musical accompaniment consisting of a series of waltzes would be a very sorry sort of picture portrayal. All bright scenes should not be fitted with the same style of selection. Serenades, intermezzos, light waltzes, mazurkas, two-steps and caprices may be used effectively to convey brightness and at the same time provide variety. Ballads, lullabyes, slow serenades, cavatinas and reveries suit slow scenes that may be tinged with sadness or regret. Here again one gets ample variety. Neutral situations must be fitted according to locations, conditions, or plot development, and, if many of them appear, the music should be sufficiently varied to dispel any idea of an integral connection one with another.

Do not use too much music composed by one man. Each has a certain style and technique which is noticeable to an almost incredible extent, even among the masses. The melodies may be different, the *tempo* changed and the harmonic treatment may be widely divergent, but we hear people say, "That sounds like Debussy"—and it is Debussy. Every composer is stamped with his hallmark, and no one knowing his Grieg could be told that "Morning" was by Massenet.

Thus, to obtain variety in its widest sense, the choice of composers enters largely into the question, although the composer should not be sacrificed for the sake of variety, if the selection be different in *tempo* and arrangement, but peculiarly characteristic of the composer.

In conjunction with variety, we must have a standard style to our musical settings. Classic or non-classic music must prevail for the entire picture under ordinary conditions. It is unwise to mix into a musical setting, comprising excerpts from grand opera or symphonies, the popular "Shoo-fly" one-steps of the day. They have their place in many light comedy dramas, and the intrusion of Grieg's Peer Gynt Suite into this class of musical material would be equally foolish. . . .

Then again the music must be selected with an eye to its sonority or volume, and graded upward to the climax and downward to the anti-climax of the picture. Taking it for granted that the climax is reached in the fourth reel of a five-reel feature, the music should follow the development of the play, gradually increasing in sonority and massiveness until the climax number is reached, when it should die down with the photoplay. This gives us a mountain with a long grade upward and a rapid descent from the peak. . . .

Thus we find three elementary principles for the selection of incidental music that have proved their worth:

First. Get a variety in *tempi* and composers.

Second. Use a uniform style or class of music.

Third. Obtain a graded sonority; up toward, and down from, the climax of the picture.

Naturally, the duration of incidental numbers must depend upon the length of scene for which they are used. The key matters only so far as it gives a smooth progression from one piece to the next. Synchrony and key-sequence are the technical requirements that enter into the playing of all music for the pictures.

No doubt many new rules regarding the choice of incidental music will be evolved and developed in the future, but the leader of to-day can safely follow the three enumerated in this chapter. They will save him from many a pitfall and, when memorized, will smooth out the manifold difficulties which he now encounters in score making.

CHAPTER XII. SYNCHRONY

Synchrony as applied to picture playing means the exact timing of the accompaniment to the score. It is an absolutely essential feature of a musical score arranged for motion pictures. Everybody in the audience appreciates it in a way, although probably few, except musicians, recognize the factor which obviates sudden stops and jarring changes in the musical setting.

Synchrony, however, has not yet been reduced to its ultimate perfection. It is at present comparative, depending largely upon the intelligence of the orchestra leader. A correct knowledge of *tempo*, the completeness of the film as originally set to music, the steadiness of projection and the care of the operator are all contributing factors.

Synchrony is only a matter of a stop-watch with a knowledge of addition and subtraction so far as the viewing of the picture in the projection room is concerned. But the idea back of synchronization goes further than that simple problem in mathematics.

In selecting a number for a score, allowance must be made to overcome the changes of speed of the operating machine. It is almost impossible to take a given number of bars of a "Hurry" and make it fit. If the conductor is fortunate in striking the right tempo—one which corresponds with the speed of the film—he may carry it no further than the following cue, but that is purely a matter of luck. The difficulty lies in the fact that a fast Allegro is not elastic. For perfect synchrony, numbers with pause notes, change of *tempo*, or drawn-out endings, are the most desirable. These act as a block signal and insure against overrunning the cue. To properly gauge these blocks, the ability does not lie solely in mathematics, but requires considerable musicianly art as well.

The secret of synchrony is not so much in careful timing of the selections as in the accurate judgment of the musical director. Music need not be cut to fit the situation; but, if care be taken in the finishing of phrases, the musical setting becomes cohesive—one complete whole that conveys to the audience that sense of unity so essential to plot portrayal.

Tempo is, of course, comparative. Many leaders have their own individual conception of *Andante, Allegro, Moderato,* etc. But metronome-marks are of the utmost importance and should always be relied upon wherever quoted.

If the film has been cut, certain scenes will be shorter than the music assigned. This is a frequent occurrence, as the producing companies know to their sorrow. In different States, certain portions of film are not allowed because of censorship. These portions vary according to the varied minds of the censors. Thus the timing of a musical setting with the scenes may be absolutely perfect in Pennsylvania and entirely at odds in Ohio. Also, there have been operators so enamored of certain scenes from a film that these portions were found to be among the missing when the film reached its next exhibitor.

Another problem in connection with synchrony is purely a mechanical one. The change of the "load" in the electrical current supplied to the projection machines will vary the speed of projection and upset the synchrony of the music. Should the operator, while shifting reels, carelessly thread twenty feet of action through, the music will outrun the scene for which it was intended. Synchrony is usually based on a schedule projection of one thousand feet in fifteen minutes. Again we find that projection is comparative, and the judgment of the operator is called into play. A difference of one minute per one thousand feet for five reels may seriously disturb the unity of both setting and scene.

Furthermore, in synchronizing the original score in the operating room, there is usually a double projection machine, and consequently no time is lost between reels. In showing pictures, however, where there is only one machine available, there is necessarily a loss of several minutes consumed by the changing of the film. This has a tendency to destroy synchrony, unless the leader is watchful.

With a live leader who takes an intelligent interest in this work at the head of the orchestra, these difficulties can be overcome; but any man who runs through the score, regardless of consequences, will find that the scenes on the screen do not coincide with the music assigned in the score. Admittedly, the synchronizing, or exact timing of music and picture, has not yet reached a state of perfection. The method of achieving perfect synchrony may still be open to improvement, but the method now employed will yield wonderful results if faithfully followed. . . .

We have now reached what may be called the Synchrony Era. All the larger theatres make it a special feature of their settings. The Rialto and Rivoli orchestras in New York have raised this department to a very high standard. Not only is the musical setting synchronized for the feature picture, but the Pictorial Review and the Scenic receive just as careful treatment. The pleasure derived by the auditors is thus materially increased. There is no breaking of phrases, no harsh clashing of extraneous keys. Every number fits the situation upon the screen, each theme is clearly defined, and, as the curtain rings down upon the picture, one feels that the music has been cohesive and coherent.

From *Musical Presentation of Motion Pictures* (New York: G. Schirmer, 1921), pp. 61–80 and 101–4.

Selections from *Encyclopaedia of Music for Pictures*

Erno Rapee

(1925)

CHAPTER 2. THE OVERTURE

The Overture and its selection depends largely upon the general lay-out of the program. If you have a Spanish picture and you are building a Spanish prologue and you happen to have a Spanish scenic it is obviously desirable to choose a Spanish Overture to keep the program in the same vein throughout. Establish your atmosphere with your Overture and keep the same atmosphere leading up to your feature picture, which is assumed to be the strongest number on your program. Should the picture have no particular local color and no bearing upon the make-up of your show as a whole, then the selection of the Overture should be made with the idea of having your program as diversified in character as possible, or it may be determined by the particular taste of your audience.

The size of the orchestra is, of course, a very important question. Where there is an orchestra of thirty-two or more pieces the performance of most works of such standard composers as Wagner, Liszt, Tschaikowsky, Verdi, etc., if well performed, will invariably meet with success. Several years ago, the playing of two or three Movements of a Tschaikowsky Symphony (with cuts, of course) in a movie house, was considered a sort of an experiment; today the stage of experiment with Tschaikowsky and his Symphonies is a matter of the past. The 2nd and 4th Movements of the 4th Symphony or the 3rd and 4th Movements of the 6th Symphony are in the repertoire of every fair size movie orchestra. The same could be said of excerpts from the Wagnerian Operas such as the Valkyries' Ride, Wotan's Farewell, etc.

Christmas and Easter Holidays would naturally suggest particular types of Overtures, such as Christmas Carols, or Easter Chimes in Russia, etc. American

Holidays should, of course, be marked by the use of Yankee Doodle, Dixie, Southern and Northern airs, etc.

The Jubel Overture by Weber has been found particularly useful, as towards the end it develops a big climax to the strains of "God Save The King" which lends itself well to patriotic tableaux. Victor Herbert's American Fantasie is always a satisfactory Overture and can be well used for covering three or four different tableaux during the various sections of the composition.

For Irish Holidays—Victor Herbert's Irish Rhapsody or his Eileen Selection will always be an appropriate overture. A warning word must be said to the ever-anxious Musical Director to choose only such works as the number of men at his disposal can do justice to. Although there are modern orchestrations of practically all the big symphonic works, it is not a pleasure for an intelligent audience to listen to one lone trombone playing English Horn, French Horn and Bass Clarinet parts, which, although they are cued in the Trombone part as a rule, will not give the desired coloring and effect. On the other hand, with an orchestra of fifty men or more it would be wasted energy to play an Overture like "Jolly Robbers."

Recently Rossini's antiquated "Semiramide" was performed by an orchestra of thirty men in one of the larger theatres of New York City but was done so exquisitely that it received round after round of applause, which would show that it is not what you play but how you play it.

I have been asked several times to supply a list of Overtures so the various musical directors throughout the country would not have to weekly go through the worry of finding an Overture, but would only have to consult the list to be covered each and every week. It would be an impossible task to select fifty-two compositions and denote them as "the" Overture to be played in fifty-two weeks of the year, because, as I mentioned before, the size of the orchestra, tastes of your audiences and the general make-up of your program will be important factors in determining the number to be used as an overture. Sometimes a collection of old time songs or a fantasie prepared by the musical director consisting of the most popular hits of well known composers will prove to be good Overtures.

By mentioning these two possibilities we have reached ground too dangerous to tread on extensively, as the solution of the problems presenting themselves in compilations of that sort will depend largely upon the ingenuity and versatility of the musical director.

CHAPTER 5. VOCAL OR DANCE ARTISTS

If your theatre employs vocal or dance artists and builds prologues to the feature picture, the selection of this type of entertainment should be governed by the same principles as those of selecting the Overture. The question as to whether a vocal or dance prologue should be used for any particular picture depends largely upon the atmosphere and the main character of your picture. A Spanish or Italian picture as a rule will lend itself to a dancing prologue, while a western picture, with, perhaps, a "waiting mother" for a "wandering boy" will offer good material for a vocal prologue with a clean western back ground.

I found the following a very satisfactory plan: Start your prologue with off-stage singing drawing nearer and interrupting some kind of pantomime on stage. This will prove particularly effective if done behind the scrim and when the picture is flashed on. Let the singing and dancing continue by dimmed lights until the picture on the screen occupies the complete attention of your audience and your orchestra has drowned the singing on stage. Some pictures have scenes, holding the keynote to the story, which if reproduced in life on the stage will make effective prologues. Building prologues, of course, is a field depending entirely upon individual endeavor, ability, vision, taste and also upon the equipment and staff at the disposal of the conceiver. I want to suggest here a few drops and accessories which can be used in many forms, shades and varieties with a minimum expenditure:

Black Velvet with black border and black legs.

A Silver drop with border and legs of the same or contrasting material.

A Batik drop with border and legs of the same material.

A Sky drop.

A drop with a little house on top of a hill, the foreground being occupied by a lake.

Your black drop is adaptable to many different presentations, either as background for a fine soloist, or when split in the center with a door-way, giving the impression of distance, or with a painted panel representing any number of things according to what your vocal or dancing act may demand. In one particularly effective scene I remember the blacks were used with a church window placed in the center, the window painted on the front side and lighted from the rear. The singer singing "Ave Marie" in the front of the panel was lighted by a blue lamp from above, giving the impression of a person standing outside of a Cathedral. If you have an organ or a harmonium back-stage your effect should be complete.

The Silver curtain will lend itself particularly well for specialty scenes, such as a "Music Box" dance with full lights or Grotesque dance with blue or green lights. Your Batik will be mostly useful for interior sets, particularly by splitting it a little off center and putting in a window, behind which you can use your sky drop. A piano, a vase of flowers, parlor furniture, etc. etc. placed in front of this batik and using dim lights will give a realistic homelike atmosphere.

It is your sky drop which is the most important part of your outfit as it will lend itself to any number of outdoor scenes which can be made very realistic by just using some rocks, flowers or hedges in front in artistic disorder. Stars, moon, sun, cloud, or ripple effects will all enhance the atmosphere. A sky drop will also lend itself to all kinds of silhouette effects. Cut a trap behind the drop and put your lighting strip into it. Either a dancing act or an orchestra in front of the drop with the rest of the stage and house in darkness, will give you a complete silhouette effect. Of course the ideal condition is where you do not have to fit your acts to the drops or hangings on hand, but can go to work and decide what scenery you want to give to the act and then order it.

However, most theatres are not in a position to spend several hundred dollars every week on scenery, so it will depend upon the ingenuity of the producer to make his two or three drops look as attractive as possible by his versatility and by surrounding it with props. The amount of props to carry depends upon the amount of money you can invest or can spend from week to week. Property such as platforms of various heights and sizes, runway, windows of different sizes, some circular, some oblong and some square, a moon, stars, benches, hedges, grass, mats, trees, flower baskets, etc. are absolute necessities in staging acts. No matter how many or how big an act you use or what outlay you can afford for new scenery and property, the one thing to be constantly borne in mind is to avoid sameness of productions. Do not have similar type of singers appear too often in succession; if you have a permanent ballet corps, vary their numbers as much as possible; sometimes bring in a jazz band for the sake of spice. If your orchestra plays a serious symphonic work one week, for the sake of diversity have them play a musical comedy selection the next week. If one act works in an outdoor scene with moonlight, be sure that your next act is surrounded by glowing amber.

CHAPTER 6. MUSICAL ACCOMPANIMENT
TO THE FEATURE PICTURE

A great deal has been written on how to arrange music to feature pictures. Experience and observation have taught me that the simplest procedure is as follows: Firstly, determine the geographic and national atmosphere of your picture; secondly, embody every one of your important characters with a theme. Undoubtedly there will be a Love Theme and most likely there will be a theme for the Villain. If there is a humorous character who makes repeated appearances, he will also have to be characterized by a theme of his own.

It will happen quite often that two characters, each having a theme, will appear together, in which case it will be necessary to write original music for that particular scene treating the two themes according to the rules of counterpoint.

After your atmosphere is established and your characters are endowed with their respective themes, determine if either the playing of atmosphere music or the individual theme will suffice in portraying happenings on the screen or if the psychologic conditions are such that the emotional part will have to be portrayed in preference to atmospheric or characteristic situations. Now you can start setting each scene: if you have a picture playing, for instance, in China, you will have to find all your accompaniment material in existing Chinese music, both to cover atmospheric situations as well as to endow your characters. If there happens to be two Chinese characters and one English, you will of course cover your English character by English music for the sake of contrast.

The choice of the Love Theme is a very important part of the scoring as it is a constantly recurring theme in the average run of pictures and as a rule will impress your audience more than any other theme. Special care should be taken in choosing the Love Theme from various angles. If you have a Western picture dealing with a farm-hand and a country girl, you should choose a musically simple and sweet ballad. If your Love Theme is to cover a relationship between society people, usually portrayed as sophisticated and blasé, choose a number of the type represented by the compositions of such composers as Victor Herbert or Chaminade.

It will often happen that the situations on the screen require the Love Theme being used for an extraordinary length of time, in which case you may have to play four or five choruses. This situation should be handled by varying your orchestrations; play one chorus as a violin solo, then have all the strings play it; the next one can be played on the Oboe or Cello and so forth. If you have exhausted all variations and particularly if the situation is of a dramatic sort, have your men play that same chorus 1/2 a tone higher or lower. As long as you vary your instrumentation or your tonality, it will not get tiresome. The danger of monotony is often encountered playing an oriental picture, as the playing of oriental music for an hour or longer will naturally get on the nerves of almost any listener, more so as oriental music is of a very specific type. In that case grasp every opportunity the picture will afford and play some English, French, Italian or American music to break the monotony.

The Villain ordinarily can easily be represented by any Agitato, of which there are thousands. Distinction should be made between sneaky, boisterous, crafty, powerful and evil-minded villains. A crafty villain who does not exhibit any physical villainy in the course of the picture can be easily described by a dissonant chord being held tremolo and very soft. If the Villain happens to be of the brute type who indulges in lots of physical activities, a fast moving number would be more apt. Sometimes you have a villain whose power to do evil is mighty but he achieves his evil deeds without any physical activities, in which case chords slow and heavy should be a proper synchronization.

The portrayal of humorous characters seems to be rather hard as there is very little music written which in itself sounds humorous and you very often will have to fall back upon your own ingenuity for the creation of such themes. Emotional and dramatic characters and situations are the hardest to fit, firstly because it requires that the music should swell and diminish in accord with the emotional moods portrayed on the screen, and it is a rare good luck to find a piece of dramatic music which will rise and fall simultaneously with the action; secondly because that very dramatic music we have reference to ought to play around the themes which are identified with the characters and within whom the emotional or dramatic situation exists. This also very often necessitates the writing of original music.

The use of Silence will prove very often highly effective in situations like the appearing of an unexpected person, committing a crime, in fact all unexpected happenings which are followed, as a rule, by stillness. The recitativo, to be effective, should also be built on the theme or themes of the characters. Very often the arranger of the music for the picture will not have time to cover every little detail in the manner here suggested, but he can help a great deal by shaping the orchestra's playing. A good musician can take an ordinary 4/4 Andante and as readily make it into a misterioso as into a recitativo. This is purely a case of ingenuity and adaptability on the part of the leader.

The flash-backs seem to be a continuous source of trouble to the inexperienced leader. If the flash-back is not of extreme length and the scene preceding the flashback is of such character that it will hold attention even during the flashback, I would not advise changing the music but would advise bringing it down to "PPP."

Another source of trouble I found is the making of musical endings. The brutal procedure of breaking your music no matter where you are just because the cue for the next number is flashed on the screen is an antiquated procedure not in use any more in first-class theatres. If you train your orchestra sufficiently and arrange for some kind of a signal for your men, you will not have to go more than 8 or 10 bars in most compositions before you can come to a tonic close. The finishing of most numbers during a feature picture should not be in a decisive cutoff manner but more of a dying-away effect. The more segues you can arrange between your numbers, the more symphonic the accompaniment will sound.

The turning of pages in the orchestra is a comparatively easy matter, if you have more than one man to each instrument. It is important that the out-side men religiously stick to playing only and have the turning done by the inside-men. In theatres where you have time to prepare a score, most of your numbers will not start at the beginning but with certain passages which you think will fit particular scenes. The number on your music and the place where it should start should be marked very plainly by an arrow so that the eye can grasp it in a second. If you have more than one theme, it will be an easy matter if you will carry out the following suggestions: If theme No. 1 is also 7–13–18 and 24, put all these numbers on top of the page and have the music sticking out in the center of your stand above your other music; if theme No. 2 is also 3–14–29 and 34, put that number also on top of your music and have that piece sticking out of the right or left side of your stand. If you will then mark on the bottom of No. 6 that the next number is Theme No. 1, I think you will find no difficulty in handling two or more themes.

If your film breaks, which nowadays is a rare happening, I advise keeping on playing the number and if necessary make a D.C. If you were playing your number soft and with strings only, bring in your brass and woodwind and play the number in concert form. Fortunately, these breaks never last more than 10 or 15 seconds. Should there be a fire in the booth, which may necessitate a wait of several minutes, I advise bringing up the house lights and having the men play any popular hit of the day which they may know by heart. It is advisable to keep in mind some such selection for use in case of emergency. The main object is to prevent the audience from getting nervous and to keep them entertained.

The effects in the percussion section and back stage can be made very effective if used judiciously. I only advise the use of effects if they are humorous or if they can be made very realistic. The shooting of the villain, unless a real shot can be fired back stage and can be timed absolutely, will be much better handled by stopping your orchestra abruptly and keeping silent for a few seconds than if the attempt of a shot is made with a snare drum. In one of the foremost theatres in New York City, I saw a picture in the course of which the villain jumped through the window and immediately after was slapped on the face by the heroine. The effect-man back stage was supposed to drop some glass at the proper moment to imitate the breaking of the window. As it happened the man was asleep on the job and the dropping of the glass occurred when the heroine slapped the villain, so what would have been a tolerably descriptive effect turned out to be the cause of hilarious laughter on the audience's part.

Effects which can be worked most satisfactorily are storm effects, obtained by the use of batteries of large square head drums and wind machines back stage.

In theatres where singers are available, vocal selections back stage will occasionally prove very effective. The most effective incident of such type I remember was applied in the Capitol Theatre in New York City during the presentation of the "Passion" where during the scene of the funeral of the French King a mixed chorus chanted the Funeral March from Madame Sans Gene. The effect was almost uncanny, as outside the death chamber there were a multitude of people assembled.

It is the Vaudeville theatres throughout the country which commit the grossest insults to feature pictures for reasons I was never able to quite understand. If the musicians are too tired after having played the vaudeville to play music to the feature picture, then there should be an organist who is alive to the possibilities. If it is ignorance on the leader's part, it is up to the management to see that the accompaniment to the feature picture is placed in proper hands. Happenings like one I witnessed where Dvořák's "Largo" was played from beginning to end with frightful tuning and wrong tempo during a reel of snappy events depicting dancing cannibals, Italian Army, Streets of New York, etc. indicated a condition which ought to be remedied if for nothing else but for the sake of music and its masters.

In choosing your orchestrations I would advise the use of arrangements which are so cued that if necessary they can be played with strings alone and will sound full, for in three quarters of the average feature picture music of very soft quality is required. The "Over-playing," by which is meant playing so loud that it attracts the ear more than the picture attracts the eye, has killed many a good picture.

CHAPTER 10. THE LIBRARY

In installing a library in a theatre particular care should be taken that the selections representing various moods should be represented numerically in accordance with their importance. Andantes, Marches and Agitatos will need most consideration as they are most in demand. . . . If your library is only of medium size, it is not necessary to go into . . . many classifications. . . . Happy and Neutral Andantes could be put in one book and if the library is very small even the Pathetics could be placed in the same collection with the Andantes. . . . For quick reference work in the library I found a double index system the most efficient. On one set of cards I would arrange composers alphabetically and put on their respective cards all of their compositions, indicating also their classification and library number. On the other set of cards I would put the various moods in alphabetical order and put on each card all compositions classified under that mood.

The use of wooden shelves or steel cabinets is largely a question of expenditure. Wooden shelves can be built by your carpenter to fill all vacant wall space in your library, but it will have the disadvantage of necessitating climbing and besides that these shelves cannot very well be dust proofed. Steel cabinets are somewhat more expensive but are absolutely dust proof and will indicate on the outside card very readily how many hundred numbers you have in each cabinet. When much music is composed on the premises, I would suggest a book containing nothing but manuscripts, regardless of their classification, as in future uses you will easily recall that a certain number you are looking for was written by you or by your staff and as such is easily traceable through the manuscript folio.

The erasing of marks on your music after the orchestra is through with it is an important factor; if the proper methods are not used the music will be ruined after having been used only three or four times. In marking the music a soft pencil should be used with as little pressure as possible as an eraser will remove any slight marking as long as there are no grooves. An erasing machine with a small dynamo, very much on the principle of an electric vibrator, will prove a great time saver. It means a small investment and can be made by your house electrician.

Although the classification of music is a Musical Director's job, it is the work of the Librarian to keep it under correct headings and properly indexed. If you classify each Movement of a suite or selection separately, it will be necessary to buy additional piano parts, but it will prove a satisfactory investment since you will put one piece of music to 3 or 4 different uses. Overtures containing Hurries, Agitatos, or Misterioso Movements should each, after being classified as Overtures, also be classified under above mentioned respective headings, and marked just where those classifications begin in the composition. The saving up of old time popular hits is of great importance as they can always be used. If your orchestra only consists of Violin, Piano or Cello, I, nevertheless, would advise the buying of a small orchestration because not only does it cost just as much as three or four parts, but should you increase your orchestra you will have the extra parts in readiness and will not have to go to the trouble of buying one 2nd violin or one flute or trombone part.

I would advise every Leader to lay aside a certain amount of money every month for buying new music, particularly of the descriptive type, since it is just as necessary to offer your patrons new music as it is to offer them new pictures. The type of new music to be purchased will have to be determined mainly by the type of picture you play. If you play mostly Western pictures you will have to buy Hurries, Agitatos, and Misteriosos. If your house plays more society dramas, the replenishing of your Intermezzos and Andante Folios will be more necessary. The offering of new picture music from time to time will not only please your audiences but will instill a new interest in the members of your orchestra.

CHAPTER 13. HOW TO ORGANIZE AND
REHEARSE AN ORCHESTRA

After you have decided upon the number of men for your orchestra, the selection of the individual players requires a great deal of consideration. It is essential that the men employed in your orchestra should not only be able to read well, as new music comes along all the time, but that they should also have a standard, symphonic and operatic repertoire. The necessity of knowing the style of popular music is becoming more and more essential every day. The choice of your most important instruments, like the Concert Master, Celloist, First Horn, etc. who are the pillars of your orchestra, will more or less determine the fate of your orchestra. True, you can take a number of mediocre men, rehearse them incessantly for a long period and sooner or later get some fine ensemble playing, but if you have artists on your first chairs you will get that individual distinction which is so effective in the numerous compositions containing solo passages, as for instance "Scheherezade."

It enhances your feature picture considerably to have the theme played by one violin or to have a cello solo with harp accompaniment, which again can only be done if the instrumentalists are artists and not mere orchestra musicians. Featuring your first chair instruments occasionally as soloists on the stage will add greatly to the reputation of your orchestra. In most motion picture theatres there is only one rehearsal a week allowed, either by the union or by the management, which generally ranges from 2 and one-half to three hours. In this comparatively short time you will have to rehearse your overture, the accompaniment to all your entertainment and verify the rotation of your picture music. If you have not a first class orchestra at disposal the only way to achieve any kind of a result will be to rehearse the high spots only and smooth out the rest of the show as you go along during the performances. This will require understanding and sympathy between the leader and his men. Although one of the greatest conductors the world has known is reported to have said:—"There is no such thing as a good or bad orchestra—there is only a good or bad leader," let us modify this to the extent that although there are such things as good and bad leaders, there is no such thing as a bad orchestra if rehearsed properly.

The placing of musicians in the pit should be governed by the size of the pit and by the old principle of having your strings on the out-side and the noisy instruments further back. I generally prefer the wood-wind to the left and the brass to the right in front of the percussion. The proper place for the harp for acoustic reasons would be on the conductor's left, but in that position it hides the face and greater part of the player's body so for the sake of showmanship it is advisable to place it on the right side. For a concert orchestra to be most effective it is essential that your audience see every member and not only their heads but also the upper part of their bodies. The average theatre goer will want to watch the mere mechanics of the playing quite as much as to listen to the results of the musicians' endeavors. Just how high you can place your orchestra will depend upon the height of the stage opening, but it should under no condition be so high as to interfere with the vision of your audience while the picture is on. The same holds true for the placing of the leader, who in very many instances spoils the sale of several seats directly behind him as he is placed right in the direct line of their vision. Where it is financially possible I would advise the installation of a hydraulic pit which would elevate the musicians above the audience during the overture and would lower them sufficiently during the picture or stage numbers to permit unobstructed vision. I shall endeavor here to suggest combinations for various numbers of men for an orchestra:

3—men—Piano, violin and cello
4—men—add obligato violin
5—men—add flute
6—men—add cornet
7—men—add drums
8—men—add trombone
9—men—add clarinet
10—men—add one 1st violin

From 11 to 25 it will be the leader's discretion as to the requirements of the theatre if it needs stringy or brassy type of music.

With 26 men the ideal combination would be

6—firsts	1—bassoon
2—seconds	2—clarinets
2—violas	2—horns
2—cellos	2—trumpets
1—bass	1—trombone
1—flute	1—drummer
1—oboe	

1—harpist—preferably one who doubles on piano and a Leader.

The combination I used in the Rivoli Theatre in New York was as follows:

8—firsts	1—oboe
4—seconds	1—bassoon
4—violas	2—horns
4—cellos	3—trumpets
3—basses	2—trombones
2—flutes	2—drummers
2—clarinets	1—harp

The combination I used at the Capital Theatre in New York was:

16—firsts	2—bassoons
10—seconds	4—horns
8—violas	4—trumpets
7—cellos	3—trombones

6—basses	1—tuba
2—flutes	3—drummers
2—oboes	and harp.
2—clarinets	

This last combination only differs from full symphony size in so far as symphony orchestras use more strings all around and three in each section of the wood-wind. The one point I would like to impress on the leader who has only a few men at his disposal is that whereas the brass and wood-wind instruments are more or less one sided by having a very distinct tone quality of their own, the strings can be used in a more diversified way and will always constitute the nucleus of any orchestra.

CHAPTER 14. THE MISSIONARY OF GOOD MUSIC AND THE MOTION PICTURE THEATRE

If you consider that only ten years ago there were not more than a half dozen symphony orchestras in this great country of over a hundred million inhabitants and that it is just exactly ten years since the first Cinema palace De Luxe opened its doors to the public, it will not be hard to see the connection between the two. It would take many pages to enumerate all the compositions performed in the big movie theatres of this country in the last ten years, so let it suffice that every form of music from Irving Berlin to Richard Strauss has been played.

This movement for better music reached its culminating point in the year 1921 when I had the honor of producing for the first time in the history of any movie theatre, Richard Strauss' "Till Eulenspiegel" and then one year later the same composer's "A Hero's Life." Some of these performances were witnessed by such judges as Paderewski, Grainger, Jos. Hoffman, Alexander Lambert and Krehbiel and although they were played with some cuts, what was attempted as an experiment proved in their judgment a huge success and a distinct step in giving to the multitude that which was written for the select few. It is this remarkable progress which music has made in the movie theatres which has made it possible for artists of worldwide reputations, like Percy Grainger, John Philip Sousa and Tom Burke, to appear without impairing their high standards in artistic circles.

Another beneficial effect the large orchestra in movies has had upon smaller communities is that fake music teachers who have been ruining untold promising talent have had to leave such communities and hunt for newer and less educated sections.

Another fact achieved by this same advancement of good music was the chance given the American singers and particularly young American composers, such as Griffes, Mortimer Wilson and others, to have their works performed, and the important part of this arrangement is that while symphony orchestras will perform a new work once or twice a year, the same work on the program of the movie theatre will be heard by 24 to 28 different audiences in one week. What this means in figures is hard to state, though I would like to quote as a record the attendance at the largest movie theatre in New York City having exceeded 80,000 in one week.

From *Encyclopaedia of Music for Pictures* (New York: Belwin, 1925), pp. 8–9, 11–16, 18–21, and 24–25.

Two Thematic Music Cue Sheets

A. *The Thief of Bagdad* (1924).
Music compiled by James C. Bradford. United Artists Corporation.

1. Personnel of Direction, ETC..Midsummer Night's Dream (Mendelssohn)............................2 3/4 Min.

2. Douglas Fairbanks in the Thief of Bagdad..Balham (Vitalis)..1 1/4 Min.

3. A Street In Bagdad......................................Balham (Vitalis)..1 1/4 Min.

4. Thief Grabs Man At Well.................................Overture Comique (Keler Bela).................................1 1/4 Min.

5. Thief Walks Away Laughing.................................Thief Theme: Carnival March of the Gnomes (Schroeder)...................2 Min.

6. Magician With Basket.................................Orientale (Amani) (Oboe Solo)..1 1/4 Min.

7. Woman Appears on Balcony.................................In Minor Mode No. 2 (deKoven)..1 1/4 Min.

B. Non-Taxable Musical Cue Sheet for
***Dame Chance* (1926).** ACA Pictures.

No. (T)itle or (A)ction	Selection	Tempo	Publisher	Style	Time
1 At Screening	Unfinished Symphony (Schubert)	3/4 Mod.	Photo Play	Spinningwheel	1— Min.
2 (A) Wheel Fade-out	Roses and Butterflies (Celfo)	2/4 Mod.	Cundy-Bettoney	Light	1¾ Min.
3 (T) Gail	Sirene (Viola)	3/4 Andno	Photo Play	Pensive	2— Min.
4 (A) Dial of Clock	THEME: Solitudine (Mule)	2/4 Ande.	Cinemusic	Serious	2¼ Min.
5 (A) Insert—Letter	Love's Miracle (Festoso)	3/4 Ande.	Photo Play	Emotional	1¼ Min.
6 (T) Memories	Tender Question (Felix)	3/4 Tempo di Valse	Amer. Compos.	Tender	1— Min.
7 (T) Six Years	Aubade Fleurie (Ganne)	2/4 Alltto.	Ascher	Animation	1— Min.
8 (A) Gail Looks at Mother's Photograph	Repentance (Kempinski)	3/4 Expres.	Photo Play	Tender	1— Min.
9 (T) One Long Part after Another	THEME: Solitudine (Mule)	2/4 Ande.	Cinemusic	Serious	2— Min.
10 (T) Why Don't You Go Home	Traumerei (Schumann)	4/4 Expres.	Cundy-Bettoney	Tearful	1¼ Min.
11 (T) A Long Dreary Hunt	Hope's Awakening (Kempinski)	4/4 Ande.	Photo Play	Despair	2— Min.
12 (A) Clancy in Office	Recitative and Aria (Kempinski)	12/8 Larg.	Photo Play	Agitation	1½ Min.
13 (T) Mrs. Downing	THEME: Solitudine (Mule)	2/4 Ande.	Cinemusic	Serious	1¼ Min.
14 (A) Nina in Dressing Room	April Breezes (Floridia)	2/4 Alltto.	Cundy-Bettoney	Animation	1¾ Min.
15 (A) Gail Enters Room	Andante (Mendelssohn)	6/8 Ande.	Cundy-Bettoney	Reverie	1— Min.
16 (T) Grace Vernon	Prelude (Chopin)	6/8 Alltto.	Ascher	Despair	2— Min.
17 (A) Vision	Tender Question (Felix)	3/4 Tempo di Valse	Amer. Compos.	Tender	½ Min.
18 (A) Mr. Stafford Picks Up Telephone	THEME: Solitudine (Mule)	2/4 Ande.	Cinemusic	Serious	1— Min.
19 (T) The Great Surgeon Operated	Sirene (Viola)	3/4 Andno.	Photo Play	Pensive	1½ Min.
20 (A) Maid in Room	Radotages (Gabriel Marie)	4/4 Mod.	Ascher	Comedy	2¼ Min.
21 (A) Gail and Sims Enter Room	Reverie (Luz)	4/4 Andno.	Photo Play	Despair	2— Min.

22 (A) Dial of Clock	THEME: Solitudine (Mule)	2/4 Ande.	Cinemusic	Serious	4¾ Min.
23 (A) Wheel Appears	Songe d'Amour (Ascher)	3/4 Tempo di Valse	Ascher	Neutral	2½ Min.
24 (A) Gail Rises to Leave	Ronde de Bachi-Bouzoucks (Gabriel Marie)	2/4 Mod.	Ascher	Humorous	2½ Min.
25 (T) Busy Days	Slumbering River (Siewert)	6/8 Alltto.	Photo Play	Coquettish	2½ Min.
26 (A) Wheel Shows Again	Roses and Butterflies (Celfo)	2/4 Mod.	Cundy-Bettoney	Light	2½ Min.
27 (A) Gail Walks from Dresser with Flowers	Reverie (Fabre)	3/4 Expres.	Cundy-Bettoney	Sentimental	1½ Min.
28 (T) I Can't Sign That	In the Dell (Frommel)	4/4 Ande.	Photo Play	Emotional	3¾ Min.
29 (T) In Answer to Gail's Summons	The Swan (St. Saens)	3/4 Ande.	Cundy-Bettoney	Placid	2— Min.
30 (T) What Is It You Wish to Say	Berceuse (Karganoff)	4/4 Lento	Ascher	Dramatic	2— Min.
31 (A) Lloyd in Room	Nature's Awakening (Kempinski)	12/8 Appass.	Photo Play	Passionate	2— Min.
32 (A) Gail Reading	THEME: Solitudine (Mule)	2/4 Ande.	Cinemusic	Serious	1½ Min.
33 (T) The Weeks Have Gone	Repentance (Kempinski)	3/4 Expres.	Photo Play	Tender	3½ Min.
34 (T) Gail's New Secretary	Chopin (Godard)	3/4 Tempo di Valse	Cundy-Bettoney	Happy	1½ Min.
35 (A) Insert—Card	Social Chat (Eugene)	6/8 Alltto.	Ascher	Comedy	1½ Min.
36 (T) The Wheel of Chance	Try Me (Schertzinger)	4/4 Mod.	Photo Play	Light	1¾ Min.
37 (A) Wheel Shows Again	Love's Fantasy (Frommel)	4/4 Ande.	Photo Play	Suppressed	2½ Min.
38 (A) Stafford at Desk	Hope's Awakening (Kempinski)	4/4 Ande.	Photo Play	Despair	2— Min.
39 (A) Maid Enters	Air de Ballet (Wachs)	2/4 Alltto.	Cundy-Bettoney	Light	¾ Min.
40 (A) Gail Greets Stafford	Barcarolle (Rubinstein)	3/4 Expres.	Cundy-Bettoney	Love	¾ Min.

THE END

NOTE: This picture was cued August 23, 1926, at which time all of the above musical selections were TAX-FREE.

Music and Motion Pictures

Hugo Riesenfeld

(1926)

If it were possible to see at a glance every city of 50,000 inhabitants and over in France, Italy and Central Europe, one would be struck by a certain similarity. However widely these cities may differ in architecture, in language, in the appearance of their people, they have one element in common. Each has its own municipal theatre where the entire population goes regularly to hear opera and light opera. And each has its promenade concerts where the symphonic works of the great masters are played.

Here in the United States we have no such institution for developing an appreciation of good music among the people. With the exception of the Metropolitan, the Chicago Opera Company, and one or two touring companies, we have no organization which furnishes us with operatic performances. We have twelve symphony orchestras of first order for a population of one hundred million.

Were it not for a substitute that has sprung up in the last twelve years or so, a vast number of Americans would never hear the finer musical works. This substitute is our motion picture theatre—an institution in which the United States rules supreme—which more or less duplicates the work of the European musical organizations.

Early in its existence the motion picture discovered that its growth could be materially aided by grafting to itself the sister art, music. Each of them has benefited. Whenever there is a film theatre of any size, there is now a good orchestra. When one considers that there are about 18,000 such theaters in the country, one realizes what an influence the industry can exert on the musical life of America.

The development of motion picture music in the short space of ten or twelve years has been remarkable. Those who were adventurous enough to go to the much-maligned movies a decade ago will recall what a miserable musical accompaniment was furnished. A single pianist drummed mechanically on a tuneless instrument. The same threadbare melodies tinkled in one's ears whether the screen showed a tender romance or the villain getting his just reward. During the supper hour the music would stop altogether while the pianist slipped out for a bit of nourishment.

Turn the pages from yesterday to to-day. Many of the country's finest instrumentalists are now playing in motion picture houses. The palatial theatres in the larger cities often have orchestras of eighty or more players. They spend hundreds of thousands of dollars annually on music alone. In fact, in some cases the cost of music totals a third of the total running expenses. The best organists and conductors are engaged. Music—and music of the highest caliber—is considered indispensable.

The dignity that has been achieved by the motion picture industry from a musical standpoint is indicated by the important musicians who have entered the field. Henry Hadley, well known associate conductor of the New York Philharmonic Orchestra, appeared on the program at the presentation of *Don Juan*. Such recognized artists as Percy Grainger, Orville Harrold, Hans Kindler and Sascha Jacobson have frequently played in motion picture houses. Film theatres, because of their ability to pay large salaries, can attract the best musicians, where sometimes concert managements are loath to take the risk.

KINDS OF MUSIC

Motion picture music may be divided into two groups. There is the program music, which includes the overture, solos, ballet and dance music, and the like. And there is the accompanying synchronized score, which forms the background of the film.

As to the former, the taste of the public is in a state of flux just now. American passion for jazz is at its height. The public—at least the motion picture public—cannot seem to get enough of it. It is like a child with a new toy, unable to see anything else.

So, for the time being, jazz predominates in our film theatres. However, I believe it is only a matter of time before the wheel of public favor again turns, bringing the better type of music to the foreground again. Above all else America wants variety, and in time it will again want its jazz tempered by classical music. A jazz selection is old and discarded in a single season. A Beethoven overture or Chopin nocturne is eternally new.

Jazz, that native American product, should by all means be encouraged. It has proved itself worthy of admission to the field of modern music. It has undoubtedly a permanent place in the world's store of fine music. Such modern composers as Gershwin, Harling and John Alden Carpenter have helped to dignify and perpetuate it.

On the other hand, there is still a vigorous minority of theatre-goers who want classical music, who loudly express regret that it has been dropped from some programs. I believe that the motion picture theatre should cater to the desires of this minority. From a commercial standpoint it would be worth while because it would serve to hold these people to the theatre. From an artistic standpoint it would be invaluable, since it would keep alive in this country a love of finer music. There is no reason why classical and modern music cannot be combined on the same program. Some of our finest symphony orchestras do this in the concert halls.

AID TO MUSICIANS

Much has been done by the motion picture theatre already to aid the cause of good music. It has offered to new singers and instrumentalists an excellent means of developing their art. The practical experience of singing before a film audience for a week is equivalent to months of secluded practice at home. It develops poise and stage presence, so that when the performer is at last ready for his ultimate goal, the opera house or concert hall, there is less probability of stage fright.

As a training school for singers, American's motion picture houses more than take the place of the provincial opera houses of Europe. The standards of the former are higher in most cases, and certainly they offer better compensation. Salaries for soloists at the major metropolitan theatres range from a hundred to four hundred dollars a week. This money enables numbers of new performers to continue with their studies, where without such financial help, it might be necessary for them to give up the struggle, with success a short but unspannable distance away.

A number of successful artists have graduated from the motion picture stage to that of the coveted Metropolitan Opera House. Among those who served their apprenticeship in the film theatres are Mario Chamlee, lyric tenor, Anne Roselle, dramatic soprano, Vincente Ballester, baritone, Jeanne Gordon, contralto; also Mary Fabian of the Chicago Opera Company and Emanuel List of the Berlin Opera and La Scala, Milan. For the young and striving artist, this is an invaluable stepping stone to a broader career.

ARRANGEMENT AND USE OF SCORES

Now as to the scores. The hit-or-miss musical accompaniment furnished by the bored pianist in the old days has long since been abandoned. Nowadays no important picture is released without a specially prepared score. Nearly every large theatre has a musical director who arranges the scores of the lesser films from week to week.

Infinite care is taken and sometimes weeks spent in the preparation of a score, so that every emotion and every bit of action on the screen will be exactly reproduced musically. As long as six months has sometimes been spent on certain of the more important scores.

The chief difficulty in score writing or arranging is keeping the music subordinate to the action on the screen. It must never obtrude itself. The audience must never be conscious of hearing a familiar tune.

To achieve this, the musical director who is obliged to prepare a new score every week must have at his disposal a limitless supply of music. For this purpose the metropolitan theatres maintain enormous libraries, some of them containing 25,000 pieces of music. These are all catalogued, not only by titles and authors, but also by the type of emotion or kind of action which they suggest. When the score writer wishes a piece of music giving the atmosphere of the opening scene of *Macbeth,* he refers to the sections marked "Witch Dances" or "Ominous Music." In the same way he may instantly put his hands on music which suggests the sound of an aëroplane, anger, a runaway horse, a canoe drifting down a quiet stream.

A staff of trained librarians is required to keep this stock of music constantly replenished with fresh works. The larger musical publishing houses have a standing order to send everything that comes off their presses. Material is sought in France, Germany, England, Italy, and even the Orient.

The musical stores of every country are assiduously combed for melodies that will create just the right illusion. When that remarkable film *Grass* was being prepared for public presentation, the services of an authority on the music of Eastern tribes were called upon. For *The Vanishing American,* rare and little known songs of the Indians were utilized. In *Deception,* original music written by Anne Boleyn and Henry VIII was dug out of the forgotten archives.

The compiler or arranger of scores searches down every possible alley, in every corner for something that will give just the right effect. He knows the vital importance of an appropriate score. A good film can be made even better by a good score. An inferior film does not seem nearly so bad if it has an excellent musical background.

In preparing the music for a film, the director first has the picture run off while he makes notes. He then consults his library for selections which he believes will produce the proper atmosphere. With these before him he again calls for a running off of the film, and working at a piano, he tries out the music he has selected. Now and then he presses a button which notifies the projectionist to stop the machine while he looks for a different number or makes further notes. After the music is assembled and timed to the film, it is turned over to copyists who prepare a complete score for the musicians. Usually three or four days are devoted to rehearsals.

Very often, if the arranger cannot find satisfactory music for a certain bit of action, he is obliged to compose some himself. The musical ability required for this work is of such a high caliber that only the larger theatres are able to afford it. It cannot be expected that the musical head of a theatre in a small town will be able to write as good a score as an expert employed by a metropolitan theatre. For this reason many scores are syndicated, and sent with the film all over the world.

The most recent developments along the line of making the best music available to smaller communities is the Vitaphone. This invention is the best so far in reproducing synchronized music and films. It makes it possible for artists and orchestras of the first order to be heard in the smallest towns. The reproduction of the voice and music is very fine. It seems almost as though the performers were in the same room as the listener. It is not probable that the Vitaphone will ever entirely replace the orchestra, but it does make it possible for certain films requiring the finest musical accompaniment to be shown in places where there is no orchestra available.

FIELD FOR COMPOSERS

Before leaving the subject of scores, I wish to touch on a matter about which I have often been questioned. That is: Do motion pictures offer a new field for composers? What future does this new art form offer to the creative musician? Tales have been spread of fabulous sums paid to certain composers for original scores. It is true that a few of the larger films have employed composers for original scores, but these can almost be counted on one hand. *Civilization, Puritan Passions, The Thief of Bagdad,* and *Little Old New York* are among them. At present, at least, the field is too limited to insure a promising outlet for composers.

There is also this difficulty: The average super-film, which lasts about two hours, requires as much music as an opera. Think of the physical effort of writing such a work! The life of even important films hardly exceeds two years. It is then put aside and forgotten, except for rare revivals. Will the composer of first rank be willing to devote his best effort and energy to something whose death is doomed before its birth? From what I know of composers, they would rather starve with the hope of creating a great symphony that will live through the ages, than grow fat off the proceeds of an excellent but short-lived film score.

If, however, the film world has not made serious inroads into the ranks of the better composers, it has encouraged a larger number of Americans to take up music as a profession. A short time ago the life of a musician—an orchestra player—presupposed great financial sacrifice. Even the first-rate symphony player did not earn as much as the average second-rate business man.

GROWING DEMAND FOR MUSICIANS

With the growing demand for musicians, however, their value has gone up. The musician to-day is in demand as he never was before. Think of the army of them necessary to man the orchestras in our 18,000 film theatres, to say nothing of the requirements of the dance halls, cabarets and legitimate theatres. The American musician has become a commercial asset. In the larger of our motion picture theatres the minimum salary is eighty-three dollars a week, and almost half of the players get one hundred dollars. First stand players and concert masters usually are paid from $7000 to $10,000 a year. The organists get from $6000 to $20,000, depending on their individual performances. Is it any wonder with our American love of luxury that the ranks of musicians have increased so enormously during the last few years? We have more musicians and better ones. Men who are naturally musical are no longer forced to become clerks or traveling salesmen in order to earn an adequate living.

AMERICAN LEADERSHIP

In this country we are supreme in utilizing music in the motion picture theatre. While traveling in Europe during the past summer, I saw little that could compare with our methods of presentation. European countries themselves are aware of this and are beginning to send over representatives to study our methods. Theater owners abroad are amazed at the way we use music in our houses. They are eager to learn from us. They are engaging our conductors to go over and take charge of presentations in their theatres.

By no means do I wish to imply that America has achieved the peak musically, any more than it has reached the limit in the development of motion pictures. There are still limitless possibilities. It is certain that the next decade will see still greater strides made by the motion picture industry. Lately large Wall Street banking firms have been allying themselves with motion picture companies, thus demonstrating their faith in the industry. With millions invested, great progress is certain. And there is no reason why music, now inseparably linked with motion pictures, should not also benefit.

From *The Motion Picture in Its Economic and Social Aspects,* November 1926 issue of *Annals of the American Academy of Political and Social Science,* pp. 58–62.

Publishers Win Movie Music Suit

(1924)

Proprietors of motion picture theatres are required to pay publishers a license fee for using copyrighted music according to a decision of Judge J. Whittaker Thompson in Federal Court here [Philadelphia] today.

The movie men were taken into court two years ago when they refused to pay a "performing right fee" of 10 cents a seat a year to the music publishers, members of the Society of Composers, Authors and Publishers.

The songs alleged to have been played for profit, thus infringing the copyright, have long since passed from current fancy, but the issue survived. Judge Thompson decided in favor of Irving Berlin and nine other New York music publishers, who were awarded $250 damages and $150 counsel fee from each of the thirty-one Philadelphia motion picture proprietors.

Eleven other suits were begun, but in some of them the music publishers sued the wrong persons and there was no hearing in the remaining cases.

It was revealed in testimony taken before Walter V. Douglas Jr., as Special Master, that the larger motion picture houses here and elsewhere have been paying an annual license fee of 10 cents a seat to the song writer's organization, and hotels, restaurants, cabarets and dance halls from $5 to $15 a month.

Rather than pay the fee, the smaller movie houses said they would play classical music or no music at all. Some of the defendants contended they had no control over the music their pianists chose, and if the latter dashed off a sentimental tune at a crucial moment in a love-making scene, the employers were not responsible.

Furthermore, several of the defendants declared they had been asked by the publishers to "plug," or popularize, current songs.

Judge Thompson dismissed these arguments in one of the three cases he heard personally before referring the others to the master with the statement that "music selected because it is fitting and appropriate to the action of that portion of the motion picture at that precise moment being shown upon the screen, and continuously changing with the theme of the motion picture, is played for the additional attraction to the audience and for its enjoyment and amusement."

EXPECT $300,000 IN NEW ROYALTIES

The decision of Judge Thompson was hailed here yesterday by the members of the American Society of Composers, Authors and Publishers, at 56 West Forty-fifth Street, as "one in a daily string of victories" by which they expect eventually to compel the 15,000 motion picture theatres of the country to pay royalties to musical composers.

The decision, like many other recent decisions, was based on the ruling made on May 13 by Federal Judge Ernest F. Cochran, in the Eastern District of South Carolina, in the case of M. Witmark & Sons vs. the Pastime Amusement Company.

Judge Cochran said that a composer had a right to assign a copyright, and that to constitute an infringement it is not necessary that the whole or even a large portion of the work shall have been copied. The defense had contended that there was no infringement of the song "Kiss Me Again," because only the chorus was used.

Of the 15,000 motion pictures [theatres] in the United States approximately 7,000 have obtained licenses to use the compositions of members of the American Society of Composers, Authors and Publishers, according to E. C. Mills, Secretary of that body.

The license rate is 10 cents a seat annually. The remaining 8,000 theatres, according to the 1922 report of Will H. Hays, Commissioner of the Motion Picture Industry, average 507 seats, so that the annual license for the remaining theatres would be in the neighborhood of $50.70 each. The aggregate royalties are estimated at approximately $500,000 from the remaining 8,000 motion picture houses still to be licensed.

In commenting on yesterday's decision, Mr. Mills said:

"This decision only confirms what the Society of Composers, Authors and Publishers has maintained as the legal rights of composers and authors since it came into existence in 1914.

"The composer's enjoyment of the rights in copyright are limited to twenty-eight years under the law. During those twenty-eight years he must reap whatever harvest is possible from his work. Many songs are written, but few achieve commercial success, and the song writer, upon whose shoulders rests the entire responsibility of public amusement and without whose creative musical genius the theatre, dance hall, cabaret, broadcasting station and all other forms of public amusement cannot exist has not been and never will be overpaid."

Besides Irving Berlin the victorious music publishers are T. B. Harms and Francis Day and Hunter, the Broadway Music Corporation, Jerome H. Remick & Co., Leo Feist, Inc., Shapiro, Bernsteinn & Co., Inc., McCarthy-Fisher, Inc., and Waterson.

PART TWO

All Singing, Dancing, and Talking

Music in the Early Sound Film (1926–1934)

INTRODUCTION

In the history of the cinema, the period between 1926 and 1932, the transition from silent to sound film, has been written and revised by cinema scholars many times over and for good reason. In the space of a brief half-decade, profound technical and aesthetic changes were introduced to both film production and film exhibition practices. Because the changes were global and dramatic, demanding that studios and exhibitors alike invest in entirely new production and projection equipment, some of the first histories that were written about this transition period presented the coming of sound film as instant, decisive, and as a long-desired or even inevitable event. This view of sound film prevailed for decades, not only in critical histories of film but even more powerfully in the cinema itself. As late as 1952, popular films like *Singin' in the Rain* presented the introduction of the "talkies" as a kind of overnight sensation, as a revolution that was slowed only by technological shortcomings that were quickly overcome.

In recent decades, this "instant revolution" or "overnight sensation" model of the transition period has been challenged by a number of cinema scholars and several large-scale critical observations. One of the most significant challenges to this model has come from an interest in constructing a more complete understanding of the history or evolution of sound film technology. August 1926, it is now commonly understood, was not the first time audiences had been exposed to moving pictures with synchronized sound. From the beginning of film history, inventors had experimented with giving film real, synchronous sound. In fact, the history of sound film is simultaneous with film history itself. From

William Dickinson's 1898 Kinetophone and Oskar Messter's 1900 Phonocinema to Edison's 1913 Kinetophone and Lee de Forest's 1922 Phonofilm, at the same time that silent film was flourishing and maturing, inventors were experimenting with sound film technology. There were often several reasons why these devices failed to become anything more than a novelty. Some, like de Forest's beautifully synchronized Phonofilm, suffered from poor sound reproduction (in terms of range of sound especially). Webb's Electrical Pictures, shown in New York's Fulton Theater in 1914, did not have an effective or consistent means of synchronizing sound and picture. Others, like Edison's 1913 Kinetophone, were well synchronized but were not projected and required instead to be viewed individually through a viewfinder in a free-standing machine. Rather than being seen as an alternative film experience, as the early Vitaphone films were in 1926 and 1927, these earlier sound film experiments were described as novelties. They were classified as peep show oddities, fodder for fairgrounds and amusement parks, and not film experiences.[1]

The overnight sensation model of the transition has also been diluted by a more detailed description of the change in exhibition practices, particularly between 1926 and 1932. The premiere of the first Vitaphone sound film, *Don Juan,* in 1926 did not trigger either an instant demand for sound film or an instant abandonment of silent film. Two years later, sound film, although growing in popularity, was still viewed as an alternative film experience, not a replacement. There was still plenty of discussion of silent film, and of silent and sound film co-existing side by side. Even as late as 1930, studios were producing some silent versions of sound films for those theaters that had not yet converted to the new projection equipment.[2] This is not to say that the industry, especially when the commercial potential for sound film became evident, did not act swiftly to replace silent film with sound. Overall, the pace at which the studios adopted a single production technology (sound-on-film rather than sound-on-disc in 1928), and the pace at which theater owners converted projection equipment to accommodate the new film medium, was indeed quite fast. That much of the change was accomplished within roughly six years is stunning. But when considered alongside the hesitation and lack of uniformity that also characterized the early years of sound film, the best term to describe the process is *transition* and not *revolution.*[3]

Sustaining the overnight sensation model, as many historians of film theory have pointed out, also means overlooking the resistance effort that marked the early years of the transition. Not everyone was convinced that the new technology was superior or even desirable. Several prominent film directors, in fact— including Eisenstein, Clair, Vidor, and Chaplin—made public statements criticizing sound film and rejecting its hyper-literal concept of sound. The range of nationalities of these directors betrayed this resistance not as an isolated event, but as an international movement. The great Soviet director Serge Eisenstein questioned the usefulness of direct or literal sound in favor of the more oblique or contrapuntal connection offered by the marriage of the visual narrative with virtual or recorded orchestral accompaniment. "ONLY A CONTRAPUNTAL USE of sound in relation to the visual montage piece will afford a new potentiality of montage development and perfection."[4] René Clair, the respected French director, was even more direct in his condemnation, deploring what he described as the

> effects of a barbaric invasion. . . . Although the talkies are still in their first, experimental stage, they have already, surprisingly enough, produced stereotyped patterns. We have barely "heard" about two dozen of these films, and yet we already feel that the sound effects are hackneyed and that it is high time to find new ones. Jazz, stirring songs, the ticking of a clock, a cuckoo singing the hours, dance-hall applause, a motorcar engine, or breaking crockery—all these are no doubt very nice, but become somewhat tiresome after we have heard them a dozen times in a dozen different films."[5]

Several in the industry, Chaplin most notably, articulated their resistance not just verbally, but visually as well. Chaplin continued to make silent films, conceding to sound only in terms of adding a recorded orchestra part to his films, as with *City Lights* (1931), or orchestra and sound effects, as with *Modern Times* (1935). "I shall never speak in a film. I hate the talkies and will not produce talking films," Chaplin said.[6] These directors were not alone. As witnessed by continued patronage of silent film houses into the late 1920s and early 1930s, many in the audience, too, preferred the art of the silent cinema to the stilted performances and garbled dialogue of the early sound film.

Outlining the scientific or technological changes that came to the movies between 1926 and 1932 tells only half the story of sound film, however. The revolution was also an aesthetic one. The task of adding dialogue, sound effects, and music to the film presented not just recording and synchronizing challenges, but also conceptual challenges. Dialogue, sound, and musical accompaniment needed to be made audible, but they also needed to be made believable. Certain sonic concepts, such as those suggesting proximity and distance, had to be constructed, as did distinctions between foreground sound and incidental background noise. These challenges were technical, to be sure, and in many cases evolved with advances in microphone and recording technology. But with these technical advances also came choices. It was not just a matter of whether the microphone *could* capture a sound but whether it *should* capture it, whether a given sound or noise would be perceived as realistic. This decision-making process required the addition of a new member to the filmmaking team, the sound engineer; it also required time and experimentation. The introduction of sound meant not just the recording of sound, but the conceptualization of sonic space.[7] It meant the introduction of sound design.

Most cinema scholars, in seeking to enrich our understanding of this complex and technically challenging period, have focused primarily on the evolution of visual style and sound design—how the camera and the microphone evolved technically and conceptually to form our modern concept of sound in film. Yet to date, music has received little attention in this discussion. Few scholars have sought to understand either how music participated in the development of sound design or its own evolution as an independent component of film.[8]

Music was affected by many if not most of technical advances of the period. On-screen musical performances especially were subject to the technical exigencies of early sound recording. Some advances in microphone technology were launched specifically to address the problems of recording music. But music by nature had a different path to pursue, one separate from the other elements of the soundtrack. Film had never had synchronized dialogue before, but it had always had music. Because music was not a new part of the film experience, instead of being conceptualized fresh, it was subjected to reconceptualization to fit the new medium. Unlike dialogue and sound, music was a familiar element that had to be reapproached and revised.

While this revision process followed the technical and aesthetic development of sound in general, in some ways its trajectory was also separate. Many of the milestones and achievements in sound design, many technical advances that shaped the recording and treatment of sound, affected music as well. But music also faced some technical and aesthetic questions that were specific only to it. As this set of documents reveals, some problems that composers and musicians in the early sound film confronted were unique. Some were also distinctive because they continued to evolve well after 1932, well after other aspects of the soundtrack had been normalized and aesthetically and practically established. The evolution of music in the early sound film follows not only a separate trajectory from the evolution of film sound, but also a longer trajectory than is described by typical transition chronologies and histories.

Music was an integral part of film before the transition to sound, and accordingly, it played a crucial role in the exhibition of the first sound film. For the first several years, in fact, sound films were much more musical than they were verbal: they sang more than they talked. The first impulse when implementing the new technology was not to facilitate speech but primarily to facilitate music, which was done by simply recording the musical parts of the movie palace program that previously had been performed live. The first stage of the evolution of sound film involved, to use Donald Crafton's term, "virtualizing" the orchestra.[9] The new synchronized sound was used to record or "can" versions of both the individual musical acts that preceded the feature film and the orchestral compilation score that accompanied the feature film.

This is not to suggest that there was no talking in the earliest sound films. When Warner Brothers premiered their new Vitaphone sound films at the Warners Theater in August 7, 1926, the historic evening began with a short filmed speech from the president of the Motion Picture Association, Will H. Hays. But as **Document 13,** a review of the evening from the music serial *The Etude,* points out, the rest of the exhibition was given over almost completely to musical performances.[10] After Hays's speech came a musical extravaganza that featured a variety of musical performers to suit a variety of audience tastes. In typical movie palace fashion, the first film short pictured an orchestral overture, although in this case it was performed rather untypically by what was considered the nation's finest orchestra, the 107-piece New York Philharmonic under the direction of Henry Hadley. The film also featured performances, designed to cater to more refined tastes, by internationally renowned concert hall artists, including violinists Mischa Elman and Efrem Zimbalist, pianist Harold Bauer, Metropolitan Opera stars Giovanni Martinelli and Anna Case, and the eighteen-year-old opera sensation Marion Talley. For those viewers craving more populist fare, there was vaudeville star Roy Smeck performing on the banjo, ukulele, harmonica, and Hawaiian steel guitar; a chorus performing a medley of Russian songs and dances; and the Cansinos, a family of Spanish dancers popular in vaudeville circles, who performed along with Case's Spanish number.[11] In typical movie palace fashion, this parade of musical "shorts" lasted about an hour and served as a prelude to the feature film. This first sound film feature, *Don Juan,* a historical epic starring John Barrymore, featured a "canned" or "virtualized" accompaniment, an orchestral score compiled by Hugo Riesenfeld and performed by the New York Philharmonic Orchestra, as well as recorded sound effects.

To make these first sound films, Warner Brothers had invested in the Vitaphone system, a sound-on-disc technology that synchronized the film visuals with a wax recording of accompanying sounds and music. At virtually the same time that Warners, one of the smaller studios at the time, was putting Vitaphoned films into production, Fox Studios was developing its own technology. Based on the Case-Sponsable method of recording film sound, Fox's Movietone sound system derived in part from de Forest's Phonofilm technology (Case had worked with de Forest before developing his own method). Fox's Movietone system recorded sound not on an accompanying disc but directly on the film itself. There were obviously advantages to Fox's sound-on-film system, especially in terms of editing and synchronization. But until 1928, the two technologies existed side by side. Fox initially used its sound-on-film technology to specialize in newsreels, speech-heavy Movietonews "shorts," but by the following year it too was producing feature films with virtual orchestral accompaniments. By 1928, most of the other major studios had joined the sound revolution, producing sound films with at the very least synchronized or virtual accompaniments.[12] In utilizing the synchronized score approach, the studios not only kept the traditions of silent film accompaniment alive, but they also kept several of silent film's most prominent musicians and compilers employed. Many of the sound films from late 1926 and 1927, like *The Better 'Ole, Seventh Heaven, What Price Glory, Four Sons, When a Man Loves,* and *Old San Francisco,* featured virtual but traditional compilation scores, as well as a few hit theme songs, from silent film composers like Erno Rapee, Hugo Riesenfeld, S. L. Rothapfel, J. S. Zamecnik, William Axt, and David Mendoza.[13]

By 1927, the year following the premiere of *Don Juan,* the virtualized orchestral accompaniment was not the only use Warner Brothers was making of its new sound film technology. They were now using the technology to feature musical performances and moments of spoken dialogue within the feature film itself, a production style that quickly became known, even though it was mostly part-music, as the "part-talkie." A mere year later, in 1928, Warner Brothers, again at the forefront of sound film conceptualization, launched a film that had dialogue throughout, a style that quickly came to be referred to as an "all-talking" film.

In short order then, filmmakers found several ways to use the new technology, with no single approach displacing another. Instead, between 1926 and 1928 studio production was incredibly diverse. Each studio was offering films in an array of formats, some mixing as many as four different approaches at once. Most studios were still producing fully silent films, many of those films being silent versions of sound films, and they were also producing sound films that were either silent with virtual accompaniments, part-talkies, or fully talking films.[14]

Like the film with only virtualized accompaniment, the brief second generation of sound films known as the part-talkie was as backward looking as it was forward thinking. Although this hybrid film offered one significant addition that feature films in particular had not had before, namely synchronized spoken dialogue, it continued to deliver the traditional compilation score of the silent film, albeit in recorded form. The early sound film also virtualized performance of the musical acts that had been part of the live musical program in silent theaters, in the form of Vitaphone "shorts" shown before the feature film. In this short-lived presentation of sound film, film alternated between formats, between a silent film with a recorded accompaniment and short films that featured musical performances.

Virtualized synchronized music and live synchronized dialogue were not the only innovations the part-talkie offered. In most cases, the narrative structure of the film was altered to accommodate the new emphasis on live musical performance. One of the most significant features of the first part-talkie, *The Jazz Singer* (1927), for instance, was not that Al Jolson sang, or that he improvised some dialogue while doing so,[15] but that the plot of the film was designed around the singing. Where *Don Juan,* the first sound film, was an epic drama with little need for diegetic music, *The Jazz Singer* was a film *about* music—about the life of a singer, both his personal life and his performances. It offered a narrative that allowed and eventually demanded that characters sing or perform, an innovation that inspired a new genre: the film musical. Most of the early "musicals" grounded musical performance visually on the screen through plot devices like the "backstage" musical or the musical-within-a-musical. Some of the first part-talkies, like Warner Brothers' *Tenderloin, Glorious Betsy, The Lion and the Mouse,* all from 1928, used interpolated moments of synchronized sound to highlight speech. But many others, like *The Jazz Singer,* Al Jolson's second feature *The Singing Fool,* Fox's *Mother Knows Best,* First National's *The Divine Lady,* and Pathé's *Show Folks,* from 1928 as well, used synchronized sound to highlight musical performances, making music a central feature not just of the soundtrack but of the visual action on the screen.

Even as early sound films sought to preserve aspects of music in the silent film experience, they were busy dismantling one musical feature in particular. Part of the lure of sound film was that, by making music a part of production and not exhibition, it promised to replace the hugely varied aspect of live musical accompaniment with a single recording of high quality. Movie palace–quality music would now be available to even the smallest theater in the smallest town. As the reporter for *Etude* recognized, "In smaller theatres it will take the place of small orchestras in some cases. . . . The indifferent and unworthy players may well look to their laurels. The public would far rather listen to an accompaniment by the New York Philharmonic than to a few scratchy fiddles and squawky saxophones. The general effect of the Vitaphone will be to compel higher standards of performance."

The elimination of live music was a boon for theater owners, for the money they saved could be applied to the cost of installing the new and expensive sound film projection equipment. But the egalitarian dream that canned film music offered had a serious side-effect: unemployment. The audible picture might be a great cultural equalizer, but it was also a great labor-saving device, the labor in question being that of the theater musicians. As a *New York Times* article from June 30, 1928, entitled "Musicians to Fight Sound-Film Devices" **(Document 14)** emphasizes, if there was a group that resisted the coming of sound film more tenaciously than silent film directors, it was the large number of musicians who in various configurations, from orchestras to organists, had been accompanying the pictures in cities large and small across the country for the last two decades. Joseph Weber, the president of the American Federation of Musicians, stated that the theater musicians union was not resisting sound film per se, but rather the inferior product that canned music represented. "Music at best reflects the mood of the artist," he observed. "You cannot mechanize an art. If synthetic harmony comes to supersede the services of musicians, the public will be the loser." The very aspect that critics initially praised as culturally affirming, the ability of sound film to bring high art and music to the masses, was now seen as aesthetically destructive. Musicians, especially, saw sound film as "a serious menace" to the country's "cultural growth."

While Weber professed to resist recorded music for aesthetic reasons, the Federation's battle was most certainly motivated by the dire unemployment figures that affected a large part of its membership—a situation that continued to worsen over the next few years. A study conducted by the U.S. Bureau of Labor Statistics revealed that whereas in 1928 over 20,000 musicians had been employed in movie theaters across the country, by 1931 that number was only 9,885, a decline of more than 50 percent.[16]

Even before the Bureau of Labor Statistics' figures were released, the American Federation of Musicians had mounted a full-scale campaign to resist what they described as sound film's inferior mechanization of music. They also established the Music Defense Fund, a charity organization to administer to the needs of unemployed theater musicians. Full-page ads for the Defense Fund campaign, complete with cartoon illustrations depicting a compliant womanly "Music" in the clutches of the "robot" of mechanized music, appeared in journals like *Metronome* and *Musical America* throughout 1931.[17] As these advertisements reveal, the American Federation of Musicians was resisting sound film not because it would bring patrons a uniform product or a loud, one-dimensional concept of sound, but because recorded music was devoid of life, bereft of "artistic nutrition."

In depicting sound film as cold and mechanical, an inadequate substitute for the living musical accompaniment of silent cinema, these documents convey the aesthetic and practical fears that many musicians had of sound film. For their part, the studios sought to allay these fears, held both by musicians and moviegoers, claiming that sound film would not replace silent film but that the two would coexist side by side, with patrons being able to choose their preferred style of musical accompaniment. The musicians remained hopeful throughout the early 1930s as theaters intermittently announced that they were restoring their live music programs and pit orchestras to the program. Indeed, the large metropolitan movie palaces, like the Capitol and the Roxy theaters in New York, had never gotten rid of their music programs but continued to employ large orchestras and feature live musical performances between shorts and before the feature film, even as they began exhibiting sound films. As late as 1934 there was still hopeful talk in the music journals that the movie palace model would return to film exhibition in small towns too, and that the employment of musicians would return to silent film levels. Yet the reality was that by 1932, when most theaters, in big cities and rural towns both, had installed the new sound film technology, the unemployment of most film musicians was complete. By 1935 optimism for the persistence of silent film and live musical accompaniment had all but vanished.[18]

While live music was slowly being eliminated from film exhibition, on the production side of filmmaking music was undergoing complex changes, thereby gaining a prominent place in the sound film. In 1928, Warner Brothers and Fox were each still using separate technologies—the Vitaphone sound-on-disc and the Movietone sound-on-film systems. As the other studios pondered which system to use, the advantages of having a single, industry-wide format inspired the five biggest studios—MGM, Universal, First National, Paramount, and Producers Distributing Corporation—to form a consortium and settle on a sound standard. Sound-on-film technology was deemed the superior approach, and by 1931 Western Electric's version had been adopted by all the major studios, Warners included.[19]

Meanwhile, studios continued to experiment with the conceptualization of sound. Based on the success and popularity of its part-talkies, Warner Brothers introduced the first "100% Talkie" in July 1928, a gangster picture called *Lights of New York*. This film had the distinction of having not just interrupted moments of synchronized dialogue but continuous dialogue throughout. While this new format allowed studios to pursue more dramatic genres like detective pictures and thrillers, it also allowed them to expand on narrative formulas that had already proved popular, the music-centered part-talkie in particular.

Starting in 1929, the all-talking sound film introduced a new approach to film music, one that saw a marked increase in the use of live musical performances. Perhaps because it was in closer keeping with film's aspirations of realism, or because it came closer to realizing the non-canned ideal so strenuously argued for by musicians, diegetic, and especially performed music suddenly began to play a dominant role in feature film production. Between the 1929 and 1930 seasons especially, the studios produced an abundance of film "musicals."[20] Much like the part-talkies, these films featured a great deal of music through a variety of narrative contrivances and formulas borrowed from Broadway and the stage—the revue, the European operetta, and the musical comedy in particular. The all-talking, all-singing musical was a significant because it continued to give music a prominent place in the visual construction of the film. But it was also significant because it offered a new conceptualization of filmic space.

The earliest sound films with virtualized orchestral scores offered little recognition of diegetic space, and the part-talkie had only problematized that concept by alternating long sections of nondiegetic-music-only texture with brief moments of diegetic-only music and speech. The all-talking format offered a compromise. It stabilized filmic space but at the cost of limiting it to the diegesis of the film—or in terms of the music, limiting it to diegetic music performances only.[21]

One common observation about the all-talking film is that the new emphasis on dialogue sent silent actors either to vocal coaches or to the unemployment line. Those with bad or unmanageable voices struggled to make their voices cinematic, whereas those with distinctive voices, or at least unproblematic ones, flourished in the new medium.[22] Less remarked upon is the fact that the new sound film also forced actors to be overtly musical. Because of a still limited concept of filmic space and an emphasis on realism, if a film was going to have music, it had to be seen as emanating from the characters on the screen. Actors needed to speak, but they also needed to be able to sing or perform a musical instrument—or at least be shown doing so. **Document 15,** an article by Mark Larkin entitled "The Truth about Voice Doubling," is a good reminder of the conceptual emphasis on diegetic music and the practical and technical solutions that surfaced to serve it. Published in the early fan magazine *Photoplay,* which was devoted to revealing the secrets of screen stars, but also revealing the technical secrets and innovations in film production, the article is also reminder of how popular the film musicals were.

By 1929, there was little question that film, whether part-or all-talkie, would feature musical performances; the only question was how that performance would be achieved. Some actors were already musically accomplished. Larkin mentions Bessie Love, who did her own ukulele playing in the popular musical *The Broadway Melody* (1929), and Barry Norton, who played the piano in the part-talkie *Mother Knows Best* (1928). The most famous example of a silent actor with secret musical talent was the matinee idol Ramon Novarro, who in several early musicals revealed a much-admired singing voice.[23] In the absence of natural talent, Larkin points out, an actor could get coaching. "A surprisingly large number of players in the film capital are now training their voices, in diction as well as singing, for the express purpose of avoiding the necessity of voice doubling. . . . Stars are rapidly learning to sing and play. It won't be long now until a majority of players can boast of these accomplishments."

Film stars also took on musical training to respond to the needs of a specific screenplay or scenario. Actress Corinne Griffith, for instance, learned to play the harp for close-ups of her musical performances in the part-talkie *The Divine Lady* (1928), although her voice was dubbed, and Laura La Plante had to learn to correctly finger and play the banjo for her performance in *Show Boat* (1929). What Larkin observed regarding the earliest musicals held true for even Hollywood's biggest silent stars. Gloria Swanson, for instance, took a good deal of voice instruction to be able to sing the theme song herself in one of her first talkies, *The Trespasser* (1929), and many other silent screen veterans, including Joan Crawford, Clara Bow, Myrna Loy, Bebe Daniels, and Noah Berry, learned to sing, though with varying degrees of success.[24]

In those cases where film stars were not musically inclined, rather than altering the aesthetic need for music to be performed or visualized, filmmakers developed technical solutions to address the problem. With the help of a good sound engineer and the technical trick of "doubling," any actor could fake it as an accomplished musician. One method of doubling had an actor mime his or her performance for the camera, mouthing words or moving fingers over the keys of a piano while a real musician performed the music just off camera. "In that worthy picture

Alibi," Larkin reports, "Virginia Flohri, a widely known radio singer, doubled for Irma Harrison, who, you remember, sang a song in the cafe as Toots, the chorus girl. Miss Harrison simulated singing while Miss Flohri actually sang into the microphone off stage." Sometimes the business of live substitution got fairly complicated, as in the case of *Weary River,* where it took two musicians, pianist Frank Churchill and singer Johnny Murray, playing into microphones just off camera to create actor Richard Barthelmess's on-camera performance. With the help of doubling and some intentionally distant camera shots, even Greta Garbo was able to "sing" in her second sound picture, *Romance* (1930). Microphone and camera placement was an essential part of music production in the early sound film.

Another method of doubling that could render even the least talented stars musical involved substituting a superior musical performance for an inferior one not on-set but after the performance had been photographed. As Larkin describes it, "Voice doubling is often done in the monitor room after the production is complete, the double playing the designated instrument or reading the lips of the player and timing his words to fit these lip movements." The substitution or dubbing trick of playback, another device sound engineers developed to improve the quality of diegetically performed music, worked in a similar way. Although Larkin only mentions it briefly, the use of playback was also exploited in the early development of the musical. This technique involved reshooting the visual portion of a film, but synchronizing it with a previously recorded segment of the soundtrack. Later the practice involved intentional pre-recording of the music for the performance off-set in a studio and then allowing performers to perform to it to get a better-quality performance. Scenes where the actors were both singing and dancing, in particular, were often reshot with the actors lip-synching to the playback, usually to a pre-recording of their own musical performance, so that the quality of the visual and the soundtrack could be maintained separately.[25]

These practices had a profound effect on both the visual and sonic construction of the film. Removing music to a studio liberated the camera. With sound now a separate component, complementary to the visual part of the film, the camera was free to move around the set—or even, on location, outside it. The impact on music was even more pronounced. In the short term, it was primarily technical. Moving the recording of music to a studio and synchronizing it later meant more control. But the displacement also allowed filmmakers to aesthetically revise filmic space, to reconceptualize diegetic space and give nondiegetic space new shape. "The unlinking of the microphone from the live event," as historian Crafton puts it, "opened the door to unlimited intervention in the construction of the music track."[26]

In the short term, this unlinking meant greater an emphasis on control and quality. No doubt because close synchronization was difficult to achieve, and because a stigma began to be attached to the doubling process for both the actor and the musician doing the covering, the studios quickly began to shy away from faking. They now favored drafting musicians to become stars rather than training stars to become fake musicians. Between 1928 and 1930, the musical established a number of successful musical formulas and techniques as well as propelling a number of new screen stars to fame. Many vaudeville and Broadway stars, such as Marion Davies, Anita Page, Janet Gaynor, Jack Benny, and Stan Laurel and Oliver Hardy, were imported directly to the screen in stage revues like *The Hollywood Revue of 1929, The Fox Movietone Follies of 1929,* and *Paramount on Parade* (1930). With the operetta came operatic baritone Lawrence Tibbetts in *The Rogue Song* (1930) and *New Moon* (1930). *The Desert Song* (1929) and *The Vagabond King* (1930) were also successful, but the most popular of the early operettas were the Paramount fairy tales *The Love Parade* (1929), *Monte Carlo* (1930), and *Love Me Tonight* (1932), which introduced audiences to singers Jeanette MacDonald and Maurice Chevalier. Cabaret was also an important part of the early sound musical, a performance style that brought the famous German chanteuse Marlene Dietrich to the screen by way of *The Blue Angel* (1929) and *Morocco* (1930). MGM's musical comedy *The Broadway Melody* (1929) made stars of Bessie Love and Anita Page and popularized the formula of the backstage musical.

If the reconceptualization of music between 1928 and 1931 especially motivated technical changes in recording, it also required practical changes in the style and composition of music. The foregrounding of diegetic music meant a new emphasis on contemporary music and contemporary composers. Whereas orchestrally trained Europeans like Riesenfeld and Rapee had played a major role in the construction of musical style during the silent period, compositional style now shifted noticeably. To be sure, these big-name music directors were still recruited to compose or compile the earliest virtual orchestra scores, and Rapee had some success as a song composer for several part-talkies; however, because of the emphasis on diegetic song, the Hollywood studios now began to recruit composers not from the silent movie palaces but from Broadway. As **Document 16,** "Westward the Course of Tin-Pan Alley" from the September 1929 issue of *Photoplay,* suggests, the most influential and successful composers for the 100 percent talkie sound film came from New York's Tin Pan Alley and from Broadway theaters. The most sought after film composers now included Irving Berlin, Nacio Herb Brown, Arthur Freed, Louis Silvers, Harry Akst, and writing teams like DeSylva, Brown, and Henderson, in addition to hundreds of song-writers who wrote one-hit wonders only to fade back into obscurity. Hollywood was so thick with song-writers, author Jerry Hoffman writes, that it was "impossible to cross the lobby of the Roosevelt Hotel without wading waist-deep through them." Hollywood and Broadway had become so closely aligned, he notes, it was difficult to determine which industry was controlling whom. "Is the motion picture industry a subsidiary of the music publishing business,—or have film producers gone into the business of making songs?"

As Hoffman's article also highlights, it wasn't just the early aesthetic emphasis on diegetic music that triggered the Broadway migration. The shift was also motivated by commercial concerns, copyright law, and the hope of increased profits. The new sound film had a novelty and visibility that even the relatively new medium of radio could not compete with. "Within a month of a film's release, the average motion picture song with commercial possibilities will sell from 100,000 to 500,000 copies [of sheet music] plus an equal number of records. Formerly, the average good number . . . would be fortunate to sell 30,000 copies in three months." Studios and exhibitors had a working relationship with Tin Pan Alley in the silent period, but with sound film the connection became more direct and overt as studios not only engaged Broadway composers but also bought the companies that published the music. This gave Hollywood the additional profits from the sheet music and record sales for a song used in one of their films, and it gave them copyright control as well. With Warner Brothers' purchase of Witmarks, Inc., for instance, came the rights to songs in the publisher's catalogue and control over future music produced by composers contracted to it. MGM had the same arrangement with the Jack Robbins Music Company, as did Fox Studios with the publisher-songwriters DeSylva, Brown, and Henderson and their stable of composers.[27] These new arrangements were both profitable and expedient. Not only could film studios use or rearrange old musical numbers, but they could commission composers to write new songs directly for their movies.

In reconceptualizing sound film music between 1928 and 1931, one final important correction took place. In this instance, a problem surfaced not with the recording of music but with music's connection to the narrative structure of the film. In large part because of the profits associated with the publication and sale of songs, the studios began to flood all films, regardless of genre, with music. Songs, often in different styles, were inserted randomly, and characters would burst into song for little or no reason. This momentary excessive and gratuitous use of music, along with the reforms this excess triggered in the narrative structuring of film musicals, is documented in an essay from August 1930 titled "What's Wrong with Musical Pictures" **(Document 17)**.[28] Its author, composer Sigmund Romberg, was a prominent and well-respected Viennese composer, and many of his stage operettas had been made into successful films, including *The Student Prince* and *The Desert Song*. In the early 1930s, as he was engaged in writing several operettas directly for the screen, Romberg paused to reflect on the film musical's problems and to pose some possible solutions.

One of the most pressing problems, in his view, was the overuse of songs and singing in contemporary films. "At every opportunity," whether narrative conditions warranted it or not, or whether the film's star was even capable of singing, producers and directors were inserting songs. For Romberg, this excess was symptomatic of a larger conceptual problem. It was not enough that music be performed to be real; it also needed to be validated by the film's narrative setting. Romberg articulates the problems of the prevailing unintegrated or piecemeal approach by drawing a distinction between a song and a musical score. Musical performances inserted without justification, he argued, were just songs, whereas a *score* presents the music from a consistent perspective, whether a melodic one (in the case of the operetta) or a narrative one.

> Nobody knew, or cared, that in a score, a composer, from the opening note to the closing bar, through skillful manipulation of different tempos, with different instrumentations, through different songs, plays for two and a half hours with an audience and sells them something so satisfactory that, by the end of the evening, they go out whistling his numbers and recommending the show to their friends. Songs, of course, are also part of a score. But not even a successful song will make a bad score good; while, in a cleverly manipulated score, one or two songs written, of course, by the same composer who writes his own score, will stick out and satisfy the demand.

The phenomenon Romberg describes is one that film scholars have documented well. During the 1931 season, film musicals saw a sharp drop in attendance as audiences wearied of the gratuitous use of music. In 1930 Hollywood had made over seventy film musicals, but by 1932 that number had fallen to less than fifteen.[29] The studios responded not by abandoning the genre but by reforming it. Those reforms were both practical and conceptual. One answer was to give the musical score unity by having a single composer or a composer-lyricist team write it, in coordination with the scriptwriter, instead of having six or seven composers and lyricists work on individual songs in isolation from one another. This meant a new sense of authorial consistency, apparent in operettas like *Naughty Marietta* (1935), by composer Victor Herbert; *Rose-Marie* (1936), by Rudolf Friml and Herbert Stothart; *Maytime* (1937), by Romberg; and in MGM's eight-picture series from 1933–38 featuring the team of Jeanette MacDonald and Nelson Eddy.[30]

The idea of producing fewer but more carefully constructed musicals was one response. But the new emphasis on narrative responsibility triggered another reform that affected the structural context for diegetic musical performance. As many film scholars have noted, the reform effort resulted in the rise of a new generation of musicals whose plots were devoted to grounding the musical performance in some kind of visible musical reality. With the musical comedy it meant a plot adjustment, a narrative focus on the business of music itself. It also meant a renewed interest in the backstage musical, in plots whose main characters were themselves musicians or dancers. This musical-within-a-musical formula thrived, while the revue format, that vaudeville-like parade of diverse and unconnected musical acts, faded in popularity. The reforms fueled the resurgence of the backstage musical formula and popularized films like *42nd Street* (1933), *The Gold Diggers of 1933,* and *Footlight Parade* (1933), three films that featured the innovative choreography of Busby Berkeley. The reforms also inspired the RKO hits *The Gay Divorcee* (1933) and *Top Hat* (1935), which featured the famous coupling of Fred Astaire and Ginger Rogers. Both pictures complied with the reforms in the sense that they featured song-and-dance man Fred Astaire as a song-and-dance man. Many post-1931 musicals, in fact, revealed continued emphasis on making performed or visualized music narratively viable.

Not all music for early sound films involved the composition and performance of songs. Attempts were made early on to use music in a nondiegetic context as well, as background or mood music for dramatic scenes, for instance. Such efforts, however, were intermittent and rather insubstantial, primarily because of technical limitations. Early on-set recording practices and omnidirectional microphones in particular made the practice of underscoring, the use of music behind dialogue, difficult to execute.

Although the status of nondiegetic music would not change significantly until almost the mid-1930s, that is, until well after the musical had established the popularity of diegetically contained music, two innovations in sound editing made its eventual emergence possible. The first change, as mentioned above, came with the relocation of music production to a studio off-set where sound could be manipulated and recording controlled more easily. In other words, the sound track had to first be separated, quite literally, from the image track before sound editing could be practiced.[31]

The second innovation involved microphone technology and multitrack recording. Starting in January 1931, with the introduction of the RCA "ribbon" microphone, the studios adopted the use of directional microphones, replacing the ultrasensitive omnidirectional mikes that recorded all sound unselectively, including the whirring of the camera. It now became possible to insert clarity and balance into the soundtrack, as well as a sense of stratification or differentiation, as directional microphones facilitated the development of multitrack recording, the practice of separating the different elements of the soundtrack—dialogue, effects, and music—onto separate recording tracks. When coupled with re-recording techniques borrowed from radio and record production, the new multitrack recording technology meant that each element could be layered together, or "mixed" and balanced, in postproduction.[32]

Aspects of this differentiated or "well-tempered" soundtrack, including the use of nondiegetic music, began to surface as early as 1931.[33] The emergence of sound editing brought significant changes to the theoretical understanding and practical negotiation of all the elements on the soundtrack, but the effect it had on music was particularly striking. **Document 18,** Verna Arvey's 1931 article "Present Day Musicals and How They Are Made Possible" from *Etude* magazine, describes not only how the new technology was affecting the recording of music, but also how it was affecting the conceptualization of music in the early sound film. An accomplished Los Angeles–based journalist and concert pianist who later married William Grant Still, a well-known concert hall composer and sometime Hollywood orchestrator in the 1920s and 1930s, Arvey makes several essential observations. She confirms, for instance, that as of January 1931, music was no longer captured live on-set but was recorded and engineered in a studio either before or after the film had been shot and edited. "In synchronizing and scoring, a projector and screen replace the camera and stage," she writes. Once the music had been separated from the rest of the soundtrack elements, it could be synchronized with dialogue and sound effects. While composition and performance were still in the hands of the musicians, control over the way the music sounded in the final film was now given over to the sound editor, who, it is hoped, was also "an accomplished musician." By mixing the music and balancing it with the other elements of the soundtrack, the sound engineer became a third participant in the realization of the film's musical character.

If sound editing allowed filmmakers to exercise control over music in a way not possible before, it also allowed them to reconsider the conceptual limits of music in film. Specifically, it allowed them to experiment with a presentation *not* tied to diegetic musical performance and cinematic realism. In Arvey's article, this alternative conceptualization is glimpsed briefly in a discussion of the familiar glut of unnecessary musical performances then plaguing the sound film musical. "No sooner had this all occurred," she notes, describing the studios' tendency to exploit the performance and publication of music for commercial gain, "than the public began to tire of the music that was seemingly thrown into every picture without rhyme or reason. Now music is used mainly in the beginning of feature pictures and for the end." One solution to the fatigue moviegoers were experiencing with musicals, she posits, lies in the use of extra-diegetic music to "frame" the main body of the film. Although the scope of her solution is limited, it reveals that nondiegetic music, music with no apparent connection to action on the screen, is starting to inform the discussion and practice of film music.

In Arvey's discussion, the concept of nondiegetic music is also present in the emerging distinction between sound effects and music. The practice of using music to describe or illustrate discrete physical actions, she notes, was a holdover from the silent era, and in the early sound film it became a particular conceit of the animated film. In cartoons, "nine-tenths of the story centers around the music. . . . Perfect synchronization is secured by mathematical means. Every frame of film has to account both for a certain action, and also for music to accompany that action." If sound editing liberated sound from the image, it also helped liberate music from a visualized-music-only policy. Music could emerge from beyond the diegesis if it was used to illustrate or accompany action.

One final technical innovation resulted from this particular early practice of nondiegetic music, Arvey notes. In order to illustrate an action musically in the sound film, composers needed to coordinate the image and sound with split-second precision. Although Arvey doesn't specifically describe the "click-track" or any of the devices animation composers used to synchronize musical effects with screen events, she does refer to the animated films that first popularized this type of musicalized sound effect, the "Silly Symphony" cartoon series. Because Disney's cartoons were some of the first sound films to make use of nondiegetic music in the form of musical illustration, this kind of musical illustrative technique later became known as "mickey-mousing."[34]

Arvey's article documents how limited the use of nondiegetic music was as late as 1931, well into the transition period. But this undeveloped conceptualization of nondiegetic space was also clearly manifest in early sound film theory. The problem of nondiegetic music, for instance, is given relatively substantial consideration in one of the first theoretical texts to consider sound film, Rudolf Arnheim's *Film* (1932). Between 1925 and 1932, Arnheim, who would later become well known for his texts on aesthetic theory, was a film critic for several weeklies in Berlin, Germany. In Arnheim's estimation, not only was the diegetic singing in film musicals unnatural and artistically invalid, but other kinds of music, nondiegetic music (or "film accompaniment," as he called it) especially, were equally intrusive because they lacked the narrative grounding to validate their presence on the soundtrack.[35] Without a visible source, such music contradicted the reality and naturalness to which film aspired. Nondiegetic music only confused the audience, who wondered where the music was coming from and why. Only under very limited circumstances does Arnheim find nondiegetic acceptable. Music, he states, should be used only in those moments where there is no dialogue, that is, where it has a kind of "stop-gap" function or, like Arvey's "music for action," is used to fill a hole or empty space in the soundtrack. Otherwise, for Arnheim non-diegetic music is unacceptable.

The hesitation over the use of nondiegetic music continued into the early 1930s, occupying not just theoretical but also practical discussions of filmmaking. In a 1933 interview published as "Alfred Hitchcock on Music in Film" **(Document 19),** the famous director revealed a similar hesitancy to use nondiegetic music, or musical accompaniment.[36] Although Hitchcock is best remembered today for the great psychological thrillers he directed for Hollywood in the 1950s and 1960s, films like *Vertigo* (1958), *North by Northwest* (1959), and *Psycho* (1960), he began his career in England directing silent movies for Gainsborough Pictures. His 1929 film *Blackmail,* shot silent, had been converted to sound film and released to great success. Talking here to Stephen Watts for the British film serial *Cinema Quarterly,* Hitchcock was on the eve of signing with England's Gaumont studios to make a series of thrillers that would soon attract the attention of Hollywood. His recent foray into sound film, however, had also afforded him a rare and uncharacteristic detour into the genre of the musical. Having just directed *Waltzes from Vienna* (1933), Hitchcock offers pertinent observations on both the practical uses and the aesthetic boundaries of diegetic and nondiegetic music.[37]

Hitchcock begins his consideration of music from a conceptualization rooted in the cinematic ideal of realism. Music should participate in the construction of reality, in the sense that it should have a visible source on screen. It should also be carefully placed so as not to interfere with the film's dialogue. Hitchcock agrees with Arvey and Arnheim that a separation of soundtrack elements—sound effects and dialogue—is necessary because "an audience cannot listen to and appreciate both words and the musical background at the same time." At the same time, Hitchcock challenges some of the then-current assumptions in the practice of music. The diegetic-music-only policy of the musicals, he argues, is artificial, its use of music interrupting the narrative flow of the film. There is another kind of music, he points out, one similar to Arnheim's "stop-gap" music and Arvey's "music for action" which he calls "dramatic" music, though it too must negotiate around dialogue. "The only dramatic use of music in talkies," Hitchcock observes, "—leaving out of account the 'musicals' which interpolate 'numbers' rather than employ music—is the crude instance of slow music for love scenes. Anything else has been an odd stunt and not a properly worked out scheme." While Hitchcock confirms that nondiegetic music has a regular presence in the early sound film, that presence is still severely limited, its main use being "atmospheric," to take the place of missing dialogue.

Although Hitchcock stops short of considering additional uses for nondiegetic music, such as *under* dialogue, the fact that he considers it at all shows clear development toward the theoretical and practical conception of nondiegetic music within filmic space. "Music can also be a background to a scene in any mood and a commentary on dialogue," Hitchcock concludes, "but, frankly, I have not yet made up my mind about the function of music in relation to dialogue in general." As ambivalent as Hitchcock was with the as yet untested idea of "underscoring," that is, inserting atmospheric music not just around dialogue but with it, he is equally uneasy with the limited use of music in current film soundtracks. "There are lots of things I have not made up my mind about," he concludes. "But I do think that any intelligent attempt to harness music to films is a step forward. Words and incidental noises and 'song numbers' are surely not all the sound track was invented for." Hitchcock's clear but frustrated desire to incorporate music for not just realistic purposes but for emotional and narrative reasons as well are a good reminder that even as late as 1933 filmmakers were still struggling with the conception of the soundtrack, with the construction of filmic space and music's place in it. Although the practice of continuous "atmospheric" music or orchestral underscoring would soon become a ubiquitous part of the Hollywood soundtrack, during the transition period it was only beginning to be tested.

Arvey's and Hitchcock's observations document the conceptual problems and practical limitations that nondiegetic music in particular faced in early sound film. In many ways their commentaries apply not just to the early Hollywood score in general, but more specifically to the early scores of film composer Max Steiner. Steiner (1888–1971) was born into a musical family in Vienna, with its the rich traditions of orchestral composition and operetta. Before he left Austria he wrote several successful operettas himself, and he put his song-writing skills to use in both London, in 1909, and the United States, where he settled at the outbreak of World War One. He established his career orchestrating and arranging for such Broadway composers as George Gershwin and Jerome Kern, and conducting the orchestra at one of Rothapfel's silent movie palaces, the Riverside Theater, when Hollywood came calling. Steiner was part of the great immigration of Broadway composers and orchestrators to the California studios with the advent of the sound film. His work on the early musical *Rio Rita* (1929) secured him the position of music director at RKO studio, and throughout the early 1930s he continued to compose and arrange scores for musicals, most notably for Fred Astaire and Ginger Rogers's first RKO pictures, *Flying Down to Rio* (1933) and *The Gay Divorcee* (1933).[38]

Early in his tenure at RKO, Steiner began to experiment with nondiegetic music for dramatic pictures. His first trials were quite limited. The score for *Cimarron* (1931), a film of Edna Ferber's classic about the Oklahoma land rush for which he received an Oscar nomination, for instance, consisted primarily of "extra-diegetic" music—Arvey's "credit" music that played with the opening and closing titles. In subsequent films, however, Steiner experimented with nondiegetic music, particularly the "stop-gap" or "action sequence" music that Arnheim and Hitchcock describe. Three films from 1932 and 1933, all with exotic themes and locations, reveal this new but still somewhat limited use of nondiegetic orchestral music. *The Most Dangerous Game* (1932), *Bird of Paradise* (1932), and *King Kong* (1933) all have fairly lengthy scores, but much of the music occurs around the dialogue, not under it. *King Kong* especially, with its extended action sequences that pit the giant ape against other oversized animals, indigenous humans, and finally a Hollywood movie crew visiting the mysterious Skull Island, is a good example of this early approach to scoring. Most of the score strives not to interfere with the dialogue or even, as in Kong's battle with the airplanes on the Empire State building, with sound effects. The most extended passages of scoring come in the action sequences of the film.

Steiner's technique also reflects Arvey's discussion of the blurred line between sound and music in the early sound film score. In many of his early scores, Steiner is unconcerned with drawing a clear distinction between sound effects and music, preferring instead to "musicalize" sound, especially in action sequences. Capitalizing on the synchronizing techniques and technology pioneered in anima-tion, the click-track especially, Steiner frequently used music to illustrate and punctuate discrete events within action sequences—downward glissandos when the hero and heroine jump from a cliff into the water below, for instance, rhythmic drum beats to heighten the menace in the steps of an approaching tribal chief. Such "mickey-mousing," in fact, became a signature feature of Steiner's orches-tral scores and an important element in the early sound film score in general.

Evidence of Hitchcock's "atmospheric" music, the limited use of nondiegetic music in a psychological way to create a kind of narrative subtext for dialogue, is also evident in Steiner's early film scores. On a very limited basis, the composer experimented with creating a more continuous musical background and with having that orchestral background play under dialogue. In the RKO drama *Symphony of Six Million* (1932), about a New York City physician's rise from impover-ished circumstances to social prominence, Steiner writes sustained passages of underscoring where the orchestra plays at a diminished volume during dialogue.[39] In general, however, Steiner's early scores follow Arnheim's and Hitchcock's res-ervations about the use of nondiegetic music. Like most composers working with the developing sound film, Steiner did not pursue the practice of "underscoring" with any consistency. Until the mid-1930s, when for technical, aesthetic, and practical reasons composers began to more actively engage in orchestral under-scoring, the Hollywood score and the use of nondiegetic orchestral music in gen-eral would remain something of an experiment.

NOTES

1. The most detailed history of sound film, including these early or alternative technologies, is Harry Geduld's *The Birth of the Talkies: From Edison to Jolson* (Bloomington: Indiana University Press, 1975). See also David L. Parker and Burton J. Shapiro, "The Phonograph Movies," *Journal of the Association for Recorded Sound Collections,* July 1975, pp. 6–20, 75. An important discussion of early sound film technologies and of some of the financial arrangements they inspired can be found in Douglas Gomery, "The Coming of Sound: Technological Change in the American Film Indus-try," in *Film Sound: Theory and Practice,* ed. Elisabeth Weis and John Belton (New York: Columbia University Press, 1985), pp. 5–25. Worthy summaries of the period are also offered in a few film music histories; see, e.g., Miles Krueger, ed., *The Movie Musical: From the Vitaphone to 42nd Street* (New York: Dover, 1975), pp. ix–xi; and Laurence E. MacDonald, *The Invisible Art of Film Music: A Compre-hensive History* (New York: Arsdale House, 1998), pp. 5–21 ("The Evolution of Synchronized Sound").

2. See Donald Crafton, *The Talkies: American Cinema's Transition to Sound, 1926–1931* (Berke-ley: University of California Press, 1997), pp. 1–22 and 169–70.

3. Some scholars even describe the conversion to sound film as uniform and uneventful. "Despite the challenges," Robert Sklar notes, "the talkie revolution was smooth, progressive, and generally beneficial" (*Movie-Made America: A Cultural History of American Movies,* rev. ed. (New York: Vintage Books, 1994), pp. 154–55.

4. Perhaps one of the most famous and most analyzed documents from this period, this statement signed by Sergei Eisenstein and his colleagues Vsevolod Pudovkin and Grigori Alexandrov can be found in numerous sources; see, e.g., Weis and Belton, eds., *Film Sound: Theory and Practice,* pp. 83–85.

5. Ibid., pp. 92–95.

6. Quoted in Crafton, *The Talkies,* p. 374.

7. Aspects of the evolution of sound design have been reconstructed in various places and by various scholars. Two works central to the topic are Rick Altman's *Sound Theory, Sound Practice* (New York: Routledge, 1992) and James Lastra's *Sound Technology and the American Cinema* (Durham, N.C.: Duke University Press, 2000). See also Crafton, *The Talkies,* pp. 225–50 ("Inaudible Technology: The Trail of the Lonesome Mike"); David Bordwell, Janet Staiger, and Kristin Thompson, *The Classical Hollywood Cinema: Film Style and Mode of Production to 1960* (New York: Columbia University Press, 1985), pp. 298–309; and David Bordwell and Kristin Thompson, "Technological Change and Classical Film Style," in Tino Balio, *Grand Design: Hollywood as a Modern Business Enterprise, 1930–1939* (Berkeley: University of California Press, 1993), pp. 109–43.

8. Some of the prominent film music histories have given the transition period some consideration. See, e.g., Roy M. Prendergast, *Film Music: A Neglected Art,* 2d ed. (New York: W. W. Norton, 1977), pp. 19–35 ("Music and the Early Sound Film"); and MacDonald, *Invisible Art of Film Music,* pp. 1–21 ("The Evolution of Synchronized Sound"). Other than overviews, however, the period has received little specialized attention. Only one article stands out in this regard: Rick Altman, McGraw Jones, and Sonia Tatroe, "Inventing the Cinema Soundtrack: Hollywood's Multiplane Sound System," in *Music and Cinema,* ed. James Buhler, Caryl Flinn, and David Neumeyer (Hanover, N.H.: Wesleyan University Press, 2000), pp. 339–60.

9. Crafton, *The Talkies,* pp. 63–88.

10. *Etude* magazine, a long-established music journal, had never been particularly interested in movie music, even during the silent period when other journals such as *Musical America* and *Musical Courier* joined *Metronome* to provide regular reports on musical events at the New York movie palaces. Strangely, though, it was one of the only music journals to report on the premiere of Vitaphone at the Warner Theater. The mainstream press covered the event, of course, though not with the same attention to musical detail that the *Etude* reporter did. See, e.g., the review titled "Audible Pictures" in the *New York Times,* August 8, 1926, sec. E, p. 6.

11. For a detailed account of this first program of sound films, see Geduld, *Birth of the Talkies,* pp. 103–43 ("The Voice of the Vitaphone").

12. Ibid., pp. 144–94 ("You Ain't Heard Nothin' Yet!"), deals specifically with the sound film in its first year of existence, 1926–27, as does Crafton, *The Talkies,* pp. 101–26 ("Enticing the Audience: Warner Bros. and Vitaphone").

13. Crafton, *The Talkies,* pp. 76–100

14. Many of the part-talkies, in fact, were "goat-glands," that is, silent films to which sections of synchronized dialogue were added to make them into sound films (the term was derived from a treatment for male impotence). For a good overview of the diversity of film formats, styles, and offerings between 1927 and 1929, see Richard Barrios, *A Song in the Dark: The Birth of the Film Musical* (New York: Oxford University Press, 1995), pp. 41–59 ("1928: Breaking the Sound Barrier"); and Crafton, *The Talkies,* pp. 165–79.

15. Crafton, *The Talkies,* pp. 108–13.

16. Several scholars have described the great displacement of theater musicians that the sound film brought. See e.g., James Kraft, *Stage to Studio: Musicians and the Sound Revolution, 1890–1950* (Baltimore: John Hopkins University Press, 1996); and Geduld, *The Birth of the Talkies,* pp. 252–60; and Crafton, *The Talkies,* pp. 218–21.

17. See, for instance, the January and September 1931 issues of *Metronome.* The theatergoers in these cartoons were also depicted as innocent children or helpless women being menaced or seductively lured by the robotic artifice of canned music.

18. This transition is clearly illustrated in *Metronome,* for instance. As late as 1934 the column once devoted to discussion of silent film practices was still reporting on the state of music in film exhibition and on the continued use of musicians in large, metropolitan movie houses; in 1935, after a series on the new Radio City Music Hall in New York City and Rothapfel's role in designing it, the discussion of live music at the movie theater abruptly stopped.

19. The moment in the transition to sound film is described in full in Crafton, *The Talkies,* pp. 127–65 ("Battle of the Giants: ERPI and RCA Consolidate Sound"). For a more digestible overview, see Bordwell and Thompson, *Film History,* pp. 193–224.

20. Crafton, *The Talkies,* pp. 355–80. See also Edwin Bradley, *The First Hollywood Musicals: A Critical Filmography of 171 Features, 1927–1932* (Jefferson, N.C.; MacFarlane, 1996).

21. Much of the discussion of the large aesthetic and conceptual issues surrounding the film musical has been influenced by film historian Rick Altman; see his book *The American Film Musical* (Bloomington: Indiana University Press, 1987), esp. pp. 110–28.

22. See, e.g., Crafton, *The Talkies,* pp. 445–80 ("The Voice Squad").

23. Barrios, *A Song in the Dark,* p. 140.

24. Ibid., pp. 132–42; and Crafton, *The Talkies,* p. 455.

25. Barrios, *A Song in the Dark,* pp. 115–16. "What seems like an obvious tactic was in fact a huge advance that saved time and money, helped to liberate musical films from technical paralysis, and ultimately defined a leading difference between musicals on film and on stage" (ibid., p. 65). See also Crafton, *The Talkies,* pp. 235–36.

26. Crafton, *The Talkies,* p. 236.

27. Jeff Smith, *The Sounds of Commerce: Marketing Popular Film Music* (New York: Columbia University Press, 1998), pp. 30–31. Warners eventually acquired all or parts of several other music publishing concerns, including Max Dreyfus; Harms Music Publishing; Remick Music Corporation; DeSylva, Brown, and Henderson; and several other small music publishing houses. See also David Sanjek, *American Popular Music and Its Business,* vol. 3: *From 1900 to 1984* (New York: Oxford University Press, 1988), pp. 91–114.

28. The essay was originally printed in *Rob Wagner's Script,* a literary periodical that catered to the intellectual communities in Hollywood and Beverly Hills. Launched in 1929 and folding shortly after Wagner's death in 1949, the *Script* featured a mix of columns, fiction, profiles, and humor, much of it authored by well-known Hollywood and literary figures of the day, including Charlie Chaplin, Ernst Lubitsch, Ray Bradbury, and Upton Sinclair. See *The Best of Rob Wagner's Script,* ed. Anthony Slide (Metuchen, N.J.: Scarecrow Press, 1985), pp. 9–13.

29. The statistic comes from Tino Balio, "Production Trends," in *Grand Design,* p. 211. For an overview of the temporary interruption in the production of musicals in 1931, see ibid., pp. 211–35; Crafton, *The Talkies,* pp. 357–60; and Barrios, *A Song in the Dark,* pp. 342–70.

30. For a detailed description of the evolution of the operetta in early sound film, see Barrios, *A Song in the Dark,* pp. 278–308; also Balio, *Grand Design,* p. 223; and Crafton, *The Talkies,* pp. 334–38, 365.

31. The importance of this first step—that of liberating sound from image and separating it out for special consideration—is reflected most immediately in technical articles on sound recording that surfaced in a central trade journal of the day. See J. P. Maxfield, "Technic for Recording Control

For Sound Pictures," and K. F. Morgan, "Dubbing Sound Pictures," in *Cinematographic Annual,* 1930, pp. 409–24 and 424–31, respectively.

32. Two chapters in Crafton, *The Talkies,* describe the development and impact of these technological advances in the soundtrack; see chapter 10, "Inaudible Technology: The Trail of the Lonesome Mike," esp. pp. 235–49, and chapter 14, "The Well-Tempered Sound Track: 1930–1931," pp. 355–81. See also David Bordwell and Kristin Thompson, "Technical Change and Classical Film Style," in Balio, *Grand Design,* pp. 123–25; David Bordwell, *The Classical Hollywood Cinema: Film Style and Mode of Production to 1960* (New York: Columbia University Press, 1985), pp. 298–308 ("The Introduction of Sound"); and Mary Ann Doane, "Ideology and the Practice of Sound Editing and Mixing," in Weis and Belton, eds., *Film Sound: Theory and Practice,* pp. 54–63. In addition, several cinema scholars have pointed out the connection between the technical innovation of multitrack recording and the rise of nondiegetic scoring; see, e.g., Kristin Thompson and David Bordwell, *Film History: An Introduction,* 2d ed. (New York: McGraw Hill, 2003), p. 219; and Kathryn Kalinak, *Settling the Score: Music and the Classical Hollywood Film* (Madison: University of Wisconsin Press, 1992), pp. 68–69.

33. Two important contemporary articles well cited in the critical literature remind us that aspects of multitrack recording, including the further innovation of multichannel recording, were still being introduced as late as 1938: W. A. Mueller, "A Device for Automatically Controlling the Balance between Recorded Sounds," *Journal of the Society of Motion Picture Engineers* 25, no. 1 (July 1935): 79–86; and H. G. Tasker, "Multiple-Channel Recording," *Journal of the Society of Motion Picture Engineers* 31, no. 4 (October 1938): 381–85.

34. For a good description of the origins of both the term and practice of "mickey-mousing," see Daniel Goldmark, *Tunes for 'Toons: Music and the Hollywood Cartoon* (Berkeley: University of California Press, 2007), pp. 6, 19–20, and 52–53.

35. "It is obvious that a film in which the actors sing must be unnaturalistic from its very inception. It is impossible to insert popular songs several verses long into an otherwise perfectly naturalistic film" (Rudolf Arnheim, "Film and Music," *Film* [London: Faber & Faber, 1933], p. 271). The 1933 edition is long out of print, and the chapter on music is not included in the edition of Arnheim's film criticism that is available today, *Film as Art* (Berkeley: University of California Press, 1957), which combines only excerpts from the original text (published in 1932 in Germany) with some of Arnheim's other film criticism. This early work reflects the European film experience and the traditions of the Weimar cinema of the 1920s and 1930s in particular, traditions grounded in both "gestalt" aesthetics and Marxist ideology; but its observations are relevant to the discussion of Hollywood film of the period too.

36. Stephen Watts, "Alfred Hitchcock on Music in Films," *Cinema Quarterly* 2, no. 2 (Winter 1933/1934): 80–83.

37. Alfred Hitchcock has been the subject of numerous biographies and critical studies. See, for instance, Donald Spoto, *The Art of Alfred Hitchcock* (Garden City, N.Y.: Doubleday Press, 1979). For a good overview of his place in early sound film, see Thompson and Bordwell, *Film History,* pp. 208–9, 241–42.

38. Steiner's biography is available in a number of critical histories of film music, though some offer more detailed coverage of his early sound film career. See, e.g., William Darby and Jack Du Bois, *American Film Music: Major Composers, Techniques, Trends, 1915–1990* (Jefferson, N.C.: McFarland & Co., 1990), pp. 15–73; Christopher Palmer, *The Composer in Hollywood* (New York: Marion Boyars, 1990), pp. 15–51; and Tony Thomas, *Music for the Movies,* 2d ed. (Los Angeles: Silman-James Press, 1997), pp. 141–60.

39. Steiner in fact claimed that *Symphony of Six Million* was the first film to have a continuous musical underscore (see his essay "Scoring the Film," Document 22 in Part 3 of this text): "With

re-recording being rapidly improved, every studio again began to import conductors and musi-cians. At the time, I was general musical director for RKO studios. I wrote *Symphony of Six Million*, and *Bird of Paradise* soon after, the first of which had about 40 per cent, and the latter 100 per cent musical scoring. Both pictures had been shot for music. The directors and producers wanted music to run throughout, and this gradual change of policy resulted in giving music its rightful chance. One-third to one-half of the success of these pictures was attributed to the extensive use of music."

13

New Musical Marvels in the Movies

(1926)

The first exhibition of the Vitaphone in New York City exhausted the superlatives of many metropolitan critics. Here, at last, was a perfectly synchronized screen representation with the spoken word and with music. More than this, the music was not a little, frail stream of sound but the full volume of the original in a measure hardly believed credible.

The first presentation was given in the magnificent Warner Theatre in New York early in August.

We had the pleasure of being present at the pre-view on the night before the opening. The invited audience was composed of some fifteen hundred representative men and women from all parts of the country, particularly those interested in music, acoustical inventions and the stage. The applause that met the first performance demonstrated at once that a new era in the combination of the art of music and the art of the cinema had arrived.

The new invention is the result of years of research in the laboratories of the Western Electric Company and the Bell Telephone Company. The coöperation of the Brunswick-Balke-Collender Company, The Victor Talking Machine Company and the Metropolitan Opera House were all required to make the program possible.

Imagine having on one program Mischa Elman, Harold Bauer, Efrem Zimbalist, Anna Case, Giovanni Martinelli, Marion Talley—to say nothing of the New York Philharmonic Orchestra conducted by Henry Hadley—performing throughout *Don Juan,* undoubtedly John Barrymore's greatest picture!

The Vitaphone reproduction of sound was of course the chief interest of the audience as the possibilities of the screen were well-known. The first thing to astonish was the volume of the sound completely filling a theatre of ordinary size. We took the precaution to go to the top seats in the balcony and found the volume surprisingly great there. Next was the matter of verity of tone-color. This can be described only as astonishing. We have, for instance, heard Mr. Harold Bauer play many times in private. His delicious tone effects are well-known. They were as remarkably preserved in the reproduction as was his portrait playing upon the screen. The piano is one of the most difficult instruments to record. The *Vesti la giubba* of Martinelli was rendered with astonishing dramatic force and the quality of his voice was preserved in such amazing fashion we doubt whether he ever received as great an ovation from the audiences at the Metropolitan Opera House.

PERFECT SYNCHRONIZATION

Indeed the synchronization was so perfect and the effects so astonishing that one had to pinch oneself now and then to realize that this was a mechanical reproduction rather than the original. True there were occasional tonal lapses when "hollow" or "empty" tones were to be heard, and at one time the apparatus "ran down." In the orchestra it was obvious that not all of the instruments had been "caught" in recording. However, the whole effect was so extraordinary that the exhilaration of the experience more than balanced these shortcomings.

What may be the effect of this epoch-making invention upon the musical profession? Certainly it is already in a stage to be considered as a "problem" by some. Years ago, in company with the late Mr. Presser, we heard Mr. Edison's amazing attempt to bring "Talking Pictures" before the public, combining his two extraordinary inventions—the phonograph and the vitagraph. Mr. Presser, with his characteristic vision, noted then that it would be only a matter of time before the insufficient volume of the phonographic or sound reproducing principle would be amplified to any desired quantity. Now, it has actually arrived in an altogether unusual state of development. What effect may all this have upon performers and teachers?

Twenty or thirty years ago, when the methods of mechanical sound reproduction were new, thousands predicted that singers and performers and, of course, teachers would have to seek other callings. There could be no opportunity for their advancement in face of such marvelous machines. What happened? The art of music and the profession of teaching music advanced enormously. Never have singers, performers and teachers been so much in demand—never have they received such extraordinary fees. Then came the radio. This was predicted as the doom of the musical profession. Imagine anyone saying that advertising a product would injure the industry. The radio has been of prodigious value in promoting the musical interests of everyone who has anything worth while to sell. The publishers of *The Etude* have been having the best year in the history of the firm, and all of its prosperity is dependent upon the prosperity of musicians and teachers of music. Indeed, we find that our patrons are regularly employing the talking machine and the radio as indispensable adjuncts of musical culture in the home and in the studio. For years we have used them in our own work for this purpose.

EFFECT OF THE VITAPHONE

What may be the effect of this marvelous new invention upon employees in moving picture theatres? This is problematical. In smaller theatres it will take the place of small orchestras in some cases. But there will always be the need for the organ and the piano for special features. It is impossible to give an orchestral accompaniment to a flight over the North Pole unless the enterprising exhibitors send an orchestra in another airplane. At the same time there is always a demand for a fine orchestra "in the flesh." The indifferent and unworthy players may well look to their laurels. The public would far rather listen to an accompaniment by the New York Philharmonic than to a few scratchy fiddles and squawky saxophones. The general effect of the Vitaphone will be to compel higher standards of performance.

For the really worth while performers who have their vitaphonic pictures taken, the machine should prove a wonderful advertisement. We have always noticed that artists are never loath to have their pictures appear in print as frequently as possible. Therefore every vitaphonic reproduction becomes an astonishingly fine advertisement.

Many years ago, when the Victor Company was in its infancy, the famous baritone, Emilio de Gogorza, was persuaded with much difficulty to make records. He refused to make them under his own name, fearing that his professional standing would be injured. He made them under a *nom de plume*—or shall we say *nom de voix?* Soon his manager found that there were so many applications coming in for concert engagements by the remarkable singer in the name of the *nom de voix* that Mr. de Gogorza realized that there was no better advertisement for a singer than the well-made record. The vitaphonic records will, we predict, multiply the demand for the professional, concert and operatic services of the artist "in the flesh."

This great invention is being introduced by the famous moving picture producers, Warner Brothers, of New York.

From *The Etude* 44 (October 1926): 13–14.

14

Musicians to Fight
Sound-Film Devices

(1928)

Musicians all over the country are preparing to oppose the installation in motion picture theatres of machines to synchronize words and music with action on the screen. The American Federation of Musicians, comprising the 158,000 members of the national labor union, announced yesterday that such devices threaten to debase the art of music, and that it has voted a "defense fund" of $1,500,000 annually to prevent the introduction of the devices into more than the 1,000 theatres now preparing to install them.

In a statement issued yesterday by the Federation President, Joseph N. Weber, it was denied that a collision with the theatre interests by the union was imminent.

"We are not opposed to talking movies," the statement read, "because we realize that synchronization of words with actions on the screen is a scientific accomplishment of value. But if the machines are used as a substitute for vocal and orchestral music in the nation's theatres, they will become a serious menace to our cultural growth. And that just at a time when America has achieved rank as the undoubted world centre of music.

"Music at best reflects the mood of the artist. You cannot mechanize an art. If synthetic harmony comes to supersede the services of musicians, the public will be the loser. The gain, if any, will be that of the theatrical enterpriser who will be offering cheaper and inferior music for the old price of admission. This would be especially unfortunate in view of the fact that the motion picture theatre has been a great factor in promoting appreciation of fine orchestral music."

The musicians' first step, according to Mr. Weber, will be a nationwide survey to discover the reaction of theatre patrons.

Local opinion among motion picture men is that the new devices cannot greatly threaten their orchestral programs. In smaller communities, however, it is predicted that the new installations, together with organs, will gradually satisfy the public.

When informed of the contemplated action by the Federation, S. L. Rothafel, better known as "Roxy," said that as one of its few honorary members he regretted to learn of its attitude.

"The law of averages will apply to the musicians as it did for the imagined menace of the radio," he said. "This is a new sign of progress, and they should pitch it to their own uses."

A Paramount executive declared the common sense view is that people will soon decide whether they desire and approve of the new equipment. The benefit for the smaller non-metropolitan theatres, it was said, would more than offset the drawbacks to the union, and the problem would begin to find its own solution when the new industry had the chance to fit itself into the theatres.

15

The Truth about Voice Doubling

Mark Larkin

(1929)

Light travels 186,000 miles per second, but nobody cares. Sound pokes along at approximately a thousand feet per second, and still nobody cares. But when Richard Barthelmess, who is famed as a film star and not as a singer, bursts into song in *Weary River,* playing his own accompaniment, folks begin to prick up their ears.

And when Corinne Griffith plays a harp in *The Divine Lady* and acquits herself vocally, with the grace of an opera singer, people commence asking pointed questions.

And when Barry Norton does a popular number to his own accompaniment in *Mother Knows Best,* a quizzical light appears in the public's eye.

Then, too, when Laura La Plante strums the banjo in *Show Boat* and renders negro spirituals in below the Mason and Dixon line style, the public breaks out in an acute rash of curiosity which can be cured only by disclosing state secrets of the cinema.

Richard Barthelmess did not sing and play the piano in *Weary River.* A double did it.

Corinne Griffith did not sing or play the harp in *The Divine Lady.* A double did it.

Barry Norton did not sing in *Mother Knows Best.* A double did it. He did, however, play the piano.

Laura La Plante did not sing and play the banjo in *Show Boat*—at least not for all of the songs. Two doubles helped her. One played the banjo, the other sang.

And so it goes, *ad infinitum.*

There are voice doubles in Hollywood today just as there are stunt doubles. One is not so romantic as the other, perhaps, but certainly just as necessary.

Those who create movies will probably not cheer as we make this announcement. In fact, they may resent our frankness. They may even have the Academy of Motion Picture Arts and Sciences write letters to *Photoplay* about it.

Richard Barthelmess received what he considered rather embarrassing publicity in connection with the song he did not sing in *Weary River*. And, as a result of that, persons who undoubtedly know say that he is effecting a change of policy regarding future pictures. I was told on good authority that he informed Al Rockett, who heads First National's studios in Burbank, that he did not choose to sing in forthcoming photoplays. "I am not a song and dance man," he explained, "and I don't want any pictures that feature me as such."

Nevertheless, Richard will sing—or rather someone will sing for him—in his forthcoming feature, titled at present, *Drag*. That is, he will have a voice double unless they change the story. One never knows, you know, until the picture is released. There's many a slip between the screen and the cutting-room floor!

But Dick will not be seen actually in the act of singing as was the case in *Weary River*. Probably there will be only his shadow, and the expression of the man for whom he is singing, this man—in the rôle of a song producer—registering reactions to the song.

If you saw *Weary River*, you will remember that Dick sat at a piano and played and also sang. The means by which this was accomplished was ingenious, to say the least.

You will remember that it was a grand piano. Mr. Barthelmess faced the audience. You did not see his hands upon the keys, yet you saw him go through the motions of playing and singing. And you heard what you thought was his voice. But it was not his voice.

Many persons have said that it was the voice of Frank Withers. But it was not. It was the voice of Johnny Murray, former cornetist at the Cocoanut Grove, and now under contract to First National to sing for Richard Barthelmess. He is a real, dyed-in-the-wool voice double, Johnny is.

There was much enthusiasm on the set the day Johnny Murray put over the song, "Weary River." Dick threw his arm around Johnny's shoulder and said something like this: "Don't you ever die, young fella, or go East, or get run over, or anything!" And they both laughed.

Dick faced the audience during the filming of the scenes at the piano so as to conceal his hands. It has been said that a dummy keyboard was built on the side of the piano at which Dick sat, but that is not so. But the strings of the instrument were deadened with felt so that when Dick struck the keys the strings would give forth no sound. And Frank Churchill, pianist in a Hollywood theater orchestra, sat at a real piano off stage and played the accompaniment while Johnny Murray sang. The recording microphone was close to them and nowhere near Barthelmess. Dick merely faked the singing and playing, but he did it so beautifully that the results were convincing beyond doubt.

Probably the highest paid voice double in pictures is Lawford Davidson, who doubles for Paul Lukas. Mr. Lukas, an exceptionally fine actor, is handicapped for American pictures by a foreign accent. For that reason, therefore, it is necessary for someone else to speak his lines. And Davidson is said to receive five hundred dollars a week for this service.

Many individuals in Hollywood are wondering why Davidson has seen fit to submerge his own personality for this sort of work, for he is regarded as fully as gifted an actor in his own right as Paul Lukas. He is listed in all casting offices as a five-hundred-dollar-a-week man. It may be, of course, that he has an arrangement to appear in other pictures, too.

There are a number of ways of doubling the voice on the screen. Usually it is done through a method known as "dubbing." This means that it is done after the picture is shot. "Dubbing" is a term handed down to the movies by the makers of phonograph records. When portions were taken off several phonograph records to make one record, the process was referred to as "dubbing." So "dubbing" it is these days in pictures.

Most of the doubling that Margaret Livingston did for Louise Brooks in *The Canary Murder Case* was accomplished by "dubbing." Miss Livingston took up a position before the "mike" and watched the picture being run on the screen. If Miss Brooks came in a door and said, "Hello, everybody, how are you this evening?" Miss Livingston watched her lips and spoke Miss Brooks' words into the microphone.

Thus a sound-track was made and inserted in the film. And that operation is called "dubbing."

All synchronizations are dubbed in after the picture is finished. The production is edited and cut to exact running length, then the orchestra is assembled in the monitor room (a room usually the size of the average theater) and the score is played as the picture is run. The sound-track thus obtained is "dubbed" into the sound film or on to the record, depending upon which system is used.

If foreign sounds stray into the film, such as scratches and pin-pricks, they are "bloped" out. Some call it "blooping." This means that they are eliminated with a paintbrush and India ink. The method is not unlike that applied to the retouching of photographic negatives.

Voice doubling is sometimes forced upon the producers as an emergency measure. Such was the case with Paramount in connection with *The Canary Murder Case.*

They called Miss Livingston to the studio one day and said, "Miss Livingston, we are up against it and we think you can help us out. We want to turn *The Canary Murder Case* into a talkie and Miss Brooks is not available. We think you can double for her. Will you do it?"

She thought it over. Well, why not? It meant experience in the talkies, *and double her usual salary.* So she wore clothes that duplicated Miss Brooks', "dubbed" some of the stuff and played some of it straight, her profile always to the camera.

A few times she missed the timing, and as a result her words did not come out even with Miss Brooks' lip movements.

After it was all over a very amusing incident occurred. Miss Livingston was sitting in a restaurant in New York and the friend with whom she was having dinner remarked, "So you have been talking for Louise Brooks, have you?"

From a nearby table came a strange voice. "Yes," quoth the voice, "and it had better be good!"

They looked around in astonishment and there sat Louise Brooks!

Of course, they all laughed and immediately went into a huddle about Hollywood.

A surprisingly large number of players in the film capital are now training their voices, in diction as well as singing, for the express purpose of avoiding the necessity of voice doubling. Vilma Banky, for instance, spends two hours a day perfecting her English. And James Burroughs, Bessie Love, Carmel Myers, Billie Dove, Gwen Lee, Jacqueline Logan, Frances Lee, Leatrice Joy, Armand Kaliz and innumerable others are all taking vocal lessons. Most of these have sung professionally at some time in their career. . . .

Obtaining suitable voice doubles is often a difficult task. The voice must not only fit the player, it must suit the characterization as well. And good singing voices are not always easily found. One reason for this is that persons of marked vocal accomplishments are frequently reluctant to double. They are afraid their voices will be recognized, that it will cheapen them. A notable case in point was that of Marion Harris, the vaudeville headliner, who turned down an offer of $10,000 from Universal, according to one of her representatives, to substitute her voice for a film player, presumably in *Broadway.*

No end of problems develop, of course, in connection with registering the voice. When Douglas Fairbanks did his bit of talking for *The Iron Mask* his stentorian tones all but wrecked the recording apparatus.

Before beginning, he was cautioned by the sound engineers to speak softly. However, for Doug this was impossible. He could not get dramatic effect with his conversation thus cramped. As a result the first uproarious line of his speech brought the sound men pouring out of the mixing chamber like a swarm of mad hornets. Much argument ensued. Finally Earle Browne, director of dialogue, hit upon the bright idea of moving the microphone thirty feet away and turning it so that it faced *away* from Fairbanks.

Laura La Plante's problem in *Show Boat* was quite the opposite of Doug's. The most difficult thing she had to learn in working with a double was, not to sing silently, but to finger a banjo perfectly. She realized, naturally, that the eyes of countless trained musicians would be upon her in audiences the world over. In consequence, she could not fake. She had to be convincing. So she spent several weeks learning the correct fingering of a banjo.

Some of the stars, of course, actually play musical instruments, though few have done so professionally. There's Bessie Love and her ukulele, and a few others. In *Mother Knows Best,* Barry Norton actually played the piano while Sherry Hall sang his song. Sherry stood before the "mike" just outside the camera lines and Barry played his accompaniment and at the same time spoke the words of the song inaudibly, putting into them the proper timing, a thing possible to him because of his knowledge of music.

Of course, every effort is made on the part of producers to guard the secret of doubling. Picture-makers feel that it spoils the illusion, that it hurts a production's box office appeal. In this respect, however, they are wrong. I know this from my own personal experience in exploitation work. In nearly twelve years of steering the box office destinies of photoplays—especially film road shows, some of the largest of which I have handled personally—I have yet to encounter a single set-back or loss because the public had knowledge of a double's work. On the other hand, I found that it often stimulated business to let the public in on a secret or two.

Eva Olivotti, one of Hollywood's most promising voices, assured a friend that, if it became known that she doubled for Laura La Plante in the singing numbers of *Show Boat,* she would never be able to obtain another job. That is an example of the fear instilled into the hearts of the doubles by the companies for which they work. They are afraid even to breathe the nature of their employment.

The fact remains, however, that Miss Olivotti *did* sing Miss la Plante's songs, and sang them very well, indeed.

Songs for *The Divine Lady* were "dubbed" in after Miss Griffith completed the picture. An odd complication developed when it came to doubling the harp. It had been arranged for Zhay Clark to play this instrument for Miss Griffith, but when that portion of the picture was viewed, it was discovered that Miss Griffith's fingernails were longer than Miss Clark's and that her hands, therefore, could not substitute effectively for Miss Griffith's.

So Miss Clark spent two days teaching Miss Griffith the fingering of the harp, and how to come in with the orchestra. Then the star did the scene herself. The music and songs, according to those acquainted with the facts, were "dubbed" in the East—a feat easily accomplished merely by watching the picture on the screen and getting from doubles a sound-track that would fit properly.

Voice doubling is often done in the monitor room after the production is complete, the double playing the designated instrument or reading the lips of the player and timing his words to fit these lip movements.

But voice doubling seems to be on the wane. As time goes on, there will be less need for it. In rare instances, of course, it will be done where stars can't sing or play the instruments called for in the script. But stars are rapidly learning to sing and play. It won't be long now until a majority of players can boast of these accomplishments.

Then, too, microphone miracles are becoming more prevalent every day. This is due primarily to rapid improvement in equipment. Josef Cherniavsky, the musical director for one company, says: "Give me a person who is not tone deaf and I will make him ninety-five percent perfect in talking pictures." Perhaps Mr. Cherniavsky is a wee bit enthusiastic, but at least his outlook indicates the present Hollywood trend.

Bearing out his statement, it is interesting to note that if a voice has tone quality, but lacks volume, the fault can be easily corrected by the amplifier. Take Alice White. Alice sang her own songs (unless I have been terribly fooled, and I suspect I have!) in *Broadway Babies,* sang them sweetly, but in a piping little voice that couldn't be heard off the set. Yet when the "play-back" gave evidence of surprising volume in her tones, loud cheers went up from company officials. The "play-back," by the way, is a device which plays back the voices of the cast from a wax record shortly after the scene is filmed. It's an invaluable check-up.

The problem of the foreign player is, of course, difficult to solve. At first it was regarded as an insurmountable obstacle. It is being discovered by producers, however, that what they thought a hopeless liability in the beginning has actually become an asset. In the case of feminine players in particular, accent is a decided charm. Such foreign players as Baclanova, Goudal, et al. are giving up the thought of perfecting their English. Nils Asther is studying English religiously. Care will always have to be exercised, nevertheless, in casting these players.

Another instance of piano doubling occurs in *Speakeasy,* that splendid underworld picture about the prize-fighter and the gin reporter. Fred Warren, an exceptionally capable pianist, doubled at the piano for Henry B. Walthall. This was accomplished by tying down the keyboard of the real piano at which Walthall sat, so that when he struck the keys, nothing happened. You will remember, of course, that he sat facing the audience in such a position as to conceal his hands.

Warren sat off stage at a real piano, about fifteen or twenty feet away, in a spot where he and Walthall could see each other. The recording "mike" was near Warren. As he played, Walthall imitated his motions. They had rehearsed the thing to perfection.

Although voice doubling is to the public the most interesting phase of sound work—because it is hidden from public view, no doubt—it is one of the comparatively simple things which confront producers. Problems much more subtle really vex them. For instance: New caste has grown up with the advent of conversing pictures; sound engineers are competing with directors for prestige and dominance; there is often open warfare between directors and monitor men; the new terminology of the business—"dubbing," "bloping," the invention of "split sets"; the mere fact that light travels faster than sound—a circumstance frequently baffling to engineers, and one that gives them grey hairs.

Just recently sound engineers found out that perfect synchronization in a big theater is virtually impossible—all because light travels faster than sound. If you are sitting comparatively close to the screen, all is well. If you are sitting in the back of the house, or in the balcony, it's another matter. Sound vibrations reach you after you have seen the image speak. The speed with which light vibrations exceed sound vibrations will depend of course upon where you sit. And this is a problem that sound engineers are trying to solve.

So you see producers have other troubles than doubles!

From *Photoplay*, July 1929, pp. 32–33 and 108–10.

16

Westward the Course of Tin-Pan Alley

Jerry Hoffman

(1929)

That little gray home in the West is no longer for rent. The bird who first glorified it from a piano on West 46th Street has moved in—with his Mammy.

The home-cooked bacon, the sugared yams which his Mammy was scheduled to turn out, are also in the picture. Mammy, however, isn't doing the cooking, but daily you can find those who write the nation's songs gathered around tables in Wilson Mizner's Brown Derby, Henry's, and Eddie Brandstatter's Montmartre.

For ten years they've been singing the warning: "California—Here I Come!"

They've come—and how! That yearned-for Golden Gate has sprung a hinge in opening wide to let 'em in. And they'll never ask for more.

It is now a question as to which has absorbed which. Is the motion picture industry a subsidiary of the music publishing business,—or have film producers gone into the business of making songs?

To the song-writer himself, the question means nothing. All that matters is that he has never been so happy in his life. Never before were things as easy for a composer or lyricist as the present. That goes, financially, artistically and comfortably. Named in the order of importance to the song-writer.

During the so-called "good old days," the song-writer sweat agonies before an idea came for a song. There were comparatively few production writers who were given situations on which to build themes. After writing it, the trouble of getting the song marketed began. If the composer or lyricist was under contract to the music publisher, that difficulty was easily removed. Even then, his work was just starting. A staff of "pluggers" was assigned to get the song placed. This meant personal interviews with vaudeville actors, band leaders, radio entertainers, cabaret performers and even circus troupers. The function of the "plugger" was to convince such persons of the tremendous merits contained in the new song, in order to warrant their learning it and placing it in their routines or repertoires.

Individuals in all branches of the amusement industry were showered with courtesies by the representatives of the publisher or by the song-writers. These attentions varied in size, according to the artist's importance.

Many rated only a lunch. Others were given theater tickets or admissions to baseball or football games or fights. The very highest of the high were "cut in." In this fashion many of the better known orchestra leaders, black-faced comedians, revue stars and vaudeville headliners obtained a percentage of royalty on a song featured by them. Such methods were (and sill are) supposedly forbidden by members of the Music Publishers Protective Association.

The taboo was (and still is) overcome by the simple expedient of naming the singer or musician as one of the song-writers.

Some hits of the past have had as many as eight writers named responsible for a lyric or the melody.

The more bands or acts using a song, the better became its commercial value, for it reached the ears of so many more music-buyers. If a song was a "natural," the work was easier, for many performers would voluntarily use it. A "natural" in songwriterese is a number that clicks with the public the first time it is heard. It doesn't require constant plugging, for its melody is whistled and learned easily.

After he had his song with hundreds of acts, the song-writer's worries were far from ended. There was the job of keeping that song in the routine or repertoire of the performer as long as possible. Personal jealousies among actors or orchestra leaders; a sore throat or laryngitis suffered by a singer; peeves at the song-writer or his firm often resulted in a song being taken out of an act after one or two weeks.

There is a big difference in writing songs for motion pictures. To a song-writer there is no greater comfort than the knowledge that once a number is set in a movie—it *stays* in.

The song *stays* in. To a layman, the big thing in motion picture exploitation of songs would appear the increased financial returns resulting from a greater appeal. That is a minor consideration to the professional writer. The star who sang it originally may have paralyzed vocal chords a week later; the song-writer may say the nastiest things about the star's mother or wife. But regardless of what happens—once that picture is released, the song is *IN*.

Within a month of a film's release, the average motion picture song with commercial possibilities will sell from 100,000 to 500,000 copies [of sheet music], plus an equal number of records. Formerly, the average good number, with very rare instances, would be fortunate to sell 30,000 copies in three months.

For example: Last June, the *Fox Follies* opened in fifty-seven cities over the entire country on the same date. Within three weeks, "Breakaway," "That's You, Baby" and "Walking With Susie" had sold over 100,000 copies and records. Had

Con Conrad, Archie Cottler and Sydney Mitchell written those songs for a theatrical production or just as popular numbers, it would take the time for the show to play over the entire country or the acts using them to appear in the same territories to produce results probably not as good.

The first song written for a motion picture, to be sung as part of the film's action, was "Mother I Still Have You," in *The Jazz Singer*. It was written by Louis Silvers and Al Jolson, who sang it. Had the number or the picture been released a year later, its sheet music sale would have been from 300,000 to 500,000 copies instead of 30,000. The reason for this small number of sales, even with Jolson singing it, was the few theaters equipped for sound at the time of the picture's release. Incidentally, Louis Silvers may be termed the advance guard of the songwriters now flooding Hollywood. He was the first to establish permanent residence in the film colony under the new era. He came with Jolson, with whom he has been associated for seventeen years in the theater, conducting the orchestras for all Jolson shows.

However, the possibilities shown by "Mother I Still Have You" caused motion picture producers to realize that here was an element worth considering. It was further impressed a year later when "Sonny Boy" swept the country as one of the greatest selling hits in the history of popular music.

"Sonny Boy" may or may not have been a "natural." It was played and sung often enough during the course of *The Singing Fool* to stamp it indelibly on the minds of its hearers. . . . By July, "Sonny Boy" had sold one and a quarter million copies of sheet music. Two million records had been disposed of—for cash.

A music publisher's gross return on a copy of music is twenty cents. From this are subtracted royalties and all other expenses. The writer's royalty on sheet music ranges from three to six cents on a copy. The publisher gets two cents on every record sold. Two-thirds of that he keeps, the other third goes to the writers. De Sylva, Brown and Henderson were both writers and publishers of "Sonny Boy." Al Jolson added to the lyrics, made some changes and collected one-fourth of writers' royalty. Try that on your comptometer.

Is it any wonder then, that motion picture producers began to look upon the music publishing business as more than an incidental? Warner Brothers received nothing of the monies made by "Sonny Boy" the song. Having sponsored the industry's best-seller, they decided not to overlook any future possibilities and made the most expensive gesture of all producers. This was the purchase, lock, stock and barrel of Witmarks, Inc., one of the oldest music publishing firms in existence. That firm's catalogue of past hits and classics alone brings a revenue of several hundred thousand yearly to the firm. The deal involved over five million dollars for Warners, but all future song profits will go to them.

Since then, almost all the major producers have either merged or made working agreements with various publishers. De Sylva, Brown and Henderson supply the writers and own all copyrights to songs used in pictures made by William Fox. Metro-Goldwyn-Mayer and the Jack Robbins Music Company have a similar agreement.

Paramount has made an exceptionally wide arrangement. It formed the Famous Music Company as a subsidiary of the established firm of T. B. Harms, Inc., and its allied group. Old firms such as Remick's and Chappell-Harms, which is responsible for the Harms' music popularity in England and Europe, are included. There is the younger concern of Spier and Coslow in the deal. This arrangement gives Paramount call on any of the contracted writers with these music publishers, and publication of the numbers through the Famous Music Company. Hence, "Louise," which sold almost to the million mark in copies, made money for Paramount as well as the publishers. Leo Robbins and Dick Whiting collected the royalty profits due the writers.

Song writing for pictures has made every person engaged in Hollywood now a "production writer." This is different from old conditions, when one had to grope for an idea before turning out a number. The writer is given situations. The film's director and the scenarist can tell in advance what they want the lyrics to convey.

In this respect, the writers of songs have one difficulty to overcome, which seems slight, but is annoying. They have to contend with the popular impression shared by producers, scenarists and directors—that a song's lyric is written first. It isn't. In fact, it is well-nigh impossible to set a tune to a lyric. A song-writer may build a melody on a title, but never on a complete lyric. The tune is always composed first, and then the lyric set to it. If a line runs short or long one or two notes—the melody is altered.

Definite ideas are not always available—or else the producer cannot express 'em. One example in an incident at Paramount, is typical. The producer simply told the song-writing team: "We've got a picture called *Wolf-Song.* It's all about a man on a mountain. Write a song for it." From such premise came "Yo Te Amo," warbled by Lupe Velez, and "Wolf-Song" roared by Gary Cooper and the mountaineers.

There are quite a few producers, on the other hand, who have a very definite idea of what they want and know it when they hear it. The numbers in Harry Rapf's production of *The Hollywood Revue of 1929* for Metro-Goldwyn-Mayer are an exceptionally fine illustration. In this picture, the songs were not written for situations. The scenes and the numbers were built and staged for the numbers.

Seven teams of song-writers were used by M.-G.-M. in getting numbers for the revue. Rapf wanted a military finale to the first half, and assigned all fourteen writers to the task, the intention being to select the best of all submitted. For a month, various ideas and finished compositions were turned in—none of them suiting Rapf.

Many were original and novel, but didn't convey just what Rapf wanted to get over.

One day the entire group were assembled in the rehearsal hall discussing ideas. Fred Fisher finally burst out with:

"Well, Mr. Rapf, I don't know what you want. If it were twenty years ago—I'd give you something like this—" sat down at the piano and improvised a strain of six-eight rhythm (march style).

"That's it!" shouted Rapf, "that's it!"

Thus was born "Strike Up the Band," one of the most effective military finales seen in any revue. The style of composition may have been twenty years old, but the production gives it all the essence of sensational novelty. Here, it is showmanship that makes the song effective.

A number such as "Strike Up the Band" will sell very few copies. It has no commercial value in royalties to either its writer or publisher and comes under the heading of special material. In direct contrast is another song in the *Hollywood Revue* called "Singing in the Rain." This is the "plug" song of the show, meaning the one selected as having best possibilities for popular appeal. Therefore it is rendered throughout the production more than any other song. This is to thoroughly familiarize fans with it and create a demand.

"Singing in the Rain" will sell over a million copies and easily as many records. "Strike Up the Band" probably won't go to 10,000, if it goes to any fraction of that. To balance things, studios have made an unique arrangement in financial matters with song-writers.

Unique in the history of song-writing, although obvious to members of other businesses. Prior to the Hollywood era of song-exploitation, song-writers were paid strictly on a royalty basis. Every dollar they were handed was charged against the financial earnings of their songs published by the firm. If the final accounting showed they had drawn more than they were entitled, such sums were charged against future possible royalties. The writer was in debt for whatever amount was overdrawn.

The new arrangement has made Hollywood brighter than any blue heaven for the composer and lyricist. He is paid a salary plus drawing account against royalties. *The total amount paid the writer is guaranteed to the music publisher by the motion picture producer.*

No matter how much money a writer has drawn, or has been paid—and whether his songs have earned a single penny or not—he does not owe the publisher or producer a cent in the final statement!

He may draw $10,000 against royalties in one year and his total earnings in that respect be no more than $2,500. The following year, he may still be drawing $10,000 and his royalty earnings total $40,000.

The music publisher still owes him $30,000! And he gets it! The balance, supposedly due the publisher from the preceding year's statement, *is not deducted....*

Warner Brothers have been most fortunate with vocal hits. Although "Sonny Boy" didn't bring his song pennies to them, "Am I Blue?," by Harry Akst and Grant Clarke from *On with the Show,* is rapidly mounting the lists of numbers called for most in music shops. Metro-Goldwyn-Mayer cleaned up for Jack Robbins and themselves with *The Broadway Melody* by having three big sellers in the one show. This is very unusual, even for the best written Broadway reviews. "The Broadway Melody," "You Were Meant for Me" and "The Wedding of the Painted Doll" are all from the score by the same writers, Arthur Freed and Nacio Herb Brown.

Oddly enough, the writers of *The Broadway Melody* are probably the only composer-lyricist team not brought to Hollywood by producers. Arthur Freed spent ten years in Los Angeles, producing musical comedies and straight dramas which somehow never clicked. Nacio Brown composed melodies for the spasmodically produced musical shows on the West Coast, and attained prominence finally with the "Doll Dance," written for Carter De Haven's Music Box Revue in Hollywood.

With the hits from *The Broadway Melody,* "Singing in the Rain" from the *Hollywood Revue,* and "The Pagan Love Song" bringing royalties, the boys have gained sufficient confidence to embark on a music publishing business of their own.

The free-lance song-writer has little or no market in motion pictures. In fact there are but three known successful ones, and their connections in the past have made the road easy. Billy Rose, otherwise famous as Fanny Brice's husband, is one. Fred Fisher ceases to be by signing a contract at this writing with M.-G.-M., and John Milt Hagen is the third. Hagen was an established vaudeville and revue writer in New York prior to coming to Hollywood, and since has been very successful in writing the themes for independent firms and for short subjects.

It is also a fact that the very topmost of Those Who Rate are still in New York and evince little desire to join their brothers in A Paradise for Two—Or More. George Gershwin has turned down $100,000 to do a picture. Jerome Kern also remains aloof. Rudolf Friml, probably the most prolific of living composers, has succumbed to the wiles of Sam Goldwyn and will write an operetta for him.

The field for production writers seems a set-up for newcomers in New York. That is for the theater—not for pictures. Harry Ruby and Bert Kalmar, who have been banging out book lyrics and scores of shows for years, were captured by RKO and will write *Radio Revels,* which is to star all the important names of the National Broadcast System. Kalmar and Ruby will be placed in an adjoining cage to Oscar Levant and Sidney Clare, who have been holding down the entire RKO lot by themselves and have turned out songs for three pictures, *Street Girl, Side-Street* and *Half-Marriage.*

In connection with the song-writers are a few unheard of individuals known professionally as "arrangers." Their modesty is not assumed, neither need they worry about publicity. The average salary of an established arranger is more than the weekly paycheck issued to most of the song-writers. Arthur Lange, at Metro-Goldwyn-Mayer; Victor Barravalle at RKO, Louis Silvers at Warners, Leo Forbstein at First National, and Arthur Kay at Fox are said to be paid $1,000 weekly.

However, they have no accrued royalties coming, unless a composition be one of their own.

It is these people who are responsible for the orchestrations of a song. Their arrangements can make a poor number sound great and a great one—rotten.

There is still another feature of the new song era that is lovely for the Hollywood Chamber of Commerce and the members of the Motion Picture Producers Association. They are relieved of any possible rush to Hollywood by film-struck song-writers. Simply because the song-writers are not engaged by studios in Hollywood—but by publishers in New York.

It is just as well. Right now it is impossible to cross the lobby of the Roosevelt Hotel without wading waist-deep through song-writers. In Hollywood's cafes they get into your hair.

And that is the solution of why Sid Grauman finally got his famous locks sheared. He knew what was coming.

From *Photoplay*, September 1929, pp. 56–59.

17

What's Wrong with Musical Pictures?

Sigmund Romberg

(1930)

Music accompanies us from the cradle to the grave—from "Rock-a-bye, Baby," to Chopin's "Funeral March." We sing, march and dance to music. There is music in our schools, churches and play places. White men, brown men, yellow men, and black men—all are attuned to music. Music is the universal language. Music is part and parcel of life. Yes, and after death, the heavenly choir!

What, then, is wrong with our musical pictures? Why is it that music and dancing are failing on the screen? It can't be music per se; it must be the way it is being played. Perhaps a study of the stage will give the answer, for there, too, music has faced difficult problems which have been solved only by years of experimentation.

Out of fifty productions a year in New York, only ten are musicals. The reason is twofold—the cost and the scarcity of musician-composers.

An ordinary drama requires a cast of from six to perhaps sixteen characters; two or, at most, three sets; weekly expenses of from fifteen hundred to five thousand dollars, and a road try-out of two or three weeks. In case of failure, the loss may not be more than fifteen or twenty thousand dollars.

A musical show, on the other hand, requires a huge cast, a large singing and dancing ensemble, a big orchestra, innumerable sets, and a horde of electricians and stage hands. A single musical number in an operetta will often cost more than a whole dramatic production.

By the time a musical show has reached the try-out period on the road, the producer is in perhaps sixty or seventy thousand dollars. And so, of course, he must go on investing more and more in order to save his initial investment.

The possible results, of course, justify the gamble, for the musical show can demand a much higher top price than ordinary drama. If successful, it will play to the extraordinary grosses of from thirty to fifty thousand dollars a week. For every such production, however, there will be five which will just get by or fail entirely.

We now come to the sudden invention of the audible film. Realizing that music was now possible in moving pictures, the producers set forth in a mad scramble to import every song writer and dance impresario in New York to come to Hollywood and make musical whoopee for the masses. Untrained in the technique of musical construction, the executives thought all they had to do was assemble a lot of musical and dancing numbers and then let nature and the cutting room take their course. The result was a jumble of this and that with no definite score, complete absence of story, and the inclusion of songs that had nothing to do with anything, but which the producers hoped to force into popularity.

The producers next began to gather in all the musical shows and operettas that had ever seen the boards, failures as well as successes. Better grab everything in sight lest the other fellow get it. But here again, they depended upon their own staffs. They bought the productions, but not the men who had produced them. The result was added slaughter of fine material.

With an entirely new medium and no standard pattern, no new form having been invented, tried and found satisfactory, every studio had to create its own method—and bedlam reigned.

Songs, the primitive form of a musical score, were the first elements employed. Songs, songs, songs! At every opportunity a song. Stars with no voices were made to sing. Songs were written overnight by the new army of song writers. Songs of moons, songs of coons; songs of loves and songs of doves; flowers, bowers, blues and booze. No picture, howsoever dramatic, but must be punctuated with songs.

Even the successful operettas purchased in hysteria had to be broken down and operated upon to conform with the new movie technique. The new songs from the song hands on heavy salary must be included. For you must remember that one song hit, howsoever foreign to the artistic whole, might—through radio and other rights—pay for the cost of production.

Then, again, the operetta must be changed to satisfy the looks of the star or the mood of the director, or to "give the gravy" to this person or that. The score which made that operetta popular in London, New York, Paris, Berlin and Australia—which was the essential backbone of a production—was changed overnight by song writers with new songs.

Did the movie producers realize the difference between a score and a song? Did any of them stop to think that a score is a unit of melodies written after careful consideration, by graduation, to bring an audience into a certain mood, or frame of mind, as the book may require? Nobody knew, or cared, that in a score, a composer, from the opening note to the closing bar, through skillful manipulation of different tempos, with different instrumentations, through different songs, plays for two and a half hours with an audience and sells them something so satisfactory that, by the end of the evening, they go out whistling his numbers and recommending the show to their friends.

Songs, of course, are also part of a score. But not even a successful song will make a bad score good; while, in a cleverly manipulated score, one or two songs written, of course, by the same composer who writes his own score, will stick out and satisfy the demand. Compare a bungalow with a ten-story building, and you will have the same ratio as a song with a score.

But time was pressing and songs replaced the score in the hurry to produce. So bedlam broke out again, not noticed at first, on account of the rush and the newness of the whole thing. There was a rush to release, popular openings with lights and whatnot—and then the result? Apathy from the movie audiences, who, of course, didn't know and didn't care under what circumstances these musical pieces were gotten up. At first the novelty of music surmounted the handicap. But the sameness and monotony of singing and dancing in the wrong place, at the wrong time, and in the wrong way, got past the mark of endurance, and people simply refused to have anything to do with musicals.

The song writers, some of them masters in their individual art, were the first to realize that something was missing, but unfortunately, nobody else did—or even wanted to listen to them. The staggering figure of two hundred or three hundred new songs per month also became ridiculous and utterly beyond the receptivity of the picture audiences. The Broadway producer of musical shows, who took his show on the road before bringing it to New York, could change music if his author or composer were wrong. He could change his cast and keep fixing up and changing until the best results were obtained, bringing a finished production into New York.

Not so with the movie producers. Once something was recorded and photographed, it had to stay. The clamor for pictures was so great and the demand for supply so vehement that everything had to be released at once.

The break came. It came gradually until every studio realized that the procedure was absolutely wrong, and that in order to produce a successful musical picture, different technique and different knowledge must be employed. The studios learned, too, that every emotion in the picture requires thought and that only persons with experience, who have made music a life study, are the right ones to undertake the making of musical pictures.

A complete change of policy is the result. From now on, instead of producing forty musicals a year, each studio will make three or four. Instead of having six or seven writers, lyricists, and song writers prepare something for the same purpose, men like Jerome Kern, Oscar Straus, Harry Tierney, Rudolph Friml, and Richard Rodgers will compose original scores for pictures, for which the original books will be made by such outstanding artists as Oscar Hammerstein 2nd, Otto Harbach, Ernest Vajda, Herbert Fields, and Anne Caldwell.

Will the movie audiences like this new type of work? Time alone will tell. But, at least, it will be tried by the most successful writers, and if this set of authors can't make it go, nothing will.

From *Rob Wagner's Script* 3, no. 77 (August 2, 1930): pp. 6–7. Reprinted in *Rob Wagner's Script,* edited by Anthony Slide (Metuchen, N.J.: Scarecrow Press, 1985), pp. 9–13. Used by permission of Anthony Slide.

18

Present Day Musical Films and How They Are Made Possible

Verna Arvey

(1931)

"I am conscious less of present performance than of the future vision of a nation of music lovers trained by the leaders of our film industry. The level of musical appreciation is rising all over the country," declares Harold B. Franklin in his book, *Sound Motion Pictures.*

In this opinion he is substantiated by Ramon Novarro, screen star, himself a splendid musician. Novarro has watched the development of music in pictures for years—ever since the old silents were in vogue. And now, as he sees the music in them becoming more melodic instead of depending mainly on dance rhythms, he foresees the coming of opera with its finest interpreters to the screen, and the time when music will be an integral part of the picture, not incidental to it.

On the other hand, Charles Wakefield Cadman, composer, who not very long ago was employed by the Fox studios, has this to say in the *Music World* of September, 1930: "The musical taste of most of the studios is very low, and it has not improved one whit since music for sound pictures came in. I feel that we had better music with the old silents than we do right now."

Music for the old "silents," however, consisted of whatever musical accompaniment the individual theaters provided for their movies. At first, the choice of music was left largely to the organist, pianist or orchestra leader. "This resulted," says Arthur Kay, "in their buying a book of miscellaneous compositions and playing it through during the progress of the picture." To stop this, the studios began to publish "cue" sheets which largely settled the matter of what music to use. In playing these correctly, however, it was necessary for the musician to have a complete knowledge of keyboard harmony in regard to modulations and so forth.

WHERE SOUND IS WROUGHT FROM SILENCE

In actuality, making the pictures in the old days, music was always played as a sort of emotional background for the actors. Maurice Costello is responsible for the introduction of that element. Consequently, there was always an uproar of some kind around the "set" during the making of a silent picture. Now, with the talkies, each studio is as quiet as a churchyard, for the microphones are so sensitive that they record tiny sounds that are not meant for them. Airplanes flying overhead, the sound of a distant hammer, the swish of nearby silk skirts, the clatter of high heels—all would register on the microphone if preventative methods had not been discovered. In the "silents," all commands to the actors were spoken; now they are in the form of visual signals.

And yet sound recording for pictures is not so recent as one might suppose. Its success is a result of experiments begun years ago. The first talking pictures had electric sound effects manually operated at each performance. That is, they were not mechanically synchronized with the picture.

Then feature pictures plus sound brought the problems of recording, re-recording when necessary, timing, cutting the music to fit the picture, and so forth.

In synchronizing and scoring, a projector and screen replace the camera and stage. In order that the sound track may be printed in perfect synchronism with the picture, which is exposed at the same time, a marker light is placed on the recording machine and on the camera. These lamps make it possible for instantaneous exposures to be made on the sound and picture negatives. Thus the two negatives are simultaneously exposed though they are separate from each other. Afterward they are printed together, the sound track running along the left side of the film.

Film recording is, however, divided roughly into two general sections; first, variable density recording, of which the Western Electric and Fox Movietone companies are the major exponents: second, variable area recording, the chief exponent of which is the RCA Phototone system.

HOW MUSIC IS FILMED

Briefly, this is what happens when music is brought to the screen. Each studio, of course, has different methods, and each technical director different ideas; but this is a more or less composite picture of all of them.

The musical director watches the picture through, figures out the score, then goes over it with a pianist in order to time it. Then the musicians are hired. (The Union wage for this sort of work is $10 an hour for not less than 3 hours of work, $50 for 6 hours and $10 an hour for any amount of time over that.) The picture is run off, reel by reel, as the orchestra plays.

When there is only one microphone, the violins are placed nearest it in a half circle. The harp is close also, but the brasses are placed well to the back. If there is a solo instrument, it is placed very close to the microphone. When there are several microphones, however, two are placed over the string section and one over each of the different wind sections.

As far as the musicians are concerned, the work is unusually nerve-wracking. They must at all times be perfect, due to the sensitiveness of the microphone.

The next morning the musical director enters the projection room with much trepidation to hear the final result. For with all their experiments, they never quite know how the "mike" will behave. Most studios make two recordings of the sound accompaniment: one in the form of a sound track on the side of the film; and another on a large record which is equal to about one reel of film. Thus the director can play the record as if it were that of a victrola and hear, but not see, the results of his work. This is done to insure accuracy in the recording. If necessary, it is re-recorded until a perfect record is secured.

THE "MIXER"

The results of any recording depend not only on the original broadcast, but also on whatever distortions have been introduced into the sound system. The broadcast is regulated largely, too, by the "mixer" in the other room. The term "mixer" refers to the technician (who must, incidentally, be a fine musician) who regulates the way the orchestra comes over. Most of the "fixing" is done by him, not by the players themselves.

When mechanical sounds are interpolated into the music, such as those of bells, streetcars, and so forth, usually they are each recorded on a separate sound track and given to someone who will remove those sounds that do not belong, make some sounds loud, others soft, and so forth. When this person has finished his work, the sound tracks are then combined and printed as one.

But this is not all. After the music has been recorded, a copy of the finished record is sent to the Music Rights Department. This is composed of people whose business it is to know what music can be used and what cannot. Even if only ten measures of a composition are used, it is necessary to wire the publishers and get a clear title on it. Some music, though, is "public domain." That is, after a certain number of years, it is no longer necessary to pay for the use of it. Folk songs usually come under this heading.

Another problem arose in the studios. Publishing houses and copyright owners began to ask such fabulous prices for the use of their music that the studios were forced to use as much original music as possible. They found it cheaper to employ a group of composers than to pay the enormous fees required if they were to use published music. Then each studio hurried ahead in a mad dash to secure the best writers, some even going so far as to buy up some of the song publishing houses, under the impression that they would create song hits through the pictures and afterward coin money selling them.

MUSIC WITH DISCRIMINATION

There again they were disappointed. For no sooner had all this occurred than the public began to tire of the music that was seemingly thrown into every picture without rhyme or reason. Now music is used mainly in the beginning of feature pictures, and for the end. Often there are incidental songs. For those things, almost all the material used is original. Each talkie also has a silent version to go to picture houses that are not equipped with sound apparatus and also to foreign countries. It is obviously impossible and unprofitable to make talkies in every language, inasmuch as there are approximately seventy-two different languages in use throughout the world.

Sometimes a big musical picture is launched—that is, one in operetta or musical-comedy style. Music also appears in educational pictures and newsreels, short subjects, when big artists are presented in small gems (Harold B. Franklin calls them "tiny branches of the films that have grown to be very big indeed), and the sound cartoon.

It is impossible to write an article of this kind and not include Mickey Mouse. Mickey's creator, Walt Disney, also produces the Silly Symphonies. In both of these cartoons nine-tenths of the story centers around the music. In fact, from a standpoint of interpreting the music with actual movement, these cartoons are some of the most perfect things made. The recording is done exactly as it is in other studios, but the process leading up to it is quite different.

In the first place, the cartoons are the result of the united efforts of cartoonist and musician. Bert Lewis, the studio pianist, begins to work out the musical score at the same time as the plot is being formulated. Sometimes Mr. Disney gets his ideas from the music; sometimes Mr. Lewis gets ideas from Disney's description of the action involved.

RHYTHM AND ACCURACY

Perfect synchronization is secured by mathematical means. Every frame of film has to account both for a certain action, and also for music to accompany that action. Thus, Mickey's rhythm is the only perfect one, since it is mechanical. Even the boys in the studio who draw the cartoons (there are six or seven thousand drawings needed for one film) are chosen mainly for their sense of rhythm and accuracy. It is indeed a complicated matter, but Mickey's tremendous worldwide success proves that it is worthwhile.

In some film studios the music department consists only of the director. Then other musicians are hired when they are needed. In other studios there are usually a music library, copyright department, the actual performers, and a complete set of mechanical effects, such as wind machines, bells, animal and bird imitators.

Inasmuch as talking pictures have meant the advent of music, dancing and languages, almost every studio maintains a department for voice tryouts. To these come people from all walks of life, young ambitious singers, old ones who have seen their day, but who never lose hope. From these people the very best talent is chosen to fill the choruses in the musical pictures. Some of those who try out are pitiful in their anxiety. In one thousand voices, though, not more than two or three succeed. And not one of the music directors the writer interviewed knew of a case in which anyone who had received an audition had risen to stardom. Various reasons were given, but the most usual one was the fact that no one, so far, has been good enough, that most of them who try out have overrated themselves. Then, too, most of the studios look for important names before they look for ability.

VOICE DOUBLING

There used to be an epidemic of voice doubling. When a star who had been a drawing card in the silents was found to have a voice not fit for the talkies, she was given a double. The double did the singing and speaking and the star would merely be photographed moving her lips. At times it was quite convincing. But this method soon was abandoned. Audiences began to associate certain voices with certain characters, and then, well, something usually happened to the double! Also, some doubles proved to be more unsatisfactory than the star would have been had she been allowed to speak. Now, when a player is not capable of speaking and it is not possible to coach her into perfection, she is dismissed.

Hollywood then began the importation of Broadway stars of the stage, not realizing that a screen technic as well as a good voice and diction was necessary in the new medium. Nevertheless, it is notable that many of them succeeded remarkably well, and we number a few of them among our outstanding stars of today. Lawrence Tibbett was probably the most heralded and most widely successful importation. Coming, as he did, from the Metropolitan opera stage, he has meant a great deal toward the raising of standards of film music.

Yet one studio was too hasty with its dismissal of a past picture star. Bebe Daniels was under contract to Paramount. The officials said she couldn't sing. Away went Bebe, to R. K. O., and sang for Victor Baravalle. He knew at once that she had a lovely vocal quality, although her tone was very small. Where Paramount had considered it a hindrance, he thought of it as an asset. The result was that Bebe Daniels, in R.K.O.'s *Rio Rita,* was one of the hits of the season.

SOFT SINGING BEST

The very best picture singers sing softly and into the "mike." Thus they are able to decrease and increase the sound volume at will. When they can only sing loudly, the "mike" has to be placed far away, making it impossible to hear at all if the volume is suddenly diminished.

The type of music used in pictures depends largely on the grade of ability of the musical director. Some of the smaller, independent studios call in different directors for different jobs. The major studios, however, all have a definite musical director of splendid musical ability and background. The directors aren't always the orchestral conductors. Sometimes they compose; sometimes they merely superintend the various departments under them.

Several of them, Martin Broones, Heinz Roemheld, Alfred Newman and Erno Rapee were formerly widely known as concert pianists. That fact may or may not be significant. Newman, who was a child prodigy, considers his piano training a necessary part of his musical equipment.

A fairly good idea of the importance most studios attach to music is attested by the fact that one of the musical directors was placed under a three-year contract when he first entered the films. His salary was to be $135,000 a year.

Paramount studio has one of the most extravagantly set up music departments of all. All of the musical requirements are met within the studio, even to the extent of the manufacturing of their own manuscript paper. Nat W. Finston, the director, is, while he is working on something, a most intensely energetic personality. He has the opportunity of completely dictating the musical policy of every picture. After once having studied the script and having decided what effects he wants and where he wants them, his chief concern seems to be the technical means to the end—the size of the orchestra, the kinds of instruments it contains. "I try," he says, "to give the audience the feeling that it is hearing what it sees."

MUSICALES

It is true that most of the musical directors disagree with the newspaper critics, inasmuch as they (the musicians) foresee the return of musicales—each one having, of course, a different reason for his views. Bakaleinikoff, at Columbia, thinks it strange that films burst into musicales at the start of the talkies, when they hadn't the necessary technical knowledge. Now that they have it, the public has seemingly tired of musicales. There must be some sort of a compromise. "It isn't possible to have enough action in the talkies," he declares. "We must have music to sustain the interest of the audience."

The late Josiah Zuro, of Pathé, felt that the screen, which is today the best medium of entertainment, would demand music, which is a basic art. He contended that musicales would return, when they were made with greater care, with less speed and more idealism. Zuro's reason for using original music in his synchronizations was also interesting. He "cast" his music just as a casting director casts a play. Each character had a theme. When he used published music, the audience had already associated the themes with other things, thus detracting from the establishment of the characters. He delighted in taking one theme and improvising on it extensively—changing its character when necessary, and so forth.

Arthur Kay, at Fox studios, has a new and hitherto unexpressed idea of the mission of music in pictures. He hopes to see the day when every picture, whether it contains dialogue or not, will have a constant accompaniment of impressionistic, inarticulate music. All of this will be vague and descriptive—not melodic. This he gives as an alternative for the excessive use of musicales. "One can't transplant musical comedy to the screen," he says. "It hasn't the first-hand personality of the players to back it up." He also gives credit to his colleagues in the profession by saying that, in general, he considers film music to be much more intelligently handled now than ever before.

PICTURES FIRST

Martin Broones avers that, although he is head of the *music* department at M.G.M. Studios, he is primarily interested in pictures. The picture comes first, music second. Therefore, he tries to choose music that is significant, that is, music that will enhance the picture. Musicales, in his opinion, are not dying out. They simply were not handled well at first. Producers tried to give picture audiences material that only a concert audience would enjoy.

Heinz Roemheld, with Universal pictures, believes that people *do* like good music and are intelligent enough to understand it. The reason good music was formerly not in general use in films was that most producers were under the impression that the term "classical" music meant somber, church music. As a matter of fact, he believes that music should be as genuine as the picture. He feels that the public misses the musician in the pit. Whether they are willing to pay for his return is another matter. Several theaters have tried it, but with no appreciable results.

"Although music enhances some places in a picture, it detracts from others," says Alfred Newman, youthful music director for United Artists. "It should not be used in a wholesale way. I consider the most important factor in sound recording to be orchestration. The technical equipment forbids using the same orchestration as one would use in a concert. Thirteen men playing an interesting orchestration sound much better than fifty playing in 'massed' formation. I am interested in different instrumental combinations, using always as a basis the established fact that strings and woodwinds record best."

On the other hand, Victor Baravalle appears to be most interested in the interpretation of the music and the personality behind it than with the actual music. He assigns different composers to write songs for a picture, then, of course, superintends their use. Incidentally, he says, each composer is concerned with writing what he terms a "hit"—more for his own benefit than for that of anyone else. When Mr. Baravalle holds auditions for singers he looks first for correct tone production, then for artistry and temperament.

Erno Rapée, First National and Warner Brothers musical authority, has formed a recipe of his own for synchronizing pictures. First, he says, determine the geographical and national atmosphere of the picture. Then embody every important character with a theme.

And, finally, Mr. Rapée sums up the entire musical situation in pictures with this simple statement: "In everything that we do, we must always remember to use good taste and discriminating judgment!"

The author wishes to acknowledge the cooperation of the various studios in the preparation of this article.

SELF-TEST QUESTIONS ON MISS ARVEY'S ARTICLE

1. What are the duties of the "mixer"?
2. When is music "public domain"?
3. Why has voice doubling proven unsuccessful?
4. How may practically perfect synchronization be procured in the "Silly Symphonies"?
5. Why is soft singing more fitted for the "talkies" than loud singing?

From *The Etude* 49 (January 1931): 16–17, 61, and 72.

19

Alfred Hitchcock
on Music in Films

An Interview with Stephen Watts

(1934)

When the British student of intelligent cinema turns to survey the creative side of film-making in his own country the names available for reference are pathetically few. Even ranging over the whole of the talkie's short history he can probably produce a bare half-dozen, say (alphabetically for safety!) Asquith, Dupont, Grierson, Hitchcock, Korda, and Saville, and only the two last-named of these can be regarded, at the moment, as contributors to the ordinary cinema.

But the arrival of *Waltzes from Vienna* and the news that he has joined the Gaumont-British organization bring back to prominence the name of Alfred Hitchcock.

His return to active direction is almost accidental. After his term as production supervisor at British International—a regrettable, fallow period for the keen intelligence which gave us *Blackmail* and *Murder*—and his signing a contract for Korda, he was approached by Tom Arnold, the theatrical manager, to supervise the filming of *Waltzes from Vienna*. The step from that to actually directing it was taken because the subject interested Hitchcock so much.

It sounds strange that the most unremittingly cinematic of our directors, the realist and humanist, Hitchcock, should undertake what seemed like simply the rendering into celluloid of a stage musical success.

The clue is in that word "musical." He saw here a chance to do two things: to try out some of his ideas about the relation of music to the film, and try to prove that a film that *is* a film can be created out of a ready-made theatre subject.

It was of these beliefs and theories about music and the film that Hitchcock talked to me, illustrating his points with instances from the film he was then busily engaged on cutting.

"The arrival of talkies, as you know, temporarily killed action in pictures," he began, "but it did just as much damage to music. Producers and directors were obsessed by words. They forgot that one of the greatest emotional factors in the silent cinema was the musical accompaniment. They have gradually realized that action should still come first—that, talkies or not, they are still making motion pictures. But music as an artistic asset of the film is still sadly neglected.

"I was greatly interested in music and films in the silent days and I have always believed that the coming of sound opened up a great new opportunity. The accompanying music came at last entirely under the control of the people who made the picture. That was surely an advance on having a separate score played by cinema orchestras. The tremendous advantage of a film being musically accompanied had been demonstrated by 'silents' like *Ben Hur* and *Way Down East*. Yet when it became possible to blend film and music together in an artistic entity the opportunity was overlooked, or at least left undeveloped.

"The result is that the only dramatic use of music in talkies—leaving out of account the 'musicals' which interpolate 'numbers' rather than employ music—is the crude instance of slow music for love scenes. Anything else has been an odd stunt and not a properly worked out scheme.

"But that conventional soft music is the basis of the right idea—expressing the mood of the scene. It is an elementary application of it."

"Do you believe, then, that every film should have a complete musical score before it goes into production?" I asked.

"I do," Hitchcock replied emphatically. "Though by 'complete' I do not mean continuous. That would be monotonous. Silence is often very effective and its effect is heightened by the proper handling of the music before and after.

"There is, somewhere, the correct musical accompaniment for almost any scene— music which will improve the scene. But none at all is better than the wrong music."

"But how would you relate music and action? What would you say was the underlying purpose of all film-music? Can you give me an example?" I asked.

"Well, the first and obvious use is atmospheric. To create excitement. To heighten tensity. In a scene of action, for instance, when the aim is to build up to a physical climax, music adds excitement just as effectively as cutting—but I shall have more to say about that comparison later. Music can also be a background to a scene in any mood and a commentary on dialogue, but, frankly, I have not yet made up my mind about the function of music in relation to dialogue in general. I can only give specific instances where I think it might be profitably used."

"Surely the trouble there," I suggested, "is that an audience cannot listen to and appreciate both words and the musical background at the same time?"

"Partly that. But not entirely. I might argue that I do not want the audience to listen consciously to the music at all. It might be achieving its desired effect without the audience being aware of how that effect was being achieved.

"No. The problem goes deeper than that. Music with certain types of dialogue might be made to achieve a great deal, and here I can give you an apt illustration from *Waltzes from Vienna*.

"There is a dialogue scene between a young man and a woman. It is a quiet, tender scene. But the woman's husband is on his way. The obvious way to get suspense is to cut every now and then to glimpses of the husband traveling towards the house. In the silent days, when the villain was coming, you always had the orchestra playing quickening music. You *felt* the menace. Well, you can still have that and keep the sense of the talk-scene going as well. And the result is that you don't need to insist pictorially on the husband's approach.

"I think I used about six feet of film out of the three hundred feet used in the sequence to flash to the husband. The feeling of approaching climax can be suggested by the music.

"It is in that psychological use of music, which, you will observe, they knew something about before talkies, that the great possibilities lie.

"It makes it possible to express the unspoken. For instance, two people may be saying one thing and thinking something very different. Their looks match their words, not their thoughts. They may be talking politely and quietly, but there may be a storm coming. You cannot express the mood of that situation by word and photograph. But I think you could get at the underlying idea with the right background music. It may sound far-fetched to compare a dramatic talkie with opera, but there is something in common. In opera, quite frequently the music echoes the words that have just been spoken. That is one way music with dialogue can be used.

"*Waltzes from Vienna* gave me many opportunities for working out ideas in the relation of film and music. Naturally every cut in the film was worked out on script before shooting began. But more than that, the musical cuts were worked out too.

"Let me give you an example. As you probably know, *Waltzes from Vienna* tells the story of the conception, composition, and first performance of 'The Blue Danube.' Obviously there has to be a long musical sequence when the piece is first played in public—one of the big scenes of the picture. In what I have been saying about music in films I have supposed the action to be the inspiration of the music. But in this case the music had to inspire the action. All the camera has to work with is the orchestra, the conductor, and the audience. The human angle is the conductor—the younger Strauss—and the people of the story who are listening. So I arranged the cutting to match the rhythm of the music. It is difficult to describe in words. You must visualize the film moving in time with the music. In the slow passages the cutting is slow, when the music quickens the mood of the melody is followed by the quick cutting.

"Then, again, there is a good instance of the sort of thing I have aimed at in the scene when Strauss, a young baker, conceives the tune while at work. There the action—composed of simple things like bakers kneading dough and rolls falling into baskets—moves in time with the music which is forming in the young man's brain.

"Film music and cutting have a great deal in common. The purpose of both is to create the *tempo* and mood of the scene. And, just as the ideal cutting is the kind you don't notice *as* cutting, so with music."

"You think then that cutting, montage, or whatever you like to call it, cannot do all that is required to establish the mood of a film, Mr. Hitchcock?"

"Exactly. I think cutting has definite limitations. Its best use is in violent subjects. That is why the Russians made such effective use of it, because they were dealing with violence, and they could pile shock on shock by means of cutting. But have you noticed that since they started to make quieter subjects, concerned with agriculture, etc., their montage has not been so noticeable or effective? If I am sitting here with you discussing the Five-Year-Plan, no amount of cutting can make a film of us dramatic because the scene is not dramatic. You cannot achieve quiet, restrained effects that way. But you might express the mood and tone of our conversation with music that would illuminate or even subtly comment on it.

"Please make it clear that I am not laying down laws on this subject. I am simply experimenting in theory as I have done in practice in *Waltzes from Vienna*. There are lots of things I have not made up my mind about. But I do think that any intelligent attempt to harness music to films is a step forward. Words and incidental noises and 'song numbers' are surely not all the sound track was invented for.

"The basis of the cinema's appeal is emotional. Music's appeal is to a great extent emotional, too. To neglect music, I think, is to surrender, willfully or not, a chance of progress in film-making."

_____

From *Cinema Quarterly* 2, no. 2 (Winter 1933–34): 80–83.

PART THREE

Carpet, Wallpaper, and Earmuffs

The Hollywood Score (1935–1959)

INTRODUCTION

By the early 1930s, the cinema was more than just a popular form of entertainment in the U.S. It had become an important social institution and a powerful cultural force in the everyday life of many Americans. Each week roughly 80 million viewers flocked to some 17,000 theaters nationwide. A large percentage of these were repeat customers who went to the movies more than once a week. While white, middle-class females seemed to be the film industry's largest and most loyal constituency, it was the cinema's mass appeal, its ability to engage multiple demographics and age groups, that helped it generate record attendance figures that by most estimates represented a third of the country's population.[1] Even as the country was plunging into a great economic depression and industries and businesses nationwide were suffering crippling losses and foreclosures, the film industry enjoyed relative prosperity.

Part of what allowed the film industry to survive and even thrive in the early years of the depression was the sound film, still a novelty. Hearing movie stars sing, dance, and talk was an experience few could resist. Even in the face of tightening economic resources, patrons flocked to the movies to revel in the new entertainment. This success gave the film industry enormous cultural cachet, but it also caused economic upheaval, especially in film exhibition.

Movie theater ownership had always been highly profitable, but the expense of installing new sound-film projection equipment now changed that. Instead of upgrading their theaters, many exhibitors chose to sell them. The few studios that were wealthy enough to purchase these theaters or savvy enough to borrow the money and take on the costs of upgrading them suddenly assumed control not just of these profitable assets but, to some degree, of the industry itself. In 1928, RCA merged with the large Keith-Albee-Orpheum theater chain and formed a new studio, RKO.[2] A year later, Warners expanded its theater holdings by acquiring the First National theater chain. Fox Studios, which already had extensive theater holdings, bought a controlling interest in the Loews theater chain, and the Famous Players studio, now renamed Paramount, added over one thousand houses to their holdings. Despite substantially smaller budgets, Universal and Columbia studios also acquired new theaters.[3]

As of 1932, some 85 percent of theaters were still independently owned, but a majority of the most lucrative ones, the first-run theaters that produced some 70–80 percent of all theater revenues, were now "vertically integrated" with production studios. As a result, by the early 1930s the industry had consolidated from dozens of production companies to an oligopoly of eight studios. The five with the largest theater holdings were quickly deemed the "major" studios—Paramount, Warner Brothers, MGM, Fox, and RKO; the three with smaller or no exhibition concerns—Universal, Columbia, and United Artists—were designated "minor" studios. A few additional production companies, including Selznick studios, Goldwyn, Monogram, Republic, and Disney, continued to function by making various distribution arrangements with the eight largest studios.[4]

Although the payoff from theater acquisition and vertical integration was handsome, it was ultimately not enough for the studios to escape the depression permanently. By 1933, as the economic decline worsened and as the novelty of sound film wore off, the bottom fell out of the movie market. Some four thousand theaters nationwide were forced to shut down, and even though the studios laid off more than 20 percent of their production forces, the revenue losses were so great that several were forced to take drastic action. RKO, Paramount, Fox, and Universal declared bankruptcy and went into receivership. Warner Brothers, Columbia, and United Artists suffered losses but managed to stave off court action. Only MGM, by practicing tight fiscal responsibility and expertly gauging public tastes, stayed profitable.[5] Court-sanctioned restructuring and reorganization efforts kept the studios operational, and the National Industrial Recovery Act (NIRA), a piece of New Deal legislation, helped as well. NIRA sought to sustain large national industries by allowing companies to regulate competition through the creation of "codes of fair competition." Although these "codes" were often monopolistic and in violation of antitrust laws, the government overlooked them in order to keep large sectors of the economy viable.[6]

In the film industry, the studios quickly instituted distribution and exhibition practices that were more advantageous to the studios than to exhibitors. Blind and block booking, which forced exhibitors to rent a large number of films (a block) from a studio at a time, sight unseen, benefited the studios because it guaranteed income from all films, even bad ones that failed to turn a profit.[7] The major studios also created a system of "zones and clearances," which dictated where a film would play and for how long—from large and profitable first-run theaters down to small, rural, third-, fourth-, and even fifth-run theaters. A lower-zoned and typically independently owned theater did not get a film until it had first "cleared" or played for a sufficient amount of time at a higher-zoned, higher-yielding, typically studio-owned theater. This distribution system was designed to allow the studios to reap the lion's share of the profits made from exhibition.

This new system of controlled distribution in turn necessitated a more prolific "system" of production. The studios needed to produce seventy to a hundred films a year for first-run theaters, which changed their programs one to two times a week, and upward of three hundred films a year for lower-run houses, which sometimes changed programs three or more times a week. In order to consistently and quickly produce a quality product with mass appeal, the industry developed a system of production that was hierarchical and highly compartmentalized and specialized. Each studio started employing groups of six to ten "unit" producers, each of whom was responsible for developing pictures typically within a specified genre or style. Unit producers coordinated the film's director as well as the directors of various craft departments—photography, art, sound, and music. Departmental directors, in turn, distributed the work to be done within a unit to a team of specialists. This highly controlled division of labor allowed the industry to adopt a factorylike mode of production, one that could guarantee the quick, consistent creation of a large number of products each year. Production of a large number of films was also made possible by having members of both talent and crafts departments sign long-term contracts, typically covering five to seven years.[8]

The final aspect of industry success was the ability to repeatedly meet the generic expectations of the moviegoing audience. Musicals, comedies, dramas, westerns, romances, action, crime, and horror films all followed well-established narrative formulas. Production efficiency was furthered by the typecasting of actors, directors, and even crafts personnel, and by the adoption of a two-tiered economic system of production. "A" films had bigger budgets, recognizable stars and writers, more elaborate set designs, and tended to experiment more with the boundaries of genre. "B" pictures had smaller budgets, adhered more strictly to narrative formulas, and were typically used to test new talent.[9] By the mid-1930s, studios were flourishing not only by controlling film exhibition but also by employing this highly determined, industrial system of production.

While audiences flocked to the new sound film with enthusiasm, they also began to protest perceived moral laxity within the industry. Film content had always been a problem for the studios. In the silent period, it was less contentious because exhibitors could easily censor films, tailoring their programs to the tastes of their audiences by literally cutting out offensive material and pasting it back into the reel after the screening. With sound film, the site of censorship was shifted from exhibition to production. It was now up to the studios to regulate the content of films before they distributed them. In 1930, with the content of early sound film becoming increasingly risqué or violent, several large religious organizations and citizen groups threatened to boycott the industry. Not wishing to lose a substantial portion of its revenues, the Motion Picture Producers and Distributors Association (MPPDA), under president Will Hays, responded by creating a set of guidelines to censor film content, known as the Production Code.[10] Although they erected it, the studios largely ignored the code until 1933, when the Catholic Legion of Decency and several other religious groups again protested against the excessive violence and moral decay being depicted in films. The industry responded this time with the creation of a new office, the Production Code Association (PCA), appointing a head officer, Joseph Breen, a one-time public relations officer for the Catholic Church, to begin enforcing the code. In July 1934, the "Breen Office" officially began approving scripts, levying $25,000 fines against films released without certificates of approval.[11]

The Production Code, scholars caution, was not solely responsible for all the changes within the film industry after 1934.[12] Film content also changed, Robert Sklar observes, "because audience tastes changed, because American society changed."[13] A pre-code "age of turbulence" gave way to a post-code "age of order" and to a new emphasis on "prestige" filmmaking.[14] For the industry, "prestige" meant a new formula that triangulated well-known literature with star actors and large budgets. Instead of entertaining audiences with violent thrillers or risqué comedies, the studios turned to more elevated and morally unquestionable material.[15] They now were making films of classic novels like *Anna Karenina, Les Misérables, David Copperfield, Robin Hood, Mutiny on the Bounty,* and *Little Women;* Shakespeare plays like *Romeo and Juliet, As You Like It, A Midsummer Night's Dream;* award-winning contemporary plays like Eugene O'Neill's *Anna Christie* and *Strange Interlude* and Noel Coward's *Private Lives;* contemporary best-sellers such as *The Good Earth, Anthony Adverse,* and *Grand Hotel (Menschen im Hotel);* and biographies of prominent historical figures, including Alexander Hamilton, Louis Pasteur, Emile Zola, Marie Antoinette, and Henry VII—all with reputable actors and actresses such as Greta Garbo, Clark Gable, Claudette Colbert, Paul Muni, Fredric March, Errol Flynn, Katharine Hepburn, Olivia de Havilland, Bette Davis, and Norma Shearer. After the Production Code went into effect, studio filmmaking took on a higher level of seriousness and artistry.

The development of film music in the early 1930s was also affected by industrialization, the Production Code, and the emphasis on "prestige" filmmaking. Like the other craft departments, music turned to an assembly line method of composition. In its initial phase of industrialization, however, music had to attend to some lingering aesthetic questions, especially ones concerning the theoretical conceptualization and practical manipulation of music in nondiegetic cinematic space. By the mid-1930s, the sound film had matured to the point that its visual style, in terms of editing especially, and its sonic style, in terms of the negotiation of speech and sound, had largely been solidified. Yet the relationship of music to the image track, on the one hand, and to sound effects and speech on the soundtrack, on the other, had yet to be finalized. As the first two documents in this section suggest, even while the physical production of film music was moving toward industrialization, its aesthetic conceptualization, that of nondiegetic music in particular, was still being determined.

George Antheil's 1935 essay "Composers in Movieland" (**Document 20**) addresses the industrialization of music production in the vertically integrated studio system, but it also observes the still-emerging concept of nondiegetic music. In the 1920s, while living in Paris and Berlin, Antheil had developed a reputation for writing high-minded dissonant, modernist music. By the early 1930s, however, as his style changed to suit a new populist aesthetic, he joined the Paramount music department, where he worked from 1935 to 1957. He also began a career as a film music critic, writing about the practical and aesthetic challenges facing composers in Hollywood in a monthly column entitled "On the Hollywood Front" for the journal *Modern Music*.[16]

In "Composers in Movieland," one of the first of these columns, Antheil suggests that nondiegetic film music was still being conceptualized to a large degree according to Arnheim's "stop-gap" philosophy. It was being added with increasing frequency, but its placement was still guided by a general "fear of interference" with dialogue. As a result, Antheil argues, film music was something of a "pastiche," a loose collection of disparate music used to fill in non-dialogue sequences. This pastiche approach had also generated a new compositional process, an industrial or "group" formula whereby non-dialogue sequences were categorized in terms of mood or action and then assigned to a composer who specialized in writing appropriate types of music. "The work is divided; one man writes war music, a second does the love passages, another is a specialist in nature stuff, and so on. After several days, when they have finished their fractions of music, these are pieced together, played into 'soundtrack,' stamped with the name of a musical director, and put on the market as an 'original score.'"

This specialization of compositional labor according to action or mood was practical and cost effective. With several composers working at once, it ensured the quick creation of a large score, thus allowing the studios to produce several films with full scores each week. While this industrial practice might not be aesthetically pleasing, Antheil notes, it had become the industry standard because "it is cheaper to keep a staff of composers on salary, ready to produce a score overnight if necessary." This formula was also cheaper because it didn't require expensive licensing fees like compilations of preexisting music were beginning to do. "Now that copyright has been recognized as protecting composers against sound-film, it costs the movies big money to quote twelve bars from anything or anybody. . . . Think of a hundred thousand measures, and you will have some idea of the cost of a quoted score, and you will also understand the sudden new vogue for 'originals.' " Although Antheil also hints at an emerging studio practice that divides the labor not between several composers but between a single composer and several orchestrators, he admits the idea was still largely untested and not yet uniformly adopted. Because nondiegetic space was still unformed, the time for a single-author, thematically unified score had not yet arrived.

Leonid Sabaneev (Sabaneyev), the author of **Document 21,** "The Aesthetics of the Sound Film" from his book *Music for the Films,* was a Russian composer, historian, and theorist who spent much of the 1920s and 1930s championing contemporary Russian composers. After the Bolshevik revolution, Sabaneev stayed in the newly formed Soviet Union and helped found the Institute of Musical Science in Moscow; later he became head of the music division of the State Academy of Artistic Sciences and the music editor for the state-run newspaper *Pravda.* In 1926, however, he left the Soviet Union and lived in Germany, Great Britain, and the United States before settling in France.[17] During this period he contributed articles to several Western music journals, both on Russian music and on the new medium of film music.[18] His and the other book-length study of film music from the period, Kurt London's *Film Music* (1936), are evidence that while much of the practical production of film music was being solidified, the aesthetic placement of music in sound film was still evolving.[19]

Sabaneev's book addresses a host of technical matters, including cinematography, editing, synchronization, and soundtrack recording. In the chapter included here, he presents a sophisticated and expanded discussion of film music, one that gives full consideration to the still-unsettled topic of music's relationship with filmic space. Sabaneev begins by recognizing that the cinematic space of mature sound film is essentially bifurcated. He describes these two spaces as "planes" and distinguishes them as being either "photographic" or "non-photographic," a spatial distinction similar to what we refer to today as "diegetic" and "nondiegetic."

Determining the placement and function of music in and between these spaces or planes, he asserts, is "one of the most difficult problems of the sound cinema." Images, speech, and sound (which includes sound effects, noises, and performed or live music) constitute the purely photographic plane. In this space, he observes, music functions to reinforce the visual reality of the film as a literal part of the image on screen. Music, however, can also exist in the non-photographic space of the film. Although Sabaneev acknowledges that music should in general give way to dialogue, he considers the possibility of the two elements coexisting on the soundtrack simultaneously. By broadening the concept of nondiegetic space, he admits that music can exist not just in the frame of the film and in the gaps between dialogue, but it can exist "under" dialogue as well. "Music has its inertia," he argues; "it forms a certain background in the subconsciousness of the listening spectator, and its sudden cessation gives rise to a feeling of aesthetic perplexity, even though the music be kept entirely in the background."

The recognition of nondiegetic space and music, he observes, has forced a reevaluation of the conventional hierarchy that governs the sonic elements on the soundtrack. Music must still give way to the photographic elements of speech, sound effects, and live music, but it may now do so in terms of volume, not only silence. Instead of stopping completely, music may play in the background at a low enough volume that it does not obscure dialogue. In this position, music has a new function. Rather than merely illustrating or verifying the images on the screen, he suggests, this new background music acts as a kind of "psychological resonator" for them. "A film that is continuous dialogue can dispense with music altogether, except the photo-plane moments. . . . But a film of a psychological nature, with love episodes, would find it difficult to dispense with music, not merely from an aesthetic point of view, but also because the audience, accustomed to the musical tradition of the silent film, expects it."

This new, more continuous conceptualization of nondiegetic space and music also requires a reassessment of film music form and structure. Instead of a pastiche or "gap-filling" model, film music, Sabaneev argues, "should posses a musical form of its own, in some way subordinated to the rhythm[s] of the screen, but not destroyed by them." Although in other chapters he suggests that nondiegetic or background music should also make use of unifying thematic and leitmotivic techniques, here Sabaneev advocates only that music achieve some measure of autonomy from the images on the screen while at the same time supporting them and following their structure and rhythms.

Expanding the conceptualization of film music to include cinematic space, as Sabaneev does, reflects the growing need to address the complexities of the soundtrack. The early sound film, musicals especially, had negotiated the relationship between speech, sound, and music within diegetic space and it had made limited use of interstitial and extra-filmic (credit sequence) music. But it wasn't until composers began to experiment with "underscoring," extending Hitchcock's concept of "atmospheric" music to dialogue sequences as well, that the value of nondiegetic music fully emerged. Sabaneev defines the theoretical distinction between "real" and "unreal" filmic space by modifying the hierarchy between sonic elements on the soundtrack. In **Document 21,** He describes music as an element equal in narrative meaning, if not volume, to dialogue and provides a solid theoretical discussion of the emerging practice of "underscoring."

Max Steiner's essay from 1937, "Scoring the Film" (**Document 22**), also does much to articulate this new compositional practice and the aesthetic shift in thinking that it required. Steiner begins his discussion by recognizing the new conceptualization of nondiegetic space and recounting the limited conceptual consideration nondiegetic music was given in early sound film. Music, he observes, was limited to the photographic plane because of the belief that it needed to be seen as well as heard. "A love scene might take place in the woods, and in order to justify the music thought necessary to accompany it, a wandering violinist would be brought in for no reason at all." Steiner confirms that the introduction of nondiegetic music came later and developed somewhat incrementally. After experimenting with stop-gap and atmospheric music in films like *Symphony of Six Million* (1932), *King Kong* (1933), and *The Lost Patrol* (1934), he observes, the practice of underscoring began to produce a "gradual change of policy." As the conceptualization of nondiegetic space expanded and became more sophisticated, the hierarchy of soundtrack elements had to be renegotiated. Music no longer needed to stop for dialogue but could instead co-exist with it, supporting it rather than being dialogue instead of interfering with it.

Where Sabaneev outlines the aesthetic considerations of nondiegetic music, Steiner maps the practical concerns of underscoring. This new placement of music in relation to speech, Steiner observes, is accomplished in two ways, only one of which is within the composer's control. Through manipulation of the pitch, range, and timbre of individual orchestral instruments, the composer can create music that is audible but distinct from dialogue. "It pays," Steiner advises, "to watch the particular pitch in which a person talks. A high voice often becomes 'muddy,' with high-pitched musical accompaniment, and the same is true of the low pitch." Underscoring can also be facilitated by the sound engineer or "mixer," who, in blending the elements of the soundtrack together, can lower the volume of the music so that it doesn't interfere with dialogue. This solution, Steiner notes, is not ideal because it is executed by technicians and not composers. Both solutions, however, recognize an adjusted or revised hierarchy of soundtrack elements. For composers, the adjustment of placing music "under" dialogue necessitates a new compositional imperative. It requires them to observe the dialogue carefully in order to calibrate the instrumentation and orchestration of the music, its range and texture, so as not to interfere with it.

Steiner also recognizes that the underscore, physically larger and longer than the stop-gap or pastiche score, is in need of a sense of organization, coherence, and unity. Although its structure is governed by the action on the screen, certain music compositional procedures can lend additional narrative support and coherence. The practice of using recurring themes or leitmotifs, of attaching specific themes to individual characters, locations, moods, actions, or ideas in a symbolic capacity, is an old one, but Steiner advocates reactivating it to give screen action and dialogue additional narrative coherence. "While [the] cue sheets are being made, I begin to work on themes for the different characters and scenes," Steiner observes. "I [then] begin the actual and tedious work of composing according to my cue sheets, endeavoring to help the mood and dramatic intent of the story as much as possible." The expansion of nondiegetic space and the practice of underscoring was forcing composers to reassess the orchestration of their music, as well as its large-scale organization. Developing themes and placing them throughout the film in a nearly continuous, wall-to-wall carpet was Steiner's solution to giving unity to the film score.

Thematic coherence and instrumentation are not Steiner's only concerns with regard to nondiegetic music. While some procedures should be maintained or adapted, others should be avoided. He perpetuates the long-standing practice of musicalizing sound effects—for instance, using music to create or enhance sounds like the "pounding of the locomotive, a train whistle or the screeching of the brakes." The use of preexisting music, popular songs and concert-hall repertoire that summon up specific titles and texts, in contrast, should be avoided, for they disrupt the coherence of the underscore with their extra-filmic references.

Steiner also describes the new labor hierarchy needed to industrialize the underscore. By the early 1930s, most of the studios had formal music departments, with a "music director" to coordinate the activities of its large and specialized labor force. As the aesthetic conceptualization of nondiegetic music shifted from stop-gap to underscore, compositional production shifted from a group formula to a single-author approach. The industrial underscore still required a team of musicians to complete it, but the division of labor was different. While one composer now determined the general location and style of the music to be used, and composed or designed most of the musical material, he was aided in his efforts by a number of musical supernumeraries: music editors, sometimes called spotters, who created a cue sheet specifying the length and number of cues needed; orchestrators, who realized a composer's sketch in terms of instrumentation or set out melodic and harmonic ideas that the composer may have only indicated verbally; and copyists, who duplicated the score for musicians to perform during a recording session. The industrial underscore then went to the conductor, who rehearsed and recorded it with the house orchestra, typically consisting of forty to sixty musicians, and finally to the music librarian, who catalogued the score when recording was finished. Secretaries, rehearsal pianists, and proofreaders rounded out the personnel in a typical studio music department. This tightly organized and specialized labor force allowed studio music departments to produce numerous scores, ranging anywhere from thirty to sixty minutes in length, quickly and efficiently.[20]

The industrialization of the underscore also redistributed power within the departmental system, not just between songwriters and orchestral composers, but between composers and music directors, a shift that also raised the question of compositional authorship.[21] When the industry began formally recognizing film music composition at the 1934 Academy Awards, the Oscar for best score went to Columbia Pictures' *One Night of Love;* however, the statuette was presented not to the score's composers, Victor Schertzinger and Gus Kahn, but rather to Columbia's musical director, Louis Silvers. At first, moreover, little distinction was made between original compositions and arrangements of preexisting music. *One Night of Love*'s score consisted almost entirely of recrafted song arrangements and not newly composed music. The emerging practice of the single-author score soon challenged this conception of musical authorship, and in 1938 the Academy, having adjusted its criteria, gave the best score award to the composer and not the music director.[22] Underscoring forced the industry to value orchestral writing as much as songwriting, but it also forced the studios to distinguish the compositional efforts of the composer from the organizational efforts of the music director.

Steiner's own biography illustrates the organizational shift that occurred with the rise of underscoring. In 1933, after having been the musical director of RKO's music department, where his duties consisted primarily of arranging and conducting song material for musicals, Steiner relocated and became a staff composer at Warner Brothers, where he worked for nearly thirty years. He is credited with producing more than three hundred film scores over the course of his career. For the first decade or so years at Warners he maintained a hectic, even frenetic pace, averaging eight to ten film scores a year. His prolific filmography, which includes such highly acclaimed films as *The Informer* (1935), *The Charge of the Light Brigade* (1936), *Gone with the Wind* (1939), *Now, Voyager* (1942), *Casablanca* (1943), *Since You Went Away* (1944), *Mildred Pierce* (1945), *The Treasure of the Sierra Madre* (1948), *The Caine Mutiny* (1954), and *The Searchers* (1956), is a testament to the industrialization of music and the prestigious reputation he earned as one of Hollywood's most skillful composers.[23]

The development of nondiegetic space had a huge impact on film scoring in the early 1930s, but the enforcement of the Production Code also had a measurable effect. In the general shift in production style from "spectacle" to "prestige," orchestral underscoring gained both narrative significance and extra-filmic stature, especially in the hands of Erich Korngold. Korngold first came to Hollywood in 1934 at the invitation of the great Viennese theater director Max Reinhardt, whom Warner Brothers had contracted to produce a film version of Shakespeare's *A Midsummer Night's Dream.* Like Reinhardt, Korngold was engaged because of his reputation as one of the most important composers working in Europe. With no intention of becoming a film composer, after scoring *A Midsummer Night's*

Dream Korngold returned to Vienna. But when the Nazis canceled the premiere of his newest opera in Vienna the following year, Korngold, who was Jewish, changed his mind and returned to Hollywood. Between 1935 and 1948 he composed some of the most celebrated scores of Hollywood's Golden Age.

Like Steiner, Korngold reveled in the emerging practice of orchestral underscoring. In his 1940 essay "Some Experiences in Film Music" **(Document 23),** Korngold recognizes the expanded conceptualization of nondiegetic music and the new compositional choices it was affording film composers. Writing diegetic music for a film musical, he observes, is of course satisfying because it resembles legitimate compositional forms like opera and operetta. But recent developments in underscoring, or "music accompanying the spoken word," were also proving "most stimulating."

In terms of outlining a practical methodology, Korngold is less accommodating than Steiner, for he creates no clear list of dos and don'ts. But his general aesthetic is similar, especially in terms of his interest in using the underscore to bring coherence and unity to the visual aspects of the film. Like Steiner, Korngold aims to write "symphonically dramatic music which fits the picture, its action, and its psychology, and which, nevertheless, will be able to hold its own in the concert hall." Also like Steiner, his "fitting" process, especially in terms of supporting the psychology of the narrative, includes not just reducing and calibrating the instrumentation of the orchestra to accommodate dialogue, but using themes or leitmotifs to generate narrative coherence.[24]

Korngold's essay also clearly documents that the studios were using not just high-profile actors and award-winning literature to generate post-code "prestige" in a film, but highly reputable craft personnel as well. One indication that Korngold was one such person, a craftsman whose presence conferred status and transcended industrial competence, was the unusual terms of employment he enjoyed. Where staff composers typically got only a few weeks to produce, with the help of a team of spotters, orchestrators, and copyists, a working score, Korngold enjoyed several months. "I am fully aware of the fact that I seem to be working under much more favorable conditions than my Hollywood colleagues who quite often have to finish a score in a very short time and in conjunction with several other composers." This special pace likewise allowed Korngold to dispense with the team of assistants that other composers needed. He proudly rejects the assistance of an editor or spotter, for instance, in favor of sketching cues himself while "the picture is unrolling before my eyes." Whereas Steiner wrote music for some three hundred scores over the course of his thirty-five-year career at RKO and Warner Brothers studios, Korngold produced only twenty over the course of twelve years, most of which were for elevated cinematic treatments of classic literature, such as *The Prince and the Pauper* (1937), *The Private Lives of Elizabeth and Essex* (1939), and *Of Human Bondage* (1946); classic swashbucklers like *Captain*

Blood (1935), *The Adventures of Robin Hood* (1936), and *The Seahawk* (1940); or best-selling contemporary literature like *Anthony Adverse* (1936) and *King's Row* (1942).[25]

Korngold was not the only prestigious concert-hall musician brought to postcode Hollywood to elevated the content of its pictures. Several attempts, some successful, were made to lure other reputable composers and musicians into the business of film music. Paramount music director Boris Morros, it was reported, at one point "discharged more than half of the existing music staff" in order to make room for new concert-hall talent who could write "special" orchestral scores.[26] The industry was helped in this wish to elevate film through music by the increasingly unstable political climate in Europe. The looming war there brought to Hollywood two of the most famous composers of the twentieth century, Arnold Schoenberg and Igor Stravinsky, in the late 1930s.[27] Although the studios promised both men special nonindustrial work conditions and schedules, neither could reach an agreement and as a result never wrote a Hollywood film score. While this setback slowed the industry's interest in prestige composing, it didn't extinguish it entirely.[28] Just a few years later, the well-known orchestral composer Aaron Copland contributed significantly to the sound and shape of the film score.

The post-Code shift to prestige filmmaking was also evident in the construction of the film musical, as **Document 24,** Denis Morrison's 1937 *Variety* article "What Is a Filmusical?" reveals. Several studios, Morrison observes, were making room not just for new and reputable singers and dancers but for songwriters and conductors as well. The studios had already established a relationship with the world of opera, and their roster of notable opera stars was swelling to include new "warblers" like Lily Pons, Gladys Swarthout, Nino Martini, Grace Moore, and Kirsten Flagstad, who could be heard "chirping out Wagner's 'Die Walküre'" in an upcoming musical, as well as the teenage opera phenomenon Deanna Durbin. For the 1937 musical *One Hundred Men and a Girl,* in which Durbin sings Mozart and Verdi opera arias, Universal studios also imported the esteemed conductor of the Philadelphia Orchestra, Leopold Stokowski. Paramount, Morrison notes, had also signed the well-known German musical theater composer Kurt Weill. As longtime songwriter Buddy DeSylva points out, the "injection of new personalities from the stage" (and concert hall) "has meant more than any other single factor for the advancement of filmusicals."

Morrison's article also observes the degree to which the structure of the film musical was changing in the industrial age. Along with the upgrades in personnel, several studios sought to elevate their musicals with a greater degree of narrative complexity. "Film makers use to have the habit of shoving a song into a picture just because it was a pretty song. That was horrible," RKO music director Nathaniel Shilkret states. "Nowadays we know better." Indeed, Morrison confirms, the studios had developed new formulas for greater plot complexity and coherence. While Warners' musicals were still narratively thin, offering "the best and liveliest tunes [with] just enough plot to string everything together," the Fox and MGM musicals were moving away from the revue format in favor of formulas "stoutly equipped with plot." Fox's chief, Darryl Zanuck, is a "believer in story values," Morrison asserts, and Louis Meyer, the head of MGM, was likewise looking to distinguish his studios' musical production through "sound story values . . . quality music played and sung by the best artists obtainable, production values and spectacle, plus a dramatic believable story." Aspects of the early sound musical still lingered, of course. Many stories still revolved around the trusted formula of "girls, gags and tunes," and despite the increase in narrative complexity, the film director continued to occupy a position of "comparative unimportance," with the unit producer maintaining the majority of the decision-making power. But the producer's struggle to find a better balance between story and music was an indication that the industrywide desire for quality and prestige was leaving its mark on the filmusical too.

While an industrial method of production and a quasi-monopolistic control of distribution and exhibition brought the industry success and record profits, it also brought it legal and economic instability. At the end of the 1930s, the studios' system of film distribution in particular came under scrutiny. Almost immediately after the practice of blind selling and block booking was erected, independent exhibitors challenged its legality with various lawsuits.[29] The studios staved off their attacks until 1935, when the Supreme Court declared the National Industrial Recovery Act, on which the distribution practices had been based, unconstitutional. This action opened the way not just for independent exhibitors to expand their protest but for the government to take up their cause. Bundling over 130 smaller lawsuits filed by individual states together into a single class-action case, the government launched a major lawsuit against the film industry in 1938. The case, *United States v. Paramount Pictures*, did not immediately go to trial, however. Instead, the industry negotiated a "consent agreement" in 1940 which made some concessions to independent theater owners but kept many aspects of the distribution system, block booking especially, in place. The studios were still allowed to participate in film exhibition and control the majority of profitable first-run theaters, but they were forbidden from buying any new theaters.[30]

At the beginning of the 1940s, the hierarchical organization of the production system was also being challenged from within by a labor force eager to have a greater share of power. With some reservations, the studios finally allowed its workers to unionize, recognizing the Screen Actors Guild in 1937, the Directors Guild in 1939, and eventually, after much resistance, the Screen Writers Guild in 1941.[31] Although executives feared their star talents would use the guilds to make excessive salary demands, those fears went largely unfounded. Instead, directors, and writers especially, agitated for greater creative control over their work. As the power of unit producers waned, a new category of directors and writers with expanded executive powers emerged. These new "producer-directors," "writer-directors," and "writer-producers"—"hyphenates," as they were known— represented one of the most significant modifications to the industrial model.[32] Directors like Frank Capra, John Ford, William Wyler, Howard Hawks, Cecil B. DeMille, and Alfred Hitchcock and writers like Preston Sturges, Billy Wilder, and Dory Schary destabilized the industrial system by opening it up to short-term, independent freelance employment. This shift in power in turn opened studio filmmaking to greater experimentation with genre and stylistic conventions.[33]

The outbreak of the war in Europe challenged the stability of the studio system as well. Since the end of World War I, foreign rentals had accounted for 35 to 50 percent of the industry's total revenue.[34] Hitler's invasion of Poland in 1939, and England's and France's subsequent declaration of war against Germany, suddenly made this significant source of income vulnerable. Although the United States remained officially neutral, film rentals in Germany, Italy and Japan either stopped or slowed to a trickle as heavy taxes and import restrictions within those countries stifled trade.[35] Great Britain, which accounted for the greatest percentage of the studios' overseas revenues, also initially restricted trade with Hollywood, limiting the studios' ability to withdraw exhibition and production profits from the country. Germany's bombing raids on London the following year also wreaked havoc with theater exhibition.[36]

As the war raged in Europe, the economic outlook at home was uncertain. For a brief period the film industry thrived. With personal incomes rising in 1940 and 1941 thanks to expanded wartime production, movie theater revenues increased dramatically, especially in large urban markets with major defense-related industries. The industry competed successfully for the country's growing disposable income by capitalizing on people's growing interest in the war in Europe. Films that featured the war and home-front narratives were especially popular and generated big box office returns.[37] But they also generated criticism from isolationist politicians in Congress, who accused Hollywood executives of engaging in war-mongering and prowar propaganda. Several studio executives were summoned to appear before Congress to testify as to the industry's intentions. Although the hearings were eventually dropped as public sentiment began to swing in favor of intervention instead of isolation, the industry's troubles were not over.[38] In February 1940, Congressman Martin Dies from Texas and his House Un-American Activities Committee launched another government investigation into the industry, this time to examine the sympathies of Hollywood's labor force. Many actors, including James Cagney, Humphrey Bogart, and Fredric March, were investigated but exonerated, and the investigation was largely abandoned when Hitler invaded the Soviet Union, forcing the government itself into an uneasy alliance with Communist Russia.[39]

This congressional turbulence evaporated when the United States entered the war in 1941. After the attack on Pearl Harbor, many industries were converted for war production. Although the motion picture industry was not one of them, its ability to affect morale, to entertain, distract, propagandize, and instruct, made it a valuable asset to the government. In early 1942, Washington dropped its antagonistic stance toward Hollywood and became the film industry's best customer. It relied on Hollywood films to entertain and boost the morale of the armed forces both at home and on the battlefield, and it used the industry's resources to make training and instructional films for the war effort.[40] The government also drained Hollywood of a large portion of its workforce. Some 2,700 film industry employees volunteered for service, including top stars and directors Clark Gable, Jimmy Stewart, Henry Fonda, Alan Ladd, Robert Taylor, John Ford, Frank Capra, and William Wyler, and executives Darryl Zanuck, Jack Warner, and Harry Cohn.[41] While many saw action on the battlefield, some were assigned to the government's own filmmaking units. Others, including Bob Hope, Betty Grable, and Frances Langford, worked with auxiliary organizations like the USO to provide live entertainment for the troops stationed abroad.

The studios also responded to the war effort by modifying film production to suit the government's propaganda needs. It tailored the content of its films to articulate key wartime themes and to present them in what the Office of War Information considered a positive light. To galvanize public sentiment in favor of the war, the industry routinely and sympathetically featured "the Allies, the armed forces, the production front, and the home front" wherever it could.[42] To accommodate these new national imperatives, the studios largely retreated to familiar formulas, styles, and genres. The well-worn genre of the "revue musical" was reactivated and found renewed popularity during the war. These were essentially filmed versions of the live, star-studded stage shows that were used to generate support for the troops, and the studios turned them out in record number.[43] *This is the Army* (1942), *Star Spangled Rhythm* (1942), *Stage Door Canteen* (1943), *Thousands Cheer* (1943), and *Hollywood Canteen* (1944) all followed this model. Other popular musicals like *Yankee Doodle Dandy* (1942) and *Meet Me in St. Louis* (1944), while not referring overtly to the war, were generally nostalgic and patriotic. The studios also gave viewers a solid dose of realism in films that had a darker and more psychologically complex style and perspective. The gothic and horror pictures of the 1930s were the first films to explore the film noir style, but the war made troubled, anxious Americans more receptive to it. With its moody settings, voice-overs, complicated chronologies, and ambiguous representations of good and evil, film noir characteristics flourished not just in obvious places—dramatic genres, crime and detective thrillers—but also in unconventional places, including women's pictures and even comedies.[44] Films like *Double Indemnity* (1944), *Mildred Pierce* (1945), *Laura* (1944), and *The Lady Eve* (1941) took *noir* characteristics in new and innovative directions.[45]

The war also gave the studios a new style to work with.[46] The home-front drama and the combat film, especially, displayed the influence of an emerging style of documentary realism coming from war newsreels, combat reports, and battle footage. This brand of realism, which featured location shooting, unstable and unconventional frame composition, and poor sound quality, was facilitated by technology developed during the war—lightweight 16mm cameras, underwater and aerial cameras, high-speed cameras, and portable sound equipment. The gritty sense of reality that this technology allowed inspired directors like John Huston, John Ford, William Wyler and Darryl Zanuck, directors who made documentaries for the war department, to import this new aesthetic into their Hollywood films.[47] "Advances in nonfiction war coverage," Thomas Schatz observes, "encouraged Hollywood filmmakers not only to dramatize combat but to do so with a greater degree of verisimilitude and historical accuracy. In the process, the narrative and dramatic emphases of combat dramas, as well as the number of Hollywood filmmakers doing documentary work, clearly influenced nonfiction war films."[48]

The war also directly and indirectly challenged the studios' industrial process. Like most businesses, the film studios had to navigate supply shortages and rationing, which affected everything from the availability of film stock to lumber for sets and gasoline for distribution of film prints to theaters. A less visible but equally dramatic problem that plagued star talent was the exorbitant wartime income tax rates, which for many high-earning stars reached a staggering 80–90 percent. Many actors joined the ranks of directors and writers in seeking independence from long-term contracts, becoming independent producers, setting up single-picture production companies, and taking their profits from a picture as capital gains, which were taxed at a lower rate, instead of salary.[49]

In other regards, the studio system remained stable and remarkably profitable during the war.[50] Although between 1942 and 1946 the number of films the major studios produced annually actually shrank, from an average of roughly 500 to around 440, soaring attendance figures spurred by the booming wartime economy caused industry profits to increase dramatically, from $35 million in 1940 to over $60 million a year in 1942 through 1945, spiking in 1946 with record profits of $122 million.[51]

As film production in general during the war retreated into established styles and genres, film music composition remained largely split into two categories: musical songwriting and arranging, and orchestral underscoring for comedies, dramas, and all other genres. As the practice of underscoring matured, however, and as wartime filmmaking expanded to accommodate more somber realistic material, some composers began to reassess the effectiveness of current compositional methods in meeting these new visual styles, questioning the general size and shape of the conventional underscore. Aaron Copland's essay "Music in the Films" from his book *Our New Music* (**Document 25**) is just such a reassessment. The concert-hall composer, who had recently joined the Hollywood ranks by scoring two United Artist pictures, *Of Mice and Men* (1939) and *Our Town* (1940), finds many aspects of the prewar underscore limiting and in need of revision.

Copland begins his analysis by confirming the underscore's fundamental psychological function. Music is a "flame put under the screen to help warm it," he famously pronounces. While recognizing the essential usefulness of nondiegetic music in film, however, Copland is also critical of many aspects of underscoring. The convention he finds most confining is the "symphonic" sound of the film score. Copland does not object to the fact that the orchestra has become the default instrument for composers, but he does object to the style of orchestration that had become so ubiquitous. "Most scores, as everybody knows, are written in the late nineteenth century symphonic style, a style now so generally accepted as to be considered inevitable. But why need movie music be symphonic? And why, oh, why, the nineteenth century? Should the rich harmonies of Tschaikovsky, Franck, and Strauss by spread over every type of story, regardless of time, place, or treatment?" The lush and largely tonal sound of the late-nineteenth-century orchestra may be an assumed convention, he argues, but it is by no means a necessity. To suit Hollywood's expanding narrative styles, the orchestration of the underscore should be more flexible in terms of both the size of the orchestra and the style of harmonic language being used.

Another convention Copland challenges is the structure of the underscore—the practice of using leitmotifs, of creating a dense web of themes to play even under dialogue. "Another pet Hollywood formula, this one borrowed from nineteenth century opera, is the use of the leitmotiv. I haven't made up my mind whether the public is conscious of this device or completely oblivious to it, but I can't see how it is appropriate to the movies." Leitmotifs, he argues, have transformed the underscore from a series of gap-filled transitions to a nearly uninterrupted set of interconnected cues. It has given the underscore a coherence and structural independence it did not have before. But it does so, Copland argues, at the cost of being cinematic. Leitmotifs undermine the unreality of the nondiegetic realm. When repeated, motives develop a kind of semiotic independence, one that competes and interferes with the action on the screen. Their accumulated, extra-filmic meaning challenges the conceptual boundaries of nondiegetic space. The solution he proposes, however, is not to abolish this long-standing practice, but to modify it. Thematic composition, and the use of the overture or opening credit sequence to introduce themes, can be effective, he observes, if the number of themes is limited and their employment throughout the film diffuse.

"If there must be thematic description, I think it would serve better if it were connected with the underlying ideas of a picture . . . [with] something broader in feeling than the mere tagging of characters."

Copland's critique targets general industry practice, but it also at times takes aim at a specific composer, one largely considered the architect of the industrial underscore: Max Steiner. In his discussion of the leitmotivic process, criticism of Steiner and his "theme-for-every-character" approach is implied, but in his discussion of "mickey-mousing," the practice of using music to "mimic everything that happens on the screen," the references are overt. "Max Steiner has a particular weakness for this device," Copland announces, dismissing the practice as both disruptive and outdated, and certainly unnecessary. A composer with a significant concert-hall reputation, Copland articulated his vision not just in the essays he wrote but also in the seven film scores he composed for United Artists. Most were settings of classic American literature, including, in addition to *Of Mice and Men* and *Our Town*, *The Red Pony* (1948) and *The Heiress* (1949), for which he won an Academy award.[52] With their smaller, often soloistic, chamber orchestra sound, their sparse textures and abbreviated structures, and their conservative use of thematic material, they offered practical solutions to the problems he pointed to in the prewar, Steineresque model of underscoring. Their influence can be seen in the scores not only of veterans like Franz Waxman and Dimitri Tiomkin, but also of a new generation of composers including Hugo Friedhofer, Jerome Moross, David Raksin, Leonard Bernstein, Alex North, and Elmer Bernstein.

After World War II, from the late 1940s to the late 1950s, the stability and profitability of the film industry slowly dissolved. As the country struggled to convert back to a civilian marketplace, the studios struggled too. Movie theater attendance fell precipitously from 90 million in 1946, to 60 million in 1950, and again to 40 million by 1960. Sharp increases in ticket prices spurred by postwar inflation played a role in the decline, but another factor was the large-scale shift in the location of the country's population.[53] After the war, young families especially began leaving the cities for more affordable and spacious housing in newly created suburbs, encouraged, in part, by the new "in-home" entertainment medium of television, which made them less dependent on urban offerings. By the mid-1950s, a majority of Americans owned a television set and were using it as their primary source of entertainment. With the advent of television, movie theater revenues declined so steeply that by the early 1950s some 15 percent of all movie theaters had been forced to close.[54] Although the studios tried to counter these losses by building new exhibition spaces tailored to suburban needs, like the family-friendly "drive-in" theater, in general the film industry lost the war against television. Despite offering an aesthetically inferior visual experience, television was simply more convenient.[55]

In the past, Hollywood had used foreign markets to compensate for revenue fluctuations in the domestic market. But those markets, too, were in upheaval in the postwar period. Because of the enormous expense of rebuilding, England and France especially were trying to slow the outward flow of capital by imposing import taxes and quotas on Hollywood films and by restricting the amount of profits that the Hollywood studios could extract from them.[56] To circumvent some of these restrictions, the studios began importing more foreign films to the United States. Beginning in the late 1940s, American audiences saw more British films, like *Great Expectations* (1946), *Hamlet* (1948), and *The Red Shoes* (1948), and Italian films like *Shoeshine* (1946) and *The Bicycle Thief* (1949).[57] The studios also began financing foreign-made films like Britain's *The Bridge on the River Kwai* (1957) and France's *Bitter Victory* (1958). Another way the studios got around foreign constraints was to shoot Hollywood films abroad using foreign revenues that had been frozen or were restricted to in-country use. This approach was additionally efficient because in postwar Europe and Asia the costs of materials, labor, and facilities were significantly lower than at home. Known as "runaway" production, this practice also allowed the studios to make use of picturesque foreign locations—an added advantage. Runaway production explains the existence of many of the postwar period's big-budget historical epics such as *King Solomon's Mines* (1950), *Quo Vadis* (1951), *The Land of Pharaohs* (1955), *The Ten Commandments* (1956), *The Vikings* (1958), and *Ben Hur* (1959). It also explains many of Hollywood's intimate comedies and dramas from the period, including *Roman Holiday* (1953), *Three Coins in the Fountain* (1954), *Summertime* (1955), *To Catch a Thief* (1955), *Love Is a Many-Splendored Thing* (1955), *The Snows of Kilimanjaro* (1952), and *The African Queen* (1950), all of which were shot on location in Europe, Asia, or Africa. By the end of the decade, so many films were being made elsewhere that, as historian Peter Lev says, "Hollywood cinema was no longer 'made in Los Angeles'; instead, there was an expectation that large-scale productions would film in authentic locations world-wide."[58]

The Golden Age industrial system was being stretched and weakened by declining and shifting audiences at home and abroad, but it was also being weakened by renewed attack on its distribution and exhibition practices. Dissatisfied with the results of the consent agreement and inspired by the success of a number of smaller legal cases, the government resumed its antitrust suit against the studios after the war. In 1945, the Justice Department finally presented its case, the *United States v. Paramount Pictures, Inc.,* to the Supreme Court. After much deliberation, the Court sided with the government and remanded the case to the federal courts with the instruction that the lower courts require the studios to fully divest themselves of all their distribution and exhibition holdings. On July 25, 1949, the studios were formally ordered to "de-integrate" and sell their movie theaters. Although the ruling was not unanticipated and appeals were considered, the studios eventually, if reluctantly, complied. RKO and Paramount were the first to act, but it took the better part of the next decade for the remaining major studios—especially MGM, Fox, and Warners—to carry out the court's order. After having been standard operating procedure for several decades, the practice of vertical integration was not easily abandoned.[59]

The Supreme Court ruling created logistical work for the industry, but it also created a financial crisis. In their weakened state, having to rid themselves of their most profitable holdings, the studios sustained multiple buyouts and take-overs. In 1951, two lawyers, Arthur Krim and Robert Benjamin, bought the United Artists studio. A year later, Universal Studios was swallowed up by Decca Records. Between 1956 and 1959, MGM underwent significant management reorganization. Even family-owned Warners was sold to a syndicate headed by First National Bank of Boston in 1956, although Jack Warner remained the studio president for another decade. Twentieth Century–Fox, also struggling to stay profitable, eventually sold off a major portion of its production facilities in 1959. The Paramount decree also resulted in one studio's death: in 1957, after being badly mismanaged by Howard Hughes, RKO closed its doors permanently.[60]

Even as the industry's management structure was being slowly dismantled, film content in the postwar period was under heavy assault as well. Fueled by cold war anxieties and the fear of Communist aggression, the Congressional House Un-American Activities Committee (HUAC) reconvened after the war and began to investigate Hollywood once again.[61] In 1947, HUAC chairman Thomas Parnell accused the Screen Writers Guild in particular of inserting Communist propaganda into studio films. The committee subpoenaed forty-three Hollywood executives, labor leaders, and filmmakers to testify.[62] Friendly witnesses like Jack Warner assured the committee that the industry was already voluntarily purging the industry of political subversives. But it was the testimony and behavior of the nineteen "unfriendly" witnesses that created a national stir. The first nine to testify were openly hostile, arguing with the committee and refusing to answer questions about their political affiliations. The remaining witnesses—the "Hollywood Ten," as they came to be known—refused to testify at all. During an adjournment, industry executives gathered at the Waldorf-Astoria Hotel in New York City and signed a statement refusing to employ the Hollywood Ten or anyone else in the industry suspected of subversive or Communist ties. All of the Ten were eventually found guilty of contempt and fined or sentenced to prison.[63] Over the course of several more years of testimony, the list of blacklisted Hollywood Communists grew to more than two hundred.[64] Some in the industry "named names" for the committee, while others pleaded the Fifth Amendment— largely considered to be a tacit admission of guilt. Hundreds more with left-leaning or liberal sympathies or associations were put on less overt but no less damaging "graylists." As Sklar observes, "It was a dark and difficult season for the industry. For non-Communists, 'clearance' required repudiating all liberal opinions and associations; former Communists were required to perform a humiliating public ritual of expiation by naming names of other Hollywood Communists."[65]

A general climate of anxiety, over Communist infiltration and Soviet aggression as well as the rise of atomic energy, defined the country's mindset in the 1950s. But it also shaped and influenced much of the content of postwar filmmaking. Cold war fears bubble to the surface in the decidedly somber and claustrophobic tone, and in the texts and subtexts of distrust, disillusionment, and anxiety, of many films made in the 1950s. This "crisis of confidence"[66] affected dramatic genres, in particular, which were riddled with new levels of cynicism, disillusionment, and unease—as films like *All about Eve* (1951), *Sunset Boulevard* (1953), *A Streetcar Named Desire* (1951), *The Cobweb* (1955), *Rebel without a Cause* (1955), *East of Eden* (1954), *Giant* (1956), *Cat on a Hot Tin Roof* (1958), *All that Heaven Allows* (1955) reveal. The topics of adultery, alcoholism, greed, family dysfunction, and jealousy are also given more frank and detailed examination, and themes that had previously been available only as subtexts—male anxieties, mental illness, homosexuality, and racism—are given more focused attention.[67] The film noir proved fertile ground for the angst-ridden postwar psyche. Films like *The Big Sleep* (1946), *Kiss of Death* (1947), *The Naked City* (1948), *Crossfire* (1947), *In A Lonely Place* (1950), and *Touch of Evil* (1958) all reveal new levels of moral ambiguity and despair.[68]

Cold war anxieties also surfaced in typically heroic genres. Films like *High Noon* (1951), *Shane* (1953), *The Searchers* (1956), and *Rio Bravo* (1959)—"superwesterns," as André Bazin calls them[69]—were riddled with moral ambivalence, and psychological conflict. The seemingly inviolate and incorruptible genre of the war picture also saw its boundaries eroded. Battle films like the psychologically complex *Twelve O'Clock High* (1950) and home-front pictures like *From Here to Eternity* (1951), with its frank portrayal of sexuality, prostitution, and adultery, challenged moral conventions, while pictures like *Paths of Glory* (1957) and *On the Beach* (1959) questioned the validity of war itself.

The social-problem film reflected the changing atmosphere as well, with directors like Elia Kazan and John Cassavetes forging a new approach to realism that emphasized an unwavering and gritty look at contemporary working-class America. With often unhappy or conflicted endings, Oscar-winning and –nominated films like *On the Waterfront* (1954), *Marty* (1955), and *Blackboard Jungle* (1955), and others like *Shadows* (1959), made protagonists out of average Americans—dockworkers, butchers, teachers, and nightclub musicians—confronting ethical and economic challenges.

New political and social anxieties radically altered the look and content of many familiar genres, but they also triggered the flourishing of a new genre of film: "science-fiction." Although such films had surfaced sporadically before the war, after the war the genre flourished, with Hollywood churning out some five hundred sci-fi movies between 1948 and 1962.[70] "Never in the history of motion pictures," notes scholar Joyce Evans, "has any other genre developed and multiplied so rapidly in so brief a period. . . . By dislocating the narratives to different times and/or different worlds, the science-fiction genre catered to public anxiety about the bomb and communism."[71] With themes of alien invasion, extraterrestrial travel, human mutation, metamorphosis, and annihilation, films like *Invasion of the Body Snatchers* (1956), *The Thing from Another World* (1951), *The Blob* (1958), *The Fly* (1958), *The Day the Earth Stood Still* (1951), *Forbidden Planet* (1956), and *War of the Worlds* (1953) gave filmmakers a new range of narrative possibilities with which to confront the nation's insecurities. It also encouraged the development of new visual technologies and techniques to depict these otherworldly experiences.[72]

Psychological fears were not the only enemy the industry was facing. In television, the studios faced the very real threat of extinction. With television now replacing the downtown cinema as the entertainment medium of choice, Hollywood sought to distinguish the cinematic experience from the television experience by making movies bigger, louder, and more colorful. Film stock innovations made color film and larger-gauge film more affordable and special gimmicks like 3-D viewing formats possible.[73] The antitelevision campaign also fueled new widescreen viewing formats, including Cinerama, CinemaScope, VistaVision, Todd-AO, and Panavision. The studios tested these bigger formats on a number of genres, from historical epics like *The Robe* (1953), *The Ten Commandments* (1956), *Quo Vadis?* (1951), and *Around the World in Eighty Days* (1956), to contemporary dramas like *How to Marry a Millionaire* (1953) and *A Star Is Born* (1954), to musicals like *White Christmas* (1954), *High Society* (1956), *Oklahoma!* (1953), and *Auntie Mame* (1958). Most of these new imaging technologies attempted to match the bigger pictures with enhanced and more nuanced sound, typically four-track or stereophonic sound. The costs of installing new projectors and stereo sound equipment, and the lack of a single platform for either one, however, kept most theaters from converting to wide screen. By the late 1950s, the antitelevision campaign of "bigger is better" had largely been abandoned.[74]

The venerable genre of the musical also underwent changes. Although the long-standing practice of importing successful Broadway shows to the silver screen continued, the 1950s musical also indulged in new and original material, becoming the site of structural, topical, and stylistic experimentation.[75] The new "integrated" musical, which flourished in MGM's "Freed Unit" of production (so called because it was run by the charismatic and innovative producer Arthur Freed), called not only for more fluid camera work, but also for the singing numbers to be more seamlessly inserted into the narrative structure of the film.[76] It also showcased new musical, dance, and artistic styles. Newcomers like composers André Previn and Leonard Bernstein experimented with contemporary styles of atonality and Latin and bebop jazz. In terms of choreography, Astaire and Kelly were still visible, but the prewar preference for tap and ballroom dance gave way to more contemporary choreographic styles and to new dancers, like Cyd Charisse and Leslie Caron, who were imported from the more serious worlds of ballet and modern dance. The studios also stretched the musical topically to accommodate contemporary themes like cold war politics (*Silk Stockings,* 1957), beatnik culture (*Funny Face,* 1957), proto-feminism (*Gentlemen Prefer Blonds,* 1953), and sexual impropriety (*Gigi,* 1958).

The surprise success of social-problem films like *Blackboard Jungle* and *Rebel without a Cause,* films that depicted youth culture and juvenile delinquency, also made Hollywood realize it had a powerful new constituency: teenagers. Hollywood responded by tailoring its so-called teen pics to focus on youth-centered topics like parental authority, delinquency, cars, dating, and drugs.[77] Seeing the record-breaking profits the recording industry was enjoying, the studios also worked hard to incorporated the new music that teenagers were listening to: rock 'n' roll. Relying on variations of the revue musical and the backstage musical, the new rock 'n' roll musical, with performers that included Bill Haley and the Comets, the Platters, James Brown, and Elvis Presley, brought a growing audience of teens into movie theaters.[78]

After the war, a perceptible change in the visual style, tone, and temperament of many of Hollywood's most familiar genres of film could be seen. But the anxieties and insecurities that challenged the postwar film could also be *heard,* as both the underscore and the filmusical experienced a crisis of confidence that affected musical sound, style, and structure. One symptom of this crisis in film music was a verbal argument that erupted in the late 1940s between several well-known composers from Hollywood, on the one hand, and the concert hall, on the other. Fueled to some degree by Copland's erudite assessment of film music, composers from both inside and outside Hollywood began to contemplate not just the conventions of the medium, but the medium itself. As film music assumed not only a more sparing, metaphorical, and nuanced relationship with the screen, but also a more independent existence, the question of its ontological status began to surface. "Is film music, music?' asked the composer Igor Stravinsky. Instead of reiterating the typical emotional and psychological function of music in film, Stravinsky asserts a new one: "There is only one real function of film music," he concludes, and that is to financially benefit composers—or as he derogatorily puts it, "to feed the composers." Film music may have a practical function, but it has no artistic merit. Like wallpaper or perfume, Stravinsky argues, film music's function is primarily decorative.[79]

Coming from one of the century's most preeminent composers, Stravinsky's remarks triggered a hot and contentious debate in the film music community, with several film composers issuing formal responses. David Raksin offered a characteristically witty and withering attack on Stravinsky's methods and motives.[80] His colleague Dimitri Tiomkin posed a more contemplative counterargument. Tiomkin concedes Stravinsky's point that film music's function is indeed not to "explain" the action on the screen. The acting agent, Tiomkin asserts, is not the music but rather the listener. Rather than presenting the listener with a definable meaning, film music works by providing a "psychological stimulus" that triggers a conscious or subconscious reaction in the mind of the listener.[81]

While not in direct response to Stravinsky, but in general response to the lack of critical appreciation of film scoring, Copland also weighed in on the topic of film music's ontology.[82] Like Tiomkin, Copland agrees that it is not the music itself but the listener who generates film music's meaning. Unlike Tiomkin, however, Copland considers this meaning less a product of the moviegoer's psychology and more a product of previous musical experience and musical education. It is the amount of this "preparation" and the degree to which a viewer is "aurally minded" that determines whether he or she simply "listens to" the music or instead "hears" it and uses it to assign meaning to the images on the screen. This higher function of hearing the music in film, he observes, is desired, but it is conditioned on the viewer's varying "general musical perception" and not the music's inherent aesthetic value or lack thereof.

The philosophical argument regarding value and function reflected the general crisis of confidence that film music was experiencing in the postwar period. But as important and high-pitched as the debate was, it did not directly affect the style or production of film music. What did affect the medium was the equally philosophical question of film music's conceptual separation from film sound. While Copland's "neutral," thematically reduced method of underscoring was giving composers greater flexibility, it also blurred the distinction between music and sound.

In a 1947 article titled "Music or Sound Effects?" **(Document 26),** Harold C. Schonberg considers the "sonic" crisis that the revised Coplandesque underscore posed for film music. Schonberg, an emerging New York music critic who would eventually become a Pulitzer Prize–winning critic for the *New York Times* and the author of several distinguished music history books, specialized in concert-hall music,[83] but the ontological questions that recent film scores were raising caught his attention. For Schonberg, the culprit was the decline in reliance on the leitmotif. For any sounds to be considered music, he begins, they must satisfy certain conditions. Music must have "continuity," "a melodic outline," "rhythm," some small amount of "development," and be produced by musical instruments.

Many sections of contemporary Hollywood scores, however, are falling short on these requirements, for example offering sounds that are produced by musical instruments but that have no continuity or melodic outline. Instead of presenting the viewer with themes, contemporary scores now often consist of discontinuous pitches or arhythmic motives. He describes one movie's evocation of a "brooding night" by "a dissonant, low-pitched pedal point over which the high winds interjected occasional shrill pipings to imitate the sound of insects." These sonic events, though musical in the sense that they are produced by musical instruments, lack organization and continuity—a melodic outline—and so are not, "by any definition of the word," music.

The postwar confusion between music and sound was by no means an isolated phenomenon. As Schonberg observes, these experiments were being facilitated by the vicissitudes of runaway production. In the postwar economy, foreigners like French composer Georges Auric (creator of the "brooding night" music) were cheaper for studios to employ, since they were willing to work for a substantially reduced rate. And because European composers were outside the isolating environment of the studio music department, they were also freer to experiment with scoring conventions. Just as the postwar mood of introspection was encouraging composers to experiment with new sounds, the postwar economy was encouraging the studios to find this experimentation in composers working outside of Hollywood.

In the postwar period, questions about the form of the underscore also surfaced. Because it typically consisted of a series of individual cues that varied in length from several seconds to dozens of minutes, and because it did not resemble any conventional concert-hall forms like a symphony, sonata, character piece, or suite, a film score's "form" had been largely ignored. The commercialization of film music in the early 1950s, however, brought the issue to the surface. In an article titled "Movie Music Goes on Record" **(Document 28),** film critic Arthur Knight observes that composers were beginning to structure the film score in order to extract it for external consumption. The extraction process had been happening with film music for decades, especially with diegetic music. Songs used within films had long enjoyed autonomy because their short ABA form conformed to standard sheet music, radio, and 78 rpm record formats.

In the early 1950s, however, film producers and record executives began to consider making film underscores commercially available. To accomplish this, scores had to be reworked to follow not just record and printed music formats, but "the requirements of concert listening" as well. Instrumental themes were modified and rewritten to follow "song" form. They were given "gaudily symphonic arrangements" or lyrics, and had a contrasting B section added so they could be more easily consumed in sheet music and record form. Whole underscores were also being modified to resemble a conventional "orchestral suite" to be performed by concert-hall orchestras. As Knight observes, several well-regarded composers of the postwar period, Miklós Rózsa, Alfred Newman, and Victor Young among them, had recently turned their scores into orchestral suites, and the commercial success of their efforts was making the practice popular.

This extraction process had practical ramifications, for it encouraged composers to think about these external processes precompositionally, that is, to anticipate the "recorded" existence of their score by making thematic and melodic material naturally lyrical or self-contained. It also had aesthetic ramifications, in that it forced composers (and critics) to recognize that while underscores could be made to be autonomous and conform externally to concert-hall conventions, within the film proper they were dependent on the film's visual content for structural coherence.

The philosophical arguments that surfaced over the underscore's value and meaning were only one part of the postwar crisis in film music. These years were also marked by significant changes in the style and instrumentation of the underscore. Composers like Copland had already begun to loosen the underscore from its hyperthematic, hyperorchestral sound. But in the 1950s, the parameters of these revisions were expanded significantly. Hanns Eisler and Theodor Adorno's book on film music, *Composing for the Films*, discusses some of these changes in detail. Published in 1947, the text was the product of an unusual collaboration. Both authors were German émigrés who had taken up residency in Los Angeles during the war. Both had strong ties not only to leftist politics and Marxist ideology, but also to music. Eisler was a respected composer and former student of Arnold Schoenberg; Adorno was a noted philosopher, aesthetician, and cultural critic and at one time had been an accomplished musician and composer.[84] This text, one of the only book-length studies of film music to emerge from postwar Hollywood, reveals the authors' dueling interests in politics and music and reads as both a cultural critique of Hollywood's industrialization of art and an examination of the practical conventions of contemporary film scoring. Much of it also stems from Eisler's two-year project investigating the relationship between music and film, financed by the Rockefeller Foundation, that he undertook from 1940 to 1942 as a professor of music at the New School for Social Research in New York City.[85]

The book's third chapter, "New Musical Resources" **(Document 27)**, examines how the new visual style of the postwar dramatic film was challenging prewar musical conventions. In the view of Eisler and Adorno, the orchestral, leitmotivic underscore was neither suitable nor subtle enough to support the dark psychologically complexity of contemporary films. Thanks to the "new realism," with its newsreel- and documentary-inspired camera work and its narrative focus on social problems like racism, addiction, corruption, adultery, and sexuality, composers were being forced to find new sounds and compositional styles to match. The convention most in need of revision, the authors argue, is the score's harmonic language. Tonality is completely inadequate to convey subtle shades of suspense, horror, fear, anxiety, or disillusionment seen on the screen. These moods, they argue, are instead best accompanied by the dissonant, atonal, or tonally ambiguous musical language that has emerged in recent modern concert-hall music. The "unresolved" nature of atonal music, where chords exhibit "no inherent tendency to further action," and the "shocks of modern music" are perfectly suited to meet the anxiety, tension, suspense, and ambiguity of the postwar film.

With atonality, Eisler and Adorno also acknowledge, comes a similar adjustment to local musical structure and organization. Because melodic structure is tied to tonality, the period's new "irrational" pictures should be met with new linear structures—with brief or fragmented motives, asymmetrical patterns, ostinatos, and even athematicism, the complete absence of developed thematic material. Contemporary film music composers would do well, they counsel, to study and adopt the new harmonic techniques and structures being advocated by such modernist concert-hall composers as Schoenberg, Bartók, and Stravinsky. If contemporary films have liberated the score to be fully atonal, they have also liberated it to pursue new methods of motivic and thematic organization. Although Adorno and Eisler don't mention it, a new generation of composers, including David Raksin, Bernard Herrmann, Leonard Rosenman, Miklós Rósza, Elmer Bernstein, Alex North, and Leonard Bernstein, composers fluent in both traditional and modern concert-hall styles, were doing just that. Their collaborations with directors like Alfred Hitchcock, Elia Kazan, Otto Preminger, and Billy Wilder, directors who were challenging visual stylistic and generic conventions, were making atonality and ostinatos an integral part of the new postwar musical lexicon.[86]

As composer Elmer Bernstein reveals in his analysis of the score he wrote for Otto Preminger's 1955 film *The Man with the Golden Arm* (**Document 29**), the search for musical styles and sounds to suit the dark psychology of the postwar social drama was leading composers to experiment. Like Eisler and Adorno, Bernstein considers the harmonic language of the conventional underscore inadequate for meeting the demands of contemporary American filmmaking. The sound of the orchestra, he argues, is too large, inflexible, and "European," the melodies, phrasing, and tonality of the classical orchestral score too balanced and clear, to convey the visual landscape of *The Man with the Golden Arm*, with its urban decay, heroin addiction, gambling, and despair. Modern, urban social problems require an equally modern, urban, and American musical style. "I wanted an element that could speak readily of hysteria and despair, an element that would localize these emotions to our country, to a large city if possible. Ergo—jazz."

This was not the first time jazz had been a part of film music. It was prevalent in early sound film musicals, but only diegetically, to capture the jazz age's great performers on screen. But it was the first time jazz had been an integral part of the underscore. Bernstein's new "symphonic jazz" style expanded the sound of the underscore by offering an unconventional mix of orchestral and jazz instruments, techniques, and idioms, such as syncopated rhythms, abrupt meter changes, "improvisation," and "solo breaks." This new style also required a change in the personnel of the studio orchestra. To execute this improvised jazz style, Bernstein had to import drummer Shelly Manne and trumpeter Shorty Rogers to help him arrange and perform the music. Although Bernstein made use of some conventional orchestral textures and techniques, his score for *The Man with the Golden Arm* did much to give the anxieties of the postwar film a new musical signature.

Nor was Bernstein the only composer to link jazz idioms with images of postwar disillusionment—of crime, poverty, adultery, drug and alcohol addiction, domestic violence, and more. Alex North's score for Elia Kazan's *A Streetcar Named Desire* (1951) also used the sound of sultry saxophones and seemingly improvised and syncopated rhythms to describe the film's urban setting and the complex psychology and sexuality of its central characters.[87] Leith Stevens's score for László Benedek's *The Wild One* (1953), too, forged an indelible connection between jazz and the "new American realism"; it also continued the tradition of importing jazz performers such as Shorty Rogers, Jimmy Giuffre, Bud Shank, and Shelly Manne to articulate it. By the mid to late 1950s, jazz was heard underscoring many film noirs and social dramas, including *The Sweet Smell of Success* (1957, Elmer Bernstein), *Touch of Evil* (1958, Henry Mancini), *Odds against Tomorrow* (1959, John Lewis), and *Anatomy of a Murder* (1959, Duke Ellington). Just as jazz had become synonymous with urban decay by the end of the decade, jazz performers and composers comfortable writing jazz idioms had become regular fixtures in studio music departments.

The flourishing of the science-fiction film also inspired new sounds and instrumentations in the underscore. While some composers experimented with unusual symphonic writing, it was the use of electronic instruments both new and old that accounted for the most striking contributions.[88] Limited use of electronic instruments had already surfaced briefly in the postwar drama.[89] To depict the main character's amnesia in Hitchcock's *Spellbound* (1945), for example, composer Miklós Rózsa used an early electronic instrument called a theremin. Invented in the late 1920s by Russian scientist Leon Theremin, this monophonic instrument produced an eerie, ethereal warbling sound.[90] After Rózsa used it again in Billy Wilder's *The Lost Weekend* (1946) to articulate the central character's crippling addiction to alcohol, the theremin became the signature sound of mental instability and suspense.[91] Roy Webb helped expand the use of electronic instruments to film noir when he used a theremin to accompany the slow and suspenseful murder that opens *The Spiral Staircase* (1945).

As **Document 30** reveals, in the 1950s the unnatural and otherworldly sound of electronic instruments also found a home in the science-fiction film. The predominantly "B" status of the sci-fi film liberated composers to experiment, with the ethereal sounds of electronic instruments being perfect for the depiction of alien landscapes and creatures. The "score" for the film *Forbidden Planet* (1956), the first completely electronic film score, is a good example of this transfer of electronic experimentation to the sci-fi genre. Its composers, the classically trained Louis and Bebe Barron, were interested in the amateur popular mechanic and electronic movements that surfaced after the war. Louis especially experimented with newly available transistors and electronic circuitry to generate sounds and noises that Bebe would record and organize into "sonic" compositions. The electronic accompaniments that the two created for several early-1950s avant-garde and experimental films caught the attention of MGM directors, who invited the Barrons to work on an "A"-grade science-fiction film they were making called *Forbidden Planet*.[92]

In the explanation of their score, the composers describe the unconventional instrumentation as well as the unique organizational method they use. The score was a collection of unusual sounds or "electronic tonalities" generated by primitive, pre-synthesizer, electronic circuitry. Each circuit was designed to create a single ephemeral sound. The electronic sounds were then paired, much like a melodic theme, with the various on-screen characters, locations, and emotions they were designed to sonically represent. Although these electronic tonalities, the Barrons argue, occupy the same nondiegetic space as a conventional underscore, they do not technically constitute a musical score. Instead, this material is best understood as a "pure flow of sonic sensations," meant to facilitate direct and unconscious communication between composer and viewer.

This manipulation of custom-built, ephemeral circuitry was so labor intensive the Barrons never attempted a repeat performance, and neither did any other Hollywood composers. Nonetheless, the score to *Forbidden Planet* was an important contribution to the development of the postwar sci-fi score. In the 1950s, experimentation with emerging electronic instruments in sci-fi film scores was widespread (which perhaps explains the Barrons' wish not to get typecast as sci-fi composers). The alien images and landscapes inspired new sounds from a host of new electronic technologies, from theremins to synthesizers. They also encouraged composers to continue to challenge the conceptual difference between sound, noise, and music. Although the term "electronic tonalities" was not their own, the Barrons' unusual conception of the underscore as nonmusical, as an arrangement of "sonic sensations," was both groundbreaking and influential.[93]

The sound, style, and placement of diegetic music in musicals was also affected by postwar anxieties and innovations, as director and choreographer Stanley Donen later observes, in a 1977 interview (**Document 31**). Audiences still identified with the genre, but they were finding the long-standing "revue," "backstage," and "biography" formulas predictable and unappealing. As a result, according to Donen, in the postwar period the musical experienced substantial revision. Because "photography" and camera movement, not just choreography, were now considered an essential part of the visual conception of the musical performance, the role of the director—which just a decade before producer Darryl Zanuck had declared "of relative unimportance" (see **Document 24**)—was now pivotal to the conception of the filmusical. Camera positioning was now more fluid, free to observe the action more closely and from multiple perspectives. The integration of the camera into the conception of narrative was matched by additional integration of the musical performance into the narrative structure of the film. That is, whereas the prewar musical had clung to diegetic or "real" performance, where "everything happened on the stage," in the new postwar formula performance advocated a dash of the "surreal." Characters now routinely danced and sang in any setting, with no visible source for the music and no narrative explanation for the characters' desire to perform being necessary. This seamless and completely unmotivated style of performance was championed as the new "integrated" musical. Although Donen vacillates on whether to credit producer Arthur Freed with its creation, he does credit Freed with giving actors, choreographers, and directors the freedom to innovate and modify prewar formulas.

An integrated structure and more mobile visual style were not the only innovations directors and producers were experimenting with. The postwar musical was also being stretched to accommodate new narrative material. Plots that involved or processed the war experience were not new, but their conceptualization of it—like *On the Town* (1949), whose story presents a single twenty-four-hour period in the lives of three servicemen—was. Some featured contemporary topics, such as the expatriate experience (*American in Paris*, 1951; *Les Girls*, 1958), racial prejudice and juvenile delinquency (*West Side Story*, 1960), or the rise of television (*It's Always Fair Weather*, 1957).

Experimentation with new styles of choreography and music were symptomatic of the genre's crisis of confidence as well. Prewar veterans like Busby Berkeley were being phased out in favor of new choreographers from the world of modern dance. The contemporary ballet style of the great choreographer George Balanchine was being imported through the work of his protégé Jerome Robbins, and although Donen doesn't mention them by name, the work of contemporary choreographers Agnes de Mille and Martha Graham was also being used and referenced.[94] The lyricists and composers the studios were now employing represented another departure. George Gershwin and Jerome Kern, Donen observes, had been replaced by Leonard Bernstein, Stephen Sondheim, Oscar Hammerstein, Richard Rodgers, Larry Hart, and Cole Porter, a new generation articulating a new kind of "Americanism." Through this new group of musicians, the virtuosity and the tonal and metric irregularities of bebop jazz and the polyrhythms of Latin American jazz were finding their way into the postwar musical.

The studios also stretched the genre to embrace another new style of music. In the late 1950s, the youth market was generating record profits for the music recording industry with its seemingly insatiable appetite for a new style of music: rock 'n' roll. In an effort to capture some of this revenue, the film industry quickly recalibrated several of its well-worn film musical formulas to feature the popular new style of music.[95] Some, like *Rock around the Clock* (1956), *Don't Knock the Rock* (1956), *Shake, Rattle, and Rock!* (1956), and *Rock, Pretty Baby* (1956), were variations on the "revue musical" and featured a parade of live performances by emerging rock stars such as Bill Haley and the Comets, the Platters, Little Richard, and Chuck Berry. Others, like *Love Me Tender* (1956) and *Jailhouse Rock* (1957), were, as Alan Freed notes in his article "One Thing's for Sure, R 'n' R Is Boffo B.O. [Box Office]" **(Document 32),** were turning recording stars into film stars. Freed, a popular disk jockey, and film producer Sam Katzman were quick to recognize the economic benefit of not just vocally but visually recording the performances of rock stars like Elvis Presley, Tommy Sands, Pat Boone, and Fabian. This marriage of rock 'n' roll and film not only allowed the film industry to share in the recording industry's profits; it also allowed the recording industry to reap additional revenue from the increased visibility of its stars. "Never before in the history of the film business," Freed notes in a subsequent article, "has the disc jockey and the value of recorded music been so graphically evident or so vitally important."[96] While none of these films was structurally or narratively innovative, or "known to garner 4-star critiques," Freed concludes, they did end the music department's postwar crisis of confidence by opening up the genre of the musical and the industry in general to the revolutionary style of rock 'n' roll.

NOTES

1. Tino Balio, *Grand Design: Hollywood as a Modern Business Enterprise, 1930–1939,* (Berkeley: University of California Press, 1996), p. 5.

2. Ibid., p.16.

3. Douglas Gomery, *The Hollywood Studio System* (New York: St. Martin's Press, 1986), pp. 5–6; Balio, *Grand Design,* pp. 16–18.

4. As Gomery puts it (*Hollywood Studio System*, pp. 7–8), in terms of revenue, the pyramidlike structure of the industry was reversed in the early 1930s. Instead of being studios with subsidiary theater holdings, the studios essentially became large theater chains with ancillary production and distribution enterprises. See also Balio, *Grand Design*, p. 5.

5. Robert Sklar, *Movie-Made America: A Cultural History of American Movies* (New York: Vintage Books, 1994), pp. 161–64. See also Thomas Schatz, *The Genius of the System: Hollywood Filmmaking in the Studio Era* (New York: Henry Holt, 1988), p. 159; and Balio, *Grand Design*, pp. 15–17.

6. Sklar, *Movie-Made America*, pp. 165–69. See also Gomery, *Hollywood Studio System*, p. 9; Balio, *Grand Design*, p. 30; and Schatz, *Genius of the System*, pp. 159–60.

7. Balio, *Grand Design*, p. 18; Schatz, *Genius of the System*, pp. 159–60; and Gomery, *Hollywood Studio System*, p. 12.

8. Gomery, *Hollywood Studio System*, p. 9.

9. Schatz, *Genius of the System*, p. 257; see also Balio, *Grand Design*, pp. 102–5.

10. This code, authored by industry outsiders—a Jesuit priest, Father Daniel Lord, and a trade publisher and fellow Catholic, Martin Quigley—was a set of production guidelines for the studios to follow to ensure that the content of their films would match the morality of its viewers. It was initially to be reinforced by a Studio Relations Committee, which, under the direction of another Protestant layman, Colonel Jason Joy, was to screen and approve scripts for production. See Balio, *Grand Design*, p. 40.

11. Ibid., p. 61. As Balio points out, however, Breen's position at first was largely ornamental. Although his office reviewed and censored scripts, few fines were ever levied against the studios.

12. "The change was gradual rather than cataclysmic," Balio asserts, "the negotiation, by experiment and expedience, of a system of conventional representation that was constructed in the first half of the decade and maintained in the second" (ibid., p. 40). The code was also not single-handedly responsible for the noticeable change in film style and content. "The Production Code did not cause the lack of experimentation in Hollywood product," Balio continues. "Rather, it was itself a symptom of the underlying cause. The Code was a consequence of commercialism and of the particular understanding of the audience and its desires that the industry's commercialism promoted." From virtually the inception of the sound film, the industry had negotiated to maintain control of film content without alienating its audience. In an age before detailed audience research, in fact, boycotts and decency campaigns were an efficient way to gauge audience tastes (ibid., pp. 70–72).

13. See Sklar, *Movie-Made America*, p. 189. As Sklar also puts it (p. 173), the code was not as much a mechanism for censorship as it was a way for the studios to "unite religious morality with box office necessity."

14. Ibid., p. 175; see also Balio, *Grand Design*, p. 39.

15. An easy way to avoid censorship in the post-code era was to use "dignified, elevated, respectable pictures set in the past and usually drawn from the classics or current best-sellers" (Sklar, *Movie-Made America*, pp. 190–91); see also Balio, *Grand Design*, pp. 179–80.

16. Linda Whitesitt, *The Life and Music of George Antheil, 1900–1959* (Ann Arbor: UMI Research Press, 1983), pp. 50–63, 72; a complete list of Antheil's film scores is included in appendix A, sec. VIII, pp. 250–57.

17. See Rita McAllister and Iosif Genrikhovich Rayskin, "Leonid Leonidovich Sabaneyev," in *The New Grove Dictionary of Music and Musicians*, 2d ed., ed. Stanley Sadie and John Tyrrell (London: Macmillan; New York: Grove's Dictionaries, 2006), 22:61–62.

18. See "Music in the Cinema," *Musical Times* 70 (Feb. 1929): pp. 113–15; "Music and the Sound Film," *Music and Letters* 15, no. 2 (Apr. 1934): 147–52; "Technical Progress in the Music of To-Day,"

Musical Times 75 (Oct. 1934): 881–83; and "Opera and the Cinema," *Musical Times* 81 (Jan. 1940): 9–11.

19. Kurt London, *Film Music,* trans. Eric S. Bensinger, foreword by Constant Lambert (London: Faber & Faber, 1936).

20. In *Settling the Score: Music in the Classical Hollywood Film* (Madison: University of Wisconsin Press), pp. 72–73, Kathryn Kalinak observes: "The determining characteristic of the studio model was its efficiency, keeping the assembly line of production moving with a highly diversified division of labor." See also Roy Prendergast, *Film Music: A Neglected Art* (New York: W. W. Norton, 1977), pp. 35–38; and Roger Manvell, "The Music Director and the Sound Recordist," *The Technique of Film Music* (London: Focal Press, 1975), pp. 199–218.

21. See Fred Karlin, *Listening to Movies: The Film Lover's Guide to Film Music* (New York: Schirmer, 1994), esp. pp. 181–83 and 194–95.

22. Laurence E. MacDonald, *The Invisible Art of Film Music: A Comprehensive History* (New York: Ardsley House, 1998), p. 33.

23. For a good analysis of Steiner's score for *Gone with the Wind,* see ibid., pp. 50–53; Tony Thomas, *Film Score: The Art and Craft of Movie Music* (Burbank, Calif.: Riverwood Press, 1991), pp. 60–65; and William Darby and Jack Du Bois, *American Film Music: Major Composers, Techniques, Trends, 1915–1990* (Jefferson, N.C.: McFarland & Co., 1990), pp. 59–64. There is also a good general discussion of Steiner's leitmotiv method in Kalinak, *Settling the Score,* pp. 113–34. For analyses of other Steiner scores, see Peter Franklin, "*King Kong* and Film on Music: Out of the Fog," in *Film Music: Critical Approaches,* ed. K. J. Donnelly (Edinburgh: Edinburgh University Press, 2001), pp. 88–102; and Martin Marks, "Music, Drama, Warner Brothers: The Cases of *Casablanca* and *The Maltese Falcon,*" in *Music and Cinema,* ed. James Buhler, Caryl Flinn, and David Neumeyer (Hanover, N.H.: Wesleyan University Press, 2000), pp. 161–86.

24. Korngold once referred to movies as "opera without songs" (quoted in Larry Timm, *The Soul Of Cinema: An Appreciation of Film Music* [Upper Saddle River, N.J.: Prentice Hall, 2003], p. 135).

25. Korngold's biography can be found in numerous places. See, e.g., Tony Thomas's *Music for the Movies,* 2d ed. (Los Angeles: Silman-James Press, 1997), pp. 160–85, and *Film Score: The View From the Podium* (New York: A. S. Barnes, 1979), pp. 83–91; and Darby and DuBois, *American Film Music,* pp. 157–84. For good analyses of Korngold's style, especially how it differs from Steiner's, see Kalinak, *Settling the Score,* pp. 66–110; and Royal S. Brown, "Interlude I: Erich Wolfgang Korngold: *The Sea Hawk* (1940)," in *Overtones and Undertones: Reading Film Music* (Berkeley: University of California Press, 1994), pp. 97–120.

26. George Antheil, "On the Hollywood Front" *Modern Music* 14, no. 2 (Jan.–Feb. 1937): 105–8. See also Jack Jungmeyer, "Waning of Filmusicals" *Variety,* Jan. 4, 1938, p. 35: "*Variety* reported that Warners purged all 'contract cleffers' from its music department; let the option lapse on its chief songster, Dick Powell; and cut its musical schedule to lowest program in a long time."

27. Prendergast, *Film Music,* pp. 45–48; and William H. Rosar, "Stravinsky and MGM," *Film Music I,* ed. Clifford McCarty (New York: Garland, 1989), pp. 109–21.

28. Antheil, for instance, reports that attempts to replace Broadway composers with major orchestral composers—at least Schoenberg and Stravinsky—had failed: "Hollywood, after a grand splurge with new composers and new ideas, has settled back into its old grind of producing easy and sure-fire scores. . . . Many excellent composers have come out to Hollywood and returned East again. Scarcely any of them have gotten jobs. . . . The wish of Paramount to have both Stravinsky and Schönberg score pictures has not materialized" (Antheil, "On the Hollywood Front," *Modern Music* 15, no. 1 [Nov.–Dec. 1937]: 48–51). While the "prestige" movement failed to secure Stravinsky or Schoenberg, it did help secure orchestral underscoring as an established method of using music in film.

29. The policies of blind selling and block booking and the systems of zones and clearances may have brought stable prices for consumers, but they instituted significant financial instability and disadvantaged the non-affiliated theaters owners who were forced to absorb the costs of underperforming films. These owners fought back immediately and won some concessions from the industry as the code was being written. The popular depression-era practice of double features, for instance, which helped theaters entice customers with two films for the price of one, were allowed to continue and theater owners were granted limited abilities to devise and run promotional incentives and give-aways and cancel bad films or underperforming films. Sklar, *Movie-Made America*, pp. 168–69; see also Balio, *Grand Design*, pp. 26–30; and Thomas Schatz, *Boom and Bust: American Cinema in the 1940s* (Berkeley: University of California Press, 1997), pp. 13, 16–18.

30. This concession or "consent degree," delivered in 1940, abolished blind booking and the compulsory rental of short films. It allowed the practice of block booking to continue but in reduced bundles of five films or fewer. See Gomery, *Hollywood Studio System*, pp. 22–23; Balio, *Grand Design*, p. 36; and Schatz, *Genius of the System*, pp. 297–300.

31. Balio, *Grand Design*, pp. 81 and 85. See also Sklar, *Movie-Made America*, pp. 170–73; and Gomery, *Hollywood Studio System*, pp. 10–11.

32. Schatz, *Boom and Bust*, p. 81.

33. Ibid., pp. 79–83.

34. Ibid., p. 22; see also Gomery, *Hollywood Studio System*, p. 20.

35. The markets in Germany and Italy had actually been declining throughout the late 1930s, but that decline was dramatically accelerated after Hitler's invasion. See Schatz, *Boom and Bust*, p. 22.

36. With Europe destabilized, the studios immediately looked to open new foreign markets to recoup their losses. Attention was initially focused on Latin and South America, a large, untapped market that was militarily neutral. Although the studios began to produce films with Latin themes and about Latin figures, this move was not profitable and so was ultimately short lived. See ibid., pp. 25–27.

37. Ibid., pp. 27–29, 116–127. See also Schatz, *Genius of the System*, p. 297.

38. Schatz, *Boom and Bust*, pp. 37–40. In the fall of 1941, Senators Burton Wheeler (Mont.) and Gerald Nye (N.D.) launched an investigation into Hollywood's supposed "war-mongering" and political propagandizing, what they called "the most vicious propaganda ever unloosed on a civilized people." Using seventeen films as evidence, and additionally interviewing Will Hays and top studio executives, the committee sought to uncover a political bias in the production of Hollywood films.

39. Ibid., pp. 34–35. See also Sklar, *Movie-Made America*, pp. 243–46.

40. Schatz, *Boom and Bust*, pp. 144, 405–6. See also Sklar, *Movie-Made America*, pp. 249–53. Although Hollywood's involvement in the war effort may not have been entirely altruistic, by 1943, according to Sklar, the committee was expressing suspicion that "the movie industry's offer to produce government films without profit was motivated less by patriotism than by a desire to ensure that extraordinary wartime circumstances would not disturb the monopoly power of the major studios" (p. 250).

41. Schatz, *Boom and Bust*, pp. 170, 142–43.

42. According to Schatz (*Boom and Bust*, p. 142), "The OWI significantly affected Hollywood's depiction of America's social and political issues, its allies and enemies, and its role in the envisioned post-war world." As a result, the studios altered many thematic strategies and conventional narrative paradigms. As Schatz observes, in many wartime films the protagonist was made "to yield to the will of the activity of the collective (combat unit, the community, the nation, the family) and coupling was suspended 'for the duration,' subordinated to gender-specific war efforts that involved very different spheres of activity (and conceptions of heroic behavior) for men and women" (ibid.,

p. 204). See also Clayton Koppes, "Regulating the Screen: The Office of War Information and the Production Code Administration," in Schatz, *Boom and Bust,* pp. 262–84.

43. Schatz, *Boom and Bust,* pp. 223–24.

44. Paul Schrader, "Note on *Film Noir,*" *Film Comment,* Spring 1972, p. 16. See also Schatz, *Boom and Bust,* p. 235.

45. As Sklar observes, noir characteristics infected "the psychology and the look not simply of a genre, but of a surprisingly pervasive tone in Hollywood films of the 1940s" (*Movie-Made America,* p. 253). See also David Bordwell, Janet Staiger, and Kristin Thompson, *The Classical Hollywood Cinema: Film Style and Mode of Production to 1960* (New York: Columbia University Press, 1985), pp. 75–76; and David Cook, *A History of Narrative Film* (New York: W. W. Norton, 1981), pp. 467–68.

46. Between 1942 and 1944, war films accounted for roughly one-quarter of all feature films made; Schatz, *Boom and Bust,* p. 240.

47. Ibid., pp. 408–13. These feature-length documentaries, which included John Ford's *The Battle of Midway,* John Huston's *Report from the Aleutians* and *The Battle of San Pietro,* William Wyler's *Memphis Belle,* and Darryl Zanuck's *At the Front in North Africa,* enjoyed widespread cinematic release during the war.

48. Ibid., p. 248.

49. Schatz, *Genius of the System,* p. 300; and also Schatz, *Boom and Bust,* p. 178.

50. Schatz, *Boom and Bust,* pp. 143–44. Efficiency measures during the war ranged from shooting fewer takes during production to making few prints for distribution. It also meant cutting B-list film production and concentrating on A-list production, as well as just making fewer films in general and letting them run longer at high-yield first-run theaters.

51. See Sklar, *Movie-Made America,* p. 249; Schatz, *Genius of the System,* p. 298; and Schatz, *Boom and Bust,* p. 131.

52. In 1939, when Copland was first approached by Hollywood, he was a well-regarded concert-hall composer who had just scored his first film, an experimental documentary by Ralph Steiner and Pare Lorentz called *The City* (1939) written for the New York World's Fair. For more details on both his documentary and Hollywood films, see Neil Lerner, "Copland's Music of Wide Open Spaces: Surveying the Pastoral Trope in Hollywood," *Musical Quarterly* 85, no. 3 (Fall 2001): 477–515; and Howard Pollack, *Aaron Copland: The Life and Work of an Uncommon Man* (New York: Henry Holt, 1999), pp. 336–406, 428–51. See also Thomas, *Film Score: View from the Podium,* pp. 15–26.

53. Peter Lev, *The Fifties: Transforming the Screen, 1950–59* (Berkeley: University of California Press, 2003), p. 7. Ticket sales declined in spite of the fact that personal income actually increased some 22 percent.

54. Ibid., p. 9. See also Sklar, *Movie-Made America,* pp. 269–72. The growing availability, affordability, and convenience of television, the entertainment tailor-made for a suburbanized audience, was at least partially responsible for decline in theater attendance. How much of a threat it posed was debatable. Polls credited television with draining anywhere from 30 to 70 percent of moviegoers from the theaters.

55. Schatz, *Boom and Bust,* pp. 289–97.

56. In the decade and a half after the war, "national sales declined and international sales increased until, in the early 1960s, international income was substantially greater than income from the U.S. market" (Lev, *The Fifties,* p. 147). Boosted by the Marshall Plan and reinforced by the growing economic and political clout of the United States abroad, the film industry reestablished its foreign markets after the war. Given the declining revenues in its domestic market, this proved crucial to the studios.

57. Ibid., pp. 297–303.

58. Ibid., pp. 148–62 (quote on p. 162). See also Schatz, *Boom and Bust*, pp. 297–303

59. Schatz, *Boom and Bust*, pp. 323–28; and Sklar, *Movie-Made America*, pp. 272–74. As Sklar (p. 274) observes, "By 1954, the five major producing firms had divested themselves of ownership or control of all their theaters."

60. Lev, *The Fifties*, pp. 12–24.

61. The industry initially tried to forestall criticism and investigation by establishing the Motion Picture Alliance for the Preservation of American Ideals, a conservative-minded watchdog group set up to monitor politically subversive activity. When that group's assurances that the industry had been purged of Communists failed to reassure some members of Congress, HUAC took over. See Schatz, *Boom and Bust*, pp. 307–9.

62. Ibid., pp. 309–10. When Hollywood complied with the subpoenas, a new Hollywood group, the Committee for the First Amendment, which included such high-profile actors and directors as William Wyler, Billy Wilder, Katharine Hepburn, Humphrey Bogart, and Groucho Marx, formed to counter what they considered the government's overreaching censorship. They traveled to Washington to air their objections before the committee, but their actions were overshadowed by the proceedings of the sensational testimony and actions of the subpoenaed Hollywood Ten.

63. Ibid., pp. 307–13. See also Sklar, *Movie-Made America*, pp. 256–68.

64. Lev, *The Fifties*, p. 68–72. In 1951, a second wave of hearings expanded the scope of the committee's investigation through the process of "naming names." With the anti-Communist fervor being increasingly supported and the blacklisting being increasingly expanded by Hollywood executives, many complied and named names, as Lev observes, "because this is what was required for them to be able to work again in the film industry" (p. 69).

65. Sklar, *Movie-Made America*, p. 267.

66. Ibid. p. 282.

67. Ibid., pp. 235- 41, 58–62.

68. Ibid., pp. 41–44, 229–31.

69. The "superwesterns," according to Bazin, challenged the "aesthetic, sociological, moral, psychological, political, and erotic" boundaries of the conventional western (André Bazin, "The Evolution of the Western," in *What Is Cinema?*, trans. Hugh Gray [Berkeley: University of California Press, 1971], 2:151). See also Lev, *Fifties*, pp. 54–58, 232–35.

70. Ibid., p. 169. The science-fiction film was not entirely new, existing in the 1930s and 1940s primarily by way of infrequent feature films or low-budget serials like Buck Rogers or Flash Gordon.

71. Joyce A. Evans, "Celluloid Mushroom Clouds: Hollywood and the Atomic Bomb (Boulder, Colo.: Westview Press, 1998), p. 75. See also Victoria O'Donnell, "Science Fiction Films and Cold War Anxiety," in Lev, *The Fifties*, p. 169.

72. O'Donnell, "Science Fiction Films," in Lev, *The Fifties*, 169.

73. Color film innovations boosting color film production from 15 percent in 1950 to nearly 50 percent by 1955 (Lev, *The Fifties*, p. 112).

74. Ibid., pp. 124–25. For details on all the different screen and camera formats that were tested by various studios, see pp. 107–25 ("Technology and Spectacle").

75. Ibid., pp. 34–40, 219–23. See also Schatz, *Boom and Bust*, pp. 375–77. The industry made several Rodgers and Hammerstein stage musicals into successful films, including *Oklahoma!* (1949), *Carousel* (1956), *The King and I* (1956), and *South Pacific* (1958).

76. Producer Arthur Freed is typically credited with encouraging or facilitating the creation of the postwar integrated musical. He employed resourceful directors like Vincente Minnelli and Stanley Donen, who experimented with not just narrative formulas but also camera movement. Freed also utilized the best singing and dancing talents of the period, including Gene Kelly, Fred

Astaire, Cyd Charisse, Frank Sinatra, and Donald O'Connor, and as a result produced some of the most popular musicals of the period, from *Meet Me in St. Louis* (1944), *On the Town* (1949), *An American in Paris* (1951), *Singin' in the Rain* (1952), to *The Band Wagon* (1953), *It's Always Fair Weather* (1954), and *Gigi* (1960). See Rick Altman, *The American Film Musical* (Bloomington: Indiana University Press, 1989).

77. Lev, *The Fifties*, pp. 244–49.

78. Thomas Doherty, *Teenagers and Teenpics: The Juvenilization of American Movies in the 1950s* (Philadelphia: Temple University Press, 2002), pp. 54–82.

79. See "Igor Stravinsky on Film Music (as told to Ingolf Dahl)," *Musical Digest,* September 1946, pp. 4–5, 35–36.

80. Raksin was invited by *Musical Digest* to respond to Stravinsky's article, which he did in "Hollywood Strikes Back: Film Composer Attacks Stravinsky's 'Cult of Inexpressiveness,'" *Musical Digest,* January 1948, pp. 5–7.

81. See Dimitri Tiomkin, "A Film Composer's View of Film Music: Opposing Stravinsky's Ideas," *Musical Digest,* January 1948, pp. 18 and 39. A Russian émigré, Tiomkin had been an acclaimed concert pianist before becoming a studio composer, a career he pursued from the late 1930s to the 1960s.

82. See Aaron Copland, "Tip to Moviegoers: Take Off Those Ear-Muffs," *New York Times Magazine,* November 6, 1949, pp. 28–32.

83. Partick J. Smith, "Harold Schonberg," in *New Grove Dictionary of Music*, 22:611. Schonberg, senior music critic for *The New York Times* from 1960 to 1980, wrote several engaging and popular music history texts, including *The Great Pianists* (1964), *The Great Conductors* (1967), *The Lives of the Great Composers* (1970), and *Facing the Music* (1981).

84. For the biographical and philosophical backgrounds of each author, see Graham McCann's new introduction to the most recent reprint of the book, Theodor Adorno and Hanns Eisler, *Composing for the Films* (London: Athlone Press, 1994), pp. vii–xlvii.

85. Hanns Eisler and Theodor Adorno, *Komposition für den Film, mit DVD: Hanns Eislers Rockefeller-Filmmusik-Projekt 1940–1942, ausgewählten Filmklassikern und weiteren Dokumenten,* ed. Johannes C. Gall (Frankfurt: Suhrkamp Verlag, 2006).

86. Analyses of Herrmann's scores, especially for Hitchcock's films, are relatively plentiful. A good selection includes Royal S. Brown, "Herrmann, Hitchcock, and the Music of the Irrational," in *Overtones and Undertones,* pp. 148–74; Fred Steiner, "Herrmann's 'Black and White' Music for Hitchcock's *Psycho,*" *Film Music Notebook* 1, no. 1 (Fall 1974) ("Part I") and 1, no. 2 ("Part II"), reprinted in *Elmer Bernstein's Film Music Notebook: A Complete Collection of the Quarterly Journal, 1974–78* (Sherman Oaks, Calif.: Film Music Society, 2004), pp. 30–38 and 68–88; Murray Pommerance, "Finding Release: 'Storm Clouds' and *The Man Who Knew Too Much,*" in *Music and Cinema,* ed. James Buhler, Caryl Flinn, and David Neumeyer (Hanover, N.H.: Wesleyan University Press, 2000), pp. 207–47; and Anthony John, "'The Moment That I Dreaded and Hoped For': Ambivalence and Order in Bernard Herrmann's Score for *Vertigo,*" *Musical Quarterly* 85, no. 3 (2001): 516–44. Two book-length studies on Herrmann also discuss the Hitchcock scores: Graham Bruce, *Bernard Herrmann: Film Music and Narrative* (Ann Arbor: UMI Research Press, 1985); and Steven C. Smith, *A Heart at Fire's Center: The Life and Music of Bernard Herrmann* (Berkeley: University of California Press, 1991).

87. For a good discussion of jazz in American cinema, see Krin Gabbard, *Jammin' at the Margins: Jazz and the American Cinema* (Chicago: University of Chicago Press, 1996). See also Gary Marmorstein, *Hollywood Rhapsody: Movie Music and Its Makers, 1900–1975* (New York: Schirmer, 1997), pp. 306–21 ("Leave Your Worries on the Doorstep: Jazz Arrives by Streetcar"); and David Meeker, *Jazz in the Movies* (New York: Da Capo Press, 1982).

88. Bernard Herrmann's sci-fi scores are a good example of the creative use composers made of conventional orchestral instruments. His score for *The Day the Earth Stood Still* (1951) featured a theremin in places, but it was also underscored throughout with an unusual ensemble of thirty brass instruments, four pianos, four harps, electric violin, and bass. The scores he later produced for the sci-fi/fantasy films *Journey to the Center of the Earth* (1959), *The Seventh Voyage of Sinbad* (1958), and *Jason and the Argonauts* (1963), the last two of which featured the unusual animation of Ray Harryhausen, also have unconventional orchestral instrumentation. For a detailed discussion of Herrmann's early career and his science fiction scores in particular, see Randall Larson, *Musique Fantastique: A Survey of Film Music in the Fantastic Cinema* (Metuchen, N.J.: Scarecrow Press, 1985), pp. 109–31 ("Mysterious Worlds: The Music of Bernard Herrmann"; and Rebecca Leydon, "Hooked on Autherophonics: *The Day the Earth Stood Still*," in *Off the Planet: Music, Sound, and Science Fiction Cinema,* ed. Phillip Hayward (Eastleigh, U.K.: John Libbey, 2004), pp. 1–29. See also Bruce, *Bernard Herrmann,* pp. 103–15; and Smith, *A Heart at Fire's Center,* pp. 164–66.

89. David Raksin made notable use of electronic processing techniques in the 1944 film noir *Laura,* superimposing multiple recordings of the main theme to warp and warble it and suggest a hallucinatory effect. See Prendergast, *Invisible Art of Film Music,* p. 67.

90. Albert Glinsky, *Theremin: Ether Music and Espionage* (Urbana: University of Illinois Press, 2000), provides a detailed look at Leon Theremin and the instrument itself.

91. Miklós Rózsa, *Double Life* (New York: Wynwood, 1989), pp. 144–48, 206. See also Larson, *Musique Fantastique,* pp. 65–76 ("The Music of Miklós Rózsa"). For a discussion of the use of the theremin in film and television music in general, see Glinsky, *Theremin,* pp. 253–55, 279–83.

92. The pair's interest in electronic music stemmed from an electronic recording studio they created in New York City in the late 1940s that catered to avant-garde writers and composers. Prominent artists who worked there in the early 1950s included writers Henry Miller, Tennessee Williams, Aldous Huxley, and Anais Nin and composers John Cage, Morton Feldman, and Earle Brown. It was Cage who first suggested that the Barrons start conceptualizing their arranged electronic "sounds" as musical compositions. See James Wierzbicki, *Louis and Bebe Barron's "Forbidden Planet": A Film Score Guide* (Metuchen, N.J.: Scarecrow Press, 2005); and Rebecca Leydon, "*Forbidden Planet*: Effects and Affects in the Electro Avant-Garde," in Hayward, ed., *Off the Planet,* pp. 61–76; also Thom Holmes, *Electronic and Experimental Music,* 2d ed. (New York: Routledge, 2002); and Jane Brockman, "The First Electronic Filmscore—*Forbidden Planet*: A Conversation with Bebe Barron," *The Score* 7, no. 3 (Fall/Winter 1992): 5, 12–13.

93. Because the Barrons were not members of the Hollywood musicians' union, union representatives objected to their employment. The standoff was settled not by admitting the Barrons to the union but by agreeing to label their non-union work as non-music, as "electronic tonalities." See Brockman, "The First Electronic Filmscore." For a good overview of the Barrons' influence on sci-fi scoring, see Larsen, *Musique Fantastique,* esp. chap. 5: "Big Bugs in Outer Space," pp. 76–109; and chap. 13: "Electronics," pp. 266–93.

94. The niece of the legendary Hollywood director Cecil B. de Mille, Agnes de Mille was a successful concert hall and Broadway choreographer. Although Hollywood made several of the hit Broadway musicals she choreographed into films, including *Oklahoma!, Brigadoon,* and *Carousel,* de Mille was invited to choreograph only *Oklahoma!* for Hollywood. See Carol Easton, *No Intermissions: The Life of Agnes de Mille* (New York: Da Capo Press, 2000). Modern dance pioneer Martha Graham never choreographed for Hollywood, but her "modernist" style was utilized by several film choreographers, most notably Jack Cole, who studied with Graham's teachers Ruth St. Denis and Ted Shawn and colleague Doris Humphreys. Cole protégé Bob Fosse satirized Graham in one of the stage numbers in the film *White Christmas* (1954). See Larry Billman, *Film Choreographers and*

Dance Directors: An Illustrated Biographical Encyclopedia, with a History and Filmographies, 1893 through 1995 (Jefferson, N.C.: McFarland & Co., 1997).

95. Doherty, *Teenagers and Teenpics*, p. 58; see also Lev, *The Fifties*, 244–46.

96. Quote in Joel Friedman, "Spinning Wax Sells Music Movies Nowadays," *Billboard,* November 10, 1956, p. 20. For a more detailed biography of pioneer teen-pic producer Sam Katzman, see Doherty, *Teenagers and Teenpics*, pp. 55–57.

20

Composers in Movieland

George Antheil

(1935)

The technic of writing motion picture music is complicated by many elements unknown to the musician of yesteryear. First of all the average theatre, ballet or opera composer of the past had to contend only with a few changes of scene, whereas the motion picture flies out of space and time, from cut to cut and second to second. How is one to illustrate a background flashing from galloping horsemen to pastoral scenes and on to three or four other varied shots? Writing two measures gallop music, one second pastoral music, and so on to the end of the film will obviously not answer. Neither can one ignore what is happening upon the screen and work away at a symphonic form hoping somehow to secure a metaphysical background or the sense of what is going on.

It is apparent that cinema music, to fulfill its primary purpose, should be descriptive and local. Yet if it is to be music at all it must achieve organic unity, whether by symphonic treatment, or some other method of restating and developing original thematic material. Either the score stands on its own feet as music or it falls into the category of pastiche, which is the destiny of most Hollywood film music.

Now there is only one way to achieve an "authentic" original score, and that is to give its production into the hands of *one* composer, who, from his conference over the first script with the film producer, plans all his work, and solves all his problems. This is so obvious that it seems hardly necessary to reiterate or explain. Indeed it is the method which has given us the only noteworthy film music to date— Georges Auric's score for René Clair's *A nous la liberté*, Ernst Toch's music for *The Brothers Karamazov*, Eugene Goossens' for *The Constant Nymph*, Serge Prokofieff's for *The Czar Wants to Sleep*, Dmitri Shostakovitch's for *Odna*, Kurt Weill's for the filmed *Dreigroschenoper*. But these musical films are, it will be seen, all European. Until recently the method was unknown and untried in America.

For Hollywood has a group formula for making music. Every studio keeps a staff of seventeen to thirty composers on annual salary. They know nothing about the film till the final cutting day, when it is played over for some or all of them, replayed and stopwatched. Then the work is divided; one man writes war music, a second does the love passages, another is a specialist in nature stuff, and so on. After several days, when they have finished their fractions of music, these are pieced together, played into "soundtrack," stamped with the name of a musical director, and put on the market as an "original score." This usually inept product is exactly the kind of broth to expect from so many minds working at high speed on a single piece.

It is well to consider the economic factors in motion picture production which have developed this "forcing" process. If a picture needs music at all, it usually needs it badly when the film cutting time is over. It is at this advanced moment that the score must be "dubbed" into the picture, that is, run in final orchestral form into the first "soundtrack." Joining the film now, the score cannot afford to miss the mark; it must fit the picture like a glove and be fairly descriptive of the important highlights. Otherwise it will endanger a previous outlay of several hundred thousand dollars spent in taking and cutting about four hundred thousand feet of film. Every minute longer that it takes to "dub" the final score into the picture, and so delay its release, will cost the film company the interest on its tied-up capital—which may amount to one thousand dollars a day. Thus it is cheaper to keep a staff of composers on salary, ready to produce a score overnight if necessary. Since each studio produces many pictures, a music department helps to make the producer's investments immediately profitable by expediting the film releases.

But recently a new factor has come to disturb this ideal balance of speed and expense. The group method of patching up a score was developed in the early days of the sound-films, before it was necessary to write "original" music. Ten years ago existing musical scores were not protected by copyright from this medium. The only expense producers incurred was the cost of having able copyists go to the music libraries or buy sheet music. The contents were available to them without royalty costs. It was thus that the method of "pastiche" became so recognized. Nothing could be easier, less time consuming or cheaper than to have a corps of men take a little of this or that, all well tried and of proved popularity, and fit the excerpts to a picture.

But now that copyright has been recognized as protecting composers against the sound-film, it costs the movies big money to quote twelve bars from anything or anybody—an average of $100 a measure. Think of a hundred thousand measures, and you will have some idea of the cost of a quoted score, and you will also understand the sudden new vogue for "originals."

There can be little doubt that the demand for "original scores" is an excellent augur for composers. For it becomes obvious, even in Hollywood—perhaps after the spectacular successes of René Clair here and abroad—that the best original scores must be written by original composers—in other words that they must be composed. Already feelers are being put out from Hollywood in the direction of one-man scores. Naturally when such scores are tried and prove commercially popular, the mechanical organization of the music departments and studios will be adjusted to new methods of score production. And these will be developed on a sound economic basis as effective for speed and expense as the old ones—perhaps even more so.

Such an experiment, on a large scale, has been undertaken, as is already well known, by the Eastern Paramount Studios, under the direction of Ben Hecht and Charles MacArthur. Besides being successful in literary and dramatic fields, they are practiced men of the movies; since I am associated with their venture as composer and music director, it has been necessary for me to substitute a method of procedure for the standard practice of the Western studios. The method is necessarily experimental, but as it has already been put into effect, and is to be continued throughout the series made at the studios this spring, I will outline it briefly here, for those composers, motion picture people, and laymen who, I presume, have an interest in the development of the sound-film.

When one man writes the score of a film (as I did for *Once in a Blue Moon*) it is advisable to have as much of the score *finished* as is possible by the final cutting, or on the day when the music department receives the film. This reverses the Hollywood process, and for good reason—there will be no seventeen or more co-writers to rush into the job at the last moment. The first step toward this accomplishment is an exhaustive preliminary discussion with the director before the film is begun, at which copious notes should be taken of the planned situations, shots, montages, movie leitmotifs. With this as background, and the first script at hand, a musical "break-down" can be made, which is movie parlance for a work chart. The script is broken into purely musical items, timings, work-out valuations, and sequences from the viewpoint of leitmotif. The tiny changes from shot to shot should be disregarded in planning the large sections and the thematic material of the score. To avoid the creation of a commercial potpourri, it is necessary to adjust the main musical outlines to the major psychological developments of the plot.

The break-down chart finished, the whole picture can be acted out by assistants in the music department, so that the timing of each shot and sequence may be recorded by a stop-watch. Such a framework of action and time is sufficient for the composer to undertake the work of score writing. This may then be carried on during the month or months spent in shooting the picture. The composer should naturally expect to write too much music and also be prepared for many changes form the original script. Daily, yesterday's "rushes" (which is all the film taken from the cameras in the previous day's shooting) are timed and can be checked against the original timing guesses, to gauge the length of any particular scene. When the first rough cuts appear, it may be apparent that a complete read-justment of the score is necessary, but usually guess-work methodically undertaken and checked will come within a few odd seconds of the timing for the entire picture.

Thus when the final film is cut and given to the composer, a great deal of the picture is not only in glove-fitting piano score but may be orchestrated as well. A final week is devoted to writing and orchestrating new sequences introduced by the producer a the last moment, or to any other sudden breath-taking, brain-exploding movie business. The "wipes" and "dissolves" and "fades" (which are various ways of blending one shot into another) are the last thing to be cut into the film; they make a slight difference in timing and must be reckoned with in the music.

By this technic, one week after the final cutting date a composer may complete a score which fits the picture. It is then handed to the copyists in the music department, twenty-odd men who work day and night for at least five days. Meanwhile orchestra rehearsals are begun on the first reels. In the big sound recording rooms the orchestra plays and two or three "takes" of each reel are made. Sometimes the picture is played while the recording goes on, sometimes not, depending upon how many small changes in tempo are necessary to hit various high spots "on the nose." When the whole picture is "hit on the nose" musically, second for second, and each reel is "in the bag" the new sound tracks go to the laboratories and are developed, and the next day the best tracks are selected for the final "dubbing." This highly technical process involves the putting together of the silent film, the speaking and original sound track taken with it, and the new music beneath it. When there is no dialogue the orchestra plays forte enough, and when the action demands, the track can be "squeezed" to pianissimo.

The master print is then ready. The negative film is matched exactly, and from the master negative thousands of prints are prepared for thousands of sound film theatres all over the world.

From *Modern Music* 12, no. 2 (January/February 1935): 62–66.

21

The Aesthetics of the Sound Film

Leonid Sabaneev

(1935)

From the aesthetic point of view a sound film is a combination of visual and aural impressions, that is to say, of pictures, music, noises, and speech. It is a species
of synthetic art, approximately of the same type as opera and drama. Nevertheless, in spite of the external resemblance, there is a profound distinction between
the aesthetic basis of the sound film and that of these antiquated forms of art. In
order to grasp this enormously important difference, to understand the sphere to
which the cinema is restricted, we must turn to the sources of cinematography in
general.

It has to be realized that the cinema is fundamentally photography, endowed
with movement it is true, and recently with sound as well, but both movement
and sound are essentially photographic; in other words, they are based on the
reproduction of certain natural phenomena. In the realm of fantasy the cinema
has boundless possibilities; it can accomplish easily and simply that which in the
theatre is cumbersome and difficult, and to all intents and purposes there is no
impediment to the exercise of the imagination. In spite of this, it is primarily a
reproductive art, which gives us a copy of nature and hence is naturalistic (not
even realistic). The theatre, on the contrary, originated as an outlet from the
world into imaginary realms; only in the latest stages of its development has it
arrived at realism, and this is merely a transitory phase.

The public is keenly conscious of the naturalistic nature of the cinema, the
more so because the former differs widely from the theatrical public which constitutes the audience of drama and opera. First of all, it is far more democratic
(owing to the cheapness of the cinema and to the fact that the character of the
production is industrial and not "artisan") and incomparably vaster. A rough

estimate of the figures shows that the theatre audiences of the world comprise, in the most favorable case, not more than three or four millions, whereas the frequenters of the cinema have long since been reckoned in tens, or even hundreds, of millions—nearly the whole world is attracted to the cinema.

The immensity of the audience and its democratic nature impose their imprint, which is seen in its aesthetic requirements: at heart the general public of to-day is not idealistic, but naturalistic—it prefers life to fantasy. Observation reveals that pictures with a large proportion of the fantastic element, though combined with enormous artistic merit, are less successful than commonplace films of real life. The photographic nature of the cinema here plays a great part. The primary significance of the cinematograph is the reproduction of something that actually happens; it is a scrap of life printed on a film. And in thus understanding it the public displays the profundity of its view. When a non-realistic picture is shown on the screen, it always suggests the idea that it has been staged previously. Although we know that even naturalistic films are photographed from a preliminary staging, the inevitable artistic deception which is present in every art should, in the case of the cinema, prevent this fact from being noticed. The public wants to believe that what it sees on the screen is a bit of life, which somebody has watched unobserved and filmed. Hence the irruption of the typical theatre into the world of the cinema proves to be permissible only in a naturalistic form, i.e. as an actual photograph from the theatre fixed on a film, because even the theatre may be a fragment of life. On the other hand, a theatricalized film usually has a spurious look.

From the components of the cinema another of its aesthetic qualities is derived—its illustrative nature. The silent film was simply an animated illustration of the captions which represented the rudiments of literature, the text, as it were, of the romance unfolded on the screen. When the film began to talk, its nature was not thereby altered: the only difference was that the literary element of the captions was converted into the dramatic element of dialogue; the illustrative nature persisted.

Here we are interested only in the question of music for the film, and the aesthetics of that music. It was associated with the cinema from the very beginning, when its aesthetic function was, *inter alia,* to fill up the tonal void which was an inherent feature of the silent film. Here aesthetics played a real part; aesthetic custom, too, had always required that a spectacle should be accompanied by sound. Independently of this, music, in its illustrative capacity, supplied the poetry and emotion which the captions, necessarily brief and of an informatory nature, could not give. Music provided rhythm for the happenings on the screen and, as it were, interpreted the emotions of the characters and of the screen in general.

With the arrival of the sound film the role of music was altered. First and foremost, for technical reasons, it ceased to be mere improvisation and developed into strict and solid composition. Previously it had been possible to play anything one chose for the screen, but that is no longer permissible. On the other hand, whereas music was once the sole provider of sound for the cinema, it now has to share its functions with dramatic speech and various naturalistic noises. But its position has remained. Speech, pictures, and noises constitute the purely photo-graphic section of the cinema; music, whether with the silent or the sound films, supplies the romantic, irrational element illustrating emotion.

As we have said, the sounds connected with the sound film are divisible into three categories: music, speech, and noises, and to understand the aesthetics of music in the new cinema it is very important that we should know how the bound-aries of their spheres of action are delimited. It is, of course, evident that when two or three varieties of sound are proceeding simultaneously, the attention can with difficulty be concentrated on any one of them. The dialogue, which has replaced the caption, naturally occupies the first place, if only from the fact that it explains the meaning of the picture on the screen and music should therefore give way to it. The filling of the silences of the cinema was formerly entrusted to music, but speech is now employed instead. As everyone knows, it is difficult to listen to music and speech at the same time; usually one of them is lost—either the music, or the meaning and beauty of the words. On the one hand it is felt that someone is pre-venting us from enjoying the dialogue, on the other that someone is talking dur-ing a musical performance. Both are aesthetically distressing.

It should always be remembered, as a first principle of the aesthetics of music in the cinema, that logic requires music to give way to dialogue. Even if the for-mer is relegated entirely to the background and is barely audible, it still interferes to some extent with the dialogue, and, as it becomes vague and can hardly be heard, its aesthetic value is only second-rate.

The same remarks apply to music in connection with photographic sounds—noises, shouts, et cetera—which usually drown it and deprive it of any aesthetic significance.

Thus we naturally come to the following conclusions: music should cease or retire into the background when dialogues and noises are taking place. Except in rare instances it blends but poorly with them. When combined with dialogue we get a kind of melodeclamation, and then both dialogue and music are faced with the demands generally presented to melodeclamation, that is to say, coincidence of rhythm, and their artistic symbiosis, which, as we know, is usually difficult to achieve. When we have noises and music simultaneously, the former become part of the musical whole and have the effect of percussion instruments of a sort; in this case they require to be reduced to order; their rhythm must be coincident, and they must be incorporated in the musical composition and not be a mere disorderly din, drowning the music and making it meaningless.

Normally, the musical background should be suppressed on the entry of dia-logue or noises—they are incompatible planes. There is a good aesthetic reason for stopping the music on such occasions, but the precise method to be adopted is one of the most difficult problems of the sound cinema. Music has its inertia; it forms a certain background in the subconsciousness of the listening spectator, and its sudden cessation gives rise to a feeling of aesthetic perplexity, even though the music be kept entirely in the background. The substitution of dialogue and noises for music, on the contrary, does not cause perplexity. The music itself may not be noticed, but if it is stopped without being replaced by other sounds the gap becomes perceptible, as a false note and a cinematographic dissonance.

Of course it must not be imagined that the existing films always corroborate what has been said, but that signifies nothing: these aesthetic principles are gradually penetrating the consciousness of cultured directors.

Music in the cinema, occupying the position of a separate and unreal, non-photographic, plane, preserves a large measure of its individuality and its independent nature. It should possess a musical form of its own, in some way subordinated to the rhythm[s] of the screen, but not destroyed by them. Indeed music often dictates its rhythms and tempi to the screen, and this state of affairs, recognized by all directors, even appears to be normal. The rhythm of the screen is regulated by the music, and this is particularly noticeable when there is no noise or dialogue. Music in the cinema cannot sacrifice the principles governing its form: no matter what is happening on the screen, the music must have its melodic structure, its phrases and cadences, and it must not be asked to suffer dilution by the rhythms and occurrences of the picture. It expresses the general mood of the scene on the stage, and should not be required, except in a few instances mentioned below, to follow the events in detail, otherwise it is untrue to its nature and becomes anti-musical.

Sometimes, to produce an aesthetic impression, it is sufficient that the musical background should not be at variance with the mood of the screen. Very characteristic of the cinema is the use of neutral music, which fills the tonal spaces and annihilates the silences without attracting special attention to itself. In general, music should understand that in the cinema it should nearly always remain in the background: it is, so to speak, a tonal figuration, the "left hand" to the melody of the screen, and it is a bad business when this left hand begins to creep into the foreground and obscure the melody. On the comparatively rare occasions when the interest is concentrated on the music, the latter may emerge from its subordinate position for a time, but as a rule it should be subdued and should make its presence felt without effort, nor should it attract attention to itself at the expense of the screen.

This musical background serves as a sort of psychological resonator of the screen, enhancing its effect and augmenting its emotional passages. Hence it is as important that the music and the picture should synchronize and that their rhythms should coincide. If these precautions are observed, the aesthetic effect of the stage action will be strengthened. A procession gains enormously if accompanied by music with a well-marked and coincident rhythm, just as the impression will be lessened if the music and the screen do not synchronize. This applies equally to the non-coincidence of the emotional tempo and rhythm. So long as this harmony is observed the music is not noticed of itself—it merely forms part of the general effect—but in the contrary case the audience becomes aware of it as a dissonance, a disturbing element.

Music may exercise a powerful influence on the rhythm of the screen, may act as a kind of throttle-valve. Unfortunately this attribute of music has not been fully explored by film directors, who have not yet realized that, though occupying a secondary place, it is important and indispensable. They look upon it as of no consequence, forgetting that, if the cinema wants to become and remain an art, the background should be carefully thought out and thoroughly well done; in art nothing is unimportant. The rhythmizing and resonating function of music is particularly evident in comic films and animated cartoons. The congruence of the movements with the musical rhythm is always very effective and enormously emphasizes their significance. Furthermore, it may be said that music in general best and most naturally illustrates movements and gestures. The importation of a certain portion of Dalcroze's theory into the cinema would be by no means unprofitable. Then, and only then, would music be aesthetically bound up with the screen, creating an artistic amalgam, and not an amateurish improvisation round about the screen.

Another function of music, already employed in art, is the artistically stylized imitation of sounds. Musical literature knows of a vast quantity of descriptive music. Its precise role in the cinema, however, is limited, owing to the photographic nature of the latter, to which we have previously referred. The cinema has many means of accurately and photographically reproducing all the sounds of nature, and any attempts by music in this direction always seem naïve. On the other hand, this artlessness may sometimes prove opportune. The employment of cinema music to imitate sounds is most advantageous when a certain symbolism—the reflections of spiritual events in the sounds of nature—is required. Music is essentially symbolical, and this rôle befits it, but a bald, non-symbolical imitation is usually unsuccessful, and rings false. A rigid line must be drawn between these two main aspects of the cinema—the photographic, with the noises and dialogue, and the ideal, which music alone can depict. Some sounds which, though musical, belong to the photographic plane, demand a special reference. The following example will explain the writer's idea: suppose we have the sound of a horn. Being musical, it can easily be inserted in the musical background, but the director and the composer will act wisely if they realize that it belongs to the photographic plane, and therefore should not be mixed up with the other music. There are two methods of treatment: either the horn must be isolated and played solo, thus emphasizing the fact that it is of the photographic plane, or if it must be combined with the musical background, it should be made to stand out, to be at cross purposes with its setting, by entrusting to it a false or extra-harmonic note.

Again, let us imagine that we have a musical scene, such as jazz in a restaurant or cabaret. This is essentially photographic, and therefore in dealing with it we can take a course which would not be permissible in relation to a purely musical background; for instance we may, and even must, stop these sounds the moment the scene changes, so that when the jazz disappears the ear no longer hears its music. The stoppage may be sudden and occur at any point of the accompaniment, without regard to the musical construction. It is as though the sounds were cut off by the closing of a door. With an event on the musical plane we cannot behave thus; we must continue the musical texture to its natural end, to the cadence, and that cadence must be adapted to the change of scene.

The writer has often asked himself: "Why not combine music and photography by the method whereby this has been accomplished in opera?" In other words, why not create a cinema opera? Then music would be organically blended with drama, and between music and speech there would be, not inconsistency, but fusion. Practical experience shows, however, that attempts in this direction have been short-lived and unsuccessful.

The reason for this will be found in the fact that the art of the cinema, as already pointed out, is a photographic art, and is therefore obliged to be naturalistic and anti-theatrical. In the cinema anything of a theatrical nature sounds false, and opera is the theatre sublimated, is doubly theatrical. Although the cinema has vast possibilities at its disposal—possibilities which are almost beyond the scope of the operatic stage—and, by virtue of its inexhaustible scenic resources, could introduce into opera many new and artistic effects, such as changing and contrasting planes, opera does not blend with the cinema; nor does the cinema want to become opera, except occasionally in the form of operetta or extravaganza. And the sole cause for this is that the cinema is naturalistic. The conventional falsehood on which opera is based is intolerable in the cinema, and opera is admitted only in the form of photographs of it, or of excerpts from it, as operatic episodes casually photographed from life, as operatic episodes in real life. In just the same way, singing in the cinema is always real singing, the singing of the actor in real life, and not the conventional song of the operatic stage, that is, song which has captured speech and replaced it. Realistic photographs of opera in real life are conceivable and artistic, and so are photographs of singing if among the actors are included some who sing, but opera as such, as a synthesis of music and speech, is unendurable on the screen.

The cinema can make use of different planes, and is thereby endowed with a superabundance of resources wherewith to provide artistic contrasts. The aesthetics applicable to the various planes are of special importance, and it will be interesting to investigate the mutual relation between music and this problem of planes.

Normally, music, like any other sound phenomena in the cinema, supplies a tonal background for the screen. In the case of a close-up the listening spectator contemplates everything at close quarters, so to speak, and naturally the sounds issuing from the screen should be nearer and more audible to him. Therefore the dialogue of the close-up is generally louder, and of the long and medium shots fainter. When the close-up is larger than life-size, the volume of sound may be increased beyond the normal without any loss of artistry. This applies also to noises, shouts, and other sound phenomena of the photographic plane, but the musical, non-photographic plane has more license in this respect, just because it is non-photographic.

In its general features music also adheres to this principle: the bigger the plane the more powerful the sounds. But exceptions and contradictions are possible here. For example, the music accompanying the conversation in a close-up may be remote and subdued, in order that it may not interfere with the latter. In general it should accord with the mood of the scene, rather than with the plane. Again, the music of a triumphal procession in the distance may be soft, but when the procession becomes visible, the accompaniment should also be triumphal and sonorous; in the latter case it would be absurd to have barely audible music merely because it is on a common plane. The correlation of the type and dynamic of the music with the screen is usually far more complex, and is subject to much that has not yet been explained and to laws that have not been established. Hence in the given case it is better to rely on the composer's instinct. It may, however, be remarked that the more intimate scenes, the close-ups, generally suggest music of a limited range and modestly laid out. On the other hand, big episodes, such as crowds and processions, require music on a big scale, embracing all the register, from the highest to the lowest.

The cessation of music in the cinema always produces an impression of dissonance, unless it is promptly and directly replaced by other sounds. It must be remembered that the technical conditions of the cinema are such that it can never be silent—there is always the noise of the apparatus, aesthetically detrimental and obnoxious. Silence can be realized only through music, which should be the "music of silence" and not an actual cessation of sound. From this it will be seen that the discontinuance of any kind of tonal background causes an aesthetic dissonance. But a mixture of backgrounds is also objectionable, on account of their mutual interference. Hence arises the phenomenon that music often plays a very insignificant part in the contemporary cinema, and the more insignificant it is, the more prominent are the dialogue and the tonal photographs (the photographs of actual sounds). A film that is continuous dialogue can dispense with music altogether, except the photoplane moments. On the other hand, the musical background of a film with so little dialogue that it is almost silent should be correspondingly increased. Since music is a symbolical and preeminently psychological substance, it is often superfluous and ridiculous in films with a minimum of psychology. Films of savage life in Africa or of wild beasts—and, indeed, any picture of a documentary type—should be accompanied by photoplanes only, and not by music. But a film of a psychological nature, with love episodes, would find it difficult to dispense with music, not merely from an aesthetic point of view, but also because the audience, accustomed to the musical tradition of the silent film, expects it.

The cinema has a public of its own, which differs from that of the theatre. In the mass the former is aesthetically backward: its aesthetic psychology is infantile, its tastes undeveloped, its comprehension of, and ability to distinguish, musical details and texture limited. All this must be borne in mind. The cinema audience regards as vital those forms which, in the eyes of advanced art, bear the impress of banality, and on the whole its tastes are more antiquated than those characterizing the main tendencies in art. Effects long since relegated to the museum still bring tears to the eyes of the cinema-goer, and sentimentality and naïve methods of exciting him have not yet lost their sway. Hence melodeclamation, to which any dialogue to music is reduced in the cinema, offers a wide field for development. By way of comfort, however, it should be noted that, while the aesthetic tastes of the cinema audience may be primitive, they are nevertheless more refined and more elevated than is supposed by many cinema promoters, and even directors, who ascribe their own lack of artistic development to "the demands of the crowd." In the final reckoning this public appreciates anything that is genuinely good, and is presented in such a manner as to be within everybody's grasp; and it rejects all that is coarse in form and anti-artistic. This public has been badly educated: its aesthetic conceptions have not been artistically developed and it has been fed on trash, as being cheaper and more profitable. The cinema, of course, is run on commercial, and not on artistic, lines, to a far greater extent than is the case with any other branch of art.

From *Music for the Films*, trans. S. W. Pring (London: Faber & Faber, 1935), pp. 15–31.

22

Scoring the Film

Max Steiner

(1937)

Music has probably had the most hectic career, not excepting sound, of all mediums which combine to make a motion picture.

The present use of music in heightening the emotion of a film was borrowed directly from the elaborate orchestral accompaniment in motion-picture theaters during the silent days. No theater was too small to hire a regular orchestra. But with the advent of talking pictures, recorded music, both vocal and instrumental, was used sparingly at first, as was the dialogue. In some instances an entire picture would be silent, and suddenly in the fourth or fifth reel someone would burst into song, as in *The Pagan Love Song*. The theater orchestra still played the accompaniment up to the time the sound track was used, leading up to the particular key in which the song was being played. Then, as soon as the recorded music was over, the orchestra would start playing again, leading away from it gracefully.

A year or so prior to that time, the Vitaphone short subjects came into vogue. In these, a large orchestra of symphonic strength was assembled and photographed while recording the music. In some instances, close-ups of the players were shot, and vocalists added. These photographed orchestra novelties would then be shown instead of comedics, scenic subjects or cartoons.

The economic distress in which musicians found themselves after the advent of talking pictures was somewhat counteracted by a miniature gold rush to California. Well-known musicians and orchestra leaders were brought to Hollywood, and the march of recorded pictures began in earnest.

For reasons which I will later explain, there was very little underscoring (background music) in those days, but chiefly main and end titles (opening and closing music). Recorded music was deemed necessary only for musical productions, such as *Rio Rita, The Street Singer, The Rogue Song* and *Vagabond Lover*.

Almost insurmountable difficulties confronted musicians in those days in successfully transferring even a small part of the actual sound on to the sound track. The reasons were numerous: Producers and directors did not know how to handle music; sound men and musicians were inexperienced; the microphone was in its infancy; and, therefore, the entire technical staff went into contortions to reproduce, even in part, what was actually heard on the set.

I remember, during the filming of a certain picture, that it took us two days to find a suitable spot for the double bass, as the acoustical conditions on the stage were such that every time the bass player touched his instrument the sound track would *overshoot* (distort or blur). This experience with the entire company—actors, singers and musicians—on the set, cost the company seventy-five thousand dollars.

At that period the musicians were required to play very softly. The modern recording orchestra, however, plays in a normal tone, and through the use of special microphones a great part of the orchestra balance is now maneuvered by the recordist.

In the old days one of the great problems was standard (actual) recording, as dubbing or re-recording was unknown at that time. It was necessary at all times to have the entire orchestra and vocalists on the set day and night. This was a huge expense when one considers that a musician was, and still is, paid thirty dollars for three, and fifty dollars for six, hours' recording, with half-pay for rehearsals. But because of inexperience and the very undeveloped technique of sound it was impossible to work fast. Many rehearsals and many recordings (takes) were necessary before a satisfactory result could be obtained. I have known of instances where one short number, of two or three minutes' duration, would take two days to record. As sound technique gradually improved, this loss of time was considerably lessened, until it became so far advanced that today a three-minute number can easily be recorded in one hour or less, if properly rehearsed and balanced (which, of course, must *still* be done carefully).

At this time, music for dramatic pictures was only used when it was actually required by the script. A constant fear prevailed among producers, directors and musicians, that they would be asked: Where does the music come from? Therefore they never used music unless it could be explained by the presence of a source like an orchestra, piano player, phonograph or radio, which was specified in the script.

To get back to musical pictures: The success of the early musicals like *Broadway Melody, Rio Rita, The Street Singer* and *The Rogue Song* caused every company to concentrate on the production of this type of picture, and fabulous salaries were paid to singers and musicians. It was prosperity at its peak for the chosen few; but, even as at present, the cycle of musicals was OVERPRODUCED.

Through lack of sufficient good material and the ever changing taste of a fickle public, musical picture after musical picture failed, and the studios decided to call it a day and go back to dramatic pictures. It therefore became unnecessary to maintain a large staff of musicians, and so in September, 1930, I received a letter telling me that the studio would not require our services any longer and to dismiss everyone not under contract. In most instances the studios even tried to buy up existing contracts. Musical activity in Hollywood was almost at a standstill.

But in the spring of 1931, due to the rapid development of sound technique, producers and directors began to realize that an art which had existed for thousands of years could not be ruled out by "the stroke of a pen." They began to add a little music here and there to support love scenes or silent sequences. But they felt it necessary to explain the music pictorially. For example, if they wanted music for a street scene, an organ grinder was shown. It was easy to use music in night club, ballroom or theater scenes, as here the orchestra played a necessary part in the picture.

Many strange devices were used to introduce the music. For instance, a love scene might take place in the woods, and in order to justify the music thought necessary to accompany it, a wandering violinist would be brought in for no reason at all. Or, again, a shepherd would be seen herding his sheep and playing his flute, to the accompaniment of a fifty-piece symphony orchestra.

Half of this music was still recorded on the set, causing a great deal of inconvenience and expense. Whenever the director, after the completion of his picture, made any changes, or recut his film, the score was usually ruined as it was obviously impossible to cut the sound track without harming the underlying continuity of the music. Occasionally we were able to make cuts that were not too noticeable.

At this time the process of re-recording was slowly being perfected, and we soon learned to score music *after* the completion of a picture. This had two advantages. It left the director free to cue his picture any way he pleased without hurting our work, and we were able to control the respective levels between dialogue and music, thereby clearing the dialogue.

To go back to 1931: With re-recording being rapidly improved, every studio again began to import conductors and musicians. At the time, I was general musical director for RKO Studios. I wrote *Symphony of Six Million*, and *Bird of Paradise* soon after, the first of which had about 40 per cent, and the latter 100 per cent musical scoring. Both pictures had been shot for music. The directors and producers wanted music to run throughout, and this gradual change of policy resulted in giving music its rightful chance. One-third to one-half of the success of these pictures was attributed to the extensive use of music.

After that many pictures were completely scored, one of which was *King Kong*. This score I wrote in two weeks and the music recording cost was around fifty thousand dollars. The picture was successful and the studio again attributed at least 25 per cent of its success to the music, which made the artificially animated animals more life-like, the battle and pursuit scenes more vivid. After this other studios followed suit and began to score their pictures. At this time I wrote the music for *The Lost Patrol*, directed by John Ford. Mr. Ford also directed *The Informer*, and he and I conferred on the use of music for this picture before it was shot. This was not the case with *The Lost Patrol*. At first it was not intended to have any music, but after the picture was finished the producer decided that, because of the long silent scenes, it was necessary to underscore the entire production.

In order to explain the modern technique and procedure of composing, directing, and recording music for the screen, I will outline my way of scoring which may differ to some extent from the systems adopted by composers and directors in other studios: but the fundamentals are the same.

When a picture is finished and finally edited, it is turned over to me. Then I time it: not by stop watch, however, as many do. I have the film put through a special measuring machine and then a cue sheet created which gives me the exact time, to a split second, in which an action takes place, or a word is spoken, as in the following example:

EXCERPT FROM CUE SHEET OF REEL III, PART I, OF *THE INFORMER*

	MIN.	SEC.	FEET	FRAMES
Cue: The captain throws money on table....................	0	0		
1. Gypo grabs money and exits...	20	30		
2. Door slams.................	26	39		
3. CUT to blind man...........	33	49	5	
4. Gypo grabs blind man's throat	41	61	6	
5. Gypo leaves him.............	58	87		
6. The blind man's step is heard...	1	5½	97	7

By comparing the respective timing, the reader will be able to discern the method of underscoring. The music for each cue is timed exactly by the number of feet and extra frames and by the number of minutes and seconds each cue runs.

While these cue sheets are being made, I begin to work on themes for the different characters and scenes, but without regard to the required timing. During this period I also digest what I have seen, and try to plan the music for this picture. There may be a scene that is played a shade too slowly which I might be able to quicken with a little animated music; or, to a scene that is too fast, I may be able to give a little more feeling by using slower music. Or perhaps the music can clarify a character's emotion, such as intense suffering, which is not demanded or fully revealed by a silent close-up, as, for instance, the scene in *The Charge of the Light Brigade,* where Errol Flynn forges the order sending six hundred to their death.

After my themes are set and my timing is completed, I begin to work. I run the picture reel by reel again, to refresh my memory. Then I put my stop watch on the piano, and try to compose the music that is necessary for the picture within the limits allowed by this timing. For instance: for fifteen seconds of soldiers marching, I may write martial music lasting fifteen seconds. Then the picture might cut to a scene at a railroad track, which lasts for six seconds, when I would change my music accordingly or let it end at the cut. Once all my themes are set I am apt to discard them and compose others, because frequently, after I have worked on a picture for a little while, my feeling towards it changes.

Having finally set my themes I begin the actual and tedious work of composing according to my cue sheets, endeavoring to help the mood and dramatic intent of the story as much as possible. The great difficulty lies in the many *cuts* (sections; different locations) which make up a modern motion picture. For example: The first two minutes on my imaginary cue sheet consist of the arrival of a train in some little town. I would use music that conforms with the pounding of the locomotive, a train whistle or the screeching of the brakes, and perhaps some gay music to cover the greetings of people getting on and off the train. After these two minutes, the picture cuts directly to the death bed of the father in a little attic in an outlying farmhouse, the scene lasting three minutes in all. I must, therefore, devise some method of modulating quickly and smoothly from the gay music in the station to the silence and tragedy in the death room. These two scenes would consume five minutes of the ten-minute reel, and at the point of the father's death we might cut directly to a cabaret in New York where the daughter is singing, not knowing that her father is dead. Here is a transition which I would not modulate at all. Instead, it would be very effective to let a hot jazz band bang right in as soon as the cut, or *short fade,* to the cabaret was completed.

There is nothing more effective in motion-picture music than sudden changes of mood cleverly handled, providing, of course, they are consistent with the story. During the cabaret scene, while the jazz orchestra is playing, if the daughter is notified of her father's death, it would be absolutely wrong to change from the hot tune in progress to music appropriate to her mood. We must consider the jazz orchestra as actual music, not as underscoring; and, in order to make this sequence realistic, we should contrive to make the music as happy and noisy as possible. For, in the first place, the orchestra leader does not know what has happened, and would, therefore, have no reason to change his music; and, second, no greater counterpoint has ever been found than gay music underlying a tragic scene, or vice versa. The latter, of course, applies only if the audience is aware of tragedy taking place unknown to the players.

Standard symphonic music, such as Beethoven's *Eroica,* should not be used in its entirety for the same reasons stated in my last paragraph. The change of locale and cutting back and forth make it almost impossible. For example, if I were to use a funeral march from the *Eroica,* however well it might fit the scene and mood, if the picture cut on the twelfth bar to a cabaret in the Bronx, what would I do with the funeral march by Beethoven? I would have to rewrite, discontinue or break it up in some way, and I, for one, am loath to recompose the old masters.

Furthermore, it is my conviction that familiar music, however popular, does not aid the underlying score of a dramatic picture. I believe that, while the American people are more musically minded than any other nation in the world, they are still not entirely familiar with all the old and new masters' works. I am, therefore, opposed to the use of thematic material that might cause an audience to wonder and whisper and try to recall the title of a particular composition, thereby missing the gist and significance of a whole scene which might be the key to the entire story. Of course there are many in our industry who disagree with my viewpoint.

In composing a score there are certain facts which I have found important to consider. For instance, it pays to watch the particular pitch in which a person talks. A high voice often becomes "muddy," with high-pitched musical accompaniment, and the same is true of the low pitch. I rarely combine these except when I want to attain a special effect, such as matching voice and orchestra so that one is indistinguishable from the other.

The speed of the dialogue is also of great importance to the modern motion-picture composer. Fast music, over a slow dialogue scene, may help to speed up the action, but it may also ruin the mood, whereas slow music, over a slow scene, may either fit admirably or retard the action to an unprecedented extent. I rarely use fast music over fast dialogue. Instead I try to punctuate a fast-moving dramatic scene with music which seems to be slower, but which, in reality, approximates the same speed.

Pronounced high solo instruments or very low ones, or sharp or strident effects (oboe, piccolo, muted trumpets, screaming violins, xylophone, bells, high clarinets, and muted horns fortissimo) are taboo with me, because we should be able to hear the entire combination of instruments behind the average dialogue. But I have found muted strings, harp, celeste and low woodwind effects to be successful. Of course, there are exceptions to this rule, and in many of my pictures I have broken it entirely.

In fact, by now, the reader may well ask: What's the matter with Steiner? In one paragraph he gives advice and sets down a rigid rule, and in the next he reverses it. That is true . . . there are no rules, and there won't be as long as music continues to assume more and more importance in pictures, and the development of sound continues to make such rapid strides.

When the music has been composed and orchestrated, the orchestra assembles on a sound stage, especially treated for acoustics. The modern music-recording stage has soft and hard *flats* (panels) which can be moved around the stage on rollers at will to accommodate the different orchestral and vocal sounds produced. The reason for the flexibility of these flats is the varying sizes of orchestras and choruses required to score a motion picture. Naturally, inside a theater an orchestra has a different tone quality than it would have out-of-doors; and, by the same token, a singer in a fairly small room would sound entirely different than the same singer in a large concert hall. In order to reproduce these tone qualities as closely as possible, these flats are moved around either to reduce or enlarge the size of the tone space required. Often these flats are not used at all, particularly when the orchestra or chorus is very large.

The monitor booth is usually located on the first floor, out of everyone's way. That is the room in which the recordist sits and manipulates the various dials (channels) which combine the different microphones and thereby produce the final orchestra sound track. This recordist, in most instances, is himself a former musician, or at least a person who has great interest in music. His work is tedious and of great responsibility, because of the enormous expense incurred during the recording of the picture, involving musicians' salaries and film expense.

If one considers that the orchestra may have to do ten to twenty takes of the same number in order to get one good recording, one can imagine the time involved, not to speak of the thousands of feet of film needed.

A good take can easily be spoiled by the noise of an overhead airplane. Many times mail planes pursuing their duty swoop a little too low over the recording stage during a very tender violin solo; and, of course, this recording cannot be used, as the most modern microphones are extraordinarily sensitive. Also accidents occur, such as the scraping of a chair, the dropping of a mute or a bow, or even the scraping of a shirt button on a stand, the swish of music sheets being turned over, or an unavoidable cough. It is not always a wrong note or a conductor's mistake which causes a take to go wrong. Sometimes the projection machine *freezes* (gets out of order) and it may take fifteen or twenty minutes to repair. With a fifty-piece orchestra the expense is about two hundred and fifty dollars in unused salaries for this twenty-minute delay, as the musician gets paid from the time he is called until he leaves, whether he plays or not.

To get back to our first rehearsal of a new picture: The orchestra is rehearsed a little more thoroughly than other orchestras, for the better an orchestra plays, the less takes will be required and the less money spent on salaries and film. During this rehearsal the recordist places his microphones according to the wishes of the conductor, who indicates what instruments or orchestra sections shall be specially emphasized or *miked*. Then, when this is accomplished, while someone else conducts, the conductor goes upstairs to the booth to determine whether everything is to his liking. If it is, we then record our first take. Of course long association between recordists and conductors results in tremendous speed in balancing. I work with recordists whom I trust so implicitly that I rarely go up into the booth unless the recordist asks for advice, such as in the case of a special orchestral effect I wanted for the money theme in *The Informer*.

After our first take, we play it back. That means a loud speaker plays back the record that has been made on a separate recording machine, but which reproduces exactly the same result as on the film itself. It stands to reason that we cannot replay an undeveloped film; for, first of all, the negative would be spoiled, and, second, we would need a dark room for unloading, loading and re-winding. Should this playback be satisfactory, we go into our next sequence; rehearsal again, and we proceed exactly as before. We make as many takes as necessary until we get a perfect recording.

Each film is divided into sections of a thousand feet, and one such section is called a reel. A modern feature film consists of approximately nine to ten thousand feet. The latest projection machines in the theaters are able to run films of two thousand feet each, which are simply the first and second thousand-foot reel spliced together. However, the laboratories only develop thousand-foot reels. In recording music, we divide a reel into as many sections as possible, for it is much easier for musicians and conductor to remember a two-minute scene than a ten-minute one.

In writing the music and recording it, great care must be taken by orchestra and conductor that the overlaps are properly handled, so that when the film is finally completed the listener is not conscious of the "breaks."

With our first day's recording over, we await the next morning with great expectation, or, shall I say . . . anxiety . . . when the laboratory sends the developed and printed recordings back to the studio for us to hear and pick takes. We sometimes print two or three recordings of the same number to be on the safe side, and in some instances intercut from one to the other. For instance, in a composition of one hundred and twenty bars' duration, the first ninety bars may be perfect whereas the last thirty may have been spoiled by any one of the aforementioned factors.

Our profession is not always "a bed of roses," and looks much easier to the layman than it really is. The work is hard and exacting, and when the dreaded "release date" is upon us, sleep is a thing unknown. I have had stretches of work for fifty-six consecutive hours without sleep, in order to complete a picture for the booking date. The reason for this is the fact that the major film companies sell their pictures for a certain date before they have even been produced; and, if the film's final editing has been delayed through some unforeseen happening, the music and re-recording departments have to pitch in to make up for lost time.

After we have picked our developed takes which have been returned by the laboratory, and providing everything is satisfactory, these takes are turned over to the music cutter and he synchronizes them to the film and dialogue track. When these tracks have finally been set up the entire film is taken up to the re-recording room. There both dialogue and music are mixed and regulated; again numerous takes are made; and impurities of the film and sound tracks are ironed out. These re-recording sessions are every bit as tedious and painstaking as the original recordings, since they constitute the final product. The next day, when these re-recorded takes come back from the laboratory, the same procedure of picking the best takes is followed. This time, of course, more attention is paid to the ratio between dialogue, music and sound effects.

Then, some evening, the picture is given a *sneak* preview at some obscure theater, where only the highest executives are allowed to witness its initial showing. The studio management thereby wishes to prevent any unfavorable opinion from penetrating the papers before the final editing. Should the projection equipment have been in mediocre or very bad condition, the sound and music departments would be the butt of unfavorable criticism. Happily for us, all picture theaters, including the small neighborhood houses, are gradually buying or renting new first-class standard equipment. I think most of our troubles in that respect will be over in another year or so.

I have often been asked: What are the requirements that make for a competent film composer-conductor? I would answer: ability, good disposition, PATIENCE. A thousand and one things can happen to a music sound track from the time it leaves the composer's brain until it is heard by the audience. I have had pictures which did not require any music whatsoever, according to the producers. Some of these turned out to be 100 per cent underscoring jobs. On other pictures I was told that a certain film could not be released without an entire underscoring job, and I would work for weeks, day and night. When the finished product left the studio to go to the exchanges, only 60 per cent of all the music written remained. Many factors cause this: a bad preview reaction, very bad sound, the unfortunate presence of a director or producer, who might still be opposed to the use of music throughout, or dialogue that may have been recorded too softly at the outset, so that no music could be heard at the low level required to keep this dialogue intelligible.

In some instances a composer or musical director himself may feel that music did not help a particular scene. This is not always easy to recognize in the studio projection room because of the absence of any audience reaction. Besides, one who works to a film is apt to get so used to the dialogue that he knows it by heart, and, therefore, does not miss any part of it during the multitude of runnings which are required to complete the job.

From *We Make the Movies,* edited by Nancy Naumburg (New York: W. W. Norton, 1937), pp. 216–31. Copyright 1937 by W. W. Norton & Company, Inc. Used by permission of W. W. Norton & Company, Inc.

23

Some Experiences in Film Music

Erich Wolfgang Korngold

(1940)

When I came to Hollywood about six years ago, I knew no more about films and their making than any other mortal who buys his ticket at the box office. It was not even known to me that music—which happens to be my particular field—is only in rare cases recorded together with the picture, that is to say at the same time the camera photographs a scene. But my very first assignment, Reinhardt's production of *Midsummer Night's Dream,* was to make me familiar with all three music techniques. For this production, I had to make preliminary recordings, the so-called playbacks of Mendelssohn's scherzo and nocturne, which were relayed over huge loudspeakers during the actual filming. Further, I conducted an orchestra on the stage for complicated, simultaneous "takes"; and lastly, after the film was cut, I conducted a number of music pieces which were inserted in the completed picture as background music. In addition, however, I had to invent another, *new* method which was a combination of all three techniques and which was for music accompanying the *spoken word.* I wrote the music in advance, conducted—without orchestra—the actor on the stage in order to make him speak his lines in the required rhythm, and then, sometimes weeks later, guided by earphones, I recorded the orchestral part.

The playback system, which is used mostly for songs and dances in the so-called musicals, is without doubt the most satisfactory method for the composer. It not only enables him to create freely and independently but it also leaves him undisturbed by all kinds of noises such as cannon shots, ship sirens, rain and thunder storms. No dialogue—the composer's most hated rival—not even the softest footsteps (let alone galloping horses, rattling automobiles or roaring railroad trains!) interfere with his music. I myself have made only one such happy musical. Since *Captain Blood* I have been busy exclusively with the third and last technique—that of scoring. And I must confess that, despite the definite advantages offered the composer by the playback, I consider the task of composing and recording music for the completed picture the most interesting and, for the composer, the most stimulating. When in the projection room or through the operator's little window, I am watching the picture unroll, when I am sitting at the piano improvising or inventing themes and tunes, when I am facing the orchestra conducting my music, I have the feeling that I am giving my own and my best: Symphonically dramatic music which fits the picture, its action, and its psychology, and which, nevertheless, will be able to hold its own in the concert hall. And if the picture inspires me, I don't even have to measure or count the seconds or feet. If I am really inspired, I have luck. And my friend, the cutter, helps my luck along.

However, I am fully aware of the fact that I seem to be working under much more favorable conditions than my Hollywood colleagues who quite often have to finish a score in a very short time and in conjunction with several other composers.

So far, I have successfully resisted the temptations of an all-year contract because, in my opinion, that would force me into factory-like mass production. I have refused to compose music for a picture in two or three weeks or in an even shorter period. I have limited myself to compositions for just two major pictures a year.

Further, I am told that my method of composing is entirely different from that employed by other Hollywood composers. I am not composing at a desk writing music mechanically, so to speak, for the lengths of film measured out by an assistant and accompanied with sketchy notes on the action of those section, but I do my composing in the projection room *while the picture is unrolling before my eyes.* And I have it run off for me again and again, reel by reel, as often as I need to see it.

It is entirely up to me to decide where in the picture to put music. But I always consult thoroughly with the music-chief whose judgment, based on years of experience, I consider highly important. I also keep the producer well informed and always secure his consent for my musical intentions first. But in none of my assignments have I ever "played" my music first to either the music-chief, the director or the producer. And the studio heads never make the acquaintance of my music until the day of the sneak preview. The executive producer always calls me in for the running of the picture's final cut and I am invited to voice my opinion for or against proposed changes, and I may make suggestions myself.

The actual composing of the music is not begun until the final cut of the picture is ready. But most of my leading themes and general mood motifs suggest themselves to me on reading the manuscript. Only when the picture has reached the stage of the final cut can I proceed to compose the exact lengths needed for the different music spots. Changes after the preview are often painful although, fortunately, I have not suffered any particularly smarting musical losses.

I have often been asked whether, in composing film music, I have to consider the public's taste and present understanding of music. I can answer that question calmly in the negative. Never have I differentiated between my music for the films and that for the operas and concert pieces. Just as I do for the operatic stage, I try to invent for the motion picture dramatically melodious music with symphonic development and variation of the themes.

The toughest problem in film music production is and remains the *dupe* system, *i.e.* the combining of dialogue, sound and music. It is difficult from the beginning to strike the right balance between dialogue and music, but it is achieved fairly accurately in the small intimate dupe room which is acoustically ideal. However, when the film reaches the theatres which are large, noisy, acoustically uneven, often poorly equipped, this delicate balance is easily upset, and even distorted.

But I am convinced that in time better solutions will be found. Motion pictures are young and neither the public nor those who are making them have a right to be impatient or ungrateful for what has already been achieved.

From *Music and Dance in California*, edited by José Rodríguez, compiled by William J. Perlman (Hollywood: Bureau of Musical Research, 1940), pp. 137–39.

24

What Is a Filmusical?

Denis Morrison

(1937)

The picture industry this season moves definitely out of the woods on musicals.

A number of majors think that they have evolved foolproof formulas for tune features. Formulas are not all the same, far from it, but the probability is that they are all correct. Anyway, as producers have a way of doing, they put their faith in grosses more than in their own judgment.

As in every phase of this biz, the public has told Hollywood what to do and Hollywood is doing it. Trial and error all over again. The time for experimenting is over. Nowadays, when a major lot sets out to make a musical, the heads know exactly what has to be done, and the measure of success depends on how well qualified are the experts who do the work.

Proof that this thesis is correct is seen in the fact that no less than five cleffed features will go, or have gone, this year with the earmark of the hardy perennial on them. That is, they will be the first of a series, taking after the tried and true *Broadway Melody* series of Metro and *Gold Diggers* of Warners.

THE NEW CROP

New series getting the gun this season are: *Artists and Models,* Paramount (which already has *Big Broadcast*); *Merry-Go-Round,* Universal; *New Faces,* Radio; *Goldwyn Follies,* Goldwyn; *Hit Parade,* Republic; *Walter Wanger's Vogues,* Wanger.

Question comes: What makes a musical click?

Ask around and you'll get a lot of answers, the diversity of which would surprise you.

Industry has toiled long and put out many millions in learning how to wrap up musical entertainment and peddle it to the public. In the end the producers have, by and large, come back pretty closed to the familiar formula of the oldtime extravaganza, a sort of super-variety entertainment. Elements are girls, gags and tunes, with opinion almost, but not quite, unanimous in favor of sound story values as well.

How to blend these elements most effectively, and where to find the talent to do it, have been the brain-fagging problems for the film impresarios. It's got so out here that the quickest and surest way to film success is to have something that a big musical can use—as witness Buddy Ebsen, Martha Raye, Harriet Hilliard, Fred Astaire, Ella Logan, to name a few, and also the grand opera warblers such as Lily Pons, Gladys Swarthout, Nino Martini and Grace Moore.

Jack Warner and Darryl Zanuck started the search for the wining musical formula as far back as 1928 when Warners got the jump with sound. First Warner musicals socked the b.o. [box office] bell an awful wallop because, in those days, anything went that made a noise. Came the era of the theme song and the whole setup went sour. Songwriters and musicians, who had flocked around the lots in droves, slunk away again. No one wanted them. Some even declaimed openly that the public had turned thumbs down to filmusicals for good.

FAITH WINS OUT

That wasn't the case, as everyone now knows. Only trouble was the producers hadn't mastered the medium. And today Zanuck and Warner are far apart in their notions of what makes a musical show.

"The keynote of a successful screen musical is improbability," says Warner, "the best and liveliest tunes and just enough plot to string everything together."

Zanuck, on the other hand, is a believer in story values, no matter what kind of picture he's making. All the Zanuck musicals are stoutly equipped with plot.

Analysis shows that the big 20th-Fox and Warner musicals, and others as well, have one important element in common—the comparative unimportance of the director. When actual shooting time comes the layout is complete, step by step.

Most of the successful Metro musicals have had sound story values in addition to other "musts," which Louis B. Mayer lists as "quality music played and sung by the best artists obtainable, production value and spectacle, plus a dramatic believable story."

Even Metro's *The Great Ziegfeld,* which stressed spectacle more than most, had strong drama, its producer, William Anthony McGuire, points out.

"The formula of Ziegfeld himself," says McGuire, was music and beautiful girls, costumes and settings. We used all these elements, plus Ziegfeld's own story, which was essentially dramatic.

"The present-day screen public will not be content with just enough plot to hang the musical numbers on. They insist on believing the stories they unfolded, if that's possible."

Zanuck demands certain qualities in musicals, in addition to story. These he lists as "spontaneity and lightness, fresh comedy, new faces different song hits, new personalities, new backgrounds." This year, Zanuck says, 20th-Fox is going to the race track, to the gridiron, to Switzerland and to the Arabian Nights for fresh and colorful backgrounds.

Universal's musical standard bearer is B. G. DeSylva, who foresees the vital necessity of developing new talent for musicals of the future. Talent is what Buddy DeSylva is concentrating on for *Young Man's Fancy* and *Merry-Go-Round of 1938*.

He has bunched Bert Lahr, Billy House, Jimm Savo and Mischa Auer in the first as "the four horsemen of hilarity" and it will be Auer's bow as a filmusical comedian. "There are just as many clever people out of pictures as in them," is DeSylva's credo, "and it's our job to dig them up and develop their talents." It took years for the picture business to discover W. C. Fields.

Ever since the oldtime combo of DeSylva, Brown & Henderson made *Sunny Side Up* for Fox Films—one of the big all-time grossers of film biz—DeSylva has been a stickler for story. On top of sound story values he piles gals, gags and tunes, interspersed with original dance routines and musical novelties. In *Young Man's Fancy* he will introduce, in addition to tested personalities, Alice Brady, Louise Fazenda and Ella Logan; Casper Reardon, swing harpist; Larry Black, also a "hot" harpist and a comedian; "Scat" Powell, singer; and the three Diamond brothers.

"You will see that I am bringing in a lot of new personalities," DeSylva points out. "That is because I am convinced that the injection of new personalities from the stage has meant more than any other single factor for the advancement of filmusicals.

FROM AN OLD FORMULA

Nathaniel Shilkret, RKO-Radio's musical director, believes that the present-day filmusical is nothing more than an adaptation of the old Gilbert & Sullivan formula and that it's taken the picture industry seven years of trial and error to make that discovery.

"Film makers," says Shilkret, "used to have the habit of shoving a song into a picture just because it was a pretty song. That was horrible. Nowadays we know better. Music was abused in the old days and I believe it was when RKO-Radio bodily lifted *Rio Rita* from the stage to the screen that the transition was accomplished. Effect of that was electrifying."

Shilkret remembers the days when musicals were in such evil grace with audiences that *Viennese Nights* was exploited as "a musical with only one song."

Radio is going heavily for musicals this year, as witness the Nino Martini features, Lily Pons and other pix, including *Joy of Living* with Irene Dunne. In this one the Gilbert & Sullivan formula will be closely followed, with Jerome Kern, Dorothy Fields and Herbert Fields collabbing all the way on story, music, lyrics and screenplay.

The musical destinies of Paramount have been placed largely in the hands of William LeBaron, production executive and Boris Morros, music chief. Morros is another believer in complete advance preparation. Newcomers on the Paramount music talent list are Augustine Lara, George Antheil and Kurt Weill. Morros is angling for Stravinsky, Aaron Copland and Richard Hageman.

SHOT THROUGH WITH TUNES

Music will figure in 40 of Paramount's 60 production on the forthcoming season's program. Topper about to hit the theatres is Jerome Kern's *High, Wide and Handsome,* on which the studio went to town. Other ambitious musicals coming along include *Sapphire Sal,* with Mae West; *Chocolate Parade,* all-sepia tuner for which an attempt is being made to corral all the top available Negro talent (Louis Armstrong's band already pacted); *Big Broadcast,* in which Kirsten Flagstad will be heard chirping out of Wagner's "Die Walküre"; *College Swing* and *Artists and Models,* now in work. Contemplated are *The Count of Luxemburg* and *Vagabond King.* Big Crosby is down for *Double or Nothing* and *Paris Honeymoon;* Gladys Swarthout and John Boles for *Yellow Nightingale.*

Morros says, "New generation knows more about music and is more sensitive. To get what I want I take part in story discussion and remain in close touch with the producer and director from the inception of a picture until the finish. My staff has many specialists and I try to assign to each man the sort of thing he can do best."

Columbia while maintaining no staff of specialists, will spare neither expense nor pains on the musicals it puts out, especially the Grace Moores. Production assignments are passed around the staff.

From *Variety*, June 16, 1937, pp. 3 and 10. Copyright © 2009 Reed Business Information, a division of Reed Elsevier Inc. Reprinted by permission.

25

Music in the Films

Aaron Copland

(1941)

With the radio and the phonograph, the music track of the sound film must be set down as a revolutionizing force in today's music. The medium is so new, and the possibilities so vast, that this brief chapter can hardly do more than introduce the subject. Even so, it treats of little more than the Hollywood aspect of film music. Though artistically of a low order, historically the music of the West Coast is certain to loom large in any stocktaking of filmdom's musical achievements.

Everyone is so prepared to hear the worst about Hollywood that it is a pleasure to be able to start these observations on a cheerful note. The best one can say about Hollywood is that it is a place where composers are actually needed. The accent is entirely on the living composer. Day after day and year after year there are copyists, instrumentalists, and conductors who do nothing but copy, perform, and conduct the music of contemporary composers. Theoretically, at any rate, the town is a composer's Eldorado.

For the movies do need music and need it badly. By itself the screen is a pretty cold proposition. In Hollywood I looked at long stretches of film before the music had been added, and I got the impression that music is like a small flame put under the screen to help warm it.

It is this very function, however, which so often gives the composer a minor role. There is no sense in denying the subordinate position the composer fills. After all, film music makes sense only if it helps the film; no matter how good, distinguished, or successful, the music must be secondary in importance to the story being told on the screen. Essentially there is nothing about the movie medium to rule out any composer with a dramatic imagination. But the man who insists on complete self-expression had better stay home and write symphonies. He will never be happy in Hollywood.

Whether you are happy or not largely depends on two factors: the producer you work for and the amount of time allotted for completing the score. (I am assuming that the film itself is an intelligent one.) The producer is a kind of dictator, responsible only to the studio executives for every phase of the picture's production. This naturally includes the musical score. The trouble is not so much that these producers consider themselves musical connoisseurs but that they claim to be accurate barometers of public taste. "If I can't understand it, the public won't." As a result of this the typical Hollywood composer is concerned not with the reaction of the public, as you might think, but with that of the producer. It isn't surprising therefore, that all film music originating in Hollywood tends to be very much the same. The score of one picture adds up to about the score of any other. You seldom hear anything fresh or distinctive partly because everyone is so intent on playing safe. A pleased producer means more jobs. That alone is sufficient to explain the Hollywood stereotype of music.

The demand for speed from the composer is familiar to anyone who has ever worked "in pictures." The composer may sit around no end of time, waiting for the picture to be done; as soon as it's finished the director, the producer, the script writer—everybody—is in a frightful hurry; valuable time is passing, and the studio has visions of the money it is losing each day that the film is not in a theater. It is difficult to make studio executives realize that no one has yet discovered how to write notes any faster than it was done circa A.D. 400. The average movie score is approximately forty minutes long. The usual time allotted for composing it is about two weeks. For *Of Mice and Men* I had about six weeks, and I believe that other composers insist on that much time for writing an elaborate score.

The purpose of the film score is to make the film more effective; that's clear enough. But I don't think anyone has as yet formulated the perfect solution for this problem. In fact, I came away with a sense of the mysterious nature of all film music. In retrospect, I can see three important ways in which music helps a picture. The first is by intensifying the emotional impact of any given scene, the second by creating an illusion of continuity, and the third by providing a kind of neutral background music. Of these three, the last presents the most mysterious problem—how to supply the right sort of music behind dialogue.

Intensification of emotion at crucial moments is, of course, an old tradition of theater music. True, it is no more than the hearts-and-flowers tradition, but still, perfectly legitimate. The one difficulty here is to get the music started without suddenly making the audience aware of its entrance. To use a favorite Hollywood term, you must "steal the music in."

Obvious, too, is the continuity function of music. Pictures, jumping from episode to episode, from exterior to interior, have a tendency to fall apart. Music, an art that exists in time, can subtly hold disparate scenes together. In exciting montage sequences where the film moves violently from shot to shot, music, by developing one particular theme or one type of rhythmical material or some other unifying musical element, supplies the necessary continuous understructure.

But "background" music is something very special. It is also the most ungrateful kind of music for a composer to write. Since it's music behind, or underneath, the word, the audience is really not going to hear it, possibly won't even be aware of its existence; yet it undoubtedly works on the subconscious mind. The need here is for a kind of music that will give off a "neutral" color or atmosphere. (This is what creates the indefinable warmth that the screen itself lacks.) To write music that must be inexpressive is not easy for composers who normally tend to be as expressive as possible. To add to the difficulty, there's the impossibility of knowing in advance just what will work in any given scene. If one could only test the music by adding it to the scene before it is shot or have the music performed while the actors speak their lines! But this is utopian. Once the scene is done and the music is added, the result is fairly problematical. Even dubbing it down almost below the listening level will not always prove satisfactory.

If Hollywood has its problems it has also its well-known solutions. Most scores, as everyone knows, are written in the late nineteenth century symphonic style, a style now so generally accepted as to be considered inevitable. But why need movie music be symphonic? And why, oh, why, the nineteenth century? Should the rich harmonies of Tschaikovsky, Franck, and Strauss be spread over every type of story, regardless of time, place, or treatment? For *Wuthering Heights,* perhaps yes. But why for *Golden Boy,* a hard-boiled, modern piece? What screen music badly needs is more differentiation, more feeling for the exact quality of each picture. That does not necessarily mean a more literal musical description of time and place. Certainly very few Hollywood films give a realistic impression of period. Still, it should be possible, without learned displays of historical research and without the hack conventions of symphonic music, for a composer to reflect the emotion and reality of the individual picture he is scoring.

Another pet Hollywood formula, this one borrowed from nineteenth century opera, is the use of the leitmotiv. I haven't made up my mind whether the public is conscious of this device or completely oblivious to it, but I can't see how it is appropriate to the movies. It may help the spectator sitting in the last row of the opera house to identify the singer who appears from the wings for the orchestra to announce her motif. But that's hardly necessary on the screen. No doubt the leitmotiv system is a help to the composer in a hurry, perhaps doing two or three scores simultaneously. It is always an easy solution mechanically to pin a motif on every character. In a high-class horse opera I saw this method was reduced to its final absurdity. One theme announced the Indians, another the hero. In the inevitable chase, every time the scene switched from Indians to hero the themes did, too, sometimes so fast that the music seemed to hop back and forth before any part of it had time to breathe. If there must be thematic description, I think it would serve better if it were connected with the underlying ideas of a picture. If, for example, a film has to do with loneliness, a theme might be developed to induce sympathy with the idea of being lonely, something broader in feeling than the mere tagging of characters.

A third device, and one very peculiar to Hollywood, is known as "Mickey-Mousing" a film. In this system the music, wherever possible, is made to mimic everything that happens on the screen. An actor can't lift an eyebrow without the music helping him do it. What is amusing when applied to a Disney fantasy becomes disastrous in its effect upon a straight or serious drama. Max Steiner has a special weakness for this device. In *Of Human Bondage* he had the unfortunate idea of making his music limp whenever the clubfooted hero walked across the scene, with a very obvious and, it seemed to me, vulgarizing effect. Recently, Mr. Steiner has shown a fondness for a new device. This is the mixing of realistic music with background music. Joe may be walking around the room quietly humming a tune to himself (realistic use of music). Watch for the moment when Joe steps out into the storm, for it is then that Mr. Steiner pounces upon Joe's little tune and gives us the works with an orchestra of seventy. The trouble with this procedure is that it stresses not so much the dramatic moment as the ingenuity of the composer. All narrative illusion is lost the instant we are conscious of the music as such.

It may not be without interest to retrace some of the steps by which music is added to a film. After the picture is completed, it is shown in the studio projection room before the producer, the director, the studio's musical director (if any), the composer and his various henchmen, the conductor, the orchestrator, the cue-sheet assistants, the copyists—anybody, in fact, who has anything to do with the preparation of the score. At this showing the decision is reached as to where to add music, where it should start in each separate sequence, and where it should end. The film is then turned over to a cue-sheet assistant whose job it is to prepare a listing of every separate moment in each musical sequence. These listings, with the accompanying timing in film footage and in seconds, is all that the composer needs for complete security in synchronizing his music with the film. The practiced Hollywood composer is said never to look at a picture more than once. With a good memory, a stop watch, and a cue sheet, he is ready to go to work. Others prefer to work in the music projection room where there are a piano, a screen, and an operator who can turn the film on and off. I myself used a movieola, which permits every composer to be his own operator. This is a small machine that shows the film positive through a magnifying glass. Using the movieola, I could see the picture whenever and as often as I pleased.

While the music is being written, the film itself is prepared for recording. Each important musical cue must be marked on the film by some prearranged signal system that varies in every studio. These "signals" show the conductor where he is. If he wants to hit a certain musical cue that, according to the cue sheet, occurs at the forty-ninth second, the film must be marked in such a way as to indicate that spot (always with sufficient warning signals), and if the conductor is competent he can nearly always "hit it on the nose." In Hollywood this knack for hitting cues properly is considered even more important in a conductor than his ability to read an orchestral score. Another method, much more mechanical but used a good deal for Westerns and quickies, is to synchronize by means of a so-called "click track." In this case, the film is measured off not according to seconds but according to regular musical beats. There is no surer method for hitting cues "on the nose." But only the experienced composer can ignore the regularity of the beat and write his music freely within and around it.

For the composer the day of recording is perhaps the high point. He has worked hard and long and is anxious to test his work. He hears his music sounded for the first time while the film is being shown. Everything comes off just as it would in a concert hall. But if he wishes to remain happy he had better stay away from the sound-recording booth. For here all the music is being recorded at about the same medium dynamic level so that later on the loudness and softness may be regulated when the moment comes for rerecording.

Rerecording takes place in the dubbing room. This is a kind of composer's purgatory. It is here that the music track is mixed with other sound tracks—the dialogue, the "effects" track, and so forth. It is at this point that the composer sees his music begin to disappear. A passage once so clear and satisfying seems now to move farther and farther off. The instant a character opens his mouth, the music must recede to the near vanishing point. This is the place that calls out all a composer's self-control: it's a moment for philosophy.

From the composer's standpoint, the important person in the dubbing room is the man who sits at the controls. It is he who decides how loud or soft the music will be at any given moment, and therefore it is he who can make or ruin everything by the merest touch of the dials. But surprisingly, in every studio these controls are in the hands of a sound engineer. What I don't understand is why a musician has not been called in for this purpose. It would never occur to me to call in an engineer to tune my piano. Surely only a musician can be sensitive to the subtle effects of musical sound, particularly when mixed with other sounds. A Toscanini would be none too good for such a job—certainly a sound expert is not qualified.

While on the subject of sound levels, I might as well mention the unsatisfactory way in which sound is controlled in the picture theater. The tonal volume of a picture is not set for all time; no mechanical contraption permanently fixes the loudness or softness of the music. The person who decides on the sound levels is not even the film operator but the individual theater manager, who is, of course, susceptible to advice from Tom, Dick, and Harry sitting anywhere in the house. People who love music tend to prefer it played loudly. Those who don't care for it especially want to hear it only at a low level. So no matter how much care is taken in the dubbing room to fix proper tonal levels, the situation will remain unsatisfactory until a method is found to control the casual and arbitrary way in which dials are set in the theater operator's booth.

Hollywood, like Vienna, can boast its own star roster of composers. Alfred Newman, Max Steiner, Victor Young, Anthony Collins are composers created by the film industry. It is easy enough to poke fun at the movie music they turn out as so much yardage, but it would at the same time be foolish not to profit by their great experience in writing for the films. Newman, for example, has discovered the value of the string orchestra as a background for emotional scenes. Better than the full orchestra, the strings can be depersonalized. This is important in a medium where the sound of a single instrument may sometimes be disturbing. Another secret of movie music that Steiner has exploited is the writing of atmosphere music almost without melodic content of any kind. A melody is by its nature distracting, since it calls attention to itself. For certain types of neutral music, a kind of melodyless music is needed. Steiner does not supply mere chords but superimposes a certain amount of melodic motion, just enough to make the music sound normal and yet not enough to compel attention.

Composers who come to Hollywood from the big world outside generally take some time to become expert in using the idiom. Erich Korngold still tends to get overcomplex in the development of a musical idea. This is not always true, however. When successful, he gives a sense of firm technique, a continuity of not only feeling but structure. Werner Janssen, whose score for *The General Died at Dawn* made movie history, is still looked upon as something of an outsider. He shows his pre-Hollywood training in the sophistication of his musical idiom and in his tendency to be overfussy in the treatment of even the simplest sequence. Ernst Toch, who belongs in the category with Korngold and Janssen, wrote an important score for *Peter Ibbetson* several years ago. On the strength of this job, Toch should be today one of the best known film composers. But unfortunately there aren't enough people in Hollywood who can tell a good score when they hear one. Today Toch is generally assigned to do "screwy music." (In Hollywood music is either "screwy" or "down to earth"—and most of it is down to earth.) Toch deserves better. The latest addition to Hollywood's roster of "outsiders" is Louis Gruenberg, who composed a distinguished score for *So Ends Our Night*.

The men who write Hollywood's music seem strangely oblivious of their reputations outside the West Coast. I have often wondered, for instance, why no concerted effort has ever been made to draw the attention of music critics to their more ambitious scores. Why shouldn't the music critic cover important film *premières*? True, the audience that goes to the films doesn't think about the music and possibly shouldn't think about the music. Nevertheless, a large part of music heard by the American public is heard in the film theater. Unconsciously, the cultural level of music is certain to be raised if better music is written for films. This will come about more quickly, I think, if producers and directors know that scores are being heard and criticized. One of the ways they will find out what's good and what's bad is to read it in the papers. Let the press now take this important business in hand.

From *Our New Music* (New York: McGraw-Hill, 1941), pp. 260–75. "Music in the Films" by Aaron Copland is reproduced by permission of The Aaron Copland Fund for Music, Inc., copyright owner.

26

Music or Sound Effects?

Harold C. Schonberg

(1947)

Music in the movies is nothing new; good music is. Back in the nickelodeon and early silent film era the town's piano teacher had steady employment in the local theatre. So did *Hearts and Flowers,* left-hand tremolos, the *Hall of the Mountain King* and other tried and true classics. Later on, as culture and the movies advanced side by side, the town's instrumentalists plus the pianist—anywhere from ten players to an orchestra of some fifty in the larger cities—had steady employment. So did *Hearts and Flowers,* orchestral tremolos and the *Hall of the Mountain King.*

Less music is encountered today. What there is on the sound track is definitely more sophisticated. It may even be better, in some instances, though in determining the point of precedency one is reminded of Dr. Johnson's refusal to arbitrate the point of superiority of two certain winged creatures. In point of actual performance values, of course, there is no contest. Hollywood orchestras are composed of very capable musicians and enjoy the benefit of the best high-fidelity reproduction. There is, too, constant experimentation with musical sound effect—something little known a score of years ago; and here we get into something new which has been and still is confusing people.

Quantities of books and articles have been written about the problems of movie music, but nobody has ever really defined the subject they are criticizing. The scope takes in everything from the percussive, heart-beat taps in *The Fight for Life* to Heifetz and Reiner playing the Tchaikovsky concerto in *Carnegie Hall.* The trouble with much discussion of movie music, it seems to me, is that no difference is made between music as music and music as sound effects. If the difference can be cleared up it might perhaps admit of a clearer basis for criticism.

Sounds cannot be criticized musically. They may be judged from the psychological, emotional or physiological view, but not the musical. Music presupposes continuity and organization, and until we have that there is no point talking about its worth. In the motion picture much use is made of sound, whether the result of mechanical or musical instruments. Hearing the latter, one's mind has a tendency to jump to the conclusion that it is music, though with as much justification as calling an array of colors on a palette a painting.

Suppose a composer is called upon to supply background for a film featuring the atomic blast. In an effort to match the horrendous image on the screen at the moment of explosion, he suddenly juxtaposes it with a dissonant, fortissimo chord played by full orchestra. In conception it may be psychologically just, with timbres that would have ravished Berlioz. It also may be much more effective than any amount of music—but it has no continuity. It remains pure sound. This is a simple instance. To take a fuller and more concrete example, in the film *Caesar and Cleopatra* the composer, Georges Auric, was confronted with a sequence in which Caesar, at night, is contemplating the Sphinx. Auric obtained the effect of the brooding night and the brooding Caesar by a dissonant, low-pitched pedal point over which the high winds interjected occasional shrill pipings to imitate the sound of insects. Very effective, too; but again not music, by any definition of the word. In most of this film Auric used similar methods, and all any music reviewer or listener could say was that they were or were not successful emotionally or functionally. Those sounds could not be criticized as music, since they had no pattern, no connected flow, no sequence. In short, Auric did a fine job of using musical instruments to point up a mood, but he did not create music.

It so happens that the technique of sound effects has reached a high point of perfection. It could well be argued that, as film philosophy now stands, they are handled more artistically than music. They complement the action admirably, they are self-explanatory, they fill in needed gaps and are seldom in bad taste. There is nothing like poor music to take the edge off an otherwise good scene; and sound effects generally have the virtue of not offending artistically. But by the same token, sound effects (whether done by an engineer, by a Copland or Prokofieff) are of no critical concern to the music lover, who confines his attention to the genuinely musical sequences.

A genuinely musical sequence can be defined as one which must have continuity, if only for a brief while. It must attempt a definite melodic or rhythmic outline (whether jazz, romantic, classic or atonal), and must have a minimum of development, no matter how unorthodox. In short, it is more than pure sound; it is sound logically organized. The result is music—functional, often entirely different from concert-hall music—but it is still music and to be judged as such. It is not a sound effect; and when the word "music" is used in this article it refers only to sound logically organized into a recognizable sequence, as contrasted to sound used as an end in itself for emotional purposes.

Quite a few composers handle sound effects for the films very imaginatively; very few handle music imaginatively. If this sounds like an exaggerated statement, that is because most people do not pay special attention to the music that accompanies a film. Indeed, it takes training to keep one ear focussed on the sound track while the eye is focussed on the screen. Try it sometime; and if you get the knack of simultaneous concentration you soon will notice the ever-present formulae. After a while you will pray for something new; something showing even a tiny bit of originality. You will become fully acquainted with the musical customs and associations built up over the years. A bassoon and a lopsided rhythmic figure invariably accompanies the intoxicated person. An impasse in a romantic comedy is hailed by squealing flutes and burlesque harmonies. Alarums and excursions without accompany the credits. And so on. Even the melodies sound the same from one picture to the next; and small wonder. Those conventions have been played out for some years now, with precious little new added.

Thus the reviewer of film music is forced to sound sour notes. Hollywood is not creating music; it is mass-producing it. There is much music in the majority of films but it creates no great joy in the music lover's heart. What concerns him is not the number of notes per film, but the quality. If music must be used, he wants good music. Not necessarily great music, but music with at least a modicum of originality, or charm, or instrumental resource or ingenuity. Anything but the standardized product that constitutes the majority of background in the typical American product.

There are any number of excellent composers who are fully able to write movie music which would meet the highest critical standards. Few have had the chance. When Hollywood attempts something really ambitious in the way of a score, the assignment will fall into the hands of the cliché expert—one who knows film technique, one who is reliable (i.e., will not offend by anything daring), one who has every virtue but the ability to integrate his sounds into an original, consecutive musical pattern. What finally emerges is a pastiche that would be laughed out of existence in the concert hall. It is significant that the movie scores which have been universally acclaimed the best, the movie scores which the screen proudly hails as its contribution to musical culture—among them *Lieutenant Kije* and *Alexander Nevsky* (both by Prokofieff), *The Blow That Broke the Plains* (Thomson), and *Quiet City* (Copland)[1]—have achieved solid recognition as music that can be enjoyed without the artificial prop of accompanying action. With the action, so much the better; but those composers have enough innate ability to deal with the materials of music in a creative fashion. Naturally not all film scores can be as good or as self-sufficient, no more than ballet music can always stand as an entity divorced from the action; but at the very least one can look for imagination, musical probity and seriousness of purpose.

All of the foregoing scores and other good ones like *Dead of Night* (Auric) and *Odd Man Out* (Alwyn) are, incidentally, serious in nature. Very little outstanding light cinema music is encountered, one of the reasons being that good light music is notoriously harder to compose than good serious music. Hollywood's idea of light music is either cute synchronization, or built-up jazz, or dismally sentimental songs that make the Hit Parade and soon disappear forever. Only the music to a few Disney shorts shows originality in that sphere. I also remember with pleasure a film called (if memory serves) *Pardon My Past,* with a clever score by Kurt Weill which is the closest the screen has come to a genuine three-act operetta.[2]

One who knows anything about Hollywood, of course, must sympathize with the problems of the composer. It is granted that many who are palpitating to write some decent music are not allowed to do so. The producers and directors seem to know nothing about music or, worse yet, "know what they like" or, even worse, set themselves up as authorities on what the public likes. Nobody, probably, has accurately gauged the latter; it is factor X. But whatever X may be, when divided by zero it means infinity—an infinity of emptiness in this case. Hollywood magnates, confronted with X, are afraid of experimentation, are unwilling to risk a big monetary investment on untested musical idioms, and insist on imposing their will upon the composer. They are in business for money; and since it is a fact that most fine, sincere films lose money, they are afraid to take a chance. Result: stagnation.

Is there a solution? Pending a new art form for the screen (for which, they hasten to assure us, the public is not prepared) or large subsidies for the independent producer who eventually could produce the new art form, I cannot think of any. But viewing things as they are from the auditory standpoint, I only know that there is a difference between sound and sound organized into music; that we have much of the former, often very well done, and much of the latter, generally badly done. The conclusion, at any rate, is clear enough: if you want good music in films it's necessary to have a good composer; and if you want great music, it's necessary to have a great composer.

From *The Musical Digest,* September 1947, pp. 6, 9, and 14.

NOTES

1. Schonberg is confusing two works by Copland. *Quiet City* is a work for trumpet, English horn, and string orchestra fashioned from incidental music that Copland wrote in 1941 for the Irwin Shaw play of the same name. The film score Schonberg is referring to is one that Copland wrote for the documentary film *The City* (1939).—Ed.

2. Schonberg's memory is in fact not serving him correctly. Kurt Weill scored only three films between 1937 and 1944, and *Pardon My Past* is not one of them. That film, from 1945, was scored by Dmitri Tiomkin, not Weill.—Ed.

27

The New Musical Resources

Theodor Adorno and Hanns Eisler

(1947)

As we pointed out earlier, there is a striking discrepancy between contemporary motion pictures and their musical accompaniment. Most often this accompaniment drifts across the screen like a haze, obscuring the visual sharpness of the picture and counteracting the realism for which in principle the film necessarily strives. It converts a kiss into a magazine cover, an outburst of unmitigated pain into a melodrama, a scene from nature into an oleograph. But all this could be dispensed with today because, in the course of the last few decades, autonomous music has developed new resources and techniques that really correspond to the technical requirements of the motion picture. Their use is urged not merely because they are "timely"; it is not enough to demand only that the new motion-picture music should be new. The new musical resources should be used because objectively they are more appropriate than the haphazard musical padding with which motion pictures are satisfied today, and are superior to it.

We refer to the elements and techniques elaborated particularly in the works of Schönberg, Bartók, and Stravinsky during the last thirty years. What is all-important in their music is not the increased number of dissonances, but the dissolution of the conventionalized musical idiom. In truly valid new music, everything is the direct result of the concrete requirement of structure, rather than of the tonal system or any ready-made pattern. A piece full of dissonances can be fundamentally conventional, while one based on comparatively simpler material can be absolutely novel if these resources are used according to the constructive requirements of the piece instead of the institutionalized flow of musical language. Even a sequence of triads can be unusual and striking when it does not follow the accustomed rut and is conceived only with regard to its specific meaning.

Music based on constructive principles, in which there is no room for clichés and embellishments, can be called "objective" music, which is equivalent to the potentially objective music of the cinema.

The term "objective" is susceptible to incorrect and narrow interpretation, such as, for instance, connecting it exclusively with musical neo-classicism, the "functional" stylistic ideal as developed by Stravinsky and his followers. But advanced motion-picture music need not necessarily be cold. Under certain circumstances, the dramaturgic function of the accompanying music can consist precisely in breaking through the soberly objective surface of the picture and releasing latent suspense. We do not mean that the musician, in composing objective motion-picture music, must assume a detached attitude, but that he must deliberately choose the musical elements required by the context instead of succumbing to musical clichés and prefabricated emotionalism. The musical material must be perfectly subordinated to the given dramatic task. The development of modern music tends in the same direction.[1] As intimated above, it can be regarded as a process of rationalization in so far as every single musical element is at each moment derived from the structure of the whole. But as music becomes more pliable through its own structural principles, it also becomes more pliable for purposes of application to other media. The release of new types of resources, which was denounced as anarchistic and chaotic, actually led to the establishment of principles of construction far more strict and comprehensive than those known to traditional music. These principles make it possible always to choose the exact means required by a particular subject at a particular moment, and there is therefore no need to use formal means unsuitable for a specific purpose. Thus it has become possible to do full justice to the ever-changing problems and situations of the motion picture.

It is easy to see that the traditional resources long since frozen into automatic associations cannot achieve this, although even they can be used meaningfully again if they are clarified and "alienated" in the light of advanced practice. Here are a few instances of these petrified associations: A 4/4 bar with regular accents on the strong beats always has a military or triumphal character; the succession of the first and third steps of the scale, played piano, in a quiet tempo, because of its modal character suggests something religious; an accented 3/4 bar suggests the waltz and gratuitous *joie de vivre*. Such associations often place the events of the film in a false perspective. The new musical resources prevent this. This listener is stimulated to grasp the scene in itself; he not only hears the music, but also sees the picture from a fresh point of view. True, the new music does not represent conceptually mediated ideas, as is the case with programmatic music, in which waterfalls rustle and sheep bleat. But it can exactly reflect the tone of a scene, the specific emotional situation, the degree of seriousness or casualness, significance or inconsequence, sincerity or falseness—differences not within the possibilities of the conventional Romantic techniques.

In a French puppet film of 1933 there was an ensemble scene—a board meeting of industrial magnates—which required a benevolently satirical accompaniment. The score that was submitted, despite its puppet-like thinness, appeared to be so aggressive and "critical" in its use of advanced musical resources that the industrialists who had commissioned the picture rejected it and ordered another.

The "non-objectivity" of epigonous music is inseparable from its seeming antithesis, its cliché character. Only because definite musical configurations become patterns that are resorted to over and over again can these configurations be automatically associated with certain expressive values and in the end seem to be "expressive" in themselves. The new music avoids such patterns, meeting specific requirements with ever-new configurations, and as a result expression can no longer be hypostatized and made independent of the purely musical content.

The suitability of modern, unfamiliar resources should be recognized from the standpoint of the motion picture itself. The fact that this form of drama originated in the county fair and the cheap melodrama has left traces that are still apparent; sensation is its very life element. This is not to be understood solely in a negative sense, as lack of taste and aesthetic discrimination; only by using the element of surprise can the motion picture give everyday life, which it claims to reproduce by virtue of its technique, an appearance of strangeness, and disclose the essential meaning beneath its realistic surface. More generally, the drudgery of life as depicted in a reportage can become dramatic only through sensational presentation, which to a certain extent negates everyday life through exaggeration, and, when artistically true, reveals tensions that are "blacked out" in the conventional concept of "normal," average existence. The horrors of sensational literary and cinematic trash lay bare part of the barbaric foundation of civilization. To the extent that the motion picture in its sensationalism is the heir of the popular horror story and dime novel and remains below the established standards of middle-class art, it is in a position to shatter those standards, precisely through the use of sensation, and to gain access to collective energies that are inaccessible to sophisticated literature and painting. It is this very perspective that cannot be reached with the means of traditional music. But modern music is suitable to it. The fear expressed in the dissonances of Schönberg's most radical period far surpasses the measure of fear conceivable to the average middle-class individual; it is a historical fear, a sense of impending doom.

Something of this fear is alive in the great sensational films, for instance in the scene of the collapsing roof in the night club (*San Francisco*), or in *King Kong* when the giant gorilla hurls a New York elevated train down into the street. The traditional music written for such scenes has never been remotely adequate to them, whereas the shocks of modern music, by no means an accidental consequence of its technological rationalization—still unassimilated after thirty years— could meet their requirements. Schönberg's music for an imaginary film, *Begleitmusik zu einer Lichtspielszene*, op. 34, full of a sense of fear, of looming danger and catastrophe, is a landmark pointing the way for the full and accurate use of the new musical resources. Naturally the extension of their expressive potentialities is applicable not only to the realm of fear and horror; in the opposite direction, too, that of extreme tenderness, ironic detachment, empty waiting, and unfettered power, the new musical resources can explore fields inaccessible to traditional resources because these latter present themselves as something that has always been known, and therefore are deprived in advance of the power to express the unfamiliar and unexplored.

For example, *Hangmen Also Die*, after the preliminary music, begins by showing a large portrait of Hitler in a banquet hall of the Hradshin Castle. As the portrait appears, the music stops on a penetrating widespread chord containing ten different tones. Hardly any traditional chord has the expressive power of this extremely advanced sonority. The twelve-tone chord at the moment of Lulu's death in Berg's opera produces an effect very much like that of a motion picture. While the cinema technique aims essentially at creating extreme tension, traditional music, with the slight dissonances it allows, knows of no equivalent material. But suspense is the essence of modern harmony, which knows no chord without an inherent "tendency" toward further action, while most of the traditional chords are self-sufficient. Moreover, even those traditional harmonies that are charged with specific dramatic associations have long since become so tame that they are no more capable of giving an idea of the chaotic and fearful present-day reality than nineteenth-century verse forms are capable of giving an idea of fascism. To make this clear it is enough to imagine an extreme case, such as the picture of the explosion of a block buster, accompanied by conventional martial music in the style of Meyerbeer or Verdi. The modern motion picture, in its most consistent productions, aims at unmetaphorical contents that are beyond the range of stylization. This requires musical means that do not represent a stylized picture of pain, but rather its tonal record. This particular dimension of the new musical resources was made apparent by Stravinsky in his *Sacre du Printemps*.

Here are, briefly stated, some of the specifically musical elements suitable to the motion picture:

Musical Form

Most motion pictures use short musical forms. The length of a musical form is determined by its relation to the musical material. Tonal music of the last two and a half centuries favored relatively long, developed forms. Consciousness of a tonal center can be achieved only by parallel episodes, developments, and repetitions that require a certain amount of time. No tonal incident in the sense of major-minor tonality is intelligible as such; it becomes "tonal" only by means of relationships revealed in the course of a more or less extensive whole. This tendency increases with the specific weight of the modulations, and the further the music moves away from the original tonality, the more time it needs to re-establish its tonal center of gravity. Thus all tonal music necessarily contains an element of the "superfluous," because each theme, in order to fulfill its function in the system of reference, must be expressed more often than would be required according to its own meaning. The short romantic forms (Chopin and Schumann) contradict this only in appearance. The expressive power of certain aphoristic instrumental compositions of these masters is based on their fragmentary, unfinished, suggestive character, and they never claim to be complete or "closed."

The brevity of the new music is fundamentally different. In it, the individual musical episodes and the patterns of the themes are conceived without regard to a pre-arranged system of reference. They are not intended to be "repeatable" and require no repetition, but stand by themselves. If they are expanded, it is not by means of symmetrical devices, such as sequences or resumptions of the first part of a song form, but rather by means of a developing variation of the given original materials, and it is not necessary that these should be easily recognizable. All this results in a condensation of the musical form that goes far beyond the romantic fragments. Instances of this are Schönberg's piano pieces op. 11 and 19, and his monodrama *Erwartung;* Stravinsky's pieces for string quartet and his Japanese songs; and the works of Anton Webern. It is obvious that modern music is especially qualified to construct consistent precise short forms, which contain nothing superfluous, which come to the point at once, and which need no expansion for architectonic reasons.

Musical Profiles

The emancipation of each motive or theme from symmetry and the necessity of repetition makes it possible to formulate specific musical ideas in a far more drastic and penetrating fashion, and to free the individual musical events from all unessential gewgaws. In the new music there is no room for padding.

It is because of this capacity for unfettered characterization that the new music is in keeping with the prose character of the motion picture. At the same time this sharpening of musical characterization permits a sharpness of expression, which the "stylization" of the elements of the traditional music made impossible. While traditional music always preserves a certain restraint in the expression of sorrow, grief, and fear, the new style tends to be unrestrained. Sorrow can turn into appalling despair, repose into glassy rigidity, fear into panic. But the new music is also capable of expressing absence of expression, quietude, indifference, and apathy with an intensity beyond the power of traditional music. Impassiveness has been known in music only since Eric Satie, Stravinsky, and Hindemith.

The range of expression has been widened not only with regard to the different types of musical profiles but above all to their alternation. Traditional music, with the exception of the technique of surprise used, for instance, by Berlioz and Richard Strauss, usually requires a certain amount of time for the alternation of themes, and the necessity of achieving an adjusted balance between the tonalities and the symmetrical parts prevents the immediate juxtaposition of themes according to their own meaning. As a rule, the new music no longer recognizes such considerations, and can fashion its forms by means of the sharpest contrasts. The new musical language can satisfy the technical principle of abrupt change elaborated by the motion picture because of its inherent flexibility.

Dissonance and Polyphony

For the layman, the most striking feature of the new musical language is its wealth of discords, namely the simultaneous employment of intervals such as the minor second and the major seventh and the formation of chords of six or more different notes. Although the wealth of dissonances in modern music is a superficial characteristic, far less significant than the structural changes of the musical language, it involves an element of especial importance for the motion picture. Sound is robbed of its static quality and made dynamic by the ever-present factor of the "unresolved." The new language is dramatic even prior to the "conflict," the thematic development with its explicit antagonisms. A similar feature is inherent in the motion picture. The principle of tension is latently so active even in the weakest productions that incidents which of themselves are credited with no importance whatsoever appear like scattered fragments of a meaning that the whole is intended to clarify and that transcend themselves. The new musical language is particularly well-suited to do justice to this element of the motion picture.[2]

The emancipation of harmony also supplies the corrective for the requirement discussed in the chapter on prejudices: melody at any price. In traditional music, this requirement is not altogether meaningless, because the independence of its other elements, particularly harmony, is so restricted that the center of gravity inevitably lies in the melody, which is itself guided by harmony. But for that very reason the melodic element has become conventionalized and outworn, while the emancipated harmony of today unburdens the overworked melodic element, and paves the way for ideas and characteristic turns in the vertical, non-melodic dimension.[3] It also helps to combat melodizing in another way. The conventional notion of melody means melody in the highest voice, which, borrowed form the *Lied* style, is supposed to occupy the foreground of the listener's attention. Melody of this type is a figure, not a background. But in the motion picture the fore-ground is the scene projected on the screen, and permanent accompaniment of this scene with a melody in the highest voice must of necessity lead to obscurity, blurring, and confusion. The liberation of harmony and the conquest of a genuine polyphonic freedom, which is not reduced to academic conventional techniques of imitation, permits the music to function as a background in another sense than that of a mere backdrop of noise, and to add to the true melody of the picture, namely the action portrayed, meaningful illustrations and genuine contrasts. These decisive potentialities of motion-picture music can be realized only by the use of the new musical resources, and so far have not even been seriously considered.

Dangers of the New Style

The elimination of the familiar frame of reference of traditional music results in a number of dangers. First of all, there is the irresponsible use of the new resources in a hit-or-miss style, modernism in the bad sense of the word, that is to say, the use of advanced media for their own sake, not because the subject calls for them. A poor piece composed in the traditional musical language can easily be recognized as such by any more or less trained musician or layman. The unconventional character of the new musical language and its remoteness from what is taught in the conservatories make the recognition of stupidity and pretentious bungling in modern music more difficult for the average listener, although objectively such bungling can as well be spotted as it could before. For instance, certain novices might be ready to exhaust the listener with completely absurd twelve-tone compositions which seem advanced, whereas their sham radicalism would only weaken the effect of the motion picture. It is true that this danger is today far more acute in autonomous music than in motion-picture music, but the demand for new composers might lead to a situation in which the cause of new music will be so badly represented that the trash of the old guard will triumph.

The methods of new music imply new dangers that even experienced composers must take into consideration: excessive complexity of detail; the mania for making every moment of the accompanying music arresting; pedantry; formalistic trifling. Especially dangerous is the hasty adoption of the twelve-tone technique, which can degenerate into a mechanical task and in which the arithmetical consistency of the sequence is supposed to replace the genuine consistency of the musical whole—resulting in no consistency at all.

While it is unlikely that the motion-picture industry, organized as it is today, will permit wild experiments on the expensive medium of motion pictures, another danger is much more imminent. The defects of conventional motion-picture music are generally realized, more or less consciously, yet radical innovations are largely excluded for commercial reasons. As a result, a certain tendency to follow a middle course is beginning to make itself felt; the ominous demand: modern, but not too much so, is heard in several quarters. Certain modern techniques, like the ostinato of the Stravinsky school, have begun to sneak in, and the abandonment of the routine threatens to give rise to a new pseudo-modern routine. The industry encourages this tendency within certain limits, while at the same time composers who have adopted the modern idiom, but who do not want or cannot afford to spoil their chances on the market, tend to work for the industry. The hope that an advanced and original musical language can impose itself by the detour of false moderate imitations is illusory; such compromises destroy the meaning of the new language, rather than propagate it.

From *Composing for the Films* (London: Athlone Press, 1994), pp. 32–44. By kind permission of Continuum International Publishing Group.

NOTES

1. It is worthy of note that certain features of the work of Alban Berg, whose late-romantic, expressionistic instrumental and operatic music is far removed from the motion-picture and the new "functional" style, illustrate the prevalence in advanced music of objective tendencies in the sense of a rational construction which come close to the requirements of the motion picture. Berg thinks in terms of such exact mathematical proportions that the number of bars and thereby the duration of his compositions are determined in advance. It is as if he composed them with a stop watch in his hand. His operas, in which complex stage situations are often accompanied by complex musical forms, such as fugues, in order to make them articulate, strive toward a type of technical procedure that might be called a musical close-up.

2. The predominance of discords in the new musical language leads to the dissolution of tonality, for neither the separate harmonic incidents nor their functional connection and the harmonic structure of the whole can any longer be adequately represented in the pattern, however broadened, of traditional tonality. But this dissolution of tonality is furthered most by the objective formal structure of motion-picture music itself. This structure has a definite bearing upon harmony. With some exaggeration one might say that motion-picture music is driven to atonality because there is no room in it for the formally satisfactory expansion of tonality. To be sure, the individual harmonic incidents of the usual motion-picture music are almost without exception strictly tonal, or at most only "seasoned" with dissonances. But the tonality remains one of single sounds and their most primitive sequences. The necessity of following cues, and of producing harmonic effects without regard for the requirements of harmonic development, obviously does not permit of really balanced modulation, broad, well-planned harmonic canvases; in brief, real tonality in the sense of the disposition of functional harmony over long stretches. And it is this, not the atoms of the triads or seventh chords, which constitutes tonal organization. What was said above concerning leitmotifs is in a higher sense true of the tonal principle itself. If one went backwards, that is to say, from the dramaturgically inevitable breaks and deviations of the composition, something like satisfactory tonal relationships might be achieved by means of extreme care and virtuosity in composition; but according to the prevailing practice, while the separate chords are banal and overfamiliar, their interrelation is quite anarchistic and for the most part completely meaningless. True, the emancipation

of tonality does not, according to the strictest criteria, facilitate the harmonic disposition, but at least it liberates the composer from the preoccupation of restoring the basic key and the selection of modulations, which are hardly ever consistent with the extra-musical requirements of the motion picture. Moreover, the dissonances have far greater mobility and adjustability, and unlike tonal chords which are derived from the pattern and need the restoration of the pattern for their own fullfilment do not require to the same degree unambiguous definite inevitable resolutions.

3. The extraordinary effectiveness of Stravinsky's earlier works can be partly explained by his renunciation of neo-romantic melodizing.

28

Movie Music Goes on Record

Arthur Knight

(1952)

The insistent pinging of Anton Karas's zither in *The Third Man* probably did more to draw attention to movie music than all the massed orchestras of Max Steiner, Erich Korngold and Alfred Newman combined. Blasting out from every record shop for months, inescapable in the jukeboxes, on the air or in the night spots, its syncopated themes quickly made the movie-going millions acutely aware of the picture from which they came. Actually, this kind of sales assistance for the movies it springs from, has long been considered a proper function of movie music. Even before the sound track had been added to silent pictures, the ubiquitous theme song was already with us in the form of printed scores that the movie companies sent out to neighborhood pianists and organists as proper accompaniment for their epics, often incorporating a brand new love song for the picture's more lyric moments. Phonograph recordings, they found, helped popularize both the music and the picture it came from. "Charmaine" and "Diane" were only two movie heroines of the silent days whose many charms were itemized in numerous hit records.

Once sound had arrived, in a veritable rash of "all talking, all singing, all dancing" monstrosities, the rush to wax was instantaneous and overwhelming. With a major portion of all popular music now coming from their films, movie studios began incorporating into their domains whole record companies and music publishing firms. Singing stars like Chevalier, Nick Lucas ("The Crooning Troubadour") and Jeanette MacDonald became almost as popular on discs as they were on the screen. By the mid thirties, the hit tunes of all big musicals were being recorded by every company in the field, with at least one version contributed by the stars themselves. Crosby, Astaire, Dietrich, Deanna Durbin, Judy Garland,

Nelson Eddy and Jeanette MacDonald, Alan Jones were soon drawing a substantial share of their incomes from record sales of the songs they had first popularized in their pictures.

The musical scores for dramatic pictures were a lot slower in coming onto records, however, perhaps because of the widely held theory that nobody listens to film music anyway. In recent years, that idea has come up for considerable questioning, especially since—as with *The Third Man*—it has been discovered that, in recorded form, the themes of a good score can do much to recreate the feeling of the original film, and with it a strong desire to see the film itself. The actual beginnings of this type of recording, it must be admitted, were not too auspicious. As part of David O. Selznick's all-out campaign to publicize *Duel in the Sun*, RCA Victor was somehow inveigled into releasing an album of Dimitri Tiomkin's brassy, splashy music for that maizey masterpiece. Only a short time earlier the recordings of Richard Addinsell's tuneful "Warsaw Concerto" had helped turn a weak and sentimental British war film into a moderate box-office success, and Selznick was probably aware that his own picture sorely needed any such assistance it could get. But the *Duel in the Sun* album did serve to open up the field to many more recordings of motion picture scores, generally, as in the Andre Kostelanetz, Alfred Newman and Victor Young albums, featuring gaudily symphonic arrangements of the theme music from various films. Young's own "Stella by Starlight," for example, or David Raksin's "Laura" were each thus elaborated from music they wrote to be played under the romantic sequences of "The Uninvited" and "Laura" respectively.

Other Hollywood scores now on disc, notably Miklós Rózsa's music for *The Lost Weekend* and *Spellbound*, Alfred Newman's for *The Captain from Castile* and Victor Young's Byzantine-modern music for *Samson and Delilah*, are little more than suites of themes from these pictures, performed of course by full symphony orchestras. Size of the recording orchestra would seem to be a measure of prestige. The English have, on the whole, been far more energetic in getting outstanding film scores to the record-buying public, perhaps because so many of their best composers are writing for films these days. Sir William Walton's music for both *Hamlet* and *Henry V* has been extensively recorded, along with the voice of Laurence Olivier and others from the cast. The Arnold Bax score for *Oliver Twist,* a suite from William Alwyn's music for *Notorious Gentleman* and another drawn from Noel Coward's *The Astonished Heart,* the entire ballet that Brian Easdale wrote for *The Red Shoes* barely scratches the surface of recorded British film music, although it does give some hint to the range and seriousness of these works.

Actually, many of the British scores come directly from the sound tracks of the pictures in question, a practice frowned upon by Mr. Petrillo's locals in this country. This technique, stormily inaugurated here by Walt Disney in 1940 with a Victor album from his *Pinocchio,* has been revived in recent years by the new M.G.M. Records. Their issues on *Annie Get Your Gun, Easter Parade, Good News, Royal Wedding, Summer Stock* and a short time ago, *Show Boat,* make much of the fact that now you can take home with you exactly what you heard in the theatre. Victor, with Mario Lanza under contract but without recourse to M.G.M.'s sound tracks, has nevertheless recorded that redoubtable young tenor through the entire repertory of his *Great Caruso* selections, and songs from *That Midnight Kiss* and *Toast of New Orleans* as well. It all seems to tie in with the current vogue for recording everything from the Broadway hit shows, the good with the bad and indifferent. One interesting M.G.M. LP, however, is made up of ballet music from a number of their motion pictures, and featuring Richard Rodgers' memorable *Slaughter on Tenth Avenue.* The orchestrations are big and juicy, in the best M.G.M. Technicolor tradition, but the basic idea of groupings of this sort is an excellent one.

But what about serious composers—concert composers—film music? The gap is not really so wide as one might suppose, and it grows narrower all the time. A late score by Camille Saint-Saëns was written to accompany a 1907 French picture, *The Assassination of the Duc de Guise.* Jacques Ibert's popular "Divertissement" was drawn from the music he wrote as an accompaniment for René Clair's wonderful silent comedy *The Italian Straw Hat.* In a similar manner Serge Prokofiev developed his music for Eisenstein's *Alexander Nevsky* into the cantata which Columbia has recorded. Less generally known is the fact that his "Lieutenant Kije" suite was also drawn from a film score, *The Czar Wants to Sleep.* Virgil Thomson arranged his music for the documentary films *The Plow That Broke the Plains* and *Louisiana Story* into suites that have been recorded by the Philadelphia Orchestra under Ormandy; and only recently Alec Wilder did the same for the charming accompaniment Hugh Martin provided for the art film *Grandma Moses.* Aaron Copland's piano arrangement of his music for *Our Town* has been recorded by Leo Smit. With serious composers increasingly shuttling back and forth between New York and Hollywood, there will probably be more and more such music coming onto records from movie sources. Even now there is enough film music around to permit New York's music station, WQXR, to schedule a full half-hour program of it each week.

What has happened here, of course, is that these composers have taken the music they wrote originally to fit a certain sequence of pictures and ideas, and reworked it to fit the requirements of concert listening. In a radio interview during the past summer George Antheil, "the bad boy of modern music," explained the necessity for doing this. A picture may call for forty seconds of music here, a special bit of transition music there, a long sustained passage to underline a dramatic situation a bit further along. This is music written to order, timed to exactitude, its mood drawn from and dependent on the picture it accompanies. If it is a good job, Antheil went on, it is valid under those circumstances only. If it can stand alone, as a concert piece must, then it probably failed in its film function.

But such music can be—and is being—developed into serious orchestral works. Typical is the recording of Franz Waxman's music for *The Paradine Case*. Waxman speaks of it as a "recomposition" of his thematic material into a symphonic poem for piano and orchestra. In working it out, he followed the ideological development of the movie, but freely transposed and reorchestrated his original material into a unified work for concert hall presentation. With the new audiences opened to them by the record companies, film composers—whether the occasional visitor from New York or the Hollywood regulars—will undoubtedly be making more such adaptations of their motion picture music. Which is all to the good, for movies are our greatest single source of new music today, and much of it deserves more than the first cursory half-hearing it receives in the movie theater.

From *Film Music Notes* 11, no. 3 (1952): 21–23.

29

The Man with the Golden Arm

Elmer Bernstein

(1956)

First, let me clear up an important point. The score for *The Man with the Golden Arm* is not a jazz score. It is a score in which jazz elements were incorporated toward the end of creating an atmosphere, I should say a highly specialized atmosphere, specific to this particular film. In this respect I was fortunate in that jazz has heretofore been used most sparingly in this manner. Now there are a rash of unpleasant films using jazz more or less skillfully. In the future, therefore, it will be difficult, if not impossible, to create a highly specialized atmosphere merely by using jazz elements. Let us then conclude that my notion was enhanced by fortuitous timing. But enough modesty. Let us get on to more interesting considerations, and the first one that presents itself is: Why Jazz?

I told Otto Preminger, the producer, of my intentions after one quick reading of the shooting script. The script had a Chicago slum street, heroin, hysteria, longing, frustration, despair and finally death. Whatever love one could feel in the script was the little, weak emotion left in a soul racked with heroin and guilt, a soul consuming its strength in the struggle for the good life and losing pitifully. There is something very American and contemporary about all the characters and their problems. I wanted an element that could speak readily of hysteria and despair, an element that would localize these emotions to our country, to a large city if possible. Ergo,—jazz.

Before going on to specific examples from the score I would like to make some general observations. This is not a score in which each character has a theme. It is not a score which creates a musical mirror for dialogue. Nor is it a score which psychoanalyzes the characters and serves up inner brain on the half shell. It is basically a simple score which deals with a man and his environment.

There are only three themes which are exploited in a compositional manner in the development of the score. These can be loosely identified in the following manner:

1) Frank's relationship to his general environment; his job as a dealer in a cheap poker joint, to his fight against the dope habit, to the pusher who sells him the stuff, to the street itself.
2) Frank's relationship to his home environment; his neurotic wife, who feigns a debilitating illness in order to hold him, to the shabby flat with its "lower depth" inhabitants, to his own guilty lack of love for his wife.
3) Frank's relationship with "the other woman, who is a symbol to him of love, and the better life, such small hopes as he has from time to time, and his chance of making it away from the habit and even the neighborhood and its hold on him.

Before we go on to examine the music in detail you should have some knowledge of what went into getting the score on film. My first move was to avail myself of the counsel and help of two brilliant young jazz musicians, Shorty Rogers and Shelly Manne. Rogers arranged all the band numbers and was of invaluable aid as a guide to the wonders of contemporary jazz. Shelly Manne created his own drum solos where indicated and thus made a unique and exciting contribution to many parts of the score. Since time was of the essence (the score was written in twenty days), an orchestrator of the highest caliber was of great importance. In this my sketches were graced by the great talents of Fred Steiner, a fine composer in his own right, who subsequently went on to score the film *Run for the Sun,* soon to be released.

Upon completion of the score it was apparent that it would take a "super orchestra" of the finest jazz and symphonic musicians available to perform it. This job was entrusted to Bobby Helfer who, with even more than his customary magic, assembled a dream ensemble of 57 musicians from the four corners of the Hollywood symphonic and jazz scene. Perhaps the best way to indicate the cooperation and performance of these artists is to tell you than one occasion Armand Kaproff was roundly applauded by his colleagues for his performance of a four bar 'cello solo. There was much applause those days for more spectacular feats by Shelly Manne, Pete Candoli, Milt Bernhart, Mitchell Lurie, Ray Turner, Martin Ruderman, Anatol Kaminsky, but it was the reaction to a short 'cello solo that most eloquently described the degree of concentration and intensity of performance achieved during this recording session.

Once the music was on film its care was entrusted to Leon Birnbaum, who used his vast experience as a music cutter to make life easier on the recording stage, and who was most helpful in preparing the film for transfer to the record album.

Of technical matters there is little to say. The score was recorded single channel on Westrex equipment. The recording room at RKO is too small to successfully record a full jazz and symphonic ensemble playing at the same time so in one notable case we tried a short cut. Leon Birnbaum built a click track for the main title and we recorded the two ensembles separately and they were reunited in dubbing. Other than that we made no further forays into technical fields.

Ex. 1 is a portion of the main title. Here the intent was to create the atmosphere in a dramatic and straightforward way. There are no subtleties here. The repetitive bass figure gives us a sense of drive and grim monotony. At the top we have the hysterical scream of the brass and within, the chromatic triplets whirling about and circumscribing themselves in a hopeless circle from which they finally emerge, but only for the last cry of despair at the end of the title. (This material is contained in cut 1 of the Decca album from the sound track.)

Ex. 2 is the first statement of the second theme, described in an earlier paragraph. Here is a long line, faintly scented with an aura of romanticism, troubled, never quite going where you expect it to go, striving but never quite comfortable or fulfilled in its cadences. Later on in this scene as the exposition of the relationship between Frank and his wife becomes clearer we hear a lonely trumpet with a gentle rhythm accompaniment filter through the rather gentle string and woodwind setting of this composition. No matter what the specific scene dealt with we never lose our consciousness of basic atmosphere.

Ex. 3 is a treatment of the third theme. This is the least disturbed theme although even in this case the first statement in a rather halting 5/4 lest we become too pat or, by making this extremely simple theme too symmetrical, render the relationship with the "other woman" too easy or ideal.

At one point Molly (the other woman) leaves Frank when she realizes that he is once again falling before the narcotic habit. She runs from the dingy clip joint, through the slum street. Arriving at her place she hurriedly packs her few belongings as Frank pounds on the locked door. This scene presented a tough problem. The chase through the street was not the difficult part but I am presenting the first part of it (Ex. 4) as it is one of my favorite spots in the score. Being a realist I am forced to the melancholy fact that my solution of the problem is something less than genius; however, the intense, rather nervous rhythmic piano figures, string bass pizzicato and the insistent drumming of Shelly Manne seemed to me to create a kind of grim, driving excitement that suited the scene very well. One can judge the result much better by listening to the cut entitled "Breakup" in the Decca soundtrack album. The tough part of the scene was that in which we have Molly packing and Frank pounding on the door. As you already know from Ex. 3 the theme for this relationship is almost dangerously simple, and certainly devoid of great emotional impact. I wanted to use the theme in this scene and

EXAMPLE 1

project some of the tears and bitterness of the scene through some use of that fragile motif. The results are in Ex. 5 and also in "Breakup" in the album.

There are various times in the course of the film when Frank is seized by the desire for heroin. In each case the desire is fulfilled as Frank seeks out the "pusher." The music which is used throughout to characterize this situation stems from the first theme and although space would not permit reproduction of each of these sequences one can hear these treatments in cuts named "The Fix" and "Sunday Morning" in the Album. On one occasion Frank approaches the

EXAMPLE 2

EXAMPLE 3

"pusher" without money. During the tension which is growing through Frank's pleading an old jazz device, a form of "boogie-woogie" bass, was used to help increase the tension in consonance with the general atmosphere. (See Ex. 6.) Although there is no accurate way of notating it, I should mention that when Frank's pleas fail and he attacks the "pusher" in a blind rage and ransacks his room, the entire frenzied sequence was underscored by a rather remarkable drum break by Shelly Manne.

One of the most unusual scoring assignments I've run into up to now was that of scoring the so-called "withdrawal" sequence. For those of you who haven't had to break the narcotics habit recently I must explain that one manner of effecting

EXAMPLE 4

some sort of cure is to deprive the patient of his drugs suddenly and keep it up for a period of three or four days. Apparently the only problem with this cure is that the attendant pains and discomforting symptoms are so severe as to incite self-destruction, murder or death of the patient. The film pictures a most striking performance by Frank Sinatra portraying a withdrawal scene. He alternately tries breaking out of the room in which he has been locked, rolls around on the floor in agony, tries to quiet his craving by enacting self administration of the drug in a charade which is once again brilliantly underscored by Manne's drumming, and finally he's rescued as he's on his way out the window. I remember writing this sequence at four, one morning, feeling not much better than Sinatra

EXAMPLE 5

looks in the scene. The entire scene is scored by a series of disconnected, but violent outbursts, mounting in fury and intensity until the character, exhausted, collapses writhing on the floor in pain. Ex. 7 contains the opening bars of this sequence. On record it is the section entitled "Withdrawal."

In the end Frank's wife kills the "pusher" accidentally, and jumps from a fire escape in a fit of panic when apprehended. After the ambulance leaves Frank, Molly and other minor characters drift away from the scene, silently, thoughtfully, and the film ends without indicating more than the slimmest hope for the future. In the instance of this last composition I had my only serious disagreement with

EXAMPLE 6

the producer. I lost. It seemed to me that the only honest way to end this film was on a "downbeat" note, to use an industry expression. There is thoughtful feeling at this point in the film. We are left full of apprehension for Frank's future, which seems grim at best. We have seen all his dreams shattered by his addiction. It would be almost inconceivable to believe that Frank walks off into the sunset to find a pot of gold with the next day's dawning, and even if he found it, we have no reasonable guarantee that he wouldn't consume the pot, buying narcotics. In any case Mr. Preminger felt that the audience would have taken enough by that time, and to cheat the stricken spectators of Dr. Quack's quick remedy for narcotics addiction, wife's suicide, prison record and ruined lives would have been more

EXAMPLE 7

EXAMPLE 8

than a body could bear. Let us not scoff too heartily. Mr. Preminger has yet to make an independent motion picture that did not require some extraordinary courage in one way or another. This a quality which comes very dearly in our industry. In any case in Ex. 8 we have Frank dutifully walking into a better life. The composition starts after the removal of Frank's wife. The lone trumpet sounds l'envoi with the same blues motif which had started the film with Frank's walk down the same street at the opening. For one moment we get the feeling that in some wonderfully gentle way we are going to follow Frank off the screen, walking beside him quietly, thoughtfully, but then the rose glow obediently suffuses the scene and we are sent from the theater in a state of euphoria.

From *Film Music Notes* 15, no. 4 (1956): 3–13.

30

Forbidden Planet

Louis and Bebe Barron

(1956)

Electronic Tonalities came into the MGM film *Forbidden Planet* when Studio Chief Dore Schary and General Musical Director Johnny Green decided that this picture should not have a *musical* score (neither did *Executive Suite*), but should in this case express its moods and actions with a new auditory art form.

The need for a completely new art in scoring *Forbidden Planet* was intensified by the fact that MGM had never approached this kind of film before, and in their determination to make an adult science-fiction picture, had budgeted the production at two million dollars in order to make full use of all the artistic resources of the film medium in expressing the really unique dramatic values of the story and this out-of-this world locale. Dore Schary and Johnny Green both felt that these unique emotional expressions required a new aesthetic experience for the audience, creating emotional messages which they had not before received.

At this point we were called in. Although we had not yet scored a feature film with our new electronic medium, we had done several short experimental films produced by Ian Hugo and Walter Lewisohn which had been seen at European festivals. We had always avoided science-fiction themes because of the obvious danger of being type-cast, but the challenges offered in *Forbidden Planet* tempted us to chance the hazards of being professionally pigeon-holed.

Our big problem was (and still is) that we are "artistic orphans," since what we compose is not music (it is almost more like choreographing for the ear). Dore Schary christened our work "Electronic Tonalities," and Johnny Green personally took charge of us and supervised us as if we were composing a musical score.

The MGM music run, as Johnny Green has set it up, was most useful to us both in helping us orient our dramatic function and in establishing a close rapport with the producer, Nicholas Nayfack. In fact, Mr. Green's helpfulness is based on not only his wide musical talents and experience, but also a great sense of dramatic values.

Some of the themes which we worked with were Robby, the Lovable Robot; the invisible monster, serene space, playful pseudo-love, true love, 60 gallons of bourbon for two, a unicorn theme, night with two moons, suspense and terror of the unknown, comic dialogue, etc.

Electronic Tonalities are *not* music, but they are composed—in the sense that the acting and dancing of a scene is composed—differently from the manner of music which organizes and structures a sequence of individual notes. In our case we do not compose in the sense of note-by-note construction.

We design and construct electronic circuits which function electronically in a manner remarkably similar to the way that lower life-forms function psychologically. This is really a fascinating phenomenon, and there is even a young but respectable science explaining it, called "Cybernetics" and first propounded by Prof. Norbert Wiener of M.I.T. (Norbert Wiener, *Cybernetics or Control and Communication in the Animal and the Machine* [New York: Wiley, 1948]). It is found that there are certain natural laws of behavior applicable alike to animals (including humans) and electronic machines of certain types of complexity.

Although Cybernetics does not concern itself with artistic or even audible expressions, the scientific laws are there to be borrowed, and electronic nervous systems can be specifically designed with built-in behavior patterns resembling emotional personality types. When these circuits are properly designed, controlled, and stimulated, they react emotionally with strange and meaningful sounds.

If we think of these electronic personality circuits as character actors, then when we compose for them, we function like writer-director. Like writers, we first decide on a *cast of characters,* and design and build the circuits to act out the character parts. Then we structure a *dramatic plot* in which these electronic characters interact with each other as the plot unfolds. Now we become directors and see to it that the actor-circuits get their cues at the right times, and express their characters authentically and effectively. This is possible by properly understanding and controlling their electronic activity.

By amplifying the electronic activity and recording it on magnetic tape, we are able to translate the electron behavior into audible form. The most remarkable aspect of this whole phenomenon is that the sounds which result from these electronic nervous systems convey distinct emotional meaning to listeners.

The design and dramatic control of synthetic nervous systems which care nothing about symbols, but which seem to feel, and seem to express audibly the emotions which the artist intends, and which the audience *unconsciously* experiences, is the essence of what we do. We were gratified to hear people tell us after seeing *Forbidden Planet* that the Tonalities reminded them of what their dreams sound like.

Actually, this orphan art is more related to drama than it is to music, for it is governed very much by dramatic laws, and very little by musical laws. The art of "composing" an electronic-nervous-system score is largely an art of dramatic construction. Yet musical training is invaluable because this is an *abstract* art, manifesting itself in pure form and sonic sensation rather than in the literal symbols (like words and gesture) of drama.

We believe this new art is in the trend of direct communication from artist to audience—direct in the sense of coming from the unconscious (non-symbolic) emotions of the artists, and proceeding to the unconscious emotions of the audience, without translating the message into the conscious level where symbols are used to represent agreed-upon meanings. We are striving to make the audience feel a pure flow of sonic sensations unrelated either to the world we live in, or to the literary-theatrical experiences and traditions we have grown up with.

From *Film Music Notes* 15, no. 5 (Summer 1956): 18.

31

Interview with Stanley Donen

Jim Hillier

(1977)

In the 1940s, what developments were most important for you? Was there anyone who you felt was working towards a new musical style?

Well, it was very obvious . . . This may seem a funny thing to say, but in my opinion, movies like *On the Town, Singin' in the Rain, Give a Girl a Break* and so on were really a direct continuation from the Astaire-Rogers musicals; they have nothing to do with the Busby Berkeley kind of musical. The tradition they came from was the Fred Astaire world, which in turn came from René Clair and from Lubitsch, who were the predecessors of people like Astaire, George Stevens, and Mark Sandrich who made those pictures. That was the kind of musical with which we were familiar. If you can put your finger on a really broad general difference between the Lubitsch and Clair musicals and something like *Seven Brides for Seven Brothers* or *Singin' in the Rain,* it is energy, which has to do mainly with a) America and b) dancing. If you could have put into Clair's or Lubitsch's hands this American drive and dancing, then I think you would have what we brought to those films.

Dissatisfied is perhaps the wrong word for our feelings about the Berkeley kind of musical. I just thought they were dead—they had nothing to do with movies. Now, 25 years later, we look back on those big extravaganzas typified by Berkeley, and they look very funny and unusual. Even then we made jokes about it. Today everybody thinks we were *doing* one in the "Beautiful Girl" number in *Singin' in the Rain,* but we were really satirizing Berkeley there, not praising him. Everyone knew that at the time. It's only a problem now because those films have acquired a nostalgic quality.

*How aware were you of new influence in dance styles around that time, the early
1940s?*

I was certainly aware that we weren't it! I mean, we couldn't by any stretch of
the imagination be called the vanguard of the dance world at that point. Jerome
Robbins and George Balanchine were well established people by the time of
Singin' the Rain, Balanchine, of course, a long time before that. What we were
doing was light years behind these people, in terms of pure dance, I mean.

*Had you any notion that you were in any way introducing any of that into the
movies, modifying it?*

I didn't, I don't know what anybody else thought. It is quite clear that the
dancing in these movies—with the exception of *Seven Brides,* where the
dancing is quite different from the other pictures—was rather an outgrowth of
vaudeville, and that the other sort of dancing that was springing forth in
America, let's say from Robbins, was not in our pictures.

*What about other developments? Did you feel, for example, that there was a lack
of realism in the musical at that time?*

On the contrary, most musicals were "real"—what there was a lack of in the
musicals of the time was *sur*realism. I mean to say that the whole drift of the
Busby Berkeley kind of musical was towards "realism." Everything happened on
the stage and you are supposed to suspend your imagination just long enough to
believe it was happening on the stage—there was always a phonograph playing a
record, or a radio, or there was a piano in an automobile, or a banjo, or a man
picked up a harmonica, and you always saw where the music came from.
Nobody ever took off into the surrealism of the musical, the way Lubitsch or
Astaire or Clair did. What *we* did was not geared towards realism but towards
the unreal.

You shot in the streets of New York but . . .

That is not real. That is anything but real, it just happens that the street is real.
A musical is like an opera in the sense that it is anything but real. It seems to me
that the whole mistake that films made was in trying to make it believable, as if
it were happening in reality. And *I,* certainly, with Gene and a number of other
people, was not going in the direction of what you could call realism. An opera
has its own reality but it isn't what you could call day-to-day reality, and the
same thing with the musical.

Were you not interested, though, in more everyday basic subjects . . . ?

More everyday than what? The theater spectacular, not everyday? I mean, what
is un-everyday about doing a thing like putting on a show? It seems to me that
most banal idea in everyday life. The leading lady breaks her ankle—who's

going to replace her? Those were the plots. It's the same plot as *Singin' in the Rain*, actually—who's going to be the leading lady? My God, she can't sing and dance—we'll get somebody else. That seems to be the plot that everybody else gets stuck on. It's the same plot in *Funny Face*—who's going to be the girl—take the ugly duckling. *On the Town* is quite different; its plot is a quite new departure. It's three guys on a day's leave when the war is on—you've got to put yourself back into the frame of mind that everything was revolving around the fact that a war was on—in 24 hours, how much juice there is in life that people weren't living, all crammed into those hours. That's a super idea for a movie, I think.

Reference is frequently made to the "Freed Unit," but there were at MGM other active musical producers, people like Joe Pasternak, Jack Cummings. Were there distinct units reflecting different or conflicting policies? Did producers specialize in certain kinds of musicals?

Producers had a lot to say, certainly as much to say as they wanted to say—I'm talking about the producers you mentioned—and they were important in the kind of pictures they made in that *they* liked them. That's why they made them, in general. So, were they distinct units?

Actually, nothing was distinctive about anything. Nobody was assigned to anybody, nobody had any more authority than anybody else. Except what he could brag for himself. However, in practice, it worked as a sort of unit. It was Arthur Freed who thought of it as a sort of a unit, which was garbage. But he, Freed, loved film musicals, he really loved them and really wanted to promote them and really ate them, like . . . And he wanted to think of this as his group. He would say things like "my unit wouldn't do that" or "my unit did that," because he never wanted to say "*I* did that." First of all because he didn't feel that. I can only say that he made a joke once when he was walking with Vincente Minnelli down the street at Metro—in one sense it was very snotty and in another very sweet—he saw Joe Pasternak walking ahead of him and he turned to Vincente and said to him: "there but for you go I!" Arthur thought of himself as loving these people and helping them. He saw them as supporting him in his position, and he wanted to keep them together. He was always jealous of those people who were doing something, like me, and there was a sort of rivalry, which is inevitable. But there was no such thing as a "unit," except in his head. And it is precisely because of that that, in my opinion, there really was such a thing as a "Freed unit."

For Freed and Roger Edens, music seems to have been the crucial factor. . . .

Well, Freed was a lyric writer and Roger was a vocal coach—I'm talking about their origins—and a rehearsal pianist, so of course they were interested in music more than Pasternak, who was a waiter . . .

How do you feel about musicals without dance?

It's almost impossible to say. I loved *Cabaret* and I don't think it had much dancing in it. It had a lot of expertise, I suppose you can call that dancing. A musical doesn't have to have dancing in it, but I like dancing and if there's any way to get dancing into a musical, I like to put it in there. . . .

Did you and Kelly have any sense that you enjoyed a special place or prestige, along with Minnelli, in MGM's musical output or was everything regarded more or less as important as everything else?

It depends on who you're talking about, of course, but in terms of the studio or even Arthur Freed, whom I praise as highly as I possible can, he didn't say "there but for you go I" to Kelly and me, he said it to Minnelli because it was Minnelli he really loved, for whatever reason right or wrong, and Gene and I were second-stringers as far as Freed was concerned. As far as the studio was concerned I was a fifth-stringer and Minnelli was top-class, and George Sidney was very big and Berkeley was very big. But I don't think it matters. *Seven Brides for Seven Brothers,* as far as the studio was concerned, was a B picture and they didn't give a damn about it. It didn't make any difference.

As long as you had a producer who . . .

We didn't have any producer. He was in Mexico—he didn't care what we did. They left it to him. If he was away, that was his problem. There we were making a movie and that was that. He trusted us, he was away, and we made the picture. In truth, it was his picture, no matter how he arrived at it. . . .

You have worked with studios other than MGM, including Paramount and Warners. How different were the working conditions? Were your films different as a result?

No, the working conditions were pretty much fine everywhere. I have no complaints about any of the studios. When I had a fight—and I only ever had a few of them with the studios—they always, and I mean always, backed down and let you alone. I mean, you'd be hanging yourself, but they left you alone.

Now that the classic studio system has gone, do you have any reflections on its strengths and limitations?

Well, I have a lot. It had both very big strengths and very terrible illnesses about it. One could write a whole book about the system, although it was not really a system, it was simply a situation. They were trying to make as many pictures as possible and they would employ as many people as they thought could contribute in any way to a picture. But it was never clear what anyone was to contribute. We were all thrown into a giant hopper and left to try to swim our way to the top. In one sense you were thrown together with a lot of marvelous people, and in another sense you were in a sort of war. And in a third sense, you had over you a general feeling being directed from above about the kinds of films which were acceptable and what was acceptable in them. It was a very vague thing, but you were aware of it, and you were always being pushed in one direction or another. So what was always the surprise—although it's inevitable—was that you were able to do something different from what they wanted, because what they wanted was what they already had, so it was yesterday's dinner.

So if you wanted to innovate, you were always in trouble?

You were always in trouble and yet you always had to do it anyway, in order to survive. *You* knew it, and they sort of knew it too. That was the pressure cooker you were in and that's what created the situation. There were a lot of people in there struggling to beat you at it and do better than you, so you were in this marathon race.

So having a producer like Freed was extremely important . . .

Terribly important. What was directed down from him was *slightly* different, and that was his big strength. His strength was his attitude and his position. He was willing to put his job and his reputation on the line every time because his attitude was different from other people's. That's where it was.

How did you work with departments such as Art, Special Effects, Music?
Hard.

Was the collaboration always extremely intimate?
It had to be.

Was the individual influence of someone like Cedric Gibbons felt or not?

No, not as an art director. By the time I was making films he was head of the MGM Art Department and they were making forty to sixty films a year. But we did see him quite a lot. A lot of meetings were held in his office and he was present but the art director for the movie was always there. Cedric was actually a marvelous art director who could never get into it, who could never catch up, and typically because of that he would offer a suggestion which was no good or too difficult, because he didn't know enough about what you were doing.

Was there any sense that he was also passing along requirements about style?

No. Metro couldn't care less about the art direction of the film. All they cared about really was the kind of film it was and who was in it. They didn't care a damn, and they were worried about money.

How is a dance number conceived and communicated to the performers? It is easier to imagine how a dramatic sequence is directed, shaped.

Its conceived in your head. You're working with much more abstract forms. You can't do it until it's concrete, you can't direct abstractly any more than you can write or paint abstractly—it's only the *result* which is abstract. It has to be specific in order for you to do it. You can't say something vague as a piece of direction because it doesn't mean anything.

So it would be very difficult for a non-dancer to communicate an idea for a dance number.

It would be ludicrous. It would be like a man teaching English literature who only spoke Chinese or something.

Minnelli?

Vincente did get a lot of thoughts about librettos for musical sequences, like the "Limehouse Blues" number in *Ziegfeld Follies*. But a number is communicated to the performers by doing it yourself or trying to explain it or getting someone else to do it. As abstract as it may look, its got to be an absolutely concretized idea, down to the last eyelash, the last, barest detail and whisker and hair of the head. It's anything but vague.

While you're conceiving a number, at the same time you're conceiving how you will photograph it?

Yes, it all just grows and emerges together. And you keep on changing it, like the script. You keep working at it and thinking, and you get some thoughts as you're shooting it, naturally, and you get a lot of thoughts after you've done it. It's what the fellow said: "nothing's ever written, it's re-written." It's never finished, and eventually you have to stop because you just can't go on forever. You have to say "well, that's it."

There's always a point where you say to yourself that you could still improve it but you'll just have to stop?

Something always stops you.

Were the ballet sequences, "A Day in New York" in On the Town and "Broadway Melody" in Singin' in the Rain, conceived right at the start of the movies—were they always integral to your idea?

They were never an integral part; that's their problem. I don't think they are even now—I never thought they were. I'd like to take them out of the pictures. I wish they weren't there. The one in *Singin' in the Rain* is actually less objectionable because it has less phoney pretension about it than the one in *On the Town*.

They both feel like something added to me, but the one in *Singin' in the Rain* is less sort of horseshit. And it's helped by the fact that it's done with some humor. We always knew we were going to have to do something and we never knew quite what. It's true of every sequence; some of them just come out better. First of all, if they had been shorter they would have been less of an intrusion. It's because they are so heavy, in length, that they feel something of a wart.

Your collaboration with Kelly was obviously very close. Did it work out in any principled way—did you for example have more to do with the dramatic sequences?

No.

There was always a sort of confluence of ideas?

Or conflict.

How would you compare working with Kelly and Astaire? Did their differences of style mean working differently with them?

Not because of their differences in style, more because of their differences in personality.

Was Astaire more fixed in or content with a style? Kelly seems to want to innovate more.

No more than Astaire. Astaire's the fellow who started it all. He was anything but content, Fred Astaire. He would never go to the rushes, for example. He always used to say to me, "there's no point in my going to see it, it's too late now." He didn't go because it pained him so, not because he was happy with it, but because he suffered so. It's too late now not to like it.

Did Astaire tend to work in terms of steps and Kelly to make more expressive use of his body, of space? Did it mean directing them very differently?

It means *using* them very differently, and knowing what they have to offer. You have to think of a musical number that one is going to do in a different way than the other would do it. But it's like playing a game of tennis, it all happens because you're working together. Since it is a real collaboration, you offer what you've got, they give you what they've got, and you use it in the way that it works.

Was Astaire as involved in the choreography of his sequences as Kelly?

Well, they were both up to their eye-balls in it, so it's hard to measure. They were both tireless, fiends for work, and vitally interested in what they were going to do and how to do it. They had somewhat different feelings about how they could best do a musical sequence, because they're quite different people.

Was Astaire, for example, concerned about how a particular number would be photographed?

No, he would concentrate on his number.

But Kelly was always thinking about that other aspect of the dance, about the actual photographing of the number?

Somewhat, but Astaire, funnily enough, had these ideas for numbers despite his lack of knowledge of cinema. It was Fred Astaire who did the number with the fun-house mirrors, and who did the number in the rain, "Isn't This a Lovely Day to Be Caught in the Rain"; it was Fred Astaire who did the golf number; it was Fred Astaire who did the rear projection number—this was all before Kelly and I came on the scene. All these were cinematic innovations of Fred Astaire. Everybody minimizes what extraordinary cinematic ideas Fred Astaire had in those pictures. They tend to believe he was a dancer and that was all. *I* didn't do any of those pictures, but they had a gigantic impression on me. When he did "Bojangles" it was an incredible piece of film, with shadows of Astaire behind dancing with himself in front of them. I was about nine or ten years old then and I must have seen it forty times, that sequence. And it was that which made these huge impressions on me to do cinema dancing ideas; they *were* surrealistic and that's what hit me so hard. Then later Kelly and I did the double exposure thing in *Cover Girl* and the mouse thing in *Anchors Aweigh,* but the spark to me for all that was Fred Astaire, without any question. While he himself literally doesn't know anything about a camera, he knows about movies as something quite different from dancing on the stage. Even the number he did on the stage, the *Top Hat* one, is an unbelievable piece of movie, a sensational idea.

You have worked with a number of other choreographers, including Michael Kidd, Bob Fosse, Gower Champion, Eugene Loring, Nick Castle—were there any you had a special feeling for?

Yes, the ones I had—and have—a special relationship with are Kidd and Fosse, because I admire their work. I just admired them as talents, and as soon as that happens you find you can work better. If you like something, somehow it's a better collaboration. . . .

It's Always Fair Weather has often been considered as having a strange, rather downbeat, subject for a musical and perhaps because of that as marking the end of a certain era of the musical.

Actually, I looked at it again not long ago and its not cynical or downbeat—its all sugar-coated if anything. It did mark the end of an era, because it was a failure. I don't think we had anything particularly new to offer, it was a re-hash, we'd done it. You'd seen it all already and we didn't bring anything new, except

Gene did what is probably one of his best numbers—the "I Like Myself" number on roller-skates. But it wasn't a success—I don't mean commercially, I don't think it was a huge success as a film. I thought Gene did it very well, and the Dolores Gray number "Thanks a Lot, But No Thanks" is still very funny.

Does a lot of the stage versions of Pajama Game and Damn Yankees remain in the films?

A lot, yes. They were hit shows and that's what the company wanted to make.

After 1959, did you still want to make musicals but could not set them up?

I certainly didn't want to make only musicals, but yes. Even in the mid-sixties it wasn't easier. The only things I could have made would have been movies of hits shows and there's just not much to do on them. . . .

You have found Britain a good place to work?

Very, yes. In terms of everything except musical people. I like it enormously making pictures here, I like everything about it. They do lack a certain energy, which is American and which I like to see in musicals . . .

You see that resulting from a different tradition of popular theater?

I think it comes from a whole different tradition of everything. . . . The musical theater in America is really European. . . . The music writers were more or less fleeing Jews from Europe, and they've all come out of that tradition—Kern, Gershwin, and even Bernstein, while he's American born, that's his back-ground, and Steve Sondheim, Oscar Hammerstein, Dick Rodgers and Larry Hart. The only exception is Cole Porter and he's got his own kind of Americanism.

From *Movie* 24 (Spring 1977): 27–35.

32

One Thing's for Sure, R 'n' R Is Boffo B.O.

Alan Freed

(1958)

No matter how you look at it or feel towards it, rock 'n' roll is just a variation of the 4-by-4 tempo that was used by singers of the Al Jolson–Harry Richman–Eddie Cantor era. If you listen closely to Jolson's "Mammy" or Richman's "Vagabond Song," it's the same as rock 'n' roll. As a matter of technical musical fact, all rock 'n' roll numbers are based on the four chords originated by "Banjo-Eyes" in his famous theme, "We Want Cantor."

What we are hearing and playing and writing today is a reprise of the music that stirred the country three and four decades ago. Actually, rock 'n' roll is a form of music that dates back to the workers on the southern fields, before it moved into the Jolson era. But not until the teenagers of the middle 1950s adopted it as their own did it result in such a boon to the music business.

This past year, especially so. In the period from 1946 to 1950 a big sale on a record was 500,000 with a few exceptions. Then in the middle '50s along came Elvis Presley and "Don't Be Cruel." The trade was more flabbergasted than the public when it was revealed that this rock 'n' roll record sold around 5,000,000 copies. Elvis followed it with a few more in the same neighborhood. It didn't take the record business long to realize what was happening. Other platters on the rock 'n' roll style were pressed pronto and single disk sales began to broaden in scope. What had been figments of many recording companies' and press agents' imaginations became an actuality—the fabulous unknowns with the million-selling records. Today as a direct result of the rock 'n' roll trend the disk that sold 200,00 in '46 to '50 now sells about a million. The record that would stop at a 500,000 mark in another era now sells about 2,000,000.

The popularity of rock 'n' roll music has had a heavy influence on TV. Ed Sullivan and Steve Allen have used as many as three to five r & r artists on some of their shows, as does "The Big Record" and other national TV programs. Local video shows are likewise saturated wit rock 'n' roll talent, amateur as well as established names.

In the past year almost all the major motion picture studios turned out top films featuring rock 'n' roll artists like Elvis Presley, Tommy Sands, Pat Boone, et al. It is granted that musicals featuring popular recording names of the day have been made for years by major and independent studios yet the amount of monies being grossed by musicals featuring rock 'n' roll have been nothing short of fantastic. Not only here but abroad. None of the rock 'n' roll musicals has been known to garner 4-star critiques, it's true, but that too may come in time. One thing is sure—they do business at the box office.

Tours of rock 'n' roll artists go out on 12 to 15 weeks of one-nighter trips to many towns in the U.S. that seldom see live musical talent. As much as a quarter of a million profit is realized from one of these tours. The demand for rock 'n' roll talent has some of the country's best promoters scheduling big r & r jaunts for 1958.

The biggest boon, however, has been to music publishers who, not many years ago, numbered a little over 100. Today there are thousands. Through the power of rock 'n' roll popularity publishers earn money from record sales, performance fees of records on TV & radio, picture rights and, yes, even from whatever sheet music sales that result.

This much-maligned music has also been a plum to promoters of live stage shows. Musical vaudeville shows were considered kaput until in-person shows in major theatres away back in the early '50s, featuring the "big beat" of the first rock 'n' roll stars this era. As a result, disk jockeys in every big city in the country are staging similar shows.

It is in my opinion that rock 'n' roll, which has always been with us as a native American art form, is at last being accepted as part and parcel of the nation's musical form.

Which reminds of the time recently when Mike Wallace invited me on his interview show. I had to turn him down. "Why argue about rock 'n' roll?" I said. "It's Bigger than Both of Us."

PART FOUR

The Recession Soundtrack

From Albums to Auteurs,
Songs to Serialism (1960–1977)

INTRODUCTION

By the early 1960s, the anxieties that Hollywood experienced after the war had blossomed into something much more than temporary insecurity. The industry was now, as some scholars have described it, "at the nadir of a long transformation," the studios so beleaguered that the industry was in full recession and hovered, in the opinion of many, "near death."[1] The statistics outline this decline in starkly dramatic terms. In 1946, cinema attendance stood at a high of roughly 90 million, but by 1960 attendance figures had dropped to 40 million, and they continued to fall into the early 1970s, hitting an all-time low of 15.8 million in 1971. This precipitous drop in attendance was accompanied by a similarly steep reduction in film production. Whereas through the mid-1950s the studios had produced more than three hundred films a year, by the early 1960s that number stood at just over 140, and it slumped to a record low of 80 films a year in 1970.[2] In the 1960s and 1970s, the decline that marked the postwar years had turned into a full recession, with some studios hovering near or on the verge of economic collapse. It was a crisis in film production that, as historian David Cook notes, was "matched only by the coming of sound."[3]

The film industry was not the only institution experiencing crisis and upheaval in the 1960s and early 1970s. The country as a whole was enduring an unprecedented wave of social and political unrest. The decade began with the blossoming of the civil rights movement and the shocking assassination of President John F. Kennedy, and it ended with more high-level political assassinations, including presidential candidate Robert Kennedy and the acclaimed civil rights leader Reverend Martin

Luther King. The decade also saw the start of a brutal and unsuccessful war in southeast Asia. As protests over the country's involvement in Vietnam escalated, the government's reaction grew increasingly agitated, peaking in 1970 when members of the U.S. National Guard opened fire on protesters at Kent State University in Ohio, killing four students. The early 1970s were equally tumultuous. Although the government had by the middle of the decade extracted itself from the costly and unpopular war in Vietnam, the country continued to experience political upheaval with the eruption of the Watergate scandal. What began with the burglarizing of Democratic national headquarters by Republican operatives ended with the criminal conviction of several high-level government officials and, in August 1974, the resignation of President Richard Nixon.

Though for very different reasons, the film industry, too, was experiencing a period of turmoil and instability. Hollywood continued to suffer fallout from the 1948 Supreme Court divestment decree ending the monopoly the studios had over film distribution and exhibition. The buyouts, takeovers, and sell-offs that the studios endured throughout the 1950s had left them operationally in a state of disarray. Without their theater holdings and revenues, the studios were physically smaller and financially weaker than they had been throughout the 1930s and 1940s. Because most were under new management, they were also operationally insecure, experimenting with new organizational structures and production procedures that would help restore revenues to prewar levels. In this state of disorganization, the studios lost the ability to gauge audience tastes and expectations. Although some successful films were made, in general the gap between profitable and unprofitable films grew disproportionately wider. In 1961, a full three-quarters of the movies released by Hollywood lost money.[4]

The industry's finances continued to be destabilized by the increasing presence of television. In 1953, roughly 46 percent of American households owned a television; by 1960, that number had nearly doubled, to over 85 percent.[5] Although scholars caution that movie theater attendance had already begun dropping before television came into its own, there is little doubt that by the 1960s television was siphoning off a significant portion of the film audience. Its small but free pictures continued to be at least partially, if not significantly, responsible for the industry's record low attendance figures and dwindling profits.[6]

With revenues from exhibition no longer reliable, the studios were forced to find new ways to operate in order to cut costs. During the postwar period, independent production had steadily increased as the studios sought to keep star producers, writers, and actors happy with increased flexibility and creative control. With growing recession in the late 1950s and early 1960s, the number of independent production companies surged as the studios sought to trim overhead. Increasingly, the studios now contracted with independent production companies, having them coordinate or "package" all the materials and labor necessary to make a film. It was the independent production company's job to find a script, a director, actors, and major craft personnel (cinematographers, art directors, composers) for any given film project. The studios were still involved in the process, but their participation now revolved around financing and distribution. By the mid-1960s, the studios were largely "managerial entities," focused on "the securing of productions funds, the arranging of contracts, the supervising of productions, and on the marketing of the final product, rather than the actual producing of feature films."[7] From only a dozen or so independent production companies in the mid-1950s, by the mid-1960s there were over 165,[8] accounting for nearly two-thirds of all films being made in Hollywood. By the mid-1970s, the majors were producing only one-fifth of the films being made.[9]

The shift to independent production required a similar shift to a freelance labor force. With revenues at an all-time low, and with so much production being taken up by independent companies, the studios could no longer afford to keep large pools of actors or crafts personnel on staff. Two significant strikes involving the Screen Actors Guild and the Federation of Musicians hastened the transition to a freelance labor arrangement. In the 1940s and 1950s, actors had stretched the practice of long-term contracting as they sought to assume more creative and financial control of their work, and the practice remained largely intact until 1960 when the Screen Actors Guild went on strike. Although the actors were agitating primarily for a greater share of the profits from their work in film and television, the studios agreed to their demands only on condition that the actors relinquish long-term contracting, which they did. Some contracts continued to be honored—Rock Hudson's, one of the last in the system, for example, did not expire until 1965. But the strike effectively marked the beginning of freelance employment for film actors.[10]

Most of the crafts departments experienced a similar transition. In 1958, the Federation of Musicians struck, demanding a larger share of the revenues from their film and television work the studios acceded, but only in exchange for the end of long-term contracting. For film musicians this meant the disbanding of long-standing in-house or studio orchestras. Composers were still needed to score films, and orchestras were needed to record those scores, but the musicians were now contracted by independent production companies on a film-by-film basis.[11] As with the Screen Actors Guild, the musicians' improved salaries and share of royalties came at the expense of job security.[12]

As the studios struggled to solidify new operating procedures, they also worked to develop new streams of revenue. One tactic was to renegotiate relations with the television industry.[13] Although the studios still denounced television as inferior, in the 1960s they began to participate directly in television production. Several film studios, for example, sold or leased their empty sound stages and production spaces to television production companies.[14] They also profited from licensing films from their libraries for television broadcast. In 1961, some

45 theatrical films were aired on television; by 1970, that number had soared to 166.[15] In the early 1970s, the demand for feature-film material for television was so great that the networks began to make their own. Although the film studios initially objected to "made-for-TV" movies, they were soon participating in and profiting from the production and financing of them. Ironically, as film historian Paul Monaco points out, "television had taken away much of the mass audience from movies in the 1950s only to become increasingly dependent on the motion picture industry's product and production values for much of its prime-time programming by the end of the 1960s."[16]

In an attempt to generate revenue, the film industry also renegotiated its ties with the music industry. Postwar technological innovations had dramatically improved sound reproduction quality and made home stereo equipment readily available to the mainstream public. This and the advent of the long-playing record, or LP, in 1956 began to dramatically alter music consumption patterns in the United State. Between 1946 and 1969, the number of record players in American homes quadrupled, from approximately 15 million to over 60 million, and record sales likewise grew exponentially, from $250 million to $650 million.[17] Naturally, the studios wished to benefit from the record boom directly. While their methods for extracting, licensing, and commercializing film music remained more or less the same, the physical practice of recording of film music changed dramatically.[18] Now, instead of using an outside record company to produce a film soundtrack, the studios recorded it themselves, either by creating their own record companies or converting preexisting ones. In 1957, Paramount bought Dot Records, and the next year Warner Brothers, 20th Century–Fox, and Columbia followed suit, creating their own subsidiary record companies from scratch.[19] In order to more directly and efficiently control film music profits, the studios began to horizontally integrate themselves with the music recording industry. If the sale of ancillary soundtrack albums was going to substitute for severely lagging ticket sales, the studios need to wring every bit of profit out of them that they could. In-house recording was the key.[20]

In the 1960s, Hollywood also sought to boost profits by expanding the business of importing foreign films. During the postwar period, tariffs and quotas had forced the studios to import films from countries with strong national industries to protect, such as England, Italy, Sweden, and Japan. Fed a steady diet of these films, Americans' appetite grew to the point that by the mid-1960s a significant and reliable audience for foreign films had emerged. The studios encouraged the growth of this niche market by defining these films as not just foreign but as serious, artistic, and noninstitutional, descriptions that resonated especially with youthful audiences interested in countering conventional culture and in questioning authority and institutions.[21] Americans were introduced to master filmmakers such as Federico Fellini, Ingmar Bergman, Akira Kurosawa, and Luis Buñuel, as well as

emerging directors such as François Truffaut, Jean-Luc Godard, and Claude Cha-
brol, representing the French New Wave, and Alain Resnais, Jacques Demy, Claude
Lelouch, and Michelangelo Antonioni. Foreign films, typically screened at small
"art house" theaters, exposed American audiences to new and unconventional visual and narrative techniques and to new moral sensibilities. Because international
film industries abroad did not adhere to the same production code as the Hollywood studios, films made abroad often presented audiences with morally challenging subject matter and frank, graphic depictions of sex and violence.[22] While the
interest in foreign films did not replace interest in conventional Hollywood fare,
for a few years in the early 1970s the number of foreign film the studios imported
and distributed actually exceeded the number of films that were made domestically.[23] In the 1960s, as Monaco points out, the studios embraced European filmmaking because "labeling a theater an 'art house' theater or promoting a movie by
calling it 'New Wave' could translate into considerable box-office profits for niche
exhibitors in the United States" and for the studios distributing them.[24]

The revision of old partnerships and the development of new ones were some
strategies the industry pursued to generate revenue. But it also sought to counter
the recession by lowering production costs. In the late 1940s and early 1950s, the
studios had been forced to some degree to engage in the practice of "runaway
production"—shooting and producing movies overseas—by European countries
looking to protect their national film industries from the dominance of Hollywood. By the 1960s, however, with freelance labor and production costs in general growing ever more costly at home, runaway production became a highly
desirable approach. By 1960, 40 percent of all Hollywood studio productions—90
out of 164 feature films—were "runaways." Although many were shot and produced in Europe, locations and crews in Asia, Africa, and South America were
used as well.[25] Many of the era's biggest-budget historical epics, such as *Cleopatra*
(1963) and *El Cid* (1961), and musicals like *The Sound of Music* (1965), *Doctor Doolittle* (1967), *Chitty Chitty Bang Bang* (1968), *Fiddler on the Roof* (1971), and *Willy
Wonka and the Chocolate Factory* (1971) were runaways. Others, though considered foreign productions, were heavily financed by Hollywood; these included
Lawrence of Arabia (1961), *Dr. Strangelove* (1964), *Dr. Zhivago* (1965), *Tom Jones*
(1963), *A Fistful of Dollars* (1964), *A Man for All Seasons* (1966), *The Good, the Bad
and the Ugly* (1966), *Anne of the Thousand Days* (1969), and *2001: A Space Odyssey*
(1968). As historian Robert Sklar points out, where in the previous decade American companies had made "quota quickies" to satisfy foreign trade practices, by
the 1960s "overseas locations and American investment in foreign production
had become essential elements in Hollywood's financial survival."[26]

All of these new practices and partnerships kept the studios from slipping into
bankruptcy, but they didn't give them the financial stability they needed. That
solution came in the mid to late 1960s when the studios were taken over by several

large business conglomerates. In 1966, Paramount Studios was bought by Gulf & Western, a large holding company with diverse interests ranging from auto parts to electronics. Although takeovers and buyouts had been a regular part of the landscape in the postwar period, the purchase of Paramount was noteworthy because Gulf & Western had no connection to or previous experience with the film industry.[27] By the end of the decade, the other studios had been similarly bought by large conglomerates with no experience in film production or distribution. United Artists was bought by the Transamerica Corporation; Warner Brothers was purchased by Kinney National Services Corporation, whose chief activities were manufacturing shoes and managing parking lots; and MGM was sold to the hotel magnate Kirk Kerkorian.[28] While the takeovers were denounced by many in the film industry and the new CEOs were largely seen as robber barons with no creative credentials or interests, the financial benefits were swift and undeniable. As Monaco observes, "The mergers and takeovers in Hollywood during the late 1960s stabilized studio finances and quickly set feature film production in the United States back on a promising financial course."[29] The industry's financial recovery was further assured in the early 1970s when Congress enacted legislation that brought tax relief specifically aimed at boosting the economic health of the film industry. The profit shelters and investments tax credits instituted in the Nixon Administrations Revenue Act of 1971 gave the conglomerates controlling the studios increased abilities to generate and retain profits. "These measures," scholar David Cook points out, "provided, *for the first time in film industry history,* a solid base for investment" and a meaningful solution to the recession.[30]

Economic instability within the industry, combined with general political and social upheaval nationwide, had a significant impact on film content as well. The studios' retreat into production financing afforded independent producers and production companies license to reexamine both conventional style and content. But at first, because the studios were above all looking for safe, solid profits, the new independent model of production allowed only modest experimentation. Movies such as Hitchcock's *Psycho* (1960), Kazan's *Splendor in the Grass* (1961), Kubrick's *Lolita* (1962), and Lumet's *The Pawnbroker* (1965), which transgressed production code mandates for the depiction of sex and violence, and Frankenheimer's *The Manchurian Candidate* (1962) and Kubrick's *Dr. Strangelove* (1964), which challenged American audiences with new and unusual political perspectives, were more the exception than the rule.[31] Because the production code was still largely in place, narrative or stylistic innovation was sporadic and confined to a handful of filmmakers. "Rather than leading American film toward more adventurous risk-taking," Monaco observes, the new independent, picture-by-picture system initially produced "less room for experimentation and high-risk production . . . leading to greater emphasis on projects that stayed closer to tested formulas."[32]

In the late 1960s, however, film content changed dramatically when the industry adopted a new production code. Citing changing "social values" and the country's increasingly liberal attitudes toward sex, violence, and language, Jack Valenti, the new president of the Motion Picture Association of America, spearheaded the effort to establish a new and more liberal system of self-censorship for the industry. Spurred also by moral and stylistic liberties taken by foreign filmmakers, Valenti proposed significant changes to the production code that had stood unaltered since the mid-1930s. Most significantly, Valenti stepped away from the limitations that had been placed on the use of "mature content" or topics and behaviors that were deemed taboo, and instead implemented a ratings system that would inform audiences about the contents of films they were about to see. The new Code and Ratings Administration (CARA) assigned films awaiting distribution into one of four categories identified by a system of letters: G, indicating no questionable content and appropriate for general audiences; PG, signaling material that required parental guidance for young audiences; R, for mature content that was prohibited to children under 17 years of age without an accompanying adult; and X, for content unacceptable to any person under 17. By classifying films in terms of their treatment of sex, violence, and language, the new ratings system profoundly changed film production not only by allowing more mature content but also by shifting the site of censorship from production to exhibition.[33]

Filmmakers immediately exercised the stylistic and narrative freedoms allowed under the new production code. In this they were encouraged by studio executives, who reasoned that a domestic style of "artistic" filmmaking would attract audiences and so tap into the revenues being generated from the exhibition of foreign "artistic" films.[34] With the studios' permission, young directors well versed not just in past Hollywood traditions but also in contemporary European cinematic themes and trends began to experiment with more liberal content and with unconventional visual styles. Initially labeled the "New Hollywood" or the "Hollywood Renaissance," directors such as Mike Nichols, Arthur Penn, Stanley Kubrick, Robert Altman, Sam Peckinpah, Hal Ashby, Bob Rafelson, Roman Polanski, and William Friedkin experimented very successfully, if the box-office popularity of their films is any indication, with more permissive attitudes toward sex and violence and with more sophisticated narratives and innovative camera work.[35]

A second wave of young directors, most of them fresh out of newly launched university film programs, also participated in reshaping the Hollywood landscape in the post-CARA era. This so-called Film Generation, or the "Hollywood Brats," included filmmakers like Francis Ford Coppola, George Lucas, Martin Scorsese, Brian De Palma, and Peter Bogdanovich and helped define postclassical American filmmaking in the early 1970s as unique, diverse, and unconventional.[36]

As with their immediate predecessors, this group challenged audiences with more mature and graphic language and content and with more liberal social and political discourse. Both groups also borrowed heavily from the visual style of contemporary European filmmakers, especially the camera and editing techniques of New Wave and *cinéma vérité*—jump cuts, unstable camera work, natural light and sound.[37]

Throughout the late 1960s and early 1970s, the studios not only tolerated but encouraged challenging, personal styles of filmmaking from these young domestic *auteurs,* in the hope that they would generate profits as strong as their foreign counterparts.[38] Liberated by a new production code and looking to expand their successful art house market, the studios facilitated a new and diverse period of experimentation in mainstream Hollywood filmmaking.

The studios also used the new production code to pursue niche markets. The studios had discovered the "youth" market in the 1950s, but it wasn't until the 1960s and 1970s that they began to see teens as an audience worthy of A-level production status. Even before the new code was instituted, filmmakers like Roger Corman had begun to challenge the content of conventional "teen pics" by depicting youths engaging in the more serious and sensational subculture of drugs and motorcycles. With CARA in effect, similarly themed pictures like *Easy Rider* (1968) enjoyed mainstream success as well.[39] The new production code also facilitated a resurgence of the horror film, as illustrated for example by George Romero's *Night of the Living Dead* (1968) and *The Texas Chainsaw Massacre* (1974). A successful B genre in the 1950s, in the 1960s and early 1970s the horror film was legitimized by such young auteurs as Roman Polanski, Ken Russell, William Friedkin, and Richard Donner, who explored its graphic and religious (or sacrilegious) potentials in the popular films *Rosemary's Baby* (1968), *The Devils* (1971), *The Exorcist* (1973), and *The Omen* (1976).[40]

In many ways, the desire to capture the profitable youth market directly overlapped with the studios' artistic, auteur imperative. "In the unstable environment of the crumbling studio system," Cook observes, "the studios' transitional managers briefly turned over the reins of creative power to a rising generation of independents and first-time directors whose values seemed to resonate with the newly emerging 'youth culture' market." There was an "industry-wide perception," he continues, "that the youth market was the key to reviving the sagging box office" and that young directors and youth-oriented pictures that challenged the authority of cornerstone institutions like the government and the church would appeal to young audiences engaged in social and political protest.[41] The studios' interest in exploiting the emerging youth market resulted in a noticeable increase in films with youth-oriented topics like sex, motorcycles, cars, and drugs, but also, as the war in Vietnam wore on into the 1970s, in films with themes of social justice and political protest.

CARA encouraged the studios to cater to other fringe or niche markets as well. In the late 1960s and 1970s, three new "exploitation" genres flourished. Although pornography had been a part of film history since its inception, the new production code allowed filmmakers to experiment with it as a legitimate theatrical genre. Films like *Deep Throat* (1972), *The Devil in Miss Jones* (1972), and *Behind the Green Door* (1973) helped to define the industry's new X rating and identify a new and profitable viewership for adult films.[42] The studios also used the new production code to target African American and Asian American audiences, in the form of "blaxploitation" and marital arts films. *Sweet Sweetback's Baadasssss Song* (1971), *Shaft* (1971), *Superfly* (1972), and *Foxy Brown* (1974) were successful studio productions that catered to African American audiences with more graphic depictions of contemporary morality and urban crime.[43] Bruce Lee's *Enter the Dragon* (1973), with its extended and graphic fight scenes, exploited a growing national interest in martial arts and Asian culture.[44] Although these films perpetuated unflattering and even distasteful racial and ethnic stereotyping, they also created new creative opportunities for minority directors, actors, and production personnel.

Not all of the studios' energy was directed at niche markets. The industry also tried to entice audiences to return to the theater with conventional genres and topics. The film musical had become increasingly unpopular with American audiences by the early 1960s, in part because it had failed to feature new musical styles like rock 'n' roll. The unexpected and phenomenal success of *The Sound of Music* in 1965 delayed the genre's complete demise for several years. Yet subsequent attempts to recreate *The Sound of Music*'s success, big-budget projects like *Dr. Doolittle* (1967), *Camelot* (1967), *Star* (1968), *Sweet Charity* (1968), *Chitty Chitty Bang Bang* (1968), *Hello, Dolly!* (1969), and *Paint Your Wagon* (1969), were spectacular disasters. *Hello Dolly!*'s losses were so great they nearly bankrupted 20th Century–Fox.[45]

With the musical no longer a reliable method for generating profits, the studios began to search for new narrative blockbuster formulas. Although Francis Ford Coppola's *The Godfather* (1972) and *The Godfather, Part 2* (1974), based on Mario Puzo's bestselling novel, suggested the presold historical epic might be a possible substitute, subsequent epics failed to generate a bankable formula. What did succeed were "disaster pictures," dramatic thrillers with thin plots and stunning special effects such as *Airport* (1970), *The Poseidon Adventure* (1972), *The Towering Inferno* (1974), *Earthquake* (1974), and *Jaws* (1975); with their attention to improved sonic and visual effects, these films proved enormously popular with mainstream audiences, and the profit-hungry studios focused their resources on the new genre.

Now devoting more space and financing to production of blockbuster films, the studios giving less support to the more challenging and unconventional auteur

productions. By the late 1970s, studio-financed auteur filmmaking was all but ex-
tinct. The recession had taken the studios to the brink of bankruptcy, but it also
generated one of the most interesting and intellectually challenging periods of film
production, one that temporarily but irrevocably changed the visual and sonic
style of American narrative cinema.

The recession significantly reorganized film production and diversified film content, and not surprisingly, it had an equally striking effect on film music. Music
was not immune to the changes invoked in response to the recession. In fact, in
several instances it was a central element in the industry's attempts to generate
new sources of revenue and capture new viewers. Licensing theme song rights to
performers and sheet music publishers had generated extra income for the studios since the silent era. But as June Bundy's 1960 trade journal article "Film
Themes Link Movie, Disk Trades" (**Document 33**) reveals, in the early part of
the recession the sale of recordings of film theme songs was a central pillar in the
industry's recovery strategy. When the record industry began to boom in the
mid-1950s in the wake of the LP and home stereo revolution, film executives gave
fresh attention to the soundtrack, in hopes that film music recordings—theme
songs especially—would boom as well. According to Bundy, the industry did indeed enjoy a surge in profits from the sale of film score LPs. Part of that increase
came from a new strategy instituted to better control film music production and
marketing. As we saw above, instead of creating partnerships with existing record companies to re-record film soundtracks to sell as LPs, in the late 1950s and
early 1960s most of the studios either bought or started their own subsidiary record companies and began producing and marketing film music themselves.

   As before, the commercialization of film music generated income for the cash-
strapped studios, but in the 1960s it also affected the structure and instrumentation of the film score. Previously, film scores were composed with only the faint
possibility of extraction, primarily for concert-hall performance; now, the recording boom put pressure on composers to reformulate the underscore to fit contemporary popular music formats, specifically the "hit single" of 78 r.p.m. records and
radio play. Theme songs had been an important part of early sound-film scoring
formulas, but in the recession there was new interest in engineering orchestral
themes to follow contemporary commercial forms and styles. Producers pressured
composers to conceive orchestral themes as pop "singles" or album "tracks"—
roughly two minutes long, in ABA form, and with a lyrical melodic contour or
striking rhythmic pattern.[46] With ancillary revenues at stake, the film score in the
early 1960s became increasingly monothematic, anchored to an identifiable theme
or title song that repeated throughout the film. This intense refocusing of film music also resulted in a significant shift in creative control. As Bundy reports, film
executives, not composers or even directors, were dictating "which composers and

which types of material have the best potential for the singles field" and were insisting that composers build "film themes as singles hits."

Eddie Kalish's 1961 trade journal article "Mancini Debunks Album Values" **(Document 34)** likewise documents the enormous influence the music industry was having on film music in the early 1960s. The "singles" format was still central, but as the article reveals, a new style of scoring was coming into use. In 1961, Henry Mancini had just teamed with director Blake Edwards to produce an enormously popular symphonic jazz theme for Edwards's television show *Peter Gunn* and an equally popular theme song and score for his first studio film, *Breakfast at Tiffany's* (1960). For Mancini, the key to successfully commercializing film music lay not just in turning themes into pop "singles" but in altering the instrumentation of the film score to reflect contemporary popular trends. Jazz had already been incorporated into film scoring a decade earlier when "symphonic" jazz was attached to dramatic genres, specifically *noir* and social problem films. Mancini added to this convention by introducing a more "contemporary styling" of jazz to film scoring, a lighter, Latin and Afro-Cuban style articulated by smaller, six-to-ten-piece "jazz combos." Mancini also expanded the context for jazz by using it to underscore lighthearted and sophisticated comedies as well as dramas.[47]

Kalish's report also emphasizes the important contributions Mancini made to the structure of film music. Where record producers were reconceptualizing film music to fit the requirements of the 78 record and radio single, Mancini was restructuring it to suit the parameters of the new long-playing (LP) record album. As the composer himself points out, the singles format encouraged film executives to demand hit songs from composers but not to think about the commercial viability of the rest of the underscore. The rest of the score was presented as unusable, "an assortment of fragments which don't mean much musically or commercially." Mancini's solution was to redesign the film score, tailoring it to the parameters of the LP album. The whole underscore can have commercial value, he argues, if not just the title theme but all the parts of the score are made to conform to the form of a pop single or album track.[48] He composed his scores so that, when re-recorded for disk use, "each selection on the platter" could be "a separate tune with its own identity." Far from debunking the value of the new LP, Mancini reinforces it by reconceptualizing the film score as a collection of hit singles.

The new singles or LP formula, Mancini also observes, was being pursued not just by eager executives but also by composers. Previously, once a composer finished a score and it was recorded onto a film's soundtrack, the studios owned and controlled it. At Mancini's insistence, that began to change. The new preponderance of pop songs and pop instrumentation in film scoring in the 1960s, as Mancini observes, was being driven by a new financial incentive. For the first time, composers were allowed to share directly in the profits made from the commercial sale of film theme songs and soundtrack albums.[49]

This formula was successful and highly profitable for Mancini and others, like newcomers Ernst Gold and Maurice Jarre and veterans Dmitri Tiomkin and Elmer Bernstein. Some composers, however, did not thrive in the commercial, pop music environment. Veteran composer Bernard Herrmann, for instance, lamented the new dominance of the singles score. The need for extra film profits, he observes in **Document 35,** left little or no room for other scoring approaches. "Most producers . . . think that a hit title tune over the screen credits automatically means a hit picture."[50] As Herrmann saw it, film executives and producers, men with little or no musical knowledge, had assumed some of the duties of the composer by dictating what kind of music got used in a film and where. Hermann also lamented the new emphasis on novel instrumentation for theme songs. More and more frequently, composers were being pressured to experiment with unusual or distinctive instrumental combinations in their theme songs; although jazz or conventional orchestral instrumentation was still allowed, he observed, the disproportionate success of two recent film scores—Mancini's score for *Breakfast at Tiffany's* (1960), which featured "a harmonica surrounded by a choral group," and Manos Hadjidakis's score for *Never on Sunday* (1960), featuring an "electric zither"—was causing producers to agitate for scores with similarly "gimmicky" instrumentation.

Not complying with these new compositional mandates, as Herrmann quickly discovered, had dire consequences. When Herrmann refused to provide a theme song for Alfred Hitchcock's *Torn Curtain* (1966), the producers threw out his score and replaced it with a "title theme" pop song and score written by not one but three other composers. The theme-song craze not only severed one of the most important collaborations in film history—Herrmann and Hitchcock never again worked together; it also precipitated Herrmann's exit from Hollywood.[51] The need for ancillary profits also forced many other veteran Hollywood composers, including Franz Waxman, Alfred Newman, Miklós Rósza, and Hugo Friedhofer, out of the film scoring business.[52]

The significant impact the recording industry was having on the sound and shape of film music is reflected in the opening paragraph of a 1967 article by music critic Gene Lees for *High Fidelity* magazine, "The New Sound on the Soundtracks" **(Document 36).** The magazine itself was a product of the recording and stereo boom and the technological innovations that were turning the United States into a nation of "listeners." Although most of its pages reinforced the consumption of classical music, old and new, the magazine also recognized major trends in the recording of popular music. Some of the most successful recordings of 1967, Lees observes, were coming not from classical or popular music but from film music. This was because film composers had adopted new extraction formulas to fit underscores into recorded music formats. "Poor indeed," Lee observes, "is the picture that doesn't have such an album on the market, and perhaps a hit 'title' song to go along with it." The demand for pop songs was so ubiquitous, he concludes, that "at the present we are in a phase of . . . 'the Top Forty score.'" Booming LP sales were restructuring the formlessness of the in-picture score, but improved home stereo equipment was also fueling an interest in film soundtracks. The film industry, as Lee points out, was "far behind the commercial record industry in sound reproduction." As a result, interest in the commercial aspects of film music was also fueled by new recording standards. "Re-recording [the score] for disc can make it more assertive, more communicative, for the home listener."

Instead of observing the death of the orchestral underscore, as Herrmann did, Lee celebrates the Top 40 score and the new composers who were defining it. Henry Mancini, Johnny Mandel, Maurice Jarre, Quincy Jones, Lalo Schifrin, Jerry Goldsmith, Dave Grusin, and John Barry represented a new generation because not only could they write popular melodies, but they also merged new melodic formulas with old composition styles and structures. As Lees observes: "While most of the new generation of film composers have backgrounds in popular music and jazz as well as classical training, perhaps the most significant thing about them is that they are evolving, with casual skill and growing confidence, a new music that partakes of all three traditions." Lees's article documents the rise of these new "third stream" composers and the continued emphasis on the theme song format. But it also suggests the beginnings of an emerging pluralistic style. In response to the growth in auteur and niche filmmaking, composers were being encouraged to experiment with an eclectic range of styles. While knowledge of jazz and popular music idioms was still essential, knowledge of contemporary concert-hall trends was also becoming increasingly useful. An interest in serialism, a highly specialized method of atonal composition, Lees notes, was fast becoming a prerequisite for Hollywood scoring, as was eclecticism. "I like Alban Berg and James Brown, Stravinsky and Duke Ellington," he observes.

A good portion of Renata Adler's 1968 article "Movies: Tuning In to the Sound of New Music" (**Document 37**) is an examination of America's growing appetite for rock 'n' roll music. But it is also an astute critique of another significant event in the historical evolution of film music: the death of the Hollywood musical. Excessive licensing fees and production costs, as most film historians have pointed out, contributed significantly to the demise of the genre,[53] as did the studios' inability to integrate contemporary pop music styles within the format of the musical. While the underscore had been attentive to the most recent trends in recorded music, Adler observes, the film musical had not. Outside the movie theater, viewers were listening to contemporary jazz and rock, which in 1968 meant a variety of sounds—the Beatles, the Beach Boys, the Mamas and the Papas, Bob Dylan, Joan Baez, Simon and Garfunkel, Aretha Franklin, Wilson Pickett, the Byrds, the Doors, and Jefferson Airplane. In film musicals, however, viewers were still being served a steady diet of Broadway song. "It seems sad for musicals to be resolutely cut off from the attractive composer-performers of our time," Adler notes. "And unprecedented for musicals to be divorced so completely from the popular music of which they used to form such a vital part."

The film musical was becoming irrelevant not just because of the rise of rock 'n' roll, Adler argues, but also because of the rise of recorded music, which had changed the country's listening habits. The home stereo had replaced active participation in music making, singing and dancing in particular, with passive listening. "The era of the twist, the discotheque and even the dance is almost gone. The teenybopper audience has become, or yielded to, serious young adults; and it has been the era of the concert for some time," in which audiences were encouraged to listen and not move. Rock music was being integrated into films, Adler observes, but not through diegetic musical performance as in a film musical. Instead, film directors were using passive, non-diegetic presentations of popular music, interpolating recorded pop songs under extended visual montages instead of through on-screen performances, as in *The Graduate* (1964), *A Hard Day's Night* (1967), *Easy Rider* (1969), *Butch Cassidy and the Sundance Kid* (1969), and *Zabriskie Point* (1970). All of these films made use of rock music but in a "montage" or "concert" format rather than a diegetic musical performance.[54]

In the early 1960s, the studios were pouring new energy and resources into the music business to generate new sources of revenue. But the recession also pushed them to develop new audiences. In the 1950s, cheap foreign labor as well as postwar tariffs and trade protections had encouraged studios to import a steady stream of foreign films. By the early 1960s, American audiences had grown accustomed to this exotic fare, and their appetite for it was increasing. As **Document 38,** an interview with Italian composer Ennio Morricone titled "Towards an Interior Music," illustrates, the studios had a healthy relationship with several European film industries, the Italian film industry among them. One director whose films were enjoying particular acclaim and popularity with American audiences in the mid-1960s was Sergio Leone. His "spaghetti" westerns *A Fistful of Dollars* (1964), *For a Few Dollars More* (1965), and *The Good, the Bad, and the Ugly* (1966) planted American and Italian actors in European locations and used innovative visual techniques all to striking effect. Leone's films also exposed American audiences to the unconventional scoring techniques of composer Morricone.

European composers were free to innovate in ways that their American counterparts were not. To match Leone's unique visual and narrative style, Morricone experimented with musical instrumentation especially. He was particularly interested in challenging the default instrument of the Hollywood score: the orchestra. "In general the Americans use symphonic music even for Westerns, something I never do," he admits. "I find symphonic language excessive, too rich for films." Morricone describes his musical style and instrumentation as "interior" because it seeks to manipulate sounds that are literally located within the frame of the film. Instead of a full orchestra, Morricone uses whistles, anvils, whips, organs, harmonicas, carillons, ocarinas, human chants and vocalizations, and other ambient sounds as "instruments" for his score. For Morricone, "found" sounds, sounds and noises not previously considered "music," are just as capable of generating an interesting and effective score as a traditional orchestra. Although Morricone still uses conventional scoring structures and thematic practices, the instrumentation of his scores was decidedly inventive and deliberately un-Hollywood. As a result, he and other European composers, like Maurice Jarre, exposed American audiences to a kind of sonic experimentation they were not hearing in conventional studio scoring.

As the studios sought to capitalize not just on the profitable art-house market but also on the freedoms allowed by the new ratings system and production code, U.S. audiences heard new sounds from American composers as well. In the late 1960s and early 1970s, Hollywood composers were increasingly experimenting with avant-garde scoring techniques. "Keeping Score on Schifrin" **(Document 39)**, an interview with one of Lees's Third Stream composers, describes some of the new sonic and structural conditions of the emerging auteur score.

Originally from Argentina, Schifrin was a pianist who early in his career toured with jazz trumpeter Dizzy Gillespie. He went to Hollywood as a jazz composer, where his experience with popular music made him an effective composer of Top 40 scores and singles.[55] But his conservatory training, which exposed him to avant-garde and modernist concert-hall techniques, proved useful in the emerging climate of auteur filmmaking. As the interview reveals, what was most required of film composers working in the late 1960s and early 1970s was a facility with a variety of musical styles and a willingness to explore unconventional instrumentations. Auteur directors experimenting with visual style and narrative structure were asking composers to match their films with equally eclectic musical scores. Just as Morricone found the orchestra "too rich" for Leone's unconventional imagery, composers like Schifrin considered the orchestra inappropriate for many narrative settings. For *Cool Hand Luke* (1967), a prison drama set in the American South, Schifrin rejected the orchestra in favor of the banjo and folk and bluegrass idioms.[56] For the climactic scene of the revisionist World War II film *Hell in the Pacific* (1968), he experimented again with a "very wild, contemporary, avant-garde jazz . . . with the tenor [sax] attached to an electronic device with lots of 'reverb.'" In the same film Schifrin made use of aleatoric composing methods that were being popularized by contemporary avant-garde composers like John Cage. To convey a sense of nervousness, he recorded six golf balls bounding on the strings inside of a piano with the damper pedal down, then manipulated those sounds to serve as an underscore for the film. In *Eye of the Cat* (1968), he experimented with similar "extended" techniques, having the string players "rapping their instruments with their knuckles, or with their finger tips, hitting the music stands with their bows, or even rubbing the chairs they were sitting on with the heels of their shoes," to get "a sound that was quite indeterminate—a sound that came like a murmur from all over."[57] "When [a film] calls for it," Schifrin concludes, " I will experiment."

A 1969 interview with composer Jerry Goldsmith (**Document 40**) also emphasizes the eclectic range of musical styles demanded by the visual experiments of the auteur film. For Goldsmith, aleatoric and extended techniques were useful, but so was the technique of serialism. Although Goldsmith was not the first to experiment with serialism, a dissonant or atonal style of composition that manipulated a fully chromatic twelve-note collection of pitches, he was one of the few film composers to use it in films that enjoyed great popularity.[58] In three scores— *Freud* (1962), *Planet of the Apes* (1968), and *The Illustrated Man* (1969)—Goldsmith employed serial techniques extensively, while in several other scores from the period—among them *The Sand Pebbles* (1965) and *Seconds* (1966)—he explored similarly dissonant and atonal, but nonserial, styles.[59] Goldsmith's score for *Planet of the Apes* was particularly influential in weaning the sci-fi film from its dependence on electronic instrumentation, a habit developed in the 1950s. In addition to utilizing serial techniques for long stretches of the *Planet of the Apes* score, Goldsmith used an array of unconventional instruments including stainless steel mixing bowls, aluminum sheets, slide whistles, conch shells, a *shofar* or a ram's horn, and a Polynesian instrument called an *ung-lung*. Goldsmith also required several traditional orchestral instruments to be played in untraditional ways: gongs were scraped with metal mallets, for instance, French horns were played without mouthpieces, and piano chords were abruptly cut off with hand-stopping technique.[60] Goldsmith called the orchestra he used for this score "old-fashioned," but that was true only in the sense that there were no electronic instruments. In terms of instrumentation and compositional style, the score was highly avant-garde.

Although auteur and niche filmmakers were empowering composers to experiment with atonal styles and "found" sounds, what characterized film scoring as a whole in the late 1960s, Goldsmith points out, was stylistic diversity. Conventional dramas and comedies were still being produced, so there was still a need for jazz scores and for pop-infused singles scores. But for a composer to be successful, he had to be adept at a range of musical styles, from pop to classical to avant-garde. Goldsmith became part of the newest generation of composers because, as he observes, "I have a strange versatility. I can do pop, jazz, romantic, you name it. Personally, my own genre which I compose is as a serial composer."

"The Jazz Composer in Hollywood" (**Document 41**), a 1972 symposium sponsored by *Downbeat* magazine, documents this need for diversity by affirming the continued centrality of jazz and jazz composers in studio scoring in the 1960s and 1970s. This document describes Mancini's influence on the industry and the new opportunities that jazz scoring created for African American composers like Quincy Jones and Benny Carter. It also exposes the racial prejudice and stereotyping that kept African Americans from joining the ranks of Hollywood composers before the mid-1960s. The prejudices and rejection that Jones and Carter experienced are a reminder that the civil rights movement was only beginning to have an effect on hiring practices in studio music departments.[61]

The symposium participants also discuss the new pluralism of the underscore and the variety of musical styles demanded by contemporary filmmaking—everything from jazz and rock to electronic, folk, and atonal music. One additional element they discuss is the use of silence. Auteur filmmaking was inspiring the adoption of avant-garde techniques and experimental sounds, but it was also encouraging sparse textures and less music in general. Classical wall-to-wall, orchestral-thematic scoring was now more typically a feature of television, not film scoring.[62]

The symposium also documents an emerging concern on the part of musicians, who observed the tendency of auteur directors such as Mike Nichols, Dennis Hopper, and Michelangelo Antonioni to score films with music from their own record collections, revitalizing the silent-era practice of the "compilation score." The record-breaking sales of compilation soundtracks for films like *The Graduate, Easy Rider, Zabriskie Point,* and *Midnight Cowboy* only helped to popularize this scoring method with film executives. The use of preexisting music (dubbed the *"Easy Rider"* approach) was beginning to affect film music, not just because it was replacing newly composed scores with contemporary rock songs, but because it was experimenting with the absence of the composer from the film scoring process.[63] Although the composers' reaction to the return of the compilation score is at this point mild, the full displacement of the composer from the film scoring process will soon cause great concern.

Just as distressing was the incursion of a new style of rock music into the Top 40 formula. The new niche market of blaxploitation films was generating record-breaking soundtrack sales with the use of theme songs and scores that featured contemporary funk music. Melvin van Peebles's *Sweet Sweetback's Baadasssss Song* (1971), with music by the R&B group Earth, Wind, and Fire, started the trend, but Isaac Hayes's title song for the film *Shaft* (1971) cemented it. The film's funky soundtrack album generated strong profits and earned Hayes an Academy Award for Best Song, making him the first African American to win in that category. Hayes's success encouraged film executives to bypass established composers for other funk and R&B performers and composers, such as Curtis Mayfield, who wrote the score for *Superfly* (1972), which went on to become a platinum album, and Marvin Gaye, who composed the music for the critically acclaimed *Trouble Man* (1972). The success of these soundtracks encouraged executives to agitate for more funk-style hits and scores from their staff composers. That mention is made of Hayes's inability to write musical notation suggests that in the hierarchy of film composing, contemporary and highly commercial styles (like funk) were still viewed as not artistic by established jazz and orchestral composers.[64]

By the early 1970s, the rock compilation soundtrack had become a legitimate film-scoring formula. In 1971, for example, director Peter Bogdanovich used recordings of Hank Williams, Tony Bennett, and Eddie Fisher to score his film *The Last Picture Show,* set in a west Texas oil town in the 1950s. In *Mean Streets* (1973), director Martin Scorsese used prerecorded Italian art songs and classic rock 'n' roll to give his first studio picture, about petty mobsters in New York's Little Italy, sonic legitimacy. In contrast to earlier auteur soundtracks, these compilations were not presented in "concert" or montage mode but diegetically, visibly and authentically spilling out of car radios, jukeboxes, and record players. The same is true of the soundtrack George Lucas created for his film *American Graffiti* (1973), a coming-of-age story set in 1962 that follows several high-school friends during their last night together before parting ways. Lucas infused the film's narrative and visual style with a *vérité* sense of realism, a quality that marks its soundtrack as well. As Lucas points out in a 1974 profile by Steven Farber, "Stinky Kid Hits the Bigtime" **(Document 42),** the film was also influenced by rock music he heard on the radio and by the "giant rock and roll record collection—78s and 45s" he owned as a youth. The forty-one songs were written into the script to comment on the action, after first being a part of the film's *mise en scène.*[65]

Lucas didn't set any precedents in terms of the method he used to create the score for *American Graffiti.* He made the selections himself, much as Hopper and Fonda had with the less ambitious *Easy Rider* soundtrack. And he placed the music distinctively all within the diegesis of the film. *Graffiti* was also the first to collapse the auteur practice of compiling and remarketing preexisting recorded music with the marketing practices of the Top 40 pop score. As Lucas points out, it is not just the preferences of the director that shape the content of the compilation soundtrack, but legal availability of the music as well. In the case of *American Graffiti,* Lucas originally wanted to license close to fifty songs, but when some proved too expensive and others legally unavailable, he cut several out or substituted cheaper selections.[66]

According to Lucas, the compilation score and the removal of the composer from film scoring had also precipitated a change in terminology. Whereas previously "directors" created and coordinated only the film's visual material, the new auteur director was a "filmmaker" who controlled several if not all significant aspects of film production, including the film's musical score or soundtrack. Famed director George Cukor, Lucas remembers, detested the term *filmmaker,* saying it equated the act of directing with toy-making. Lucas, in contrast, embraced the term because it reflected the director's new ability to create and control all the elements of the film. "I'm very much akin to a toy-maker. . . . I like to make things move, and I like to make them myself. Just give me the tools." Spurred by the recording boom, the auteur phenomenon created filmmakers by empowering directors to make their own soundtracks, thereby removing the composer from the production process altogether.

Many auteur filmmakers, like Martin Scorsese, Peter Bogdanovich, Woody Allen, Mike Nichols, and Arthur Penn, produced compilation soundtracks using popular music. But as Elmer Bernstein's article "The Annotated Friedkin" (**Document 43**) reveals, the compilation soundtrack was not limited to popular music. At the end of the article, in an interview conducted by the American Film Institute's Center for Advanced Film Studies, William Friedkin admits that when he was directing his film *The Exorcist* he originally engaged avant-gardist Lalo Schifrin to write the score. When Schifrin failed to articulate Friedkin's ideas to his liking, the director took matters into his own hands. Citing poor communication, he jettisoned Schifrin's score in favor of a compilation soundtrack of his own making—"Music Score by Tower Records." "I was bound and determined to have the kind of music that I originally intended," he asserts. For Friedkin, that mean an interesting collection of classical music. By the mid-1970s, one of the most important retailers of classical music recordings especially was Tower Records. This was no doubt where Friedkin purchased the recordings of the avant-garde music he used to score the film with.

Friedkin was not the first director to compile a soundtrack from preexisting classical music. In 1968, Stanley Kubrick established this practice as an auteur option when he jettisoned the newly composed score written by Alex North for his film *2001: A Space Odyssey* in favor of a compilation of classical and avant-garde orchestral music by Johann Strauss, Richard Strauss, Aram Khachaturian and György Ligeti.[67] It was Kubrick's *2001* soundtrack, in fact, that most likely introduced Friedkin to the experimental music of Ligeti and his contemporaries, Krzysztof Penderecki and Hans Werner Henze.[68] Although it was pursued with less frequency than the "*Easy Rider* soundtrack," as the interview with Friedkin documents, the "Tower Records" method of compiling classical music was a valid scoring practice in the late 1960s and 1970s, one that produced some of the most memorable moments in the marriage of film and music.

While the studios looked to these new filmmakers to help resolve their financial crisis, they also tried to escape the recession by practicing economic restraint. For film music this meant continuing the practice of "runaway production," that is, of using foreign composers and postproduction facilities to record film scores. When Goldsmith, for instance, mentions in Document 39 that he prefers to work with English orchestras because the musicians are so accommodating, he is referring to the practice of runaway production and Hollywood's use of cheaper British and French orchestras. The runaway productions of the 1950s had already introduced American audiences to Italian composers like Ennio Morricone and Nino Rota and Frenchmen like Maurice Jarre, Georges Delerue, Michel Legrand,

and Francis Lai. By the late 1960s and early 1970s, however, Hollywood film music production was exercising fiscal efficiency not just by running away to Europe, but by bringing European composers to the United States to score domestically made films. There, able to enjoy better working conditions than at home,[69] they thrived, in party because they were adept at realizing the studios' increasingly pluralistic needs. Not only were they able to write creative auteur scores, but they were also adept at writing hit singles. Indeed, many of the period's most popular themes and songs were penned by European composers. Frenchman Michel Legrand, for example, won Oscars for his theme songs for *The Thomas Crown Affair* (1968) and *The Summer of '42* (1972), while fellow countryman Francis Lai wrote the popular theme for the romantic drama *Love Story* (1970). By the early 1970s, Italian composer Nino Rota—who had recently worked in Italy on a pair of runaway Hollywood productions of Shakespeare plays, Franco Zeffirelli's *The Taming of the Shrew* (1967) and *Romeo and Juliet* (1968)—was in studio system proper, where he wrote the highly successful orchestral theme for Francis Ford Coppola's *The Godfather* (1972). Ennio Morricone, too, became a fixture on studio rosters in the 1970s and 1980s.

David Raksin's humorous vivisection of the Hollywood film music industry, "Whatever Became of Movie Music?" **(Document 44)**, neatly summarizes many of the trends and innovations we have been discussing. He observes, for instance, the invasion of foreign composers into Hollywood, and the studios' attempt to tap into booming LP sales with the Top 40 singles score.[70] He also laments the popularity of the "Tower Records Score," or as he calls it, "Griffithitis" (after D. W. Griffith, who used preexisting classical music for the underscore of *The Birth of a Nation*). In his view, the auteur-directors had succeeded in eradicating the composer from the filmmaking process by substituting recorded music for a newly composed score. As a result, the recession score was filled with a variety of contemporary musical styles—jazz, pop, rock 'n' roll, funk, and avant-garde instrumental music. It had pluralistically and eclectically embraced all styles except one: the thematic orchestral underscore. As director William Wyler observed, "If a director allows a violin on today's soundtrack, he is considered something of a senile relic."[71]

Raksin points to two additional forces shaping film music in the 1960s and 1970s. One reason why film scores were full of theme songs and pop and rock music, he argues, is because composers long ago surrendered the copyright of their music to the studios. "To the extent to which we have . . . accepted the appropriation of our right to legal 'authorship' of our own music . . . we have only ourselves to blame." The conditions Mancini won, Raksin observes, had yet to be uniformly applied to all composers. Composers needed to wrestle back from the "studio barons" the copyright and legal authorship of their music, not only to maintain creative control but also to receive a more equitable share of the profits made from it. His colleague Elmer Bernstein, he notes, was currently attending to just such a legal case that would challenge the studios' ownership of film music.[72]

Raksin's observations also reveal that while the sound of the orchestral, thematic score was virtually nonexistent in recession filmmaking, it was not entirely absent from the aural landscape. The lush, tonal, and melodic orchestral underscores of Steiner and Korngold, for example, were currently enjoying enormous popularity not on screen but on commercially available LP recordings. In 1972, the RCA Victor record label began re-recording older film scores under the direction of Charles Gerhardt, releasing thirteen of them under a new series label, "Classic Film Scores." They included Korngold's score for *The Sea Hawk* (1937), Steiner's for *King Kong* (1933), Waxman's for *Bride of Frankenstein* (1935), Rózsa's for *Four Feathers* (1939), and Tiomkin's for *Guns of Navarrone* (1961). When the recordings hit the market they were unexpectedly and enormously popular. "Who could believe," recording executive Grover Hensley asks, "that a 1930-whatever score for a motion picture that had long since been forgotten would ever make the charts?"[73]

These classic film scores did much to remind audiences of the sounds of past film scores, sounds that were now little if at all heard. But they also underscored the drastic changes in film music practices over the preceding two decades. "Consider the apparent paradox," Raksin notes, "that people who buy recordings of film scores are buying music—by Korngold, Steiner, Newman and others—that is the antithesis of what is for the most part heard on the soundtracks of current films." The re-airing of these classical scores was profitable for the studios, but it also helped to articulate the differences between contemporary and past scoring conventions. The recordings fueled a recognition that there was an older and much more uniform practice of film scoring, one very different from the modern, highly divergent approach. As Raksin rightly forecasts, the aesthetic and commercial re-embracing of the orchestral score, "antiquated" though its sound may be, will not only come to define a new postclassical practice, but it will also be instrumental in ending the industry's long-standing recession.

NOTES

1. Paul Monaco, *The Sixties* (Berkeley: University of California Press, 2001), p. 11. See also Robert Sklar, *Movie-Made America* (New York: Vintage Books, 1994), p. 321.

2. See Monaco, *The Sixties*, pp. 39–40; also David Cook, *Lost Illusions: American Cinema in the Shadow of Watergate and Vietnam, 1970–79* (Berkeley: University of California Press, 2000), pp. 14–19. As Cook points out, beginning in the mid-1970s, the studios purposely made films scarce in order to demand a larger percentage of the box office take from exhibitors. As a result, production numbers fell to an all-time low in 1977, but the studios' grosses and profits actually increased.

3. "The recession of 1969 had produced more than $200 million in losses; left MGM, Warner Bros. and United Artists under new management; and brought Universal and Columbia close to

liquidation" (Cook, *Lost Illusions*, p. 9). See also John Baxter, *Hollywood in the Sixties* (New York: A. S. Barnes, 1972), pp. 7–8 and 14. Baxter also characterizes the sixties as a period of crisis.

4. Baxter, *Hollywood in the Sixties*, p. 11.

5. Sklar, *Movie-Made America*, p. 321; see also Monaco, *The Sixties*, p. 16.

6. Sklar, *Movie-Made America*, pp. 269–85.

7. Monaco, *The Sixties*, p. 12.

8. Ibid., pp. 24–25.

9. "For example, in 1973 Paramount produced ten of the twenty-two films it distributed; in 1974 it produced fourteen of twenty-five; but by 1974 it produced only five of twenty—a fairly typical progression for the majors throughout the decade" (Cook, *Lost Illusions*, p. 21).

10. Ibid., p. 19.

11. For some film musicians, the transition from the contract to the freelance system was gradual. In 1947, the studios started reducing the size of their in-house orchestras, which at that time were typically around fifty players. By 1954, that number had dropped to around twenty long-term contract players, the rest being contracted in a more or less freelance fashion. See Robert R. Faulkner, *Hollywood Studio Musicians: Their Work and Careers in the Recording Industry* (New York: Aldine Atherton, 1971), pp. 22–23; and Walter Scharf, *The History of Film Scoring* (Studio City, Calif.: Cinema Songs, 1988), pp. 59–60. See also Peter Lev, *The Fifties: Transforming the Screen* (Berkeley: University of California Press, 2003), pp. 212–14.

12. Faulkner, *Hollywood Studio Musicians*, pp. 24–26. See also "A.F.M. Steps Up Fight: Files With N.L.R.B. to Regain Control of Film Music," *New York Times*, October 17, 1958, p. 32. The studios still maintained music supervisors and department heads on long-term contracts, but by the early 1960s the composing and the performance of film music had largely been converted to what was hoped would be a less expensive, freelance system. See Monaco, *The Sixties*, p. 109.

13. Ibid., pp. 283–85. See also Baxter, *Hollywood in the Sixties*, pp. 8–13.

14. Monaco, *The Sixties*, p. 17. As Monaco observes, "By the end of the 1960s the films produced by the Hollywood majors directly for television actually outnumbered Hollywood's theatrical releases being shown on the networks."

15. Cook, *Lost Illusions*, pp. 22.

16. Monaco, *The Sixties*, p. 17.

17. Jeff Smith, *The Sounds of Commerce: Marketing Popular Film Music* (New York: Columbia University Press, 1998), p. 40.

18. Jeff Smith, *Sounds of Commerce*, pp. 59–67. The recording boom encouraged a surge in theme and title song composition and recording. Several "recording artists" like "Mantovani and His Orchestra" and the duo-piano team of "Ferrante and Teicher" preferred to record film music rather than play live concerts. They established careers recording versions of the title themes from popular films like *Exodus* (1960), *Never on Sunday* (1961), *The Magnificent Seven* (1960), *West Side Story* (1960), *Breakfast at Tiffany's* (1960), *Lawrence of Arabia* (1960), *The Alamo* (1961), and *The Sandpiper* (1964).

19. Ibid., pp. 42–44. For a complete history of the film industry's entrée into the music record business, see especially Smith's subchapter "Establishing a 'Soundtrack' Record: The Majors and Their Record Subsidiaries," pp. 32–44.

20. For a good discussion of how record subsidiaries dovetailed with the business strategies of the newly conglomerated film studios in the mid-1960s, see Tino Balio, *United Artists: The Company That Changed the Film Industry* (Madison: University of Wisconsin Press, 1987), p. 113.

21. Monaco, *The Sixties*, p. 44

22. The healthy profits foreign films generated in the recession economy often extinguished the need for them to win the Production Code Office's "seal of approval" before distribution. Starting with

Antonioni's *Blow-Up,* shown without code approval to strong box office receipts, foreign films shown in the United States for the most part evaded moral censorship. See Cook, *Lost Illusions,* p. 18.

23. Ibid.

24. Monaco, *The Sixties,* p. 54.

25. Ibid., pp. 12, 14. In 1962, Monaco asserts (p. 12), 30 percent of major studio production was undertaken overseas.

26. Sklar, *Movie-Made America,* p. 276.

27. While most conglomerates acquired film studios primarily as investments, turning the reins over to industry outsiders, there were exceptions. Gulf & Western CEO Charles Bluhdorn, for example, allowed Paramount studios to be run by the one-time actor Robert Evans. See Monaco, *The Sixties,* pp. 32–35.

28. Baxter, *Hollywood in the Sixties,* pp. 7–8. See also Monaco, *The Sixties,* pp. 30–39.

29. Monaco, *The Sixties,* p. 39.

30. Cook, *Lost Illusions,* pp. 11–14.

31. Ibid., pp. 56–60 and 188–192.

32. Monaco, *The Sixties,* pp. 26–27.

33. For an overview of the production code changes made in the 1960s, see Sklar, *Movie-Made America,* pp. 294–300; Monaco, *The Sixties,* pp. 60–66; and Cook, *Lost Illusions,* pp. 70–71. Monaco's claim that 1967, the year before the new code officially took effect, was a watershed year for the studios in terms of topically adventurous filmmaking bolsters Valenti's claim that the new code was simply articulating the changes in national tastes and mores that were already being established.

34. As Monaco (*The Sixties,* p. 3) observes, "The vitality of several film industries in Western Europe encouraged the perception that many foreign productions were setting new standards for sophistication and artistic achievement as well as increasing box-office competition for Hollywood."

35. For a detailed study of seminal auteur filmmakers, see Diane Jacobs, *Hollywood Renaissance* (South Brunswick, N.J.: Delacorte Press, 1980); Thomas Schatz, "The New Hollywood," in *Film Theory Goes to the Movies,* ed. Jim Collins, Hilary Radner, and Ava Preacher Collins (New York: Routledge, 1993); and Robert Kolker, *A Cinema of Loneliness,* 3d ed. (New York: Oxford University Press, 2000).

36. See Michael Pye and Linda Myles, *The Hollywood Brats: How the Film Generation Took Over Hollywood* (New York: Holt, Rinehart & Winston, 1979).

37. Kolker, *Cinema of Loneliness,* pp. 181–85, describes the influence of documentary and New Wave filmmaking especially on the second wave of auteurs like Scorsese.

38. Cook, *Lost Illusions,* pp. 68–69.

39. Monaco, *The Sixties,* pp. 27–30.

40. Cook, *Lost Illusions,* pp. 220–38.

41. Ibid., p. 156

42. Sklar, *Movie-Made America,* pp. 296–300; and Cook, *Lost Illusions,* pp. 271–83.

43. Sklar, *Movie-Made America,* pp. 329–32; and Cook, *Lost Illusions,* pp. 259–266.

44. Cook, *Lost Illusions,* 266–71.

45. Thomas Schatz writes that Fox studios went on a "blockbuster musical binge in an effort to replicate its success with *The Sound of Music,* and the results were disastrous: losses of $11 million on *Dr. Doolittle* in 1967, $15 million on *Star!* in 1968, and $16 million in 1969 on *Hello Dolly!,* at the time the most expensive film ever made" ("The New Hollywood," in *Film Theory Goes to the Movies,* p. 14).

46. One 20th Century–Fox recording executive, Bernie Wayne, may have had a special influence in shaping the length of the theme in the new singles or LP score. "One of Wayne's additional twists from the 20th soundtrack LPs is the editing of each band to a maximum of a two-and-a-half

minutes. That's the same running time as a pop song and facilitates the use of film by the pop disk jockeys" ("20th-Fox Label Tests New Slant on 'Track' LPs," *Variety*, April 21, 1965.

47. Smith, *Sounds of Commerce*, pp. 72–76.

48. Ibid., pp. 77–82. On the *Breakfast at Tiffany's* album, for instance, all eleven cues are distinct tunes that adhere to the length requirements for standard radio airplay (roughly three minutes). As Smith (p. 72) puts it, "Mancini was certainly not the first to use elements of jazz style, but he was among the first to develop entire scores as collections of jazz tunes."

49. According to Smith (ibid., pp. 98–99), "Throughout the 1960s, Mancini's celebrity also enabled him to negotiate very favorable terms for publishing royalties. . . . In early 1965 Mancini even publicly announced that he would no longer score a film if he did not receive the music publishing copyrights."

50. See Smith, *Sounds of Commerce*, pp. 36–40.

51. John Addison wrote the score for *Torn Curtain*, but the film's theme song, "The Green Years," was composed by Jay Livingston and Ray Evans. Hitchcock himself was partly responsible for Herrmann's exit from *Torn Curtain*. Some of the pressure to provide commercially viable music came from film directors, in other words. For a detailed description of the *Torn Curtain* incident, see Steven Smith, *A Heart at Fire's Center: The Life and Music of Bernard Herrmann* (Berkeley: University of California Press, 1991), pp. 267–74. Shortly after the *Torn Curtain* debacle, Herrmann moved to London, where he did some scoring for European directors, French director François Truffaut most prominently. He returned to Hollywood only briefly before his death, scoring Martin Scorsese's *Taxi Driver* (1976).

52. The financial incentives of successful soundtrack LPs created a whole new generation of young film composers who were adept at both scoring and writing popular songs or tuneful instrumental themes; among them were Ernest Gold (*Exodus*, 1960), Maurice Jarre (*Lawrence of Arabia*, 1961; *Dr. Zhivago*, 1965), Johnny Mandel (*I Want to Live*, 1958; *The Sandpiper*, 1965), and Jerry Goldsmith (*The Sand Pebbles*, 1966). The effect the new structural and stylistic requirements had on the older, established generation of studio composers, however, was complicated. Some, like Elmer Bernstein and Dmitri Tiomkin, who had early theme song successes—Bernstein with *The Magnificent Seven* (1960) and Tiomkin with *The Alamo* (1960), *The Guns of Navarrone* (1961), and *55 Days in Peking* (1963)—adapted fairly well at first, only to fade by the end of the decade. See Smith, *Sounds of Commerce*, pp. 57–68.

53. See Baxter, *Hollywood in the Sixties*, pp. 43–55; David Cook *A History of Narrative Film* (New York: W. W. Norton, 1981), pp. 430–31; and Monaco, *The Sixties*, pp. 37–39. Most have attributed the sudden disappearance of this genre to extraordinary production costs that could not be recouped even under the best of circumstances (costs that included extraordinary licensing fees of Broadway shows) and an emerging "counterculture."

54. For discussion of Richard Lester's *A Hard Day's Night*, especially the substitution of "concert" listening techniques for film musical techniques, see David Ehrenstein and Bill Reed, *Rock on Film* (New York: Delilah Books, 1982), p. 56: "Not since *On the Town* (1949) have music and movement meshed as infectiously as in this film. . . . [Lester] creates a *sense* of dance movement in the 'Can't Buy Me Love' number by quickly cutting between the four [Beatles] as they pose, gesture and jump about a field in rhythm to their music." See also R. Serge Denisoff and William D. Romanowski, *Risky Business: Rock on Film* (New Brunswick, N.J.: Transaction Publishers, 1991), pp. 167–75; Smith, *Sounds of Commerce*, pp. 159–60; and Monaco, *The Sixties*, pp. 86–87.

55. Harvey Siders (**Document 39**) gives a detailed overview of Schifrin's writing credits, but he fails to mention several crucial compositions, including themes for the popular television shows *The Man from U.N.C.L.E.* (1964–68) and *Starsky and Hutch* (1975–79) as well as the scores for the feature films *Bullitt* (1968), *Dirty Harry* (1971), and *Enter the Dragon* (1968). See also Tony Thomas, *Music for*

the Movies, 2d ed. (Los Angeles: Silman-James, 1997), pp. 292–300; and Lawrence MacDonald, *The Invisible Art of Film Music* (New York: Ardsley House, 1998), pp. 208–10.

56. A number of folk and hillbilly scores, including those for *Bonnie and Clyde* (1967), *Alice's Restaurant* (1969), *Little Big Man* (1970), and *Deliverance* (1972), reveal that nonorchestral folk instrumentation was a popular and appropriate alternative for many films of the period.

57. Monaco, *The Sixties*, p. 112. Just as blurring the distinction between sound and music was not new to the concert hall, it was not entirely new to film scoring either. Bernard Herrmann constructed a "score" of manipulated bird sounds for Hitchcock's *The Birds* (1963), and sound designer Arthur Piantadosi used electronically manipulated piano sounds for the film *Marooned* (1969). See S. Smith, *Heart at Fire's Center*, pp. 252–55. But Schifrin and others created similar sound effects using avant-garde techniques on conventional instruments instead of using electronics.

58. Leonard Rosenman's score for *The Cobweb* (1955) is typically credited with being the first serial film score. See MacDonald, *Invisible Art of Film Music*, p. 143.

59. John Caps, "The Serial Music of Jerry Goldsmith," in *Elmer Bernstein's Film Music Notebook: A Complete Collection of the Quarterly Journal, 1974–78* (Sherman Oaks, Calif.: Film Music Society, 2004), pp. 196–201. In his article, Caps suggests that a fourth Goldsmith film score was also serial, the score for *The Satan Bug* (1965).

60. In contradiction to Goldsmith's own description, Caps suggests that Goldsmith did use an electronic instrument briefly, although Caps does not identify the instrument in question. "The only unusual sounds," he observes, "may be in the percussion sections . . . and in the one electronic instrument which makes perhaps only two or three cries" (ibid., p. 199). No source gives a consistent or complete accounting of the score's instrumentation. See also Dale Winogura, "Jerry Goldsmith, Composer, Apes 1 and 3," *Cinefantastique* 2, no. 2 (Summer 1972): 37; and Randall Larson, "The Versatility of Jerry Goldsmith," in *Musique Fantastique: A Survey of Film Music in the Fantastic Cinema* (Metuchen, N.J.: Scarecrow Press, 1985), pp. 251–65. Larson's article contains the most detailed description of the unconventional acoustic effects he created and in what sequences they were used. Although in Winogura's article (p. 37) Goldsmith is quoted as saying, "A Polynesian instrument called Ung-lungs were used in the cave sequence," no instrument with that name, Polynesian or otherwise, appears to exist.

61. *New York Times*, March 16, 1975, p. 21. As Jones notes in this interview, when director Edward Dmytryck found out that Jones was black, "he [Dmytryck] became concerned whether I could relate to a love scene between Gregory Peck and Diane Baker."

62. Although no specific composers or films are mentioned, many of Jerry Goldsmith's scores from the early 1970s—*Patton* (1970), *Papillon* (1973), and *Chinatown* (1974) among them—are a good example of this trend. All of these scores illustrate a new interest in sparseness and economy. Film scoring, as Goldsmith saw it, had become an explication of the "less is more" philosophy. "The composer must wait," he states, "for those moments in the picture where there is something to be said that only music can say. Then the presence of music will bring that extra element you need, and if it's done right, it will elevate the scene (quoted in Tony Thomas, *Film Score: The Art and Craft of Movie Music* [Burbank, Calif.: Riverwood, 1991], p. 287). See also MacDonald, *Invisible Art of Film Music*, p. 206.

63. For a discussion of the *Easy Rider* soundtrack, see Denisoff and Romanowski, *Risky Business*, pp. 167–76. See also Ehrenstein and Reed, *Rock on Film*, pp. 65–75; Seth Cagin and Philip Drey, *Born to Be Wild: Hollywood and the Sixties Generation* (Boca Raton, Fla.: Coyote Press, 1994), pp. 62–64; and Monaco, *The Sixties*, p. 30.

64. Smith, *Sounds of Commerce*, pp. 158–63. Smith refers to this use of rock-influenced music in film as "rock scoring."

65. See Dale Pollock, *Skywalking: The Life and Films of George Lucas* (New York: Harmony Books, 1983), pp. 108–9; Smith, *Sounds of Commerce*, pp. 172–73; and Denisoff and Romanowski, *Risky Business*, pp. 177–85.

66. Pollock, *Skywalking*, pp. 108–9; and Smith, *Sounds of Commerce*, p. 173.

67. Robert Townson, "The Odyssey of Alex North's 2001," liner notes to *Alex North's 2001*, conducted by Jerry Goldsmith with the National Philharmonic Orchestra (Varese Sarabande, VSD-5400, 1993); and Timothy Scheurer, "The Score for *2001: A Space Odyssey*," *Journal of Popular Film and TV* 25, no. 4 (Winter 1998): 172–82.

68. For a good discussion of Kubrick and the use of preexisting classical music in his film soundtracks, see two articles by Claudia Gorbman: "Eyes Wide Open: Kubrick's Music," in *Changing Tunes: The Use of Pre-existing Music in Film* (Burlington, Vt.: Ashgate Press, 2006), pp. 3–18; and "Auteur Music," in *Beyond the Soundtrack: Representing Music in Cinema*, ed. Daniel Goldmark, Lawrence Kramer, and Richard Leppert (Berkeley: University of California Press, 2007), pp. 149–62.

69. European composers were not only willing but excited to be brought to Hollywood in the late 1960s and early 1970s because, despite the recession, working conditions in Hollywood were better than in Europe. For a detailed look at the film music industry in France, for instance, see David Kraft, "A Conversation with George Delerue," *Soundtrack: The Collector's Quarterly* 1, no. 2 (June 1982): 12–13.

70. Another article that acknowledges the significant presence of European composers in studio music departments in the early 1970s is Frank Werba's "Italo Cleffers Hail New Dawn," *Variety*, May 15, 1974, pp. 59–60.

71. Quoted in Fred Karlin, *Listening to Music: A Film Lover's Guide to Music* (New York: Schirmer's, 1994), p. 244.

72. See Elmer Bernstein, "Film Composers vs. the Studios: A Three Hundred Million Dollar Complaint," in *Elmer Bernstein's Film Music Notebook*, pp. 201–12.

73. Karlin, *Listening to Music*, p. 230.

33

Film Themes Link Movie, Disk Trades

June Bundy

(1960)

UA PROGRAM SPARKS TREND TO CLOSER, EFFECTIVE
TEAMWORK BY TWO INDUSTRIES

The record and motion picture industries are working in closer and more effective harmony today than they have since the golden days of movie musicals.

United Artists Records' success in building film themes as singles hits (by careful co-ordination between the label and movie firms during a film's pre-production period) has been a major sparkplug of the new trend. UA now has four best film-themed singles—"Exodus," "Never on Sunday," "The Apartment," "The Magnificent Seven," all of which were released considerably in advance of the movies.

In each case, UA producers report the films benefited strongly at the box office as the result of the long-term radio exposure and coordinated promotion (lobby displays of soundtracks, etc.) on the local exhibitor and distributor level.

Presley Movie

In line with this, Paramount Pictures has introduced a special radio merchandising campaign on Elvis Presley's movie *G.I. Blues,* currently going into national release. With the assistance of the Radio Advertising Bureau, Paramount selected 200 stations which had previously demonstrated "strong promotion-mindedness."

These stations were allocated a cash budget for a specified number of spots and told to form their own campaign based on their knowledge of their markets' needs. Thus each outlet—working, of course, with local Paramount field men and record distributors—is encouraged to devise its own contests, gimmicks, copy.

Meanwhile, veteran film composer and Academy Award Winner Dimitri Tiomkin struck a rather ominous note for film producers this month. Tiomkin is campaigning for film theme composers to be cut in on the profits from films the way that many stars, directors and producers have been for some time. Tiomkin bases his case on the growing importance of movie background music and themes—when tunes become best sellers—to a picture's box-office pull.

Picker's Part

United Artists Records executive Vice-President David V. Picker (also an executive of the parent UA company) is currently working closer than ever with UA's indie film producers—conferring with them on eight future productions (discussing which composers and which types of material have the best potential for the singles field, etc.).

At the same time UA's artist and repertoire director Don Costa, who cut the label's best-selling film theme "Never on Sunday," has recorded the theme from the forthcoming Marilyn Monroe–Clark Gable movie *The Misfits*, which will be released February 1.

Pickers has been instrumental in encouraging the producers of *Paris Blues* (the Paul Newman film) to add three new Duke Ellington songs to its score, which already feature four Ellington oldies. Ellington, who wrote the movie's score, has recorded all seven themes for UA. The three new tunes were added after the picture was already in production.

Short Score

An interesting development has been seen in the case of UA's best-selling theme-single "The Magnificent Seven" by Al Cariola (No. 67 on the "Hot 100" this week). Elmer Bernstein's film score was too short (about 20 minutes) for an album, so no sound-track LP was issued. However, UA has received so many requests for an LP as the result of the singles click that it is now planning to augment the sound track and bring out an album.

Among the forthcoming UA productions which have hit theme potential are Lana Turner's *By Love Possessed,* for which Sammy Cahn is writing a special theme; *The Naked Edge,* and the Gary Cooper–Deborah Kerr starrer with score by William Alwyn. Also Frank Sinatra's Essex Productions signed a $15 million pact with UA this month. His first film will star Dean Martin, Peter Lawford, Sammy Davis Jr., Joey Bishop and, of course, Sinatra.

Another potent source of potential hit singles should be theme music featured in a $55 million product program (including *By Love Possessed*) set by the Mirisch Company with UA for 1961 and 1962. The Mirisch Company produced *The Apartment* and *The Magnificent Seven,* which in turn produced two top-selling singles for UA.

Movie themes on the charts this week include two versions of "Exodus," by Ferrante and Teicher (No. 5) and Mantovani (No. 70); "North to Alaska," by Johnny Horton (No. 6); "Ballad of the Alamo," by Marty Robbins (No. 38); "Pepe," by Duane Eddy (No. 88); "Gloria's Theme" from *Butterfield 8,* by Adam Wade (No. 74); and "Ruby" (from an old Jennifer Jones movie), by Ray Charles (No. 32).

From *The Billboard,* December 24, 1960, pp. 8 and 10.

34

Mancini Debunks Album Values

Eddie Kalish

(1961)

What's the value of a soundtrack album? "The majority of these mean nothing commercially speaking," says Henry Mancini, prolific writer of background scores for pix and TV. In fact he feels for the most part, there shouldn't be soundtrack LPs.

By this comment he is referring to background soundtracks and not those that feature the score from a musical which do have their obvious merits. Mancini feels that the majority of the background music albums come off only to the point of establishing a main theme on probably the first band. The rest of the disk is usually an assortment of fragments which don't mean much musically or commercially.

Mancini, of course, has made several background music albums, some of which have been big sellers, so there would appear to be an inherent contradiction. But Mancini asserts there are reasons behind this. For one thing, he points out, most film scorers don't write with commercial values for the music in mind. They compose strictly for the film's requirements. Mancini says he does both. He, of course, composes to do the best job for the particular pic on which he's working, but he also considers the commercial value of the music as well.

CITES HIS REASONS

Another reason he feels that soundtrack albums aren't too valuable is that the albums are usually prepared directly from the track itself. In this instance he finds two difficulties. One, he believes, is that the quality of the recording is not all that good, and the other is that the finished product emerges mostly as assorted bits of themes which don't have any individual value.

When Mancini does a soundtrack album from either pix or TV, he re-records his music for disk use. In this way, he is able to control each selection on the platter and make it into a separate tune with its own identity. He uses the same tooters on everything he does, and notes that he runs the show much differently for the picture and the waxing.

There is more control exercised for the film, he relates, but for a record date of the same music he lets them go a lot more because he wants "excitement" to come from his recordings. In both cases he uses improvisation, but he says that a disk is "one of the few places where you can have your work come off." The result, he feels, is a more exciting package than would have been created if the LP were made directly from the film.

He adds, however, that most composers aren't in a position to work this way since their contracts with studios don't permit them to. In Mancini's case, he has an exclusive recording pact with RCA Victor, thus he has the built-in authority to proceed along these lines.

For another thing, he points out, most composers don't get performance royalties on their soundtrack LPs when they conduct them. "I don't see why the guy who conducts shouldn't get the artist royalty," he observes. As it stands, the producers keep this.

GOOD SINGLE "IMPORTANT"

Also important, Mancini feels, is that more helpful for a picture than its album is a good single of its theme or a tune from its score. This can be "infinitely more important" than an LP. It gets more play and action and does a better publicity effort for the picture. In this area he cites his "Moon River" tune from his score for Paramount's *Breakfast at Tiffany's,* which has been covered by several artists and is getting widespread action in both sales and airplay.

As far as soundtracks themselves are concerned, Mancini opines that it will be some time before contemporary stylings such as jazz are applied more often. There are several contemporary composers in Hollywood who are offered pix but the established, more traditional writers will get the big ones.

He believes that his type of music, which he says is not jazz but rather jazz influenced, can be used in more pictures like sophisticated comedies and others. But there are personalities and other outside elements, he asserts, that dictate to the composer on what should be used. He also contends that composers are paid "minutiae" by comparison to the overall budget of a film.

An example of contemporary use is his recently completed score for Paramount's *Hatari,* which is located in Africa. Among his other upcoming scores are the music to *Bachelor in Paradise* and *Experiment in Terror.* Although Mancini likes TV work, he prefers the pace of film scoring. His current aim, however, is to do the music for a Broadway musical comedy. He was in New York recently to talk with MCA about such a project.

_____

35

Herrmann Says Hollywood Tone
Deaf as to Film Scores

(1964)

As far as good musical scores for features are concerned, Hollywood is gradually becoming tone deaf, according to veteran composer Bernard Herrmann, who claims producers aren't lending an ear to this phase of the business.

Herrmann, whose first screen score was written in 1940 for the Orson Welles classic, *Citizen Kane*, recently finished his 50th, Alfred Hitchcock's *Marnie*. He has done 10 previous films for the producer-director, including *North By Northwest* and *Psycho*.

He says that fine musical scores are becoming "as rare as whales in telephone booths"; that many current producers are so anxious to hear the sound of music at the box office they pay very little attention to it on a scoring stage; and that this attitude is being out of tune with reality.

An inept score, claims Herrmann, is as bad for a picture as an inept performance by the star.

"There are still a handful of producers, " states Herrmann, "like Hitchcock, who really know the score and fully realize the importance of its relationship to a film. Hitch was in on every musical note of *Marnie,* starting with conferences long before the picture began. Another exception is Fred Zinnemann, who spends as much time with the music as he does with the actors."

However, according to Herrmann, most producers today are not so much interested in good music as they are in a good gimmick. They think that a hit title tune over the screen credits automatically means a hit picture.

"That's as wrong as a busted adding machine," snaps Herrmann. "In my 24 years in Hollywood the standard of movie music has gone down, down. A large percentage of producers, today, are so unaware of their pictures they're looking for a musical gimmick to lure the public. Like the hit title tune, a harmonica surrounded by a choral group, the twanging sound of an electric zither, or the wail of a kazoo in an espresso café. Stuff like that. It only takes away from what's happening on the screen."

The composer feels that the function of an authentic film score is not to sell a picture, but to simply make its proper emotional contribution to the story-points. He claims he's not in the business of writing a smash title tune that will sell platters like hotcakes, but not movies.

———————————

From *The Hollywood Reporter,* July 14, 1964, p. 5.

36

The New Sound on the Soundtracks

Gene Lees

(1967)

If you look at record industry sales charts in any given week, chances are that you'll find at least one motion picture soundtrack album listed near the top—perhaps several. Poor indeed is the picture that doesn't have such an album on the market, and perhaps a hit "title" song to go along with it. More and more of our best popular music is coming from films, as witness the songs of Henry Mancini with lyrics by Johnny Mercer. The biggest popular song in at least two decades—in eighteen months it piled up more than 250 recorded versions—is "The Shadow of Your Smile," from Johnny Mercer's score to *The Sandpiper*.

At the same time, soundtrack albums and songs derived from film scores have become powerful factors in the commercial exploitation of pictures. The most striking recent example is that of "Lara's Theme" from Maurice Jarre's score for *Doctor Zhivago*. Motion picture insiders say the film almost certainly would have been a box office failure had "Lara's Theme" not become a hit. The song's success gave the picture a blizzard of free publicity through its constant exposure by disc jockeys.

Jarre is one of the most successful members of a new generation of composers who in recent years have moved into the film industry. He is, ironically, one of the least respected by his colleagues. There seems to be some justification for their resentment of Jarre and the Academy Award he won for the *Zhivago* score: his melodies are ordinary and derivative, his orchestration awkward and coarse. There are far better men in this new group, such as Jerry Goldsmith, the gifted and thoroughgoing young composer whose music added so much to *The Sand Pebbles*.

Goldsmith and Jarre have one thing in common: they are not pop- or jazz-oriented. While most of the new generation of film composers have backgrounds in popular music and jazz as well as classical training, perhaps the most significant thing about them is that they are evolving, with casual skill and growing confidence, a new music that partakes of all three traditions—and other traditions as well. They have, in fact, developed the "Third Stream" music that was such a hot topic of theoretical discussion in jazz circles a decade ago.

Quincy Jones, Lalo Schifrin, and Johnny Mandel, three former jazz arrangers with extensive training in classical composition, are now established film composers. In recent months, Oliver Nelson, Billy Byers, and Gerry Mulligan each has written his first Hollywood score. The great jazz musician Benny Carter has been in the field for years, though he is only now coming into his own. From popular music have come Nelson Riddle, Dave Grusin, Percy Faith, and Don Costa. Riddle has been writing film scores for several years; Cost and Grusin have just broken into the field. Britain's Johnny Keating, another superior jazz-and-pop-rooted composer, is now in Hollywood. Meanwhile, back in London, alto saxophonist and jazz composer Johnny Dankworth has emerged as a force in British film music with his work for such pictures as *Darling* and *The Servant*. Another Englishman, John Barry, is in heavy demand, though his colleagues have as many reservations about his work as they do for that of Jarre. In Sweden, Bengt Hallberg and Bengt-Arne Wallin, also ex-jazzmen, have written for pictures. Even popular songwriters, such as Cy Coleman and Burt Bacharach, are turning out music for the movies, but their work consists mostly in contributing tunes and perhaps a little thematic material—which may or may not be well developed by experienced orchestrators and arrangers.

Not only have jazz-trained composers moved into the field—jazz players have invaded it too. A few years ago, film composers who wanted to use jazzmen for their soundtracks encountered adamant skepticism from the heads of music departments at the big studios, because of an unfounded belief that jazzmen, though superb players, couldn't read. The best of them are, of course, alarmingly good sight readers, commonly referred to as "hawks" for the sharp-eyed precision with which they can play an unfamiliar score. This is now generally recognized, and such jazzmen or former jazzmen as the great bassist Ray Brown, trumpeters Pete Candoli and Don Fagerquist, drummers Shelly Manne and Larry Bunker, and trombonist Dick Nash now are hardworking familiars of the motion picture sound stages. "As a matter of fact," says Henry Mancini wryly, "when you walk into a studio now, you may find Woody Herman's old band sitting there."

These men too are important to the evolution of the new style in motion picture music. It is useless to write jazz rhythmic figures and orchestral colorations unless you have musicians who can play them. Musicians grounded strictly in classical music usually can't handle such scores; but jazz-trained studio musicians have little trouble with "legit" music. Thus, the penetration of all these former jazz players into movie work has created a new and more versatile kind of orchestra, the kind of orchestra the Third Stream people in New York City have never been able to build.

Yet for all of the training in jazz of the new generation of composers, and for all that the studios are full of first-rate jazz players, there is little improvising permitted in film scores. The composers are wary of it. "If you let a man improvise," Johnny Mandel explained, "he may build a climax in his solo at a point where you don't want it for dramatic reasons. I wrote out every note for Jack Sheldon's trumpet solos in *The Sandpiper*. If they sound improvised, that's a tribute to Jack as a player."

Thus, it is the sonorities, the textures, the *sound* of jazz, rather than the principle of improvisation, that has penetrated into film music. When Mandel wanted Sheldon to produce a certain tight, sad, harmon-muted sound for *The Sandpiper*, he marked the trumpeter's part "Miles"—meaning, play like Miles Davis. "I once marked a saxophone part 'Charlie Barnet,'" Mandel said with a smile.

One of the reasons for the new sound in motion picture scoring, and for a wave of brilliant younger composers, is a change in the way pictures themselves are made. This, at least, is the conclusion drawn by Al Bart, an agent with General Artists Corporation who handles more than seventy composers, including an older line (many of them very gifted men, it should be noted) such as Elmer Bernstein, Bronislau Kaper, and Franz Waxman as well as new-wave writers such as Lalo Schifrin and Neal Hefti. He points out that in the days of the big studios, music was considered secondary, often very secondary, in the value scale of a motion picture.

"Sometimes," Bart explains, "they'd get a picture finished and find they had only $5,000 left for music. So the producer would call the head of the music department and say, 'Get me a $5,000 composer.' Today all that's changed, with the rise of the independent producer, who brings in the whole package for a picture— the star, the director, the writer, and often the composer. The independent producer has more control over his product, often total control, and he'll frequently have very specific ideas about what he wants in the way of music."

An example of this can be seen in the career of Henry Mancini, who is also one of Bart's clients. Mancini's fortunes rose with those of producer-director Blake Edwards, who used Mancini scores for his television series *Peter Gunn*. When Edwards went on to make big-budget pictures, he took Mancini with him. He gave the composer his head, and Mancini turned in scores and songs that became hits on records, thus publicizing the pictures and making more money for them and for Edwards.

"By now," Bart says, "music has become such a tremendous asset to films, both financially and dramatically, that you find producers are casting the composer before the film is even shot. Music is no longer an afterthought."

Though Johnny Mandel had used jazz in the score for *I Want to Live* and El-mer Bernstein had reflected its influence in *The Man with the Golden Arm* years before Mancini used it in his *Peter Gunn* music, Mancini is credited with making it acceptable in films that did not deal with the seamier sides of life. And through the sales of his record albums, he established film scores as a potent promotional dividend for a film. "We all owe a lot to Hank and to Johnny Mandel," Quincy Jones observes.

Mancini today gets more offers to do scores than he could possibly handle. He lives comfortably with his opportunities, taking on those pictures that give him enough elbowroom to write the way he likes to, turning down those that don't. This means that the level of his music is consistently higher than that of most of his recently arrived colleagues.

"There are plateaus in the business," Mancini says. "You can get stuck at a cer-tain level where you have to turn out an enormous number of scores in order to make a living. A young guy will come along and get into that position and turn out too much music—he *has* to do it. Unless he breaks through and establishes a really big reputation, he goes on until the freshness, the very quality that got people interested in the first place, has worn off."

Mancini paid his own bitter dues in the movie music business, so he knows whereof he speaks. Before achieving wide professional and public recognition with *Peter Gunn* and then such films as *Breakfast at Tiffany's, The Pink Panther,* and *Arabesque,* he labored in the salt mines of the old Universal-International studios, grinding out scores to nearly a hundred pictures, including such abomi-nations as *Francis Joins the Army,* which concerned the military adventures of a talking mule. Yet this period of pressure and hack work didn't destroy him, and it doesn't destroy a good many others. In some cases, it seems to hone the talent, though some composers sink into hack habits and a certain cynical despair.

"It sometimes occurs to me," says Hugo Friedhofer," that we work here under very much the same conditions as the old baroque opera composers. The public in those days didn't want to hear the same things over and over, so the composers had to keep on turning out new works."

Friedhofer is the composer of many memorable scores, including *The Young Lions, One-Eyed Jacks, The Best Years of Our Lives* (which won him an Academy Award, of which he is politely contemptuous), and *Boy on a Dolphin,* wherein he made stunning use of Greek musical materials. At sixty-five, he is in the odd position of being a sort of adopted member of the younger generation of compos-ers, who admire his enormous craft, his open mind and open ears, and skillful use of contemporary musical materials, including jazz—he uses jazz a good deal in the *I Spy* television series, which he scores on approximately alternate weeks with his old friend Earle Hagen.

Friedhofer, who hides a deep kindliness under a gnomish exterior and a dour and mordant wit, describes himself, somewhat unsympathetically, as "a broken-down old poop with a bit of a gray beard and an occupational stoop." In the 1920s, he worked as a cellist in theatre pit orchestras in his native San Francisco, and did some arranging. He was on the verge of trying out for the San Francisco Symphony when a chance to go to Hollywood (talking pictures were just beginning) presented itself. "I flipped a coin—honest—and Hollywood won," he says. He made the move in 1929, and began to make his mark as an orchestrator and arranger and later composer for films. Thus he has been in movie music from its beginning, always remaining alertly attuned to new musical developments.

Time is the enemy, in Friedhofer's view. "We used to get eight or ten weeks to score a picture," he said. "Now we consider we're in luxury if we get ten days to turn out the music for a one-hour television show."

When Friedhofer got into it, movie music was a crude and primitive craft. "In those days," he says, "everybody was feeling his way. Nobody knew a goddamn thing. The concept of scoring was derived from silent pictures and the kind of music the pit orchestras played. You know the sort of thing—if the man in the picture runs, the music's got to run. They didn't take into consideration all the factors we do now. You have to remember now that there's an extra instrument in your orchestra—the dialogue. Two extra instruments, really, because you also have sound effects. You can handle the problem in one of two ways. You can ignore it, as Dimitri Tiomkin used to do; or you can labor to figure out how to get things heard."

The most common irritant to film composers these days is the inferior quality of recorded sound in the movie industry. In the golden age of the movies, many of its moguls were pulling money out of the industry hand over fist. They neglected to reinvest much of it in new equipment. This means that a lot of the equipment now used is obsolete junk, and the Hollywood film industry is far behind the commercial recording industry in sound reproduction—and behind the British film industry, according to some composers. "They're improving here, little by little," Mancini says, "but when you've just finished an album in a recording studio, you're used to a certain crispness, a certain urgency, in the sound. It's disillusioning when you get on the sound stage. I just did a picture in England, and the recorded sound was so beautiful that I could put the soundtrack out on an album."

Because of this inferior Hollywood sound reproduction (it should be emphasized that this applies to movies only; the record industry in Hollywood produces some of the finest sound in the world) a good many composers go into commercial studios and re-record their scores for release on disc. Mancini does this for all his albums. There is an additional advantage in that the musical effects can be heightened. Movie underscores, after all, are necessarily subsidiary to the dialogue and scenics. Thus there is usually a certain deliberate reticence in the readings of the music. Re-recording it for disc, the composer can make it more assertive, more communicative, for the home listener. "Besides," Quincy Jones said, "if you don't do it, you're stuck with the form of the picture—without the picture to help you."

Because so many of the new composers have roots in jazz and dance music, there is a widespread belief, at least among outsiders to the industry, that they are just pragmatic arrangers who got lucky. This is untrue. For one thing, even the better popular music arrangers in the commercial recording world today are extensively studied musicians, and this is even truer in the movie music world. Mancini studied with Ernst Křenek, Mario Castelnuovo-Tedesco, and Dr. Alfred Sandry. Schifrin studied with Juan-Carlos Paz in Argentina, and later, at the Paris Conservatory, with Olivier Messiaen and Charles Koechlin. Quincy Jones studied for nearly three years with Nadia Boulanger. Most of these men are interested in serial composition, though they tend to look on it as another musical method rather than a dogma—an extension of the musical vocabulary rather than a separate language. All of them respect the work done by their predecessors in film music; and all of them retain a taste and a respect for the popular music that bred them.

Mancini says that the big-band era of American music produced a mine of musical materials that can't and shouldn't be overlooked by composers. "The bands produced some of the most dramatic sounds we've had," he claims. "What could set a better mood for a love scene than, say, the Claude Thornhill band? It was a great mood when people were dancing to it, and it's a great mood for a bedroom scene in a film. For a sense of humor, there were the great Woody Herman bands in the 1940s—things like "Your Father's Mustache." That band was loaded with wit, and it wasn't at all heavy wit. If you want power and violence, well, you get all that brass going. And then there's the simplicity of the solo jazz musician: Jack Sheldon's trumpet work in *The Sandpiper,* Sonny Rollins's tenor solos in *Alfie,* or Plas Johnson's tenor and Jimmy Rowles's piano, which I used in *The Pink Panther.*"

Most of the new composers share Mancini's philosophy. Quincy Jones says, "The classical people are still brainwashed by the European tradition. They're such snobbish bastards that they haven't tapped one-tenth of American's musical resources. There have been exceptions, of course, such as Leonard Bernstein on Broadway, and Aaron Copland. But there's so much that most of those people don't know about. I like Alban Berg and James Brown—Stravinsky and Duke Ellington. Only in films, the good ones anyway, do you have a chance to express as much as you know musically.

"The level of the music here is very high, and it's getting better all the time. Everybody's writing the best he can. Where else can you write good music for a living these days? I'm writing closer to what I want than I ever have in my life. As a matter of fact, I believe the best music being written in this country today is coming out of films."

There are fads and fashions in film music. At present we are in a phase of what Mancini calls "the Top Forty score"—music intended not so much to enhance the dramatic value of the picture or achieve high musical standards as to become prominent on records and get a lot of disc jockey air play, thereby garnering a good deal of free advertising for the picture. But fads come and fads go, and this one, Mancini suggests, may already be on its way out. The over-all level of motion picture music seems, as Quincy Jones believes, to be rising. It is the result of a new freedom that has been given to film composers. Most of them seem to be using it judiciously and well.

From *High Fidelity,* August 1967, pp. 58–61.

37

Movies

Tuning In to the Sound of New Music

Renata Adler

(1968)

A few weeks short of 25 years after *Oklahoma!* opened on Broadway on March 31, 1943, the movie *Half a Sixpence*—inflated from an earlier Broadway production—opened last month at the Criterion. *Oklahoma!* marked a revolution. The American musical had broken free of the European princeling operetta on the one hand, and the vaudeville star revue on the other. *Oklahoma!* was about just folks. It was theater, with songs growing more or less naturally out of the story line. It had, not a chorus confined in place, but a number of dance routines, freely choreographed by Agnes de Mille in the Martha Graham tradition of dance. It was new. It was natural.

Twenty-five years is about a generation and *Half a Sixpence* is what we've got. Before that, *Camelot, Mary Poppins, The Sound of Music.* It is not that these musicals in any way increase the sum of harm or boredom in the world. They have, instead, given great pleasure to an unprecedented number of people—although the size of their audiences need not be taken too seriously. Conventional musicals, although they still generate money and sentiment, hardly generate anything else any more. They no longer affect fantasies or change the character of lives—as the best of contemporary music clearly does. They still satisfy an audience with a legitimate claim; but the claim of another, probably larger, audience for the music of its own time is being ignored.

· · ·

These audiences are probably not incompatible. It is not inconceivable that someone will write a fine old-style musical again. A good tune still catches on and one of the few things people of every age still have in common is the repertory of show tunes their minds are programmed with. Show tunes cut across ages and classes; everyone knows hundreds. A great old musical, if someone should happen to write one, would be lovely. A popular tune to be sung in the car or the shower is still a nice thing. (The Beatles' "Yesterday" is one of the finest melodies of recent years.) But it hasn't happened lately and Hollywood—with forced, listless, overblown reworking of dead tunes and ideas like *Half a Sixpence*—goes on as if it had. The inspiration is simply elsewhere.

The problem with movie musicals is that they are now anachronisms in every sense. They cost a fortune—although to a generation that is most characteristically post-Depression, raised in uninterrupted prosperity (with a dawning consciousness of poverty in its midst), a lavishly overpriced musical is at best unimpressive and, more normally, downright offensive. The musicals are boring, unrelated even to the fantasies of the young. One has only to look at faces in audiences. Ten years ago every European could say all young Americans looked alike, or wanted to: crew cut, fresh-faced, conformist, untenanted. Whatever one may think of the state of the young, they are not that way now. The old musical princes and princesses are not models for them. Artists and poets are. Not alone on the grounds of musicianship, the age follows Bob Dylan and Joan Baez.

And countless other performers in other styles. The curious thing is that just when popular music is flourishing—when it is varied enough to include many genres, when a whole generation has been virtually formed by it and when its technical problems are most closely related to those of film—the movies keep betting so heavily on decadent versions of precisely those shows which have been driving audiences over and under 30 away from the theater for years. Since the movie public is simultaneously more dispersed and more accessible than the theater public is, crowds will presumably gather to gum this soggy fare till the end of time. But other audiences exist and a movie *Oklahoma!*, after 25 years, is overdue. It seems to lie, not with the theater, but with recorded music.

The creative prospects of modern recording and filming are close and there are countless ways in which a new, live tradition of movie musicals could come about. (The once new tradition of elaborate group choreography on stage in *Oklahoma!*, for example, surely has some technological counterpart in what a movie camera can do.) The Beatles' films, with a bit of far out direction by Richard Lester, were a minor innovation, but they were half in jest and did not really test the form. The enduring popularity of the Beatles (and that of Elvis Presley who, though once dismissed as a passing fad, has certainly lasted) ought to be some kind of evidence that the new musical developments are not simply going to pass away.

· · ·

There was last year an undistinguished British rock satire and allegory, *Privilege*. There were the two low budget, black and white documentaries on Bob

Dylan and the Newport Folk Festival—with folk and rock and country and western, and even a little jazz; and Miss Baez and Dylan and Donovan. (Dylan's voice still sounds a bit abrasive to an ear attuned to conventional musicals, but Ethel Merman, after all, was never the absolute lark.) From Hollywood there was silence—except for the lovely though already familiar Simon and Garfunkel track of *The Graduate*.

Some accommodation must be possible. Part of the problem seems to be that even people who feel quite strongly that conventional musicals are lifeless now seem to identify contemporary popular music mainly with rock—which they associate with guttural thuds from the rhythm section and a dance floor in crowded motion like a can of worms. But the era of the twist, the discotheque and even the dance is almost gone. The teenybopper audience has become, or yielded to, serious young adults; and it has been the era of the concert for some time.

It is a matter of which songs by which performers you hear and (since radio stations, afraid of payola investigations by the F.C.C., are increasingly programming music rigidly according to national survey charts, which are themselves spurious) of where you can hear them. The Beach Boys, in everything from their own version of "Miserlou" through "Heroes and Villains," have been distinguished, like the Beatles, in nearly everything they've done. The almost basic contrapuntal harmony groups, the Bee Gees in "Massachusetts," Spanky and Our Gang in "Makin' Every Minute Count," the Association in "Never My love," the Mamas and the Papas in "Monday, Monday," Peter, Paul and Mary in almost anything—any of these is better at changing the mood of an audience, lifting its energy and taking it in spite of itself, as musicals have traditionally been supposed to do, than any conventional musical is. They are in the tradition of music of the Elizabethan court and countryside, of madrigals and of the most cheerful baroque. The Swingle Singers in jazz-Bach and Les Paul and Mary Ford with their humming electric guitar have had their influence.

There are the balladeers and troubadours: Donovan, Janis Ian, Simon and Garfunkel, Richie Havens, Tim Harden, Judy Collins, Buffy Ste. Marie, Jake Holmes, Phil Ochs, and Noel Harrison in "Suzanne." They are in the tradition of French bitter sentimentalists Piaf, Greco and Brel, and of American Folk. Their ideological and poetic content is high: drugs, social consciousness, protest, alienation. (There are currently at least five suicides: "Day in the Life," "A Most Peculiar Man," "Ode to Billie Joe," "Insanity," and even a "Richard Corey"), countless songs about runaways, divorces, wallflowers, unwanted children, miscegenation, elderly solitaries. It is not the stuff of traditional musicals, but it is very much alive. It is in some ways as much a flight from reality as the imitations of yesterday, but it is less depressing after all. It is still affecting people; it is a going concern.

There are the soul singers: Aretha Franklin, Wilson Pickett. The regionals: the Buffalo Springfield, Scott McKenzie, Bobbie Gentry. Some extras: the Byrds,

Procol Harum, the Lovin' Spoonful, the Blues Project. Some groups—the Doors, Moby Grape, Jefferson Airplane—whose talent (like, paradoxically, the kaleidoscopically pointless musicals themselves) is accessible mainly with the use of marijuana. There is the music under eastern and western religious influence. In nearly all of them there is something that movies can use. Records which now effectively include animal calls, hoof beats, carnival sounds, laughter hysterically out of control, musical puns and anagrams, cross references to other records, and motor dissonances prolonged to obscure the precise transition into silence—all of it seems cabalistic, encoded, scrambled full of double images, paradoxes, camouflages, interstices. But artistically rich. It is a medium, *recorded music,* finding itself and its audience—as the movie musical might loosen its hold on the tradition of theater musicals and start creating a contemporary audience of its own.

There ought to be nothing dogmatic about all this. There will always be room for the hummable tune, and whatever is good is good, no matter what style it's in. But in the meantime there is no need to be humming and dancing and investing toward the return of yesterday.

It is not clear that the minstrels and troubadours would be altogether happy on celluloid. But room ought to be made. It seems sad for musicals to be resolutely cut off from the attractive composer-performers of our time. And unprecedented for musicals to be divorced so completely from the popular music of which they used to form such a vital part.

38

Towards an Interior Music

Ennio Morricone

(1997)

When Sergio [Leone] came to my house to commission the music for *A Fistful of Dollars,* I recognized him at once: we had been classmates in the third grade and I remembered that we had both been rather lively children.

Little by little we found a way of understanding each other. Sergio did not express himself in a musically very precise way. Anyway, there are always problems of communication between a director and a composer. Also, on the piano you cannot always make clear what a piece is going to sound like when it has been orchestrated. Sometimes we spent whole days getting through to each other: we were both saying the same thing, but in different ways. There were never any serious misunderstandings, however. We had long, lively talks to get our opinions across to each other, and then we reached a compromise. The danger is when there is no discussion and you do not even try to understand the other's point of view.

In composing the music for Leone's movies I deliberately ignored the American precedents. In general the Americans use symphonic music even for Westerns, something I never do. I find symphonic language excessive, too rich for films. For the main theme of *A Fistful of Dollars* I played an old Gypsy piece for Sergio which I had arranged years before for a television program, accompanying it with whip lashes, whistles, and anvils . . . He told me to leave it almost unchanged. Sometimes Sergio takes a devilish pleasure in re-evaluating certain themes that other directors have discarded, knowing that the musical discourse is different from movie to movie. I had written the melody for the trumpet piece of the finale for a black singer in a television version of O'Neill's

334

sea plays. Sergio told me to add the trumpet with a Mexican accompaniment of the "Deguello" type—which I really do not like—because Sergio and Cinquini had edited the images precisely on Tiomkin's "Deguello" in *Rio Bravo.* In the second picture, I had to use the trumpet again, though with guitar and carillon; in *the* third picture, with other things; and in the fourth we finally almost freed ourselves of it.

After the first picture I did the music before the shooting began. Sergio generally does not even give me the script: he tells me the story, the way he feels the characters, even the way the shots are composed. And I bring him the music. We talk it over and influence each other, something like a marriage where two become one flesh. Sometimes he plays the music on the set. In *Once Upon a Time in the West* it seems that this was very helpful to the actors' sense of character.

The use of the organ in *For a Few Dollars More* suggested itself to me by the fact that Volonté had his hide-out in a church and, in particular, by an almost Michelangelo-like shot of Volonté. I did not want to use just any organ music, and so I used the opening of Bach's *Fugue in D minor.* The trumpet theme starts by taking the A-G-A of the organ. My carillon is a deformation of the tenuous sound of the music box incorporated in Lee Van Cleef's watch. As in the case of the harmonica of *Once Upon a Time in the West,* we are dealing here, to use Sergio Miceli's words, with interior music, music that is born within the scene.[1]

The voice of Edda dell'Orso had already been used in *For a Few Dollars More.* In *Once Upon a Time in the West* it becomes the protagonist. It is the human voice used like an instrument. The music for *Once Upon a Time in the West* was already composed and recorded before the shooting began. I believe that Sergio regulated the speed of the crane shot when Claudia Cardinale leaves the station, to fit the musical crescendo. The Cheyenne theme came to me almost out of the blue. We were in the recording studio, I sat down to play the piano, Sergio liked it; and so I wrote it.

In *Duck! You Sucker,* the sweet music that accompanies the collapse of the bridge expresses the dynamiter's nostalgia for his youth. The roar puts an end to his Irish memories. For the march of the beggars, since I had injected some rather vulgar things—there was even some belching (the illogical thing was to put full-stomach sounds into a march of starving men)—it seemed only right to add something more refined, like Mozart.

There is a special satisfaction in working with someone like Leone. Not only does he make excellent films, but he respects the work of the composer and the orchestra. Other directors do a bad job of mixing the music, they keep it too soft or cover it with noises. But Sergio always gave full value to what I wrote for him.

From Oreste de Fornari, *Sergio Leone: The Great Italian Dream of Legendary America*, translated by Charles Nopar (Rome: Gremese International, 1997), pp. 153–54. Reprinted by permission of the publisher.

NOTE

1. A reference to a Brazilian author who has written a book-length study of Morricone's music. See Sergio Miceli, *Morricone, la musica, il cinema* (Modena: Mucchi/Milan: Ricordi, 1994).—Ed.

39

Keeping Score on Schifrin

Lalo Schifrin and the Art of Film Music

Harvey Siders

(1969)

There are as many ways to approach the subject of Lalo Schifrin as there are facets of his artistry. One could devote an entire article to his legitimate learnings and show how his earliest exposure to serious music was enhanced by hearing string quartets played in his home, and later crystallized by his father's position as concertmaster the Buenos Aires of Philharmonic Orchestra. We could follow that right through to studies with Juan Carlos Paz, the Schoenberg of South America, and subsequent training in Paris, skipping his abortive pursuit of a law degree in his native Argentina. And we could bring the "classical Lalo" up to date with a listing of the concert and chamber works he has written and is continually commissioned to compose.

We'd have to mention the cantata he fashioned from his TV score to *The Rise and Fall of the Third Reich;* the a cappella chorale *No Nation Shall Take Weapons Against Nation;* the *Double Concerto for Violin and Cello,* which Schifrin wrote for Jascha Heifetz and Gregor Piatigorsky; the *Canon for String Quartet,* which is being readied for its March 24 debut; or the work which Zubin Mehta commissioned for the 1969–1970 season of the Los Angeles Philharmonic. It is called *Encounters* and Schifrin is integrating a jazz band with the larger orchestra. And there would be the ballet *Jazz Faust,* written for a festival in Washington, D.C., in 1962.

If we stayed on a "classical" kick, we'd have to recount his conducting debut at the Hollywood Bowl: a concert that featured his own music and that of Villa-Lobos and Ginastera; the soloist was Laurindo Almeida. There was the usual amount of nervousness until the manager of the Philharmonic dropped the bomb that Schifrin would have to begin the program with "The Star Spangled Banner"! The only time he'd heard it was while watching President Kennedy's inauguration on TV. So the concert-master spent some frantic moments with him before a dressing room mirror (a session Lalo describes as "surrealistic") teaching him the anthem, stressing the opening drum roll and that crucial *fermata* near the end. Schifrin was so preoccupied with that dramatic hold that he was not prepared for the response to the drum roll cue: "The whole orchestra stood up. I almost had a heart attack and I said to myself, 'My God, what have I done?'" But he kept his cool and got through the ritual.

Turning to another facet, we could dwell on his writing and playing in the jazz idiom. Among jazz aficionados, Schifrin is best known as Dizzy Gillespie's pianist from 1960–1962. But how many know he had a big band in Buenos Aires in 1956 for which he did the charts? And when Dizzy heard it during one of his tours, he became the catalyst for Schifrin's move to New York and, ultimately, suites such as *Gillespiana* and *New Continent*. We would trace Schifrin's jazz career from his trio with Eddie de Haas, bass; and Rudy Collins, drums. We could delve into the free-lance arranging he did for Basie's band, for singer Pat Thomas (remember *Desafinado?*), for Stan Getz, Johnny Hodges, Bob Brookmeyer, Sarah Vaughan, Eddie Harris; or his gigs with Don Ellis' workshop ensemble. We could follow him to Paris, where he played with Chet Baker, or back to New York for more experimentation with Gunther Schuller and gigs with Quincy Jones, then out to the West Coast and his Grammy-winning albums *The Cat* (for Jimmy Smith) and his *Jazz Suite on the Mass Texts;* his chamber jazz album for Verve, *Marquis de Sade,* his jazz-cum-rock offerings for Dot; his concert piece, *The Sphynx,* for Stan Kenton's Neophonic Orchestra. We could also join him at Donte's or some other club where he sits in on those rare evenings when he feels the need to interrupt his ever-increasing commitments.

Ready for another Schifrin? This is the one well known to video viewers. They've heard his scores for *Mission: Impossible,* they've taken to its swaggering 5/4 the way Viennese took to Strauss's 3/4. He won two Grammies for that theme. And he earned an Emmy nomination for *Small Rebellion,* a segment of *Chrysler Theater,* in which the only instruments were the highly personalized trumpet of his former boss, John Birks Gillespie, and the bass of Ray Brown. And there was the *Mannix* theme, *T.H.E. Cat,* and specials such as *The Making of the President, 1964,* and the three-part *Rise and Fall of the Third Reich.*

There are enough credits so far for three bona fide careers. Yet they serve as a mere introduction to his basic calling and the real substance of this article. The essential Schifrin we're keeping score on is the film composer-scorer-conductor. That's the Schifrin who began in 1963, shortly after leaving Dizzy's combo. His free-lance arranging in New York included some albums for the MGM label. That company's music publishing head, Arnold Maxim, was quite pleased with what he heard, and sent Lalo to Hollywood to score two films—his first American films. Lalo had been an established film composer in Argentina, and six years earlier had won the Argentine equivalent of the Academy Award for his jazz-flavored score for *El Jefe*.

For his American film-scoring debut, he drew a low-budget Ivan Tors film, *Rhino*, which he prefers not to discuss; and *Joy House*, a Jane Fonda film shot in Paris, which Lalo feels was inferior to the score he designed for it. Subsequent assignments were more in keeping with his prodigious talents.

One talent he lacks is remembering all the movies he has scored. With a little prodding, we came up with a dozen more titles: *Once a Thief, Murderers Row, The Black Cloak, Blindfold, Cincinnati Kid, The Liquidator, Cool Hand Luke, Coogan's Bluff, The Fox, The Brotherhood, The Eye of the Cat* and one not yet finished, *Che*. In all, he has scored 21 films in this country: an impressive track record for five years. Small wonder the phrase coined by Los Angeles disc jockey Gary Owens served as the title for a recent Dot album: *There's a Whole Lalo Schifrin Going On*. There's a whole Lalo Schifrin that goes into each score, too, and Lalo seems to bask in the musicological research required of him in order to match the background of the scenario.

When he was writing the score for *The Brotherhood*, Schifrin remarked, "I'm discovering things about Sicilian music which are fascinating. Once you study that music, you realize that only in that kind of an island, and that kind of a background, could a brotherhood like the Mafia develop. There is something sinister and happy in their music. The lyrics of the love songs are about skeletons and skulls, and while much of their music is supposed to be joyous, it often has a menacing Jew's harp that sounds so ominous."

Cool Hand Luke gave the composer the prestigious satisfaction of an Academy Award nomination, and also provided him with insight into another type of music hardly indigenous to the Argentine: bluegrass. He admitted having listened to banjos prior to that assignment without paying too much attention. "They had a pleasant folk music sound, and certainly a peculiar style. But now I had the chance to discover the intricate lines—I went *inside* the banjo. A good banjo player gets those intricate lines by instinct, the way an African drummer plays polyrhythmically. They are asymmetrical, irregular and very angular. And this triggered my score."

Cool hand Lalo knew precisely what he was after, and got Howard Roberts to play that theme. He also singled out Ray Brown for his rhythmic support in that score, Mike Melvin for his "tack" piano, and Earl Palmer for his country drumming.

If the services of such swingers can be singled out for their contributions to a hillbilly score, then jazz instrumentalists must be valuable in general to a film-scorer. Schifrin was quick to agree, pointing out that the new breed of jazz-flavored film and TV composer (Quincy Jones, Dave Grusin, Shorty Rogers, Johnny Mandel, Neal Hefti, Johnny Williams, Oliver Nelson, Henry Mancini, Gil Melle, Don

Ellis, Roger Kellaway, Willie Ruff) has been aided by a new breed of director and producer. According to Schifrin, men like Stuart Rosenberg, Richard Fleischer, and Mark Rydell have provided an understanding atmosphere in which the scorer with a jazz background can feel free to experiment, or at least use the wealth of west coast jazz musicians who can be found in the studios. The last-named, Rydell, is a former jazz pianist himself. Although the score of the film he directed, *The Fox,* contained little or no jazz, Rydell was the pianist.

While the stigma has not been completely removed from jazz, it is no longer a dirty word in the film industry. An increasing number of scores are jazz-flavored, but more significantly, an increasing number of jazz musicians are getting the studio calls. They may not always get a chance to swing in the dues-paying sense, but by merely having a jazz background they have a built-in advantage. Schifrin feels their greatest asset is their ability to improvise—whether around chord symbols or in a "free" situation. Related to that is the jazz musicians' ability to play "legitimately." As Lalo put it—unaware of the double entendre—"they swing either way." In other words, the legitimate musician cannot play jazz: he cannot *phrase* the way a jazz composer desires, let alone improvise on a given harmonic pattern. But the jazz musician can and does play legitimately.

Schifrin's prime example was Ray Brown. "He is an all-around bass player. He is so incredible with the bow, it sounds like he plays cello. I had him in the bass section, with all those legitimate basses, for *The Brotherhood.* This is what counts—musicianship."

There were others cited by Schifrin for the same two-way versatility: Bud Shank, Tom Scott, Buddy Collette, Plas Johnson (he singled out Plas for his playing in *Bullitt*), Frank Rosolino, Mike Melvoin, Shelly Manne, Larry Bunker, Emil Richards (Lalo had high praise for the latter three "because they can play all kinds of percussion and mallet instruments and tympani"), Bill Plummer and, when he was still in this country, Red Mitchell.

Regarding free form, the composer has occasionally resorted to that technique— and with gratifying results. "In *Hell in the Pacific,* there was a scene which is pure fantasy. It follows the confrontation between Lee Marvin and Toshiro Mifune. In their imaginations, they kill each other. I was going to do that scene one way, then at the last minute I decided it would be more effective to use a tenor sax playing very wild, contemporary, avant-garde jazz. Free—completely free and wild—with the tenor attached to an electronic device with lots of 'reverb.' For that I called Tom Scott, and it worked out very well. All the harassment and turmoil were conveyed through that music," he says.

Another situation in which Schifrin used free form is more recent. There is a high-speed chase in one of those two-hour "movies for television" with the deceptive title, *How I Spent My Summer Vacation.* "I used Tony Ortega, Don Ellis,

Ray Brown and Shelly Manne. I didn't tell them what was going on on the screen. In fact, I didn't even let them watch the screen, because there was the danger their music would be too 'cartoonish'—you know, trying to catch every movement." (The cartoon is the one medium in which he is not too experienced, but he knows enough about it to admit it is the most difficult. As he explained: "The cartoon technique calls for the music to accompany each action. If that were used for films or TV, it would sound ridiculous.") "So I just let them play and keep the counterpoint going. It was incredible how it worked out. It was fantastic." Anyone who knows Lalo is familiar with his use of the word "fantastic." It makes an appearance about once every four minutes and comes out sounding "fahn-TAHS-teek." Lalo is continually amazed at the success of matching free improvisation with the visual happenings, but as he pointed out: "It is up to the composer to see *where* the musician is allowed to improvise."

Hell in the Pacific called for a situation in which Schifrin "controlled" an unusual free device. It occurred in the beginning of that film. The action was chaotic; there was much tension, and Schifrin hit upon an idea to convey "nervous sound": he instructed—or rather the score instructed—pianist Mike Lang to throw golf balls onto the strings of the instrument. "He held the damper pedal down, then threw six golf balls at the strings in the middle register, and he got the precise sound I wanted. When it calls for it, I will experiment. Like *The Eye of the Cat* I did over at Universal. It is a horror movie, with a script by the same who wrote *Psycho*. I tried a technique to get sounds that will precede screams. I have string players rapping their instruments with their knuckles, or with their finger tips, hitting the music stands with their bows, or even rubbing the chairs they were sitting on with the heels of the shoes.

"I have a reason for all this: it gives me an effect which is very light and very percussive at the same time. You see, no matter how softly a percussion instrument plays, it is still a percussion instrument. But by experimenting with different devices, I got a sound that was quite indeterminate—a sound that came like a murmur from all over."

Such experimentation is fascinating to hear, and fascinating to write about, but it is not characteristic of Schifrin. Basically he is a very tonal, very straight-ahead composer, whose gift for melody and orchestration adheres to the mainstream of contemporary music. One of his most successful scores, which relied on conventional means, was devoted to a most unconventional film, *The Fox*.

The D. H. Lawrence story is a study of an erotic triangle whose two female angles are caught up in the world of lesbianism. The choice of instrumentation was based on considerable thought, plus hours spent looking at the rough cuts (unedited film). Schifrin utilized a most delicate orchestral texture for a most delicate subject: a chamber ensemble comprised of a string quartet, a few woodwinds, one harp and percussion.

"I decided that a chamber approach would be best to convey the intimacy and desolation. As you know, the setting is Canada and there is lots of snow. The simplicity of the chamber music allowed me to contrast the warm emotions inside the house with the cold, bleak panorama outside."

How effective was Lalo's probing, yet indirect approach? Well, the film and its score have been wedded for posterity. Many who saw *The Fox* were probably so absorbed by the visual action that they failed to get the aural message. To Lalo, however, there are two criteria by which he was able to judge his efforts, and they are both extremely meaningful. First, his score for *The Fox* has received a preliminary nomination for an Academy Award. The recognition that accompanies the word "Oscar" is self-explanatory. There is no way to minimize its importance, and Lalo is too level-headed to do so, but even he would admit that there is a vote of approval that is more deep-rooted, more enduring and less political than any Oscar.

As he recalls it: "You know, studio musicians play all day long. They go from one studio to another—movie studios in the morning, TV studios in the evening, maybe a record date at night—and there is very little that surprises them. But when *they* get caught up in the excitement of what you are trying to do, then they get the same feeling and they all try to collaborate. Believe me, when *they* applaud after a cue (a 'cue' is a sequence of film that requires music), it means something. That doesn't happen every day. It did with *The Fox*."

It could very well happen with *Che,* his next assignment. Schifrin had remarked that in his nearly six years in Hollywood, he had scored motion pictures about the south, about Sicily, about the Pacific, but never one with a Latin American theme. Finally, along came *Che*—with its semi-documentary approach about Che Guevara. Schifrin recently returned from location in Puerto Rico and expressed his enthusiasm this way: "The picture doesn't take sides. It sees Guevara, in a series of flashbacks, through the eyes of those who loved him, and those who hated him. In a sense, the music will have to be detached and objective. It's very challenging."

Actually, if Schifrin's next assignment were to score a home movie on the sale of Girl Scout cookies, it would still be a challenge. He is a man obsessed by his art— both the aggressor and the recipient in a requited love affair. "When I'm writing music for films, some kind of chemistry happens. It's sort of magical—maybe you should call it alchemy. You have a piece of music on tape and that is one entity, and you have something projected on the screen and that is another entity. But when you combine them, the result is *not* the sum of their parts, it is something *more*.

"Let me tell you, besides music, the closest thing to me is film-making. I am a fan of films, especially the classics. I have always followed Fritz Lang, René Clair and Eisenstein. I have been influenced by the book that Eisenstein wrote in collaboration with Prokofiev: *Audio-Visual Counterpoint*."

There are other books as meaningful to Schifrin: one is by Henry Mancini on film scoring; the other, on the same topic, is by Earle Hagen, and it contains some thoughts on Schifrin himself. The reason for his concern about these books is his concern for the future of film composing. "David Raksin has a class on scoring at UCLA, and Earle Hagen is teaching it privately (Hagen, incidentally, will expand his teaching activities next fall to include a UCLA extension course), but the main thing is, a young composer shouldn't be discouraged by the technical processes involved in film synchronization. It can be learned quickly and it's really no problem. The main problem is to be a composer first and then to have a feeling for the dramatic."

He credits Stanley Wilson, head of Universal's music department, with putting him through his mathematical basic training. "More important, Stanley taught me what *not* to do."

So the negatives have been eliminated, the positives have been accentuated, and Schifrin and the whole jazz community await that fateful night in April when the Academy Awards are given out. If fortune smiles (she's been winking at him all the way from Buenos Aires to Beverly Hills) there shouldn't be a single audible complaint. Whatever Lalo wants, Lalo deserves.

From *Downbeat* 36, no. 5 (1969): 16–17 and 35. Reproduced by permission.

40

BBC Interview with Jerry Goldsmith

(1969)

Where were you born?

It is assumed, even though I tell people I was born in Los Angeles, "Certainly from New York?" There's a certain snobbism that goes on in America that if you have any sort of success, you must come from New York!

Your first real musical work was in radio, I think, wasn't it?

Yes it was. I started in radio—actually my first work was picking out records for dramatic shows, and then I graduated to writing scores for them.

And conducting or simply writing?

Yes—conducting too. I was writing cue music, picking out records, filing in the music library—I was actually sweeping up the library! But I had that marvelous opportunity of being very young—21/22—that I was learning how to apply dramatic music.

And from there to television, presumably?

Yes—*live* television. Actually I must say what had happened. I did the program called *Climax*: it was the first hour-long dramatic show that had been done from the West Coast. We were on the air for five years, had the biggest stars in Hollywood, and then from there I went on to *Playhouse 90*, which was an hour-and-a-half live dramatic show, probably the finest show that was ever done in America. Many of the properties such as *Judgment at Nuremberg, The Miracle Worker* and *Requiem for a Heavyweight* were originally done on this program.

The biggest tune/melody success that one connects with you is the Doctor Kildare theme . . .

Yes, that was the first series of my own that I did after I was "released" into the world on my own. Of course, that program was a tremendous success, interesting that it was as much an instantaneous success in England as it was in America. And of course the music was very successful, and very fortunately, the song itself took off beautifully. Do we have time for one very funny ending on that? I just didn't know at the time, but I got a call from the publishers, who said they wanted to make a song out of *Doctor Kildare* because there had been instrumental recordings that had become quite a success here in England. "We have a lyric that was sent to us from England," and they read it over the phone to me, and I said: "That's awful, I hate the lyric!" I was heavily preoccupied with something at the time, so that was about it. So now, six months later (I'd been in Europe—did a picture in Italy—*Freud*), I came back, and the publisher says: "Well, how do you like that? You've been in the charts in America for eleven weeks now with your song of *Doctor Kildare!*" Of course some American lyricist (the lyricist dismissingly referred to was another Hal: Hal Wynn, who put the lyric to Pete Rugolo's arrangement of the theme) did the lyric—O.K., fine, great, why not? So now, last year, I'm in England doing a film *(Sebastian)* and I worked with a marvelous lyricist named Hal Shaper, and I fell in love with his work. Really he was the first lyricist that I feel I can work with, because I think lyricists and composers have a very special "thing." So we did a beautiful song nobody ever heard but nevertheless, we knew it was a good one. We've just now finished another song for the picture I'm doing, then he's going to come to Hollywood and do a theme song for *Justine* with me. So we were having dinner one night, and he says: "Do you remember about *Doctor Kildare?*" and he starts to tell me this story about the lyric . . . "I was the one in England who wrote the lyric *you* hated so much!" Now here I am *fighting* for this man, because I love his work so much!

It was Hal who wrote "Softly as I Leave You" . . .

You bet it was—which has one of *the* beautiful lyrics. I really think that it's a very special thing that happens between a composer and a lyricist. I, not basically being a songwriter anyway, find it a little strange for me to work in this medium.

"And We Were Lovers"? . . .

The *Sand Pebbles* song, yes.

Talking about that song from the score of The Sand Pebbles, and incidentally the theme too from Doctor Kildare, you say that you are a composer, not a song-writer; you think, obviously, instrumentally. Yet it's true that if you're going to write for singing, you've got to keep the melody within a certain range. You must really be writing with a song in mind, even when you're writing the "theme from" . . .

That's very true, except there's one psychological hang-up—that the producer says: "We gotta have a hit song." This is the anathema of all the composers, you know right away, you tighten up, because nobody can sit down and write a hit, nobody can predict a hit song. Publishers like to *think* they can, but actually it just *happens.* I think the most "successful" thing that I've written up to this point is "And We Were Lovers." Very distinctly, when I had the assignment, Robert Wise, one of the great men in films, said to me: " I do not *want* a song for this picture!" This is an $11 million picture, so I go: "Oh, thank God, just let me write a score." What he set down was a lovely love story and I was terribly moved by this film, and I wrote, without any difficulty, a very pleasant theme for it. The logic of the material was in the ge [ch'i], it just flowed, it was natural, and of course it all happened after that. The whole thing with lyricists, I feel this sort of feeling with Hal. I've written two songs with Leslie [Bricusse]: "And We Were Lovers" was written without a lyric in mind, then Leslie came in later and did a lovely lyric. We did a song more or less together for the second *Flint* picture which was mildly successful: "Your Z.O.W.I.E. Face," which is not the greatest of titles! Then I did a song with Sammy Cahn from *Bandolero!*: to begin with, it sold an awful lot of records as it happened to be on the *right* side of a bigger bit—the *other* side! [The "Goldsmith-Cahn" song was entitled, "There's got to be a Better Way," the B-Side of Hugo Montenegro's No. 1 hit version of Morricone's *The Good, the Bad and the Ugly*.] It got a lot of play and was very successful. But I never really felt (these are all marvelous people, there are lots of lyricists I've worked with I won't mention: I don't think anybody's ever heard of them) this "Special Thing" that happens. I think the greatest example today is the collaboration of Paul Francis Webster and Johnny Mandel—this, all of a sudden, is a *unit*. They've written two of the great songs: "Shadow of Your Smile" and "Time for Love." I talked to Johnny just before I left—he'd just finished a picture, Paul was dubbing in the lyric, and said that he thought it's the best one yet. These two men have got that sort of *magic* together. You look back at Richard Rodgers and the music he wrote with Lorenz Hart, later with Hammerstein, and what he did when he wrote the lyrics himself. You find his whole *style* of music is affected, because to me, the great Richard Rodgers music was with Lorenz Hart—that has the quality and class. It's that "Certain Thing" again.

We've been talking so fully about songs, song tunes, lyric writers and so on. I should have thought with your upbringing in music, the "studio man" who produces a score for strings, woodwinds or whatever of one-and-a-half hours, would lead you to think much more about instrumental music—what I would call "pure composing" rather than songwriting.

It does. I started studying composing, harmony theory, and counterpoint when I was 14, composition at 16. I'd studied the piano when I was six years old, so all this time I was studying piano, then when I was 18 I did conducting, and I'd actually had all my *formal* musical studies by the time I was 22. Although I've never *stopped* studying: I feel every time I pick up a pencil to write music I'm learning something.

Also of course you use a lot of unorthodox, unusual orchestral sounds. I was thinking of the score for The Sand Pebbles (not the tune—the score), which used sounds that it was hard to identify. These intrigue you, do they?

Yes—well—I think that it's a difficult thing. The greatest example of that sound was *Planet of the Apes,* where, being such a strange film, everyone said we're going to use electronic music! I said "No . . . I'm not: I'm going to do this with an 'old-fashioned' orchestra because it is so capable of doing so many things." I made all of these strange sounds with just the orchestra, but I made them musically, which is the important thing.

Do you mean you're using instruments out of their normal range?

Yes. For instance, I had the French horns, instead of blowing notes, they took their mouthpieces off and just blew air through them. Then you combine that with some other effects and sounds, then you put it in a musical context and it works marvelous things.

What was the film score you most enjoyed writing? I'm thinking of the names: Studs Lonigan, The Man From U.N.C.L.E., Von Ryan's Express (that was yours, wasn't it?), Detective, Blue Max, Seven Days in May . . .

It's sort of difficult to answer that because, you see, I have a strange versatility. I can do pop, jazz, romantic, you name it. Personally, my own genre which I compose is as a serial composer.

That's not for the hit songs!

No it's not, but I've done three films: *Freud,* for which I was nominated for an Academy Award; *Planet of the Apes,* also a serial score, which I am now nominated for this year . . .

Really? . . . Good.

. . . and the last film I did that way was *The Illustrated Man,* which I think is the best score I've written, the one I really enjoyed working on. I had a lot of time to do it, and it just presented some interesting problems. But then there are other films I enjoyed equally as much—*100 Rifles,* which was all Mexico, the first chance I really had to do Mexican music, and it was a wild ball to do this because you hear these marvelous wild Mexican rhythms, and do all sorts of things that you normally couldn't do in other pictures, again using native instruments, and all that.

What kind of music do you like to listen to?

Well—I love music, I mean there are times in my life when I get totally depressed and I try and deny myself . . . it's just that I love music. I don't like *bad* music. It's difficult to say which I listen to the most—anything that's well done and well made.

You mean in the musicianly sense? You prefer jazz to pop music, presumably?

Some jazz I prefer to pop, some pop I prefer to jazz—I like pop music very much. I am not one of the cultists who believe that pop music is the "Art of Today" or the "Expression of People Today": I hardly think that.

If you put on a record at home, what might it be?

It could be Bach, Beethoven, Brahms, Burt Bacharach . . . the only records I don't buy are motion picture soundtrack albums!

You're here doing the recording of music for a film score, obviously working with English musicians. How do you like English orchestras, in general?

I just adore English Orchestras. This is the third film I've been with an English orchestra: I've done a record album over here, and *The Blue Max* with a 100-man symphony orchestra, and I did *Sebastian*, which was a jazz-type pop thing. Now on this I'm using 85 men in the orchestra—it's a dream, like driving a Rolls Royce, to conduct an orchestra like that.

They are freelance musicians, aren't they?

Yes—some are freelance, many of the musicians of the BBC are on my call, and many are from the RPO, LSO, you name it: the choice of the finest orchestras and musicians. There are so many of them over here, it's just unbelievable.

—————————

From BBC Interview, July 7, 1969.

41

The Jazz Composers
in Hollywood

A Symposium with Benny Carter,
Quincy Jones, Henry Mancini, Lalo Schifrin,
and Pat Williams

Harvey Siders

(1972)

To begin with, what are the main differences between writing for movies and writing for TV?

Q.J.: No difference, man.

OK, then the article's over. Thank you very much gentlemen.

Q.J.: You mean the tape's been running?

Of course, but I can edit out all the obscenities.

Q.J.: Well, in that case, the main difference is in the money. Another thing is in the interruptions. You know, writing music so they can hang the audience in mid-air while they stick in a commercial in the middle of somebody getting stabbed.

L.S.: Perhaps we should touch on the similarities as well as the differences. In both cases you're dealing with the visual—what's happening on the screen. In both cases you're dealing with theatrics. It's not enough simply to be a good musician. You have to have the instincts for theater. It's virtually impossible to teach this in a school, this feeling for the visual and the dramatic. It's not enough to be versed in harmony, counterpoint or orchestration. Those are merely the tools. There's something more basic: the art of accompanying.

H.M.: There's another difference: there's much more heavy scoring in television than in pictures.

P.W.: Right . . . sometimes it seems like wall-to-wall scoring.

L.S.: Oh I don't know about that. When it comes to documentaries *that's* where you are required to write wall-to-wall music, and you have a chance to used compositional devices such as development that you can't use in a TV series. All you can do in TV is use variations, or one of the oldest tools: endless repetition.

H.M.: Well, you see, the producers and directors in TV don't have as much confidence in their own ability to hold an audience. They feel if the action lags, the viewer can shut off the tube. But you can't shut off a feature if you're in the theater.

Q.J.: That's the way it is, especially with those one-twenties [referring to the 120-minute movies for television] and even some of the 90s. Every time there's nothing happening, he says "music."

Who says "music?"

P.W.: Well, I guess you'd call him the music editor. Anyway, he sits there with a bulb, you know a little bulb, and they run the picture, and you're composer number 460 for film number whatever-it-is, and they sit there all day long, show after show after show, and go "pffffft" with the bulb and you keep hearing that bulb go on and off. (Knowing laughter from all)

Wait a minute, wait a minute. What's the bulb?

Q.J.: It's something the music editor holds that starts a timer to let you know what sequences have to be scored. It gives you the rough timing for the music.

B.C. (to Pat Williams): You're doing the *Mary Tyler Moore Show,* right?

P.W.: Yeah, well, that isn't such a big deal. (general laughter) Now don't get me wrong; it's a cute show. I'm not rapping the show. It's just that we go in and record three, four shows at a time. I can write five or six of those a week.

B.C.: What's the average time of the score for one of those shows?

P.W.: Oh, I would say about 45 seconds. (loud guffaws)

And that includes the main title?

L.S.: Let's face it: a main title is very important. If you expect to lure the guy who is in the kitchen to his TV set, you have to do something distinctive. That's one of the immediate differences between TV and movie writing. In TV you have 30 seconds to establish a mood; in movies, you can take anywhere from two and one-half to six minutes. *Shaft* is an example of a long main title. But you have to be very concise in TV. It's like the difference between sending a cablegram and writing a letter . . .

OK, you have more music in TV, but wouldn't you rather write for movies so you can "stretch out" compositionally and actually develop themes?

H.M.: You can develop themes in a two-hour movie for television.

L.S.: But in documentaries you have more freedom. Like Richard Rodgers' *Victory At Sea*. Was that Richard Rodgers or Morton Gould? Anyway, he wrote an entire suite for that series. Now usually a documentary is colder. That is, there is little opportunity to underscore character development. However, I was able to, in two documentaries: *The Making of the President 1964* and *The Rise & Fall of the Third Reich*. In that one *[Rise and Fall]* I was able to take two themes and state them simultaneously while establishing a counterpoint of mood: Hitler and Mussolini, plotting and sinister; Chamberlain and Daladier, rather wishy-washy. And in *Making of the President* I was able to write a fugue to accompany a montage of Election Day scenes in five parts of the country. Now how often can you write a fugue in television—unless it happens to be for a documentary? As for movies, that's a different ballgame. They're even *more* stylized, *more* sophisticated . . . .

Let's talk about individual work habits. I've been over to your place, Quincy, and I've seen you use that Moviola [a large but portable movie projector with a footage meter and a built-in magnifier that enlarges the film and eliminates the need for a separate screen].

Q.J.: Yeah, that Moviola is a big help. That's because I don't have the time to get to the studio. This way, I can look at the movie as often as I want.

What about the rest of you?

H.M.: I can't work with a Moviola. I don't know how to run one. (to Q) You're so technical-minded.

Q.J.: Not really. Richard Brooks locked me in a room and would not let me out until I finished writing.

L.S.: I see the movie maybe two or three times at the studio, but after that I work mainly from notes provided by the music editor. If I get hung up I can always go back to the studio, but you know, it wouldn't be a bad idea to have a Moviola. That way you could try something right there with a piano to see how it would go with a certain scene. . . .

H.M.: . . . A lot of producers like to get on the stand right behind you . . . and hum. So I let them stand there and at the right moment I take a good upbeat. (swings right elbow and simulates how he "disposes" of humming producer) I sympathize with you, Benny. I know what you're going through. If you're strong, like Quincy, you know if you can carry the ball. Then you just go ahead and do it. Otherwise they hang around you like flies and it becomes a group effort. That's tough.

L.S.: I find that there is a cross-section of producers in the field. Some are hip to music, like Bruce Geller. Some aren't. Most of them just don't have the time to be too concerned with the score. They're too wrapped up just delivering the product to the network. They're too concerned with dialogue, sound effects, expenses. Usually, the first time they confront the music is at the dubbing session. And even then, their main concern is time. The dubbing room has to be clear by such-and-such a time because it has been booked by some other show . . . .

Q.J.: What cracks me up is when a producer—first or second time out—tells you: "This is a very heavy picture and it needs a score that is larger than life." I *love* that. That's a code for "I don't know what I want." And I remember doing a western one time when the cat says, "There's an Indian girl in here—a Cherokee—and she's a nymphomaniac, a Lesbian and a killer." Now the chick didn't say one word throughout the picture, but the producer wanted me to convey all that with one instrument!

How did you resolve that one?

Q.J.: Oh I mumbled something about a bass guitar that would sound weird and he went for it.

L.S.: Of course there's a serious side to that. It depends on the situation. When I did *The Fox,* I used only ten instruments. And even when they showed panoramic scenes, I managed to convey the vastness with just two or three instruments.

P.W.: You know, being the junior here tonight . . . I must admit that film scoring has taken me a long time to learn, much longer than I ever thought it would. And I feel that I've learned more about writing for movies simply by writing a lot for television. I find that I try things in TV that I don't think I would try in a feature.

L.S.: That shouldn't be. In feature movies you have four to six weeks to turn out maybe 45 minutes' worth of music. In TV, you have a week to ten days to write up to 25 minutes of music. So to write your own theme and do each segment, you have to create like a factory. Of course it's possible. I have done it, but it's very exhausting.

P.W.: Well you know, I feel who really cares out there about the music on a TV episode? But I learn by watching the shows I've done and seeing if the things work.

L.S.: I'm never as subtle on TV as I am in movies. But then again, the product given to me is not subtle. You know, a heavy is a heavy; a good guy is a good guy. There are no shades of characterization on TV . . . .

Q.J.: Well I agree with Pat: you're a lot freer on TV. It's not so permanent.

P.W.: I haven't seen as many films as I'd like to, but recently we began catching up on some of them. When you hear a good writer cutting loose with his thing in a feature, there's nothing like it.

H.M.: Of course there's a big difference in the sound quality.

L.S.: The size of the screen helps, as well as the quality of the speakers. It gives you the feeling that the musical dimension is larger.

P.W.: Yeah, I suppose so. You never get that feeling in TV.

Q.J.: You'll get that feeling in the studio, especially in a playback situation—you know the way engineers turn everything up so loud. . . .

If you know there's going to be a soundtrack album issued from a picture you're scoring, does it affect what you write? In other words, do you keep one eye on the cue sheet and the other eye on the charts?

Q.J.: I don't see how you can. Not when you're dealing with a visual medium. You'd like to think you can, but you can't separate the two if you want to do the assignment right.

L.S.: Recording is a totally different medium. I'm much too honest when it comes to the needs of the film score to be concerned about what might eventually end up in an album.

Related to that, has the Easy Rider approach of scoring hurt the business? Has it cut into your assignments?

B.C.: I think so, to answer both your questions. When they use records instead of a composer's original score, that hurts.

L.S.: I really don't see how it could hurt our business. I think it would be ridiculous to score a picture like *Easy Rider* with the techniques of the Central European composers.

H.M.: That all started with Mike Nichols's thing, *The Graduate*. Since then, everybody thinks it will work for them. Now *The Graduate* was a great success, and it may have worked once or twice after that, but that was it.

What's the consensus in the industry—or at least among yourselves—on the phenomenon of Shaft? Do the established composers tend to put Isaac Hayes down?

B.C.: How could anyone possibly put him down? What he's done has been extremely successful.

Q.J.: Well I suppose you have to see the picture to see exactly what he's done. I haven't seen *Shaft* yet, but he sure scores his records dramatically. He thinks theatrically.

L.S.: Let me tell you something interesting about *Shaft*. When we were first going over the list of eligible pictures [Lalo is on the board of directors of the Academy of Motion Picture Arts and Sciences], some questions arose as to whether Isaac Hayes wrote all the music for the score. Someone said J. J. Johnson wrote some of it. So we called J. J., and he assured us that he just orchestrated what Isaac wrote. Now Isaac doesn't really write music, but he managed to score, with timings, the whole picture with a rhythm section. Then J. J. orchestrated. So the fact that Isaac doesn't write doesn't matter. He did score *Shaft,* and I think it's a good effort . . . especially that main title. It works extremely well with the picture. He has brought some fresh ideas from his own idiom.

I'm not questioning his success; I want to know if you consider him a fine scorer like yourselves.

H.M.: Maybe he doesn't want to make a career of film scoring. Right now he has a very successful track, but he may want a couple of shots, then go back to doing his thing. It depends on him.

L.S.: Personally I hope he continues to score. I feel he's going to make tremendous improvements and learn how to create tension and discover other techniques. He is one like I was telling you earlier: he has the instinct for the dramatic . . . .

Now, in deference to our readers, what about a jazz background? Does it make any difference to a film composer?

P.W.: Would you believe, when I came out here, I actually felt embarrassed about my jazz background? I figured the way to go was the Alfred Newman–Victor Young–Franz Waxman route. If you couldn't do that, you wouldn't stand a chance out here. So I went that way on one film—a pretty good film, too—without really being true to the film. I forced that type of score in order to say, "Hey I can write like that."

L.S.: Those are the techniques I was referring to earlier—the Central European style of composition.

Q.J.: Oh I can understand that. I think we all fell in love with this business because the greatest guys had come through it, and they set an unbelievable standard. It certainly pulled me into it. So I got out of the record business, talked to Hank, came out here, and what did I find? Some of those cats getting ten-million-dollar pictures like *Little Big Man,* you know, a guitar player and a singer. I was right back to what I decided to get away from. I felt like I had bought a pumpkin farm and they cancelled Halloween. (Laughter nearly shatters my VU meter)

Almost without exception, Hank, the composers that I have talked to credit you with opening the door for the jazz-oriented composers.

B.C.: Without a doubt.

Q.J.: Hey, that reminds me. (To Mancini) Did you hear that line on the *Merv Griffin Show* the other night? I was sitting there with Little Richard and all these crazy cats . . .

H.M.: Little Richard knows me?

Q.J.: No, but he was talking about you. I made the statement that you opened the door for me, and Little Richard said, "That's right, Mancini opened the door for *all* the Italians."

H.M.: Well you know what I think about that—not Little Richard—the jazz thing. *Peter Gunn* was the first time that anybody really had a chance to write some jazz. It could have happened to any other writer. It almost happened to you, Benny. It got to *M-Squad* about two episodes ahead of you. You were attached to *M-Squad,* weren't you?

B.C.: I was, but I didn't write the theme. They used a Count Basie thing for that.

H.M.: Well what I'm getting at is that *M-Squad* could have done it. But it just so happened that I had a guy like Blake Edwards who said "go with the contemporary sound." I think it was the first time they ever recorded a walking bass on film.

P.W.: Weren't there any jazz things done prior to that?

H.M.: Oh some spot things . . .

Q.J.: I remember seeing a western with the Count Basie brass section used in the score. Man that was funny . . .

L.S.: That's part of the problem that Antonioni had with *Zabriskie Point:* bringing in, not a composer for motion pictures, but other kinds of musicians who had no feeling for the screen. There have been so many cases in the past when certain groups were brought in to score a film—rock groups, jazz writers—and you'd hear trumpets blasting away during dialogue, but it had nothing to do with what was taking place on the screen. The music itself was fantastic, great, but it failed, because it was obtrusive. . . .

H.M.: There were a few jazz-oriented things before *Gunn.* Alex North used a New Orleans sound on *Streetcar Named Desire.* Then Jerry Goldsmith, Elmer Bernstein, Johnny Mandel did some jazz things before *Gunn.* Look at *Man with the Golden Arm.* But you got to remember they were movies. *Gunn* was the first on TV.

P.W.: . . . Getting back to *Man with the Golden Arm,* I don't feel that's really jazz.

H.M.: That's so-called "dramatic jazz." We used to call it "New York Jazz" . . . you know the Leonard Bernstein school, where the roots are on the other side of the fence. You know, not jazz going to classical, but classical going to jazz.

Well it might have had a classical conception, but it still swung, right?

H.M.: Oh well, if you can't swing at 6/8, you'd better quit. You know with 6/8 you can start it like a marble and it goes by itself . . . .

Can you write leitmotifs in TV, or is the luxury of a theme for each character confined to movies?

Q.J.: Well television is a monothematic kind of thing. You don't have time to come up with a theme for every little chick who pirouettes through the screen, you know. Besides, the cat at home has gone to get more beer. He can't keep up with all that. He doesn't understand it anyway.

L.S.: Oddly enough, when *Mission: Impossible* was made into an album, I found I had just two themes—the main title and the plot. Now how do you do an album with just two themes? So for the sake of the recording I wrote *leitmotifs* for each character in the show, but I never used them in the show.

H.M.: I just did a picture for Hitchcock called *Frenzy,* and it's a first for me because no two notes, literally, repeat themselves. Every scene is different; nothing is unified. I have a main theme and never use it again. But it worked. Hitchcock sat there like a Buddha through the whole recording session and just shook his head a few times (imitates Hitchcock).

Do you score everything yourselves, or do you sketch it out and hire an orchestrator to fill in the rest?

P.W.: I really don't think that matters.

Q.J.: I agree—not at this level.

P.W.: See you're being paid to compose the music for a film. It's your responsibility to come up with a score for that picture, and however you get it there is *your* problem.

L.S.: What you're hinting at is ghost-writing, and that's a very tricky subject. I think we should avoid the question of ethics and stick to the musical side of our skills here. It might have happened in the past, but I don't think it's going on now. At least I can only say what I do—that is to write my own music. I write directly onto the score paper; I don't usually have to sketch out my ideas. But if I had to turn out, say, 30 minutes of music within 7 days and I was really panicky, I could hire an orchestrator to fill out my ideas. I once hired an orchestrator to score some source music for me: some big-band sounds of the mid-1940's, for *Cool Hand Luke* . . . .

What about the comparative size of the orchestras?

L.S.: Well in TV you have to use a smaller orchestra. It's strictly a question of budget.

H.M.: Oh I don't know about that. The trend seems to be reversing itself. TV has larger orchestras than movies right now.

P.W.: The size of the orchestra doesn't matter to me, as long as it's balanced. The ideal balanced orchestra seems to be around 27 pieces. You know, if you don't have horns and trombones at your disposal, you're going to be out in left field.

Can you request certain players other than the staff members?

H.M.: The era of the large staff orchestra is long gone.

Q.J.: Right. Today, picking musicians is as important as casting a picture.

P.W.: Look at the guys that Quincy gets. He's known them for a long time, and it becomes a personal thing.

H.M.: Exactly, like the sound Johnny Mandel was after when he used Jack Sheldon in *The Sandpiper.* I get people's sounds in my head and write for them specifically.

Like your use of Plas Johnson, right?

H.M.: Yeah, for *The Pink Panther.* Plas *was* the Pink Panther.

Quincy, when you want Toots Thielemans, do you make a formal request through the producers?

Q.J.: To get Toots, you don't request: you pray. He costs a lot of money: transportation; per diem; lodging; and a fee.

How do you gentlemen feel about using electronic instruments?

Q.J.: We've all used it. Hank, didn't you use it in *Arabesque?*

H.M.: I did that one like an Italian chef: all from scratch. Listen, I was doing tape delay when it was difficult.

B.C.: What did you do, write it out?

H.M.: No (ignoring the laughter), no, I heard someone use that effect for a flute fall-off, and it intrigued me. So when I wrote an effect that required an echo, I'd have to send out to an outside recording studio. They'd use two tape machines and record onto a third. I guess that's the principle in that little box you can buy today for $1.98.

Q.J.: I recall when the Moog started making it big. We used it in the main title of *Ironside,* but it was more like garlic sauce than a full-course meal. Then about three years later everybody started talking about the Moog like it was going to replace sex.

H.M.: Well it *does* have a nice vibrato.

Earle Hagen once told me he prefers to hear a player sweating over a sound—like the opening out-of-register bassoon solo in the Rite of Spring—than have it produced electronically. How do you feel about that?

H.M.: I like some of the effects you can produce electronically.

L.S.: It's a legitimate medium, and gives you another way to go in composing.

Q.J.: Sure, it's another instrument in the orchestra.

B.C.: A sound is a sound.

P.W.: I recall hearing a sound in the main title to *Planet of the Apes*—Jerry Goldsmith's score—that was so unusual. I picked up the album. The sound was like a big *Whaaaaaaaa* (Williams spreads his arms ape-like and emits lingering, breathy sound), and I couldn't imagine how he got it, so the next time I saw Jerry I had to ask him. It was a gong, scraped with a triangle wand, with the mike very tight on it. Then he had horns blowing air through their instruments, and the whole thing was played backwards on tape. I guess you could call that electronic.

Q.J.: Face it: take any conventional instrument reproduced by a mike, and it becomes electronic. As soon as it hits that Telefunken, man, it becomes electronic.

From *Downbeat* 39, no. 4 (1972): 12–15 and 34. Reproduced by permission.

42

George Lucas

Stinky Kid Hits the Bigtime

Steven Farber

(1974)

George Lucas's *American Graffiti* is the surprise blockbuster of the year. Made for $750,000, it has already earned over $21 million; Universal is predicting that it may even out-gross *Airport*. When he first conceived the film, Lucas could not have guessed that it would be released at the height of the nostalgia boom.

Although actually set in 1962, *American Graffiti* is the quintessential fifties nostalgia movie—a comprehensive recreation of the world of sock hops, drag races, cherry cokes, and Eisenhower complacency. The remarkable thing, however, is that the film recaptures the past without sentimentalizing it. A comedy with unexpected resonance, *American Graffiti* is neither a glorification nor a mockery of the period; it summons up the deeply conflicting feelings that we all have when contemplating our own youth and the primal experience of leaving home. . . .

American Graffiti is probably as close to an autobiographical film as a studio-financed Hollywood product will ever be. Lucas, like his characters, grew up in Modesto, California, and graduated from high school in 1962; he spent most of his teenage years on the main drag, cruising. He says, "In a way the film was made so my father won't think those were wasted years. I can say I was doing research, though I didn't know it at the time." Most of the incidents in the film "are things that I actually experienced in one way or another. They've also been fantasized, as they should be in a movie. They aren't really the way they were but the way they should have been." . . .

Over just two movies Lucas's artistic development has been remarkable. *THX-1138* was a dazzling technical achievement; it revealed Lucas's control of all the resources of film—sound as well as image. Unfortunately, it also exhibited the most common failings of the science-fiction genre: the ideas (drawn from Orwell and Huxley) were rather stale, and the whole movie was cold and arid; the zombie characters could not really stir our sympathy. *American Graffiti* has the same technical flair, but Lucas's work with the actors reveals a new talent; this film has a depth of feeling missing from *THX-1138*. Lucas claims that he wanted to surprise his critics with his new movie: "After I finished *THX*, I was considered a cold, weird director, a science-fiction sort of guy who carried a calculator. And I'm not like that at all. So I thought, maybe I'll do something exactly the opposite. If they want warm human comedy, I'll give them one, just to show that I can do it. *THX* is very much the way that I am as a film-maker. *American Graffiti* is very much the way I am as a person—two different worlds really."

Nevertheless, Lucas is quick to call attention to the themes that the two films share. *THX* concerns one man's escape from the monolithic technological society. At the end the rebellious hero THX emerges from the underground prison, into the sun; it is an ambiguous conclusion, both liberating and a little frightening. *American Graffiti* also ends with one of the teenage boys breaking out of his cocoon, leaving home and escaping the enclosed, insulated world of the fifties. And he has the same mixed feelings that THX experienced on his escape— exhilaration at the new sense of possibilities, a pang of regret on leaving the safety of the familiar world. Lucas says, "I've always been interested in that theme of leaving an environment or facing change, and how kids do it. When I was 18 or 19, I didn't know what I was going to do with my life. Where was I going to go, now that I was more or less free? What was I going to become? You can do anything you want at that age. And the kids who don't believe that are wrong. Both *THX* and *American Graffiti* are saying the same thing, that you don't *have* to do anything; it still is a free country."

Beyond the obvious autobiographical impulses in *American Graffiti,* Lucas says the film reflects his interest in sociology and anthropology: "When I was in junior college, my primary major was in social sciences. I'm very interested in America and why it is what it is. I was always fascinated by the cultural phenomenon of cruising, that whole teenage mating ritual. It's really more interesting than primitive Africa or ancient New Guinea—and much, much weirder."

The American obsession with the car is intensified in California. The kids in Modesto still cruise, and they still cruise in Petaluma, where much of *American Graffiti* was actually shot—Modesto having changed too much in just ten years. For that matter, Lucas points out, "They still cruise in Los Angeles, and it's bigger than it used to be. Van Nuys Boulevard is a big cruise street. We went down there one Wednesday night, which they call Club Night, and it was just bumper-to-bumper cars. There must have been 10,000 kids down there. It was insane. I really loved it. I sat on my car hood all night and watched. The cars are all different now. Vans are the big thing. Everybody's got a van, and you see all these weird, decorated cars. Cruising is still a main thread in American culture."

Lucas's interest in early rock music is another strong influence on the movie. Excerpts from the radio—41 pop songs and fragments of Wolfman Jack's monologue—accompany most of the action in the film. "I have a giant rock and roll record collection—78s and 45s," Lucas reports. "Mainly old rock, pre-Beatles, though I love the Beatles. I was always very interested in the relationship between teenagers and radio, and when I was at USC, I made a documentary about a disc jockey. The idea behind it was radio as fantasy. For teenagers the person closest to them is a fantasy character. That's the disc jockey. It's like younger kids who have make-believe friends. A lot of teenagers have a make-believe friend in a disc jockey, but he's much more real because he talks to them, he jokes around. Especially a really excellent disc jockey like Wolfman Jack. He's part of the family. You listen to him every day, you're very close to him, you share your most intimate moments with him."

Lucas remembers listening to Wolfman Jack when he was growing up in Modesto in the late fifties and early sixties. "When we were cruising, we could get Wolfman Jack from Tijuana. He was a really mystical character, I'll tell you. He was wild, he had these crazy phone calls, and he drifted out of nowhere. And it was an outlaw station. He was an outlaw, which of course made him extremely attractive to kids."

The 41 songs in *American Graffiti* were actually written into the script. When it came to editing the film, Lucas found that some songs he wanted to use were either unavailable or too expensive, so he had to make substitutions and shift some songs around. Even so, he spent $80,000 purchasing music rights, probably a record sum. "Walter Murch did the sound montages, and the amazing thing we found was that we could take almost any song and put it on almost any scene and it would work. You'd put a song down on one scene, and you'd find all kinds of parallels. And you could take another song and put it down there, and it would still seem as if the song had been written for that scene. All good rock and roll is classic teenage stuff, and all the scenes were such classic teenage scenes that they just sort of meshed, no matter how you threw them together. Sometimes even the words were identical. The most incredible example—and it was completely accidental—is in the scene where Steve and Laurie are dancing to 'Smoke Gets in Your Eyes' at the sock hop, and at the exact moment where the song is saying, 'Tears I cannot hide,' she backs off, and he sees that she's crying.

"In a way you could trace the film through the Beach Boys, because the Beach Boys were the only rock group who actually chronicled an era. We discovered that you could almost make a whole Beach Boys album out of just *American Graffiti* songs. The blonde in the T-bird is from 'Fun, Fun, Fun.' 'I Get Around' is about cruising. You listen to the words of that and think of the movie. It wasn't intentional, but they were chronicling that period so true that when we came back and redid my childhood the way I remembered it, their songs blend right into the movie. 'Little Deuce Coupe' could be about John and his deuce coupe. 'All Summer Long'—which is sort of the theme song of the film—talks about T-shirts and spilling Coke on your blouse. '409' is about dragging. 'California Girls.' I always loved the Beach Boys because when we'd cruise, we'd listen to their songs, and it was as if the song was about *us* and what we were doing. It wasn't just another song about being in love. They got more specific."

Although *American Graffiti* is a highly personal film, it was not a one-man show, and Lucas is quick to point out the important contributions of his collaborators. His co-writers, Willard Huyck (whom he met at USC) and Huyck's wife, Gloria Katz (a graduate of the rival film school at UCLA), worked with Lucas on the original treatment and on the final draft screenplay. "I'm really quite lazy and I hate to write," Lucas confesses. "Bill and Gloria added a lot of very witty dialogue and wrote all the scenes that I couldn't find my way to write. In my script, the characters of Steve and Laurie didn't work at all, and I couldn't make them work. The Huycks saved that. And they brought a lot of character to the hoods. My screenplay was much more realistic, and they added a lot more humor and fantasy to it, and improved it a great deal." . . .

An equally important collaborator was Haskell Wexler. The entire movie was to be shot at night, and that created unusual difficulties. Lucas explains, "We'd start at 9:00 at night and end at 5:00 in the morning. In a regular movie, if you don't get what you're supposed to shoot one day, you can just throw up a few arc lights and shoot for another hour. On *Graffiti,* when the sun came up, that was the end of the ballgame. We couldn't get one more shot. It was very hard on the crew. Nobody gets any sleep, so everybody's cranky. And it was very cold—like 40 degrees. We had to shoot it in 28 days, and sometimes we'd do as many as 30 setups in one night. So we had a horrendous problem." Lucas had originally asked Wexler to shoot the film, but Wexler did not want to work in widescreen. However, the two cameramen Lucas hired could not find the visual style he wanted, and Wexler finally agreed to come to his aid. Lucas pays tribute to Wexler: "He's really, in my estimation, the best cameraman in this country. Essentially he was working in a medium he hated—widescreen. He hated Techniscope because it's very grainy and doesn't look very good. I wanted the film to look sort of like a Sam Katzman beach-party movie, all yellow and red and orange. And Haskell figured out how to do it. He devised what he calls jukebox lighting. He has his own company in Los Angeles that shoots commercials, and he was working at the time. So he'd fly up here to San Francisco every night, shoot the picture all night, sleep on the plane down to Los Angeles, shoot all day on commercials, then fly back up here. He did that for almost five weeks. It was just an incredible gesture, and he did a fantastic job. The movie looked exactly the way I wanted it to look—very much like a carnival." . . .

Lucas also points out that the film is about moving forward, not backward: "The film is about change. It's about the change in rock and roll, it's about the change in a young person's life at 18 when he leaves home and goes off to college; and it's also about the cultural change that took place when the fifties turned into the sixties—when we went from a country of apathy and non-involvement to a country of radical involvement. The film is saying that you have to go forward. You have to be Curt, you have to go into the sixties. The fifties can't live."

At the same time, Lucas admits that he is hoping to revive some of the values of the fifties: "Everybody looks at the fifties as complacent, but I look at the fifties as optimistic. Well, the film isn't really about the fifties anyway. It's about 1962. The Kennedy era is really when I grew up, and that was an era of optimism, not complacency. It was the era of Martin Luther King.

"I realized after *THX* that people don't care about how the country's being ruined. All that movie did was to make people more pessimistic, more depressed, and less willing to get involved in trying to make the world better. So I decided that this time I would make a more optimistic film that makes people feel positive about their fellow human beings. It's too easy to make films about Watergate. And it's hard to be optimistic when everything tells you to be pessimistic and cynical. I'm a very bad cynic. But we've got to regenerate optimism. Maybe kids will walk out of the film and for a second they'll feel, 'We could really make something out of this country, or we could really make something out of our lives.' It's all that hokey stuff about being a good neighbor, and the American spirit and all that crap. There *is* something in it." . . .

Lucas hopes to do more experimental work in the future, but he is amused that many people think of him as an arty director. "Francis [Ford Coppola] is really the arty director," he comments wryly. "He's the one who likes psychological motivations, Brecht and Albee and Tennessee Williams. I'm more drawn to Flash Gordon. I like action adventure, chases, things blowing up, and I have strong feelings about science fiction and comic books and that sort of world." It is the process of making films that thrills him most: "Some of my friends are more concerned about art and being considered a Fellini or an Orson Welles, but I've never really had that problem. I just like making movies. I was at a film conference with George Cukor, and he detested the fact that everyone called us film-makers. He said, 'I'm not a film-maker. A film-maker is like a toy-maker, and I'm a director.' I'm very much akin to a toy-maker. If I wasn't a film-maker, I'd probably *be* a toy-maker. I like to make things move, and I like to make them myself. Just give me the tools and I'll make the toys. I can sit forever doodling on my movie. I don't think that much about whether it's going to be a great movie or a terrible movie, or whether it's going to be a piece of art or a piece of shit. I never thought of *Graffiti* as a really great movie. I thought of it as a goofy, fun movie."

His next two projects are more obviously "commercial" projects than his first two films. He describes *The Star Wars* as "a space opera in the tradition of Flash Gordon and Buck Rogers. It's James Bond and *2001* combined—super fantasy, capes and swords and laser guns and spaceships shooting each other, and all that sort of stuff. But it's not camp. It's meant to be an exciting action adventure film."

From *Film Quarterly* 27, no. 3 (April 1974): 2–9. Reprinted by permission of the author.

43

The Annotated Friedkin

Elmer Bernstein

(1974)

The relationship between the composer of a film score and the person or persons to whom he or she is responsible in the course of the work is a difficult one at best. Now you must understand at the outset that this relationship is as complicated as a pentagonal marriage therefore requiring some definition of terms right now. During the period beginning approximately with the beginning of sound and ending approximately 15 to 20 years later, there existed a buffer between the composer and the producer known as the music director of the studio. This was an estimable group of many who were themselves excellent musicians. At the end of this halcyon period of such music directors there was Morris Stoloff at Columbia, Constantine Bakaleinikoff at then RKO, Ray Heindorf at Warners, John Green at MGM and Alfred Newman at 20th Century Fox. These were men who were fully qualified to discuss the considerations of a score much in the same way that a doctor and a consultant discuss a patient's case. These were men whose abilities were highly valued by the heads of the studios and whose advice was generally respected. In the days of that system the composer had less contact with his producer and almost no contact with the director of a film. Since the demise of this system, the composer works directly with the producer and/or director and enjoys no buffer.

Now for a definition of terms. Let us first discuss music. It may come as a *shock* to *laymen* to learn that of all the arts, music is possibly the most scientific and exacting. A well trained composer knows the exact sound that will be produced by a particular combination of instruments. He knows precisely what each instrument is capable of doing and precisely what is impossible on the instrument. A well trained composer can look at a four bar motif and anticipate what it might be able to be worked into after 20 minutes or so of development during the course of a score. A composer is not a person who works in poetic verbal concepts or in casual inspirations or in a constant search for the bizarre. The composer's tools are a hard acquired knowledge of harmonic and contrapuntal theories acquired through years of doing routine exercises in these areas in very much the same way than an athlete does calisthenics. His tools are a knowledge of compositional construction acquired by the teaching of masters and the examination of hundreds of years of music works. The tools are a precise knowledge of the orchestra, acquired through listening to thousands of hours of concerts and the study of thousands of scores. When he goes into his studio he is not going to his studio waiting for some lucky inspiration, he is going into his studio, really his workshop, to use those tools to serve his conception and imagination to produce the best product he can. He is of course limited by how well he has learned his lessons over the 15 to 20 year period required to gain his knowledge and of course he is limited by the degree to which he is able to conjure up a noble vision or concept. In the field of motion pictures he may be limited by one further factor. That factor is of course the producer or director. It is rare even in this more enlightened age to find a producer, or even a director, with a long and disciplined career in any field of the arts. More often than not the producer is a person whose background includes experience in the agency business, the law or "big" business. Although the motion picture director should be a person who has a thorough-going acquaintance with all the arts and techniques of making motion picture films, he is quite often ignorant of all of these. The best school for motion picture directors appears to be film editing or cinema-photography and many distinguished and intelligent directors have come from these fields. From these definitions it will be rather easy to understand that the getting together of such a well-trained composer and producer and/or director is often akin to having a heart specialist try to convince an Amazonian tribesman to submit to open heart surgery. While the analogy may at first glance seem a bit bizarre, it is a very good analogy. In both cases we are talking about highly trained experts attempting to improve the quality of life in one way or another. In both cases the people are fearfully ignorant and if they refuse the treatment they endanger their lives and frustrate the practitioner in the process. Obviously there are exceptions on both sides. There are many producers and directors that are highly knowledgeable in the use of music in films and many composers who pass as such but do not possess the tools they should have to ply their trade. For instance in the case of Cecil B. DeMille as producer/director, he knew exactly what he wanted musically. He had developed a cogent theory of the function of music in films and was able to communicate this to his composer. His theory was simple, direct and Wagnerian. It was that he wished the music to be used in his film as a story telling device with a motif for each character and force and for these motifs to be used appropriately as the various characters and forces appeared on screen. It was a method admirably suited to his kind of picture making, and although it is not my concept of what is the best use of music in films, I was able to function within his concept because he was able to state it clearly. Of course Cecil B. De-Mille was a man of erudition and had spent a great deal of his adult life in the field of the theater and in the arts. I remember my first meeting with Otto Preminger on the score of *The Man with the Golden Arm*. I had started to go into a dissertation of my intention to create the score as a *concerto di camera* for a jazz orchestra. He stopped me immediately and said, "That is your business. That is the purpose for which you are engaged", and in spite of Otto's reputation for sometimes being tyrannical and difficult, he found no difficulty in respecting the advice of a fellow artist. John Sturges is a director who has a great fondness for music, does not attempt to direct the composer in any technical sense, but will inspire him by the way in which he tells the story of his film. In the case of Alan Pakula and Robert Mulligan, I found them both to have tremendous sensitivity toward what music could do for film and a never ending desire to help the composer, whether through discussion or encouragement or the patience to wait for something good. Of all my good experiences with directors, I guess the funniest one concerns George Roy Hill. The first score I did for him was for a picture he directed called *The World of Henry Orient* After relatively little discussion with Mr. Hill, I went off and did the score. During the scoring session, that is the actual recording of the music, things went well for a time. At a certain point George did not like something that I had done. He walked me over toward the piano, and sitting down at the instrument he began to play quietly and said, "I would rather have something like this." I was astonished as I had no notion at that time that George Roy Hill was quite a fine amateur musician. Needless to say we were able to communicate on quite a different level.

There is of course no question that the overall concept of a film is the province of a director. In a very general way this also includes the music. In recent times the field has been invaded by some younger men whose egos far exceed their talent and there is then a tendency to treat the composer as some sort of mechanic who produces some sort of product by the yard and can or is willing, on demand, to produce three yards of this or three yards of that. Once again I must go back to the operating room with the patient on the table for open heart surgery, the question being where, when and how to treat him and what type of anesthesia to use, if any. As a matter of fact it has often been on my mind to volunteer to let the producer/director do my music if they would allow me to do their surgery. Of course all of this raises a very legitimate question which is, "How does a director or producer, ignorant of the technicalities of music, communicate with the composer in order to get what he wants?" Well, obviously they can only communicate in generalities. The situation is not too very much different from engaging an artist to do a portrait. You may say to the artist that you would like the portrait to be realistic, perhaps even photographic or even abstract. If the artist then disagrees with the concept there will be no meeting of the minds and he then walks away. The music situation is rather similar. Hours and hours of meetings using four syllable words, analogies and hyperbole exercise the producer's and director's vocabulary but do very little to help the composer. Once again the communication must be on a very simple level. The producer or director may use other sources as examples of what he wants, or he may, in a very general way, say in which way he wants the music to function . . . as with DeMille, he wanted the music to act as a story-telling device. After these discussions the best chance that the producer or director has to get a creative and original score is to hope that he has hired the right composer and to let him do his job without further interruption. He should also discipline himself to listen to a new score more than once before deciding as to whether or not he has made an error. As frightening as it may seem to many people in "the business," a piece of music is an art work, and to try to judge it by "instinct" in four seconds has about as much validity as trying to evaluate the worth of a woman by the size of her bust. Just in case you all think I am just an old, prejudiced composer, I want you to know that all of this has been a preface to a real, honest-to-goodness interview which took place at a seminar at the Center for Advanced Film Studies of the American Film Institute and with whose permission this interview is now about to be reprinted and annotated.

. . .

QUESTION: *On* The Exorcist, *the music, at what point did you realize you weren't going to use Lalo Schifrin or was it your choice?*

FRIEDKIN: When he gave the downbeat.[1] My original choice was Bernard Herrmann. And I had a meeting with Bernard Herrmann in New York. He flew in from England. I showed him the rough cut and he loved the picture and he wanted to do it, except he said he would not work in California. He didn't like California musicians. He didn't want to work in Hollywood. He had been through all that and to hell with it. He had to record it in London and he had to get St. Giles Church which has the greatest sound in the world. He was going to record it in there. I thought that was a marvelous idea if I had six months to finish the movie and let him just mail me a score. You know, through the mail one day, I'd get his score.[2] But I was making changes in the picture throughout. I figured I can't—and I wanted to dub the picture out here and do the effects here and I was doing the looping here and I couldn't be in London and here, so I had to not use Bernard Herrmann. I didn't know who the hell to use then. Noel Marshall, who's the executive producer on the movie—he's Bill Blatty's agent or manager—suggested Lalo Schifrin and I knew Lalo 15 years ago. I met Lalo when he first came to this country, when he was Dizzy Gillespie's pianist, and he was a really great guy and I liked him and I knew he had great experience and integrity as a musician, quite apart from these movie scores that he was doing, *Mission Impossible*,[3] and stuff.

Anyway, I met with Lalo and I thought, "Jesus, the guy works too much[4] but he is a talented guy and I think I can communicate with him." We had a couple of meetings. He saw the picture, loved it. We discussed the kind of music I wanted[5] and he completely agreed. The kind of music I wanted was, number one, nothing scary,[6] no so-called frightening music. No wall-to-wall music, which is to say, starts with one cut and ends with another. I wanted the music to come and go at strange places and dissolve in and out.[7] No music behind the big scenes. No music ever behind dialogue, while people are talking. Only music in the montage sequences, and the music should be like a cold hand on the back of your neck, like a chill presence[8] that would never assert itself, except for the final musical statement over the credits. I wanted "The Rites of Spring" [*sic*], you know, very little quiet, Anton Webern–like[9] oh, crystalline, oh, soft, hush, quiet stuff, no melody, and then at the end of the picture, voom! Full orchestra, big statement, send the people away like this. Lalo agreed.

We got in the studio and we did a few cues and it was really Carnegie Hall.[10] It was big, loud, scary, wall-to-wall, accent, accent, a guy picked up, his accent, accent. I don't like any musical accents. So we just came to a parting of the ways, reluctantly. It pained me to do it, but I would rather have Lalo Schifrin denounce me on the front page of the *Los Angeles Times*, every day for the rest of my life than use one note of his score in my picture. I just threw it out. It's nothing against him. I still think he's an extremely talented, resourceful, sensitive man. It was a matter of either a difference—bad communication between the director and the composer or interpretation on the composer's part. I don't know.[11] I don't give a damn.[12] I was bound and determined to have the kind of music that I originally intended.

So I went out and got the music off the records that I wanted, Penderecki and Henze and Anton Webern, and I found a few little other things along the way and it really is Music Score by Tower Records, you know, Music Composed and Conducted by Clyde Wallich. Like that, I heard Penderecki and all these guys would write this nice quiet stuff that gets in your brain, you can't hum a bar of it, but it's like somebody's cold hand on the back of your neck and we tried to bring it in the best use of music in a film, outside of Bernard Herrmann's stuff that just wipes me out. *Psycho, Citizen Kane, North By Northwest*, beautiful, even *Sisters*. Good music. Is this guy, I don't even know who the hell did the score for *Weekend*. Did you ever see Godard's *Weekend*? All of a sudden, some strange kind of orchestral thing, melodramatic out of nowhere, comes in the middle of a scene and then goes where it's least expected, and that's what I like about music. I don't want to telegraph something in music. You know, "Here's music. Uh-oh, be scared. Here it comes." That's what most of these guys'll give you.[13] Music X4783 out of the library and it's ba-ba-ba-boom-boom. That's what I was getting there, so I said, "Broom this stuff, eighty-six. You know, let's go with the real thing." I'd rather have the original Penderecki than bad Penderecki or rip-off Stravinsky or something.

From *Film Music Notebook* 1, no. 2 (Winter 1974–75): 10–16. Copyright © The Film Music Society. Reprinted by permission of The Film Music Society.

NOTES

1. Not being a George Bernard Shaw, it is difficult to find a witty analogy for this piece of egotistical nonsense but it would be rather like saying that you decided you don't like the person when you heard the doorbell ring.
    For those of you who are not musicians, a downbeat is that part which represents the first beat of a bar. It is entirely possible that on the down beat there may be a rest and that no music will be played at all. In any case, on a downbeat, the most you would be likely to hear is a sound. It is obvious from this that Mr. Friedkin has knowledge vastly superior to those of the great masters of composition who have to spend hours on the works of their students to find out if they have any worth. I would judge from a composer's viewpoint that what I know of Lalo Schifrin's abilities and Mr. Friedkin's abilities that Mr. Schifrin obviously had the wrong director.

2. I think Mr. Friedkin has a marvelous idea here. Obviously the only way a composer is ever going to be able to make a contribution to a film of his is if he allows it to be mailed to him. We can say one kind thing of Mr. Friedkin, at least he chooses two very estimable composers to show his ignorance to.

3. As far as the commercial success of *Mission Impossible* being a manifest of lack of integrity it would occur to me to wonder whether Mr. Friedkin's devotion to sensationalism in *The French Connection* and even more in *The Exorcist* evidenced a concern for artistic integrity or a superior commercial sense for what sells in the market place.

4. I would imagine Mr. Schifrin is in demand as a result of proven excellence—if Mr. Friedkin's matrix of excellence is manifested by non-productivity he should have no problems finding such people. I dare say he would find that Penderecki whom he admires so much would be too busy for him.

5. "We discussed the kind of music I wanted and he completely agreed." We must note here that Mr. Schifrin apparently never got to discuss the kind of music he wanted here. I believe he was the musician.

6. This is the kind of logic that really intrigues me. Of course it is obvious that we would not want to put any scary music in a picture like *The Exorcist,* which was like a "fin de siecle," mid-west, church picnic. I guess he is saving the scary music for when he does a children's bedtime picture.

7. This is one of Mr. Friedkin's more lucid statements. It indicates that, not being able to deal with the purpose of the music in film in any intellectual way, he is reduced to treating it in a random sentence that defies intelligent analysis.

8. My goodness, the man is not even consistent. Did he not just say that he wanted nothing scary, or is a "cold hand on the back of the neck" and a "chill presence" a normal way of life for Mr. Friedkin?

9. "The Rites of Spring" [*sic*] is a very aggressive, assertive and descriptive early work of Stravinsky, very concrete, fleshy and full of melodic content for those with ears good enough to hear them. It is a mercy that Mssrs. Stravinsky and Webern are not alive to see their names used in this context.

10. Obviously much too good for Mr. Friedkin. Apparently Mr. Friedkin does not see Stravinsky, Penderecki, Webern and all the other composers he admires in Carnegie Hall.

11. "I don't know." Mr. Friedkin finally tells the truth.

12. "I don't give a damn." Ditto.

13. This calumny on screen composers everywhere in the world comes poorly from the director of *The Night They Raided Minsky's* and had subsequently had the good fortune to deal with two dynamite stories. I doubt that people will be looking at Mr. Friedkin's films as long as they will be listening to the music of the film composers he has treated herewith so disrespectfully and ignorantly. Your dyspeptic annotator will leave you now to finish this bit of nonsense for yourself and if you think that the life of a film composer is easy, just remember what we have to work with.

44

Whatever Became of Movie Music?

David Raksin

(1974)

The new director turned out to be an amiable roughneck, about my own age, bright and shrewd, talented, and still New Yorkish enough to need to let me know that he was not about to have "any of that Hollywood music" in his picture. What he wanted was "something different, really powerful—like *Wozzeck*." A string of three-frame cuts of the aurora borealis flashed in my head. To hear the magic name of Alban Berg's operatic masterpiece invoked by the man with whom I would be working was to be invited to be free! To hear it correctly pronounced was to doubt the evidence of my ears: here was a non-musician who was not only aware that *Wozzeck* existed, but actually thought of his film as one to which so highly expressive a musical style might be appropriate. It was too good to be true; but after all those years of struggling to be honest with people who couldn't understand why I was reluctant to compose pretty music for their violent and ugly movies I was ready to believe every word. I invited him out to my farm for dinner so that we could discuss the film, away from studio distractions.

So there we were in the living room, with drinks in hand, the phonograph playing and the conversation taking its time to get under way. I remember thinking that his was the way things ought to be: I liked his script, I admired him, and I couldn't wait to hear what he had to say and to get working on musical material for the score. Suddenly irritable, he said, "What's that crap you're playing?" "That crap," I replied, "is *Wozzeck!*" That was twenty-five years ago, and if there is a story that tells more about why film composers sometimes despair of their profession, I have yet to hear it.

So here we are in 1974, and I am wondering what has changed. Having been invited to discuss the state of music in films, I find myself in the uncomfortable position of the tailor asked to give his opinion of the king's new clothes. If I am to be truthful, I have got to give up the neutralist, no-involvement copout that has enabled me thus far to avoid taking what is certain to be an unpopular stand. For there is no way to write about film music today without acknowledging the powerful current of revulsion toward many aspects of their own profession that is explicit in the words and attitudes of my most valued colleagues. I am not talking only of those who have been to some extent deprived of regular employment because of changing fashions in film scoring, and who might therefore be expected to look unfavorably upon present trends, but of leading figures who are as busy and successful today as ever they were—and yet seem to find the situation unacceptable: their talk is of getting out, somehow. Why?

The answer is not simple. To begin with, there is the state of the Industry; it should be news to no one that many people believe the Industry has been plundered, ruined by incompetence and left to twist slowly in the wind by men whose principal interests—whatever they may be—do not lie in film-making. The disastrous unemployment resulting from this circumstance has become worse as film companies have made more and more pictures abroad; American composers find it difficult to believe that the use of foreign composers is not related to the fact that they work for less money. As to the remaining available jobs, they are further curtailed by relegation of the film soundtrack to the humiliating status of an adjunct to the recording industry. In too many cases, the appropriateness of the music to the film is secondary to getting an album, or a single, and the voice of the A & R man is heard in the land.

All of this has become so much a part of the film music scene that anyone who challenges the propriety or, *perish forbid,* the artistic integrity of the process is sure to start heads shaking with concern for his sanity. Artists and Repertoire tycoons sit in the control rooms (how aptly named!) and freely render judgments upon the viability of film scores as commodities on record racks; these opinions are as freely transferred to apply (as though they were pertinent!) to the function of the music *in the picture,* and nobody seems to question the competence of these people to decide what is "right" for a sequence or for a film. Where are the proud directors and producers, formerly so zealous to ensure that all components of their films interacted to fashion the synergistic marvel that is a motion picture? (I suspect they are to be found standing in line at Tiffany's to ask, "Where do you keep your chrome?")

There are times these days when I suspect that my students at USC and UCLA are trying to provoke me into "putting down" Rock or Pop film scores indiscriminately. And I feel absurdly virtuous when I ask them whether they can imagine pictures like *Easy Rider* or *The Last Picture Show* or *American Graffiti* with any other kind of music. The fact is that the music in those films was just what it should have been. But I do not find this to be equally true of all films in which such music is used. For unless we are willing to concede that what is essentially the music of the young is appropriate to *all* of the aspects of human experience with which films are concerned, we must ask what it is doing on the soundtracks of pictures that deal with other times and generations, other lives. It is one thing to appreciate the freshness and naivete of Pop music and quite another to accept it as inevitable no matter what the subject at hand. And *still* another to realize that the choice is often made for reasons that have little to do with the film itself. *One:* to sell recordings—and incidentally to garner publicity for the picture. *Two:* to appeal to the "demographically defined" audience, which is a symbolic unit conceived as an object of condescension. *Three* (and to my mind saddest of all): because so many directors and producers, having acquired their skills and reputations at the price of becoming elderly, suddenly find themselves aliens in the land of the young; tormented by fear of not being "with it," they are tragically susceptible to the brainwashing of Music-Biz types. What is one to think of men of taste and experience who can be persuaded that the difference between a good picture and a bad one is a "now" score that is "where it's at"?

As though that were not bad enough, the situation has deteriorated further because of an epidemic of *Griffithitis,* a term which I derive from the action of D. W. Griffith, who threw out the score originally composed for *The Birth of a Nation* and substituted a hodgepodge of mismatched pieces. My favorite boss, Alfred Newman, used to say that the trouble with Hollywood was that "everybody knows his own job—plus music!" These *plus-music boys,* as he called them, have never been more in evidence than they are today. Although I want to believe that an art of multiple components such as film should be guided by a single hand, and that that hand ought to be the director's, that belief has been sorely tried by the ignorance of music, as applied in films, and the uncontrollable willfulness which my colleagues and I so often encounter. When I first suggested that any composer who had not had at least one score thrown out was either a novice or a hack—or unbelievably lucky—even my friends thought I was merely setting up defenses. Now that so many of the better composers have suffered the humiliation of seeing their talent and experience defeated by the tin ear with the power behind it, they are beginning to wonder about the validity of an art that is at the mercy of so many untutored minds.

It would be ridiculous for me to contend that only we, and not the men who make the films—and who know, or ought to know what they require of the music—are always right. But it would be equally foolish to believe that the most talented and skilful composers who ever wrote music for films could possibly strike out as often as recent statistics appear to suggest. I think that what has happened is that we have fallen into the hands of some ungovernable men whose ability to comprehend the language of music and its function in film lags far, far behind their other, often substantial skills, and who are unable to see in this shortcoming a compelling reason for abstaining from judgment in an area in which their competence is minimal. Directors scream their pretty heads off about the imposition of raw power by insensitive men who alter the delicate balances and destroy the subtle rhythms of their precious footage; then they put on their Dracula hats and go to work on our music! What is especially disheartening about this phenomenon is the compulsion of such people to discredit what they cannot make subservient to their purposes. (Here I must pause to acknowledge gratefully those who were themselves free enough to grant me the freedom to do my best, and that would include the director who had second thoughts about *Wozzeck*.)

To repeat, I do not suggest that we composers are without fault. To the extent to which we have "bought" the propaganda of those who misconstrue the meaning and importance of our contribution to the art and business that is film making, to the extent that we have put up with the most consistently inhumane work schedules within the frame of film employment and accepted the appropriation of our right to legal "authorship" of our own music (would you believe that Twentieth Century–Fox Film Corp. is the "*author in fact*" of *Laura?*) we have only ourselves to blame. And we ought, among other things, to have been more persistent about reminding the studio barons that we are the *only* group among those who contribute to films who defray the costs of their own employment—by that portion of the royalties from the performance and sale of our music which goes into studio treasuries.

It was withal a noble profession—by which I do not mean to suggest that the present situation is all bad or that movie music as we knew it is finished. For one thing, there are certain new, young composers in whose talents one can rejoice, and to whose future careers one can look—and listen—with hope. Even if one did not admire the more reserved kinds of musical utterances affected by some of today's brightest new lights, and more often than not I do, it would be necessary to concede that they are generally as appropriate in style to present modes of film making as some of the more florid kinds of music would be inappropriate. But consider the apparent paradox that people who buy recordings of film scores are buying music—by Korngold, Steiner, Newman and others—that is the antithesis of what is for the most part heard on the soundtracks of current films. The smartest money seems to believe that it is more than "nostalgia" which impels new audiences to seek out films in the Hollywood tradition, with their concomitant musical lyricism, and to buy recordings of such music. Perhaps the audience is about to realize that it is not necessary to choose among different modes of filmic expression as though they were irreconcilable alternatives, that we are free to enjoy as much of the spectrum as the spirit can accommodate. If the process runs true to form, the Industry will be about half a generation in catching up.

It is just possible that (to quote Brahms) there is someone I may have forgotten to offend. Therefore, a few last shots from the hip. Today we are witnessing a disquieting situation in the Arts; in music this manifests itself through an abnormal polarization, in which the masses throng to the Inglewood Forum to enjoy the equivalent of finger painting, while the avant garde responds with ecstasies of anal retention. Nevertheless, valid and genuine musical languages are taking form, and it is up to those who aspire to leadership in the film arts to learn to understand these languages, so that our music is free to bespeak the substance of the film instead of being forced by the ignorance of those in whom the ultimate control of the soundtrack lies to lag generations behind, aesthetically.

Finally, I will be surprised if this article does not provoke pious rebuttals from certain of my *Uncle Tom* colleagues, one of whom found it necessary to state for publication that, contrary to the notion that music can "save" a bad picture, it is good pictures that save bad music. Since that quaint notion originated in the abuse of music by film makers to attempt to repair *their* sins, music has too often been called upon to create miracles—and has come closer to achieving the impossible than anyone had a right to expect. Therefore, it was unseemly for a member of a proud profession to seek to ingratiate himself with prospective employers by being the first fellow on the block to demean his art. It is easy to see why some men who are deeply immersed in the process of *making it* feel compelled to rationalize away uncomfortable questions which threaten their continuing complicity in what is all too often a dirty game, because they see it quite correctly as the only game in town. However, to understand such behavior is one thing; to condone it is something else.

Composers (and others) of my generation have been reluctant to speak out for a number of reasons, not the least of which is that candor is a fine device for terminating one's "employability." And when one has reached that point at which, having finally learned something about the profession he has been practicing, he must come to terms with the fact that the largest chronological part of his work has been accomplished, it seems very poor grace to turn sour on that profession. To speak unfavorably of much that is currently being done—no matter with what wisdom, or forbearance, or inherent desire to appreciate what is worthwhile and disregard what is not—is certain to be interpreted in the worst possible light. Well, it may not convince any except those who know me (and who ought therefore to need little convincing), but I have always taken pleasure in the achievements of my talented colleagues, and I disavow envy—conscious or otherwise. (It is a matter of record that I have called to the attention of studio music executives certain film and television scores that might otherwise have been taken for granted.) And I would remind skeptics that the celebration of talent is traditional in our profession: said Robert Schumann on first hearing the music of Frederic Chopin, "Hats off, gentlemen, a genius!"

The gentlemen needed reminding and so do we; and, most of all, so do those men with whom and *for* whom we work. They need to be reminded that *they* need us quite as much as we need them, that it is time they abandoned their reliance upon the score that presupposes a jukebox as a human appendage and came to terms with the evocative power of dramatic music—and their fear of that power. We must (said the French politician, Jean Monnet) attack our problems instead of each other. While we are waiting for that to happen, we can do a lot worse than to keep an eye on the king's new clothes. Can it be that he is a *streaker?*

From *Film Music Notebook* 1, no. 1 (Fall 1974): 24–30. Copyright © The Film Music Society. Reprinted by permission of The Film Music Society. An earlier version of this article, titled "Raskin Raps State of Art," appeared in *Variety,* May 15, 1974, pp. 59 and 70.

PART FIVE

The Postmodern Soundtrack

Film Music in the Video and Digital Age
(1978–Present)

INTRODUCTION

While opinions vary on how to define the postwar and recession period, especially in terms of assigning solid beginning and end points, there is general critical agreement that a new and distinct practice, one that in many ways remains valid today, began to form in the late 1970s.[1] Several scholars have described this change as a "revolution," one on par with the coming of sound film in the late 1920s. What event or innovation was most responsible for sparking this revolution, and just what label best describes it, remain matters of debate; however, it is generally agreed that in the late 1970s the recession ended as new practices in film production, distribution, and exhibition emerged.[2]

Most scholars point to a change in distribution as having an especially significant effect on filmmaking practices. In the mid-1970s, the industry had already found a successful and profitable narrative formula in the disaster picture. When Universal studios decided in 1975 to produce another disaster film, this one about the appetites of an unnaturally large shark, it was not the film's creative blend of suspense and horror genres that was precedent setting, but rather the way in which the film was distributed. Instead of releasing *Jaws* to limited viewing in select, first-run theaters, Universal blanketed the marketplace, opening the film on 464 screens nationwide.[3] The idea of having a film play at all theaters on its opening day was a variation on an existing marketing formula known as "dumping," which helped weak films recover some production costs by having them play widely at second- and third-run theaters for a short period.[4] Yet because *Jaws* was a high-budget, highly anticipated film based on a wildly popular novel, the strategy was not to "dump" the film but to saturate the marketplace with it. Although the new strategy was expensive, requiring an extensive and well-coordinated advertising campaign, it produced record-breaking profits. The film's well-crafted narrative and sensational content were also certainly responsible for generating large audiences and profits. But it was the revolutionary new distribution practices of "saturation release," "saturation advertising," and "front-loading" that led to quick and massive revenues. More than any aesthetic or technical change, this new approach to film distribution defined the contemporary "blockbuster" formula, and *Jaws,* as historian Thomas Schatz observes, was the film that "brought an emphatic end to Hollywood's recession."[5]

The success of saturation release was made possible by significant changes in film exhibition. In the late 1970s and early 1980s, the movie theater itself was being radically transformed in terms of both size and number. In 1975, for instance, the number of indoor theaters in the country stood at roughly 11,500, with around 1,000 of those being large first-run theaters.[6] By the early 1980s the number of theater screens had increased to around 14,000, and by the end of the decade that number had swelled dramatically to over 22,500. The surge in numbers did not represent additional movie theaters but rather more viewing screens, in a new kind of exhibition space known as the *multiplex.* Pioneered by an exhibitor who realized that theater overflow could be captured and retained if patrons were offered several movies at the same location, the multiplex clustered as many as twelve or more small auditoriums under a single roof.

By the end of the 1980s, multiplex design dominated theater construction, to a large extent because of the boom in shopping mall construction.[7] As real estate developers sought both to consolidate and expand consumer and leisure activities within a single localized space, the multiplex with its multiple screens became a cornerstone of shopping mall construction.[8] While developers were realizing huge profits with multiplex construction, the moviegoer initially had a diminished experience. Early multiplex auditoriums often had flat floors, small screens, and bad soundproofing that frequently made for an awkward, noisy, and unpleasant viewing situation. They did make films more accessible, however, which is why, with some modifications, this new exhibition structure persisted and eventually thrived. By the mid-1990s, with a revised construction model that included larger screens and stadium seating, the number of multiplex theater screens in the country had increased to nearly 30,000.[9]

Big changes were also surfacing in the late 1970s and early 1980s in the film industry's well-established secondary exhibition space—television. Since the 1950s, television had been an important ancillary market for the film industry, giving films a life after their theatrical release, albeit on a smaller screen. Although television had become ubiquitous by the 1970s, its "space" was limited to a handful of channels dominated by the three national networks, ABC, NBC, and CBS. This broadcast space changed dramatically in the late 1970s with the introduction of cable television, which for a modest fee brought a host of additional channels to television viewers.

This expansion had a profound effect on television production, but it also had a major effect on the film industry. Several of the first channels launched on cable were devoted to offering movies without two of the annoyances that had plagued the exhibition of films on broadcast television: advertisements and delayed release dates (long clearance times). Although viewers would have to pay for the privilege, cable channels offered to show a film only a few months after it had left the theaters and to show it without commercial interruption. Home Box Office (HBO) was the first to start broadcasting, in 1975, and it was quickly joined by Showtime in 1976, the Movie Channel in 1979, Cinemax in 1980, and numerous others.[10] These channels paid the studios to let them broadcast a film for a certain amount of time to their paying audience before the studios could sell the film to network television or any other exhibition space. In the earliest days of cable, this arrangement allowed the studios to net an additional $5 to $7 million per picture, for an average of $100 million a year in new revenue.[11]

As cable subscriptions grew, so did licensing profits. By the early 1980s cable television was generating an extra $2.4 billion for the film industry through licensing fees.[12] Early entrant HBO controlled a stunning 60 percent of the cable business by the middle of the decade; indeed, it commanded so much market share that it began exerting control over the studios, demanding lower rental rates or refusing to buy films it deemed unworthy of showing. The studios initially countered this threat by launching their own cable channel, but a costly antitrust lawsuit eventually caused them to abandon the project.[13] Their failure to establish direct control over cable television only underscored how powerful and profitable cable television had become as a new film exhibition environment in the early 1980s. Although cable revenues never eclipsed theatrical box office receipts (in 1983, for instance, theater receipts stood at $3.7 billion, compared to $2.4 billion for cable profits),[14] this new outlet nevertheless represented an important source of income for the industry. Like the multiplex movie theater, it expanded the need for film material.

Channels devoted to movies were not the only cable networks affecting the film industry. MTV, which began broadcasting in 1981, was conceived around the novel idea of reconceptualizing television as a "visual radio." Exhibiting a continuous twenty-four-hour stream of popular music, MTV pioneered a new presentation format, the music video. While the length of each video conformed to the radio convention of roughly three minutes, the visual style of most videos represented a clear departure from previous conventions of musical performance. Static, concertlike performances of pop songs soon gave way to visually constructed montages that borrowed heavily from the vocabulary of avant-garde and experimental film.[15] With little serious competition, MTV quickly became one of the most popular networks on cable, establishing itself in 22 million homes by 1984 and growing to well over 30 million by the end of the decade.[16]

MTV and the music video had a strong impact on film marketing and production. Because MTV quickly replaced radio as the essential tool for advertising and promoting film soundtracks and films themselves, and because MTV targeted the same demographic group long identified as the most profitable—12–25-year-olds—the studios began to invest directly in the production of music videos, especially in videos of songs featured on film soundtracks. Directors also began to adjust the structure and visual style of their films to accommodate the new fast-paced rhythm and disjunct editing of the music video.

The introduction of cable television was not the only change affecting the exhibition space of film in the early 1980s. The introduction of the VCR (video cassette recorder) and "home video" also had a major impact on the film industry, distribution in particular. Unlike cable television, the VCR allowed individuals to record broadcast films and then watch them at a time of their choosing, at home on their own television set. The technology had been around since the early 1970s, but it gained momentum in 1976 when VCRs became available at affordable prices.[17]

The home video market grew slowly at first. In the early 1980s, fewer than a million homes had VCRs. An initial nonuniformity of platform design (Matsushita's cheaper VHS technology soon won out over Sony's superior-quality Betamax to become the industry standard) accounted for some of the stagnation, but a serious legal battle over the technology's potential for copyright infringement restrained its growth as well. Although most studio executives saw the home video as a new market, an extra-theatrical space that could increase profits, some feared that the VCR would bring a loss of control, piracy, and the unauthorized reproduction of films.[18] In 1976, Universal and Disney studios filed a lawsuit again Sony charging that its videotaping machines violated copyright laws. The case went all the way to the Supreme Court, which in 1984 ruled against the studios, stating that home videotaping fell within "fair use" practices. Although the decision represented a technical defeat for the studios, it hardly resulted in a loss of revenue for them. As soon as video technology became both affordable and legal, the studios began reaping record profits from the purchase and rental of films on videotape. By 1985, VCR units were installed in more than 11 million U.S. homes, and over 50 million films were being sold each year on videotape.[19] That number quadrupled by the end of the decade, with tape sales topping 200 million a year in 1989. By now home video was so successful that it had displaced the theater as the studio's most profitable point of distribution for a film. In 1989, for instance, the studios earned $5 billion in theater box office receipts but over $11 billion in videotape sales. As one studio executive succinctly put it, the VCR represented "the most staggeringly fast penetration of households by any electronic appliance in history—including television in its halcyon days."[20] The home video redefined exhibition space by permanently expanding it to include the home as well as the movie theater.

The home video was more than just a new means of distribution. It was also a new visual medium, one with very different properties than celluloid. Half-inch videotape projected at a different speed—30 frames per second instead of the 24 frames per second of film. Video was also designed to be projected onto television screens, with different aspect ratios than a theater screen. This difference in image size became problematic for the industry, especially in the transfer of film to videotape. Because the whole film image often could not fit on the television screen, transfer operators had to decide what parts of the image field they would make visible. With the aid of a semi-automated process called "pan-and-scan," transfer operators essentially edited films, cropping characters out of scenes, reframing scenes, and changing color saturation and contrast, to make films viewable on videotape."[21] The "videoization" of film did more than just increase the distribution and viewership for films. It changed the nature of film from a reel of celluloid to a multi-formatted "film product."

The commodification of film into film-related merchandise also increased substantially in the 1980s. From the very beginning, the studios had hawked a variety of film-related products—postcards, souvenir booklets, fan magazines, sheet music and recordings—to memorialize and prolong the film experience. Revenues increased substantially in the early 1980s, partly because of saturation booking practices, which were giving blockbuster films additional exposure, but primarily through the introduction of new film-related merchandise. One movie in particular redefined the ancillary marketplace in both size and scope. In 1978, *Star Wars* took in over a half a billion dollars at the box office worldwide, but the revenues from merchandise were three times as much. The film made an additional $1.5 billion because the studios expanded the licensing operations to include not just typical merchandise like posters and soundtracks but a huge range of new home products, including sheets, underwear, lunchboxes, board games, and action figures.[22] In 1989, *Batman* likewise generated merchandise sales of over $1 billion, a figure that outpaced the film's box office revenues four times over.

These extraordinary profits did more than enrich studio coffers. They dramatically affected film production by redefining the blockbuster formula. To be considered for production, a blockbuster film now had to be able to generate huge and fast profits at the theater box office, and it had to be merchandise or "ancillation" ready. As one historian puts it, "George Lucas and his film *Star Wars* fundamentally changed the balance between original film and supplementary spin-offs by recognizing that the money that could be earned from tie-ins and franchising could be more than that earned from the film itself."[23]

All of these changes—the multiplex theater, the home video, and the expansion of exhibition space to include cable television—had a significant effect on film production. By the mid to late 1970s, film executives were encouraging directors not to chase after niche audiences with challenging subject matter and avant-garde techniques, but instead to capture large audiences with familiar narratives and spectacle filmmaking. High-grossing, entertaining blockbusters spelled an end to Hollywood's recession, but they also spelled an end to the highly artistic and experimental filmmaking that had flourished in the previous decades. As historian David Cook observes, "In the long run . . . the idea that American directors, working within the world's most capital-intensive production context, could somehow approach the European ideal of authorship as incarnated by the French New Wave was doomed to fail from the start: and it proved especially intractable in the business climate that prevailed after *Jaws* and *Star Wars*."[24] The industry emerged from its recession not by establishing an artistic tradition of filmmaking but by recovering a more valuable asset: a mass audience.[25] "America's youth," Cook concludes, "transferred its allegiance from the cinema of rebellion to the 'personal' cinema of the seventies *auteurs,* without realizing how corporate and impersonal it had become."[26]

The spectacle blockbuster with high-profile celebrities thrived in this new atmosphere, but the studios also developed other formulas and styles of filmmaking specifically tailored to the growing "ancillated" marketplace. Drawing on contemporary television advertising techniques, the "high-concept" film consolidated most aspects of production into a stylized "look" that would be easily marketed and merchandised to a large audience and that would transfer easily to home video screen.[27] Films like *Flashdance* (1983), *Footloose* (1984), *Beverly Hills Cop* (1984), *Top Gun* (1986), and *Days of Thunder* (1990) paired established or rising movie stars with simple plots, calculated cinematography, and prominent soundtracks of popular music.[28]

The structural accommodations these films made for popular music were especially distinctive. Like the film musicals of the 1930s, '40s, and '50s, the high-concept film was frequently interrupted by the spectacle of a popular song. Instead of presenting a live performance, however, the high-concept film typically used music as the accompaniment of a fast-paced visual montage, one that resembled the audio-visual style of a music video. These musical interruptions, or "modules," as historian Justin Wyatt calls them, were set apart from the rest of the film by their lack of diegetic sound and by their editing tempo, which changed temporarily to articulate the rhythm and meter of the song.[29] The idea of interrupting the narrative to feature a musical performance was of course not new. Since the beginning of sound film and before, Hollywood had used film to promote popular songs. What was new was the use of the MTV aesthetic, the interruption of conventional cinematic style to accommodate the visual style and rhythm of a music video.[30]

The new video technology also had a visible impact on film production. In the early 1980s, a new practical aid for filmmaking called "video assist" was introduced, which allowed a filmmaker to see what the camera had captured instantly, enabling more immediate visualization of narrative structure. Film editing was also improved by advances in video and computer technologies. Editing a movie on videotape and then transferring it to film made the process cheaper and easier. The introduction of computer editing software in the mid-1980s, especially random-access editing programs, also altered film postproduction. These programs allowed editors to move easily and quickly from one point in the footage to another, while the coordination of edge code numbers with shot descriptions allowed them to record their movements precisely.[31] As a result, filmmakers were freed from linear thinking; they could now conceptualize narrative structure in entirely new ways and at entirely new speeds. By making all footage so accessible, the new technologies facilitated faster editing tempos, bringing the "MTV aesthetic" with its fast-paced montage of images within easy reach. As historian Stephen Prince observes, "Computer-based systems offered a powerful solution to the enduring problem of minimizing expensive post-production time and these systems maybe also have played a role in helping establish the ferociously fast-paced tempo of American film in the nineties."[32]

Just as visual style and tempo were being modified, significant innovations were being made to the production and exhibition of film sound. Before the late 1970s, the industry had tried to improve both the clarity and the reality of film sound. Between 1952 and 1954, for instance, the studios had made several attempts to replace monaural or single-source sound with "stereo" sound.[33] The lack of a uniform platform, the fact that some systems were magnetic while others were optical, and the expense of installing new projection equipment and speakers, however, prevented any one system from proliferating and becoming standard.[34] All of these problems were solved in the late 1970s with the introduction of Dolby sound. Dolby's noise reduction capabilities gave film sound greater clarity, and its four-channel technology could articulate direction better and give a much wider range of sounds. Most important, the Dolby system was inexpensive. Because it was affordable and easy to install in theaters, the system was adopted widely and by the late 1970s was all but standard.[35] It was also adopted quickly after filmmaker George Lucas used the new Dolby sound system in his film *Star Wars* (1977) to achieve a louder, more layered, more directional concept of sound.

The changes that film music experienced between roughly 1978 and 1989 were in many instances tied directly to the changes taking place in film production and distribution. Popular music, rock 'n' roll in particular, continued to occupy an important place in film soundtracks, especially because it appealed to that most profitable moviegoing demographic, the youth audience. But as new blockbuster formulas emerged, the design and marketing of the music soundtrack changed as well. Just as film executives and directors sought to load their blockbusters with recognizable stars, they also looked to incorporate recognizable or "pre-sold" musical talent on the soundtrack. They also relied on "saturation release" practices to increase soundtrack distribution and revenues. In the late 1970s, the process of extracting music from the film for repackaging as an LP was largely the same, but the process of marketing it was being carried out on a much grander scale.

The expansion of blockbuster strategies to film music, and to pop soundtracks specifically, was mainly the work of two film music executives, Robert Stigwood and Al Coury. Stigwood had been manager and promoter for rock groups like the Bee Gees and Eric Clapton and had produced the hit Broadway rock musical *Jesus Christ Superstar;* in the late 1970s he established a new film production company, RSO (Robert Stigwood Organization), for the express purpose of marrying rock music with film. The first two films his company produced, *Saturday Night Fever* (1978) and *Grease* (1979), set box office records, and they also set records for soundtrack album sales. Much of this double success was attributed to RSO's president, Al Coury, a former executive with Capitol Records. Coury's ties to the industry meant that he, like Stigwood, was well qualified to identify "pre-sold" music talent and material, singers and songs that would make a hit soundtrack. But as the article "Selling a Hit Soundtrack" (**Document 45**) reveals, Coury also had a new strategy for marketing the film's music. Borrowing a page from the concept of saturation film booking and advertising, Coury engineered the schedule so that both the singles and the soundtrack album for *Saturday Night Fever* hit record stores and radio stations five to six weeks before the film opened. Flooding the airwaves, the album was an instant hit, and when the film became a hit too, albums sales soared again. In addition to earning over $74 million in box office revenues, the studios sold more than 25 million soundtracks, with four singles from the album reaching number one on the *Billboard* charts. Coury, though not the first to use these techniques, played a central role in establishing early release of the soundtrack as a standard part of the blockbuster formula.[36] Yet as this article also emphasizes, the saturation formula could not have succeeded without the promotional power of radio. The repeated airplay on Top 40 radio stations gave film music quick circulation to a very wide audience.

Although the blockbuster soundtrack initially identified rock and pop music as most capable of producing large profits, that stylistic precondition proved malleable. **Document 46,** a reflective interview with composer John Williams from 1997, shows that director George Lucas and Williams radically altered the blockbuster soundtrack by revitalizing a style long absent from feature filmmaking: the thematic orchestral score. With *Star Wars* (1977), which was patterned after sci-fi adventure films of the 1930s and 1940s, Lucas extended his nostalgia not just to narrative structure and visual style but to music scoring as well. Since the 1950s, the scores of sci-fi films had largely been given over to electronic or avant-garde techniques. Lucas's neoclassical, character-driven narrative style, however, needed an equally classically minded film score, and so Williams created an orchestral-thematic score to match the film's emotionally familiar narrative. Although Williams refers to opera composer Richard Wagner as his musical source, his theme-for-every-character approach, combined with strong harmonic style and instrumentation—ominous brass for evil characters, heroic marches for good characters, gentle lyricism in the strings for female characters—suggests more specifically the scoring techniques of Max Steiner. *Star Wars'* orchestral thematic score is more Steineresque than it is Wagnerian in another convention from the past as well: the use of preexisting musical styles. In the film's "cantina scene," alien musicians regale a crowd of interstellar ruffians with the familiar sound of jazz, reinforcing the long-standing musical cliché of jazz accompanying images of alcohol, crime, and social alienation.[37]

Because Williams composed his orchestral score explicitly to support the film's narrative structure, the merchandising success of the soundtrack caught everyone by surprise. No one anticipated that a thematic orchestral score would perform like a pop soundtrack, much less reach the *Billboard* top twenty list. The *Star Wars* soundtrack didn't just "bring back the symphonic score"; economically speaking, it made the orchestral score virtually indistinct from the rock soundtrack in terms of both marketability and profitability. Thanks to *Star Wars,* directors were now free to consider a range of musical styles, from pop to classical, when designing their soundtracks. The sound of violins, to refer back to Wyler, was no longer "senile," but a viable scoring option. "I think after the success of *Star Wars* the orchestras enjoyed a very successful period," Williams observes.

While innovations like the return of orchestral underscoring were inspired by changes in film style and production, other film music changes were influenced by musical innovations. In "Scoring with Synthesizers" **(Document 47),** music critic Terry Atkinson discusses the introduction of this new electronic musical instrument into contemporary film music. Throughout the 1970s, pop and classical musicians had been making substantial use of the synthesizer for its enormous range of conventional and unconventional sounds. Film composers were quick to follow suit, though many of the initial successes with synthesized film scores involved rather conventional uses of the new instrument. *Chariots of Fire* (1981), which won an Academy Award for film composer Vangelis, "had a fairly conventional score, mostly a pretty typical keyboard sound," despite being created entirely on a synthesizer. The placement of the lyrical main melody in the title credits as well as during important internal montage sequences helped turn the score's synthesized instrumental theme into a hit single on the pop charts.

Film composers soon began to capitalize on the synthesizer's ability to generate a whole range of sounds, both musical and nonmusical. "The synthesizer can imitate a large number of other instruments," Atkinson points out, "but it can also make sounds all its own. In particular: pulsating beats that seem to echo the human heart; low, buzzing sounds that for bone-shaking vibrations beat conventional instruments like the bass viola; and high, screechy tones rivaled only by the upper registers of violins." Film composers in the 1980s also experimented with synthesizer sounds in the underscores of sci-fi and horror films and thrillers. For *Cat People* (1982), composer Giorgio Moroder used a synthesizer to articulate an unusual range of sounds that were closer to sound effects than music. Although this was not the first time composers had encroached on the sound engineer's territory, the accessibility and range of the synthesizer was making it much easier to do. As Atkinson puts it, a film score could now consist of "eeks, squonks, oing-boings, and waah-oooms," simply by altering the frequencies, shape, and amplitudes of sound waves instead of composing melodic themes or motives.

In the wake of Vangelis's and Moroder's success, both of whom had roots in techno-punk rock bands, the studios turned to well-known rock musicians who used synthesizers for a little "pre-sold" value. As Atkinson notes, Led Zeppelin's Jimmy Page and Keith Emerson of the band Emerson, Lake, and Palmer composed film scores. Their efforts were overshadowed, however, by established film composers like Morricone, Jarre, and Williams, who were better able to incorporate the "electronic" sound of the synthesizer into conventional scoring formulas.

While the primary innovation of the synthesizer was sonic, it had a significant effect on the ontology of the film score as well. At the touch of a button, the synthesizer allowed film composers to "hear full arrangements, as well as endless variations on a single theme; they could compress or extend a phrase, slow it down or speed it up." The synthesizer also changed the physical nature and location of the film score. Vangelis notes, "I work straight onto the keyboard, and when I have what I want, I can record it directly on tape. My score is my tape." For the first time in the history of film music, both scores and performing musicians had been rendered unnecessary. Although the synthesizer didn't replace the studio orchestra completely, as many industry musicians feared it would, it was certainly responsible for reducing their numbers in the 1980s.[38]

The rise of cable televisions channels like HBO and Showtime affected film production in the 1980s not only by generating demand for new material but also by expanding the employment opportunities for young filmmakers. But the introduction of one cable television channel in particular, MTV, and the rise of the music video had an especially profound impact on film music production. As music critic Marianne Meyer observes in *Rolling Stone* in 1985 **(Document 48),** MTV and music videos were first prized by the industry for their marketing value. Because "promotional clips" of songs featured in films often incorporated contextual footage from the film itself, making for excellent advertisement, the studios paid the new cable channel careful attention. Whereas radio airplay aimed primarily at selling soundtracks, MTV music videos could be used to sell both soundtracks and films. "With the introduction of music videos," notes one studio executive, "it was clear nothing sells film better than film." The music video altered the industrial model of soundtrack and film promotion by consolidating both to a single site. With a minimal financial investment, a music video could turn a soundtrack into a hit record and, in certain cases, could help create a blockbuster film. As Meyer puts it, "1984 dawned with a new equation: Movie + Soundtrack + Video = $$$!!!" Where radio had once reigned supreme, now MTV music videos became the marketing medium of choice for the film industry, facilitating a new synergy between film production and cable television. Saturation airplay on the radio was no longer sufficient to achieve blockbuster status; now a blockbuster music video was necessary too.[39]

Music videos did more than just alter how films and their music were promoted, however. They also affected film structure and cinematic style. Part of what made *Flashdance* so successful, Meyer observes, was the way the film adjusted its editing and narrative tempo to accommodate the distinctive rhythm and editing style of music videos. The film's "paper-thin story" was frequently interrupted by "quick-cut montages of film imagery set to a driving beat," the tempo being dictated by the rhythm and structure of a popular song instead of by conventional cinematic tempos. Clocking at three minutes, a length determined decades earlier by radio play, these interpolated montages gave films a noticeably "modular" structure.[40]

As Meyer observes, the visual resemblance of these musical moments to music videos was no accident. In the film *Footloose,* for instance, "the dance-and–romp sequences were modeled after the fare on MTV, which director Herbert Ross confessed to watching religiously throughout production." Many esteemed film directors, such as John Landis, Nicolas Roeg, William Friedkin, and Brian de Palma, even participated directly in the making of music videos, and likewise many young filmmakers—Russell Mulcahy, Julien Temple, Alan Metter, David Fincher, and Michel Gondry among them—got their start directing music videos.[41] The "music videoization" of film structure did not always lead to synergistic success, though, as Meyer also chronicles. Nonetheless, the formula persisted well into 1990s thanks to films like *Flashdance, Footloose, Ghostbusters* (1984), *Purple Rain* (1984), *Top Gun* (1986), *Beverly Hills Cop* (1985), and *Dirty Dancing* (1987), whose soundtrack singles were heavily promoted on MTV, producing significant ancillary profits for the studios.

In the late 1980s and early 1990s, the film industry again witnessed significant changes to its organization and marketing strategies, changes that posed even more challenges to its identity as a provider of entertainment. Film was already a heavily ancillated product that included home videos, soundtracks, music videos, toys, clothing, magazines, books, and more. In the 1980s, the list of film-related merchandise expanded yet again with the addition of theme parks. Disney, for many years the only studio with an amusement park, expanded its operations from California to Florida, while several other studios, such as Universal, opened competing amusement park facilities.[42] In the early 1990s, the studios added yet another important new product to their merchandising list: the video game. Studio executives enthusiastically began licensing film characters and scenarios to the game industry for use in video and computer games. Although games based on popular science fiction and action adventure have been the most successful (*Fantastic Four, X-Men, Spiderman, Harry Potter, King Kong, The Lord of the Rings, Pirates of the Caribbean, Titanic*), games based on classic films (*Star Wars, Scarface, Godfather*) and family films (*Toy Story, Finding Nemo, The Incredibles, Cars*) have also proved profitable.

Game developers turn to film "properties" because they represent good economics. Licensing fees can take up a significant portion of a game's development budget, but by using familiar narratives from films, a game's "marketing costs are drastically reduced because the most expensive marketing work—building awareness—is already done." [43] The relationship has proved beneficial for the studios, too. Since the late 1990s, the game industry's revenues have consistently exceeded the film industry's, and since 2003, with revenues in excess of $20 billion, video and computer games have become the most profitable entertainment medium on the planet.[44] The game industry's power is not just economic, however. As one scholar notes, "Not only does the video game industry now make more money than the film industry, but video games often take up more of the audience's time than films do."[45] Because video and computer games have become the entertainment medium of choice for a huge demographic that includes both men and women, the film industry is a willing ancillary to the game industry, seeking to forge as many synergistic connections with it as possible.

This new attitude was triggered as well by the development of new audiences and marketplaces. As the studios began to enjoy increasing economic stability and a renewed sense of internal stylistic uniformity, reliance on foreign films and cheaper foreign labor waned. The studios no longer needed to "run away" overseas in order to produce profitable films, but it did still need to engage as large an audience as possible if it wanted its revenues to continue to grow. In the early 1980s, the studios began to renegotiate their relationship with European and overseas industries, many of which still had tariffs and restrictions against Hollywood in place. However, what stymied the circulation of American films overseas, special effects–driven blockbusters especially, was not protectionism. Foreign countries wanted to profit from the popularity of American films, but poor sound and screen quality in theaters abroad made this difficult. As theater quality improved in foreign countries, often at the direct intervention of a Hollywood studio, the industry saw a measurable increase in the success of their films abroad. In the late 1980s, revenues from foreign theatrical rentals of Hollywood films grew exponentially,[46] and in Japan the appetite for American films became so large that several Japanese companies purchased Hollywood studios or entered into lucrative financing arrangements with them.[47] By the early 1990s the market abroad for U.S. films was such that several films—*Pretty Woman, Total Recall, The Little Mermaid,* and *Dances with Wolves* among them—generated greater profits overseas than they did domestically.[48] In 1994, Hollywood's marketplace became truly global as overseas theater box office receipts exceeded domestic ones for the first time.

The marketplace had expanded not just for the theatrical release of film, but also for movies on cable television, network television, and home video. In 1990, home video sales in Europe alone netted $4.5 billion, a majority of which went to the purchase of Hollywood films.[49] Although Hollywood's reach has yet to see significant penetration into Russian, Chinese, and some Asian markets, the circulation of its films has become so broad that the conventional distinctions between domestic and foreign markets have all but disappeared. Hollywood films now routinely open in theaters worldwide and are released on cable television and home video abroad at virtually the same time they are released within the United States.[50]

As film transitioned to a hyper-ancillated format in the late 1980s, its definition had to be adjusted. The downgrading of the movie theater as the primary cite of the cinematic experience caused a terminological if not ontological crisis. Because domestic theatrical box office revenues now accounted for only 20 percent of the average film's revenues, the remainder coming from nontheatrical and nonfilm sources, the once simple question "What is cinema?" had suddenly become difficult to answer. By the 1990s, a Hollywood film was no longer a single product (celluloid film) existing in a single space (the theater) and having a single market (U.S.); instead, as one scholar puts it, it had become a "small subset of interlocking, auxiliary markets . . . and multiple modalities."[51] "Movie production," as another historian puts it, should now "be seen as the creation of entertainment software that can be viewed through several different windows and transported to several different platforms maintained by the other divisions of tightly diversified media corporations."[52]

The evolution of film from celluloid to "entertainment software" happened because of technological innovations but also because of savvy industrial reorganization. In order to better control the record profits being generated from a growing range of film-related products,[53] the industry majors embarked on a fresh round of sales, mergers, and acquisitions. Where the "conglomerate" model of the 1960s had centered on diversification, in the 1980s and 1990s the studios adopted a business model that was more narrowly focused on film and ancillary products. The new tight, single-minded focus in many ways resembled the pre-war model of vertical integration. One of the first studios to downsize, or "de-conglomerate," was Warner Brothers. In 1982 it sold off most of its non-film-related holdings (including a dishware company, an electronics company, and a soccer team) in order to focus more narrowly on its media concerns: film, television, recorded music, and print publishing.[54] Gulf & Western, Paramount's parent company, followed suit, divesting itself over the better part of the decade of its auto parts, sugar-growing operations, home furnishings, and financial services companies and becoming in 1989 Paramount Communications, with entertainment and publishing concerns only.[55] Other more media-centric alignments came not through deconglomeration but with old-fashioned mergers and acquisitions. In 1985, the Australian publishing magnate Rupert Murdoch bought the Twentieth Century–Fox studio and, over the course of a few years, enough television stations to launch a new network, Fox Television. In 1989, the Japanese electronics giant Sony acquired Columbia Pictures and Matsushita bought MCA, which owned Universal Pictures and several record companies and television stations. All of these purchases were made with the idea of greater media-focused integration in mind.[56] Warner Brothers Communications' merger with Time, Inc., in 1989 became the model of this new kind of synergy. Through this purchase, Warner Brothers gained access to a vast network of book and magazine publishing companies, which it used to promote its films, videos, cable networks (HBO), cable providers, record labels, and movie theater chains.[57]

This new model of vertical integration could not have succeeded without government intervention. "The Reagan administration," historian Robert Sklar observes, "may have made its greatest contribution to the movie industry by taking a benign view of industrial takeovers and combinations."[58] In 1985, the government vacated the Supreme Court's 1948 decision against Paramount, an action that allowed the studios not only to coordinate and control film exhibition again, and on a much larger scale. As a result, many studios began purchasing theater chains again.[59] Further deregulation of the cable and network television marketplaces brought more synergistic mergers in the 1990s. In 1993, Viacom, a cable network company, swallowed up Paramount Studios and Blockbuster Video stores, making it the second largest media and entertainment corporation behind Time-Warner. In 1995, Disney acquired ABC network and its cable affiliates, including ESPN, while Westinghouse Electric, which already had vast television and radio station holdings, bought CBS. Murdoch News Corporation, the parent company of Twentieth Century–Fox, continued to expand its global media concerns in the 1990s by buying satellite television companies throughout Europe and Asia.[60]

In addition to producing synergistic media mergers, the growing appetite for film and film-related products spurred the growth of many independent production companies. Between 1983 and 1988, the number of films produced in the United States jumped from 350 films a year to 600.[61] Some of this increase was taken up by companies devoted to diversifying the marketplace with challenging material from young experimental directors like Spike Lee and Steven Soderbergh.[62] Other independent companies were formed specifically to compete in the blockbuster market, producing such hits of the late 1980s and 1990s as *Rambo: First Blood Part II* (1988), *Total Recall* (1990), *Basic Instinct* (1992), *Terminator 2* (1991), and *City Slickers* (1991). Their success created a new phenomenon known as the "mini-major" or "mini-studio," independent production companies with the economic resources and clout of a major studio. Although many of these companies—Carolco, Vestron, Orion, De Laurentiis, Cannon, New Line, Morgan Creek, Castle Rock—were short lived, some survived long enough to be acquired by major studios.[63]

Film sound, in both production and exhibition, also witnessed serious modifications in the late 1980s and 1990s. Since the introduction of Dolby sound in the late 1970s, both film and theater sound continued to develop. In the early 1980s, director George Lucas again improved theater sound with the introduction of THX, a new system that added greater range and volume to the conceptualization of sound. At the end of the decade new digital systems like *DTS, Dolby Digital SR-D,* and *SDDS* brought even greater clarity and directionality to film sound.[64] With an increasing number of separate, mixable channels, these systems have allowed filmmakers to create a sense of sonic space that is highly nuanced, having multiple layers and perspectives. The revolution in film sound has also been marked by an unprecedented degree of coordination between production and exhibition. As film sound has changed, theater speakers systems have been reconfigured to be both multichannel and multidirectional. With the ability to layer and direct sound at the point of exhibition, film sound has acquired sophisticated aesthetic sensibilities and is no longer a single, undifferentiated element. There has been "a definite shift away from the old sound hierarchies," historian Gianluca Sergi notes, "in which speech and music were accorded unconditional priority."[65]

In this new global marketplace and hyper-ancillated atmosphere, film production has also changed. In the late 1980s and early 1990s, the studios made noticeable modifications to the blockbuster formula to interface it even more closely with subsidiary marketplaces. This newest strain of blockbusters has relied almost exclusively on "pre-sold" material, material with characters or subject matter that could be easily commodified, or turned into toys, action figures, or Happy Meal fodder. While it continues to used print literature and classic novels for inspiration, as witnessed in the wildly profitable production of Tolkien's *Lord of the Rings* trilogy (2001, 2002, 2003) and the *Bourne* trilogy (2002, 2004, 2007), more commonly it is comic books and television shows, preexisting material that is predominantly visual, that drive new movie narratives. The list of films based on television shows is extensive; it includes *The Brady Bunch* (1995), *Star Trek* (1979, 1982, 1984, 1986), *Star Trek: The Next Generation* (1996, 1997), *Mission Impossible* (1996, 2000, 2006), *Charlie's Angels* (2000, 2003), *Starsky and Hutch* (2004), *The X-Files* (1998, 2008), *The Simpsons* (2007), *Get Smart* (2008), *Reno 911!* (2007), and *Sex and the City* (2008). The cinematic treatment of television shows has also been highly serialized, with some franchises reaching up to six sequels. Comic book–based films include *Batman* (1989, 1992, 1995, 1997, 2005, 2008), *Catwoman* (2004), *Dick Tracy* (1990), *Spiderman* (2002, 2004, 2007), *The Incredible Hulk* (2003), *Superman Returns* (2006), *Daredevil* (2003), *X-Men* (2000, 2003, 2006), *Elektra* (2005), *The Fantastic Four* (2005, 2007), and *Iron Man* (2008, 2010).[66] A number of blockbuster films have also been based on the characters from the billion-dollar video game industry. While the first group of these films—*Super Mario Brothers* (1993), *Street Fighter* (1994), *Mortal Kombat* (1995), *Wing Commander* (1995), and *Final Fantasy: The Spirits Within* (2001)—generated only fair or even disappointing revenues, the enormous success of *Lara Croft: Tomb Raider* (2001) reenergized the game-to-film formula. In 2006 alone, the industry slated no less than seven films based on video games for production, including *Silent Hill, DOA: Dead or Alive, Halo, Spy Hunter, Alice, Resident Evil: Extinction,* and *Castlevania.*[67] Even more recently, big-budget action films like *Hitman* (2007), *Max Payne* (2008), *Street Fighter: The Legend of Chun-li* (2009), and *The Prince of Persia: The Sands of Time* (2010) have been based on popular video games as well. The ancillary industry of video games has made film directors and game producers increasingly interested not only in shortening the release time between films and their games but also in making the game experience match the cinematic one and vice versa.[68] In all of these films, the blockbuster formula has been articulated not just with an enormous amount of special visual effects, made possible in most cases by the advent of computer graphic imaging (CGI), but also with a newly designed soundtrack that includes an ever-expanding array of sophisticated digital sound effects.

Both the reconglomeratation of the industry and the hyper-ancillation of film in the late 1980s and early 1990s affected the production and marketing of film music. In his article "How Rock is Changing Hollywood's Tune" **(Document 49)**, *New York Times* critic Stephen Holden describes the emergence of a new aesthetic formula from the post–*Star Wars* and music video landscape. By the late 1980s, film music had become an either/or proposition, he observes. Directors either commissioned an orchestral score from a composer or fashioned, often with the help of a music supervisor or film executive, a pop compilation soundtrack. If some kind of merging of the two styles was attempted, the pop song was usually tacked onto an otherwise conventional orchestral score in extra-filmic spaces like the opening or closing credit sequence. *Batman* (1989) marked a departure from this conventional separation of musical styles, Holden notes, because it integrated both styles, pop and orchestral, within a single film. Composer Danny Elfman's "post-Wagnerian action music" is heard throughout much of the film, but at key moments pop songs are prominently accommodated within the score. Although Holden finds the inclusion of Prince's "shallow ditties" unmotivated and narratively weak, part of "a long pop tradition of respected pop composers tossing off slick, impersonal product for the Hollywood entertainment machine," their presence was economically stimulated by the extra revenue pop soundtracks were capable of generating. More noticeable than their missing narrative validity, however, was the interruption the songs created in Elfman's score. As Holden concludes, *Batman* shows that "today the means for accomplishing the task [of scoring] is no longer a single vocabulary"; rather, it is "more pluralistic than ever before." [69]

This double-styled pluralism had an audible effect on film music, for by the late 1980s films were once again full of wall-to-wall music, but now the carpet consisted of both pop songs and orchestral-thematic music. The new scoring model also had a visible effect of film structure. In *Batman,* for example, because there was not enough physical space to accommodate a full-length orchestral score and a whole album of pop songs, only two Prince songs were featured in the narrative part of the film itself. Four more songs were included either over the end credits or as brief snippets of ambient background noise at busy party scenes and were barely audible. Two additional songs, though not heard in the film, were included on the soundtrack album as "inspired by" the film.[70]

The new pluralism meant altering or abandoning the idea that the pop soundtrack be entirely narratively integrated. It also meant altering conventional soundtrack formulas. With *Batman,* Warner Brothers made the unprecedented decision to release two separate soundtracks, one of the film's underscore and one a pop compilation of Prince songs. While the singular stylistic approach was still widely available, as Holden notes it too showed "the warring strains of symphonic and pop film music merging into something that is neither one." But as the experiment with *Batman* proved, not only could film accommodate more and stylistically incongruent styles of music, but the excess of music could also produce not one but multiple commercial soundtracks, allowing the music to be marketed to separate, specialized film music audiences.

Document 50, an interview by Randall Larson with composer Danny Elfman, confirms many of Holden's observations about the new double-style model. Elfman, for instance, describes tailoring many of his orchestral scores to accommodate pop songs by well-known pop stars. He also mentions the growing number of rock musicians entering the field of film scoring. In addition to hiring two quite stylistically different musicians to author a single film's music, studio executives were experimenting with consolidating those efforts by asking successful pop musicians to compose both songs and underscores.[71] Elfman himself, a pop musician from the rock band Oingo Bongo, represented just such a consolidation. For Elfman, scoring meant not only learning to read and write music, but also writing for a large classical orchestra of seventy or more musicians. It also meant using classical scoring conventions—"mickey-mousing" for comic effect—but also the use of harmonic language and instrumentation, combinations of low brass and percussion to create feelings of alienation and suspense, for example. Elfman admits to modeling his style and method of scoring after classical orchestral composers like Nino Rota and Bernard Herrmann.

Elfman's underscoring style follows the conventional orchestral model of the 1940s and 1950s but with one important exception, and that is in his approach to nonthematic material. Where the classical model made room for nonthematic underscoring, what Copland called "neutral" music, Elfman's orchestral model is hyperthematicized. He uses themes to underscore narrative action, but he also "soundtracks" them by simultaneously conceiving of them as marketable tracks on a record album or CD. In *Batman*, he engineered the main characters' themes, with the help of film executives, to be as commodifiable as a pop song. As Elfman describes it, when the producer for the film, Jon Peters, agitated for a "Heroic Theme," he took a theme he had composed and "turned it into this march, and did it in a certain way—changed the key around a little bit—and all of the sudden he [Jon] leapt up out of his chair, and it was completely obvious that I had found the Batman hero theme!" John Williams's score for *Star Wars* may have reintroduced the orchestral score to a filmmaking landscape saturated with pop music, but Elfman's scoring techniques reformulated it. By hyperthematicizing or "soundtracking" themes from the orchestral underscore, Elfman was instrumental in turning the orchestral underscore into the pop soundtrack's narrative and economic equal.

At the same time that the boundaries between scoring and soundtracking have become more porous, as films has stretched to accommodate both newly composed orchestral scores and pop selections, the compilation soundtrack has persisted, becoming more stylistically diverse and flexible. This persistence is documented in a roundtable discussion of directors, producers, music supervisors, and musicians included here as **Document 51.** As excerpts reveal, the industrial merchandising of film music was still to a large extent controlling the size and content of the pop compilation soundtrack, with producers and executives making many soundtrack decisions. For example, the producers of the film *Say Anything* (1989), said director Cameron Crowe, "told me at the last minute that if I didn't have hit music on the soundtrack then it wouldn't be marketed, so we were running with extra money . . . trying to find hits." Similarly, when Penelope Spheeris was hired to direct *Wayne's World* (1992), she was told even before filming that her musical selections would be limited to the songs of pop musicians currently under contract with the studio's subsidiary record companies. Director Quentin Tarantino was likewise forced to include some songs in his film *Reservoir Dogs* in order to finance other more expensive ones he wanted to use on the soundtrack. Indeed, even today licensing fees and copyright permission continue to determine what music gets used in a film.

The pop compilation soundtrack of the 1990s was not motivated entirely by economic concerns, however. A general discomfort with orchestral music and the loss of control over newly composed music also motivated directors to use new and preexisting popular music. For some directors, like Crowe and Alan Rudolph, the discomfort can be traced to the difficulty a musically untrained director has communicating with a trained composer. For others, like Tarantino, the discomfort has to do with the loss of directorial control, recalling the pop soundtrack's auteur roots. [72] An important factor in the question of control has to do with the centrality of popular music in contemporary culture and in the experiences of young filmmakers. As director Allison Anders notes, "Popular music is the only cultural reference we hold in common any more." Popular music is able to generate instant filmic meaning by providing a precise referential marker—a "Where was I when I heard this song" phenomenon, as Anders puts it, which gives directors a range of extra-filmic information that newly composed orchestral music cannot generate.

This roundtable discussion also reflects the tremendous impact the music video continued to have on film style and structure. Director Isaac Julien, for example, describes the importance of MTV and music videos to contemporary visual style, while director Penelope Spheeris mentions her practice of shooting music video–like montage sequences that will later be edited to fit the style and rhythm of the songs to be included on the film soundtrack. According to music supervisor Bob Last, the videoization of the pop soundtrack has resulted in noticeable rhythmic disruptions and a modular sense of film structure. "There are a lot of mainstream movies where you can see the MTV moment coming up. . . . There's a change in the pace, it adjusts itself, sometimes very subtly." Tarantino also confirms the ubiquity of the music video model and the high-concept or "module" form of filmmaking it demanded. Both he and Crowe acknowledge the extra-filmic pressure to include montage sequences in their films in order to showcase and market the soundtrack.

As this discussion observes, pop compilation soundtracks were witnessing an expansion of style and instrumentation beyond the sonic limitations of conventional pop music, in particular into the realm of "world music." While escalating permission fees are cited as the motivating factor behind directors turning to less expensive, non-Western pop music, stylistic diversity is also an aesthetic choice. Where before, non-Western musical styles and instrumentations were included only as source music or as geographic markers, in the 1990s world music styles were beginning to share the interpretive space with Western pop musical styles in the contemporary pop soundtrack. As director Rudolph observes, the industrialization of the pop compilation was driving filmmakers away from commercial synergies and toward the construction of more personal and noncommercial soundtracks, compilations that contained, for instance, Bulgarian vocal music, pop songs from Mali, and Norwegian folk fiddling.

The auteur soundtrack was showing signs of greater stylistic diversity as well.[73] In recent auteur filmmaking, the use of preexisting music has been distinctive not just because the compilations are larger than their industrial counterparts, or more fragmented and inventively placed, but also because their content has become more eclectic. Veteran auteurs like Scorsese have led the way in this expansion of compilation practices.[74] Whereas before compilation selections were typically limited to a single style (pop or classical) or confined to the period of time depicted in the film, in the last decade especially those conventions have been increasingly disregarded. Scorsese begins his film *Casino* (1995), for instance, with an extended excerpt from J. S. Bach's *St. Matthew Passion,* music that is not only temporally inappropriate but also stylistically at odds with the crowded soundtrack of popular music that follows. In *He Got Game* (1996), Spike Lee likewise experiments with stylistic contrast. Two wildly divergent styles of music, the orchestral music of Aaron Copland and the rap music of Public Enemy, take center stage in the soundtrack and occupy a central position in the film's narrative content. In the work of more recent auteurs like Wes Anderson, Sofia Coppola, and Paul Thomas Anderson, stylistic diversity has only increased. In the soundtracks to films like *The Royal Tenenbaums* (2001), *The Life Aquatic with Steve Zissou* (2004), *Marie Antoinette* (2005), and *There Will Be Blood* (2007), the musical selections are insistently diverse, with the soundtracks quickly transitioning between vastly different styles of both contemporary and historic pop and classical music.[75]

In **Document 52,** an interview by Philip Brophy, composer Howard Shore also discusses the stylistic diversity of his sonic palette. His early scoring work in the 1980s was innovative not only through the inclusion of ethnic, non-Western musical instruments, but through unusual instrumental combinations. With both orchestras and synthesizers now cliché, Shore turned, like Herrmann, Morricone, and Goldsmith before him, to alternative instrumentation and performance techniques. In the case of *Crash* (1996), he used six electric guitars, three harps, and prepared piano, all of which were additionally "processed" or manipulated electronically with amplification and delay units.

Most significantly, Shore's comments address the extent to which innovations in sound technology, Dolby digital and THX especially, were affecting film music in the 1980s and 1990s. To some extent his discussion of film sound recalls the comments of Korngold and Copland in the 1930s and 1940s, who talked of needing to negotiate music around the dialogue. For Shore, the element that music must now negotiate around is not dialogue but sound—specifically, sound effects. In the Dolby age, the tracks of film sound have become not only more numerous but more nuanced. "Quite often," Shore notes, "the sound design might be 40, 50, 60 tracks." The sheer complexity of contemporary sound design requires that it be closely coordinated with the other elements on the soundtrack, and that the composer and sound designer communicate well so that their individual design concepts do not interfere with one another or create redundancies. The fact that the score must be built around the film's sound means that the composer's relationship with the sound designer is as important as his relationship with the film director, if not more so.

The profound changes in film sound design over the last two decades have required significant changes in musical instrumentation as well. The need for composers to build a score around elaborate sound structures requires that music work not just under dialogue but also over loud and detailed sound effects. For Shore, especially in his scores such as the *Lord of the Rings* trilogy, as well as for many composers scoring blockbuster action films, this has meant using a very large orchestra with greatly expanded brass and percussion sections. The tremendous growth in the size of the orchestra in contemporary film scoring has been motivated not just by the widespread use of new visual computer technologies and computer-generated special effects but also by technological developments in the construction of film sound.

This new necessity of negotiating cinematic space with sound design has worked to blur the ontological distinction between sound and music. In many contemporary films it is difficult to determine the difference between, for instance, a "processed" percussion instrument and a designed sound effect. In *Crash* (1996), the blurring was often intentional. Shore notes "a scene which takes place inside a carwash. I constructed a *musique concrète* piece with the sound designer. I took his sounds and built a piece around his carwash sounds." In the post-Dolby age, and especially in the last decade of filmmaking, this blurring has become more ubiquitous and profound. As new technology has allowed sound to become more expressive and nuanced, film music has responded by becoming more sonically varied to fit around it. Shore's approach to recording is a direct expression of this conceptual collapse. As Shore explains, he prefers to record only one part of an orchestra at a time and then manipulate those recordings in postproduction, commenting that "I think of [recording an orchestra] like a big sound gathering session."

In the complex world of film sound, music has in many ways become theoretically indistinct from sound and sound design. For composers like Don Davis and Charlie Clouser, film music has also become more sonically driven and percussive, especially in the sci-fi and horror genres. As the scores for the *Matrix* trilogy and the *Saw* series reveal, the use of a more percussive, techno-rock style of musical composition makes it more difficult to distinguish the music score from the highly designed and layered digital sound effects it is integrated with. Recent dramatic films have also played with this greater unification of sound and music, as in Dario Marianelli's inventive score for *Atonement* (2007), where nondiegetic percussion and diegetic typewriter at times overlap, becoming indistinguishable.

The final document reprinted here, video game sound designer Rob Bridgett's "Hollywood Sound" (**Document 53**), describes the influence of music written for new interactive and digital entertainment media, video games in particular, on film music in the twenty-first century. This dialogue between game and film media stems from a large-scale shift in video game production in the last decade that has increasingly recognized film as an ideal model not just for visual style but for sound and music production too. In the early decades of game history, in the 1970s and 1980s, when computer graphic capabilities were less developed, borrowing film was not possible because of severely limited memory space. In the 1990s, however, with improved computer processing speed and memory, new graphic and sonic capabilities have allowed cinematic conventions to be imported directly into video games—everything from narrative modeling and genre formulas, to shot selections, editing styles, and reconceptualizations of time and space.[76] Conversely, as video game revenues have risen exponentially in the last two decades, the film industry has looked to video games as a source of both narrative inspiration and ancillary revenue. At the same time that the studios have been licensing selected film scenarios and characters for video games, they have also been making feature films based on video games.

This increasingly symbiotic relationship between the film and game industries is visible on a musical level as well. Recent technical innovations have given game sound designers the ability to work with high-quality cinematic sound and music. As Bridgett asserts, "the convergence" between the Hollywood film industry and game development has arrived. One important manifestation of this convergence is the number of famous film composers crossing over from film scoring to game scoring. Bridgett mentions two prominent crossovers—Howard Shore and Danny Elfman—though he qualifies their work as being used primarily for "cut scenes" or title theme music and not "in-game" or underscoring purposes. Bridgett's observations outline a pattern of migration being established by high-profile film composers like Shore, Elfman, Harry Gregson-Williams, Graeme Revell, and others. Similarly, game composers, like Bill Brown, Garry Schyman, Jesper Kyd, and Paul Haslinger are likewise crossing over into film composition. In fact, as Bridgett notes, the description of these composers as "crossover artists" is fast becoming obsolete. In the near future, he predicts, "there will be no categorization of either 'game' or 'film' composers but simply 'composers.'"

Another manifestation of the convergence of film and game music can be seen in the instrumentation of game music. Because game makers have the financial resources and the technical capabilities to demand cinematic standards for music, they are employing the best composers, arrangers, and the largest orchestras in or outside of Hollywood. While in some instances that cinematic sound means composing for a ninety-piece orchestra, in other instances it means the use of expensive pop compilation soundtracks. Many games are using "big-name licensed music content," the same kind of compilation pop soundtrack as a high-budget blockbuster Hollywood film.

The influence of game music on film music is just as strong. While that influence can be heard in instrumentation, particularly in those film scores that feature electronica and ambient music, it can also be heard in the structure and texture of the underscore.[77] The "interactive microstructures" of game scores echo the characteristics that film scholars find in the "game-inspired film score." Some parts of game scores, the music for "intros" and "outros" and "cut-scenes" for instance, which resemble opening and closing credit sequences and transitions, are rooted in traditional film scoring models. But a video game's highly flexible and repetitive "in-game" music, Bridgett asserts, is not. Bridgett calls this reiterative kind of music "evolving state" music and defines it as consisting of "stems" of music that are layered together. In this kind of music, linear thematic development has been replaced by horizontal layering. Intensity and complexity are built "across stacked layers [of stems] rather than through linear temporal movement" and are invoked not by the composer but by the player, in reaction to choices made in the game. Although film scores are not and cannot be interactive, as historian Anahid Kassabian observes, they can and have assimilated many structural and stylistic aspects of in-game music, particularly the repetitive and layered used of stems. This style of music has been surfacing increasingly in scores of films based on video games, particularly in long action sequences within those films.[78]

Another indication of the increasing convergence between film and game music lies in the autonomy that game music as recently attained. The push for equality and autonomy is visible both at the record store and in the concert hall. With increasing frequency, game music is being soundtracked, extracted from its game and marketed in a separate package. Game music is also being commodified though live performances. In the 1980s and 1990s, techno bands like the Yellow Magic Orchestra, the Minibosses, and the NESkimos established their reputations covering electronic video game themes. More recently, symphony orchestras have begun offering live performances of game music. In 1987, for example, composer Koichi Sugiyama arranged his music for the popular game *Dragon Quest* for concert performance with the Tokyo Philharmonic. More recently, Nobuo Uematsu had his music for the game *Final Fantasy* performed by the Los Angeles Philharmonic and the Detroit, San Diego, and Minnesota symphony orchestras, all to sold-out audiences. If game music has begun to influence film music, it not just because film and game composers are crossing territories. It is also because game music has become an established and autonomous genre of music.

NOTES

1. This critical agreement may come from the fact that this period of film history falls within the living memory of most historians or critics and that many of the changes that define this period are still visible in studio films being produced today. But it is certainly also because new technical innovations and marketing strategies introduced in the late 1970s early 1980s brought profound and indisputable change to the industry. For a general discussion of the aesthetic and technical basis of contemporary cinematic practice, see Murray Smith, "Thesis on the Philosophy of Hollywood History," in *Contemporary Hollywood Cinema*, ed. Steve Neale and Murray Smith (New York: Routledge, 1998), p. 3. Smith considers a variety of descriptive classifications—postclassical, postmodern, postwar, post-Ford—that film production after 1945 has been given.

2. Explanations vary as to the changes, or in some cases "revolution," that brought the recession to an end. For Robert Sklar, for instance, "The similarities between the 1930s and the 1970s went beyond crisis to consolidation. . . . What separated the two eras was nothing less than a revolution in film distribution" (Sklar, *Movie-Made America: A Cultural History of American Movies,*" rev. ed. [New York: Vintage Books, 1994], p. 323). Although Stephen Prince describes the change as more ontological—"film stopped being [Hollywood's] primary product"—he too describes the late 1970s and early 1980s as a period of profound transformation for the American film industry (Prince, "Introduction," *A New Pot of Gold: Hollywood under the Electronic Rainbow, 1980–1989* [Berkeley: University of California Press, 2000], p. xi). And Douglas Gomery suggests that, based on economic models of conglomeration, Steve Ross's and Warner Brothers' acquisition of Time in the 1980s should define a "second" or "new" New Hollywood period (Gomery, "Hollywood Corporate Business Practice and Periodizing Contemporary Film History, in Neale and Smith, eds., *Contemporary Hollywood Cinema,* p. 48). Murray Smith, for his part, finds merit in the terms *postclassical* and *neoclassical* ("Thesis on the Philosophy of Hollywood History," pp. 10–16).

3. Thomas Schatz, "The New Hollywood," in *Film Theory Goes to the Movies,* ed. Jim Collins, Hilary Radner, and Ava Preacher Collins (New York: Routledge, 1993), p. 18.

4. Sklar, *Movie-Made America,* p. 323. Although these practices to some degree "confirmed or consolidated various existing industry trends and practices," as Schatz ("The New Hollywood," p. 19) observes, they also significantly altered long-standing industrial models." See also Michael Allen, *Contemporary U.S. Cinema* (New York: Longman Press, 2003), pp. 18–22

5. The film also helped bring an end to the recession because it triggered significant shifts in production values, "usher[ing] in an era of high-cost, high-tech, high-speed thrillers" (Schatz, "The New Hollywood," p. 17).

6. Ibid., p. 20.

7. Prince, *New Pot of Gold,* p. 82.

8. Toronto exhibitor Nat Taylor was one such pioneer. As Taylor recalls, "Nobody in those days [the late 1970s] could conceive of the idea that you could put two theaters in one location" (ibid.). For additional statistics on theater construction in the late 1970s and early 1980s, see Jim Hillier, *The New Hollywood* (New York: Continuum, 1992), p. 14.

9. Prince, *New Pot of Gold,* p. 83.

10. Douglas Gomery, "Motion Picture Exhibition in 1970s America," in David A. Cook, *Lost Illusions: American Cinema in the Shadow of Watergate and Vietnam, 1970–79* (Berkeley: University of California Press, 2000), p. 415.

11. Ibid., pp. 415–16.

12. Prince, *New Pot of Gold,* p. 26.

13. Ibid., pp. 27–31.

14. Ibid., p. 26.

15. Several scholars have placed the music video in a longer history of visualized musical performances, including Andrew Goodwin, *Dancing in the Distraction Factory: Music Television and Popular Culture* (Minneapolis: University of Minnesota Press, 1992); R. Serge Denisoff and William D. Romanowski, *Risky Business: Rock on Film* (New Brunswick, N.J.: Transaction Publishers, 1991); and Charles M. Berg, "Visualizing Music: The Archaeology of the Music Video," *OneTwoThreeFour: A Rock 'n' Roll Quarterly,* no. 5 (Spring 1987): 94–103. The unique visual style of the music video has been heavily analyzed. See, for example, Andrew Goodwin, "From Anarchy to Chromakey: Music, Video, and Media," *OneTwoThreeFour: A Rock 'n' Roll Quarterly,* no. 5 (Spring 1987): 17–32; Marsha Kinder, "Music Video and the Spectator: Television, Ideology, and Dream," *Film Quarterly* 38, no. 1 (Autumn 1984): 2–15; Will Straw, "Music Video in Its Contexts: Popular Music and Post-Modernism in the 1980s," *Popular Music* 7, no. 3 (October 1988): 247–66; and Carol Vernalis, *Experiencing Music Video: Aesthetics and Cultural Context* (New York: Columbia University Press, 2004).

16. Initially, MTV had some competition from the NBC program *Friday Night Videos* and TBS's *Night Tracks,* but its twenty-four-hour programming soon allowed it to dominate. See Maira Viera, "The Institutionalization of the Music Video," *OneTwoThreeFour: A Rock 'n' Roll Quarterly,* no. 5 (Spring 1987): 80–93; and Denisoff and Romanowski, *Risky Business,* pp. 345–57. See also R. Serge Denisoff, *Inside MTV* (New York: Transaction Publishers, 1988), p. 2; and E. Ann Kaplan, *Rocking Around the Clock: Music Television, Postmodernism, and Consumer Culture* (London: Methuen Press, 1987), pp. 1–2.

17. See Prince, *New Pot of Gold,* pp. 99–111; and Cook, *Lost Illusions,* pp. 4–5.

18. As a VP at Columbia Pictures in 1972, for instance, Peter Gruber anticipated a "limitless" new market thanks to the home video, and Charles Bludhorn, president of Columbia's parent company, saw home video as "open[ing] a tremendous market." Others, however, like Jack Valenti, president of the Motion Picture Association of America, likened the VCR boom to "millions of little tapeworms" eating up studio profits (quoted in Prince, *New Pot of Gold,* p. 100). See also Cook, *Lost Illusions,* p. 5.

19. Prince, *New Pot of Gold,* pp. 94–95; Hillier, *The New Hollywood,* p. 33.

20. Prince, *New Pot of Gold,* p. 97.

21. Ibid., p. 126. As one operator observed, the transfer of film to video articulated a separate aesthetic agenda: "It's more important to fill the TV frame than it is to maintain cinematic composition" (ibid.).

22. Richard Maltby, "Nobody Knows Everything: Post-Classical Historiographies and Consolidated Entertainment," in Neale and Smith, eds., *Contemporary Hollywood Cinema,* p. 24.

23. Allen, *Contemporary U.S. Cinema,* p. 19.

24. Cook, *Lost Illusions,* pp. 156–57.

25. See Schatz, "The New Hollywood," pp. 17–25. Although Schatz credits Spielberg's *Jaws* in particularly with retooling the industry blockbuster standard in 1975, he acknowledges that "*Jaws'* release also happened to coincide with developments both inside and outside the movie industry in the 1970s which, while having little or nothing to do with that particular film, were equally important to the emergent New Hollywood" (ibid., p. 17).

26. Cook, *Lost Illusions,* pp. 156–57.

27. Mark Crispin Miller, "Hollywood: The Ad," *Atlantic Monthly,* April 1990, pp. 49–52.

28. As Justin Wyatt describes it, these films were defined by a series of predesigned, market-tested criteria known colloquially as "a hook, a look and a book. . . . The look of the images, the

marketing hooks, and the reduced narratives form the cornerstones of high concept" (Wyatt, *High Concept: Movies and Marketing in Hollywood* [Austin: University of Texas Press, 1994], pp. 20–22).

29. Ibid., pp. 36–44.

30. Kay Dickinson, "Pop, Speed, and the 'MTV Aesthetic' in Recent Teen Films," *Scope* (June 2001), available at www.scope.nottingham.ac.uk/article.php?issue=jun2001&id=275&section=article; an edited reprint on this article is in *Movie Music: The Film Reader,* ed. Kay Dickinson (London: Routledge, 2003), pp. 143–52. Other scholars of 1980s and 1990s filmmaking have also observed the effect music videos had on film structure and style. See, e.g., Denisoff and Romanowski, *Risky Business,* pp. 399–468; Jeff Smith, *The Sounds of Commerce: Marketing Popular Film Music* (New York: Columbia University Press, 1998), pp. 196–209; and Serge Denisoff and George Plasketes, "Synergy in 1980s Film and Music: Formula for Success or Industry Mythology?" *Film History* 4, no. 3 (1990): 257–76.

31. Prince, *New Pot of Gold,* pp. 112–15.

32. Ibid., pp. 114–15.

33. Michael Allen, "From Bwana Devil to Batman Forever: Technology in Contemporary Hollywood Cinema," in Neale and Smith, eds., *Contemporary Hollywood Cinema,* pp. 116–17. Systems like Cinerama, CinemaScope, and Todd-AO offered better-quality, multichannel sound, but they were difficult to use and expensive to install in theaters.

34. Ibid., pp. 117–18. By the late 1950s, only 25 percent of American cinemas, most of them first-run theaters, had stereo sound. This was true as late as 1974, when the movie *Earthquake* could only be fully experienced in those theaters having the new low-spectrum heavy sound system called Sensurround.

35. Allen, "From Bwana Devil to Batman Forever," p. 118; and Gianluca Sergi, "A Cry in the Dark: The role of Post-Classical Sound," in Neale and Smith, eds., *Contemporary Hollywood Cinema,* p. 158.

36. For further discussion on Stigwood and Coury and synergistic strategies in the late 1970s, see Hugh Fordin, "Rock Calls the Tune," *New York Times,* March 12, 1978. See also Smith, *Sounds of Commerce,* pp. 186–229; Alexander Doty, "Music Sells Movies: (Re)New(ed) Conservatism in Film Marketing," *Wide Angle* 10, no. 2 (1988): 70–79; Denisoff and Romanowski, *Risky Business,* pp. 201–82; David Ehrenstein and Bill Reed, *Rock on Film* (New York: Delilah Books, 1992), pp. 92–99; and Melissa Carey and Michael Hannan, "Case Study 2: *The Big Chill*," in *Popular Music in Film,* ed. Ian Inglis (New York: Wallflower Press, 2003), pp. 162–77.

37. Detailed examination of Williams's neoclassical style can be found in Kathryn Kalinak, *Settling the Score: Music in the Classical Hollywood* (Madison: University of Wisconsin Press, 1992), pp. 184–202; James Buhler, "*Star Wars,* Music and Myth," in *Music and Cinema,* ed. David Neumeyer, Caryl Flinn, and James Buhler (Middletown: Wesleyan University Press, 2000), pp. 33–57; Caryl Flinn, *Strains of Utopia: Gender, Nostalgia, and Hollywood Film Music* (Princeton: Princeton University Press, 1992), pp. 152–53; and William Darby and Jack Du Bois, *American Film Music: Major Composers, Techniques, Trends, 1915–1990* Jefferson, N.C.: McFarland, 1990), pp. 521–45.

38. As music scholar George Burt notes, "The near monumental surge of the digital synthesizer in the 1980s tragically forced innumerable musicians into unemployment. Some highly accomplished players had to leave Los Angeles altogether in the hope of finding work elsewhere. It was sad to see an entire generation of specialized performers—and, along with them, a specialized performance practices—fade into relative obscurity" (Burt, *The Art of Film Music* [Boston: Northeastern University Press, 1992], p. 241).

39. For further discussion of the impact music videos and cable television had on the promotion and marketing of films, see Denisoff and Plasketes, "Synergy in 1980s Film and Music"; Smith, *Sounds of Commerce,* pp. 200–201; and Denisoff and Romanowski, *Risky Business,* pp. 399–468.

40. Wyatt, *High Concept*, pp. 36–44; Prince, *New Pot of Gold*, pp. 132–41; Dickinson, "Pop, Speed, and the 'MTV Aesthetic' in Recent Teen Films," pp. 143–52; and John Mundy, *Popular Music on Screen: From the Hollywood Musical to Music Video* (Manchester: Manchester University Press, 1999), pp. 221–47.

41. The cross-pollination of film and video continued to produce high-profile exchanges. Martin Scorsese, for instance, directed the video for Michael Jackson's hit song "Bad" (1987), and well into the 1990s film directors were still getting their start in music video direction, including David Fincher, Spike Jonze, Lasse Hallström, and Michel Gondry.

42. Murray Smith, "Thesis on the Philosophy of Hollywood History," in Neale and Smith, eds., *Contemporary Hollywood Cinema*, p. 14; Prince, *New Pot of Gold*, p. 11.

43. Stephen Kline, Nick Dyer-Witheford, and Greig de Peuter, *Digital Play: The Interaction of Technology, Culture, and Marketing* (Montreal: McGill–Queen's University Press, 2003), p. 226. Recent estimates of licensing fees show the film industry to be receiving $3–5 million and 9 percent of gross profits per game. See Ronald Grover, "Game Wars: Who Will Win Your Entertainment Dollar, Hollywood or Silicon Valley?" *Business Week Online* (February 28, 2005); and Laura Holson, "Blockbuster with a Joystick," *New York Times*, February 7, 2005.

44. "Introduction," *Handbook of Computer Games*, ed. Joost Raessens and Jeffrey Goldstein (Cambridge: MIT Press, 2005), p. xii. For statistics on the demographics and profits of the game industry, see also Arthur Asa Berger, *Video Games: A Popular Culture Phenomenon* (New Brunswick, N.J.: Transaction Publishers, 2002), pp. 24–26; and "Designing Militarized Masculinity: Violence, Gender and the Bias of the Game Experience," in Kline, Dyer-Witheford, and de Peuter, *Digital Play*, pp. 146–268.

45. Mark Wolf, "Introduction," in *The Medium of the Video Game*, ed. Mark Wolf (Austin: University of Texas Press, 2001), p. 20.

46. Tino Balio, "A Major Presence in All of the World's Important Markets: The Globalization of Hollywood in the 1990s," in Neale and Smith, eds., *Contemporary Hollywood Cinema*, p. 60. The studios also financed theater improvements in foreign countries by forming less visible alliances with national companies as a way of circumventing tariffs.

47. Hillier, *The New Hollywood*, pp. 26–27.

48. Schatz, "The New Hollywood," p. 26.

49. Balio, "A Major Presence in All of the World's Important Markets," pp. 61–64. The 1990s also saw several Hollywood majors engage in partnerships with foreign television, cable, and satellite communication companies as a way of circumventing foreign tariffs and other trade barriers to U.S. films and television programs. See also Hillier, *The New Hollywood*, pp. 32–33.

50. Geoff King, *New Hollywood Cinema: An Introduction* (New York: Columbia University Press, 2002), pp. 59–62.

51. Prince, *New Pot of Gold*, pp. xi and xiv.

52. Maltby, "Nobody Knows Everything," p. 24.

53. Home video sales, cables rights, merchandise, and foreign rentals could amplify the success of a blockbuster or cushion the losses of a poorly performing film. By 1995, with only 20 percent of a film's revenue coming from domestic theater ticket sales, making movies was only a small part of the industry's business. See Allen, *Contemporary U.S. Cinema*, p. 19; and Maltby, "Nobody Knows Everything," p. 24.

54. Balio, "A Major Presence," pp. 62–63.

55. Prince, *New Pot of Gold*, pp. 60–64.

56. Ibid., pp. 69–70; Balio, "A Major Presence," p. 63.

57. Prince, *New Pot of Gold*, pp. 64–69. Gomery, "Hollywood Corporate Business Practice," pp. 52–55; and Schatz, "The New Hollywood," p. 29.

58. Sklar, *Movie-Made America,* p. 340.

59. Hillier, *The New Hollywood,* p. 23; Prince, *New Pot of Gold,* pp. 84–89.

60. Balio, "A Major Presence," pp. 67–68.

61. Ibid., p. 58.

62. Prince, *New Pot of Gold,* pp. 117–21. Films like *Kiss of the Spider Woman* (1985), *She's Gotta Have It* (1986), and *Sex, Lies, and Videotape* (1989), the last two of which turned Spike Lee and Steven Soderbergh into star directors, were independent productions.

63. Hillier, *The New Hollywood,* p. 18; and Justin Wyatt, "Independents, Packaging, and Inflationary Pressure in 1980s Hollywood," in Prince, *New Pot of Gold,* pp. 142–59.

64. Wyatt, "Independents, Packaging, and Inflationary Pressure," pp. 159–64.

65. Ibid., p. 161.

66. Schatz, "The New Hollywood," pp. 26–29.

67. Mike Snider, "More Video Games Leap to Film," *USA Today,* April 26, 2006.

68. Hillier, *The New Hollywood,* pp. 32–33.

69. For a more detailed examination of the stylistic pluralism initiated by *Batman,* see K. J. Donnelly, "The Classical Film Score Forever? *Batman, Batman Returns,* and the Post-Classical Film Score," in Neale and Smith, eds., *Contemporary Hollywood Cinema,* pp. 142–55. Donnelly also discusses "collage-like" anticipations of this model in his article *"Performance* and the Composite Film Score," in *Film Music: Critical Approaches,* ed. K. J. Donnelly (New York: Continuum Publishing, 2001), pp. 152–66.

70. Wyatt, *High Concept,* pp. 49–52.

71. The reverse also happened with some success, with orchestral film composers being given the opportunity to write pop theme songs for films they were scoring, including James Horner ("My Heart Will Go On," *Titanic,* 1997) and Howard Shore ("Into the West," *The Lord of the Rings: The Return of the King,* 2003).

72. For more on Tarantino's musical auteurism, see Ken Gardner, "Would You Like to Hear Some Music?" Music In-and-Out-of-Control in the Films of Quentin Tarantino," in Donnelly, ed., *Film Music: Critical Approaches,* pp. 188–205; and Ronald Rodman, "The Popular Song as Leitmotif in 1990s Films," in *Changing Tunes: The Use of Pre-Existing Music in Film,* ed. Phil Powrie and Robynn Stilwell (Burlington, Vt.: Ashgate, 2006), pp. 119–36. Another discussion that foregrounds the use of pop compilation soundtracks in contemporary film, especially soundtracks designed by auteur-directors like the Coen Brothers and Paul Thomas Anderson, is Jeff Smith, "Popular Songs and Comic Allusions in Contemporary Cinema," in *Soundtrack Available: Essays on Film and Popular Music,* ed. Pamela Robertson Wojcik and Arthur Knight (Durham, N.C.: Duke University Press, 2001), pp. 407–30. The problem of allusion and re-appropriation of songs in film is the general theme of *Pop Fiction: The Song in Cinema,* ed. Steve Lannin and Matthew Caley (Bristol, Eng.: Intellect Books, 2005). The essays in this book consider songs in films such as *O Brother, Where Art Thou?* (2000), *The Deer Hunter* (1978), *Ghost* (1990), *Trainspotting* (1996), *Reservoir Dogs* (1992), *Risky Business* (1983), and *Grosse Pointe Blank* (1997). The appropriation of song texts for narrative commentary is also the subject of Ian Garwood's essay "Must You Remember This? Orchestrating the 'Standard' Pop Song in *Sleepless in Seattle,*" in Dickinson, ed., *Movie Music: The Film Reader,* pp. 109–18.

73. Part of what defines a director as an auteur, scholars observe, is the essential role that music plays in the construction of their distinctively personal filmmaking styles. See Claudia Gorbman, "Auteur Music," in *Beyond the Soundtrack: Representing Music in Cinema,* ed. Daniel Goldmark, Lawrence Kramer, and Richard Leppert (Berkeley: University of California Press, 2007), pp. 149–62.

74. See Martin Scorsese, "Without Music I Would Be Lost," *Cahiers du cinéma / Numéro spécial musique* (1995).

75. Several authors have started to address the issue of stylistic eclecticism in recent auteur soundtracks. See Claudia Gorbman, "Eyes Wide Open: Kubrick's Music," in Powrie and Stilwell, eds., *Changing Tunes,* pp. 3–18; Julie Hubbert, "Bach and the Rolling Stones: Scorsese and the Postmodern Soundtrack in *Casino,*" in *Tonspuren: Musik und Film, Musik im Film, Studien zur Wertungsforschung,* ed. A. Dorschel (Vienna: Universal Edition, 2005), pp. 43–69; and Ken Gardner, "I've Heard That Song Before: Woody Allen's Films as Studies in Popular Musical Form," in *Musicals: Hollywood and Beyond,* ed. Bill Marshall and Robynn Stilwell (Portland, Oreg.: Intellect Books, 2000), pp. 14–22. See also Pauline Reay, *Music in Film: Soundtracks and Synergy* (New York: Wallflower Press, 2004), pp. 49–55.

76. Mark Wolf, "Introduction," *Medium of the Video Game,* p. 3.

77. Anahid Kassabian, "The Sound of a New Form," in *Popular Music in Film,* ed. Ian Inglis (New York: Wallflower Press, 2003), pp. 91–95.

78. Ibid., 95–101. Kassabian finds these highly iterative structures particularly in the action sequences in films like *The Cell, The Matrix,* and *Lara Croft: Tomb Raider.* Her description of the structure of these scores echoes Bridgett's description of the microstructures essential to interactive game music.

45

Selling a Hit Soundtrack

Susan Peterson

(1979)

Commercially viable music. Timing. Film company cooperation on advance planning and tie-ins. Music that's integral to the movie. A hit movie. A hit single. A big-name recording star. A big-name composer. These are a few of our favorite things, sing the marketing people at record companies, when it comes to selling a soundtrack.

RSO president Al Coury feels timing is of the "utmost importance" and he should know whereof he speaks. Under his guidance in 1977–78, RSO notched up the two biggest selling albums in the history of the music business, both soundtracks, both still on the charts as 1979 draws near to a close (*Saturday Night Fever* and *Grease* in case anyone has forgotten). These were followed almost immediately by one of the industry's most publicized flops—the infamous *Sgt. Pepper*. Almost all of the initial ingredients were there for all three—in fact *Pepper* seemed to have it all in spades (Lennon/McCartney music, the Bee Gees, Peter Frampton, an extravagant cross-merchandising campaign) with the also-fatal inception of "hit movie." But keep in mind, *Saturday Night Fever* and *Grease* were already hit records before the movies ever opened. Enter timing.

Recalls Coury, "With *Fever* and *Grease,* the timing of the release of the albums (five to six weeks before the film), the timing of the release of the singles (before, during, and after the album's release) were what we laid out, what proved to be a successful formula. But when we got into the situation with *Pepper,* we did not have the luxury of that kind of planning, because everything was pushed up to an early date. The film was originally scheduled to come out Christmas of 1978, but Universal wanted the film out in the summertime, so the production schedule was really rushed. We got the album out four or five days before the picture came out, so consequently we did not have a chance to use the music of *Sgt. Pepper* to pre-sell the motion picture.

"In looking back, when we released the album, we had absolutely unbelievable acceptance on radio. Every major station from coast to coast put the album on immediately and played almost the entire album, the minute they got their hands on it. Then a few days later, the picture came out and got terrible reviews, and immediately radio backed off. If we had done it the way we had before, giving the record an eight to 10 week lead, we would have had a much greater chance to saturate the marketplace, and it would have guaranteed a greater opening for the motion picture.

"Of course," Coury adds, "it couldn't guarantee the picture would be a great success over a long period of time, but a healthier opening. Now it could very well be that if we did everything right, it still would have wound up being a disaster. I can't say that. All I can tell you is that the timing is of the utmost importance."

Meatballs, containing the danceable David Naughton hit "Making It" and Mary MacGregor's "Good Friend," is currently doing well for the label, benefiting also from a lot of advance planning with the movie side, and some imaginative promotional tie-ins. Meatball eating contests have been held at seven Los Angeles Tower Records branches with an "eat off" taking place at the famed Sunset Blvd. branch.

According to label sales manager Mitch Huffman, "Similar contests are taking place across the country. We also cross-merchandised with the motion picture, offering a discount on the album, with a movie stub, and vice versa. We watch the box office and at the same time try to gauge if we are getting the reaction at the box office into the stores. If we see that happening in several markets, we will pursue it."

Coming attractions from RSO include a rock-oriented soundtrack for *Times Square,* a salsa-flavored package for *Angel,* and probably the brightest prospect, *Star Wars* follow-up *The Empire Strikes Back. Empire,* due out on record by March of 1980 and on film in April or May, is already being mapped out to benefit from "a lot of advance time, a lot of pre-sell time, a lot of time to work on the music, with the people who are making the motion picture (George Lucas, with John Williams on the music side)," states Coury.

At Columbia, a label that was synonymous with soundtracks way back when fever was still something to be treated with aspirin, Top 40 airplay is the first key that comes to mind for sales vice president Joe Mansfield. Putting that idea to work with the current *Americathon* campaign, Mansfield states, "We're putting together a Top 40 campaign for radio. If there's nothing Top 40 to play, you are not going to sell any records, so you don't spend any money, except trade announcements to let them know the soundtrack is available on this label.

"On *Main Event* we were lucky with a top record from Barbra Streisand. *Americathon* will probably be one of our biggest, with the single from Eddie Money, then cuts from the Beach Boys, Elvis Costello, Nick Lowe, Tom Scott."

Then with *Manhattan* there is George Gershwin. Not exactly a familiar name in the top 40 these days, but obviously still a magic one. This soundtrack's success was apparently a pleasant surprise for Columbia.

Says Mansfield, "New York was a focal point because of the setting, but to some degree, it was a passive campaign. The record is not getting airplay, though. It's crazy. Word of mouth is selling it. We've done some print and radio advertising, but it got up to 50,000 (now over 100,000) real quick."

Columbia also tries for lots of lead planning time with the film company, and looking ahead, will make use of it for the *Star Trek* release, slated for December. "We've already had three or four meetings with the Paramount Pictures people on that. The more lead time you plan together and cross-promote each other, the better off you'll be." Obviously delighted to have landed the Jerry Goldsmith–penned music, Mansfield says, "Every company bid on this one, and we ended up with it." Already a publicist's dream, the premiere in Washington D.C. in December is to be co-sponsored by no less than NASA.

The biggest soundtrack so far in 1979 has been MCA's top 10 *The Kids Are Alright,* and although MCA is certainly no stranger to hit soundtracks, marketing director Sam Passamano Jr. describes this Who package as "a marketer's fantasy."

The reason for his enthusiasm is the double LP's "double-pronged package, marketable both as a movie soundtrack and as a greatest hits package—and on top of that, the Who's first greatest hits package."

The dual impact had definite advantages—where the movie hadn't opened yet, MCA went the greatest hits route in its marketing strategy. Additionally, Passamano notes, "During the Christmas season, we will market it everywhere again as a greatest hits package, so it will continue to enjoy a sales bonus."

Another biggie for the Universal sister company is "More American Graffiti," which features hits from the sixties. It also enjoys a double whammy impact, both as soundtrack and nostalgia/greatest hits package. Comments Passamano, "In a soundtrack like 'More,' where the songs were chosen because of their sequencing in the movie, the soundtrack in the first place was marketed to enhance the success of the movie, not just as nostalgia, since filmgoers were predicted to be a younger audience for whom the music would not be nostalgia. We tied in very heavily with the Universal people in going after that younger audience." And again, the 24-year-old and up group can be hit now and at Christmas through the nostalgia appeal.

Passamano agrees that Top 40 airplay is desirable, but not always possible. In lieu of that route, he suggests, "You have to follow the openings at the theatres, work with tie-ins. With *More* we had tie-ins with retail stores and fast food chains, contests for beach towels, books, tickets to the movie. This was all done to enhance the initial success of the movie, since if the movie hits big, chances are better for the soundtrack." The budget for this massive campaign, carried out in 35 markets, was amortized through pooling with the book and film companies.

Overall Passamano feels, "The most important thing in marketing soundtracks is to take them individually, look at the potential audience both for the movie and the music, and deal with it that way."

Coming up from MCA is music from *Yanks* a 1940s period piece, a single, "Love Rhapsody," from *Concord: Airport '79*; and the next big campaign, Loretta Lynn's autobiographical *Coal Miner's Daughter,* due for 1980 release.

Another veteran in the soundtrack field, Warner Bros., naturally works closely with Warner's film company on many projects, and certainly not all have been as natural a candidate for chart success as last year's *Last Waltz.*

They've discovered a lot of trouble areas for the non-commercially oriented film music, as product manager Nina Franklin explains. "Often, the soundtrack is the last thing that I put together for a film. To maximize the impact of a soundtrack, you want to have it available at the same time the film opens. Often we can't do that because we don't get the materials quickly enough. So we'll have a film that opens in December and an album that comes out in the middle of January. Even three weeks later, the impact is gone."

On a major project such as the recent *Superman* extravaganza, however, it was a well-orchestrated and timed campaign. Franklin recalls, "Warner Communications coordinated a massive cross-marketing event with all of its subsidiaries, the book company, records, film, television, doll and novelty items manufacturer, even DC Comics. We spent a lot of money, and I'm not sure you could say how successful that expenditure was." She estimates that at approximately 380,000 units sold to date, the expense averaged at about $1 per unit. So how could the best-laid plan go astray?

"There were really two mitigating factors," Franklin believes. "The music wasn't an integral part of the story, and really, the movie didn't do as well as expected."

Coming up for Warners is the soundtrack from Monty Python's *Life of Brian*, a package that contains only two musical cuts and a lot of the British comedy team's bizarre humor. Product manager Barry Gross says, "We are going to follow the film in every market that it opens, supporting through the various WEA branches." As for any unusual merchandising approaches, Gross offers, "the film itself. Basically there is an active cult of Monty Python fanatics out there and this, they feel, will transcend that, because there is a great deal of American humor in the film. Of course we're not going out as if it's a *Saturday Night Fever*. We have a very special type of product here, appealing initially to a very special audience."

Over at Motown, along with RSO and Casablanca, a recent entry into the record-company-forms-its-own-film-company sweepstakes, sales vice president Mike Lushka feels soundtrack success has "a lot to do with the music itself, if it's going to be commercially acceptable. There's a lot of good movies out there whose soundtracks don't sell. The exceptional ones are the ones on the charts right now. If the movie end goes in and gets a good viable producer who is tied into what's happening in today's music, and you have a marriage of those two, you'll have a viable soundtrack.

"Then add to that a major artist that can sing a title song. If you tie it all in together, you'll have a hit soundtrack and also help the movie."

A good example of the above is Motown's biggest soundtrack to date, *Lady Sings the Blues,* that tied Diana Ross, the music and story of Billie Holiday, into a major success. Lushka recalls, "That was one of the first ones that was really advertised on television in conjunction with a movie."

Currently Motown has had *Fastbreak* as a major promotion. With its basketball theme, Lushka reports, "We even tied it in with the NBA. We advertised in the NBA book and got the album played during NBA games. We also had contest tie-ups with radio stations where we had one night that the winners would go to an NBA game. There would be a dribbling contest, to win prizes. We also did a lot of cute little things, had sweatshirts made up and our displays featured backboards with little baskets and little balls to throw through them. We worked very closely with the movie side, went national right away, and it worked very well."

Music and movies go together like the proverbial horse and carriage. It's a familiar refrain that is being sung in unison by virtually every major record company as each gears up to spread a little "fever" for its soundtracks.

From *Billboard,* October 6, 1979, pp. ST-6 and ST-12.

46

Interview with John Williams

Craig L. Byrd

(1997)

How did the Star Wars project first come to your attention? How did you become involved?

My involvement with *Star Wars* began actually with Steven Spielberg, who was, in the '70s when these films were made, and still is, a very close friend of George Lucas's. I had done two or three scores for Steven Spielberg before I met George Lucas, *Jaws* being the principal one among them. I think it was that George Lucas, when he was making *Star Wars,* asked his friend Steven Spielberg who should write the music, where will he find a composer? The best knowledge I have is that Steven recommended me to George Lucas as a composer for the film, and I met him under those circumstances, and that's how it all began.

How did you feel when you were first contacted about this project? Was it about one film at the time, or all three?

The first contact had to do only with *Star Wars.* I didn't realize that there would be a sequel and then a sequel after that at that time. I imagine George Lucas planned it that way and perhaps even mentioned it to me at the time, but I don't remember. I was thinking of it as a singular opportunity and a singular assignment.

What was your reaction when you read the script?

I didn't read the script. I don't like to read scripts. When I'm talking about this I always make the analogy that if one reads a book, a novel, and then you see someone else's realization of it, there's always a slight sense of disappointment because we've cast it in our minds, and created the scenery and all the ambiance in our mind's imagination. There's always a slight moment of disappointment when we've read a script and then we see the film realized. Having said that I don't even remember if George Lucas offered me a script to read.

I remember seeing the film and reacting to its atmospheres and energies and rhythms. That for me is always the best way to pick up a film—from the visual image itself and without any preconceptions that might have been put there by the script.

When you first saw an assemblage of footage, what were you looking at and how did that inspire your work?

Well, along with others involved with the film I was surprised at what a great success it was. I think we all expected a successful film. In my mind I was thinking of it as a kind of Saturday afternoon movie for kids really, a kind of popcorn, Buck Rogers show. A good, you know, sound and light show for young people, thinking that it would be successful, but never imagining that it would be this world-wide international success, and never imagining and even expecting that the sequels would (a) be along and (b) be as successful as they all were.

I can only speculate about it along with others. I remember Joseph Campbell, the great mythologist and teacher and author, who was a friend of George Lucas's and who went to Skywalker Ranch and talked to George Lucas about the films. He began to write about the mythology, or pseudo-mythology if you like, that formed the basis of these films. I learned more from Joseph Campbell about the film, after the fact, than I did while I was working on it or watching it as a viewer.

Having said all that, I think the partial answer to your question is the success of this film must be due to some cross-cultural connection with the mythic aspects of the film that Campbell described to us later. The fact that the Darth Vader figure may be present in every culture, with a different name perhaps, but with a similar myth attached to it. The films surprised everyone I think— George Lucas included—in that they reached across cultural bounds and beyond language into some kind of mythic, shared remembered past—from the deep past of our collective unconscious, if you like. That may be an explanation as to why it has such a broad appeal and such a strong one.

You would also have to assume that the hero's journey then would be a part of that.

That's right. All of these aspects of journey and heroic life and aspiration and disappointment, all of the great human subjects that this seems to touch and tap in on, must be one of the reasons for its great success. I suppose for me as a composer for the film, these forces that I'm struggling to put my finger on must have been at work subconsciously. The music for the film is very non-futuristic. The films themselves showed us characters we hadn't seen before and planets unimagined and so on, but the music was—this is actually George Lucas's conception and a very good one—emotionally familiar. It was not music that might describe terra incognita but the opposite of that, music that would put us in touch with very familiar and remembered emotions, which for me as a musician translated into the use of a 19th century operatic idiom, if you like, Wagner and this sort of thing. These sorts of influences would put us in touch with remembered theatrical experiences as well—all western experiences to be sure. We were talking about cross-cultural mythology a moment ago; the music at least I think is firmly rooted in western cultural sensibilities.

It's interesting that you brought up opera and Wagner. On a certain level it seems like the three scores are almost your "Ring Cycle." How did it become so interwoven when you originally were only scoring one film?

I think if the score has an architectural unity, it's the result of a happy accident. I approached each film as a separate entity. The first one completely out of the blue, but the second one of course connected to the first one; we referred back to characters and extended them and referred back to themes and extended and developed those. I suppose it was a natural but unconscious metamorphosis of musical themes that created something that may seem to have more architectural and conscious interrelatedness than I actually intended to put there. If it's there, to the degree that it is there, it's a kind of happy accident if you like.

That may be sound deprecating—I don't mean it quite that way—but the functional aspect and the craft aspect of doing the job of these three films has to be credited with producing a lot of this unity in the musical content the listeners perceive.

The album itself was in the top 20 on Billboard's charts. That was relatively unheard of for a non-pop score. How did you respond to that?

I don't think we ever had in the history of the record industry or a film business something that was so non-pop, with a small "p," reach an audience that size. I have to credit the film for a lot of this. If I had written the music without the film probably nobody ever would have heard of the music; it was the combination of things and the elusive, weird, unpredictable aspect of timing that none of us can quite get our hands around. If we could predict this kind of phenomenon or produce it consciously out of a group effort we would do it every year and we'd all be caliphs surrounded [laughs] with fountains of riches.

But it doesn't work that way, it's a much more elusive thing than that. Any composer who begins to write a piece would think, "This will be a successful piece." But you can't and we don't pull them out of the air that way. It also reminds us that as artists we don't work in a vacuum. We write our material, compose it or film it or whatever, but we're not alone in the vacuum, the audience is also out there and it's going to hit them. With all the aspects of happenstance and fad, and the issue of skirt length for example, which is to say style and fad, and what is à la mode? When all of these things come together and create a phenomenon like this, we then, as we're doing now, look back on it say, "Why did it happen?" It's as fascinating and inexplicable to me as to any viewer.

It's also got to be intensely gratifying.

It's enormously gratifying and it makes me feel very lucky. I'm not a particularly religious person, but there's something sort of eerie, about the way our hands are occasionally guided in some of the things that we do. It can happen in any aspect, any phase of human endeavor where we come to the right solutions almost in spite of ourselves. And you look back and you say that that almost seems to have a kind of—you want to use the word divine guidance—behind it. It can make you believe in miracles in any collaborative art form: the theatre, film, any of this, when all these aspects come together to form a humming engine that works and the audience is there for it and they're ready for it and willing to embrace it. That is a kind of miracle also.

It also changed the shape of film music. A lot of filmmakers had really abandoned the idea of big full orchestral scores.

Well, I don't know if it's fair to say the *Star Wars* films brought back symphonic scores per se. We've been using symphony orchestras since even before sound. Anyone interested in film knows that music seems to be an indispensable ingredient for filmmakers. I'm not exactly sure why. We could talk about that for days, but mood, motivation, rhythm, tempo, atmosphere, all these things, characterization and so on—just the practical aspect of sounds between dialogue that need filling up. Symphony orchestras were enormously handy for this because they're elegant and the symphony orchestra itself is one of the greatest inventions of our artistic culture. Fabulous sounds it can produce and a great range of emotional capabilities.

I think if the use of symphony orchestras went out of fad in the '50s and '60s for some reason it was just that: it was out of fad. Someone would have brought it back. It's too useful and too successful not to have it back. I think after the success of *Star Wars* the orchestras enjoyed a very successful period because of that—wonderful, all to the good. I don't think we can claim that it was a renaissance really, more than just a change of fad if you'd like.

Or a little goose if nothing else.

Right. A little helping push.

All three scores were recorded with the London Symphony Orchestra. Was there a particular reason why that orchestra was chosen?

We decided to record the music for the films in London. I say we, I think George Lucas decided that. He shot some of the film in Africa and England and did some of his post-production work there. It was part of the plan that we would record there and that was fine with me. I had done *Fiddler on the Roof* and some other large-scale productions in England and I knew the orchestras very well and liked them; I was very comfortable recording there.

We were going to use a freelance orchestra, as I had done with Fiddler and other films. I remember having a conversation with the late Lionel Newman, who was then the music director of the 20th Century Fox studios, and we were talking about the practical plans of when to record and where and so on, booking facility stages and the rest of it. He suggested to me, "Why don't we just use the London Symphony Orchestra for this recording? We won't have to be troubled with hiring freelance players, we'll just make one contractual arrangement with the London Symphony."

It also happened at that time that our friend from Hollywood, Andre Previn, was then the music director of the London Symphony. I rang him up and said, "How would it be if we borrowed your orchestra for this recording?" Andre was very positive and very excited—he had no idea what *Star Wars* was going to be about or what the music would be like, but just the idea that the orchestra would have that exposure seemed to be a good plan for him. So, it was a combination of a lot of nice things. I had worked in England for years and knew the orchestras well; I knew the London Symphony well. They had played a symphony of mine under Previn's direction a few years before, and played other music of mine in concerts and so on. It was a coming together of a lot of familiar forces in a nice way and I had a good time.

At the risk of sounding like someone from Entertainment Tonight, it sounds like the Force was with everyone involved.

[laughs] The Force did seem to be with us, yes.

How do you see the score changing from one film to another, through the three films?

The scores do seem unified to me, now that I look back on the four, five or six years involved in making the films, with the distance of time making it seem to be one short period now in my mind. The scores all seem to be one slightly longer score than the usual film score. If that contradicts what I said earlier about writing one at a time, I hear that contradiction, but given the distance of time now I can see that it's one effort really. The scores are all one thing and a theme that appeared in film two that wasn't in film one was probably a very close intervallic, which is say note-by-note-by-note, relative to a theme that we'd had.

I mean we would have the Princess Leia theme as the romantic theme in the first film, but then we'd have Yoda's music, which was unexpectedly romantic, if you like, in the second film, but not such a distant relative, musically speaking, intervalically/melodically speaking, to Princess Leia's music. So you can marry one theme right after the other. They're different, but they also marry up very well and you can interplay them in a contrapuntal way, and it will be part of a texture that is familial.

I'd like to touch on some of the characters' themes. A lot of people remember the Darth Vader theme. What was the idea behind Darth Vader and how do you see his theme?

Darth Vader's theme seemed to me to need to have, like all of the themes if possible, strong melodic identification, so that when you heard it or part of the theme you would associate it with the character. The melodic elements needed to have a strong imprint.

In the case of Darth Vader, brass suggests itself because of his military bearing and his authority and his ominous look. That would translate into a strong melody that's military, that grabs you right away, that is, probably simplistically, in a minor mode because he's threatening. You combine these thoughts into this kind of a military, ceremonial march, and we've got something that perhaps will answer the requirement here.

And then also the hero, Luke Skywalker. What about his theme?

Flourishes and upward reaching; idealistic and heroic, in a very different way than Darth Vader of course, and a very different tonality—a very uplifted kind of heraldic quality. Larger than he is. His idealism is more the subject than the character itself, I would say.

And Han Solo?

I would make similar comments there about Solo's music. Although they overlap a lot; I mean it's one thing really in my mind, a lot of it. And of course the Luke Skywalker music has several themes within it also. You'd be testing my memory to ask me how I used them all and where. [laughs]

At the Star Wars Special Edition screening in December, when the main theme came on, the audience responded. What were you looking for in the main theme?

The opening of the film was visually so stunning, with that lettering that comes out and the spaceships and so on, that it was clear that the music had to kind of smack you right in the eye and do something very strong. It's in my mind a very simple, very direct tune that jumps an octave in a very dramatic way, and has a triplet placed in it that has a kind of grab.

I tried to construct something that again would have this idealistic, uplifting but military flare to it. And set it in brass instruments, which I love anyway, which I used to play as a student, as a youngster. And try to get it so it's set in the most brilliant register of the trumpets, horns and trombones so that we'd have a blazingly brilliant fanfare at the opening of the piece. And contrast that with the second theme that was lyrical and romantic and adventurous also. And give it all a kind of ceremonial . . . it's not a march but very nearly that. So you almost kind of want to [laughs] patch your feet to it or stand up and salute when you hear it—I mean there's a little bit of that ceremonial aspect. More than a little I think.

The response of the audience that you ask about is something that I certainly can't explain. I wish I could explain that. But maybe the combination of the audio and the visual hitting people in the way that it does must speak to some collective memory—we talked about that before—that we don't quite understand. Some memory of Buck Rogers or King Arthur or something earlier in the cultural salts of our brains, memories of lives lived in the past, I don't know. But it has that kind of resonance—it resonates within us in some past hero's life that we've all lived.

Now we're into a kind of Hindu idea, but I think somehow that's what happens musically. That's what in performance one tries to get with orchestras, and we talk about that at orchestral rehearsals: that it isn't only the notes, it's this reaching back into the past. As creatures we don't know if we have a future, but we certainly share a great past. We remember it, in language and in pre-language, and that's where music lives—it's to this area in our souls that it can speak. . . .

Are there any scenes that stand out for you?

Well I have stand-outs in my mind because of the music that we play in concerts more recently: the asteroid field I remember from, I think it was the second film. It had a musical piece that was like a ballet of flying spaceships and asteroids colliding. That was a very effective and successful scene in my mind both musically and visually.

I remember the finale of the first film, which had that stately procession, where I made a sort of processional out of the middle theme of the main title music—for the beginning, I took the second theme of that and made a kind of imperial procession. And that was a very rewarding musical scene also. So many things, but I would say those two just right off the top of my head.

A lot of people have said that their favorite scene is the cantina scene in the first film. And they often speak of the music.

The cantina music is an anomaly, it sticks out entirely as an unrelated rib to the score. There's a nice little story if you haven't heard this, I'll tell you briefly: When I looked at that scene there wasn't any music in it and these little creatures were jumping up and down playing instruments and I didn't have any idea what the sound should be. It could have been anything: electronic music, futuristic music, tribal music, whatever you like.

And I said to George, "What do you think we should do?" And George said, "I don't know" and sort of scratched his head. He said, "Well I have an idea. What if these little creatures on this planet way out someplace, came upon a rock and they lifted up the rock and underneath was sheet music from Benny Goodman's great swing band of the 1930s on planet Earth? And they looked at this music and they kind of deciphered it, but they didn't know quite how it should go, but they tried. And, uh, why don't you try doing that? What would these space creatures, what would their imitation of Benny Goodman sound like?"

So, I kind of giggled and I went to the piano and began writing the silliest little series of old-time swing band licks, kind of a little off and a little wrong and not quite matching. We recorded that and everyone seemed to love it. We didn't have electronic instruments exactly in that period very much. They're all little Trinidad steel drums and out-of-tuned kazoos and little reed instruments, you know. It was all done acoustically—it wasn't an electronic preparation as it probably would have been done today.

I think that may be also part of its success, because being acoustic it meant people had to blow the notes and make all the sounds, a little out of tune and a little behind there, a little ahead there: it had all the foibles of a not-very-good human performance.

In the Special Editions there's some added footage. Did that require any rescoring?

George has changed the lengths in some of these films for the reissue because of his improved animatics and so on. It required some changes in the music, mostly additions and subtractions of a small sort. This was all attended to by Ken Wannberg who was originally a music editor and still is today.

The only thing I had to re-record was a short finale for *Return of the Jedi*, the very end of the film where George created a new scene of Ewoks celebrating. He had some ideas for new music and gave me a film without any sound but with a tempo, with Ewoks dancing and reacting and reveling in their success. You and

I are now talking in January 1997; just a few weeks ago, the end of '96, I went over to London and recorded that music for the new finale. And as a matter of fact this very day that we're talking, George is dubbing that new music into the final reel of the reissue.

From *Film Score Monthly* 2, no. 1 (January/February 1997): 18–22.

47

Scoring with Synthesizers

Terry Atkinson

(1982)

What goes *eek, squonk, oing-boing,* and *waaah-oooom,* and has won two Academy Awards in the last four years? Clue: It's neither Jamie Lee Curtis nor R2D2—though the second is closer.

Give up? The answer is synthesizer movie scores, and the Oscar winners for best score were last year's *Chariots of Fire* by Vangelis and 1978's *Midnight Express* by Giorgio Moroder. In both, the music was provided not by an orchestra, but by an electronic instrument long used by rock bands. Electronic scores are still relatively rare. But some critics, weary of classical and jazz-oriented scores, welcome them and predict that by the end of the decade, synthesizers will provide the music for most movies. Others, instead, regard the music as a fad, likely to exhaust its potential—and moviegoers' ears—well before decade's end.

The synthesizer debate is succinctly summarized in Jerzy Kosinski's latest novel, *Pinball.* Rock star Jimmy Osten defends the synthesizer, writes Kosinski, "as being not just another specialized musical instrument, but a creative multiuse musical erector set, and he quoted Stravinsky, who had once said the most nearly perfect musical machine was a Stradivarius or an electronic synthesizer. Osten then speculated that the instrument would be a boon to composers and performers; at the merest touch of a button, they could hear full arrangements, as well as endless variations on a single theme; they could compress or extend a phrase, slow it down or speed it up. All this seemed to him an invaluable enrichment of the musical tradition—as well as a means of transcending it."

But Osten's girl friend, a classical pianist, disagrees. "For all its presets, custom voice ensembles, special effects, and computerized rhythm and sequence programmers," she says, "a synthesizer is nothing but a hybrid of a jukebox and a pinball machine."

Actually, the synthesizer is a bit more complicated than that. Essentially, it's a musical computer—played both with a keyboard that allows a pianolike performance and with a series of knobs and buttons that permit all sorts of variation in pitch, tone, and decay. It suggests electricity turned into music. The synthesizer can imitate a large number of other instruments—and still add its own distinct personality. But it can also make sounds all its own. In particular: pulsating beats that seem to echo the human heart; low, buzzing sounds that for bone-shaking vibrations beat conventional instruments like the bass viola; and high, screechy tones rivaled only by the upper registers of violins. Some of the synthesizer's effects can be duplicated by the electric guitar and other instruments, but none has the same range or flexibility.

In a master's hands, a synthesizer can produce memorable film scores, like those for *Sorcerer* and *Thief* by the German band Tangerine Dream and for *Midnight Express, American Gigolo, Foxes,* and *Cat People* by Giorgio Moroder. But the highest kudos have gone to the "synth track" of *Chariots of Fire,* an unlikely candidate for an electronic score.

"Vangelis hit it dead center with *Chariots,*" says *Newsweek* critic Jack Kroll. "It wasn't period but it worked. There was a universality to the score—and it starts right away. That first shot when they're running on the beach—the music tells you what's going on. There's a deep, subliminal suggestiveness." Kroll is also high on Moroder's *Cat People* score. "Essentially, *Chariots* had a fairly conventional score, mostly a pretty typical keyboard sound. What Moroder does with a synthesizer is very different and much more interesting. The score for *Cat People* shows what the synthesizer can do that other procedures cannot so easily do. There's a suggestion that you're listening in on the vital processes of other organisms—of other places, other worlds."

The synthesizer sound has "turned out to be a terrific thing," declares Los Angeles pop music critic Robert Hilburn. "*Midnight Express* really displayed its potential. In *Thief* the music was so strong that it was hard for the director to keep pace with the dynamics of the score in a couple of scenes. In *American Gigolo* the sensual, decadent quality was especially well conveyed by Moroder's music." To Hilburn, a synthesizer score can heighten the drama. "The synthesizer is usually used to build tension—with, of course, the big exception being *Chariots of Fire.* The synthesizer is starker, punchier, and fresher than conventional instruments right now. It pulls you into the scene like nothing else."

But Hilburn and others worry that moviegoers may be in for a surfeit of synthesizer sounds. "It's going to be tempting," says Hilburn, "to use a synthesizer every time someone does a dramatic film." But, he adds, "you can't keep putting the same synthesizer sound behind every nerve-racking scene. Besides, even Moroder may run out of ideas."

New York Times critic Janet Maslin observes, "Already you can hear synthesizer effects too much in horror movies, where they capitalize on those sounds and repeat them over and over without developing them. That nervous-pulse synthesizer sound is just numbing after a while." And to Maslin, the synthesizer sound has built-in limitations. "The synthesizer can certainly add an ominous quality that is hard to create any other way. But when it's used in a more general way, as in *Chariots of Fire*, it's a little cold, a little impersonal."

Kroll, too, has reservations. "It's surprising that it took as long as it did for there to be synthesizer scores," he says, "but we may get sick of them." The critics aren't alone. Even synthesizer-sympathetic filmmakers worry about overuse. "There's a very great danger," says David Puttnam, who produced *Chariots* and coproduced *Midnight Express*. "It would be very sad if that happened." Nevertheless, more and more producers are using synthesizer scores, and some are turning, naturally, to the rock music world. *Death Wish II*, for example, was scored by Jimmy Page of Led Zeppelin, who employed a good deal of both electric guitar and synthesizer; *Nighthawks* by Keith Emerson, who, as keyboardist for Emerson, Lake & Palmer, pioneered the use of the synthesizer in live rock shows; and *The Long Good Friday* by Francis Monkman, keyboardist and composer for the early seventies British band Curved Air.

Before Robert Moog developed his Moog synthesizer in 1964, various electronic noise machines existed, but none with such sophisticated capabilities. The Moog's powers were first fully demonstrated in *Switched-On Bach*, the Walter (later Wendy) Carlos album issued in 1968 that became the biggest classical-music seller of all time. Carlos's classical rearrangements for synth played a memorable role in Kubrick's *A Clockwork Orange* (1971). And rock scores for synth go back at least to 1970, when Pink Floyd songs were heard in Antonioni's *Zabriskie Point*.

The synth sound increased in the seventies—both for rock bands and for movies. It's heard, in varying degrees, in *The Exorcist* (where William Friedkin used portions of Mike Oldfield's *Tubular Bells* album), *Tommy, Lisztomania* (with multikeyboard interpretations of Liszt by Yes's Rick Wakeman), *Quadrophenia, Stardust, The Secret Life of Plants* (a little-seen Stevie Wonder–scored work), *White Rock* (a 1976 documentary that was "the official film of the XII Winter Olympics"—Wakeman again), and disco-scored movies like *Saturday Night Fever, Thank God It's Friday,* and *Looking for Mr. Goodbar*.

However, it was with *Midnight Express* that the synthesizer came into its own. Moroder, as it happened, was not producer Puttnam's first choice. He wanted the

English rock band Electric Light Orchestra, but negotiations broke down. "Then we heard some things that Vangelis had done," Puttnam recalls. "We collected all his albums together and actually cut the film to existing Vangelis material"—but contractual problems arose. Puttnam and director Alan Parker, stuck for a score, turned for help to Neil Bogart, then head of Casablanca Records. Bogart, who had brought Euro-disco to American prominence by signing Donna Summer, recommended Moroder, the producer of Summer's synthesizer-backed hit "I Feel Love."

"Alan went to Munich to meet with Giorgio," continues Puttnam, "and played him the last cut of the film with the Vangelis material on it. Giorgio developed his own score in about a month. He called when he had the main theme done. None of us could make it to Munich just then, so we listened to it over the phone. Later Alan and the editor went to Munich and worked with Giorgio for about a week, and that was it." It was the first rock-oriented score to ever win an Academy Award for Best Original Score.

However, Puttnam adds, "I'm not trying to diminish the unquestionable quality of Giorgio's score, but I'm quite convinced that we won the Academy Award because there was absolute hysteria the year before when *Saturday Night Fever* didn't even get nominated for its score. Too many questions were asked of the Academy's attitude toward modern music. So, to an extent, Giorgio had the Bee Gees to thank for that."

Born in northern Italy, Giorgio Moroder got into music as a bass player. By the late sixties, he had settled in Munich, producing records with his partner, lyricist Pete Bellotte. Influenced by all the synthesizer pioneers around him—Kraftwerk, Tangerine Dream, Popol Vuh—Moroder eventually started putting the pulsations of the instrument behind the voice of young disco singer Donna Summer. Then came the worldwide success of *Midnight Express,* followed by a couple of solo albums—and more film work: a song-oriented score for Puttnam's *Foxes* (including the Donna Summer hit "On the Radio"), as well as the scores for *American Gigolo* (Blondie's hit "Call Me" was the basis for the sound track) and *Cat People.*

Recalling *Gigolo,* director Paul Schrader says, "The idea of that film was to have the visual style of Milan and the musical sensibility of Munich. Even though it was set in Southern California, I wanted it to have the look and feel of northern Italy and a brutal, metallic sound. In terms of people coming out of Germany at that time, Giorgio was the most commercially oriented, unlike Kraftwerk and others. He works very quickly and he's very easy to work with."

These days Moroder, who is thirty-six, is far from both northern Italy and Munich, but the synthesizer still occupies his life. Looking sleek and tan in aviator-frame glasses and white tennis shirt and shorts, Moroder sits on a white sofa in his white-walled house overlooking Los Angeles and announces that he, too, is skeptical about the electronic instrument that brought him fame. In fact, a couple of years ago, he says, he was determined to avoid synthesizers on his next film score and compose for a conventional orchestra. But that next film—*Cat People*—simply growled for a synthesizer sound track. Nevertheless, there are synth sounds that Moroder will not contemplate.

"I hate those sounds which are typical synthesizer—all that *oing-boing* that a lot of rock bands use," he says. "It's especially harmful to a score. You have to balance the sound so that it's not too much like an obvious synthesizer and not too much like just another instrument. It should be unexaggerated, subtle, and as natural as possible. We spend a lot of time getting that right, adjusting the knobs." But don't ask him how the knobs work. "I don't know about that technical stuff. I know there are some knobs that give me more highs or less decay, but I'm no good at describing them. I'd rather not know. I just listen to it."

But Moroder knows what he wants, though he seldom plays keyboards himself. "I'm not a very good keyboard player," he admits. Instead, he works closely with other musicians, mainly keyboardist Sylvester Levay and percussionist Keith Forsey. "With synthesizers, anyway," he says, "you have sequencers, so you just push a button." He chuckles. "I can do that." Moroder believes that an influx of synthesizer film scores will probably take a while, if it happens at all. That's because, he says, "there's a tendency on the part of producers to go for eight or nine big, established composers, who all use orchestra." They include John Williams (who scored *E.T.*), Ennio Morricone (*The Thing*), and Maurice Jarre (*Firefox*), and it explains why the synth sound was largely missing from the summer's big-budget, sci-fi-oriented films. Two exceptions were *Blade Runner,* scored by Vangelis, and *Star Trek II: The Wrath of Khan,* scored by James Horner, who mobilized an eighty-eight piece orchestra that included four synthesizers.

Unlike Moroder, Vangelis plays his own keyboards. "I work straight onto the keyboard," the bearded thirty-nine-year-old composer explains from his home in London. "And when I have what I want, I can record it directly on tape. My score is my tape."

Even before *Chariots of Fire,* his first film assignment, Vangelis's music was a staple of television commercials and of shows like PBS's *Cosmos,* which used extracts from the several albums he had recorded. On those albums he plays all instruments—often several synthesizers and percussive instruments, including a grand piano. Vangelis, who was born in Greece—his full name is Evangelos Papathanassiou—worked with two European techno-rock bands, Formynx and Aphrodite's Child, before launching his solo career.

Even after three film scores (including *Missing*), he's still a little baffled by the world of film. The pressures of a big-budget movie, he says, are especially challenging, worrying, and exhausting. "But you do the best you can in the time given. Still, whatever I do I can always think of doing in a different way. Given more time, I'd like to do things over."

Even some of *Chariots?* "Maybe the whole thing." But then Vangelis laughs and says, "No, really I'm quite pleased with that. It was my biggest challenge, being a period film. I didn't want to do period music. I tried to compose a score which was contemporary and still compatible with the time of the film. But I also didn't want to go for a completely electronic sound. That was my main difficulty: how to accomplish that." He accomplished that by mixing synthesizer and grand piano.

Vangelis works in self-imposed isolation, avoiding the influence of others. He has, for instance, yet to see any of the films scored by Moroder—even *Midnight Express*. "I don't try to shape my career or my music by following what other musicians do. I don't try to avoid all those things on purpose—I really must get around to seeing *Midnight Express*—but I'm very busy in the studio all day. So when I come home at night I'd usually rather do some painting or fool around with some sounds than go to the movies."

He doesn't share Moroder's reservations about "typical synthesizer" sounds. "There's nothing wrong with the sound of a synthesizer any more than there's something wrong with a trumpet or violin. What's wrong is to hear any instrument played badly. Of course, there *are* people who use the synthesizer in ways that make it sound silly. But that's the fault of the player." Nor has he tired of using the instrument, though he also likes to play others, like the grand piano. "I like changing from one to another—each has its own sound and adds its own color. The synthesizer is an extension in musical history the way automobiles were an extension in transportation history. It's a very flexible instrument, and there's nothing faster for scoring a film."

This is one reason that synthesizer composers, working swiftly with dials and buttons and tapes, are increasingly attractive to producers. That synthesizers may indeed be the shape of things to come is ironically illustrated by Moroder's latest project. He is working on it in his small home studio that somehow accommodates not only six of the computer-hearted machines—including the aptly named Jupiter-8 and Prophet 5—but also the amplifiers, recorders, and other support equipment. The composer sits at an impossibly complex looking twenty-four–track control board, where he gives instructions to his keyboardist, Sylvester Levay, who stands with fingers ready on the keys of the Synclavier II.

Moroder's eyes are fixed on the video before him. There's the image of a worker in a great mechanized city of the future operating a huge clocklike machine. But the worker is unable to keep up and collapses as he vows, "I will stay at the machine." Another man takes his place, desperately trying to keep up with the machine's demands.

Fifty-six years after it was made, *Metropolis,* Fritz Lang's dark vision of the future, is finally getting a most suitable score—from an electronic machine.

From *American Film* 7, no. 10 (September 1982): 67–71.

48

Rock Movideo

Marianne Meyer

(1985)

It began as coy flirtation, way back in 1955, when director Richard Brooks inserted "Rock Around the Clock" under the opening credits of *Blackboard Jungle,* but the on-again, off-again romance between rock music and the film community wasn't really consummated until the past year. If money makes strange bedfellows, 1984 saw film producers, feature directors and music video makers between the sheets for a near orgiastic display of financial backrubbing. A total of eight soundtracks were certified platinum, more than in 1981, '82, and '83 *combined.* With a few exceptions, music videos helped make both the films and the songs into big hits.

Film companies, which previously treated many soundtracks as mere accessories, have seen the light—neon, marquee, dollar signs. Music videos are their most cost-efficient advertising tool. "It had always been that you'd try to get a top recording act to do your title song, so that you get that additional support," says Stuart Zakem, senior publicist at Columbia Pictures. "With the introduction of music video, it was clear nothing sells film better than film. You just have to think what advertising time costs. If you do a four-minute video for $150,000 and it gets played five times on (commercial) television, you've already made your money back."

The new age began in April, 1983. No one at Paramount Pictures really expected *Flashdance* to usher in a whole revolution in film marketing: It was little more than a major-league exploitation film, modestly budgeted ($8 million), with a paper-thin story line of *Rocky*-like perseverance. Part of the film's marketing strategy was to make five videos in the MTV style—quick-cut montages of film imagery set to a driving beat—and release them to dance clubs to drum up advance word of mouth. The title track by Irene Cara flew to #1 on the pop charts, as did the soundtrack LP. Michael Sembello's "Maniac" also went to #1 courtesy of a video with a sexy female who huffed and puffed, humped and pumped in heavy rotation on the video channels. That's when the light dawned—each airing of the "Maniac" clip was, in essence, a free commercial for the film. Although critics universally panned *Flashdance,* nothing could stop what Paramount marketing VP Gordon Weaver called its "invisible marketing." The soundtrack sold five million copies and the film grossed over $100 million.

And so 1984 dawned with a new equation: Movie + Soundtrack + Video = $$$!!! Paramount, home of *Flashdance* and album/movie matings like *Saturday Night Fever, Urban Cowboy* and *Grease,* took the new marketing idea to the limit with *Footloose.* Dean Pitchford, a lyricist for *Fame* and *Flashdance,* wrote the script and, after the movie was edited, co-wrote the songs. He called it "a rock video in reverse. The idea was to mold the music to fit the visual images." With the entire package complete, Columbia Records and Paramount Pictures started an aggressive cross-marketing campaign, making the title song's video nearly indistinguishable from a saturation ad campaign aimed at MTV-ers.

Before the film's February opening, Columbia had released three singles (Kenny Loggins' soon-to-be chart-topping title song, a 12-inch dance mix of Shalamar's "Dancing in the Sheets" and Bonnie Tyler's "Holding Out for a Hero") and the soundtrack album from *Footloose.* The first video, consisting of nothing but film footage, got "Footloose" in heavy MTV rotation so quickly that the movie's star, Kevin Bacon, was mobbed by teenage girls at *sneak previews.* The film opened simultaneously in 1,340 theaters nation wide—a tactic employed when a studio wants to generate quick opening weekend sales before the reviews take hold. (*Footloose* made back its $8 million budget the first weekend.) But with *Footloose,* the momentum grew, even after a majority of critics dismissed the movie's screwloose plot.

Footloose was, quite simply, a hit record with pictures. The stars were cute, the story's mild-mannered rebellion appealed to teens, and the dance-and-romp sequences were modeled after the fare on MTV, which director Herbert Ross confessed to watching religiously throughout production. The movie/video interplay spawned three more Top 40 singles (including a second #1 for Deniece Williams' "Let's Hear It for the Boy"). The soundtrack album went quintuple platinum and knocked *Thriller* from the #1 position for ten weeks. The film grossed over $80 million. When film or record company dealmakers see figures like that, they salivate.

Director Walter Hill described the plot of his *Streets of Fire* as "a rock 'n' roll fable in which the Leader of the Pack steals Queen of the Hop and Soldier Boy comes home to do something about it." The result was a film about as deep as any 90 minutes of MTV, on which it was heavily promoted. Between constant showings of "I Can Dream About You" (in which white singer Dan Hartman's off-camera voice competed for recognition with on-screen black performance group, the Sorels) and the repeated commercial trailers, the marketing was as subtle as the film's sledgehammer showdown. Still, the album stalled shy of gold (about 300,000 copies sold) while the film received pitiful reviews and poor initial word-of-mouth, but managed to attract a portion of the teen audience.

In contrast to *Footloose* and *Streets of Fire,* where music was used as a marketing ploy, the year's slew of street dance movies—*Breakin', Beat Street, Body Rock*—were created because of the music itself. And while Charlie Ahearn's shoe-string (under $500,000) *Wild Style* from 1983 remains the purest look at the rap/graffiti/breakdance culture, Hollywood doesn't generally value purity as a virtue. This clearly was a subculture ripe with opportunity—both as a curiosity item for mainstream moviegoers and as a multimedia bonanza. *Breakin's* soundtrack is closing in on sales of three million, no doubt aided by its title theme, "Breakin' . . . There's No Stopping Us" by Ollie & Jerry, a Top 10 record with a spin-filled video in heavy rotation (pardon the pun), and "99½," a song/video by Carol Lyn Townes. Poly-Gram Records VP Russ Regan admits that the album was pulled together in an unprecedented four weeks to capture the initial sales of the breakdance phenomenon that might have gone to *Beat Street.* Although second to arrive, the *Beat Street* soundtrack went gold, and a *Beat Street, Vol. II* was released later in the year.

As for latecomer *Body Rock,* the *New York Times* described it thus: "[it] looks not like a theatrical film but like a series of music videos that have been spliced together to make a feature-length presentation." That makes sense: director Marcelo Epstein is among the growing ranks of promotional clip directors moving up to helm feature films. And why not? If MTV-type musicals can draw the kids into the theatres, why not put them in the hands of the people initially responsible for the style?

Mark Robinson ("Brass in Pocket," "What's Love Got to Do with It") is soon to make his feature debut with *Roadhouse.* Russell Mulcahy ("Allentown," numerous Duran Duran location extravaganzas) is waiting to see his horror tale, *Razorback,* released. Julien Temple, whose film school thesis was the notorious *Great Rock 'n' Roll Swindle,* is balancing work on clips ("Undercover of the Night" among them) with the completion of *Absolute Beginners.* Bob Giraldi ("Beat It," "Love Is a Battle-field") is developing projects, and MTV veteran Alan Metter is (get this) scheduled to do a musical comedy based on "Girls Just Want to Have Fun."

Steve Barron was the first graduate of video film school to break through with 1984's summer release of *Electric Dreams,* a bizarre love triangle—boy/girl/computer. Barron, with over a hundred clips to his credit, including "Billie Jean" and

"Don't You Want Me," came up with a charming, visually daring feature that died quickly in general release despite a strong soundtrack (Culture Club, Phil Oakey, Giorgio Moroder) and a classy video Barron directed for the film's title theme. *Electric Dreams* was financed by Virgin Pictures, itself an offshoot of British-based Virgin Records, so it comes as no surprise that Virgin Atlantic Airways (yes, they're related) shows the film on its budget-priced trans-Atlantic flights. So don't count it out just yet—there's always cable.

Eddie and the Cruisers offers an odd variation on the film/music marketing mix, and an example of the strange twists it can play on a new group caught in the middle. The movie grossed a disappointing $4.7 million when released in late summer '83. As of July 1, 1984, the soundtrack had sold a mere 175,000 copies. Two months later, the album had passed 600,000 copies and entered the Top 20; the LP eventually went Top 10 and platinum. The reason was simple—HBO had run the movie eight times, The Movie Channel had shown it twice, and it had numerous plays on local and regional cable channels.

It was a mixed blessing for the Beaver Brown Band led by Springsteenesque John Cafferty, composer of music for the film. Because of the movie, Beaver Brown had an album, a single and two videos out, but their picture was not on the album, their name was not on the single, and the videos featured actors from the film lip-synching to their music. To much of the viewing audience, Eddie and the Cruisers was the band they loved. Beaver Brown, meanwhile, having recorded their own album in early 1984, saw its release delayed indefinitely when cable showings revived interest in the *Eddie* soundtrack. CBS records started a campaign to "give credit where credit is due" and released a new video of Beaver Brown doing the first single, "On the Dark Side." Two clips of the song, one with Brown, one with star Michael Paré's movie band, alternated play on the video channels.

Eddie director Martin Davidson may not have realized at the time that he was doing a maxi-promotional clip, but other feature film directors have willingly taken to the form. Citing the creative freedom and more immediate gratification of working on music videos, a number of top directors are following the example set by John Landis ("Thriller") and Tobe Hooper ("Dancing with Myself") and turning their talents towards videos. According to Bob Giraldi, "Short-story telling for a feature film director who's worked on a long-form is a nice relief . . . All directors worth their salt want to do a music video."

Lindsay Anderson, British creator of *If, Britannia Hospital,* and *Oh, Lucky Man* (itself an extraordinary example of music, by Alan Price, integrated into plot), directed the debut video for Carmel, "More, More, More." Nicolas Roeg (*The Man Who Fell to Earth, Don't Look Now*) directed a clip for Tom Robinson and one for Roger Waters' "5:01 AM (The Pros and Cons of Hitch Hiking)." William Friedkin, who won an Oscar for *The French* Connection and made boffo bucks for *The Exorcist,* used surrealistic sets and special effects for Laura Brani-gan's "Self Control." Brian de Palma (*Carrie, Scarface, Body Double*) finally brought Bruce Springsteen to video with his classy performance shoot of "Danc-ing in the Dark." (*Not* based on an obscure Alfred Hitchcock rock video.)

One of the most fascinating entries of the year was directed by Zbigniew Rybczynski—the Polish filmmaker who won 1983's Academy Award for Best Animated Short Film (*Tango*). His first video clip—for the Art of Noise's "Close (to the Edit)"—was a "New York Chainsaw Massacre" with a six-year-old *Rocky Horror* punkette leading the rhythmic destruction of orchestral instruments.

All the film/video matings did not prove successful, though. *Up the Creek,* a poor boy's *Porky's* set on rafts, sank into oblivion despite an AOR soundtrack and a cute title video with Cheap Trick and cheap shots from the film. *Two of a Kind* was promoted by footage-heavy videos, but even with a platinum soundtrack and Olivia Newton-John and John Travolta making cutesy, the film did not live up to expectations. (*Grease,* the duo's first on-screen coupling, remains a box of-fice champion.) And even Rick Springfield's fans agreed that the *Hard to Hold* LP (also platinum) and videos (including "Bop 'Til You Drop" with special effects from George Lucas' International Light & Magic) were superior to the film.

"Take a Look at Me Now," the slap-dash video made around Phil Collins' theme from *Against All Odds,* didn't prevent the record from going to #1 but drew few music lovers to the film. And, in a rare example of second thoughts, Eddy Grant's "Romancing the Stone" video had to be reshot and all of the film footage removed when it was decided to downplay Grant's vocal in the film. Once the song ceased to be a promotional tool, the record company/film company romance was over.

As long as the promotional potential is alive, however, cooperation is vital. In the case of *Streets of Fire,* according to MCA Records executive director of adver-tising, Glen Lajeski, "They (Universal Pictures) didn't just put it together and hand it to us. We're actively trying to work much closer with each other."

Not so ironically, the year's three most critically successful rock movies were cre-ated outside the Hollywood film community. While all three used film footage in video clips, they did so organically and were not pulled together by anxious pro-ducers looking nervously at the bottom line.

The first was *This Is Spinal Tap,* Rob Reiner's "mockumentary" about an aging British heavy metal band. Put together on a mere $2.2 million budget and impro-vised before handheld cameras in a matter of a few weeks, *Spinal Tap* is a surpris-ingly subtle, frequently hilarious lampoon of the pretensions and absurdities of the music industry. The film's marketing people had a field day promoting the band, the music, and the documentary as if Spinal Tap really existed. (And for a few moments, at New York's CBGB and on *Saturday Night Live,* it did.) Though their tongues were firmly in cheek, the reaction to Spinal Tap's videos—"Hell Hole" and "Big Bottom" among them—was so strong that the line between reality and parody was nearly erased. Some people never got the joke, and therein lies the warning in the cross-media promotional push.

Proven masters of innovative video, Talking Heads avoided the "music video look" on their first feature film, *Stop Making Sense*. It is, plain and simple, a concert film stunningly directed by veteran filmmaker Jonathan Demme (*Melvin and Howard, Swing Shift*), with Jordan Cronenweth (*Blade Runner, Altered States*) as director of photography. Demme is a self-confessed "fan of long, sustained takes. I look for camera angles that can play for a long time and let the performance speak for itself." In his film it is the Heads and not the editing that supplies the excitement of the show. *Stop Making Sense* does not use quick cuts and montage—the common visual language of rock videos—but works its magic with smooth camera glides, a brilliant performance and direct-to-film digital recording that sets new standards in film sound. (It also provides the best onscreen credit of the year: "Mr. Byrne's Big Suit Built by Gail Blacker.")

Although the Heads' record company, Sire/Warner Bros., put up a small portion of the film's $1.2 million budget, the band took on the lion's share of financing to keep the project under their control. Byrne seems to be pleased with his first foray into features—rumors have him working on a second already, a narrative set in a town where all the inhabitants are characters out of *National Enquirer*-like tabloids.

For *Purple Rain*, Prince managers-cum-film-producers Bob Cavallo, Joe Ruffalo, and Steve Fargnoli also took an alternate route, shying away from traditional studio funding to safeguard the film's artistic freedom. (They gleefully accepted the R rating although studios consider PG the key to the youth market.) Directed by 30-year-old first-timer Albert Magnoli and shot in seven winter weeks in Minneapolis, the film was a resounding success, financially (grossing more than $60 million so far) and critically. The videos for "When Doves Cry" and "Let's Go Crazy" leaned heavily (the latter exclusively) on moments from the film, and both songs shot to the top of the singles charts. "Doves" went platinum; the *Purple Rain* album multi-platinum. Except for running time, it became nearly impossible to tell the film's commercials from its music videos, but no matter: Seeing either on the tube was a chance to see the charismatic Prince in action. Warner Distribution president and general sales manager D. Barry Reardon called the textbook triple-media marketing of *Purple Rain* "an ideally balanced campaign between Warner Bros. Records, MTV and our film division.

When "Doves" was finally knocked out of first place on the charts, and before "Let's Go Crazy" took over, Ray Parker Jr.'s theme for *Ghostbusters* took the spot. A silly bit of fluff on first hearing, "Ghostbusters" only truly came alive upon viewing. The video was directed by the film's own Ivan Reitman and immediately made the song's chorus ("Who you gonna call? *Ghostbusters!*") a catch phrase to equal "Where's the beef?"

The film surpassed both *Gandhi* and *Tootsie* as Columbia's most successful release to date, $206 million and still counting. Not surprisingly, producers Cavallo, Ruffalo, and Fargnoli (who also manage Parker) announced new film projects which will use modest budgets and a marketing sequence of album and video promotion prior to theatrical releases. One will star Ray Parker Jr., another concerns the disappearance of a rock star, and a third is about a creator of *music video clips*. The circle, indeed, will be unbroken.

For all the variations on the theme, 1984 didn't come near to exhausting the possibilities of the film/music marriage. Giorgio Moroder's restored, rescored *Metropolis* turned a profit, so no doubt there will be more classic silent movies MTV-ed with rock soundtracks. Music Motions, a Manhattan-based company geared to creating music clips specifically for theatres, is now working on taking existing videos and revitalizing them for the big screen. The Music Theatre Network is offering concert clips to movie houses as a new kind of short before the main feature. Television shows are trying their best to be hip with fast-paced action shows and glamorous evening soaps unrolling to the sound of rehashed pop. And of course, as Elton John sings it, "Sassons say *so* much" when you recut a promo video to become your tour-sponsor's commercial.[1]

"I want my MTV?" It doesn't matter anymore whether you do. Heading into 1985, you're gonna get it, wherever you turn.

From *The Rolling Stone Review, 1985,* ed. Ira A. Robbins (New York: Scribner, 1985), pp. 168–71.

NOTES

1. A reference to the Elton John song "Sad Songs (Say So Much)," which was modified and used by Sassoon Jeans to sell their product.—Ed.

49

How Rock Is Changing Hollywood's Tune

Stephen Holden

(1989)

Jack Nicholson's fiendish joker and Michael Keaton's Caped Crusader aren't the only forces that collide in the smash-hit move *Batman*. The film's noisy soundtrack presents a pitched battle between the two strains of music that have accompanied movies since the dawn of the sound era: one derived from high culture, the other from pop. The majority of the film's score is loud, post-Wagnerian action music composed by Danny Elfman. Sly, subterranean funk songs by Prince make up the rest.

Until recently, movie directors, in choosing the music for a potential blockbuster, tended to opt either for music like Mr. Elfman's, composed of carefully edited orchestral cues, or for compilations of prerecorded pop tunes like Prince's contributions. When both approaches were used in the same movie, pop tunes were typically tacked on to the credits, while the main body was composed of musical fragments synchronized with the images. In adapting both approaches at once, *Batman* spawned enough original music to prompt Warner Bros. Records to release two separate *Batman* albums. Prince's nine-song soundtrack—a product of the cross-marketing mentality that has infected Hollywood since *Saturday Night Fever*—is soaring on the charts, and an album of the music by Mr. Elfman is scheduled for release late next month.

For years many in the film industry have worried that the rise of the pop compilation might spell the demise of the traditional score. But it hasn't happened; nor is it likely to. Artistically, the late 80's are a very healthy period for movie music. Major directors like Martin Scorsese have the power to see their personal, offbeat musical visions reach fruition in their films.

And they are calling on the art-rock fringe. Besides Peter Gabriel's score for Mr. Scorsese's film *The Last Temptation of Christ*, the last year has seen distinguished iconoclastic movie scores by Scott Johnson for *Patty Hearst* and Philip Glass for *The Thin Blue Line*. Jonathan Demme's *Married to the Mob* used a peppy nontraditional score by David Byrne. Woody Allen has the freedom to make movies that carry forward the austere European modernist esthetics of Bergman and Antonioni in which music, though used very sparingly, was chosen with exquisite care.

Led by *Batman*, the soundtracks for this summer's major movies show Hollywood film music to be more pluralistic in style than ever before. On the more traditional end of the spectrum, *Indiana Jones and the Last Crusade* boasts a muscular symphonic score by John Williams, whose big, bustling soundtracks for Hollywood's adventure and science-fiction epics have established him as the most distinguished successor to the grand symphonic tradition of Erich Wolfgang Korngold, Franz Waxman, Max Steiner, and Alfred Newman. On the trendy pop side of the fence, the music for *Ghostbusters II* is an up-to-minute collection of potential hit singles by Run-D.M.C. (the rap group that re-recorded Ray Parker Jr.'s *Ghostbusters* theme song—which went to No. 1 in 1984—for the sequel), Bobby Brown, New Edition and others.

The soundtrack of Spike Lee's *Do the Right Thing* uses an exhortatory rap song, "Fight the Power," by Public Enemy, which is played repeatedly and deafeningly on a boom box to dramatize aggressive black power. Bill Lee, a jazz musician and the director's father, provides the interstitial music cues.

Although *The Last Temptation of Christ* was released last year, Mr. Gabriel's music for the movie did not come out on record until a month ago, when it was released under the title *Passion*. Mr. Gabriel's groundbreaking score is a world-music suite that features noted musicians from India, Latin America, Africa and the Middle East performing in electronic settings.

THE SCORE GAINS RESPECTABILITY

It wasn't until the early 70's that movie scores began to be recognized as a serious genre. At around the same time that Bernard Herrmann scores for Alfred Hitchcock's films and *Citizen Kane* began to acquire a cult following, RCA records began releasing a series of classic Hollywood film scores (*Now Voyager, The Sea Hawk, Spellbound* and *Gone with the Wind,* among others), sumptuously re-recorded with contemporary studio technology. Before that, movie music had been generally regarded as a semi-respectable genre, the cinematic equivalent of new-age music.

That is not to say that the field did not occasionally attract serious composers. Prokofiev, Copland, Honegger and Thomson, among others, all composed eloquent film music. But in the typical Hollywood movie the composer is often the last person to be hired, and writing the music is often little more than a matter of filling holes with sounds that inconspicuously set and maintain a mood. Where listening to most film scores is about as interesting as watching television without the sound, the more ambitious soundtracks have also had enough color, textural richness and melodic clout to stand on their own.

Scores that are made up of pop songs work a bit differently from those old-time Hollywood scores. Instead of seeming to come from out of thin air as a spur to the action, pop music, when used with discrimination, often emanates from a real source in the world of the movie, like a car radio. Where the old-time Hollywood film score uses the vocabulary of classical music to evoke a timeless romanticism, pop songs, which are inextricably tied to our sense of nostalgia, automatically convey a specific sense of time and place. Run-D.M.C.'s theme song for *Ghostbusters II,* for instance, stamps the movie as an ultracontemporary comedy of the late 1980's.

ROCK STORMS THE BARRICADES

The more ubiquitous pop music has become, the more it has served as an instant identifier of time and place in movies. And recording stars whose music is featured on soundtracks are increasingly considered lures to the box office, even if they don't appear in the movie.

It is only in the last decade that pop-rock music, by its sheer saturation of movies, has finally dissipated much of the lingering resentment felt by Hollywood's old-guard musical establishment at the intrusion of rock.

Especially in the late 1960's, when a generation of performers lacking academic musical credentials began invading Hollywood sound studios, the field of movie music became embattled. The soundtracks for *The Graduate* (1967), with songs by Simon and Garfunkel, and *Easy Rider* (1969), the first major movie hit with a multi-artist rock compilation, brought the generation gap to Hollywood movie music, just as the films did to the screen.

The dust finally began to settle when a younger generation of directors ascended to power, led by Steven Spielberg and George Lucas. Mr. Spielberg and Mr. Lucas had both grown up with rock music (Mr. Lucas's 1973 *American Graffiti* had the first major movie soundtrack built around rock-and-roll oldies), but they both also maintained a keen appreciation for the musical showmanship of the past.

And in John Williams, with whom they have both worked over the last 12 years, the two directors have found a composer whose forceful eclecticism transcends generational differences in taste. Mr. Williams (the present musical director of the Boston Pops Orchestra) made his name in the early and mid-70's as a film composer scoring such disaster epics as *The Poseidon Adventure, The Towering Inferno* and *Earthquake.*

Working for Mr. Spielberg and Mr. Lucas, he moved to higher ground with the *Star Wars* and *Indiana Jones* trilogies, *E.T.—the Extraterrestrial,* and *Close Encounters of the Third Kind.* He has dragged the best of the past—deliberately grand movie music that aggressively pushes emotional buttons—into the present and modernized it by cutting down on its lachrymose excesses. And instead of creating pastiches of Rachmaninoff, Mahler and Strauss, Mr. Williams has moved a little further ahead to Prokofiev, Bartok and Stravinsky for stylistic inspiration, and even added dollops of electronic pop.

ROCK AROUND THE CLOCK

The history of Hollywood film music directly reflects the profound changes in the roles of both rock music and movies in American life. Music has never been as ubiquitous as it is today. The proliferation of high fidelity and car radio and more recently music video, boom boxes and walkabout stereos have made urban and suburban life a nonstop musical soundtrack. Music is now as portable and erasable and disposable as the technology of the audiocassette. And in the abundance of its availability, music has lost much of its traditionally hallowed mystique.

An important part of day-to-day reality, especially for those born after 1945, has been pop-rock music. And since the 1960's, the most influential movie soundtracks have tended to be those that have furthered the incursion of pop-rock. As early as 1964, the first Beatles film, *A Hard Day's Night,* presaged the music-video era with its jump-cut editing and very loose organization of action around the songs.

But it wasn't until 1978, when the soundtrack for *Saturday Night Fever* became the best-selling album in history (only Michael Jackson's *Thriller* has since outsold it), that movie producers and record executives recognized the full economic potential of cross-marketing movies with records.

From that moment, the race was on in the record industry to create blockbuster soundtrack albums for potential hit movies. The albums for *Urban Cowboy, Flashdance, Footloose, Beverly Hills Cop, The Big Chill, Top Gun, Cocktail, Dirty Dancing* and *Beaches* are among the many soundtracks that have sold in the millions. But with these hits, movies, television, home video and records— even lunch boxes—all began to become adjuncts of one another in a regulated chain of products. Merchandising, movies, and music became inseparable.

Flashdance, in 1983, introduced a short-lived spate of movies inspired by the look and feel of music videos at the moment the cable channel MTV was enjoying its first flush of success. But what was predicted to become a new genre of instant musicals built around music-video technology has yet to establish itself.

One reason for the genre's failure may be that it was exploited so cynically. Even in a hit film like *Footloose,* pop energy, fancy editing and camera work instead of reinforcing dramatic momentum became a flashy substitute for it. Long before the flop movie *Sing* was released earlier this year, the public had wearied of the gimmick.

In traditional scoring, meanwhile, the most significant trends to affect movie music have come out of evolving musical technology. In movies like *Midnight Express,* the European disco producer Giorgio Moroder developed a new vocabulary of melodramatic synthesizer effects that has added garish new colors to the palette of horror-movie music. Mark Isham, a Miles Davis–influenced trumpeter and electronic impressionist has popularized a moody, new-age-influenced sound in his scores for Alan Rudolph's *Trouble in Mind* and *The Moderns.*

THE GOOD, THE BAD, AND THE PRODUCT

With the infusion of pop, rock and other elements of contemporary music, movies have become louder, just like the rest of the environment. Audiences who have grown up going to rock concerts, listening to rock radio and to MTV expect a relentless barrage of images and sounds. In the contemporary pop movie, the hits follow one another as quickly as the car chases and explosions in a James Bond movie.

Pop movies like *Batman* and *Ghostbusters II* are instant media events created less with any eye on cinematic history than on maintaining a commercial momentum. And their catchy, disposable pop scores epitomize and to an extent have even come to define their esthetics. Prince's shallow ditties for *Batman* continue a long pop tradition of respected pop composers tossing off slick, impersonal product for the Hollywood entertainment machine.

Pop songs, however, can be used to pointed dramatic effect. Both musical and cinematic esthetics are best served when a sensitive director matches a self-contained musical piece to the emotional core of the drama, as Spike Lee does with Public Enemy's "Fight the Power" in *Do the Right Thing.*

In Martin Scorsese's segment of *New York Stories,* Procol Harum's "Whiter Shade of Pale" both inspires and distills an artist's obsession. Dean Martin's 1953 recording of "That's Amore" set the comic-romantic tone for *Moonstruck.*

But in the end, movie music that is made the old way—underscoring the image moment by moment—still does a more complete job of transporting us into the world of a film than the pop compilation. Today, the means for accomplishing that task is no longer a single vocabulary, practiced by a small Hollywood coterie of academic composers.

From the modern symphonic action music of Mr. Spielberg's pop epics to the tingly electronic music of the contemporary horror movie, to the sleek pop-jazz of sophisticated comedies, good movie music can now be tailored to the genre and to the mood of the moment, with a fine-tuned precision made possible by technological advances. And certain scores, like Mr. Gabriel's world-music suite for *The Last Temptation of Christ* show the warring strains of symphonic and pop film music merging into something that is neither one, but that has characteristics of both, and that opens up new approaches to scoring. For ultimately in film music, what's good is what works, what seduces us to hop on a celluloid magic carpet and take a ride to a place where sound and image, dream and reality, meet and momentarily merge.

50

Danny Elfman

From Boingo to Batman

Randall D. Larson

(1990)

Briefly, would you outline your background in music and how you got involved in Oingo Boingo?

I spent a number of years with Oingo Boingo's predecessor, The Mystic Nights of the Oingo Boingo (although we were known as The Mystic Nights); it was a musical theatrical troupe, a very strange dark cabaret, I guess you'd call it. I was the musical director and my brother was the director and founder, and he kind of drafted me. Over the course of those eight years it was kind of real wild and strange and I taught myself different musical styles, a little bit about writing, rudimentary music, and more a chance to experiment with a lot of musical styles that I liked. Oingo Boingo started in '79, as a band, and there really isn't too much to tell about that.

Had you studied music at all before you go involved with that group?
No.

How did you make the shift from being in a rock group to getting involved in film scoring?
It was kind of by accident. I'd always loved film and film music; as a teenager, if you'd have asked me what I wanted to do, I always wanted to work in film. I imagined myself a cinematographer working towards being a director, or maybe an editor. I'd always thought that some way or another I'd end up in film, but somehow, I ended up in music. I did music, although I wouldn't call it real scoring, it was for The Mystic Nights and some supplementary musicians for a cult midnight film that my brother did years ago, in '78, called *The Forbidden*

Zone. It's one of these very weird, low-budget midnight oddities. And I didn't do anything else in film, really, until '84, when I got called in for *Pee Wee's Big Adventure.*

Coming from a rock background, how did you teach yourself to write, not only symphonic music, but to endure the many kinds of restrictions and special things to write for film scores? Did you work with other people or study other composers?

I've always been very critical of rock and roll artists turned film composers, and I didn't want to fall into their category. I took the attitude of: forget everything you've done with the band over the last eight years, go back to yourself as a teenager, watching and loving films. I just tried to approach those wonderful movies that I loved—all those great Bernard Herrmann scores and all the Fellini films that I adored. I just went back to those sources which were and still are so much a part of me. Even though I spent a lot of years in rock and roll, I would just as likely have the music to Fellini's *Casanova* or Bernard Herrmann's *Journey to the Center of the Earth* going in my mind as any rock and roll music.

You've got to realize, even as a rock and roll artist, I came out of musical theater, and so those roots were helpful. All during the '70s, until I started the band, I didn't listen to *any* rock and roll, so I don't consider that a strong part of my musical roots. In fact, the only reason we started the band in '79 was because we *detested* contemporary music in the '70s and we started as a reaction. I stopped listening to rock and roll when I was in high school, and I discovered Stravinsky and people like that. I literally did not listen to another rock and roll song between then and when I started to get reactivated again in the late '70s. So there wasn't a lot of baggage that I was carrying around, preconception-wise. I've listened, probably, in my lifetime to more Kurt Weill than I have Rolling Stones.

How would you describe the music that you wrote on Pee Wee's Big Adventure?

I would really describe it as a cross between Nino Rota-ish and kind of Hollywood '50s almost '60s, going for that overly dramatic type of musical style, where there aren't many subtleties; you know, he sees the bike stolen, he encounters this, it's just like BUH-BA-BOMM, just really big. I just took that very direct approach, I took everything from the eyes of Pee Wee, the character, so when he was happy I just made it really happy, just happy like a six-year-old would be happy, and when he was sad I tried to make it *really* sad, and I tried to purposely give the character a very wide dynamic that way, and treat it like a child, heavy is too heavy and happy is too happy, you know. . . .

On Pee Wee's Big Adventure, *what kind of orchestration did you use there? Did you combine electronics with symphonics, or what?*

There really wasn't much electronics. I try to minimize the amount of synthesizers used because synthesizers are so slow in trying to achieve sounds while the whole orchestra's waiting, and you're under enormous pressure. I learned that on the first movie, on *Pee Wee's Big Adventure,* that the pressure of being with a big orchestra is just enormous, especially when you have to go for a lot of minutes per session, and the last thing you need to do is be sitting there screaming up and back, nervously, with a synthesizer player, "No, a little more of this, a little more of that!" There's so few boundaries with synthesizers, it can take a long time to get the sound the way you want it, so I try to bring in my own sounds whenever I can, for the synthesizer players to download, and if there's a lot of parts I just lay them down myself. On *Beetlejuice,* I pre-laid a half-dozen cues on synthesizer and just brought them in and had the orchestra play over that.

How did you try to approach Beetlejuice, *as far as capturing its many different kinds of flavors?*

When I watch a film for the first time, I try to keep a real open attitude, and I saw right away that the Beetlejuice character had this playfulness to him, yet he was twisted; he wasn't really threatening, really heavy, so right when I was watching the film for the very first time, I already formulated the Beetlejuice theme, and already heard the kind of Stravinskyesque violins. Of course, there's a wonderful history of using violins for demons, going all the way back to *L'Histoire du Soldat,* which was a big inspiration for *Beetlejuice,* and was also a very favorite piece of mine. So for *Beetlejuice* I either kept it really boisterous, with a big horn section like in the opening credits, or I'd use this kind of fluid violin type of fun but minor-key kind of stuff for his character, which just seemed to fit. For Lydia, immediately I honed in on her character, I liked that a lot, and I just felt something more sad and melancholy and melodic. And then, for the rest of the score I would just kind of alternate between playing it strange or playing it fun or playing it serious or playing it comical or cartoony, just depending on what was happening.

There aren't many films like that and I'm sure I won't, musically, be able to do anything quite like that for quite a while. I'm just lucky I had the chance to do it. It's the type of movie that, if I hadn't scored it and I saw it, I'd just be enormously jealous of whoever had.

How big of an orchestra did you use on Beetlejuice?

That was about sixty-something, sixty-three. . . .

How long did it take you to write the music to Beetlejuice?

I usually take a little over four weeks. *Beetlejuice* went a little longer because there was a lot of re-cutting and I had to do some re-scoring, so it was more like five, a little over five weeks.

Did any of the special effects delay a lot of that?

Yeah. Unlike most movies, which put a temp score in to do their previews before they do their final cut and the composer gets a final locked print, in *Beetlejuice* Tim didn't even want to put in temporary music. He decided right in the beginning that the music was very important, and that there wasn't a lot of music out there that would match the mood of the movie. So he held off, and we scored first, before they even did their first preview, which was very unusual. Naturally after four or five previews, they decided, "Oh, we gotta change this, we have to change that, we have to add a little footage there"; they had to re-shoot one scene, so things got stretched out and we had to go back and do one more session to re-adapt a lot of the music around some of the new stuff and I had to write four or five more cues. But normally, like I say, a score, without getting into any re-doing stuff, is a little over four weeks.

That's good that you weren't locked in to a temp track, because so many composers get stuck with that temp track and wind up having to do a carbon copy of that.

I know, it is really hard. I was just talking about that with Randal Kleiser, the director of *Pee Wee's Big Top*, how hard it is for them to hear something for like a month, locked to a scene, and then to hear a completely different piece of music all of the sudden, so it's unenviable on both sides, really. The composers hate it, but I can understand how hard that would be for a director. You really get used to a piece of music and it works for them, and then to hear something totally off the wall. I'll listen to the temp music once with the director, just to get an overall feel for what he's looking for, and particularly if there's a scene that he thinks it works very well with, but I won't listen to it again. I tend to not go to previews or advance screenings, anything with the temp music. I don't want to hear it. . . .

A lot of the films you've done have seemed to be fantasy, science fiction oriented. Do you like that particular appeal, or are there other kinds of films you'd like to do?

Well, I mean, naturally fantasy is the most fun to work with, but I've been trying to do as many different types as I could, by doing, like *Back to School,* for example, or *Hot to Trot,* which is a completely different ball game. Working in *Big Top Pee Wee* or *Pee Wee's Big Adventure* or *Beetlejuice,* naturally, I get to let my imagination run wild. But I also did *Wisdom,* for Emilio Estevez, which was 80 minutes of all synthesizers, all performed by me, and a serious film, and that had its own completely unique challenges, and was a good experience. I did a De Niro film, *Midnight Run,* which is blues-based and more contemporary, and that, again, is a hundred percent different, I have to intentionally *not* catch action. My instincts always tell me to catch everything, catch all the movement, and I had to purposefully *not* do that in this movie, that's one of my little disciplines of this film. And for *Pee Wee's Big Top,* naturally, that's more in line with the style that people associate me with now, fun, wacky stuff, although the tone of the movie, parts of it are close to *Pee Wee's Big Adventure* but parts of it aren't, so there'll be musical similarities. No themes are being repeated.

Other than that I've just tried to keep myself as varied as possible. I'm under unique restrictions, as a composer, since I can't take most of the jobs I'm offered, because I work with the band nine months out of the year.

What were your first impressions of Batman, *when you first came onto the project?*

It was really just talking with Tim [Burton]. As always, I look at the movie, and I talk with the director. The critical thing is: "Am I thinking what the director is thinking?" Now, with Tim, the reason why we've had a successful relationship is that we always seem to be thinking the same thing. He flew me to London and I walked around Gotham City and I looked at a rough-cut of half the movie; we went out to dinner that night, and we both had the same word on our lips, which was "opera"—not literally but figuratively, more of a Wagnerian quality or an operatic quality to the music. Working with Tim is really great that way, because the hardest part of being a film composer is not writing the score, it's climbing inside the director's head and seeing the movie through their eyes and yet still giving it your own identity. And one of the great joys of working with Tim is that climbing inside his head is not that much different than being inside my own head, there are definitely a lot of common links there.

How did the Batman *score evolve? It seems to match a lot of dark, brooding music with a heroic, adventurous theme.*

The first thing I remember seeing when I looked at the movie was Gotham City, and Gotham City dictated the feel of the Batman Theme, I heard The Titles the first time I looked at it.

I had written all this dark music, and [producer] John Peters was saying, "Look, this is fine, but you know, we're talking about a *Hero* here!" I played him all these pieces, and Tim [Burton] was there, and he had confidence in me, but, at this point, it was essential that I came up with this one heroic theme. I just took the same basic theme and turned it into this march, and did it in a certain way—changed the key around a little bit—and all of a sudden he leapt up out of his chair, and it was completely obvious that I had found the Batman hero theme! And John actually started conducting, you know, he was waving his arms, and we knew that there was simply no question!

What can you tell me about Nightbreed?

Nightbreed was great fun. I loved working with Clive Barker. The year before that, there were two movies that I saw—*Hellraiser* and *Evil Dead 2*—where

I immediately called my agent and said I must work with these guys. I didn't know I'd be working with them back-to-back a year later! But I loved *Hellraiser* and I really wanted to work with Clive and I've read all his books. So when I got a call from Clive to meet him, I was really pleased.

It was fun but it was a real difficult score, 75 minutes with a lot of different styles, very dense, difficult music. It was very challenging, but as always, the harder it is the more I love it. I'm glad there's a soundtrack out, I'm really proud of it. I do some really fun, really crazy stuff on the music with children's voices. I'm really, really fond of the End Credits, in fact it's the first time with an orchestra that I felt I was getting kind of close to Oingo Boingo, because I have these driving marimbas, children's voices and all these drums going. I enjoyed doing the scene where they went down into the underground. There are certain kinds of music which, as I'm writing it, I know I've never been able to write this and I'll never be able to write it again, and that alone make it worth whatever hell I go through.

About Dick Tracy, *what were some of your first musical impressions when you became involved in this project?*

When I first heard about it, I didn't want to get involved with *Dick Tracy* because I didn't want to repeat myself. After I talked to Warren [Beatty], he got me a little more interested, but I was already on a movie called *Darkman* at that time, and I wasn't available. Then *Darkman* moved back five weeks, and all of a sudden I had my first time off in about two or three years . . .

When I looked at *Dick Tracy,* I got very interested, because I saw immediately that it really wasn't *Batman,* it had a much lighter tone, and the side of it that really intrigued me was the romantic side. That is something which I rarely got to write in—the big, classic romantic style, which I really love. I love Gershwin, and I love big corny old-fashioned film scores. I think that, along with the look of the film, is what really hooked me.

How closely did Warren Beatty involve himself in the film's music?

Warren was really concerned about the music. When I first came in, he said, "I've never had a full-blown score before"—because *Reds* and *Heaven Can Wait* were very minimally scored, and he knew that this movie was going to take the full treatment. He'd never done it before and was very uncertain about how to approach that. I had to go through a lot of different pieces of music and styles; I worked up a presentation, and the presentation connected. It gave him ideas.

The area that was the hardest was the romantic side. I immediately hit on the Tracy Theme and all the Crook Music. For the Breathless Theme, we had to meander around a little bit, but basically it was the first thing that I wrote; it just took a little longer to fall into. The one that we had problems on was the big, romantic Tess Theme. He liked where it started, but he didn't like where it went, so for the next two weeks, I must have worked on 20 different variations! I met him at the studio and I played through everything and he was kind of frowning, and I thought, "Well, this is it. I'm outta here. But I'll play the *last* idea." And the last idea immediately connected and that is what is now the big Tess Theme. So it was one of those great film music stories: composer almost ready to toss in the towel, then composer hitting on The Theme! On *Batman* it had been a similar situation with the Batman heroic theme.

Warren was very, very picky—I mean, every cue had to hit it just right for him. It was not uncommon to do two or three versions of a cue or to change start points around and change how a cue ends and where it got big. I knew, from Warren's reputation, that that would happen, so that didn't surprise me.

Now, Dick Tracy, *as in* Batman, *emphasized a lot of vocal music, which seemed to intersperse with some of your score, Prince in* Batman *and Madonna in* Dick Tracy . . .

It was more in *Tracy* than *Batman*. *Batman,* I had to deal with two spots, so there really wasn't anything for me to have to be aware of. In DICK TRACY, there was a lot more. I still think it's one of the weaker sides, musically. Some of them are great, but I think there are about two or three songs too many. I did write pieces of music for some songs, but they were all thrown out!

Any particular challenges that Dick Tracy *confronted you with?*

The biggest challenge was time and dealing with, again, a big production where there was a lot of focus on the music. Everybody was very concerned, like on *Batman,* about the music; it wasn't just "give us a little background music." That always puts a lot more pressure on the project. And working with Warren was an interesting challenge. As I was ridden hard on *Batman* to come up with things that I'd never really done before, Warren rode me really hard with the romantic side of *Dick Tracy,* and I'm not sorry that he did. I work well under pressure, and basically, if somebody rides me real hard on a piece of music and I have to go through hell to get it to sound just right for them, but they treat it well in the movie, I'm never disappointed. I'll go through hell and back, and I'll get dragged over the coals ten times over if I can come up with music that I like and it will be dubbed well in the movie. I would much prefer that to the situation where everybody leaves me alone and it's fun and it's enjoyable and it's easy but then it's fucked over in the dub! I think the dub for *Tracy* is good.

How did the stylization of the film, and its period, affect the music that you wrote? Did you play with that or against that?

Actually, both—the Tracy Theme and the Bad Guy music were not really period-oriented, they're just big, hero music. And even though I think that style centers around the '40s and '50s, where you have a lot of your big, heroic action scores, it wasn't really paying attention to the [fact of the] movie being in 1939. There's nothing about it that would go back that far. On the other hand, on the Tess Theme, which is still the biggest theme and my favorite in the movie, it's very period-oriented.

When I first saw the movie, I remember seeing the rooftops in all these rooftop scenes, and the rooftops reminded me of Gershwin and New York, and so I went very intentionally for a very Gershwinesque, old-fashioned style, which could have, in fact, taken place in 1939.

You worked, again, with Steve Bartek to orchestrate the Dick Tracy *score?*

Yeah, and also, as on *Batman,* I used Shirley Walker.

I guess she conducted, then?

Yeah, and I used her for orchestrations on both. Steve has been my primary orchestrator on all my scores. When you're a composer, you can get yourself into a certain high-pitched writing frenzy, but the orchestrator can't go past a certain pace, and on both cases Shirley came in and took a number of pieces.

How much music, all told, did you write for Dick Tracy?

Probably wrote about 60 minutes, although there's only about 40-something in the score.

How much time did you have to do that?

I don't know, it was pretty tight. I didn't have as much time as on *Batman* or on *Darkman.* Top-to-bottom, from when I first met him to finishing the score, was about two months.

What size orchestra did you use?

Oh, it always varies. All four of the last big scores—which would be *Nightbreed, Darkman, Batman* and *Dick Tracy*—average around 75.

Your latest score is for Darkman. *What can you tell me about this score?*

Darkman is kind of a tragedy—it's more tragic than horror, although the monster is the hero. It's kind of in the vein of *Phantom of the Opera* or *Hunchback of Notre Dame,* of a horribly disfigured hero. But [director] Sam Raimi has this wonderful visual sense of humor too, and what I love in this film is that he's done big, long sequences with no dialogue, that are pure visual, which you hardly ever see, outside of Hitchcock. In *Dick Tracy,* most of my cues were like 35 seconds, very rarely much over a minute! That was probably the most frustrating part of that. Here in *Darkman* I get to write 6½-minute cues, which is really, really great, I've just been dying to do that. Again I've got an over-70-

minute score, and I tell you, I'm really ready to get back to a normal-length film score!

But I'm real happy with the score, it's really big. Of course, it ranges from very wild to very morose and very tragic in a kind of old-fashioned, corny sense that I just love, writing these long, tragic string cues. I had a wonderful time, and I can really identify with the Darkman character.

What kind of instrumentation are you using there, anything unusual, as in Nightbreed?

No, I'm switching around a lot. In *Nightbreed* the more unusual side was incorporating all these ethnic instruments. I had a lot of percussion going. In *Darkman* I'm leaning much more just on the strings and woodwinds. I'm going back to my love for Bernard Herrmann, with the contrabassoon and bass clarinets and harp, which is the "sound" that I loved from my childhood. There's a couple of pieces I've written featuring harp and low woodwinds, and that's fun, but then there's a lot of just, a lovely kind of romantic, dark strings. . . .

And you're still doing TV work, like The Simpsons *and* Tales from the Crypt?

I just wrote their themes, I don't have anything to do with the weekly shows. I don't have time!

From *Soundtrack!,* September 1990, pp. 20–27. Reprinted by permission of the author.

51

Selections from
The Celluloid Jukebox

Interviews with Allison Anders, Alan Rudolph, Michael Mann, Isaac Julien, Wim Wenders, Bob Last, Penelope Spheeris, Ry Cooder, Quentin Tarantino, Cameron Crowe, and David Byrne

Jonathan Romney and Adrian Wootton

(1995)

THE UNHOLY ALLIANCE

These days, it's largely taken for granted that pop music and cinema have a tight-knit relationship, but beyond the fact that they both belong to popular culture, we rarely examine the reasons. What are the affinities that film-makers feel with pop, and why do musicians learn to make themselves at home in the visual field?

ALLISON ANDERS: It's just the basis for communication in our culture. I think that we can have common reference, a common sort of "Where was I when I heard this song?" It's so evocative and coded so deeply in our psyche, it's a whole world culture. I remember Wim Wenders talking about doing *The Scarlet Letter*, and he said, "It was just a drag—there were no jukeboxes, no pinball machines—I couldn't do it." I totally understand that—when I read something, I go, "OK, now where can I put in the popular songs?"

But popular music is the only cultural reference we hold in common any more. We are not all the same religion, we don't hold the same views on whether we eat meat or we don't eat meat, whether we are monogamous or we're not. There's no common ground except for pop culture, so in a way it's what's holding it all together, it's the new myth. And when songs can live on, it's such an amazing thing, considering that they're not created for that. They're marketed in a capitalistic way to not survive, and be replaced by the next new thing. So when they live on, it's so amazing, it's more powerful than anything, that creative spark in a two to five-minute song.

ALAN RUDOLPH: You can make an argument that music is the soul of the film. In movies it's like a flavorizer—it heightens, it sharpens, and it's contradictory presentation of action and emotion. Sometimes the best things that work in film are things that are undercurrents and other meanings, and music allows you to do that more than almost anything because you don't have to explain anything. It instantly becomes an emotional event.

An audience will trust music before they will trust narrative, before they will trust actors. When they hear music it's something they're comfortable with. I think we are starting to think in soundtracks. People think in soundtracks before they think in films. With movies you are sort of trusting something else, but with music it's yours. It's the people's art and it makes everyone more dynamic.

MICHAEL MANN: From the very start I always wanted to mix my love for rock with film-making, and my first major short in the late 60s has that in it.

ISAAC JULIEN: Music always plays a central role in my films—that's to do with the generation I'm from, the post-punk generation, and also to do with the influences of advertising, MTV, etc. They've all become central preoccupations in thinking about images.

WIM WENDERS: I woke up when I heard rock and roll and it has accompanied me and it has helped me a lot. I work with it and I travel with it. I feel I would have probably turned into someone else if it wasn't for Dylan or the Kinks or Van Morrison, because it woke up something in me and it made me get in touch with what I was able to do. Rock and roll and movies really have something in common. They are both contemporary at the same time, more than other forms of expression or languages. They are both able to really feel the pulse of the time.

BOB LAST: At the time of *Rock Around the Clock,* it wasn't part of people's memories. Now you've got this whole generation of film-makers who've been surrounded by popular music from their youth, and it's therefore very resonant for them. It's such a condensed form, you can very efficiently bring a lot into something. As it's become part of that memory, it's become possible to use it in a way that doesn't undermine the music you're using, doesn't make a fool out of it. And because it's part of everybody, there are textures—a certain type of guitar or whatever—that is a universal language. You can introduce those genre textures and use them.

PENELOPE SPHEERIS: Given the fact that it seems to be impossible to be creative with rock music, it's probably difficult to be creative with rock music in a film. What's surprising is that a lot of directors and studios will allow real kind of cutting-edge music to take a prominent place in big movies. Like for example, *Terminator 2*—didn't they have Guns 'N' Roses as their title song? Whereas in the days when Axl and Slash were hanging out on the street up there at the Whisky a Go Go, you would never have thought that they'd be affiliated with $60 million movies.

RY COODER: See, you just have to begin to understand where music is in a film—it's sub-textual and it's an interior sound. When Jack Nitzsche started doing that on films in the 60s, the engineers didn't like it, the producers didn't like it, everybody said, "This guy's nuts. He's crackers, what do you want him for? He's gonna ruin your film." But quickly that changed and the people who made the films got younger all of a sudden and they expected to hear something from their own experience in there. And if their own experience wasn't necessarily a German, compositionally trained disciple of Wagner, why then, they were having other thoughts. Michael Mann, for instance.

I found that I could think in images, because I didn't care about stories at all, I just wanted to see something start to happen in terms of visual rhythm, the look of light, faces, to let your mind wander.

But I don't know about rock and roll in films. Personally I don't have much use for it. Only because it's so one-way all the time. I like rock and roll all right once in a while, but to me it's a narrow path that you're going on because it has more to do with performance than some kind of style and some progression. . . .

When they start putting these pop songs into films, to me it just stops the film. It crashes, everything goes crash unless the film is about pop song. I've worked on some films that have pop songs and they weren't good, they hurt the film even though they were thematic.

The trouble with rock and roll is it's so much about that phoney heroism. I really mistrust that. In a film you don't want that, you don't want to send the message "We're winning with our bad trip and our guns and our shit." Let them work on TV. The bad guy wins, then the good guy wins, then the bad guy wins, then the good guy wins. But that's not a movie, that's a TV show.

FILM-MAKERS ON MUSICIANS

Film-makers often choose to work with the musicians who have inspired them and fueled their own visual music in the head. But from the film-maker's point of view, too, getting the right sound can be a complex process.

WIM WENDERS: It is one of the biggest pleasures in the movie-making process that you produce certain images and then you get to the editing table and you actually ask these people whose music you listened to while you were shooting the film if they couldn't help you finish it. And the biggest kick in the whole process for me is not shooting and not preparing and not finishing the film, but the moment when the tape arrives with the songs. It's really the most fantastic moment. Like the moment that Ry Cooder started with the first note of the song we had chosen, at the front of the screen, and for the first time playing the subject of *Paris, Texas*. It was like he was really cranking the film once more, but on his guitar not on the camera. I remember that moment. I had a shiver on my back. And it is still one of the most exciting things I feel.

ALLISON ANDERS: For me it's just another exciting interpretation—somebody else interpreting the movie you're making, helping you to make the movie you're trying to make. It's no different from trying source cues and them not working. The composer writes some stuff and you're like, "That doesn't work," or, "Oh, my God, I can't believe . . ."—the exciting thing is, like, "Oh, my God, that's exactly it, I can't believe what you added here, how much that process brought the movie out!"

J. Mascis' score for *Gas Food Lodging* did exactly what the score is supposed to do. It brought out the emotions without knocking people over the head— which I think rock musicians can do so much better than guys who are used to working on TV and all that stuff. When they are used to being composers for film or TV they tend to be far more heavy-handed and not go with the feel of the piece as much.

QUENTIN TARANTINO: I'm a little nervous about the idea of working with a composer because I don't like giving up that much control. Like, what if he goes off and writes a score and I don't like it? I don't like using new music that much because I want to pick what I know. *Dogs* wouldn't have benefited from having a score, it would have broken the real-time aspect of it. *Pulp Fiction* has score but again I didn't work with a composer. We used surf music a lot as score.

MICHAEL MANN: I used Tangerine Dream for *Thief* because although the film was set in Chicago, my home town where I grew up in the 60s listening to Muddy Waters and Howling Wolf at Curly's Place [a famous neighborhood bar], the thematic values of *Thief* as a high-tech political metaphor needed more abstract form and the specificity of ethnic music wouldn't work. Hence the need for an electronic score. I had known about the interesting origins of Edgar Froese as an early 60s blues guitarist, which gave a blues composition base to Tangerine Dream's work. So there was a link between the sound I needed and the film's Chicago setting. I started off by selecting from their earlier work material I liked prior to shooting and it was that, with some variations, we subsequently recorded in Berlin.

CAMERON CROWE: It's hard when you're a huge fan of your scoring artist and you're both kind of on a journey together. You'll be in the studio one night with

Paul Westerberg—who scored *Singles*—and he plays one of the great instrumental passages, and you as a fan love it, but you as the guy who made the movie know it's not right. It's hard to say, "Paul, that's not quite right—but can you put it on a tape so I can have it myself?" Which I did do so many times that I think by the end he felt he was doing a tape collection and not a score.

ALAN RUDOLPH: I work completely unconventionally with Mark Isham. He will give me all the elements and then sometimes I'll ask him to redo something or to look and listen and maybe make a cleaner version. But you just *discover* with music, and that's really the key to it. Mark is a very, very gifted musician and composer, but without his horn he would lose an edge for me.

For *Return Engagement,* I worked with this guitarist Adrian Belew. I got him on the phone and I said, "Listen, we made a documentary, are you interested in doing the music?" I said, "Come to this garage where we are working in New York and I'll teach you everything you need to know about putting music to movies." "Oh, OK." So we had this one scene on the editing machine and we watched it and put on this piece of music of his and we played this scene. It was great, it was kind of a bouncy thing and it played against what was going on. Then we put on a ballad, one of those spacey kind of things, and played the same scene. And he says, "Oh, my God—that's all you need to know about music and movies."

PENELOPE SPHEERIS: For me there are obvious places when I'm working on a film which ask very specifically for a song. And then there are obvious places which ask specifically for score. So for me there's never a question as to which I would use. If I show a film to a composer and I say, "There needs to be a source cue here," and he says, "But I could write some great score," I say, "OK, then go ahead and write it and then we'll put them both up next to each other and we'll decide." And sometimes I'll test it one way and the other. But I normally shoot montage sequences so that I can have places to put source music.

THE CELLULOID JUKEBOX

Whether it's a director programming his or her personal Top 10 into a film, or trying to get the right tracks to fit a place, a time or a subculture, there's an infinite repertoire of music available on CD and vinyl to be plundered—as well as the possibility of having music specially written. How do those difficult choices get made?

QUENTIN TARANTINO: I started realizing how much I liked pop music and how much I listened to it. I'd hear music and I would imagine a scene for it—this would be a great opening credit sequence in a movie. One of the things that I do as a film-maker now is if I start to seriously consider the idea of doing a movie, I immediately try to find out what would be the right song to be the opening credit sequence even before I write the script. When I find the right one, it's like OK, boom, OK, I got that. It's not that the personality of the movie is in that song, but it really gives me a good handle on it. I did the opening credit sequence for *Reservoir Dogs* and I think it's one of the best scenes of the entire movie, just all those guys walking out in their black suits with "Little Green Bag" on the soundtrack. Does "Little Green Bag" have anything to do with the movie? No. But it's just the right sound, and the right feel.

If a song in a movie is used really well, as far as I'm concerned that movie owns that song, it can never be used again. And if it *is* used again . . . You know, they used "Be My Baby" in *Dirty Dancing* and it's like, that's *Mean Streets'* song, how *dare* you use "Be My Baby." If you use a song in a movie and it's right, then, you know, you've got a marriage. Every time you hear that song you'll think of that movie.

I've seen movies where they put music all the way through and it's worked very well. Phil Kaufman did it great in *The Wanderers,* he had music all the way through and it was clever. But the problem is that nowadays you're trying to sell soundtracks and what they'll do is just pay for a movie with music all the way through it. So basically the record company is just trying to put music in wherever they can: "Is there a reason why we can't have music playing in this scene?" What happens is it tends to dull the effect. Unless the intention is to throw you back into another time—Richard Linklater's *Dazed and Confused* has music all the way through it from the beginning to the end but that's perfect. It takes you all the way back to '76 and all the different songs playing there and they're very cleverly used. He never has a sequence built around a song, necessarily—a lot of it is just hearing Bob Dylan sing "Hurricane" or something out of the corner of your ear. But it's cool. The movie does what it's supposed to do. You see the opening credits and you walk out of the movie singing "Sweet Emotion" by Aerosmith.

ISAAC JULIEN: My approach to music has a lot to do with memory. My memories are usually to do with past chart hits. In *Young Soul Rebels,* songs are used to evoke memory, but it's more than that. We're talking about the signifying practices of black popular culture—if you have no representations of your own as you're growing up, then obviously black popular culture has a pivotal link for you with American culture. So using "One Nation Under a Groove" was a pun on the 1977 Silver Jubilee; the nation Funkadelic are talking about is the black nation, of a particular kind. But with reference to the Silver Jubilee, it's another nation, the British nation, the Commonwealth, the Empire. So it's an example of music being used to read against the grain of the hegemony.

BOB LAST: There are structural reasons why it's almost impossible not to deal with the repertoire. But you use it for the associations it brings with it. In that sense the repertoire, even if it's very recent, is twice as efficient as anything that's completely new. It's because of the resonance of pop and its presence in everyone's life that you're now able to use it in movies in a particular kind of way.

If you're using popular music, part of its meaning is that it's popular. Pop music that isn't popular is no longer pop music, it's something else. So you're forced to make that jump—you've got to say, we'll make those calculations for a UK market, or we'll make them for a U.S. market. It's easier to make them for a US market because it moves at a rate that's comparable with that of film-making; you can't make them for a British market.

It's no good just gluing a piece of music on at the end, saying, "There's a radio on in this scene, we'll put it in here." The most interesting example of that was *Touch of Evil,* where 90 percent of it is done with source, it's all on jukeboxes. Obviously there was that excitement at the time about jukeboxes and the radio—Mancini did endless fake jukebox tracks and it's fantastic.

CAMERON CROWE: The best part of the process for me is when you finally get the film back and there are pieces of scenes and you get to try the music that always worked in your head. Very rarely is that the music that ends up working.

ALAN RUDOLPH: One thing I learned is that anything that has ever been produced on CD, I don't care who, a Malian guitarist or whoever, is owned by some big company. If it got to a CD, believe me, Island or EMI or somebody is behind it. I go to the International section of these esoteric record stores in any city I go to, I find these albums, and I take a chance on them like you do with pop albums. I came to my producer David Blocker with about ten songs and I said, "OK, here's what I'm interested in." And he said, "Wow, what *is* this—Bulgarian, guitars from Timbuktu, Norwegian?" and I said, "Well, it's, it's . . . you'll love it."

ALLISON ANDERS: Making *Mi Vida Loca* was pretty wild. These Chicano gang kids have this whole repertoire of music that they listen to, and they have their own standards, from the 50s up until now. They continue to add music on to their subculture, so they'll like 50s stuff and Motown, then James Brown, then in the 80s they're into disco, and Rick James and Zapp and stuff like that. Then with the new stuff, they're actually reluctant to take something on—they were the last kids to come around to rap. I have this sense that because when it is taken on in the subculture, it is taken on forever, it has to prove itself to be really good—it's just gonna stick around for another four, five generations.

John Taylor from Duran Duran wrote the score—he was perfect, because he could do the melodic stuff, but he could also do the total street, like Chick sort of street stuff, and dance rhythms. In fact, he turned me on to the song that becomes sort of the theme of the movie, "Girls it Ain't Easy" by the Honeycombs, and he sampled it for one piece that he wrote for the film. I also gave him the tapes that the kids had made for me. He just thought that the soundtrack that the kids had basically dictated was just great, so he totally understood where to go for sources to sample.

PACKAGING THE SOUNDTRACK

The work of putting music to film can be considerably complicated—or occasionally facilitated—when record companies take a hand. Striking that lucrative soundtrack deal can be decisive in ensuring a film's box-office success—or even in getting it made at all. Here, though, is where matters get complicated for the film-maker, whose own sound agenda might not match the requirements of the record company with their eye on promoting their own catalogue.

CAMERON CROWE: A lot of times, music in movies is the poor stepchild of the film process. People slap it on at the last minute, and directors who don't know what "hit music" is phone up a music supervisor at the last minute and say, "Let's jam on these soundtrack hits. OK, why don't we just have two seconds of it while the cop's coming out of the car?"

On *Say Anything*, they told me at the last minute that if I didn't have hit music on the soundtrack then it wouldn't be marketed, so we were running with extra money from 20th Century–Fox, trying to find hits. It was such an odd thing to be throwing money at Cheap Trick for a B-side, but that was what the marketing department wanted, and it gave me such a bad taste in my mouth that it did create a situation in *Singles* where it was all unheard music. I think because of the success of *Singles* that they're going to leave me alone musically.

The quest is always to get your video on MTV and to get a hit single out there in the marketplace before your movie comes out. It creates a situation where you have a middle-level artist who has rough cuts of every movie in town! They're basically shoving videos into their VCR and going, "Coppola's *Frankenstein*—that looks pretty good, maybe we should do a song." That's so off the mark when you think of music that really mattered in a movie—Scorsese put the Rolling Stones in *Mean Streets* and we know that was a choice that came from the heart, not from somebody at the last minute saying, "Let's get a Rolling Stones song, Marty."

BOB LAST: It seems unfortunate that film-makers who may have an interesting strategy like that resist it because it's so much associated with the crassest form of packaging in the States. The financial dynamic is, we haven't got a music budget, we'll scam a couple of hundred thousand dollars off the label, the label says, "We'll give you the money but we're going to put in who we want." So film-makers who may have an interesting strategy tend to back off from relying on source in any kind of intelligent way.

PENELOPE SPHEERIS: When I was hired for *Wayne's World,* I was just told it was going to be a Warner Bros. album, so I never questioned it. Then I met the Warner Bros. people and they were sort of vaguely interested in the movie and then when we had our first preview and our scores came up in the 90s they took this incredible interest, to the point of forcing me to use the music that I really didn't want to use, and that's when it got tricky. I think Eric Clapton is a cool guy and everything but I thought his music got really soft of recent years and I didn't find it to be appropriate head-banging music, so I didn't really want to put it in the film. But that was it, that's the way it happens and I've got my platinum record at home from the sales and, you know, my job is a series of compromises, what can I tell ya?

RY COODER: It happens a lot. The executives would like to see some marketing in place. They like to see some soundtrack but you get a hit like *The Bodyguard* or *Sleepless in Seattle,* they go mad. The feeding frenzy is on—they want some of the goddamn money and they want it now. So you come in and say, "Well, I'm gonna do this cute little job and I'll do my thing," and they say, "Oh, Christ. He's gonna do another *Paris, Texas*—silly-sounding guitars with rusty strings, we can't use that. We want hits, we want the big orchestra." Well, why didn't you say that? You insult me. Had one on *Geronimo:* "What's he gonna do, one of those *Paris, Texas* scores?" Now why would I . . . You know, a cavalry charge and two hundred Indians and I'm gonna go "Weeooougghh"? I resent that, you know, I really do.

ALLISON ANDERS: In my film *Border Radio,* we used the underground punk scene in LA. We got John Doe from X, Dave Alvin from the Blasters did our score, with Steve Berlin. We had songs by Green on Red, Los Lobos, Lazy Cowgirls, I mean, just everybody. In fact, our soundtrack was what gave us money to finish the film. We went to Enigma Records and they gave us money to finish, because they could get songs by John Doe and Dave Alvin that they could never possibly afford otherwise—they couldn't get those guys. They gave us finishing funds to finish the film, plus took care of all the licensing and everything for us. So the soundtrack was the only thing that we had.

On *Mi Vida Loca,* it was hilarious, because Mercury Records would start pitching me on somebody and it is such a sexist thing, because they would send me some rapper, or some guy with no teeth, some ugly motherfucker, and they would go, "This guy is really great." And then, instead of sending me the tapes of the girl singers, they would send me the pictures first—they would say, "These girls are really cute." But they would do these heavy pitches, and I said, "The bottom line is, the kids in the neighborhood in the movie are the music consultants."

QUENTIN TARANTINO: We needed a record deal to pay for the rights to the songs to *Reservoir Dogs*. We had different screenings of the movie for record executives and they all said, "There's not a soundtrack here," and they all turned us down. Then we had one more screening and three labels were very interested. Then Kathy Nelson at MCA stepped up to the plate and said, "We'll do it if you put in one of our artists, so we can have something to push." Bedlam were a group that MCA signed; they actually disbanded soon afterwards. But what happened was, MCA had them and they wanted to do the album, but we had picked all the songs already and they were, like, "We could do a remake of 'Stuck in the Middle With You,'" and I was, like, "Oh, no . . ." So MCA go, "We'd like to have something to promote, how about these guys—if you'd be interested, maybe we'll do the album." So they played me their CD, and I thought, "These guys ain't so bad." They wanted to do "Magic Carpet Ride" and I thought, fine. But unfortunately their group disbanded a little bit after that.

COMPOSERS—IN THE TRADITION

Although some film-makers have developed firm alliances with particular soundtrack composers, others are deeply suspicious of the artistic compromises entailed in letting another artist "hear" their film for them. At the same time, many of our interviewees, however skeptical about traditional film scoring, paid homage to some of their favorite composers, sometimes revealing unexpected affinities.

AMOS POE: The worst sin you can do with music and movies is where the music says exactly what is happening on the screen. You know, it's a love song when they're making love. Sergio Leone is very good at avoiding that. There's a violent scene, he has this pretty little music going on. But the tendency usually is to use music that's just like what's going on—the Joel Silver approach, which is to underline it, underline it, underline it.

DAVID BYRNE: I remember in the early 70s becoming familiar with the Fellini movies and Nino Rota scores. That kind of thing, where you notice the music, whereas in a lot of other films, the music may have been an essential part but you didn't notice it. It remained kind of an invisible support. Then there are the obvious soundtrack ones—Morricone, and new composers like Steve Reich or Phil Glass, Robert Ashley. Lots of very quiet music I tended to be attracted to, things that really had a strong mood attached as opposed to music that was dramatic and oriented toward cues. After I'd done music for a little bit of film here and there, I started to notice, say in Spielberg films, that some of those were wall-to-wall music. Like in *Indiana Jones,* music started at the opening credit and didn't stop till the last credit, maybe one little bit of silence for a reel change or whatever but that was about it. And it was almost all cued for hits in the action, punches and explosions.

QUENTIN TARANTINO: Of course, Morricone, that goes without saying. If I were seriously considering doing a movie with a composer, I would consider Joe Jackson. His score for *Tucker* was really good. And I guess Jerry Goldsmith and Elmer Bernstein, they're great. They do probably too many movies, but if I could get Jerry Goldsmith and know he was going to do a score as good as he did for *Under Fire,* which I think is one of the most beautiful scores ever in the history of film, I would say, "Yeah, wow." I talked with John Cale at one point to do the score for *Dogs.* I thought he did a good job of the *Caged Heat* score.

RY COODER: I always loved Georges Delerue, for what he did in those Truffaut pictures. They've got beautiful melodies in them. For me, melodies are the thing. It may be considered schmaltzy by the post-modern era but I like melodies pretty good. Romantic melodies, I like them. And Morricone's great at that, he's got this funny sense of humor—so cool. Fearless guy, just totally fearless. But he was also coming from a place of real high understanding. He's not so rustic that he uses a bad accordion because that's all he knows. He uses a bad accordion or crackly electric guitar because it makes the difference. And Mancini is just awesome. He's maybe my favorite of all. Anyone who writes "Peter Gunn" is a goddamn genius of the highest sort.

CAMERON CROWE: I've noticed that a real hack syndrome has developed among a lot of these guys. They come in to meet you and they say, "I'll give you whatever you want—what do you want?" It's like they're selling you music by the yard. A lot of it isn't very inspired—I know it's a tough job, you have to please directors who change their minds all the time, but I was surprised when I met traditional scoring guys, how little soul they put into it.

ALLISON ANDERS: I think there is little place any more for the classic film scores. Film has become so coded now that you don't need as much for the emotions to come through. Sometimes you have to work with rock musicians, in terms of packing and stuff like that, because I find that they understand the feelings a whole lot better. Theirs is a kind of innocence that doesn't crowd, they don't add on so much that you are distanced from the feelings. I think that's what an overblown score would do now. Somebody who used it really well, who could work with great composers, was Douglas Sirk; he even used pop songs—in *There's Always Tomorrow* the score is variations on the song "Blue Moon," which is very important to both of the characters and their past hopes.

MTV MOMENTS

With film-goers becoming as literate about the shorthand language of pop video as they are about more traditional movie language, cinema has come to cater increasingly to the new tastes which that shift has nurtured. Many films now contain—some are even composed predominantly of—song-anchored sequences that are effectively videos-within-the-film, in which narrative needs are subjugated to the rhythms and iconography of the hit. Our interviewees tended to be deeply suspicious of this tendency—but we found it has its defenders as well.

BOB LAST: There are a lot of mainstream movies where you can see the MTV moment coming up, and the worst are those that pretend not to—it's better just to go for it. How do you tell it's coming up? There are subtle cues in the pacing of a movie. If I was looking in a rough assembly and thinking about source, I would spot it a mile off. There's a change in the pace, it adjusts itself, sometimes very subtly. "OK, this is our MTV moment, we need to go through the chorus twice or else they won't notice it." Directors should take much more account of the underlying rhythm of music. You can cut pictures to even unheard musical rhythms, but that's not the same thing as your MTV moment, when it clearly just changes gear for this external "actor." An audience can spot it a mile off. But if you're completely blunt, you can have a musical moment, and then it becomes more like a musical. Real MTV moments are fine by me.

QUENTIN TARANTINO: It's like, "Let's put a familiar song in—let's put 'Pretty Woman' on the soundtrack or some old ditty that everyone knows and then build a little montage around that song . . ." It's mostly lazy film-making—unless you're doing it for a specific reason, I don't think you should do it. After Scorsese working with music brilliantly his entire career, I didn't like his use of music in *GoodFellas* at all. I waited my whole life for someone to use "Layla" in a movie and then you barely even notice that he does. Scorsese is probably the best that there is at the use of music in movies, and it's interesting that the movie he wallpapered with music is the one that is the least effective. But my editor Sally Menke completely disagrees with me, she loves the use of music in that movie.

FINALLY . . .

You can theorize endlessly about the complex decisions that result in a particular piece of music finding its way into a film. But it's worthwhile noting that there can also be a wonderful randomness about matters—as Cameron Crowe points out, reminiscing about his film Say Anything.

CAMERON CROWE: This illustrates the situation where artists that have made some personal and moving music get inundated with offers to use that song in a movie. In *Say Anything,* the pivotal scene is where John Cusack is holding up a boom box and you hear Peter Gabriel's "In Your Eyes." But it was written to be Billy Idol, "To Be a Lover," with this guy making a defiant stand outside his girlfriend's window, and it was really bad. Cusack was in love with the band Fishbone at the time, and he wanted to play "Party at Ground Zero," so we did it again and that was actually what was used in the movie . . . But when we showed the movie, it was like a crazed Fishbone fan was serenading outside the window, and it destroyed the meaning of the movie. So I had a tape that I made for my wedding, and by now I was so desperate that I was just rummaging through my car—let's try anything, anything! Nothing worked except "In Your Eyes," which was on this wedding tape, and it was so perfect it even told the story of the movie. It matched everything about the shot, it was great.

We tried to get it, the word that came back is, "This is a very personal song to Peter Gabriel, it's about his wife, it's a sad situation for him, he will not sell it." We tried to go back—"OK, he'll watch a tape of your movie, and maybe he'll think about it." So we sent a rough cut to Germany or wherever he was recording. A few days went by and they set up a phone call with Peter Gabriel. He comes on the phone and he says, "I've seen your film, and I'm afraid the song is too powerful, too important to me, I can't let you have it, I really didn't think it worked at the time when he took the overdose." *Overdose?* Nobody dies in my movie! And he goes, "This isn't the John Belushi film?" No, no, this is the love-crossed teenagers film. "Oh, oh, right. I haven't seen that movie." So he watched the film and we worked it out and everything was great. But I'm haunted by this image of Peter Gabriel in Germany watching John Belushi overdose to "In Your Eyes," and how close I came to never getting that song.

From *The Celluloid Jukebox: Popular Music and the Movies Since the 1950s,* ed. Jonathan Romney and Adrian Wootton (London: BFI Publishing, 1995), pp. 119–21, 126–28, 130–37, 139, and 147.

52

Composing with a Very Wide Palette

Howard Shore in Conversation

Philip Brophy

(1999)

How did you get into composing for films?

It was something I thought about while I had different careers. I had a rock 'n' roll career when I was young and on the road for years. Then I did television in Canada and eventually the United States, where I did *Saturday Night Live*. As I was doing that I thought television was really not something I was going to stick with. I had also done some music for theatre and had developed ideas about writing pieces. I wrote them in my head but didn't have an avenue for them, so I thought film scoring might be a good way to express some of my musical ideas: like, for example, the idea for the score to *Crash* [1996] with the electric guitars, harps, prepared piano and so on. If I had an idea like that, I didn't know how I could get to perform it, so I looked at films to do it. That's how I got into scoring music, through this sort of experimental level. The early David Cronenberg films like *The Brood* [1979], *Scanners* [1979] and *Videodrome* [1983] are all pretty experimental. I thought of movies as being film scores. That's what I was interested in, so that's how I got into composing.

Could you say something about your musical influences for Crash?

I was certainly aware of the composer Toru Takemitsu who did a lot of work with sound and electronics as well as composed music. That influenced me a lot in the sixties when I started listening, on one hand to rock 'n' roll and on the other to a lot of avant garde material, so a bit by accident I started listening to electronic music. He [Takemitsu] might have had an influence on me to write something like *Crash* because he was doing it many years ago.

How do you and David Cronenberg work together? When do you come in on one of his projects?

David and I work pretty close together. He sends me a script as soon as he writes it. In fact, I may well be the first or second person who gets his writing after he has completed it, and from that point we start our dialogue about the film. His most recent film, *Existenz,* is an original science fiction script. After he sent me the script we talked about many things besides music and making movies, from casting onwards. Once the shooting starts I always visit the set. *Existenz* was shot in Toronto so I went up there and hung around the set for a day to get the feel of it. We have some more talks about the movie, but not so much about the music. That comes a little later on.

After he finishes shooting he does his director's cut and that is where the process resulting from our early dialogue starts. I will look at David's director's cut and then we start formulating what we might do. About a month later we do a spotting session where we get inside the movie and talk about it scene-by-scene, and how we might use the music in the scenes. When I started composing music for David's movies in the late seventies, it was like guerilla movie-making because of their low budgets. We didn't know what it was like to have money to make movies, so we just did what we could and created the work that we could within the budgets that we had.

Later we actually had money when we made our first studio-financed picture, *The Fly* [1986]. It was a big symphonic/operatic type score and we went to London to record the London Philharmonic. After that we did a lot of orchestral scores: *Dead Ringers* [1988], *M Butterfly* [1983], *Naked Lunch* [1991]— all done with the London Philharmonic, and all fairly expensive recordings. Not expensive for films in general, but for once we had sizable budgets to do what we wanted with orchestras.

When we got to *Crash* we were back to the earlier ways of working. The smaller non-orchestral ensemble was built out of necessity, because this time we couldn't afford the London Philharmonic. Once you go outside the realm of both orchestra and electronics—but still want to do something *acoustically* in preference to using synthesizers and the like—you find some interesting solutions.

For *Crash,* I found it was better to go with numbers, so instead of using one guitar I used six guitars and so on. The original piece was written for three harps, which still remain the backdrop in the whole piece, and each pair of guitars functions like the amplification of the harp parts, transposed up an octave. All the "electronics"—the amplified sounds of the guitars, the delay units through which they are playing—are applied to the guitars alone. The guitars then perform a "harp sound." When I recorded the harps in the studio, I amplified them along with the guitars. So this was a piece that was created in the studio using acoustic instruments like harps, whereas the orchestral scores for David's films previous to that were all done live. *Crash* is like *Scanners* and *Videodrome,* and *Existenz* follows along similar lines.

How do you conceive the relationship between image and sound when you are composing music for a film?

It's a fairly intuitive thing, and not too intellectual. When you look at a scene in a movie, there is a visceral feeling you can have, particularly with Cronenberg. I sometimes watch the movie once and then get so stimulated musically and creatively that I just go and write a piece based on what I have seen. *Naked Lunch* was certainly like that, and with quite a lot of David's movies, my process starts as soon as I have seen the movie.

From that point, a whole chain of events is set in motion which is not so much about sound, but more about notes. Ideas for scores originate compositionally for me: it's not about what the sound is, but about what the *notes* are and how should they relate to the movie. *Crash* was written as a long piece that I analyzed *after* I wrote it so as to make it work in the film. This is opposed to the method of looking at a scene and wondering "what does this scene need?" and then writing 40–50 minutes of music to organize the movie. There were certain pieces which were moved around because I would hear them differently in the studio from how I wrote them, or where I thought they should go. The opening section which is used for the titles was originally written for a scene where they recreate the Jayne Mansfield crash. But then once I heard it performed and recorded, I thought it would be really good for the opening of the movie, and another version of it was used for the Mansfield crash.

So, to answer your question about the sound-image relationship, I perceive it as a gathering process: you see the image, ideas start to flow, and you should not restrict them in any way. I just let it all flow and then, on a more analytical level, I try to figure out what the ideas are. David writes in the same way, with a very wide palette where everything is possible. We keep narrowing it down, editing it until we end up with the score of the movie. Actually, movies are about editing, which is generally a reduction process. You have a lot of film that's slowly made into a ninety minute piece, and the score is reduced in the same way. Having said that, I should point out that not all movies are the same. I've done movies in Hollywood where it is a very different process. You look at it in maybe a more traditional way, and you think about how to use music in this scene or that scene, and the director may not be as experienced as David Cronenberg, so you are dealing with different types of things in different movies. Cronenberg has an extremely creative sensibility, which is the best situation that you could have as a composer. I am lucky to have worked on so many of his movies. . . .

I'm interested in the relationship between sound design and your work. How do you view that in relation to the music you write?

That's a good question. Often it depends on the relationship the composer has with the sound designer. Skip Lievsay—who has done a lot of very good work with Scorsese, the Coens, and so on—worked with me on Jonathan Demme's *Silence of the Lambs* [1991]. We first started working together on a documentary by Diane Keaton called *Heaven* [1987], and there we devised a method whereby we actually *built* the score. I had a sixteen-track machine and we dubbed the score and the sound design on the same sixteen-track. That was the ideal way of working. So when we got to *Silence of the Lambs* we did exactly the same thing, and quite often I would take my score to the studio on my twenty-four-track tape, and Skip would bring his twenty-four-track tape and we would lock them together and listen to them both and start eliminating things. He'd say, "I don't need that because you're doing that," and I'd say, "I see what you're doing now, so I won't even play my cue there," and so on.

Before we even got into the dubbing session—where we decide on what sounds will be used for the final mix—we had everything figured out. And in a way, that's an ideal position. As a composer, you do not want to be at a dubbing session with the sound designer and the director hearing the sound design *with* the music at the same time. Quite often the sound design might be 40, 50, 60 tracks. How can a director listen to 60 tracks *and* listen to the music at the same time, plus try to understand how all of it fits together? It can lead to disaster. So I recommend a unity between the composer and the sound designer wherein they can figure out what they are going to do. Sometimes it's not always possible due to distance and time, and now the schedules of movies are incredibly tighter. But there are situations in which the relationship between the composer and the sound designer works out very well. In *Crash* there is a scene which takes place inside a carwash. I constructed a *musique concrète* piece with the sound designer. I took his sounds and built a piece around his carwash sounds. . . .

You have obviously enjoyed a special working relationship with David Cronenberg, but you have worked with many other directors. Do you find it more difficult to work with them, are some jobs more bread and butter work, or do you enjoy working on any project that shows up?

Yes, I have worked with many different directors, but nothing quite matches the relationship I have with Cronenberg. That work constitutes some great, fantastic, years. Composers like to work with directors who do not get too involved in the music, and who they can really trust. Tim Burton was wonderful to work with on *Ed Wood* [1994]. He just loved anything I did. During the recording sessions, I would want to give it another take and he would say, "No, we got it, it's great." Composers like to work with directors who have good ears and who know how to use film music without being afraid of it. . . .

Did the location recordings of a particular film affect the final outcome of your compositions?

Well, with the example I mentioned from *Crash,* the location recording became the piece. I thought of it like sampling: I would sample certain sounds and compose with them. For the score to *Crash* I sampled maybe 25 percent of it after I had recorded it and manipulated it in the studio—you can hear it all on the CD. So with the last few movies I did, like *Copland* [1997] and *The Game* [1997] I used a similar process.

I actually stopped recording in a full orchestral context because I had done so much of it. After fifteen years I felt I had reached a point where I had done as much as I could in a live situation. Of course, there is certain joy in just having an orchestra there and conducting it: you do a take and it is finished. It is a wonderful thing. But the technique I have been using since *Crash* is to record *part* of the orchestra. I think of it like a big sound gathering session. I will then go in and spend six or seven hours working with different sections of the orchestra and then take it back to the studio and do quite a lot of post-production work on the recordings. At least a quarter of *Crash* was created after the initial recording.

A lot has been made recently about how over half of the best-selling albums in the US are movie soundtracks. Do you think this is a good time for film soundtracks generally?

It is a good time for composers because it's now easy to get a performance of one's music because of what has happened with the popularity of film music in general, and, say, *Titanic* [1997] in particular. James Horner obviously benefited from the movie and the score, but I think it has had an effect on the whole business of film music.

For somebody like me who is on the fringe of it, this is okay because I am not trying to do something on such a mass and popular level. Yet this success of film music filters out. The record companies are now interested in film composers, so, as somebody who has had experience in that field, if I say I want to do a piece, there is some interest. If you were in the recording business I think you would probably want me to keep on doing something because it's perceived that people are interested in film music. Whether it's true or not I don't know, but the interest from huge record labels is currently there. . . .

What happens if you come across a scene where your gut feelings tell you that no music is required, but the director insists on some being there? How do you creatively deal with that type of situation?

It is a real struggle. When you are trying to score a scene that you do not think needs music, it has to be a struggle. There are so many different situations in front of you when you are composing music for a film, and so many different ways to approach them. If you have a director who insists there should be music in a scene, it's best to try and write music for the scene. Then later you might be able to successfully suggest that the scene does not need that music. All in all, you have to go along with what is asked of you.

I learned quite early on in spotting sessions with directors that is best just to listen to what they say and try to sort it out later, because if you try telling him that this music is needed in a particular scene, you might have picked a scene with which he has a problem due to bad acting or bad writing. In fact, directors usually complain about the writing, and ponder: "Maybe music could help it here?"

Could you tell us about the music you did for Ed Wood? *What instruments did you use and how did you create the score?*

Ed Wood was a fifties project and a real labor of love for Tim Burton. So I wanted to recreate music from the era, to retain that flavor, and I decided to use instrumentation typical of the jazzy exotica of the period. I thought that a theremin simply *had* to be incorporated, but I needed a classically trained theremin player who could read the parts I had written. It transpired that the only trained theremin player was Lydia Theremin—the daughter of Leon Theremin, who invented the instrument.[1] But she lived in Moscow. I told Tim this, and he agreed to get her into a studio to record the session. I certainly loved him for that. One of the great things about working in Hollywood is that you could come up with something that wild and it was okay. I got used to it, you know.

So the production people arranged visas—it is not that easy to get a player from Moscow to come to London, where we were doing the recording sessions. Anyway, we had started the recording sessions and Lydia still had not arrived, so I had hired somebody to cover for her—Cynthia Miller, who had played the ondes martenot on some Elmer Bernstein scores in the fifties. Now, the ondes martenot is a keyboard instrument with a ribbon strip which you press with your fingers. It *sounds* like a theremin, but it is kind of cheating, because the theremin you play without actually touching.

So Cynthia did three sessions before Lydia arrived. I figured that if Lydia did not show up I would at least have the ondes martenot on the score. But I kept assuring Tim that Lydia was coming, that she was going to make it, and I even kept showing him pictures of the theremins. But I showed him pictures of the models RCA made in the twenties, huge things with dials and rings, with people playing them and everything. He was amazed with all the designs, because he loves those sort of things. Finally, through a series of motorcycle couriers across East Germany, Disney managed to get Lydia to London. So she showed up for the last session in the studio, alone with just a knapsack. Tim looked at her and he was obviously thinking, "Where's the theremin?" and Lydia goes, "Here it is." She takes it out of her *knapsack*. One of her uncles had made it for her. It was a very fifties-looking thing, like a cross between a radio receiver and a hot plate! Tim looked at it, then he looked at me, and I thought, "Oh, God"—and then after a second he said, "That's cool!"

So she did a day of recording with the orchestra live, and then we went to a studio on the other side of London and recorded a lot of solo stuff with Lydia. We loved her; she was wonderful. And she could really play—she is a virtuoso and maybe one of the best theremin players in the world. She tours and writes her own pieces for theremin and orchestra, and she also plays the ondes martenot.

One other thing about *Ed Wood*. It is essentially a Latin score and it has a very big percussion section. There are nine percussionists on the score—and they are all very square. To me it is the most wonderful part of the score because that squareness is the real "Ed Wood" part of it. I used a very small orchestra to try to capture the sound of film music you would have with those Universal Studio orchestras from the fifties. I really tried to replicate that Universal sound by organizing the orchestra in a very special way and even miking it in a very special way.

The music of the fifties in America is so interesting to me—the convergence of Cuban music with American jazz, the great creations of Bernard Herrmann. My score is dedicated to one of the masters of that period, Henry Mancini. In all respects I realize that this was a great opportunity to express my ideas about this particularly wonderful period of music and filmmaking.

From *Cinesonic: The World of Sound in Film,* ed. Philip Brophy (Sydney: Southwood Press, 1999), pp. 1–15. Reprinted by permission of the author (www.philipbrophy.com).

NOTE

1. The player's name is actually Lydia Kavina; she is the grandniece of Leon Theremin.—Ed.

53

Hollywood Sound

Rob Bridgett

(2005)

In the film industry, or more specifically *Hollywood,* convergence within game development has arrived. It's happened fast, and in a very big way. The next generation landscape promises even more integration and spectacle in this direction.

NEW MUSICAL STRUCTURES:
COMMUNICATING INTERACTIVE STRUCTURES TO
TRADITIONALLY LINEAR FILM COMPOSERS

Migration from, *Not* to *Hollywood*

For designer, producer or sound director, working with composers, not to mention big name Hollywood composers, can be a challenge. Here we consider the inherent differences between content and structure in both cinema and video game music.

It is often said that the game industry is perceived by composers as a stepping stone, where one can train, or at the very least *get paid,* until film or *real* work comes along. Over the last five years the stepping stone has transformed and now offers far easier navigation in the opposite direction. Being a small budget game composer has never really represented a clear path into linear post-production of mainstream cinema, whose roles and employment hierarchy are rigidly defined after over 100 years of industrial history. The most talented Hollywood film composers are instead migrating to games, larger audio budgets enable publishers to bypass the "sample based" and employ the best composers, arrangers and orchestras working in Hollywood. This allows the games industry unprecedented access to the highest quality of cinematic music.

Danny Elfman's recent work on Big Blue Box's *Fable,* and the more recent mention of Howard Shore's involvement in Webzen's *SUN,* instigates a trend for name composers that is equally becoming established for Hollywood voice talent, sound effects creation and screen writing. Hollywood's finest actors for example are now lured to games by the fact that, among other incentives, rather than embarking on a year-long training and pre-production schedule, and rigorous and tiring location shooting on a film, they can earn similar money for doing a few days of voice work in a comfortable sound studio.

There is a proven economic advantage to employing name actors and name composers on a video game; it gives public relations a hook to grab on to and to generate much larger PR budgets, this directly equating to increased revenue. Ask any producer how sound can sell more copies of a game and you will get the same answer: big name voice talent. Now that the score is moving into that realm—it is time for the composers in our industry to integrate on a much larger scale.

The incentives for the Hollywood composer are evident. Working on a game actually affords the composer a temporal luxury in that the development time on a large game far outstrips the small amount of time they would have to work on a feature film. Traditionally a feature film commission requires that the entire score is written, arranged and recorded as soon as a temp edit of the film is created. There are exceptions to this—the film composer Gabriel Yared works exclusively on a film title from day one of a project until it is completed; however, not many composers have this luxury. A final edit may result in a few changes to the timings and structure of the piece, but that period of time between the temp edit and the final edit is pretty much all the time the composer has to fully flesh out the score. So let's take a look at the videogame/film music landscape.

Bill Brown, composer for videogames such as *The Incredible Hulk: Ultimate Destruction* and *The Lord of the Rings: The Battle for Middle Earth* as well as motion pictures such as Michael Mann's *Ali,* Oliver Stone's *Any Given Sunday,* and recently the television series *CSI New York,* suggests:

First, I think something that is worth sharing is how, qualitatively speaking, games, film and TV music are merging. Over the past 10 years, we have been slowly bringing the consciousness of the value of the live orchestra (that is taken for granted in films now) into games. . . . Another thing that comes to mind is the "cinematic" approach to video games. This to me means more attention is being paid to how music is working to support the narrative of the game—music is now taking the next step in gaming to become a deeper part of the story-telling experience. Game developers are truly interested in the depth and dimension music brings to their product and are willing to invest more now than ever to take their project to that next level. Developers really understand that a 60–90-piece orchestra sounds better than orchestra samples, and that makes a difference in the impact of their game. Triple-A titles and A-list films are enlisting some of the same players today. Howard Shore, one of my favorite composers, is included in that new crossover group of artists. This concept of crossover artists is becoming more and more the standard for our industry.

The fact that names like Howard Shore and Danny Elfman are mentioned with such excitement in game music circles reveals a great deal about music in games, especially as Elfman only wrote a main theme for *Fable*. Why aren't we talking about the other composers on *Fable* who adapted, fleshed out and integrated this "theme" into the core mechanics of the game? This is again representative of the way that games are marketed, in a similar way to films. There is probably little difference in terms of quality between the "non-name" composers on *Fable* and the work that Elfman did; however, Elfman's name is the currency. It is *his* name that is used as an index of quality in the public mind.

Garry Schyman, composer of music for both the games *Destroy All Humans* and *Voyeur* and the films *Lost in Africa, Horse Player* and *The Last Hour,* argues:

> When truly creative opportunities present themselves, composers, even Hollywood's most famous, will want to get on board. Games have evolved to a point where game music has become as important an element to games as it is to films, and the quality expected by game companies is very high now. I think game music is the place to be at the moment for any composer interested in plying his or her trade. What is likely is that composers will cross over back and forth between the two genres.

This idea of a crossover artist is something that both Bill Brown and Garry Schyman see as clear for the future of composers. A future where there will be no categorization of either "game" or "film," but simply "composers."

There are some interesting reasons why the games industry would look to a composer of Elfman's caliber. It can be viewed as a sea change for game composition that breaks down some previous boundaries—in the eyes of gamers, critics, and the composers themselves, games are becoming recognized as serious cultural artifacts. This is intensified by the huge sales the medium is generating, not to mention the maturing and stratification of the overall core demographics of gamers and game creators.

Structure

There are vital structural differences between the music required for a motion picture and the music required for a video game. Nonetheless, both film music and video game music are aesthetically close.

Garry Schyman:

> In film music you are writing to underscore and enhance the action or emotional experience the scene creates, or perhaps you are even finding a deeper meaning to

the emotions the actors are portraying. But with films, or television for that matter, the scene and the music accompanying it, once locked, never change. Additionally, in a film score repetitive music can be an attribute, as the score will likely only be heard once. In games, repetitive music can get turned off. Because in a game the player's choices determine the experience to a significant degree, what the player is seeing and experiencing is somewhat unique each time they play. This means that music is rarely accompanying the exact same visuals twice and can easily get boring if repetitive, or hard to listen to if abrasive. So I find that the approach is quite different, though there is the obvious similarity that you are using music to enhance the emotional experience of the viewer or player.

Bill Brown:

Structurally, where film is static and games are dynamic, the two can share most other aspects [aesthetically] speaking. The score can follow an overall arc in both mediums; it can develop themes, underscore action, communicate exotic locations, and add dimension to the emotional landscape of either medium using similar tools.

From a technical and structural perspective, delivery formats in games and film are also moving closer together.

Garry Schyman:

With films and television the norm is to deliver a Pro Tools session with the music placed in time locked to picture. Music could be mixed as stereo tracks (still common in TV) or 5.1 mix (in nearly all films). Additionally, music could be delivered with separate stems (still Pro Tools session locked to picture), with various elements of the music separated out, giving the mixing stage the option of increasing or decreasing the volume of a particular musical element. With games it is common to deliver individual stereo WAV files that the audio lead will mix into the game. 5.1 mixes are beginning to be more common as well. Finally, it is common to deliver the music broken into separate musical stems so that different elements of the score can be brought in and out as gameplay dictates.

Bill Brown:

Even the formats delivered to the developer and dubbing mixer can be the same. I deliver stems (separate instrument groups in tracks for each cue) both to my music editor for films and TV, as well as to some developers for use dynamically in games. This also gives them both an opportunity to mix in 5.1 where applicable.

Working with a solid system and solid implementer is critical to the success of any interactive score.

Garry Schyman:

It is my experience that in games the music implementation has become a critical element in how you write the score. Film music implementation was settled 75 years ago and has changed little since. But I've found that with games the implementation creates challenges and can literally dictate the approach one takes. Music must be flexible enough to change with the players' experience and yet it is not possible to write and implement dozens of hours' worth of music to fit every possible game scenario. The audio lead is often the first person you will play music for as you are writing the score. Because they have most likely been involved from the game's inception they have a very good idea of the style and approach that the developer is looking for.

Bill Brown:

In film, I work most closely with the director, film editor and my music editor. Ideally, the director has a clear vision that he or she can communicate to me as we collaborate on the project, and/or an open sense of creativity and collaboration that we use to the advantage of the film. This isn't always the case, so sometimes producers are involved creatively as well—hopefully, the conversation stays positive, creative and focused. My intention is to bring as much harmony to that process as I can for myself and others, because the more cooperation there is on all fronts, the better the end result will be—not to mention how much easier and more graceful the process will be for everyone.

  In games I most often work directly with the head sound producer and several of the people from the creative team on the project (designers, artists, writers, etc.), which helps me get a feel for the overall vibe of the game—similar to the creative process I have with a film editor and director.

Scott Morgan, the sound director for Radical Entertainment who worked with Bill on *The Incredible Hulk: Ultimate Destruction* in order to implement his score within the game, concurs:

As sound director and music implementer I really bookend the music production process. I cull as much information as possible about the game, its story, characters, and structure, from the design team. With this information I provide the composer with a framework within which to work. I also act as a bit of a filter for the composer, ensuring he/she is not inundated with too much information or information that may not be critical to his/her process. After this, I have little impact on the music other than providing both technical and aesthetic feedback. Once the music is written, I then begin the process of implementation, which is comparable to the role of music editor in film. I edit and arrange the music to fit within the dynamic of the game, mostly sticking to the agreed-upon framework set up at the beginning of the process, but occasionally grabbing from other pieces or requesting additional elements from the composer to make it all work within the interactive nature of the game.

Notes on Interactive Microstructures

Music in cinema, despite its sophistication in terms of content, is rigidly defined by, primarily, the film's stylistic aesthetics and, secondly, its visual editing structure; this is why so much frustration can be experienced by composers who have to rework their content to accommodate a new edit of a scene. However, once the edit and structure are locked and the information about the emotional content of the scene is communicated by the director, the composer's work is relatively straightforward.

Structural systems represent different concerns to those of musical language, and defining and communicating the structure to the composer beforehand is essential to success in game audio. With cinema, the editing language is more transparent. In games, it is not so easy for an outside composer to instantly understand the systems that might be in place under the hood of the game—it is through neglect of this that many scores fail to be truly interactive. Of course, scores fail in many other ways too—by being poorly technically executed, by being too literal, even by being too interactive.

In film music, the editing structure of a scene controls the length of the music required, the action even dictating the pace and the tempo of the music, dividing the score up into scenes and phrases therein; there is no real difference to applying the structures of interactive music to a composer's commission, merely a few more structural units which require the composer's initial understanding.

Here are some examples of elemental "states" and "units" of interactive music's microstructure that need to be communicated to, and understood by, composers.

A **Narrative State** is a piece which plays straight from beginning to end without the need to be interrupted by user input. A good example of this would be a cut-scene movie in a game, as these sections work in a predictable and linear fashion, the old rules of film composition can be applied: the exact timings and lengths of events, once locked, are predictable.

The second type of state, the **Continual State,** is basically a piece of music that needs to keep playing until a user interrupts it. A good example would be a simple static theme on a menu awaiting input, or a particular section of a game in which the length of time for that section is an unknown parameter dependent upon many other factors.

The third, which is an **Evolving State,** is slightly more complex, and can consist of several stems of differing intensity. Here building intensity across stacked layers rather than linear temporal movements is required. In linear narrative terms, this state is an unknown quantity: the length of time this music is to play for could be anything from ten seconds to an hour—the same as for the simple continual state. However, there may be many game-side factors which influence this piece of music. A good example would be a combat situation within a game.

Entering the combat would trigger the continual state related to this, but then variables of how well or badly the player is doing in combat could be required to give audio feedback to the player and modify the music. If the fight is joined by two more enemies, the music may need to become more intense, and if the player runs to the side of the arena away from the fight to recover for a few moments, the music could again be required to reflect this less intense period of activity.

Transition to **Narrative Specific Units** or **Objective Specific Units** may also occur within an evolving state, if an objective is accomplished, such as collecting a critical piece of a puzzle. Transition to a short appropriate piece of music may be required to underscore the importance of that event.

The **Transitional Unit** is a short piece of music that bridges the two differing evolving states together. It may consist of a drum roll, a buildup of some kind which allows smooth exit of any piece at an time and into the next unit.

The **Inaugural** or **Resolving Unit** is a short transitional piece, usually only played once, which can be played at any time during the looping continual or evolving states and which signifies an end to the particular piece of music. If the player is successful in combat the combat music will fade out while the triumphant ending to the piece is played over the top, if the player was unsuccessful then a more tragic piece could be played. What you hear and when you hear it, is therefore totally dependent upon the way the use interacts with the system.

This is not by any means a *definitive* system; it is intended as a simple structural guide for building a "music map" of the game system. It should encourage communication of these structures to composers who are in fact more familiar with such structures than one may think, although under a myriad of different names. The key here is communication of the music structure. This can only be done when that system is locked down, and that lockdown can only happen when the game itself has been locked down. There may be an initial communication of style, but there should be a communication of structure only when there is confidence that it will not change.

Once the system and design have been defined and laid out, the scope of the score structure can be communicated to the composer in these or similar terms, and this can even happen in terms of a template. The states and units mentioned here will of course evolve over time, yet they do form the core units for any interactive piece of music or ambience. From this a map of the musical scope can begin to emerge. This is where the choice of composer will pay off—he/she should be able to fully realize the score according to the system. Any further changes need to be communicated as soon as possible to the composer, in the same ways as in the changing edits of a film. If a major character were to be cut or changed, the composer should know, as this would potentially affect the entire score.

Film composers have long had their music defined by a predetermined structure. Every film has a different structure and a different musical approach, and these differences are defined even more clearly and stylistically through genres. Video games function in much the same way.

Once style and structure are understood, there is very little else the composer needs other than the talent to deliver. If a game requires something innovative and different in terms of its score, it will be evident. The project itself must make these decisions. Game structures will prove the primary evolutionary force in redefining music for games. The structure and styles will evolve with the game-play and emotional content needs of the project, emerging as new genres emerge, as before with cinema on a film-to-film basis.

The interactive arts may not represent the great breakthrough in the stylistic avant-garde some seem to be pushing for. The extant models of interactive music and their relationship with content, or "image," have already been solidified into a mainstream phase. This is of course not to say there will always be stylistic and structural alternatives to any notion of a mainstream. Hollywood composing talent seems currently restricted within an exclusively orchestral context, and is arguably an initial phase of attaining critical currency on par with the film in-dustry. Everywhere in the industry this push for "equality" is prevalent, through specific BAFTA interactive awards, and in Grammy categorization. This will, in turn, open up more opportunities for established and successful composers from other media to enter the game development environment.

The Music Industry—Licensed Content

In much the same way that bigger-name composers are being enticed into the interactive realm, the potential to make use of big-name licensed music content is also gearing up as the next-generation platforms all promise online compati-bility. Hollywood films have, for many years, succumbed to the inclusion and cross-promotional value of licensed music material, as in *Flashdance*'s "high-concept" marketing marriage of both film and music content. Licensed music can, of course, be used extremely artistically, in the case of Scorsese's *Goodfellas* and the majority of Woody Allen's filmic output. However, this does often hap-pen as an artistic decision, but more a decision on the part of executive promo-tional pressure on a project.

Licensed music content already has a similarly checkered history within the video game industry.

Garry Schyman:

> Licensed music makes sense in games when it is appropriate. In sports games and racing games it's an obvious choice—it works and sounds right. In any game that needs source music, it would make sense to license the songs rather than have the composer write new ones. What I think is a big mistake is thinking that "kids" will buy a game because this or that band has contributed tracks to it. If a game is good they will come, and if the songs actually are wrong creatively for the game, then put-

ting them in will make the game less appealing. Kids are smart and know intuitively when they are being condescended to. Songs do not entice people to buy a game, and filmmakers have learned that lesson over and over again. When you look at the top 100 box office films over the last twenty years, the list is nearly entirely populated with films with lush orchestral scores that droves of kids paid money to see.

Used again as a predominantly promotional tool, licensed music has often sat uncomfortably within the video game's interactive content realm. The idea that the tracks were not interactive or "reactive" to gameplay could be espoused as a reason why they would not survive. With the dawn of the iPod came the notion of *user-defined* playlists and *user-defined* music content, notions already opened up by the Xbox. There is now a whole universe of downloadable content waiting to be hooked up to your interactive experience.

The structural potential to adapt music content to gameplay is huge. Players become creators. We can use the analogy of a DJ, within the sampling and pod-cast culture, re-appropriating cultural content as the user sees fit, in order to create new unintended (at least on the part of the original creators) juxtapositions, in order to illustrate where this phenomenon fits in a cultural context. . . .

The sound implementers can be clever about how they set up the structures for any customizable content to fit into the game. They could automate the breaking up of any track into the interactive components mentioned above in the structural composition section. Identifying intros, outros, high intensity looping sections, as well as calmer sections or sections from different songs in the same key, musically educate the console to transition in a "musical" way from a track in the same key to a related key. Programmatic stripping of audio data into usable chunks and re-appropriating of that data is ripe for exploitation in online consoles that allow for user defined musical content to be used in any game. The old notion that licensed music wasn't adaptive will become a long-forgotten adage.

In terms of music content, this could mean that the soundtrack a game ships with is only given a cursory listen before the user decides to utilize their custom content. This, in fact, makes it more and more critical that the user is given a hook on the music that is included in the game. Big-name composers and exclusively licensed content may be the only way to do this. The notion that a game is a complete cultural artifact, a *gesamtkunstwerk* (or "totally integrated work of art"), in that its music, sound, performances, and visual style are all part of the experience, has yet to be seen. One cannot imagine, for example, removing Howard Shore's score from such a fully integrated work as the *Lord of the Rings* movies and replacing it with user-defined content. Maybe this is because the very interactivity of a video game encourages a variety of individual playing styles, problem-solving techniques, tastes, and is in direct contradiction to the experiencing of a story being told in "one way."

The sense is that future games will offer an "authentic" experience with score and visual styles intact, as well as a modified option of the same game which offers users total freedom via customizable content. We are, indeed, already seeing these shifts being made in this direction.

While game sound and, more broadly speaking, video games in general begin to adopt a Hollywood action genre model, in terms of both content and marketing, one can only hope that the games industry will truly mirror the film industry in that there has always been an independent and underground vein which the mainstream feeds off. Where this will come from in the post-goliath, publisher-centric battlefield remains to be seen. Most independent game companies currently exist to be groomed and bought up by the big publishers. Only time will tell how the "independent video game" will compete with the giant publishers, and how their musical needs will be serviced and created by a Hollywood or Independent sound production sector.

From *Gamasutra.com*, September 16, 2005. Reprinted by permission of the author.

INDEX

compared with, 477; working-class
audiences, 10
Cinema Quarterly, 126
cinématographes (short films), 2, 3
cinematography, 50, 174, 213
cinéma vérité, 296
Cinemax, 381
Ciné Multiphone Rousselot, 6
Cinemusic, 98
Citizen Kane (1941), 321, 369, 438
City, The (1939), 247
City Lights (1931), 111
City Slickers (1991), 393
Civilization (1916), 31n53, 104
Clair, René, 24, 110, 111, 209, 211, 260, 277,
278, 342
Clapton, Eric, 386, 460
Clare, Sidney, 150
Clark, Zhay, 142–43
Clarke, Grant, 150
classical music, 10, 12, 15, 25–26, 31n36, 101, 102,
106, 162, 387
"classicization" project, 2, 12, 13, 19, 25. *See also*
"better" music
Cleopatra (1913), 14
Cleopatra (1963), 293
click-track, 125, 128
climax, approaching, 72, 81
Clockwork Orange, A (1971), 425
Close Encounters of the Third Kind (1977),
440
Clouser, Charlie, 399
Coal Miner's Daughter (1980), 412
Cobweb, The (1955), 189
Cochran, Ernest F., 107
Cocktail (1988), 440
Code and Ratings Administration (CARA),
295, 296, 297
Coen, Joel and Ethan, 468
Cohn, Harry, 183
Colbert, Claudette, 172
Colburn, George, 14, 30n40
cold war, 188–89, 191
Cole, Jack, 206n94
Coleman, Cy, 324
College Swing (1938), 237
Collette, Buddy, 340
Collins, Anthony, 243
Collins, Judy, 332
Collins, Phil, 434
Collins, Rudy, 338

Columbia Pictures, 170, 237, 292, 365, 392,
410, 431
comedies, 11, 26; comedy dramas, 66–67; effect
playing by pianists and, 51; exhibition
programs and, 16; musical, 78, 87, 117, 122,
162; music for, 51, 59; narrative formulas
and, 171; popular music and, 12, 17, 19;
special effects and, 71; underscoring and,
184
comic books, 393, 394, 412
Communism, 183, 188–89, 190, 204n62
compilation scores, 25, 33n73, 114
composers, 24, 27, 30n40, 81; copyright laws
and, 107; foreign, 373; motion pictures as
field for, 104; music directors and, 365;
re-recording sessions and, 242; retained
by film studios, 210; specialization of
compositional labor, 173–74; Third
Stream, 303, 324; time allotted for
composing musical scores, 239; tradition
of film scoring and, 461–62; underscoring and, 176, 194; video games and, 400
Composing for the Films (Eisler and Adorno),
194
computer graphic imagining (CGI), 394
Concorde: Airport '79 (1979), 412
conductors, 16, 17, 20, 23
Conrad, Con, 147
Constant Nymph, The (1933), 209
Cooder, Ry, 454, 455, 460, 462
Coogan's Bluff (1968), 339
Cook, David, 294, 296, 384
Cool Hand Luke (1967), 303, 339, 356
Cooper, Gary, 148, 316
Copland (1997), 469
Copland, Aaron, 180, 191, 203n52, 237, 246, 260,
328, 398, 438; on music and dialogue,
398; on music in films, 238–44; on
"neutral" music, 396; *Quiet City* score,
247; underscore and, 185–86, 194
Coppola, Francis Ford, 295, 297, 308, 363, 459
Coppola, Sofia, 398
copyright laws, 25–26, 106–8, 121, 158, 210,
308, 382
Corman, Roger, 296
Costa, Don, 316, 324
Costello, Elvis, 411
Costello, Maurice, 157
Cottler, Archie, 147
Count Basie, 355
Count of Luxembourg, The, 237

COMPOSITOR	Westchester Book Group
INDEXER	Alexander O. Trotter
TEXT	10/12.5 Minion Pro
DISPLAY	Minion Pro
PRINTER/BINDER	Thomson-Shore, Inc.